Second Edition

AWAKENING

An Introduction to the History of Eastern Thought

Patrick S. Bresnan

DeAnza College

Prentice
Hall

Upper Saddle River, New Jersey 07458

Library of Congress Cataloging-in-Publication Data

Bresnan, Patrick, (date)
    Awakening : an introduction to the history of Eastern thought / Patrick S. Bresnan—
2nd ed.
      p. cm.
    Includes an index.
    ISBN 0-13-098908-8
    1. Asia—Religion. 2. Philosophy, Asian. I. Title.

BL1032 .B74 2003
200′.95—dc21   2002070043

Senior Acquisitions Editor: Ross Miller
Editorial Director: Charlyce Jones Owen
Senior Production Editor: Barbara DeVries
Cover Design Director: Jayne Conte
Cover Designer: Bruce Kenselaar
Prepress and Manufacturing Buyer: Brian Mackey
Line Art Supervisor: Guy Ruggiero
Maps: © C. S. Hammond & Co., New York

This book was set 10/12 Galliard by DM Cradle Associates and was printed by
RR Donnelley & Sons Company. The cover was printed by Phoenix Color Corporation.

Prentice Hall

© 2003, 1999 by Pearson Education
Upper Saddle River, NJ 07458

Printed in the United States of America
10 9 8 7 6 5 4 3 2 1

ISBN 0-13-098908-8

Pearson Education Ltd., London
Pearson Education Australia PTY. Limited, Sydney
Pearson Education Singapore, Pte. Ltd.
Pearson Education North Asia Ltd. Hong Kong
Pearson Education Canada, Ltd, Toronto
Pearson Education de Mexico, S.A. de C.V.
Pearson Education—Japan, Tokyo
Pearson Education Malaysia, Pte. Ltd.
Pearson Education, Upper Saddle River, New Jersey

Contents

Preface

PREFACE TO THE FIRST EDITION

We humans struggle to make sense out of a world that often seems chaotic and meaningless. In every age men and women—at least some men and women—have sought to go beyond the appearances of everyday life and discover a transcendent truth in which reality is seen as it really is. Such an experience is often called "awakening"—it is the opening of consciousness to the light of perfect understanding.

This great quest has been an important part of the history of both East and West, and in both worlds much attention has been given to uncovering a fundamental principle of unity that underlies the manifold expressions of nature. There has, however, been a difference in emphasis. Speaking very broadly, the West has emphasized the rational and scientific approach, whereas the East, again speaking very broadly, has tended to emphasize the introspective approach, an intuitive opening of consciousness that goes beyond the limits of the rational mind. Such a state of consciousness, in which the underlying oneness of Being is personally experienced, is known as the "unitive state." The search for a way of life that will result in this kind of awakening is at the heart of the history of Eastern thought.

This book tells the story of that search. It is a search that unfolds slowly over nearly four millennia. And, of course, it is still unfolding today; the present age is merely the cutting edge. There is something especially exciting about the present age, though. As the global village takes form, the traditions of East and West are coming together. Who can imagine what wondrous offspring may result from this marriage?

The evolution of Eastern thought grows from many roots. Those of India and China are especially strong and deep, reaching back before the beginnings of recorded history. We will take up this study at the source of the tradition, in India. It is appropriate to begin in India because so much of the spiritual and philosophical foundation of Eastern thought is to be found there. And, it was out of the amazingly fertile Hindu tradition that Buddhism was born. From India, Buddhism would spread to all parts of the Eastern world, sometimes merging with other evolving traditions to create new directions of growth. In China, Buddhism would confront the already established traditions of Confucianism and Daoism, and in Japan, the ancient tradition of Shinto. These too are important parts of this study.

The history of the development of Eastern thought is far too vast to be reduced to the pages of any single volume. The purpose of this work, therefore, is not to tell everything; that would be impossible. Rather, in this book my primary aim is to help you form a comprehensive overview of the subject, a "Big Picture." In the pages that follow

I will introduce you to this important part of the story of humankind's search for awakening. It is my goal to include all that is essential to a broad understanding of the subject and to clarify all major concepts no matter how complex they may be, in a way that is clear and engaging. It is my deepest hope that you, the reader, will come away from this book hungry for more, and that you will choose to become a lifelong student of this fascinating subject.

PREFACE TO THE SECOND EDITION

In recent years the study of Eastern philosophical and spiritual traditions has become a very active field. Ongoing research is constantly generating new interpretations and understandings. And, my own involvement in the field has continued to grow as well. Out of this, a new edition of *Awakening* has emerged. It improves on the original by having a more accessible overall organization, by incorporating up-to-date scholarship, and by the addition of an expanded treatment of several topics, including the subject of Tantra, which encompasses a whole new section in this edition. In addition, I have used only my own photography for the photo illustrations. I believe that this will result in illustrations that fit more tightly with the text.

The growing threat of international mayhem in the present age underscores the need for greater understanding of and sensitivity for differing religious and philosophical traditions. By embarking on this study you are helping to achieve that goal. Thus, the overarching aim of *Awakening* remains essentially unchanged. If I may quote from the Preface to the First Edition: "It is my deepest hope that you, the reader, will come away from this book hungry for more, and that you will choose to become a lifelong student of this fascinating subject."

I am grateful to many people for their help in completing the second edition of *Awakening*. I wish to acknowledge before all else the valuable contributions of my students. They continue to be a rich source of insight and feedback. Everything is tried out on them initially; nothing goes into the book that doesn't pass the classroom test first. My wife, Elizabeth, also gets a special "thank you" for her patience and support. And, a big thanks to the folks at Nilgiri Press for their generous permission to quote extensively from Eknath Easwaren's excellent translations of the *Upanishads* and the *Bhagavad Gita*.

It's been my good fortune to work with some exceptional people at Prentice Hall, and no doubt the book shows it. Ross Miller, Senior Acquisitions Editor for Philosophy and Religion, has been very helpful to me, and I appreciate it. Editorial Assistant Carla Worner has been unfailingly gracious and efficient.

The critical analysis and suggestions of the Prentice Hall reviewers provided invaluable insights for this revision. My sincere thanks to Maxine Freed, *Monterey Peninsula College* and Carla D. Grady, *College of San Mateo*.

I consider myself to be very fortunate to have been able to work again with Barbara DeVries, the Production Editor for this book, who also steered the first edition through the complicated process of production. Thank you, Barbara, for your sound advice, your good will, and your skillful handling of the entire process.

As a final note I'd like to thank the many people who have used the book and have communicated with me about it. Your support for the book, and your suggestions, have made a big difference. This book is dedicated to all students with an interest in this fascinating subject. Don't be reluctant to send me an email; I'd love to hear from you.

Patrick Bresnan
Los Gatos, California
January 6, 2002

BresnanPatrick@fhda.edu

South Asia

PART 1
Hinduism

Hinduism is a hard word to pin down. It refers to far more than a specific religion or philosophy. Some argue that the word *Hinduism* refers to the entire culture and traditional way of life of the people of India. For our purposes, the word Hinduism designates that tradition of thought which arises from, and accepts the sacred authority of, the Vedas, the earliest spiritual and philosophical compositions of Indian civilization. This leaves room for other "non-Hindu" traditions within the history of Indian thought, and we shall examine the most important of these in Chapter 5. The greatest part of the story, though, concerns the evolving tradition that began in the Vedas and progressed through stages to the sublime mystic philosophy expressed in the *Upanishads* and the *Bhagavad Gita*. In Part 1, we concentrate on this main line of development.

1

India before the Vedas

Veda is a powerful word. It is derived from the ancient Sanskrit word *vid*, which means "to know," as in the sense of knowing the truth. *Veda* thus means "knowledge of truth." More specifically, it refers to a supreme *god-given* knowledge of Truth.

In ancient times, the Brahmin priests were the custodians of Veda; it was their responsibility to preserve this sacred knowledge and to use it for the well-being of all. To a large degree, this was accomplished through the performance of religious ritual. Over time, these ritual celebrations grew to include long chants, which came to be known as the Vedas, religious compositions that expressed the essential truths of Veda. The Vedas, composed more than three thousand years ago, are the earliest recorded expressions of the Indian tradition. They were, nonetheless, the product of a culture that was far older still.

The earliest evidence of urban civilization in India appeared more than five thousand years ago, and even that grew out of still older roots. Of course, history knows little of what was going on in those early days. Our historical knowledge of this emerging tradition starts with the Vedas, and it is thus with the Vedas that our study properly begins. But before we get to that, it would be valuable to go back and take a somewhat closer look at the background out of which the Vedas took form and that influenced them in many important ways. Most fundamental of all is the physical character of the Indian subcontinent—the stage, so to speak, on which the drama would take place. Accordingly, that is where we shall begin.

THE LAND OF INDIA

The huge subcontinent of India appears on the map to hang gracefully from the southern flank of Eurasia. Its generally triangular shape extends for a thousand miles into the Indian Ocean, dividing that sea into the Arabian Sea on the west and the Bay of Bengal to the east. Just off the southern tip of India, and almost connected to it by a land bridge, is the beautiful teardrop-shaped island of Sri Lanka. Called Ceylon for centuries, Sri Lanka has always been intimately connected geographically and culturally with India.

Approximately one-third the size of the United States, the Indian subcontinent is effectively isolated by geography from the rest of the Eurasian continent. In the south, India confronts the sea; in the north, it is divided from what lies beyond by the greatest system of mountains on Earth. The vast Himalayas and their associated ranges stretch out across the entire northern frontier from west to east. On a map, the northern mountains have the appearance of a great curtain draped gracefully across the entire reach of the Indian subcontinent. The mountains and the sea have defined India geographically and have, to a degree, isolated it from the rest of the world.

India has not always been a part of the Eurasian continent. Many millions of years ago, the continents were joined into one great landmass. At that time, India was an integral part of what would become both Africa and Antarctica. The ceaseless movement of the earth's crustal plates eventually broke loose the land we know as India, just as today the great rift system of East Africa is evidence that the slow process of plate movement is again separating another piece of that continent from the mainland.

Over millions of years the India plate moved in a generally northeastward direction, eventually colliding with the southern side of Eurasia. There were no great mountains then, but as the India plate relentlessly tunneled under the Eurasian plate, the land began to rise. In time, the high plateau of Tibet took form. The leading edge of what had once been a low coastal plain was eventually thrust as much as thirty thousand feet into the sky. Over the ages, the forces of erosion have sculpted this geology into the magnificent chain of mountains we know as the Himalaya, which literally means "house of snow."

Where there are great mountains, there are great rivers. Many rivers flow out of the northern mountains. Eventually, they merge into two great river systems. In the west is the Indus system, from which India derives its name. Several rivers gather in the northwest to form the Indus, which then flows to the south, emptying into the Arabian Sea near the modern city of Karachi. In modern times, the Indus flows mostly within the nation of Pakistan.

The other great river system is the Ganges, "Ganga" as the people of India call it. The Ganges gathers several major tributaries and flows in a generally eastward direction across the north of India, finally meeting the sea not far from the modern city of Calcutta. For more than 1,500 miles, this great river winds its way through the fertile plain of North India. It is in the enormous Ganges plain that most of the history and most of the people of India are to be found. The Ganges, "Mother Ganga," is a sacred river in the Hindu tradition. Along its banks are many hallowed sites in the history of Hinduism, including the holy city of Varanasi (formerly known as Benares).

The great Ganges basin is known to geographers as the North Indian Plain. South of it the land rises somewhat, becoming a hilly plateau that extends for a thousand miles, all the way to the southern tip of India. This plateau, which encompasses almost all of southern India, is called the Deccan. It rises gently in elevation from east to west, until it reaches the west coast, whereupon it erupts abruptly into a long line of low coastal mountains known as the Western Ghats.

India is, for the most part, a tropical country. It knows great heat. In the south the environment is lushly tropical and warm, but in the mountainous north a totally different environment is to be found. In fact, just about every kind of climate is to be found somewhere in India, but tropical heat is definitely the most common environment. From June to October, the wet monsoon winds from the south bring almost constant heavy rainfall to much of India. During the rest of the year, dry winds from the north are the rule.

After merging with Eurasia, India became an integral part of its geology. For millions and millions of years, this varied and beautiful subcontinent evolved in a perfect state of nature. Every conceivable kind of flora and fauna flourished in India—every kind but one; and in the course of time, that one, too, would come to India and establish itself there.

DRAVIDIAN INDIA

No one knows when the first of our human ancestors entered India. Over the ages, there must have been many waves of migrations. Eventually, a more or less stable human population took form. The original proto-Australoid population was largely supplanted or reduced to a subservient status by a later wave of lighter skinned people known to historians as the Dravidians. In time, the Dravidian languages and culture became dominant in most parts of India. Although Dravidian culture was undoubtedly made up of many discrete groupings, with different customs and languages, historians are still accustomed to lumping them all together, referring to these people simply as "the Dravidians."

Part of the reason for this is that—with the exception of one region—practically nothing is known about the life and history of these people. The Dravidians were a pre-literate people. There is no historical record to turn to. We can surmise that they lived out their lives close to the earth in small, widely dispersed communities. Apparently, they practiced a simple form of agriculture, undoubtedly supplemented by hunting and gathering. About their religious beliefs, their art, and their philosophy of life, we can only make wild guesses. We can be sure, though, that some of their religious beliefs and practices have left a large and permanent influence on Indian culture.

The one exception was indeed impressive. In the northwestern part of the subcontinent, in the Indus and associated river valleys, social evolution did not stagnate at the level of the small farming community. Here, urban life germinated. Genuine cities took form, with well-laid-out streets and strong defensive walls. Archaeologists are finding numerous urban sites, not only in the vicinity of the Indus and its tributaries, but also along the banks of the Sarasvati, east of the Indus. Now almost entirely dried up, the Sarasvati was a great river in ancient times and is mentioned prominently in the Vedas. Although not technically accurate, it is customary to lump all of these sites together, referring to the whole as Harappan civilization, or Indus valley civilization.

What is most exciting to the historian about these Indus valley cities is the time when they came into being: They were among the earliest in human history. Much is known about early civilization in the Tigris–Euphrates valley of Mesopotamia and in the nearby Nile valley of Egypt. City life and the accompanying elements of civilization had taken shape in these places before 3000 B.C.E. Archeological excavations in the Indus River Valley at such sites as Mohenjo-Daro and Harappa are now revealing that early civilization in the Indus valley was contemporaneous with those of Mesopotamia and Egypt. Mesopotamia is often referred to as the "cradle of civilization"; Egypt joined it in the cradle very early on. We are now discovering that there was a third baby in that cradle: the early civilization of the Indus valley.

The excavations at Mohenjo-Daro and Harappa give us a fascinating glimpse into the culture of these people—but only a glimpse. They possessed a pictographic form of writing, but it resists being deciphered. Nevertheless, some things are clear. Their cities, constructed mostly of mud brick, were marvels of engineering. They were especially clever in the technology of water management, with municipal drainage systems that surpassed anything the world would see again until Roman times. The streets were broad, paved with brick, and laid out in a grid fashion that divided the city into an efficient pattern of blocks. It seems that the standard of living was generally high. Many decorative pieces have been recovered from these sites. A few of them suggest yogic themes that would become important later on in Indian history. It is tempting to speculate that, even though the cities of the Indus valley civilization were eventually deserted and forgotten, some important parts of the spiritual legacy lived on in the ages that followed.

It is a sad fact of history that this exciting and promising beginning in the Indus valley came finally to a dead end. Civilization in the Middle East continued to grow, flourish, and spread, but in the Indus valley it declined, and by the middle of the second millennium B.C.E. it was reduced to rubble. There are many possible explanations for this decline and death. One of the more plausible theories concerns the slow, but relentless, destruction of the natural environment by the generations of people who lived in these cities and towns. As the population continuously grew, and the resources of the environment were plundered without being restored, the time must eventually have come when urban life would no longer have been tenable. Sound familiar?

We do not know for certain what caused the disappearance of the Indus valley cities. Their demise may have been due entirely to natural causes. Or, possibly, warfare may have been the cause. One popular theory holds that the *coup de grâce* may have been delivered by nomadic invaders from the north. This theory, known as the theory of the "Aryan Conquest," holds that relatively fair-skinned invaders, referred to by historians as Aryans, migrated into India in successive waves during the early part of the second millennium B.C.E. Eventually, their numbers became a force great enough to overwhelm and plunder the cities of the Indus valley and, beyond that, to conquer and subdue all of North India. According to this theory, it was these conquering people—the Aryans—who created the Vedas.

Although highly speculative, the theory of the Aryan Conquest has been widely popular since its inception in the early nineteenth century. It originated in the field of linguistic studies. As mentioned earlier, the Vedas were composed in the ancient language known as Sanskrit. Those who created the Vedas referred to themselves as "Arya," a Sanskrit word loosely translated into English as "noble." They were the noble ones—members of the ruling class within the feudal structure of the time.

When, in the late eighteenth century, European scholars began serious study of Indian culture and history, they made the startling discovery that strong affinities exist among the Sanskrit language of ancient India, classical languages such as Latin and Greek, and many modern languages, including English. It became apparent that a large "family" of languages exists that stretches from India and parts of the Middle East all the way across Europe. This group came to be known as the Indo-European language family, or the Indo-Aryan language family. The word *Aryan*, in this case, referred to the nomadic source people whose migrations had carried the root language to such widely separated places.

Belief in the existence of a nomadic source people, the "carriers" of the root Aryan language, became an article of faith among Western scholars in the nineteenth century. Out of this was born the concept of the "Aryan Conquest," a theory fashioned to explain the origins of the Sanskrit (Aryan) language in India, and the subsequent development of Hindu civilization, beginning with the creation of the Vedas.

The theory of the Aryan Conquest was basically unchallenged for more than a century. Today it is very much challenged; indeed, the whole field is full of controversy. Owing to its long dominance, though, and the fact that it is still widely accepted, it would be appropriate for us to briefly examine the character of the theory of the Aryan Conquest. Following that, we will look into modern theories that seek to replace it.

THE THEORY OF THE ARYAN CONQUEST

If you look at a map of the Eurasian continent, you will notice that the centers of urban civilization hang around the periphery of the continent like large jewels on a necklace: Europe, the Middle East, India, Southeast Asia, and the Far Eastern world of China, Korea, and Japan. The interior of the continent, the part that physically connects these different culture areas, is a vast expanse of forest, grassland, desert, and great mountains. This has been the traditional homeland of nomadic peoples who from time to time have launched incursions into the various civilized areas. Such incursions have, of course, seemed violent and destructive to their victims, but from the serene view of history, we can see that it hasn't been all bad: The barbarous newcomers have stimulated change and added vigorous new blood.

The western part of central Eurasia was the homeland of the Aryans. This is a vast and ill-defined area. On a map, we can locate it generally as the region north of the Black and Caspian Seas. It is wide-open, "big sky" country: endlessly rolling grasslands broken only occasionally by rivers and streams. This is believed to be the setting in which the Aryans developed. They were a Caucasian people whose distant ancestors had first migrated to the grasslands north of the mountains as the last great ice sheet slowly retreated. Probably, they were simply following herds that moved farther and farther north. Climate changes opened up a new world to the north, which they readily moved into and exploited.

The way of life of the Aryan people was essentially pastoral. Although it would appear that they raised a little barley from time to time, agriculture was not to their liking; they preferred the nomadic lifestyle following the herds. In time they came to possess herds of their own. The Aryans were horse breeders—which would give them a tremendous advantage in later struggles—and they raised cattle. Wealth was measured in horses and cattle. This way of life bred a strong and hardy people.

Although rough and simple by later standards, the language of the Aryans would become the root mother tongue of a large number of modern languages stretching from Europe through parts of the Middle East to India. As mentioned, these languages are sometimes collectively referred to as the Indo-European, or Indo-Aryan, language family. One interesting result of this relationship is that many words in European languages have similar-sounding "cousins" (cognates) in the languages of India. The explanation for the linguistic ties is to be found in the fact that the nomadic Aryans began migrating all over the map, eventually reaching lands very distant from their ancestral homeland in the steppes of central Eurasia.

For a thousand years, slow-moving waves of Aryan migrations rolled out into the regions adjoining the ancestral herding lands. Later migrants would often push the descendants of earlier ones further on. Wave after wave filled all of the European subcontinent. The Greeks of ancient times were of Aryan descent; so, too, were the Romans, and the Celts, and the Slavs, and the Germanic people.* Other Aryan peoples moved south through the mountain passes into Asia Minor and the high plateau of Iran and Afghanistan. (*Iran* is, in fact, a variant of the word *Aryan*.) Where possible, they continued the old herding way of life. Where it was not possible, they adapted to the new conditions. It was from the Persian–Afghan highlands (*Persian* is an alternative term for *Iranian*) that bands of Aryan horsemen would have invaded India. Their route would undoubtedly have followed the Khyber Pass, that famous pass through the Hindu Kush Mountains that has witnessed the passage of so many would-be conquerors over the ages.

When the Aryans had to fight for possession of new land, they proved themselves to be most formidable. They had a number of advantages in a fight. They were, to begin with, a very hardy people, used to a rough and simple life. The kin group structure of Aryan society gave them a ready-made military organization and a rough-and-ready chain of command. They had the horse and could put their mobility to good advantage. Men did not ride on the backs of horses until much later; rather, the Aryan warriors harnessed the horse—often two horses—to a lightweight two-wheeled chariot. Two men rode in the chariot. One was the highly skilled driver. The other—with both hands free for fighting—attacked the enemy with the deadly fire of his bow and arrows.

---

*Adolf Hitler and his followers temporarily gave the word *Aryan* a very bad connotation, due to their misunderstanding and misuse of it.

The Aryans loved the bow; they preferred it to the sword, the lance, or any other type of weapon. To an Aryan warrior, his bow was a close friend, and he gave it a name. Arjuna, the hero of the *Bhagavad Gita*, referred to his miraculous bow as "Gandiva." From the *Rig Veda*, the earliest work composed by the Aryans in India, come these stirring words:

> With Bow let us win the contest and violent battles.
> The Bow ruins the enemy's pleasures;
> With Bow let us conquer all the corners of the world.
>
> She comes all the way up to your ear
> Like a woman who wishes to whisper something,
> Embracing her dear friend.
>
> Humming like a woman,
> The bowstring stretched tight on the bow
> Carries you safely across in the battle.[1]

These, then, were the Aryans. According to the theory of the Aryan Conquest, it is reasonable to conclude that by sometime around 1800 B.C.E. their far-flung migrations reached as far as the northwestern corner of the Indian subcontinent. The early arrivals, few in number, must not have seemed very threatening, but the lure of the rich and populous land of India would have been a powerful magnet to the Aryans.

According to the traditional view, over time the original trickle of Aryan invaders grew to become a torrent. The Harappan cities and towns of the Indus Valley, already well into their years of decline, must have been among the first conquests of the Aryan warriors. There is some evidence that the Indian armies would have been able to mount a strong defense, but the Aryans, with their war chariots and death-dealing arrows, were too much for them. The Aryans may have swept onto the scene in much the same fashion as would their distant descendants, the Vikings, 2,500 years later.

According to the theory of the Aryan Conquest, the Aryans moved eastward from the Indus Valley into the great Ganges plain of North India. Presumably, they would have followed the great river courses that eventually merged in the Ganges itself. Here the scattered agricultural population would have been no match at all for the invaders. Surely they would have tried as best they could to defend their homes, but the most they could hope for was to slow down the advance. The conquest of the Indian lands was a campaign spread over at least a full century. Several generations of Aryan warriors were involved before it all was over. But the broad picture is one of an invincible Aryan horde pushing relentlessly through the entire range of the Indus and Ganges valleys, plundering and conquering everything in its path.

By the time the dust finally settled, sometime around 1500 B.C.E., the human character of India was changed forever. The invaders from the north had succeeded in conquering and imposing their rule on the native people of much of the subcontinent. Much, but not all—the Aryans never really penetrated very far into the Deccan, the vast region south of the Ganges basin. It is widely believed that even to this day the Indians of the far south are the direct descendants of the pre-Aryan native people.

Again, let it be stated that, according to this theory, the Aryan conquest of India was not a unified affair. The Aryans broke up into units based on their tribal relationships. The various tribes carved out domains for themselves, the map of North India became a vast patchwork of independent little kingdoms of different sizes, and before long, as you might expect, they were fighting among themselves. But the first order of business after the conquest was complete was the construction of a new and stable social order.

Like the Spanish in Latin America, the conquering Aryans inserted themselves at the top of the social order. They were the warrior ruling class. They controlled all power, all wealth, all land, and even the lives of the native people whom they had conquered. Like feudal aristocrats, the Aryans lorded it over the native people, who, in the eyes of the Aryans, became merely a population of laborers to be exploited.

But things weren't quite that simple. For one thing, the native Indian people existed in vast numbers, and they were engaged in many different kinds of work, some of which were considered to be of higher status than others. The Aryans wanted a rigid social order where everything was in its place and their own place was securely at the top. This was achieved for all time by the creation of the caste system. (The word *caste* rhymes with *fast*.) The Sanskrit word for caste is *varna*. At the top of the caste system were the Aryans, the arya-varna. Below the Aryans were the dasa-varna, the vastly more numerous conquered people.

This, then, is the essential argument of the theory of the Aryan Conquest. It remained the unchallenged explanation of the origins of the Sanskrit language and the rise of Hindu civilization for more than a century. In more recent times, the theory of the Aryan Conquest has been strongly challenged by scholars who believe that no such series of events ever occurred. Those who support the revised interpretation (which may be called the "Diffusion Theory") argue that not only is there no solid evidence for an Aryan Conquest, but there also is no logical need for it. The rise of the Sanskrit language in North India during the second millennium B.C.E. can best be explained through linguistic and cultural diffusion, a common process occurring in all historical eras.

Supporters of the Diffusion Theory argue that the theory of the Aryan Conquest was born of nineteenth-century European ethnocentrism. However appealing this explanation may have been to nineteenth-century Westerners, it simply isn't true. As David Frawley comments, "The Indo-Aryan invasion as an academic concept in eighteenth- and nineteenth-century Europe reflected the cultural milieu of the period. Linguistic data were used to validate the concept that in turn was used to interpret archaeological and anthropological data."[2]

For one thing, these indigenous people, far from being uncivilized "lesser" beings, had created one of the world's earliest urban cultures, as we have seen. Excavations at Mohenjo-Daro and other sites in the Indus Valley reveal that this Indus Civilization, evidence of which stretches back to at least 3000 B.C.E., was the equal of early civilizations in Mesopotamia and Egypt. Quite obviously, the native ability to create the works of civilization was present in the Indian people themselves. There was, in other words, no need for hypothetically more advanced northerners to enter India and do the work of creating the Vedas: The indigenous people of India were quite up to the task themselves. The North Indian ruling class had adopted the word *Arya* (the noble ones) to identify themselves, and it was they who created the Vedas:

> The descendents of the Aryans—the Hindus—have no memory whatsoever of having invaded India! There is no record of such an invasion in the ancient scriptures of the Hindus, nor in those of non-Vedic religions like Jainism and Buddhism. The most archaic document in any Indo-European tongue—the *Rig Veda* composed in an early form of Sanskrit—does not look back on a homeland outside India.[3]

Still, even if linguistic diffusion, at least among the feudal ruling class, is the way Sanskrit and Hindu civilization actually spread, how did the process begin in the first place? Even supporters of the Diffusion Theory will allow that some incursion by Aryan invaders was a historical possibility. Perhaps there actually was an "Aryan Conquest" of sorts, limited to only a relatively small region in the far northwestern part of the subcontinent. Such an event is easy to imagine: Many would-be conquerors have invaded India through the mountain passes of the northwest. Some have held land for a time, but their conquests have tended to be short lived in history. Eventually, the region would be reabsorbed into the North Indian environment, although some influences of the invaders might linger on. Aryan northerners may have accomplished something like this and in that way might have initiated a process of linguistic and cultural diffusion. Such a conquest, though, is a far cry from the exaggerated claims of the traditional Aryan Conquest theory. Prasad Gokhale, writing in "Antiquity and Continuity of Indian History," argues that "The unobservant reading of the *Rig Veda* and its subsequent misinterpretation led to the doctrines of 'class' and 'color' struggles among the ancient Indians; an appropriate tool to justify Marxist ideals and European racial theories. . . . As opposed to any racial connotation, the word 'arya' is a honorific title and was used for people who were cultivated in mind and character."[4]

The Diffusion Theory, however reasonable it may be, is based largely on conjecture. Clearly, this subject offers a fertile field for future research. And so it goes: Determining historical truth is a never-ending and always-changing challenge. Perhaps the truth will be found to lie somewhere between the two extremes, a viewpoint taken by the noted British anthropologist Colin Renfrew: "Renfrew considers the possibility that actual history can be explainable by a combination of both hypotheses: while proto-Indo-European speakers may have been a prominent presence in Anatolia, Iran, and northern India prior to the rise of the great civilizations, there also may have been later invasions of the civilized areas by Indo-European nomadic tribes."[5]

Whatever the case may be, some things seem to be beyond controversy. Following the decline of the Indus valley cities, Indian culture underwent profound changes, and out of these changes, including the rise of the Sanskrit language, the historical social order took form. *Varna*, the caste system, would become its most defining element.

VARNA: THE CASTE SYSTEM

The entire population of the Indian subcontinent came to be organized into a vast hierarchy of castes, each caste determined by the kind of work that a particular family engaged in. Over time, the system grew to include literally thousands of separate castes. Every conceivable kind of work came to be a caste unto itself, and the members of that caste, wherever they lived, inherited an exclusive monopoly in that area of work.

The caste was much more than just an economic thing—an area of work. The caste was economic, religious, political, and social; it was a little world unto itself. One's whole life was bound up in the caste. All marriages were arranged by the family, and only among other families within one's caste. The men performed the work of the caste and no other work; there was no such thing as social mobility. The concept of "bettering oneself" was unknown and would have seemed absurd. The only way to move to a higher caste was to die and be reborn in it, and that was believed to be guaranteed only to those who accepted the present life and did the best they could.

Varna, the caste system, certainly encouraged a stagnant and inflexible social order, but there are some positive things to be said about it. For one thing, it guaranteed a very stable social order. The individual, though presumably lacking the excitement of a more independent life, at least was spared its anxieties as well. No one had to worry about the future, which was all laid out for a person from the time he or she was born. There was no anxiety about finding the right job, the right spouse, or the right kind of home. The caste system sank deep roots in India. Although discrimination due to caste is against the provisions of the constitution of India, the tradition continues as it always has in many parts of the country, especially in rural areas.

In some fundamental way, the caste system probably grew from very ancient Dravidian roots. The caste hierarchy came to be organized into certain large "families" of castes. At the bottom of the pyramid, and by far the most numerous, were the *Shudras*, the caste engaged in tilling the land; its members were essentially reduced to a class of landless serfs. Theirs was a life of never-ending toil in the heat and dust of land that belonged to feudal overlords. It should be noted, though, that there was a class even lower than the Shudras: the *pariahs*, so low that they were not even considered a caste. Presumably derived from the original proto-Australoid population, they lived like slaves, doing only the filthiest work. Because they were regarded as being unclean, and not born into a legitimate caste, pariahs were not allowed to enter Hindu temples and in some places were forbidden even to come into the villages during the daytime. There is some evidence that this class had already existed in their suppressed state in Dravidian times.

Above the Shudras were the *Vaishyas*, a family of castes, vast in number, that made up all of the craft and trade occupations. These families often resided in towns instead of farming communities. Every occupation you can think of—from candle maker, to wheelwright, to harness maker—was to be found in one of the Vaishya castes. Here, too, the hierarchy persisted: Each caste had its niche, its place on the great stairway that led from lower to higher. The families of the warrior class made up the *Kshatriya* caste. They held themselves aloof and jealously guarded their superior status; they were the lords. They ruled their domains like an armed feudal nobility.

One part of the population was special—very special. This group of families was the highest of all of the castes, higher even than the Kshatriyas. These were the *Brahmins*, and no one except the gods were above them. The reason for their lofty status was that the Brahmins were the priests. They were man's link to the gods, and the entire society depended on them.

THE BRAHMIN CASTE

The consolidation of the Brahmin caste is an example of the kind of development that takes form within virtually every early human culture. A special group of individuals, call them priests or shamans, become the custodians of the sacred rites and traditions of the community. Seen through coldly practical modern eyes, these individuals might seem to be rather like parasites; they are neither fighters nor producers, and yet they are held in the highest esteem. In all cultures, they have been supported, protected, and honored. Why? What is it that makes this special class so special? What do they *do* for the community that the others can't do perfectly well for themselves? Let's take a moment to look at this question.

The men and women of an early society—such as the early Hindu society—would be acutely aware of the play of the forces of nature in their daily lives. By necessity, these people lived "close to nature." Unlike those of us who enjoy the way of life of modern times, they would have been acutely aware of how much they were at the mercy of the natural environment. Sometimes things went well: The weather was fair and the food supply abundant; sometimes things did not go well at all.

Perhaps it was the very fact that men and women of earlier times possessed some small amount of control over nature that made them aware of how much more they did not control. But—and here is the critically important point—they would inevitably conclude that *somebody* did possess that control!

Why make this assumption? Consider how the forces of nature operate. Seen from the grand view, they are not chaotic and unpredictable. On the large scale, nature operates with great order and regularity. Patterns are the rule, not the exception, and from them comes the predictability without which there could be no science. The sun always rises in the east and moves, with a certain predictability, throughout the daily cycle. So, too, for the moon, the tides, the seasons, and the life cycle of all things. Deer produce baby deer, and ducks produce baby ducks. A deer never gives birth to a duck, and the sun never rises in the west.

The point is that the regularity and predictability of the operations of the forces of nature can be seen to imply a grand order that simply cannot be explained by the working of blind chance. Modern science may take a different view, but to the minds of thinking men and women of the distant past, order in nature implied, of necessity, an order giver. Thus, out of the fertile human imagination were born the gods.

In this view, a god is simply a being who, by common consent, is responsible for the operation of any one or more of the forces of nature. There will be a god for rain, a god for wind, a god for the Sun, a god for the Moon, a god for birth, a god for death, and so on. In a fully developed pantheon, there must be some god for every one of the myriad forces of nature. The "person" of the god need not be conceived to be in human form: Very often, the god was imagined in the form of some animal whose character suggested the particular power of the god—a hawk, for example, to guide a celestial body, or a snake, whose ability to molt suggested renewed life. But of course, many of the gods—especially the most powerful—were created in the image and likeness of man.

And even the gods need a place to live. Befitting their lofty status, a mountaintop would do very nicely. The Greeks of ancient times lodged their gods on the summit of Mount Olympus; their contemporaries in India chose a mythical mountain named Mount Meru. That there are many similarities between the Greeks and the Hindus should come as no surprise, since both peoples are presumed to be descended from the same original Aryan source population. Though distant in geography, they are both members of what is called the Indo-Aryan (or Indo-European) language family.

So, in the worldview of ancient India, nature was organized into a vast hierarchy, an analogue of Mount Meru itself. At the bottom of the order was the world of brute animals, which had a hierarchy within themselves, ranging from the simplest creatures to the greatest, such as cattle and monkeys. Next came the world of human beings. The caste system with its myriad gradations was the reflection of the natural hierarchy among men. At the top of the worldly pyramid were the gods, who also were organized into greater and lesser. The very greatest of the gods were analogous to the tip of the pyramid, the summit of Mount Meru.

From Mount Meru, the immortal gods ruled their domain, each one manipulating that aspect of the natural order over which he or she held power. What they did they did for their own reasons; they were incomparably greater than the miserable creatures beneath them, from which they remained serenely aloof. At least this would seem to be the logical state of affairs in the early part of the story.

The difference between gods and humans was as great as the difference between human beings and insects. Consider, for example, the relationship between ants and ourselves. It is not that we despise ants, nor do we want them to suffer. It's just that we regard ants to be so far below us that we tend to ignore them; we're unconcerned about the affairs of their daily lives. But we may assume that the affairs of their daily lives are as important to them as ours are to us. We may assume that they do not feel indifferent when a great rainstorm threatens to flood their nest. At the risk of sounding a bit silly, I would like to continue this analogy in order to make the point.

If it were somehow possible for the ant colony to make contact with you—suppose that a certain few had learned how to send a message in Morse code—would you continue to remain aloof and uninterested in their affairs? Not likely. Most likely, you would be glad to use your powers to help them out in a time of need, especially if they were very nice about the way they asked for help. Presumably, they could persuade you to go out and cover their nest during a downpour.

Men, like ants, were by and large at the mercy of the forces of nature. The gods controlled the forces of nature and all too often seemed to be unconcerned about the effects on the lives of human communities. If only there were a way; if only there were a way to somehow make contact with the gods and persuade them to use their powers over the forces of nature in ways that would be beneficial to mankind—or, at the very least, to exercise their powers to prevent the worst disasters. If only this were possible, men could be free at last from the tyranny of fear. But how? Enter the priests.

The Brahmins were the priests. It was their job to make contact with the gods. So long as they succeeded in making contact and getting the desired results reasonably often, it is easy to see why they would be held in such high esteem. Their importance was second to none, and, of course, the great majority of their contemporaries did not question whether the Brahmins were in fact able to establish contact with the gods. It is what the people *believed* that counts; belief, not necessarily truth, is what inspires action. So how did the Brahmins make contact? What did the people see them do that accounts for this great faith in their abilities?

As in virtually all early societies, sacrifice was seen to be the reasonable way of attracting the attention of the gods. An offering was made to the gods, often consumed by fire so that the smoke could carry the gift to the heavens. Surrounding the performance of the sacrifice would be a ritual of some kind, which in time would become enshrined in tradition. Over the centuries, the Brahmins, too, evolved a great body of such tradition. There were appropriate rituals for everything imaginable.

Ritual, therefore, correctly performed, became the operative tool by means of which the Brahmins would make the all-important contact with the gods and persuade them to exercise their powers on the community's behalf. It's no wonder that the performance of sacrificial ritual came to be a matter of obsessive interest among these people.

But what gave real power—real, sacred power—to the ritual ceremony were the prayers spoken by the Brahmin priests. Throughout the entire ceremony, the priests would loudly and passionately call upon the gods to witness and accept the sacrifice, to hear their prayers. Such prayers were designed to be sung or chanted in a long and repetitious fashion. These sacred chants constituted the real lifeblood of the ritual.

Over the centuries, the most beloved of the sacred chants were preserved in great collections that were committed to memory by the Brahmins and passed on from generation to generation. These collections came to be known as the Vedas, which laid out the prescription for the correct performance of ritual and also the correct way of addressing the gods. The Brahmins created the Vedas, and the Brahmins used the Vedas to establish their all-important connection with the gods.

Notes

1. Wendy D. O'Flaherty, trans., The *Rig Veda* (London: Penguin Classics, 1981), copyright © Wendy Doniger O'Flaherty, 1981. Reproduced by permission of Penguin Books Ltd. RV: VI.75.
2. David Frawley, *The Myth of the Aryan Invasion* (New Delhi: Voice of India, 1994), p. 50.
3. Georg Feuerstein and others, *In Search of the Cradle of Civilization* (Wheaton, IL: Quest, 1995), p. 156.
4. Gokhale Prasad, "Antiquity and Continuity of Indian History" (article appearing on the World Wide Web, April 1997).
5. Quoted in Feuerstein and others, p. 55.

Study Questions

1. What gives historical significance to Mohenjo-Daro and Harappa? What was the cause of their decline and disappearance?
2. What is the nature of the controversy over the role of the Aryans in the development of Indian culture? What is your own conclusion regarding this issue?
3. How did the Brahmins presume to make contact with the gods?
4 What does it mean to say that Mount Meru was an analogue of all of Nature?

2

The Vedas

VEDA AND THE VEDAS

As mentioned in Chapter 1, the word *Veda* is derived from the Sanskrit root *vid*, which means "to know" (which, incidentally, is also the root of such English words as "vision" and "video"). Specifically, *Veda* refers to supreme, god-given knowledge.

Ordinary truth emerges from the practical experience of the community—the stuff of daily life. It is added to by everyone over time. Veda, on the other hand, concerned matters of great moral and religious importance—the meaning of life and death, for example, and man's proper relationship to the gods. Veda was divinely inspired knowledge. By way of analogy, we could say that in a Jewish or Christian community, knowledge about weather forecasting would be ordinary truth, but the Bible would be Veda.

The truth of Veda was given expression in the ritual chants known collectively as the Vedas. *Veda*, then, is Truth itself; the *Vedas*—the sacred hymns chanted by the Brahmin priests at ritual events—were the means by which the truth of Veda was given concrete expression in words.

It is likely that the roots of what would become the Vedas stretch far back into the distant past of the Indian people, long before the Sanskrit language appeared on the scene. As the Vedic tradition matured, undoubtedly various practices of both Aryans and Dravidians came to be combined in the Vedas. Members of the Brahmin caste were the sole guardians and interpreters of the Vedas. Brahmins alone managed the great events at which the Vedas were sung, events that were intended to result in a coming together of gods and men.

The Vedas took form during the earliest historical period following the spread of the Aryan language, roughly between the years 1500 and 1000 B.C.E. This historical era is called the *Vedic Age*. With very few exceptions, the Vedas were produced by members of the Brahmin class and, in particular, by an elite group of holy men referred to as *rishis*. A rishi is a seer, an especially learned holy man who has become the teacher of others. An unusually brilliant rishi is called a *maharishi* (literally, a "great teacher").

The Vedas were organized into four great collections, among which there is much similarity. Still, each of the four has its own general emphasis. The earliest, and by far the most significant, is the *Rig Veda*, a long and loosely organized collection of hymns and chants associated with sacrifices to the various gods. *Rig* comes from the Sanskrit root *rc*, which means simply "to praise" or "to shine." Composition of the *Rig Veda* probably began as early as 1500 B.C.E.

When completed, the *Rig Veda* consisted of 1,028 separate sections usually referred to as hymns. Each hymn was a long collection of verses meant to be sung or chanted aloud. The hymns were in turn organized into ten megasections called *mandalas*. This kind of organization was an aid to memorizing, much needed before the advent of writing. All verses quoted in the sections that follow have been taken from the *Rig Veda*.

The groundwork for the great sacrificial rituals was laid down in the *Rig Veda*, but it was followed in time by other Vedas. Two other Vedas closely associated with the *Rig Veda* were the *Sama Veda* and the *Yajur Veda*. In the *Sama Veda*, certain verses of the *Rig Veda* were arranged for chanting in the form of song. The *Yajur Veda* was essentially a collection of formulas and instructions concerned with the correct arrangement of the ritual. It was essential that everything be done correctly.

The fourth of the Vedas is the *Atharva Veda*. It stands apart from the other three and was composed considerably later than they were. The *Atharva Veda* is concerned mainly with magic formulas, spells, and mystical incantations. It is widely believed that pre-Aryan Dravidian traditions are "peeking through" in the *Atharva Veda*. Nonetheless, it, too, came to be part of the great sacrifice rituals, and a priest called the Atharvan had the role of incorporating the appropriate chants from this Veda.

Thus, the Vedas—Rig, Sama, Yajur, and Atharva—provided the Brahmin priests with all the sacred verses they needed to conduct the great rituals of sacrifice properly. The Vedas were their link to the gods, and in the Vedas, the gods are praised endlessly. (It sometimes gets a bit monotonous to the modern reader.) But behind all the praise, of course, is the real point of it all: the request.

Let's not lose sight of what this grand ritual was all about. The gods had something the people wanted—power over the forces of nature—and the Vedic rituals were the people's instrument for getting the gods to use that power in the "right" way. But we must not assume that men and women of the Vedic Age were a dismal lot, living in a state of constant worry. On the contrary, they seem to have been an optimistic, energetic people. They worshipped the gods in order to maximize the good things of life. True, they knew the weight of fear, and they prayed for freedom from illness and drought, but most of the time they were beseeching the gods for long life, success in battle, lots of healthy children, the pleasures of wealth, and abundant food and drink— those sorts of things. The overall impression one obtains is of a people who enjoyed life and wanted to get the most out of it.

The Vedas passed from generation to generation in the grand oral tradition. The art of writing did not enter India until after the beginning of the first millenium B.C.E., but even after the introduction of writing, initiates to the Brahmin priesthood would have continued to commit to memory the entire corpus of the Vedas. We can be thankful, though, that the Vedas were eventually written down: Without the written record, this study would not be possible.

If the Vedas were nothing more than lengthy collections of prayers and formulas for ritual sacrifice, they would be of only passing interest to us. But our concern is to examine the evolution of a philosophical tradition in India, and it is with the Vedas that it all begins. True, for the most part, the Vedas are not concerned with what we would call philosophical matters: They are clearly religious works. But they are not entirely religious: Threaded throughout the Vedas are questions and speculations that are like the seeds from which the lush garden of Hindu thought would later grow. In other words, the Vedas are "square one."

THE VEDIC FIRE SACRIFICE

Our modern way of life is so scrubbed clean of ritual that it is difficult for us to imagine what life was like in earlier times when practically everything involved some sort of ritual. Vedic society, like most ancient cultures, was seemingly obsessed with ritual. There were ritual-laden ceremonies for virtually everything of significance: for coming of age, for marriage, for death, for planting the crops, for going to war, for preparing food, and on and on. Ritual touched just about everything. The head of the family might officiate at minor rituals, but really important rituals were reserved for the Brahmin priests.

For sheer drama and excitement, nothing could have surpassed the great ceremony of a ritual sacrifice. In a time of crisis, or perhaps on the occasion of some special celebration—when one or more of the gods was to be approached directly—the Brahmin priests could put together a thrilling event. A great bonfire was almost certainly a part of these ceremonies, and therefore it is customary to refer to such an event as a Vedic Fire Sacrifice.

The place where the sacrifice was to occur was holy ground, a special piece of land presumably set apart from the living area of the community. There the Brahmins would begin by carefully laying out a great _mandala_ on the ground. A mandala is any design that starts with a point or empty circle at its hub and then builds out from there in concentric layers of geometric shapes. A rose is a simple example of a mandala. The mandalas used by the Brahmins were considered sacred, with the complex forms full of symbolism and mystic associations. Many other cultures, including the Native American, have used mandalas in connection with religious celebrations.

The creation of the mandala would begin with a simple wooden stake being driven into the ground. The _Rig Veda_ informs us that this stake would then be anointed and adorned with colorful ornaments. From this anointed center—this fulcrum—a great circle perhaps a hundred feet in diameter would be etched into the ground. Everything inside the circle would be part of the mandala—sacred ground that only the Brahmin priests could enter. The circle, together with all of the other lines that made up the mandala, was highlighted with colored sand or earth.

A very basic mandala—to give you an idea of the kind of work the people who made them did—could be constructed by inscribing a square inside the circle and then two intersecting triangles inside the square. The triangles would form a six-pointed star on their outer surface and a hexagon on the inner surface. A circle drawn inside the hexagon would form the hub of the mandala, and it was here that the sacred fire was built. The fire might be on a large altar constructed for the purpose, or it might be directly on the ground. Before the fire, the victim would be ritually sacrificed and its body hurled into the flames so that the spirit of the victim could be carried to the gods. There is some evidence that human sacrifice was practiced in the early days, but it would seem that it was not the usual form. Noblemen of the Vedic Age were horse-breeding people, and cattle-raisers. In their eyes, no sacrificial offering could be more valuable than a fine stallion or a bull. The ritual offering of a fine horse was common.

The event began with the lighting of the fire and the sounding of horns, which may well have been large conch shells. The priests then entered the mandala dressed in their ceremonial costumes, often including headdresses of antlers or bull's horns. The Brahmin who presided over the affair was called the *Hotri*. He was the high priest and was assisted by priests of lesser rank, including the *Udgatri*, who chanted verses from the *Sama Veda* and whose special function was to summon the gods to the celebration with the hypnotic beauty of the song. The Brahmins believed that certain musical tones held magical qualities. The *Udgatri* was skilled in droning in these tones for a very long time. Another priest, the *Adhvaryu*, held the responsibility for overseeing the whole production. In a sense, he was the stage manager, and as he went about his work, he chanted aloud verses from the *Yajur Veda*.

This was high drama—the great mandala marked out on the sacred ground, the huge roaring fire at the center, the Brahmin priests in their spectacular costumes, and the endless droning of the chants summoning the gods to the celebration. What a spectacle it must have been—and that, of course, is what it was all about: elevating consciousness from the mundane to the transcendental so as to make contact with the gods. It was the gods who held power over the forces of nature. Men lacked that power, but needed it. It was the job of the Brahmins to make contact with the gods and influence their use of power. Ritual sacrifice, prescribed in the Vedas, was the way to make that contact.

Soma

One more element in these rituals remains to be considered. The modern reader might find it somewhat shocking, but to the Vedic priests it was the all-important ingredient. It played a major part in virtualy all of their sacred rituals; they called it *soma*.

Soma was a drug, a powerful drug that produced states of ecstasy and of wildly expanded consciousness. We don't know for sure what it was. There are lots of clues in the Vedas, but nothing that pins it down for sure. Soma went out of use after the Vedic age, and the source plant may have become extinct. Modern research has focused on a variety of the fly agaric mushroom as the best candidate among still-existing possibilities. This fungus, although potentially quite poisonous, produces a compound similar to psilocybin and could very well have induced the states described in the Vedas.

Whatever it was, the Brahmin priests loved it—and so, too, according to them, did the gods. Liberal consumption of soma was a part of virtually every fire sacrifice. There was great ritual in its preparation as well as in its consumption, all of it lovingly detailed in the *Rig Veda*. The Brahmins alone were entitled to use soma, although some of the precious liquid was shared with the gods, presumably by being dripped into the fire.

Use of the soma plant probably predates the Aryans in India. Soma was not a domesticated plant; it grew wild in hilly or mountainous country. Apparently, it was gathered only at night, and according to some, only by the light of the full moon. The Indologist A. L. Herman describes the method of preparing soma:

> The plant was brought to the place where the soma ritual was to be carried out, and there it was washed and cleaned. Then the stalks of the plant were crushed in a stone mortar by a wooden pestle, and the bruised and crushed remains were laid between stones and pressed. As the pressing stones, or wooden boards, were brought together, the juices trickled out onto a cleansing sieve, usually lamb's wool. Next the juice was strained and, finally, consumed by the priest or priests. The priestly celebrants chanted exuberant hymns to the soma to accompany both the crushing and the pressing ceremonies, hymns which invited Indra to come to the sacrifice and partake of the sacred soma juice, and which ecstatically anticipated the drinking of the juice.[1]

Naturally, the soma plant was considered sacred, and the name was applied not only to the plant, but also to the god, Soma, who was the personification of the spirit of the plant. After a person drank the juice of the plant, the spirit temporarily inhabited the person, taking over his consciousness. The Brahmin priests were convinced that soma was a vehicle—*the* vehicle—that could take them spiritually to the place where contact with the gods was possible. In the incredible ecstasy of soma, they were themselves like gods; soma made it possible for them to share in the divine mode of being—or so they believed. Thus it was that soma became the heart of the ritual, the vital link between gods and men. Consider these verses from the *Rig Veda*:

> Drink thou of this [soma] . . . for power and rapture.
> The men, the pressing stones, the cows, the waters
> Have made this soma ready for thy drinking.[2]
>
> We have drunk soma . . .
> And in the wild raptures of the juice . . .
> We have become immortal;
> We have attained the light and discovered the Gods.[3]

Apparently, partaking of soma was not always an unmixed blessing: The bad trip was ever a worrisome possibility. The *Rig Veda* even seems to suggest the possibility of heart failure:

> Be kind and merciful to us, Soma;
> Be good to our heart, without confusing our powers in your whirlwind.
> King Soma, do not enrage us; do not terrify us;
> Do not wound our heart with your dazzling light.[4]

Soma became the *sine qua non* of the Vedic fire sacrifice. It produced ecstasy, and in this state of mind the Brahmin priest truly believed that he had achieved freedom from the mundane plane and had ascended temporarily to the realm of the gods:

> These glorious drops that give me freedom have I drunk.
> Closely they knit my joints as straps secure a chariot.
> The soma brings wild delight . . .
> In the wild joy of soma the Gods wrought their glorious deeds.[5]

These verses are but a small sampling of the almost endless paeans to the delights of soma found in the *Rig Veda*. So what are we to make of all of this? What was really going on at these gatherings of Brahmins?

One thing, I believe, is unarguable: The Brahmins did not take soma merely for the fun of it. No doubt they enjoyed it immensely, but to them it was a religious experience, not a social event. They were amazed beyond understanding that such an effect could be produced by consuming the juice of a simple little plant that grew wild in the hills. They reasonably concluded that the gods had infused the plant with a sacred nature—a spirit—and that that spirit could enter into them if they consumed the juice of the plant. They treated it with the greatest respect and limited its use solely to the sacred ceremony. In this they were much like other cultures, such as the Native Americans of the U.S. Southwest, who use peyote for certain ritual purposes. The Brahmin priests believed that soma produced a state of mind in which they could commune directly with the gods. After all, that was their job.

After the Vedic age the use of soma declined, and eventually it died out altogether in India. Men became interested in other ways of achieving transcendent consciousness. Whether or not the Vedic priests really spoke to the gods is not the point; they believed that they did, and in connection with that belief they created a vast corpus of ritual prayer that was passed on from generation to generation. They called this corpus Veda—sacred knowledge—and it is the solid foundation stone from which the tradition of Indian thought would grow.

All of this drama was designed to attract the attention of the gods and make contact with them. So who were these gods who were such important characters in the lives of men and women of Vedic times? We turn next to a brief consideration of the major deities addressed in the Vedas.

THE VEDIC PANTHEON

Hindu mythology is an incredibly complex subject. It recognizes a vast number of gods and goddesses, and their many stories are convoluted almost beyond imagining. But that fascinating story is not the subject of this study. Here, we simply introduce some of the major deities, ones that are prominently mentioned in the Vedas, and we include a sampling of pertinent verses from the *Rig Veda*.

In The Beginning

In the beginning was the One, the Ultimate Reality, which took the form of a golden cosmic egg, or embryo. The embryo became the earth and the sky, the most fundamental dual aspects of the one reality.

The earth was personified as Prithivi, the mother of all, and the broad and luminous sky was personified as Dyaus, the male counterpart of Prithivi, whose name is derived from the Sanskrit root *div*, which means "to shine." From Dyaus and Prithivi were born the gods and all other living beings, including humankind.

So we see that at this most fundamental level the dual character of nature, male and female, is honored in the personifications of earth and sky, which were not regarded as being distinct. Rather, the earth and sky were said to be like two hemispheres that were joined at the horizon to become one whole. The underlying unity of the two was often expressed by joining the two names together into one: Dyausaprithivi.

Mount Meru

Mount Meru, the mythical golden mountain, was the splendid dwelling place of the gods of India. When the gods were not engaged in some grand adventure, they relaxed in their golden and ivory palaces at the summit of Mount Meru, which was regarded as being the center of the universe.

Mount Meru was much more than just an abode for the gods: It was the analogue par excellence for the hierarchical order of nature. The Brahmins did not see the world around them as a chaotic mélange. On the contrary, they saw an inner order expressed in everything. In their eyes, creation took the form of a vast hierarchy. Everything that exists could be assigned to its proper place on the ladder of perfection. This ladder—or better yet, staircase—ranged step by endless step from the lowest of living things to the highest of the gods.

Seen in this way, Mount Meru is an analogue of the hierarchy of all creation. The gods occupy the highest part of the mountain because they are the most perfect beings. Mankind is lower down, near the base. And the roots of the mountain that stretch down into the earth are associated with the world of brute animals. Altogether, the mountain is whole and perfect; everything in creation has its place.

Visualized from above, Mount Meru is the universal mandala. The summit of the mountain is the perfect center of the mandala. Naturally, that is where the gods are to be found. Everything ranges out from that center, becoming less perfect as distance from the center increases. Not only was the entire world (universe) seen to be a reflection of Mount Meru, but so was every individual thing in the world. The human body, for example, was itself regarded as a perfect analogue of Mount Meru.

Principal Gods of the Vedic Pantheon

If everyone was home at the same time, Mount Meru could be a very crowded place. According to legend, there was a grand total of 33,333 gods and goddesses. Fortunately, only a few of these were prominent enough to be mentioned in the Vedas, but even among the prominent ones, their roles are a little blurry. Each of the Greek and Roman gods seemed to have fairly precise responsibilities, but the Indian deities were more casual about who did what. Among the chief gods, it almost seems that everybody did everything. One sometimes gets the feeling that the people of India were more concerned with the *personality* of the god than with his or her actual "job description."

Indra   Indra held the title of first among the gods, though he was certainly not a king or ruler over the other gods. Indra was an awesome god, much like Zeus in the Greek pantheon. He was identified with great strength and sexual prowess, and thus he was often associated symbolically with the stallion and the bull. Indra carried the *vajra* with him as the symbol of his power. The vajra has often been identified as a thunderbolt, but in fact it is a short metal rod with a stylized trident head at both ends. Whether this was meant to be seen as a thunderbolt is debatable; perhaps the assumption is due to the resemblance of Indra to Zeus.

Indra's origins go far back into the tribal past. He was regarded as a great warrior god, and he was also believed to be tremendously generous if you found him in the right mood. Many were the sacrifices performed to Indra beseeching him to grant numerous sons and to increase one's material welfare. Perhaps most important of all was the need for Indra's help in time of drought. India is a land that has always known terrible recurring droughts. During such times, the sacrificial fires would light the sky. Indra was believed to be able to destroy the power of *Vritri*, the demon who caused drought. It was Indra who brought the monsoon rains on which everything in life depended. No wonder he was chief among the gods. Among the many appeals to Indra in the *Rig Veda*, consider this one sample.

> Indra is sovereign lord of earth and heaven;
> Indra is lord of waters and mountains.
> Indra is master of those who prosper and the wise;
> Indra must be invoked at work and at rest.
>
> Greater than days and nights;
> The Giver of all is greater than the earth and the ocean's waters,
> Greater than the limit of the earth and the wind's expanse,
> Greater than all rivers and all our lands;
> Greater than all of these is Lord Indra.[6]

Indra, like the other gods, was no stranger to the delights of soma. It would seem that he was especially fond of the experience:

> They are pressing out the impetuous, exhilarating Soma juices
> For you, Indra. Drink them!
> They are cooking bulls for you; you will eat them, generous Indra,
> When they summon you with food.
>
> Wildly excited like a bull, Indra took the Soma for himself
> And drank the extract from the three bowls in the three day Soma ceremony.[7]

Varuna   Varuna was much like Indra—equally ancient and with powers that were almost indistinguishable from Indra's. But whereas Indra was more responsible for warring and "making things happen," Varuna's job was more a matter of "maintaining," especially maintaining the great Order of Nature.

It was believed that everything in nature behaved in accordance with an inner natural law known as *rita*. Varuna was responsible for maintaining rita. Applied to human behavior, rita became the inner moral law that properly guided all action. Thus, Varuna was the supreme maintainer of all law, natural and moral. Varuna watched over the affairs of men and punished those who violated the sacred law of rita.

> Keep fear away from me, Varuna,
> And hold fast to me, O emperor of Order [rita].
> Set me free from anguish
> As one would free a calf from a rope.
> I cannot bear to live apart from you,
> Not even for the blink of an eye.[8]

Agni   In some ways, Agni was the god that the Brahmins felt personally closest to, for he was the personification of the great fire that was the centerpiece of the ritual sacrifice. No matter which of the gods was being addressed, Agni was always involved. He was like the messenger—the go-between—in the sacred dealings of gods and men.

The ritual fire was, of course, no small affair; it was a huge, roaring blaze. The sound alone must have been awesome. And Agni, the god of fire, was often symbolized as a great horned bull, roaring his message to the gods. The sacrifice would be consumed in the fire and taken in the rising smoke to the gods for which it was intended:

> To you, Agni, who shines upon darkness,
> We come, day after day, bringing our thoughts and homage.
> To you, the king of sacrifices, the shining guardian of Order,
> Be easy for us to reach, like a father to his son.
> Abide with us, Agni, for our happiness.[9]

> Now get dressed in your robes [of fire],
> Lord of powers and master of the sacrificial foods,
> And offer this sacrifice for us.[10]

Agni, too, was no abstainer when it came time to pass out the soma. Presumably, some would have been poured into the fire at the appropriate time in the ceremony:

> Let Agni's bellowings reach to heaven
> As piercing weapons to destroy the demons.
> His angry glare breaks forth in the ecstacy of Soma.
> The obstacles of the godless cannot hold him back.[11]

Surya   Naturally, the sun, ultimately the most important of all of the elements of nature, would be personified as a god. The reason that Surya, the sun god, is not chief among the gods is that, to the Hindus, it is not the sun itself, but *power over* the sun, that is most important, and that power is held by such as Indra, Varuna, and Agni. Still,

Surya, who guides the sun in its daily path, is a highly significant god, and verses directed to him are among the most beautiful and poetic in the *Rig Veda*:

> His brilliant banners draw upwards the god who knows all creatures,
> So that everyone may see the sun.
> The Constellations, along with night, steal away like thieves,
> Making way for the sun who gazes on everyone.
>
> The rays that are his banners have become visible from the distance,
> Shining over mankind like blazing fires.
> Crossing space, you are the maker of light, seen by everyone, O Surya;
> You illumine the whole wide realm of space.[12]

Usas   Usas, the goddess of dawn, is one of the few female deities of high status in Vedic times. The Aryans, whose influence is so much to be seen in the Indian pantheon, were a nomadic, warrior society. Like their distant cousins who settled in Greece, they were a male-dominated people, and this was reflected in their gods. As the Greeks became civilized, they adopted female deities from other civilizations they encountered, but there is no parallel to this approach among the Aryans in India. All of the male gods did, however, have wives, generally referred to as "consorts." Sometimes these consorts were influential, but all in all, the Vedic goddesses get pretty short shrift in the Vedas. Nevertheless, Usas is much beloved, and verses dedicated to her in the *Rig Veda* go beyond even those praising Surya in poetic beauty. The Indologist V. M. Aptel puts it this way:

> In the case of Usas, the goddess of dawn, the personification is light, the poet never losing sight of the beautiful physical phenomena behind the deity. Gaily attired like a dancer with a garment of light, she rises in the east and exhibits her graces. She is ever-youthful, being born again and again. Her association with the sun is naturally very close, He is her lover, but as she precedes him, she is also said to be his mother. She is the sister of the night.[13]

In the *Rig Veda* it is put this way:

> Like a dancing girl, Usas puts on bright ornaments;
> She uncovers her breasts as a cow reveals her swollen udder.
> Creating light for the whole Universe,
> Dawn has opened up the darkness as cows break out from their pen.
>
> Her brilliant flame has become visible once more:
> She spreads herself out, driving back the formless black abyss.
> As one sets up the stake in the sacrifice,
> Anointing and adorning it with colored ornaments,
> So the daughter of the sky sets up her many-colored light.[14]

Rudra   Almost the extreme opposite of Usas was the god Rudra. Whereas Usas was light, delicate, and very feminine, Rudra was dark, fearsome, and stormy tempered. Like Indra, Rudra was a god associated with the storm clouds that brought the life-giving monsoon rains. The reason for this duplication is that Rudra was presumably a major

Dravidian god of very ancient origins who was simply incorporated into the emerging pantheon of gods with Sanskrit names. We know that the Dravidians had worshipped a god of storms who carried the thunderbolt and was known as the "Red God," and the Sanskrit root of Rudra is *rud*, which means red. A rain giver would be too important to pass up, so he may have been taken into the family and merely given a new Sanskrit name.

Alone among the gods, he could sometimes show a malevolent streak. True, Rudra could bring the life-giving rain, but sometimes, for no apparent reason at all, he would send the rain as fierce storms that indiscriminately devastated the countryside. The raging typhoons and floods of India were blamed on the unpredictable ferocity of Rudra's temperament. The people of Bangladesh know Rudra all too well. Rain, the very thing that made life possible, was also the thing that sometimes devastated life. Rudra, the personification of this dichotomy, united within himself both the beneficent and the dangerous aspects of nature. To Vedic man, Rudra represented the unconquered and unpredictable character of raw nature.

Rudra was a fearsome god, dark and unpredictable; he was the embodiment of wildness in the male nature. Rudra was something of a misfit among the divine residents of Mount Meru. He wore his black hair long and tied in braids. Like the other gods, he got around in a splendid war chariot, but one gets the feeling that if Rudra were alive today, his vehicle of choice would be a Harley.

Prayers for rain in the *Rig Veda* are generally addressed to Indra. Invocations to Rudra seem more directed simply at keeping his anger at bay:

> Praise him, the famous young god who sits on the high seat,
> The fierce one who attacks like a ferocious wild beast.
> O Rudra, have mercy on the singer, now that you have been praised.
> Let your armies strike down someone other than us.
>
> Let the weapon of Rudra veer from us;
> Let the great malevolence of the dreaded god go past us.
>
> O tawny and amazing bull;
> O God, do not become incensed or kill us.
> Be here for us, Rudra, and hear our call.[15]

Yama Unlike the gods, men and women are mortals and must eventually know death. But the Vedas gave assurances of an afterlife, and Yama was the king of this afterworld. Yama was not exactly a god; he was the first mortal to die. The gods had granted him near-divine status and allowed him to find his way to the realm of the afterworld, over which he would preside until the end of time. His task was to conduct the dead to the realm of their ancestors:

> Yama was the first to find the way for us,
> This pasture that shall not be taken away.
> Where our ancient fathers passed beyond,
> There everyone who is born follows, each on his own path.[16]

Although he was the personfication of death and the afterlife, Yama was not imagined as negative and morbid. Yama's role was an important part of the total scheme of reality. Something of the notion of heaven and hell entered into the picture. Those who were faithful to the moral order of rita in their lives could expect a happy place in Yama's kingdom; the lot of those who had been unfaithful to rita was darkness and suffering.

It was not Yama, but the gods—particularly Varuna, the maintainer of rita—who decided what a person's fate would be. Yama merely carried out the judgment of the gods. Even if the afterlife should turn out to be joyous, it was still death, and like people in all times, the men and women of the Vedic age were terrified by death and begged their gods to help them.

> Go away, death, by another path that is your own,
> Different from the road of the gods.
> I say to you who have eyes, who have ears;
> Do not injure our children or our men.[17]

> Let me not yet, King Varuna, enter into the house of clay [the grave].
> Have mercy on me, spare me, mighty Lord.[18]

The goodwill of Yama was understandably very important to men and women of the Vedic age. At the time of one's death, he could intercede with the gods, particularly Varuna. Perhaps for that reason, the Brahmin priests were especially generous with their soma where Yama was concerned.

> For Yama press the Soma; to Yama offer the oblation;
> To Yama goes the well prepared sacrifice,
> With Agni as its messenger.

> Offer to Yama this oblation rich in butter, and go forth,
> So may he intercede for us among the gods,
> So that we may live out a long lifespan.[19]

AN OVERVIEW OF VEDIC COSMOLOGY

The men and women of early Vedic times were fundamentally no different from people in any other time. They yearned for security and meaning in a world that is often violent and unpredictable. The awesome forces of nature dominated their lives, but uncontrollable though they were, the forces of nature were seen to operate in orderly ways. This could be the key to finding an underlying meaning to the great drama of life.

In response to this very human need for meaning, the religious leaders of the society created the gods—the controlling personifications of the forces of nature that shaped the destiny of human life. Along with identifying the gods, there were, of course, appropriate rituals of worship and sacrifice designed to entice the gods into using their powers in beneficial ways.

Over time, an elaborate body of religious tradition grew, until it spread into every nook and cranny of life. Presiding over this scene were the Brahmins, the elite priest class of Vedic society. They were the custodians and preservers of the religious tradition, the essence of which was consolidated into a body of god-inspired knowledge known simply as Veda. Veda was given verbal expression in the sacred hymns of the Brahmins, hymns that we know as the Vedas.

Giving order and meaning to life is no casual concern: Veda proclaimed the truth with an authoritarian voice born of the belief in its divine source, and the truth proclaimed by Veda described a world organized into a rigid hierarchy of ascending levels of perfection. Humankind was in the middle, brute animals below, and the gods above, and in each of these there was further classification by rank. In human life, the caste system was seen as the god-ordained order of society that conformed to essential differences in perfection among the member families that made up the larger community. Each had its place, guaranteed for all time, and appropriate responsibilities that went with that place. (Meaning and security have their price!) The highest place, of course, was occupied by the Brahmin caste. They alone spoke to the gods—but they did so on behalf of everyone.

The pantheon of the gods was a splendid creation of the human imagination. The Hindu pantheon represents man's poetic and mystical imagination at its best. In no way is this statement meant to imply that this was a foolish or erroneous pursuit. If Veda was to supply the much-desired order and meaning, the pantheon was its necessary capstone—and given the nature of human society at that time, the pantheon was both inevitable and reasonable.

The Vedas—practically our only source of information about the time—describe a society that was rigidly controlled by its own belief in a divinely inspired order. Altogether, life was seen to be like a great elaborate wheel slowly turning round and round. Everything and everyone, including the gods, had its proper place on that wheel, and its appropriate responsibilities corresponding to its place.

A person's sacred duty was to live his life in harmony with the customs and responsibilities of his caste and to worship the gods faithfully in the ways prescribed by tradition. If one did this (and nurtured a generous supply of the virtue of acceptance), his or her hunger for order and meaning would (probably) be satisfied, and from that would grow the all-important sense of security. Such a person was not a helpless twig tossed about in the chaotic stream of life, but rather a dignified and meaningful part of the whole, and that person's destiny, assuming that he faithfully played the part expected of him (or her), was a happy afterlife in the kingdom of Yama. Death must inevitably come, but it was no cause for terror or despair.

To the people of Vedic times, the gods were as real and as present as were other men and women. The stories of their adventures and their involvement in human affairs were endless. Invoking the favor of the gods—and staying the malevolence of demons—was the warp and woof of daily life in Vedic times. Numberless rituals were addressed to numberless gods. India, then as now, was a land passionately devoted to the worship of its many deities. We may safely assume that sacred shrines and statues were an important part of every village. Celebrations, festivals, and, above all, the great fire sacrifices were the highlights of an otherwise very mundane existence. Religion, richly laced with magic and superstition, was what gave daily life a special meaning and excitement.

What we have here is a relatively unsophisticated agricultural society that in Vedic times was really not significantly different from other early cultures. The foregoing description applies to many other human societies in historical times. Traditional forms of belief and worship were the stuff of life for the vast majority of Indian men and women in Vedic times, and, it must be stressed, the situation has not substantially changed for the masses even down to the present day.

Our concern in these pages, however, is not primarily with the religious beliefs of the masses; rather, it is with the contribution of a tiny minority of men and women who struck off on a different path. They hungered for something that could not be satisfied with the customary menu. Out of their search came new answers to old questions. If the evolution of Indian thought had ended with the Vedas, the philosophical side of the Hindu tradition would not occupy an especially important place in the history of human thought. But it did not end there; the Vedas were just the beginning. Much, much more was to be built on this Vedic foundation. So the question is, What was there in the Vedas, apart from the purely religious, that provided the germ for later speculation?

To answer this question, we must look very carefully into the Vedas and do some reading between the lines. Woven through all of the much-repeated proclamations and entreaties are some subtle philosophical themes that appear to evolve and become more important with the passage of time. Chief among these themes is the yearning for something that stands behind the myriad things of life—something that underlies it all and gives order and unity to existence.

Unity is the key word here. A sense of underlying unity is the hallmark of so much of Eastern thought. Like seeds just beginning to sprout, this theme appears in the Vedas, but it will not grow to maturity until a later age. Nevertheless, the interest is there and shows up in different ways.

The concept of Mount Meru is a unifying theme. Mount Meru organized all of creation into the symbolism of a mandala. By its very nature, a mandala stresses unity: The importance of the parts is seen in their relationship to the whole. It is the whole, perceived as one great unity, that is the special beauty of a mandala. In the myth of Mount Meru, Vedic man was giving expression to a belief in an underlying unity that joined together all of the multiple parts of creation.

Among some of the rishis, there was a developing awareness that the One was fundamentally more real than the Many. The universe began as the One and eventually would return to the primal state from which it had emerged. Between this alpha and omega, the One would propagate itself as the myriad creatures that temporarily made up the great hierarchy of being. This point of view is certainly not prominent in the Vedas, but here and there in the *Rig Veda* we find tantalizing little nuggets such as "To what is One, sages give many a title" or, in the same vein of thought, "that One wherein abide all things existing."

A final point concerns the doctrine of rita. Many came to believe that a natural law was immanent throughout all of creation. Even the gods did not exercise their powers capriciously. Like all other creatures, the gods must act in accordance with the universal order of rita. The rising and setting of the sun was seen to be an example of rita, the changing of the seasons was rita, and birth and death were the workings of rita. Applied to human behavior, the grand order of rita became moral law. Whatever one's caste, the proper goal of life was to live in accordance with rita.

Rita assures harmony and wholeness, the orderly evolution of life. Rita is the grand unifying order of Nature. Mount Meru is the natural expression of rita. In the concept of rita, the rishis gave form to the idea of a rational order that underlies and unifies all of Nature.

Again, it is worth stressing that, for the most part, the Vedas were not concerned with such philosophical matters. Still, there were stirrings—hints—of what was to come. Undoubtedly, some were toying in the Vedas with the concept that the multiplicity of creation is really a secondary, ephemeral sort of reality. This is what we see with our unenlightened eyes, but at a more transcendent level of consciousness, it is possible to see that, fundamentally, all of reality is One. This insight opened the door to a vastly richer meaning of Veda. In the age that followed, there were some who could not resist the maddening temptation to give up everything and dedicate their lives to the search for that higher truth.

Notes

1. A. L. Herman, *An Introduction to Indian Thought* (Englewood Cliffs, NJ: Prentice-Hall, 1976), p. 42.
2. Herman, p. 43, quoted in Ralph T. W. Giffith, *The Hymns of the* Rig Veda, 3d ed. (2 vols.) (Benares, India: E. J. Lazarus and Co., 1920–1926) (*Rig Veda*: VI.40.1–2).
3. *Ibid.*, p. 43 (*Rig Veda*: VIII.46.14).
4. Wendy D. O'Flaherty, The *Rig Veda* (London: Penguin Classics, 1981), p. 121 (*RV*: VIII.79.7-8). Hereafter referred to as *RV*.
5. Herman, p. 43 (*RV*: VIII.48.5, and I.85.7, 10).
6. O'Flaherty, p. 144 (*RV*: X.89.10–11).
7. *Ibid.*, pp. 146, 149 (*RV*: X.28.3, and I.32.3).
8. *Ibid.*, p. 218 (*RV*: II.28.6).
9. *Ibid.*, p. 99 (*RV*: I.1.7-9).
10. *Ibid.*, p. 100 (*RV*: I.26.1).
11. *Ibid.*, p. 103 (*RV*: V.2.10).
12. *Ibid.*, pp. 189, 190 (*RV*: I.50.1–4).
13. R. C. Majumdar ed., *The Vedic Age* (Bombay: Bharatiya *Vidya* Bhavan, 1971), p. 372.
14. O'Flaherty, pp. 179, 180 (*RV*: I.92.4–5).
15. *Ibid.*, p. 222 (*RV*: II.33.11, 14–15).
16. *Ibid.*, p. 43 (*RV*: X.14,1–2).
17. *Ibid.*, p. 52 (*RV*: X.18.1).
18. *Ibid.*, p. 216 (*RV*: VII.89.1).
19. *Ibid.*, p. 44 (*RV*: X.14.13–14).

Study Questions

1. What is the difference between Veda and the Vedas?
2. Exactly what was it about soma that the Brahmin priests loved so much?
3. What does it mean to say that Mount Meru "is an analogue of the hierarchy of all creation"?
4. Why isn't Surya, the god of the sun, "first among the gods," instead of Indra?

5. Why do you suppose that Usas was one of the very few female deities to receive attention in Vedic times?

6. "Given the nature of human society at the time, the [Hindu] pantheon was both inevitable and reasonable." How do you feel about that statement? Was it really both inevitable and reasonable? Could a "scientific" response have been possible instead?

7. In what significant ways does the yearning to uncover "a sense of underlying unity" appear in the Vedas? How is it that the concept of rita is the most significant of all in this regard?

3

The Upanishads

INTRODUCTION TO THE UPANISHADS

The Upanishads are an outstanding addition to humanity's search for meaning and beauty in life—and in death. The Upanishads have been a rich source of inspiration throughout the ages and seem to speak with special eloquence to men and women of modern times.

The word *Upanishad* is a combination of three Sanskrit root words, *upa-ni-shad*, which literally means "sit down close to." This undoubtedly refers to the fact that the Upanishads were "secret teachings" in the early days. They were passed along orally within the groups that created them, and the initiate had to "sit down close to" the master to receive the teaching. It was a personal transmission not meant for the ears of others.

Like the Vedas the Upanishads are a part of that great body of sacred knowledge known simply as Veda. In all, there are four parts to Veda. First, of course, were the Vedas themselves, which were complete by about 1000 B.C.E. Next came the Brahmanas, which were appended to the Vedas, and were intended to clarify some of the more abstruse passages in them. Third in the order of time were the Aranyakas, which consisted of various esoteric rules for meditating properly on verses from the Vedas. The Aranyakas were of special interest to an expanding group of "forest dwellers" who chose a life of solitude in the wilderness in order to pursue spiritual growth.

The Upanishads form the final part of Veda. They were composed over a very long period stretching from about 1000 B.C.E. to 200 B.C.E. Most of the really creative work, though, was limited to the spiritually dynamic time between 800 B.C.E. and 500 B.C.E. Strictly speaking, the Upanishads are further commentaries on the Vedas, but the philosophical and mystical depth of the Upanishads goes far beyond anything that is presented in the Vedas. We could say that the Vedas contain the seeds, but the flower comes to full bloom in the Upanishads.

Each Upanishad was the product of the spiritual and philosophical tradition of a distinct group. Consequently, taken as a whole, the Upanishads do not present a systematic, coherent philosophy. However, during the age that followed, a philosophical move-ment gradually took form that sought to interpret the Upanishads and to see in them a unified system of thought. This movement came to be known as *Vedanta*, which liter-ally means "end of Veda." The teaching of the Upanishads, in other words, was seen as a coherent whole that amounted to a culmination of the great search for truth that began in the Vedas. What had begun in ritual honoring of the gods culminated in a lofty inquiry into the true nature of ultimate reality.

The term *Vedanta*, therefore, became the name of a fully developed school of thought that offered a comprehensive interpretation of the teaching of the Upanishads. Such a school is known as a *darshana* in Sanskrit. The darshana of Vedanta evolved over several centuries; there is no single founder that we can point to. Some important names, though, do stand out along the way. Sometime after 200 C.E., for example, a sage named Badarayana condensed the teaching of Vedanta into a literary work known as the *Brahma-Sutra*, and in the eighth century C.E., the great Indian scholar Shankara brought the teachings of Vedanta together into a philosophical system that would become the very bedrock of Hindu thought from that time to the present. Although he lived for only thirty-two years, Shankara was a highly influential thinker. He estab-lished Vedanta firmly on the central teaching that, at bottom, all reality is one. (Shankara's interpretation of Vedanta is referred to as *Advaita Vedanta*, meaning "monistic" Vedanta, to distinguish it from certain other interpretations that would emerge later.)

Although Vedanta would become the dominant darshana with respect to the teach-ings of the Upanishads, it is not the only school of interpretation that came to be accepted as legitimate. Over time, other schools of thought came to be recognized as darshanas in their own right. Ultimately, six distinct "orthodox" schools of Hindu thought, known as the *astika darshana*, took form. In addition to Vedanta, there are the darshanas of Samkhya, Yoga, Purva Mimamsa, Vaisheshika, and Niyaya. These other schools originated in the teachings of specific historical founders. All sought in various ways to establish the teaching of Veda on a philosophically sound foundation. We will examine each of these darshanas in Chapter 5.

In the pages that follow, our examination of the Upanishads will be based largely on the interpretation of Upanishadic thought as elucidated in the teaching of Vedanta. Certain specific contributions of other darshanas, especially Samkhya and Yoga, will be included where appropriate. In this way, we can construct a coherent exposition of Upanishadic thought—an exposition that conforms to what is broadly accepted as the orthodox interpretation of the Upanishads. In addition to being the name of one of the six orthodox darshanas, the term *Vedanta* has, in fact, become something of a general-ization that refers to the philosophy of the Upanishads as a whole.

The Sanyasin Tradition

It is safe to say that during the Vedic age the only ones devoted to the search for tran-scendent knowledge were the rishis, most of whom were members of the Brahmin class. Their search was defined pretty narrowly by tradition, consisting for the most part in

Sadhus at the holy city of Varanasi. (P. Bresnan)

studying the Vedas and participating in ritual sacrifice—and this, of course, was influenced enormously by the effects of soma. The rishi was not a rebel; he was a functioning member of the social system. Not only was he shaped by tradition; he was the *upholder* of tradition. Undoubtedly, this situation was perfectly satisfactory for many, but definitely not for all.

During the late Vedic age, an exciting new movement began to emerge. Like so many other things, it probably had roots in the Dravidian past, but we can only guess about that. The thirst for transcendent knowledge, engendered in the Vedas, began to take a new turn. Some few men were willing to give up everything and totally dedicate their lives to a search for spiritual enlightenment. Ordinarily, such men took the vow of *sanyas* and were thus known as *sanyasins*, or renunciates, because they were willing to renounce everything—all material wealth, family, even their caste status—and go off into the wilderness, living like hermits in order to dedicate their lives to the all-consuming search for transcendent knowledge. The wilderness was essential because the sanyasins had voluntarily become literally out-castes and also because they wanted to get far away from the lures and distractions of ordinary life.

Many renunciates were Brahmins, but perhaps even more came from the Kshatriya class. Tradition excluded the Kshatriyas from becoming Vedic priests, but nothing could exclude them from this new way. Shakyamuni Buddha, the most famous of all renunciates, came from a Kshatriya family, but he would not appear on the scene until long after the tradition had matured. In ancient times, women did not become renunciates—they simply did not have the opportunity—but that has changed dramatically in modern times.

The sanyasin gave up ordinary life in order to search for transcendent spiritual knowledge—self-realization or "enlightenment." His was a very hard life; few could endure it. Much of the renunciate's time was given to spiritual study, prayer, and, most important of all, meditation, to the practice of which he might give many hours of each day. All renunciates lived a life of severe self-denial, and many endured rigorous ascetic practices as well, such as long fasting or going about in the coldest weather with little or no clothing. All of this was intended to burn out the deep longing for comfort and ego-satisfaction that stood in the way of spiritual growth.

As you might expect, some renunciates were more successful in their way of life than others. Some were so remarkable, and their spiritual growth appeared to be so impressive, that they acquired a reputation. Other renunciates then sought them out, if only to gain something from simply being in their presence. A holy man who attracted a following of disciples was called a *guru* by his followers. A guru is the leader of a spiritual community—its guide and teacher. The title is conferred out of respect by the disciples, never by the man himself.

The disciples of guru were called *sishyas*. The relationship between guru and sishya was one of mutual acceptance and love; it had to be like the relationship between a loving father and son. The sishya gave himself entirely to the guru; the guru's will became his will—absolute, uncompromising trust was essential. Given this kind of relationship, it is obvious that only a genuinely enlightened master was appropriate for the role of guru. Anything less could lead to disaster. (In India, where the tradition is ancient and deeply engrained in the culture, safeguards have evolved to protect against the possibility of an impostor posing as guru. In the Western world, however, where the tradition is new, no such safeguards exist, and the naive have sometimes been exploited.)

Together, the guru and his disciples formed a tightly knit spiritual community called an *ashrama*. We in the West refer to it as an "ashram." Originally, the term *ashram* meant only the community itself—a community that was usually on the move. The ashram wandered about in the mountains or forest, acquiring its meager needs from the bounty of nature or, occasionally, from begging. Unlike its status nowadays, begging was perfectly respectable during the time of the Upanishads; it was considered a noble act to share one's food with the holy men.

During the rainy season, the community would have to settle down in one place. India's myriad rivers, swollen by monsoon rains, made travel virtually impossible. Over time, many of these communities acquired donations of land and gradually gave up their wandering ways. Thus, in time, the word *ashrama* came to refer to the place—the "hermitage"—of a particular guru and his disciples. Once established, an ashram might continue to exist for many generations—even centuries. The disciples cycled in and out, with new ones replacing old ones, and the guru typically would appoint a successor. Continuity was thus assured.

But much more than mere temporal continuity was at stake here: It was the spiritual tradition of an ashram that was its real, enduring soul. The reason ashrams existed at all was that the individual members believed that such an arrangement was the best way to further their quest for spiritual enlightenment. Sharing life with other searchers in a close relationship with a guru was considered to be a much richer life than the way of the hermit, and what energized the community, in a spiritual sense, was its tradition of sacred teachings passed down from one generation to the next. This tradition was the community's treasure, and it was jealously guarded. It was "secret teaching" in the sense that sishyas believed that only those initiated into the community and guided by its guru were capable of really understanding the truth contained in it. But that truth was the key which could unlock the gates of paradise.

Most of the Upanishads began as just such secret teachings, enshrined in the tradition of various spiritual communities and handed down over many generations. Eventually, they were committed to writing and became available to all.

KEY ELEMENTS OF THE UPANISHADS

The purpose of studying the Upanishads will best be served by treating them as a collection of writings, rather than examining the principal ones individually. Taken as a unified collection, the Upanishads give expression to a complete and harmonious system of thought, one that addresses virtually all of the basic questions of life. Using appropriate selections from various Upanishads, let us try to identify the key themes of the Upanishads and show how they join together into one comprehensive whole.

The place to begin such a study is right where you are. Consider the world around you. There's always a world around you, and as far as your own perception is concerned, you're always right at its center. It doesn't matter what the condition of the world around you is at the moment; any condition will do. This "world around us" is what we ordinarily call reality. What can we say about this reality simply by observing it? What basic observations are always true about the world around us?

The first thing to be said about reality is that there is a lot of it. We are surrounded by a seemingly infinite number of "things." Anything you can put a name on is a thing, anything that can be a noun: a chair, for example, a tree, a garbage can, a guitar, a dog, a telephone, a hat, an eel-skin belt, and so on ad infinitum. All of these myriad things are constantly interacting, and one of them—the most important one to me by far—is myself. I am a thing among other things, interacting with them and changing with them as we all go along in the flow of time.

Change is the key concept here. Reality, as we perceive it, is constantly changing. *Everything is in a state of change, all of the time!* Reality is a never-ending flux, and nothing in the universe is exempt from it. With some things—clouds of smoke, for example—the process of constant change is obvious. With other things, such as granite boulders, it's not so obvious, but we know change is occurring anyway; it's just that it's slow to manifest itself. If we could see a time-lapse film of a boulder over some long span of geologic time, the boulder would almost appear to be liquid, or if it were possible for us right now to peek in at the atomic level of the boulder, we would see a whirlwind of movement and change. The appearance of unchanging solidity is only that: a superficial appearance.

This matter of constant change has troubled philosophers since the Greeks of ancient times first pondered its implications. If everything is always changing, always becoming something else, how can we say anything really definite about anything? How can we have a dependable science if nothing sits still for even an instant? The Greek philosopher Heraclitus complained that you can't put your foot into the same river twice. (Because the flowing body of water is constantly changing its form, it's really a new "river" every instant.) This is quite a problem for someone who wants to be able to make definite, enduring statements about reality. As if that weren't bad enough, another Greek philosopher made it even worse: He pointed out that you can't even put your foot into the same river *once* (because not just the river, but the pattern of flow itself, is changing even as you put your foot into the water)!

So we live in a world made up of things that are in a constant state of change. But there is more: These things are constantly *inter*changing; everything is constantly becoming something else. Here again, this is sometimes easy to see, as when a fire changes wood to smoke, and sometimes not so obvious, as when the surf changes a rock into sand. But here, too, it is simply a matter of time: Given enough time, everything decays, and out of that, new things take form. The tree dies and becomes the soil. Out of the soil grows a blade of grass. The grass becomes the worm that eats it, and the worm becomes the bird that eats it. The bird dies and decays into the soil, becoming one with it. Out of the soil grows a tree, and so on.

That brings us to the next point about change: Change is not capricious and meaningless, although it may sometimes seem that way. Change is always orderly, always reasonable. What this means is that change always conforms to the laws of nature. Change is always bound up in the process of cause and effect, wherein the effect follows the cause in a lawlike manner. That is to say, deer do not give birth to baby ducks, and falling apples do not fall upward.

The important point is that everything—every *thing*—is the result of some prior thing that caused it. Everything is the *doing* of something else. An apple is what an apple tree *does*; an apple tree *apples*. Apples are an *appling* of the apple tree, and the apple tree itself is a *treeing* of the soil, and so on. Looked at in this way, there really are no such things as nouns, which imply a static, set reality. In truth, everything is in movement, constantly in a state of becoming. Alan Watts used to suggest, tongue in cheek, that we should replace all nouns with verbs (really, gerunds): "The horsing ate an appling from the treeing." I suspect that that's not likely to happen, though.

Our concern here is with the fact that everything is the doing of something else. You are the doing of your parents, they are the doing of their parents, and so on. The apple is the doing of the tree, the tree is the doing of planet Earth, the Earth is the doing of the galaxy, and on we go back in time. No matter what you start with, you can—in fact you must—trace the chain of cause and effect back to the starting point of the universe. Everything ultimately goes back to the Big Bang (and maybe before long, science will reveal that the Big Bang itself was the *doing* of something that preceded it!).

Everything is the doing of something that preceded it in an unbroken chain of cause and effect back to the beginning of the universe. So the ultimate question is, What's doing the universe? If everything in the universe is the *doing* of something else, what is doing the *universe*? (Notice that the question is not What *did* the universe—that is, what *started* the universe? Whether the universe really began with the big bang is not our present concern. It's an interesting question, but it's not the right question.)

Given the fact that the universe exists—*given* the fact that all of this "stuff" around us exists—there is a perfectly reasonable explanation for why it has all evolved in the way it has: The laws of nature explain it fully. But that requires a "given the fact," and why should we be willing to do that? Everything, including the universe itself, has to have a reasonable explanation. So again, the ultimate, bottom-line question is this: *Why does anything exist at all? What's* doing *the universe?!*

What is it that holds the universe in existence? What is it that is *doing* the universe? Every cosmology must answer this all-important question. In Vedanta, the answer to the question can be summed up in a single word, and that word is—*Brahman.*

Brahman

Brahman is the Fact of Existence. Brahman is the underlying reality and root cause of all that is. The name, as you might suppose, is closely related to Brahma, the principal deity of the late Vedic Age, in which there was a gradual evolution of thought, at least among the rishis, in the direction of monotheism. Brahma, the Creator, came to be seen as the personification of the creative source from which all of nature continually emerges.

The next step in this process of thought was to go beyond the anthropomorphic personification—a mythic figurehead—and identify the impersonal reality itself, the ultimate creative force that Brahma merely represented. Verbally, this was accomplished by changing the masculine gender *Brahma* to the neutral form, *Brahman.* Both words are derivitives of the Sanskrit root *brih*, which means "to grow." Thus, Brahman is the ultimate root of existence from which the entire universe "grows" and continues to exist.

It is very important to resist the temptation to let the imagination cast the word *Brahman* in the form of some personal being, especially a godlike being. Brahman is not a god. Neither is Brahman a he; indeed, Brahman is not any *thing* at all that can be identified and separated out from all other things. Brahman is the Fact of Existence, pure and simple. Brahman is the *reason* things exist. Brahman is the ultimate inner essence of all things that exist. In the *Mundaka Upanishad*, Brahman is described as being invisible, ungraspable, eternal, and without any qualities whatsoever. Brahman is the imperishable source of all things.

In the Upanishads, Brahman is often referred to as "the Self," with a capital S, meaning the innermost Self of all that exists. From the *Katha Upanishad*,

> The supreme Self is beyond name and form,
> Beyond the senses, inexhaustible,
> Without beginning, without end,
> Beyond time and space, and causality,
> Eternal, immutable.[1]

The preceding quote reveals the frustration in trying to define Brahman in words. By definition Brahman transcends everything that can be a matter of experience, and that's what words are all about. Perhaps the best verbal definition of all is given in the *Mundaka Upanishad*. A sage being questioned about the nature of Brahman keeps answering, "Neti, neti, neti" (not this; not that; not this; not that). In other words, we can identify Brahman only by negating every possible *thing* that we can imagine. What's left is Brahman. But what *is* left? Well, that's why the sages call it "ungraspable." The most that we can say in words is that what's left is pure, undifferentiated existence itself—not some thing that exists:

> Him our eyes cannot see, nor words express;
> He cannot be grasped even by the mind.
> We do not know, we cannot understand,
> Because he is different from the known
> And he is different from the unknown.
> Thus have we heard from the illumined ones.[2]

Don't let the use of the masculine pronouns in this passage confuse you. Writers of the Upanishads were fairly casual about that sort of thing. Brahman clearly transcends gender; there's no question about that. But "it," nonetheless, is often referred to as "he" in the Upanishads. Perhaps it's a desire to make things seem less impersonal.

In trying to describe the admittedly indescribable, sages use many words—*pure spirit, eternal, infinite, immutable, uncreated, unchanging*, and so on. So far as they go, all of these are good words. But words are like "fingers pointing at the moon": fine if they direct your attention to the moon, but just don't mistake the finger *for* the moon.

In attempting to define Brahman, I think we can do no better than the statement in the first paragraph of this section. Brahman is the fact of Existence. Brahman is the underlying reality and root cause of all that is. Brahman is the doer of the universe. Thus do we answer the question posed at the end of the last section: What is it that holds the universe in existence? What is it that is *doing* the universe? It is Brahman.

So Brahman is pure existence. Pure existence is infinitely passive and undifferentiated. But the world of our experience is not passive; it is highly active. A multitude of things is constantly coming into existence and passing out of existence. These *things* are the manifestations of existence. In other words, the universe of things is the way pure existence expresses itself—*manifests* itself. In Vedanta philosophy, the reality of Brahman is conceptualized in two ways. In its pure, unmoving, essential suchness, Brahman is known as *nirguna* Brahman, absolutely perfect and absolutely passive (at least conceptually speaking). As the active source of creative power, though, Brahman is known as *saguna* Brahman. It is *saguna* Brahman that creates the universe—in the beginning and for every continuing moment—as an expression, a *manifestation*, of itself. In this way Brahman, the ultimate source of all that is, *does* the universe:

> As the web issues out of the spider, and is withdrawn;
> As plants sprout from the earth,
> As hair grows from the body,
> Even so, the sages say,
> This universe springs from the deathless Self,
> The source of life.[3]

There is an excellent Sanskrit word, *lila*, which means "play," as in "to play a musical instrument." The creative act of Brahman is often referred to as *lila*. Rather than say that Brahman *creates* the universe, many sages prefer to say that Brahman *plays* the universe. (It sounds so much more appealing put that way.) After all, *why* does Brahman do the universe? There really can't be any purpose to the universe outside itself; nothing exists outside itself. Is it going too far, then, to say that when you come right down to it, Brahman *plays* the universe for the fun of it? I don't mean to sound flippant; nor, though, do I wish to pretend that this is all heavy and serious business. It is what it is, and what it is—what everything is—is the *lila* of Brahman.

Brahman-Dharma

Brahman, the Fact of Existence, manifests itself as the universe. Everything that exists is the *lila* of Brahman.

> Brahman, attributeless Reality . . .
> Casts his net of appearance over the cosmos
> And rules it from within through his divine power.[4]

Brahman "projects" and "rules" the universe. By "rule," it is simply meant that the *lila* of Brahman is not whimsical, not erratic. From the beginning of time, the universe has been unfolding in a grand and orderly fashion. This orderly evolution of the universe, the *lila* of Brahman, is known as *Brahman-Dharma*.

Dharma—derived from the Sanskrit *dhar*, which means "to hold"—is the inner law of creation that upholds the order of Nature. We see it around us as the expression of Natural Law, and over time it is expressed as the awesome unfolding of the evolution of the cosmos. Brahman projects the universe from itself, but does so in accordance with the order of Dharma.

Brahman, then, is pure existence, the source of all that is. *Lila* (or *maya*) is the creative act of Brahman, expressed as the evolution of the universe. And Dharma is the inner law of Brahman that causes the evolution of the universe to unfold in an orderly and harmonious way. Dharma is what gives unity and harmony to all of nature. To be in accord with Dharma is the proper state of all things.

Until human beings appeared on the scene, there was no problem concerning Dharma: Everything in nature automatically acted in accordance with it. The apple falling from the tree is Dharma. The Earth turning on its axis is Dharma. The lion pouncing on the antelope is Dharma. The balance of nature, the working out of the good of the whole—that, too, is Dharma. But human nature has the capacity for self-reflection and therefore the capacity to frustrate Dharma by willfully substituting personal desire for the good of the whole. Thus, it becomes the moral responsibility of men and women to transcend selfish desire and deliberately choose to live their lives in accordance with Dharma. The word *Dharma*, therefore, refers to transcendent Natural Law and also to moral law. The concept of Dharma is in many ways an outgrowth of the Vedic concept of *rita*. Both are concerned with the inner order of reality.

Prakriti

The evolution of the universe—the *lila* of Brahman—began in a state that is commonly referred to as "undifferentiated materiality." This simply means that the basic substance of matter and energy existed, but it had not yet taken any definite form. It was still just primal "stuff," full of unactualized potential. This primal material essence is called *prakriti*. (The concept of *prakriti*, as well as the related concept of *purusha*, are given a central place in the teaching of the darshana known as Samkhya.)

Prakriti may be thought of as being ultimately the simplest state of matter and energy—the *power* that generates materiality in its primal state. The Upanishads are not precise about this point, nor does it really seem to matter. In any case, we can say that, in giving birth to the material universe, Brahman's act was the expression of itself as *prakriti*, and from the very first moment of time, *prakriti*, being imbued with the character of Dharma, became involved in the process of movement and change that we envision as the evolution of the universe.

One of the amazing things about Vedanta is the harmony that exists between the insights of this ancient philosophy and those of modern science. Contemporary physics is enchanted with the quest for the primal, fundamental components of materiality. In a sense, we could say that modern science is trying to get as close as is humanly possible to an understanding of the fundamental nature of *prakriti*. From the modern point of view, we could say that *prakriti* took the form of primal energy that "froze out" into the elementary particles of nature. According to this view, a quark is a form of *prakriti*, and so is a photon. Such a view does no violence at all to the original meaning of *prakriti*; in fact, it seems to develop the original concept and make it even more meaningful.

Prakriti is not static: It constantly responds to the forces of nature, and out of this dynamic come all of the forms which we recognize as the world around us. The fundamental forces of nature, elucidated in the Samkhya tradition, are threefold and are referred to as the *gunas*.

The three *gunas* are *tamas*, the character of inertia; *rajas*, the character of energy, activity, and passion; and *sattva*, the character of equilibrium and harmony. Everything that exists is said to be a result of the interaction of these three forces, although one will always dominate and will establish the nature of a particular thing. In a seed, *tamas* dominates, but when the seed sprouts, *rajas* takes command. A healthy, mature tree exhibits *sattva*. Dharma, taken as a whole, is perfect *sattva*. The *guna* forces are always and everywhere in movement and interaction, shaping the character of the forms that *prakriti* assumes.

To sum up, the Dharma evolution of the universe began in a state of undifferentiated material reality. We call that state *prakriti*. Responding to the ever-present influence of the basic forces of nature (the *gunas*), *prakriti* has evolved, and continues to evolve, all of the myriad *forms* ("things") that make up the constantly changing character of nature. We call this evolutionary unfolding of forms, *maya*.

Maya

Insofar as the material order is concerned, *prakriti* is all that exists. The things that we can see and name are forms that *prakriti* has taken. Like a slowly drifting smoke cloud, *prakriti* is constantly assuming myriad forms—forms that take shape and then dissolve into other forms. For billions of years, the cosmic dust cloud produced by the Big Bang has been slowly evolving new and ever more complex forms. We put names on these forms and call them galaxies, stars, planets, trees, eel-skin belts, and so on. But all of them remain at root that original cosmic dust, which has simply been good at evolving more complicated molecular forms over time. The term *prakriti* will serve here as well as any. Everything that exists is simply a temporary *form of prakriti*—and that brings us back to *maya*, the world of changing forms. *Prakriti*, so to speak, is what the forms are made of.

An analogy will help. Imagine a potter at work. The first thing the potter needs is a tub of clay. Then he or she will shape the clay into various artifacts. If one is for holding flowers, it will be called a vase. Another meant to hold soup will be called a bowl. I say "will be called" because, strictly speaking, there is no such thing as a vase or a bowl. Those words are just agreed-upon practical descriptions of what essentially is still clay. The clay hasn't changed; only its form has changed. Now some of it has become clay *in the form of* a vase, some clay *in the form of* a bowl. The names refer to the forms. If we break the vase, only the form has been destroyed. All of the clay is still there, although now it is in the form of shards.

In this analogy, the clay, of course, represents *prakriti*, and the forms that the clay temporarily assumes are *maya*. When we give names to forms, we seem to confer a sort of reality on them that goes beyond the character of transient forms. The name creates an illusion. Our mistake is to confer on the things of our experience a kind of reality unto themselves, rather than see them as the fleeting expressions of a deeper reality.

One more analogy is apropos; we'll use the cloud again. Lie on your back on a summer day, and watch a big puffy cloud drift slowly overhead. It doesn't take much imagination to pick out all kinds of familiar shapes. A chicken slowly turns into an alligator; a face becomes a chair. The cloud is *prakriti*; the forms it takes are *maya*. The forms are real; you are not hallucinating, but their reality consists in being forms of the cloud, not in being substanding things with their own separate reality. If you thought that it really was a chicken or an alligator, you would then be a victim of illusion, but it would be your own illusion, not inherently the fault of *maya*. Vedanta maintains that this is a mistake that we often make.

Maya is derived from the very basic Sanskrit word *ma*, which provided the root for English words such as "matter" and "measure." The English word "magic" is derived from the same root, and magic was an early Sanskrit meaning of *maya*. In Vedic times, *maya* referred to the magical powers of the gods, but in the Upanishads, *maya* has come to refer to the (seemingly) magical power of Brahman to evoke the appearance of the many out of the One. The word *maya* thus refers both to the creative power of Brahman and to what it is that appears to be created:

From his divine power comes forth
All this magical show of name and form;
Of you and me,
Which casts the spell of pain and pleasure.
Only when we pierce through this magic veil
Do we see the One who appears as many.[5]

Know him to be the supreme magician
Who has become boy and girl, bird and beast.[6]

Brahman is pure spirit. Through the creative *lila* of Brahman, the universe comes into existence and unfolds through time. What is unfolding are the myriad forms of nature, the countless, ever-changing *things* that make up the world around us. This is *maya*, our perception of the totality of the myriad *forms* (things) that make up the constantly changing character of nature. Maya is the particular way in which Brahman manifests itself in its creative action. The *Shvetashvatara Upanishad* puts it this way:

[Brahman] is the sun, and the moon, and the stars.
He is the air and the sea.
Brahman is the Creator, Prajapati.
He is this boy, he is that girl.
He is this man, he is that woman,
And he is this old man, too, tottering on his staff.
His face is everywhere.[7]

The same point is made in the *Katha Upanishad*:

The Self is the sun shining in the sky,
The wind blowing in space;
He is the fire at the altar and in the home the guest;
He dwells in human beings, in gods, in truth,
And in the vast firmament;
He is the fish born in water, the plant growing in the earth,
The river flowing down from the mountain.
For this Self is supreme.[8]

To sum up, the orderly evolution of the universe is the play of Brahman; we call it *Dharma*. The Dharma evolution of the universe began in a state of undifferentiated material reality that we call *prakriti*. Responding to the ever-present influence of the basic forces of nature (the *gunas*), *prakriti* has evolved, and continues to evolve, all of the myriad forms ("things") that make up the constantly changing character of nature. This evolutionary unfolding of nature is what we know as *maya*.

Maya is the totality of the "things" (including sense impressions and thoughts) of the material world. *Maya* is reality in that, through the Dharma evolution of *prakriti*, it is the manifestation of Brahman. *Maya* is illusory only to the extent that its forms (things) may be mistaken for having a reality of their own, rather than being the expression of a deeper reality.

As a final point on this subject, consider that, among the myriad forms of *maya*, two distinct kinds can be seen to exist: those which exhibit consciousness and those which do not. The ones that exhibit consciousness (or at least exhibit the potential for consciousness) are called *sentient beings* (an animal, for example). The ones that do not exhibit consciousness are called *insentient beings* (a rock, for example). This difference is, to say the least, momentous.

Purusha

Brahman is pure spirit. In the view of Vedanta, pure spirit and pure consciousness are one and the same. Pure consciousness is not to be confused with ordinary thinking or feeling. In the sense used here, "pure consciousness" refers to transcendent, infinite awareness. It is in itself totally inactive. The word for it is *purusha*.

Purusha is a tricky word to nail down. (Aren't they all!) The meaning of the word changed enormously from Vedic times to the age of the Upanishads. In the Vedas, *purusha* refers to a mythic primal male whose body enveloped the entire cosmos. From the various parts of his body were derived the different castes. Obviously, the meaning has changed a lot, but the connotation of maleness was not entirely lost. In their more poetic moments, the authors of the Upanishads refer to the male–female dichotomy of nature by representing *purusha* as the male aspect and *prakriti* as the female.

Brahman is pure consciousness and as such, enters directly into its own *lila*. Recall that, among the myriad forms of *maya* there are two distinct kinds: those which exhibit consciousness (sentient beings) and those which do not exhibit consciousness (insentient beings). *Purusha* is therefore the conscious essence of Brahman, revealed directly in *maya*—that is, in those forms of *maya* (sentient beings) which are sufficiently evolved to allow purusha.

Your body, for example, is one of the forms of *maya* that is sufficiently evolved to allow purusha. Your brain, because of the kind of material organization it has, is capable of expressing consciousness. A rock, which might possess all of the same chemical elements as your brain, is not capable of expressing consciousness, because it lacks the appropriate form to permit it. Your brain, if damaged, could become like the rock and lose the ability to express consciousness. In the Dharma evolution of the universe, *maya* (*prakriti*) eventually reached a level of maturity that made possible the direct revelation of Brahman itself (*purusha*) through the appropriate forms of *maya* (sentient beings).

Another common misunderstanding concerning Vedanta has to do with the division between Brahman and the Universe. Here is how it might be stated: The most fundamental tenet of Vedanta philosophy can be summed up in three little words: All is One. Brahman is the One. Brahman is pure spirit. But the universe—the *lila* of Brahman—is matter. Matter is not spirit: Matter is matter, and spirit is spirit. How, then, can Vedanta maintain that all is One? It would seem that the basic dichotomy of matter and spirit would reduce Vedanta philosophy to asserting, not that all is One, but that all is Two: spirit (Brahman) and matter (the universe).

This fine distinction was to become the source of a major problem dividing Vedantists. Some, the dualists, have held simply that both matter and spirit are real and separate. Others, the monists, maintain that *maya* is essentially illusion: Spirit alone is ultimately real.

One much-favored solution to this dilemma lies in the definition of "matter." From the viewpoint of Vedanta, matter is *prakriti* (which evolves the forms that we see and name). *Prakriti* is not to be understood as something that Brahman created separate from itself—as, for example, in the Judeo–Christian view, God created the world separate and distinct from Himself. In the Vedanta view, *prakriti* does not have a distinct reality unto itself; rather, it is the *expression*, or *manifestation*, of Brahman. There is no dichotomy: *Prakriti* is the manifestation of Brahman.

To bring out the point, consider this analogy. When you sing a song, is the act of singing you, or is it something separate from you? Is not your behavior—what you do—a fundamental part of what it is that defines you? Singing is a modified form of breathing; it's a way of *expressing* yourself. In the same way, the universe could be said to be the song, the *lila*, of Brahman. Stars and clouds and trees are the "notes" of Brahman's song. Seen in this way, there is no separation. All is One; all is Brahman.

Nevertheless, this way of reconciling the issue seems overly subtle to some. *Purusha*, being Brahman itself, is *pure spirit*. *Prakriti* (the raw material of *maya*), being the manifestation of Brahman, is matter. In the judgment of many philosophers, Vedanta does in fact maintain that reality is of two basic kinds: spiritual reality (Brahman) and material reality (the manifestation of Brahman). In this dichotomy, spiritual reality is perfect and eternal. Material reality is imperfect and transient.

There is an all-important relationship between *prakriti* and *purusha*—matter and spirit—in that material forms (for example, the bodies of animals) provide the necessary means by which Brahman itself enters directly into its *lila* play, the Dharma evolution of the universe. It may be said that in the long run, the role of *prakriti* is to free *purusha*.

Brahman-Atman

The doctrine of *Brahman-Atman* is the quintessential feature of Vedanta. This philosophy holds that at the core of your being—and at the core of every other sentient being—is *atman*. *Atman* is not a *creation* of Brahman; *atman is* Brahman. The Brahman-*Atman*, although individualized in each sentient being, is Brahman. *Atman* is the true inner Self of each sentient being—hence the powerful verse from the *Chandogya Upanishad* that ends with the Sanskrit words *Tat tsvam asi*! ("You are That!") The word "That" refers to the ultimate, unspeakable reality of Brahman:

> In the beginning was only Being,
> One without a second.
> Out of himself he brought forth the cosmos
> And entered into everything in it.
> There is nothing that does not come from him.
> Of everything he is the inmost Self.
> He is the truth; he is the Self supreme.
> And you are that, Shvetaketu; you are that.[9]

You are That! You are Brahman! You are not a *creature* of Brahman; you-are-Brahman! To really know this, to discover and know the *atman* within oneself, is the ultimate goal of life. Nothing else compares in significance. Let's look at how this works out logically.

As we have seen, *prakriti*, through the ceaseless play of the *gunas*, produced and continues to produce all of the *maya* forms of the universe. Each of us finds one of these forms, one of these entities, to be of very special interest. That particular form is, of course, "myself." I am a physical being, a part of the world of *maya*, just like all other physical beings. But in an important way, I am unlike most of the other "things" of my experience: I am a *conscious* being. A conscious being is known as a "sentient" being. In the Hindu view, all animals, being possessed of consciousness, are sentient beings. The plant kingdom, however, is insentient.

Consciousness is not just another attribute: It is the nature of Brahman itself. Brahman as pure consciousness is known as *purusha*, and *purusha* is perfect and undivided; that is to say, *purusha* is universal, one and the same as Brahman itself—it is not divided into discrete parts. *Prakriti*, in the myriad evanescent forms of *maya*, is perceived as a manifold, but *purusha* is the purely spiritual reality of Brahman itself and is One. Thus, my physical self is *prakriti*—an aspect of the play of *maya*—and is subject to all the conditions of unconscious *prakriti*. But the conscious self is not *prakriti*. We customarily recognize the importance of this distinction by spelling the *purusha* "Self" with a capital "S."

The Self—the indwelling conscious core of every sentient being—is known by the term *atman*, which is derived from an early root word that means "to breathe." In many ancient cultures, the principle of life—the soul—was associated with the breath. This is understandable; a baby *seems* to come to life when it takes its first breath and remains vital and warm throughout life so long as it continues breathing. "Breath" is also the meaning of the Latin *spiritus*, from which is derived our word "spirit."

Atman, then, *is* Brahman! *Prakriti*, through the appropriate forms of *maya*, provides the means through which Brahman (*purusha*) can enter directly into its *lila*. The Dharma evolution of the universe is the play of Brahman, the creation of Brahman, the manifestation of Brahman. But *atman is* Brahman. This cannot be stressed too strongly: *atman* is not a *part* of Brahman; Brahman is pure spirit and cannot be divided into parts. *Atman* is not a role of Brahman. *Atman is* Brahman:

> This Self who gives rise to all works,
> To all desires, all odors, all tastes,
> Who pervades the universe,
> Who is beyond words,
> Who is joy abiding,
> Who is ever present in my heart,
> Is Brahman indeed.[10]

Thus, in a manner of speaking, there are two important aspects to the nature of my being. The conscious core of my being (and of all sentient beings) is the Brahman-*Atman*. This is the Self, which, participating in the nature of *purusha*, is pure spirit, eternal, and non-acting. The much more familiar self, though, is the ego, the *maya* role that is identified with what I do. This is the *prakriti* self, active, constantly changing, ephemeral, and not in itself conscious.

Atman (*purusha*) is the conscious *subject* of all that the ego (*prakriti*) does and experiences. *Atman* is the "hear-*er*" of what is heard, "see-*er*" of what is seen, and "think-*er*" of what is thought:

> The Imperishable is the seer, though unseen;
> The hearer, though unheard;
> The thinker, though unthought;
> The knower, though unknown.
> Nothing other than the Imperishable can see, hear, think, or know.
> It is in the Imperishable that space is woven, warp and woof.[11]

> That which makes the tongue speak, but cannot be spoken by the tongue,
> Know that as the Self.
> This Self is not someone other than you.[12]

The *Self* is not someone other than you—a profound notion, indeed, but unfortunately, far from apparent to us. In the normal course of development, the *atman* (pure consciousness) becomes entranced, as it were, with the ego role of which it is the conscious subject. So entranced, so enchanted does it become, that it gets absorbed in the game, going so far as to falsely identify with the ego role that it observes. This is the understandable, but fatal, mistake that we all make early in the game. By way of a very loose analogy, we may compare the relationship of *atman* and ego to the viewing of a film in which the camera gives you the impression that you are seeing the action through the eyes of the main character. If you get very absorbed in the action, you might forget that you are a separated observer and temporarily think that you really are that actor—that role. If the character in the film faces danger, you would feel that you were the one in danger. In your entrancement, you have identified with the experience. In like manner, when *atman* falsely identifies its being with that of the ego role, all of the troubles of the world are the result. To reveal this error, and to correct it, is the central thrust of Vedanta philosophy:

> Like two golden birds perched on the selfsame tree,
> Intimate friends, the ego and the Self, dwell in the same body.
> The former eats the sweet and sour fruits of the tree of life,
> While the latter looks on in detachment.[13]

There are some very profound implications in all of this, in this assertion of Vedanta that the real me is Brahman. For one thing, there is no essential difference between me and all other sentient beings. We are all Brahman—the one, indivisible Brahman. We are simply different expressions of Brahman, all manifest at the same time. You and I are one! The terrible feeling of separateness is only an illusion. At root, all is One.

Also, death has no reality; there can be no such thing as death. Brahman cannot die; Brahman is eternal. And *atman* is Brahman. Therefore, the real enduring me cannot die. Only the role—the ego—can die. The *atman* does not die. Let's go into both of these points in a bit more depth.

Avidya

We say that everyone is a unique individual, and it's true: No two persons are exactly alike. But what we see, what we identify as a person, is in fact the "persona," the personality, which is the ego role that that individual plays. Through practice, we get so good at playing the role that it becomes second nature. It's easy to see why people would identify with their roles and fail to see that the roles really are just that—roles. According to Vedanta, that is exactly what we're doing; we're all actors going about our business, totally wrapped up in the roles we play. "All the world's a stage," said Shakespeare, "and the men and women are players on it."

The analogy of a play is not a bad one. An actor on the stage is clearly an "actor," but we don't want him (or her) to *appear* to be an actor. An actor gives a good performance to the extent that he really gets into the role. Wouldn't it spoil the role, though, if the actor was continually looking over his shoulder and winking at the audience? We want the actor to get into role, but definitely not to the extent that he starts believing that he *really is* that role! That is going too far. It would take the fun out of the play, and it might be dangerous; there could be real murders on the stage!

If an actor comes to believe that he really is the role that he plays and adopts that personality as his own, we would judge that he had lost his mind. Such a person would be committed to a mental hospital for his own safety—and ours. Well, . . . should we not all be committed then? Are we not all doing exactly the same thing? Typically, we all identify totally with the ego roles that we play, and we believe with all our hearts that "this is what I am" (not something I do). If we fall for our own act, are we not just as insane as the stage actor who falls for his?

In Vedanta, this great illusion about the nature of self is called *avidya*. The word is derived from the Sanskrit root *vid*, which, as mentioned earlier, means "to know." This is the same root that gave us Veda. Another derivative is *vidya*, which means "knowledge"—knowledge of the highest sort, knowledge of Brahman. Veda is Truth, and *vidya* is knowledge of the Truth. In Sanskrit, the prefix "a" has the effect of negating the word to which it is attached. (This is often the case in English, too, as in "moral" and "amoral"). Thus, *avidya* comes to mean "ignorance," ignorance of the truth that the real Self is Brahman.

Avidya is the common condition of mankind; it is the "human problem." *Avidya*, the Upanishads contend, is responsible for all suffering. Note that the contention is not that *avidya* is responsible for *most* suffering; rather, the Upanishads proclaim that *avidya* is responsible for *all of the suffering of mankind*—what a statement!

In the view of Vedanta, the real self of every individual is Brahman, the Brahman-*Atman*. *Atman* is the conscious core. The "person," which includes everything from the functioning of the body to the behavior of the personality, is *maya*. It is part of the *lila* of Brahman, and no matter how wonderful it may be, it remains true that it is something you *do*, not what you *are*. *Atman* is what you *are*. To fail to see this is *avidya*. In the long view of Dharma, the destiny of evolution is to ultimately transform every trace of *avidya* to *vidya*.

We can sum up the matter of *avidya* in the following manner: To identify my being with the role that I play is fundamental ignorance. It is called *avidya*, the powerful illusion that my reality consists in the "person," the *role* that I play. This ego identification results inevitably in a sense of personal separation, personal insecurity, and angst regarding the unavoidability of personal death. *Avidya*, the common condition of mankind, is responsible for all suffering.

To see through the illusion of the separate self and to come to know the real Self, the Brahman-*Atman*, is the proper goal of life. This is true Knowledge. This is *vidya*:

> The Self is indeed Brahman.
> But through ignorance people identify it with
> Intellect, mind, senses, passions,
> And the elements of earth, water, air, space, and fire.
> This is why the Self is said to consist of this and that,
> And appears to be everything.[14]

The Self is the "eye of the eye." The eye (i.e., the body) may die, but the eye of the eye cannot die. It is *atman*; it goes on forever.

Samsara

> The world is the wheel of God,
> Turning round and round with all living creatures upon its rim.
> The world is the river of God,
> Flowing from him and flowing back to him.
> On this ever-revolving wheel of being
> The individual self goes round and round through life after life.
> Believing itself to be a separate creature,
> Until it sees its identity with the Self,
> And attains immortality in the indivisible whole.[15]

The Vedas held that death is followed by an afterlife, a sort of heaven or hell, but the Upanishads proclaim that the *atman* will be reborn over and over until, finally, it bursts through *avidya* and awakens perfectly to its own Brahman identity. This may take aeons of time and millions of rebirths. It is Brahman's way of playing hide-and-seek with itself, and time is of no consequence.

Presumably, an individualized Brahman-*Atman* begins its career spontaneously at the absolute lowest level of sentient life, whatever that might be. Whatever it is, that minute speck of consciousness is the first step in the *atman*'s long journey. In accordance with the unfolding of Dharma, the *atman* will ascend one lifetime at a time through the vast hierarchy of sentient life-forms. As the "wheel of life" turns round and round, the *atman* will have played the role of many an animal by the time it first is born in a human body.

The particular nature of each rebirth is determined by karma, which has been accumulated by the *atman* in its previous lives. Karma must not be confused with a system of reward and punishment. Vedanta does not hold that some sort of celestial police force is watching us, ready to pass out negative karma citations for our selfish acts. Karma is the natural outcome of the play of Dharma. It is purely and simply a matter of cause and effect. If I eat more calories than I burn, I will inevitably gain weight. It has nothing to do with morality; I'm not being punished. It's simply the natural play of cause and effect. At the time of ego death, the state of one's karma is carried over into the next life and determines the character of the next rebirth.

Progression upward is natural and, as it were, "automatic," until the *atman* reaches the level of human life. The hierarchy continues, of course, through the various castes, but now there is a difference. The human animal, unlike all previous species, is capable of fouling the machinery of Dharma. This is because the human life-form provides the *atman* for the first time with the capability of creating a role that is self-reflective—and as we have seen, therein lies all the trouble. The ego can choose to stand in conflict with Dharma by putting its own selfish desires in place of the good of the whole. Depending on its severity, this mode of behavior creates negative karma, which must inevitably influence the nature of that *atman's* rebirth.

Sufficient negative karma at the time of ego death can even result in an *atman* falling backward and being reborn at a lower level of sentient life. Given this belief, it was inevitable, I suppose, that someone would attempt to work out what kind of rebirth would result from certain types of negative karma. It was widely believed that an unfaithful wife, for example, would be reborn as a scorpion. (There was no mention, so far as I know, of what would happen to an unfaithful husband.)

We can summarize the doctrine of *samsara* thus: It is obvious that sentient beings on Earth exist in a multitude of different kinds, a vast hierarchy stretching from the lowest forms of animal life to mankind, which we take to be the highest. Throughout all of this hierarchy, there is a constant cycling of death and birth. The body, being *maya* and material, dies. But the *atman*, being Brahman and spirit, is eternal and can never die. Each Brahman-*Atman* enters the Dharma evolution at the most elementary level and is reborn over and over in successive bodies. This cycle is the ever-turning wheel of *samsara*.

The doctrine of *samsara* is beautifully stated in several of the Upanishads, such as the following extract:

> As a caterpillar, having come to the end of one blade of grass,
> Draws itself together and reaches out for the next,
> So the Self, having come to the end of one life,
> And dispelled all ignorance,
> Gathers in his faculties,
> And reaches out from the old body to a new.
>
> As the skin of a snake is sloughed onto an anthill,
> So does the mortal body fall.
> But the Self, freed from the body,
> merges in Brahman; infinite life, eternal light.[16]

Moksha

In the grand unfolding of Dharma, *samsara* is the slow progression of the Brahman-*Atman* to ever higher levels of consciousness through the procession of successive rebirths. Each rebirth presents the *atman* with the potential for a new and higher level of consciousness, of gradually dawning Self-awareness. *Samsara* is Brahman's long quest for the ultimately perfect rediscovery of Self:

> As long as we think we are the ego,
> We feel attached and fall into sorrow.
> But realize that you are the Self,
> And you will be freed from sorrow.
> When you realize that you are the Self,
> Supreme source of light, supreme source of love,
> You transcend the duality of life
> And enter into the Unitive State.[17]

"Enter into the Unitive State"; "be freed from sorrow." To be freed from the turning wheel of *samsara*—that is what it's all about. The Upanishads proclaim that the unquenchable yearning for perfect bliss can finally be satisfied, fully and completely. The only thing that stands in the way is ego: the grip of the illusion of ego. It is like a dream that holds us in the bondage of fear, and fear is the essence of suffering:

> When one realizes the Self,
> In whom all life is one, changeless, nameless, formless,
> Then one fears no more.
> Until we realize the unity of life, we live in fear.
> For the mere scholar who knows not the Self,
> His separateness becomes fear itself.[18]

But it is possible to awaken from the dream of ego. *Moksha* is awakening. In *moksha*, the ego—the illusion of the separate self—dissolves into the sea of peace that is Brahman:

> As a lump of salt thrown in water dissolves
> And cannot be taken out again,
> Though wherever we taste the water it is salty,
> Even so, beloved, the separate self dissolves
> In the sea of pure consciousness, infinite and immortal.[19]

The awakened man or woman—the person in whom the *atman* has broken through to the experience of *moksha*—lives daily life in a state of perfect peace, free from fear and suffering. Such a one is free to see himself in all and all in himself.

In the time of the Upanishads, there was some variety of opinion regarding the exact nature of *moksha* and how it was achieved. Many believed, for example, that the working out of *samsara* denied the possibility of *moksha* to all but high-caste Hindu males. Some would even go so far as to say that only the elite among the Brahmin caste were eligible. It might be necessary to be reborn many times even in spiritually perfected families before the *atman* was cleansed entirely of negative karma and thus became ready to make the final step. All agreed, though—or so it seems—that liberating oneself entirely of all selfish desires was the essential precondition of *moksha*—hence the emphasis on the life of the renunciant for those who sought this highest of all goals.

The attainment of *moksha* means release from the great wheel of *samsara*—from the cycle of birth, and death, and rebirth. In *moksha*, the *atman* awakens fully to its Brahman nature. Like a river returning to the sea, the *atman*—liberated from *avidya*—awakens perfectly to its Brahman identity:

> He is the eternal Reality, sing the scriptures,
> And the ground of existence.
> Those who perceive him in every creature merge in him,
> And are released from the wheel of birth and death.[20]

AN OVERVIEW OF VEDANTA COSMOLOGY

The Upanishads came into being as the "secret teachings" of various forest communities living in remote parts of India as long as three thousand years ago. The Upanishads were part of the private heritage of these ashrams, lovingly preserved and handed down orally for generations. How amazed those spiritual seekers would have been if they could have foreseen the present-day legacy of their teachings. We can read and ponder their thoughts as if it were all of us who were "sitting down close to" the guru.

Now, why are we still reading and pondering the thoughts of such an ancient tradition? What is it that connects us so vitally with the genius of ancient India? We certainly don't share a similar way of life; it would seem that ours and theirs couldn't be more different. Superficially, that is obviously true; but at a deeper level it's not true at all. Men and women of all times and cultures are alike with respect to the basic needs of life. We all face the same questions with regard to the meaning of life and the nature of death. People in every age—at least *some* people in every age—have yearned to get beyond the confusing complexity of ordinary life and find out what existence is really all about. That is exactly what the Upanishads attempt to do, and they are as alive and provocative today as they ever have been in the past.

The Upanishads are a major contribution to the fund of human wisdom. Technically speaking, they were composed as commentaries on the Vedas, but they go far beyond the Vedas: The Upanishads are to the Vedas as a flower in bloom is to a seedling. Taken as a whole, the Upanishads present a complete synthesis of insight regarding the true character of human life. This is the philosophy of Vedanta. Allow me to attempt a brief summary of this synthesis.

We began by raising this question: Why does anything exist at all? (What's *doing* the universe?) The Upanishads answer that it is Brahman, the root cause of all that is, the Fact of Existence. But Brahman is perfect and complete unto itself; there is no need for Brahman to act. Then why does Brahman begin to act? For what reason does Brahman *do* the universe? There is no purpose outside itself; there can't be. Brahman does the universe purely for its own sake. The universe is the "play," the *lila*, of Brahman.

The play of Brahman is not a haphazard affair. The universe unfolds in a rational and orderly fashion. This is due to the working of Natural Law, which is inherent in the *lila* of Brahman. We call this Natural Law Dharma. It is Brahman-Dharma that accounts for the orderly evolution of the universe. It is Brahman-Dharma that accounts for the harmony and balance that we observe in nature from one day to the next.

The Dharma evolution of the world that we know (the universe) began in a state of undifferentiated material reality. Whatever that may be—and it may not be directly knowable to human reason—it was, and always remains, the fundamental substrate of all material reality. We know it as *prakriti*. Responding to the ever-present influence of the basic forces of nature (the *gunas*) *prakriti* has evolved, and continues to evolve, all of the myriad forms ("things") that make up the constantly changing character of Nature.

The totality of all of these "things" of the material world is what we know as *maya*—reality that, through the Dharma evolution of *prakriti*, is the manifestation of Brahman. *Maya* is illusory only to the extent that the *forms of maya* (things) may be mistaken for having a reality of their own, rather than being the expression of a deeper reality.

Among the myriad forms of *maya* are two distinct kinds: those which exhibit consciousness (sentient beings) and those which do not (insentient beings). Consciousness is fundamentally different from materiality, although it can be *affected* by materiality, as, for example, in the case of thought and feeling. But consciousness itself is spiritual reality. Pure consciousness is the nature of Brahman.

Pure consciousness is known as *purusha*, the conscious essence of Brahman, revealed directly in *maya*—in *those forms of maya* (sentient beings), which are sufficiently evolved to allow it. In the Dharma evolution of the universe, *maya* (*prakriti*) eventually reached a level of maturity that made possible the direct revelation of Brahman itself (*purusha*) through the appropriate forms of *maya* (sentient beings).

Purusha, being Brahman itself, is pure spirit. *Prakriti*, the raw material of *maya*, being the manifestation of Brahman, is matter. Thus, Vedantic philosophy maintains that reality is of two basic modes: Spiritual Reality (Brahman) and Material Reality (the manifestation of Brahman). In this dichotomy, Spiritual Reality is perfect and eternal, and Material Reality is imperfect and transient.

There is an all-important relationship between matter and spirit (*prakriti* and *purusha*) in that material forms—for example, the bodies of animals—provide the necessary means by which Brahman itself enters directly into its *lila* play, the Dharma evolution of the universe. It may be said that the role of *prakriti* is to free *purusha*.

When it is indwelling in a sentient being, Brahman is called Brahman-*Atman*. Thus, Brahman-*Atman*, though individualized in each sentient being, is still Brahman. The *atman* is Brahman, not a role of Brahman. *Atman* is the Brahman seed of each sentient being, the true inner Self of each sentient being.

Atman is the conscious core of the ego role of each individual. The role is everything which makes up that distinct person, body as well as behavior. The role includes the "personality," the ego. Ego is the role; *atman* is the conscious *subject* of the role.

To mistake the role for the *atman* is fundamental ignorance, called *avidya*—the powerful illusion that my reality consists in the "person," the *role* that I play. This ego identification results inevitably in a sense of personal separation and personal insecurity and is responsible for the universal dread of personal death. *Avidya*, the common condition of mankind, is responsible for *all suffering*!

To see through the illusion of the separate self and to come to know the real Self, the Brahman-*Atman*, is the proper goal of life. This is true Knowledge. This is *vidya*.

It is obvious that sentient beings on Earth exist in a multitude of different kinds, a vast hierarchy stretching from the lowest forms of animal life to mankind, which we take to be the highest. Throughout all of this hierarchy, there is a constant cycling of death and birth. The body, being *maya* and thus material, dies, but the *atman*, being Brahman and thus spirit, is eternal and can never die.

Each Brahman-*Atman* enters the Dharma evolution at the most elementary level and is reborn over and over in successive bodies. This progression of rebirths, this turning of the wheel, is known as *samsara*. In the grand unfolding of Dharma, *samsara* is the slow progression of Brahman-*Atman* to ever higher levels of consciousness through the procession of successive rebirths. Each rebirth presents the *atman* with the potential for a new and higher level of consciousness, of gradually dawning Self-awareness. *Samsara* is Brahman's long quest for the ultimately perfect rediscovery of Self.

The great wheel of *samsara*—of birth, death, and rebirth—culminates finally in the *atman* awakening fully to the knowledge of its Brahman nature. Perfect, final awakening is referred to as *moksha*. Like a river returning to the sea, *moksha* is the state wherein the *atman* is liberated from *avidya*, awakening perfectly to its Brahman identity.

In the final end of Dharma, every *atman* will be reabsorbed into Brahman, and the play of *lila* will come to an end. Thus does Brahman, by "playing the universe," evolve eventually to perfect knowledge of Self, completing the Great Cycle of Creation.

At this point, the only question remaining is this: How does one achieve the awakening of *moksha*? What does one do? How does one live in order to prepare oneself for the experience? The answer is simply this: One practices *yoga*. The discipline of yoga offers the indispensable path that can lead one from the darkness of *avidya* to the light of *moksha*. In reality, the practice of yoga calls for a total transformation of life. The great *Bhagavad-Gita*, a work that draws together the teachings of the Upanishads, focuses on the nature of yoga, our next area of study.

I would like to end this chapter by returning briefly to the *Chandogya Upanishad*. In this work, a young man named Shvetaketu has returned to his father's home after formally studying the Vedas for twelve years. Uddalaka, his father, observes that Shvetaketu seems very proud of all this learning. "But," Uddalaka asks his son, "did you ask your teacher for that special wisdom which enables you to hear the unheard, think the unthought, and know the unknown?" A surprised Shvetaketu replies that he did not. "What is that wisdom, father?" he asks. Uddalaka then uses several magnificent analogies to describe to his son the nature of the Self, the *atman* within. Each of these analogies, of which the following is one, ends with the stirring words, *Tat tsvam asi*! (You are That!):

> As the rivers flowing east and west
> Merge in the sea and become one with it,
> Forgetting they were ever separate rivers,
> So do all creatures lose their separateness

When they merge at last into pure Being.
There is nothing that does not come from him.
Of everything he is the inmost Self.
He is the truth; he is the Self supreme.
And you are that, Shevetaketu; you are that.[21]

Notes

1. Eknath Easwaren, *The Upanishads* (Petaluma, Calif.: Nilgiri, 1987), p. 122.
2. *Ibid.*, p. 68 (*Kena Up.* I.3.4).
3. *Ibid.*, p. 110 (*Mundaka Up.* I.1.7–8).
4. *Ibid.*, p. 222 (*Shvetashvatara Up.* III.1–2).
5. *Ibid.*, p. 225 (*Shvet. Up.* IV.5).
6. *Ibid.*, p. 226 (*Shvet. Up.* IV.11).
7. *Ibid.*, p. 225 (*Shvet. Up.* IV.2,3).
8. *Ibid.*, p. 93 (*Katha Up.* II.2.2).
9. *Ibid.*, p. 183 (*Chandogya Up.* VI.2.2–3).
10. *Ibid.*, p. 178 (*Chandogya Up.* III.14.4).
11. *Ibid.*, p. 41 (*Brihadaranyaka Up.* III.8.11).
12. *Ibid.*, pp. 68, 69 (*Kena Up.* I.5, 7).
13. *Ibid.*, p. 115 (*Mundaka Up.* III.1.1).
14. *Ibid.*, p. 48 (*Brih. Up.* IV.4.5).
15. *Ibid.*, pp. 217, 218 (*Shvet. Up.* I.4–7).
16. *Ibid.*, pp. 47, 48, 49 (*Brih. Up.* IV.4.3, 7).
17. *Ibid.*, p. 115 (*Mundaka Up.* III. 1.2–3).
18. *Ibid.*, p. 144 (*Taitiriya Up.* II.7.1).
19. *Ibid.*, p. 38 (*Brih. Up.* II.4.12).
20. *Ibid.*, p. 218 (*Shvet. Up.* I.7).
21. *Ibid.*, pp. 184, 185 (*Chandogya Up.* VI.10.1; 10.3).

Study Questions

1. What is an ashram? What critical role did it play in the origin of the Upanishads?

2. "The place to begin such a study [the study of Vedanta] is right where you are." What does this mean?

3. "The ultimate question is, What's *doing* the universe?" Why is that the ultimate question, and what does it mean to say that it is the ultimate question?

4. Why do you suppose that the concept of Dharma (Brahman-Dharma) is taken up in the Upanishads second only to Brahman itself? What is it about the concept of Dharma that makes it so primary, so fundamental?

5. What do you think of the assertion that Vedantic philosophy and modern science are in wonderful harmony?

6. Is a thought *maya*?

7. How do you feel about the issue regarding matter and spirit? Is there truly a dichotomy between them, or does Vedantic philosophy succeed in reconciling the two as only an apparent dichotomy?

8. What profound philosophical assertions are implied in the doctrine of Brahman-*Atman*?

9. "*Avidya* is responsible for all suffering!" What in the world does that mean?

10. Why is it that the grip of the illusion of ego is the only thing that stands in the way of ultimate and perfect *moksha*?

4.

The Bhagavad Gita

The *Bhagavad Gita* opens on a battlefield where a most decisive battle is about to begin. Two great armies have assembled to decide once and for all who will rule the North Indian kingdom of Bharata. Will it be the Pandavas or their kinsmen, the Kauravas? After much bloodshed on both sides, the noble-hearted Pandavas will eventually prevail over the evil-hearted Kauravas, but that is far in the future, and as the first battle is about to begin, the excitement is building.

The preparations for battle have been nearly completed; the sacrifices have been made, the armour has been strapped on, the battle trumpets are sounding, drums are pounding, and the warriors on both sides are shouting and getting themselves emotionally keyed up for battle. At this point, Arjuna, the leader of the Pandavas, asks his charioteer to wheel him out into the no-man's-land between the armies so that he can get one last good look at the enemy's forces:

> O Krishna, drive my chariot between the two armies. I want to see those who desire to fight with me. With whom will this battle be fought? I want to see those assembled to fight for Duryodhana, those who seek to please the evil-minded son of Dhritarashtra by engaging in war.[1]

The driver of the chariot is none other than Krishna, an incarnation of the divine Vishnu. When they reach the center of the battlefield, Arjuna, shielding his eyes from the sun, peers over at the army that he will soon attack. It suddenly dawns upon him that he is about to order the slaughter of old friends, former teachers, and kinsmen. The realization hits him like a bolt of lightning, and he totally loses his nerve. Numbed with sorrow, he actually *sits down* on the floor of his lightweight war chariot and refuses to fight!

> "This is a great sin! We are prepared to kill our own relations out of greed for the pleasures of a kingdom." . . . Overwhelmed by sorrow, Arjuna spoke these words. And casting away his bow and arrows, he sat down in his chariot in the middle of the battlefield. . . . with the words, "I will not fight," he fell silent.[2]

To say the least, this is a dramatic moment. Krishna, ever wise and calm, must think of something to get Arjuna back into the fight; leading the army is Arjuna's duty. And Krishna had better come up with something fast! What follows in the *Bhagavad Gita* is a dialogue between Krishna and Arjuna that makes up all of the remainder of the work. In the course of this dialogue, Krishna accepts Arjuna as his disciple and explains the teachings of yoga to him. Naturally, a conversation of this sort—particularly one that rambles on for eighteen books (i.e., chapters)—would not ordinarily take place in the middle of the battlefield, but this story is being told in the epic style, and in an epic anything can happen.

The name *Bhagavad Gita* literally means "Song of the Lord." The Lord in this case refers to Krishna, who, as mentioned, was the mythical incarnation of the god Vishnu. Krishna, a compassionate and loving god, is a favorite among the Hindus. The word "song" might better be translated as "discourse" or "chant." The *Bhagavad Gita* (often referred to simply as the *Gita*) was composed in verse form and was intended to be chanted aloud. In this respect, the *Gita* was much like the epics of other ancient cultures. Homer's *Iliad*, for example, was originally composed in verse form and was meant to be chanted. Like the *Iliad*, the *Gita* was handed down in the oral tradition for many generations before it was eventually committed to writing.

The *Bhagavad Gita* represents the grand climax of the richly creative period that saw the creation of the principal Upanishads. In a way, the *Gita* is a synthesis of the philosophy of the Upanishads, which, generally speaking, were concerned with elucidating the difference between *vidya* (awareness of truth) and *avidya* (ignorance). The *Gita*, while reaffirming the truths of the Upanishads, goes beyond that and attempts to describe the way in which one actually makes the ascent to awakening. This is the way of yoga; the *Bhagavad Gita* is, in effect, an exposition of yoga.

The *Bhagavad Gita* was not composed as an isolated work. It is a part—actually, a very small part—of a much larger work known as the *Mahabharata*. The *Mahabharata* and the *Ramayana* are the two great epics of Hindu culture. They were to early Indian culture what the *Iliad* and the *Odyssey* were to the culture of ancient Greece.

THE *BHAGAVAD GITA* AND THE *MAHABHARATA*

The *Mahabharata* is a vast work; it seems that everything which makes up the culture of India is somehow included in it. The struggle between the Pandavas and the Kauravas is the central theme of the story, but woven in with that theme are a great many other substories. In the words of Sri Aurobindo,

> [The *Mahabharata* is] not only the story of the Bharatas, the epic of an early event which had become a national tradition, but on a vast scale the epic of the soul and religious and ethical mind and social and political ideals and culture and life of India. It is said popularly of it and with a certain measure of truth that whatever is in India is in the *Mahabharata*.[3]

History has virtually nothing to say about the composition of the *Mahabharata*; what we know is more a matter of legend than history. Presumably, there was a single author of the epic, but we know nothing of the life of that person. According to legend, the *Mahabharata* was written by a famous sage named Vyasa. He composed the entire work in only three years and dictated it to the popular, elephant-headed god Ganesha, who was the only one with a quick enough mind to follow the swiftness of Vyasa's thoughts. (Some believe, incidentally, that Vyasa never died. He lives to this day, so they say, in a secret hermitage somewhere back among the Himalayas.)

For our purposes, the name *Vyasa* will do as well as any. A literary genius named Vyasa, it shall be agreed, was the author of the *Mahabharata*, just as it is agreed that Homer was the author of the *Iliad*. Determining when the *Mahabharata* was created is also a tricky problem. Like Homer, the author of the *Mahabharata* undoubtedly pulled together many traditional legends and stories, some of which had been in existence for centuries. We can reasonably conclude, though, that this was done sometime between the fifth and fourth centuries B.C.E., because it seems very likely that that was the time when the *Bhagavad Gita* was composed, and the *Bhagavad Gita*, remember, was included within the *Mahabharata*. The overall tenor of the *Gita* suggests strongly that it was composed as a response to certain spiritual movements, including early Buddhism, that had come into existence at that time in Indian history.

The *Bhagavad Gita*, then, is a small, but key, part of a much larger work, the *Mahabharata*. Writers on the subject almost invariably say that the *Gita* is set like a precious jewel in the midst of the *Mahabharata*. Some have speculated that this jewel was not always there, that the *Gita* began life as an independent Upanishad and was appropriated by the author of the *Mahabharata*; it's a beautiful addition, they say, but extraneous to the story of the epic. Most scholars today feel that this interpretation is highly unlikely. The integrity of the style of the *Mahabharata* continues evenly through the *Gita*, and far from being a brilliant departure from the main theme of the *Mahabharata*, the dialogue that makes up the *Bhagavad Gita* provides the critical element necessary for making sense of the symbolism inherent in the story of the epic conflict that is recounted.

Nevertheless, the principal reason why some believe that the *Gita* might have been a later addition to the *Mahabharata* is that it can stand so well on its own. Except for that small part which we call the *Bhagavad Gita*, the *Mahabharata* does not play a crucial role in our understanding of the evolution of philosophical thought in India during the post-Vedic age. We can lift the *Gita* out of the *Mahabharata* and ignore the rest, and that is what I intend to do. However, the setting of the *Gita* is intimately connected to the larger story, and I feel that it would be helpful to take a few moments here to outline the character of the story up to the opening of the *Gita*.

Vyasa, the legendary author of the *Mahabharata*, assigns himself an important role in the story. It all started one day when his father, Parasara, a renowned Indian sage, hired the services of a ferryboat girl to carry him across a river. The girl, Satyavati, was so maddeningly lovely that Parasara found himself consumed with lust. She politely spurned his heated advances, but Parasara was quite a charmer, and Satyavati finally yielded to him when he promised her that she would not lose her virginity. He magically conjured a fog by the riverbank, and they made love, hidden from view by the dense mist. Later that same day, Satyavati gave birth to a son. All of this happened without Satyavati's losing her virginity. (Quite a day!)

The son, of course, was Vyasa. Like his father, he became a highly respected sage. Concerned about the deteriorating state of human life, Vyasa resolved to dedicate his life to collecting and explaining the spiritual lore of the Indian tradition. Meanwhile, his mother became the wife of Santanu, ruler of the Kuru kingdom. Since Satyavati was committed to lifelong virginity, Santanu was depending on his only son by a previous marriage to produce sons and continue the family line. Unfortunately, the son died young, leaving two childless wives. Satyavati, feeling compassion for her grieving husband, summoned her son, Vyasa, and begged him to help out. Vyasa reluctantly (or so we're told) agreed and slept with both beautiful young widows. Both girls conceived, and in the course of time each gave birth to a son.

Vyasa was said to be strikingly ugly. As he approached the first of the young widows, she was so revolted by the sight of him that she turned her face away and closed her eyes. This infuriated Vyasa, and he responded by putting a curse on the girl. (Apparently, though, he was not so angry that he declined to sleep with her.) As a result of the curse, the first girl's son, Dhritarashtra, was born blind. The other girl, being kind and noble hearted, did not look away. Her son, Pandu, born shortly after Dhritarashtra, was perfectly healthy.

Since Dhritarashtra was the first to be born, he would have been the successor to the throne. However, his blindness disqualified him, and the rightful line of succession went to Pandu and his descendants. From an early age, it was obvious that Pandu was uncommonly good and noble, whereas Dhritarashtra was a more average sort of person—that is to say, scheming and self-centered. With his two wives, Kunti and Madri, Pandu had five sons, the Pandavas, who like him were strong and courageous young men. Dhritarashtra, demonstrating that blindness was his only infirmity, produced one hundred sons. These hundred are referred to as the Kauravas, which literally means "The sons of Kuru," Kuru being the name of the kingdom. All of Dhritarashtra's sons were, like their father, mean-spirited and selfish young men. But the kingdom was secure; after all, it was Pandu and his sons that would inherit the crown. But that wouldn't make a very good story.

Pandu unexpectedly and tragically died young. His five sons were still only boys. The eldest, Yudhishthira, was the rightful heir to the crown, but he couldn't wear it until he became a man. In the meantime, his uncle, the blind Dhritarashtra, seized the throne and ruled as regent. This might have been technically unlawful, but all things considered, it could be argued that it was a reasonable move at the time. Dhritarashtra merged the two households, raising the five Pandu boys along with his own hundred sons.

The court of Dhritarashtra was a large and active one. The courtly education of so many boys called for many teachers. In addition, there were seers, court officials, military men, and countless relatives. It wasn't long before everyone was aware that the five Pandu boys stood out from the rest. They were excellent young men; the comparison was stark and embarrassing, especially to Dhritarashtra.

Dhritarashtra had hoped that in the course of time his own claim to the throne would be legitimized and that *his* firstborn son, Duryodhana, would be accepted as the next king. To forestall this eventuality, the leaders of the court pushed through a proclamation recognizing the young Yudhishthira as the rightful heir apparent. Now the sons of Dhritarashtra were consumed with jealous hatred. They decided privately to solve their problem by killing their five Pandu cousins. This decision set in motion a spectacular and complicated plot designed to do away with their rivals.

We need not go into the details here. Suffice it to say that at one point, pretending to want to bury the hatchet and have good relations again, Dhritarashtra's sons presented the Pandava brothers with a splendid palace built entirely of ivory. The modest-minded brothers really didn't want something so extravagant, but to be polite, they accepted the peace offering. Well, it wasn't ivory at all, but was constructed of pure beeswax—very beautiful and also highly flammable. While the Pandava brothers slept, the Kaurava brothers set fire to the palace. As you might guess, the Pandus escaped, but only by the skin of their teeth. They used a secret underground passage that led into the nearby forest, but to save their lives, they had to remain in the forest disguised as holy men.

Here, too, the story might have ended, but again a dramatic event came to the rescue of the story line of the epic. Drupada, the ruler of the neighboring Panchalas, sent out the word that all of the nobles of North India were invited to a great festival at which he would select a husband for his beautiful young daughter, Draupadi. The Pandava brothers heard about the festival and decided to go. Everyone who was anyone was there, including the divine Krishna, who was there as the leader of a powerful clan named the Yadavas.

In the spirit of a good Robin Hood story, Drupada designed an archery contest for the would-be suitors. The winner, using a monster bow fashioned by Drupada himself, would have to hit a moving target, shooting through a revolving ring that was mounted high off the ground. As you might guess, it was a Pandava who won the prize. In fact, it was the noble Arjuna, destined to be one of the two central characters of the *Bhagavad Gita*.

As a result of Arjuna's victory, the consequent alliance of the Pandavas with the Kingdom of the Panchalas, and their new friendship with Krishna and the Yadavas, the Kaurava brothers were more or less forced to sit down and settle their differences with their cousins. They reached a compromise settlement: The kingdom of the Kurus would be divided into two parts. The Kaurava brothers would keep the largest and best part along the Ganges River, and the Pandavas would receive an inferior piece of land along the tributary Jumna River.

Before long, trouble was brewing again. The industrious Pandavas developed their poor parcel, transforming it into a rich and attractive land, thus arousing the greed of their Kaurava cousins. Enter the wily Sakuni, an uncle of Duryodhana. He knew that the noble Yudhishthira had one weakness—one that he shared with noblemen throughout history: He was a reckless and passionate gambler. Sakuni enticed Yudhishthira into a game of dice wherein he skillfully cheated him out of everything. Yudhishthira lost his entire kingdom and all of the possessions of his brothers as well. Penniless, they had to retreat back into the wilderness again, forced into exile for thirteen years.

The Pandava brothers accepted the terms of the loss without complaint, but at the end of the thirteen years they demanded the restoration of their kingdom. Naturally, the

Kauravas rejected the demand. Krishna interceded on behalf of the Pandavas, but got nowhere. Ultimately, it became apparent that the conflict could have only one resolution: war. The sons of Pandu did not want war for the sake of their own personal gain. They would have been willing to accept exile and poverty for the rest of their lives rather than visit the horror and suffering of war on their kinsmen. However, much more than personal satisfaction was at stake. This was a conflict between justice and injustice, between good and evil. It was the Pandavas's duty as members of the warrior class to uphold the honor of their family and the good of the social order. For this reason, they sadly agreed to shoulder the awesome responsibility of war, in which Arjuna would be their leader.

Both sides began the long and arduous preparations for battle. Both sides petitioned Krishna for his help. Representatives of the Kaurava brothers went to him first. Krishna declared that he would not fight, but that he would offer instead the services of his splendid army or his own personal counsel. The Kauravas greedily accepted the army. With the help of Krishna's fighting men, they reasoned, their army would be invincible in battle. To counter the superior strength of the Kauravas's warriors, Krishna offered his services as charioteer to Arjuna, and that is how the two men, Krishna and Arjuna, happened to be together in the war chariot in the middle of the battlefield at the opening of the *Bhagavad Gita.*

As noted much earlier in these pages, the Aryan warriors of ancient India loved the bow and arrow, as well as the horse-drawn war chariot. The chariot was a lightweight two-wheeled vehicle, probably made of wicker and leather. Pulled by one or two well-trained horses, it was a deadly weapon. The chariot carried two men. One was the fighting man, with both hands free to rain the killing fire of his arrows on the enemy. The other, of course, was the driver of the chariot. This man was no servant: He was a highly skilled and highly respected warrior. One false move could mean instant death for both.

There is a profound symbolism in the fact that Krishna was a charioteer in this story. Krishna's role in the *Bhagavad Gita* will be to instruct Arjuna in the ancient teachings of yoga. The word *yoga* was derived from the Sanskrit root *yuj*, which originally meant "to bind things together." The English word "yoke," as in "to yoke oxen," is a cognate of *yoga*. One who seriously practices yoga is called a *yogi*. There is some speculation that in its original meaning, *yogi* referred to the man who trained the semiwild horses and harnessed them (yoked them) to the war chariot that he himself would drive into battle. In other words, he was a charioteer. The profession became a powerful symbol for yoga, which demands that the yogi harness the wild horses of his own nature and drive the chariot of his own person into the battle against self-will and ignorance.

DEVELOPMENT OF THE *BHAGAVAD GITA*

The Opening Scene

Thus we come to the gathering of the forces at the great battlefield of Kurukshetra, field of the Kurus. The army of the Pandavas is on one side, led by Arjuna. Facing them is the powerful army of the Kauravas, led by the eldest brother, Duryodhana.

Dhritharashtra, now old as well as blind, does not travel to Kurekshetra. The battle, however, will be described to him by Sanjaya, his personal driver. Sanjaya will be Dhritarashtra's eyes and ears; he will describe for him all that occurs on the battlefield. For the occasion, Sanjaya has acquired magical powers of perception. With the power of clairaudience, he can hear everything that is said, even though the speakers be far away. The author of the *Mahabharata* uses this device to make Sanjaya the narrator of the entire dialogue that is about to take place between Krishna and Arjuna. Sanjaya is relating the conversation to Dhritarashtra. It is for this reason that the opening line of the *Bhagavad Gita*, delivered by Dhritarashtra, reads thus:

> O Sanjaya, tell me what happened at Kurukshetra, the field of dharma, where my family and the Pandavas gathered to fight.[4]

As we saw at the beginning of this chapter, Arjuna asks Krishna to take him out to the center of the battlefield, where he can get one last look at the enemy before ordering the attack. What he saw, of course, were "grandfathers, teachers, uncles, sons-in-law, grandsons-in-law, and friends. Arjuna was overcome by sorrow. Despairing, he spoke these words":

> O Krishna, I see my own relations here anxious to fight, and my limbs grow weak; my mouth is dry, my body shakes, and my hair is standing on end. My skin burns, and the bow Gandiva has slipped from my hand. I am unable to stand; my mind seems to be whirling.

> O Krishna, what satisfaction could we find in killing Dhritarashtra's sons? We would become sinners by slaying these men, even though they are evil. The sons of Dhritarashtra are related to us; therefore, we should not kill them. How can we gain happiness by killing members of our own family? Though they are overpowered by greed and see no evil in destroying families or injuring friends, we see these evils. Why shouldn't we turn away from this sin?[5]

Paralyzed with sorrow and confusion, Arjuna slumps to the floor of his chariot, utterly unable to stand and lead his men into battle. "I will not fight," he says. In the heavy silence that follows this declaration, the attention turns to Krishna, who now must find a way to get Arjuna back into the fight. He must persuade Arjuna to do his duty and lead his men into battle against the enemy.

The *Bhagavad Gita* as Metaphor

This is an appropriate place to consider a most significant question regarding the *Mahabharata* in general and the *Bhagavad Gita* in particular. Was it the intent of the author of the *Mahabharata* that the story of the war be taken literally, or is the battlefield of Kurukshetra meant to be seen as a metaphor for a very different kind of conflict? Is Krishna, as his words clearly seem to indicate, encouraging Arjuna really to join battle with his Kaurava kinsmen and visit slaughter on them? Or do the words hold a different meaning—a metaphorical meaning—and is the battle that Krishna has in mind of a totally different sort from what is being literally described?

These questions have no easy answers. From the historical perspective, it is likely that the battle described in the *Mahabharata* is based on an actual event that occurred in northern India sometime around the tenth century B.C.E. We know very little about this great conflict, but it became enshrined in folk legends and would eventually become the unifying theme around which the *Mahabharata* was composed. In this way, that battle was very much like the Trojan War, an actual historical event that became the basis for Homer's *Iliad*. But the *Iliad* was not a documentary retelling of the Trojan War, and neither was the *Mahabharata* a retelling of its Indian war. Both epics used a dramatic event popularized in the traditional legends to provide a highly charged setting for a story about human strength and weakness.

Throughout the centuries, some scholars have argued that the *Mahabharata* is meant to be understood in a literal sense—that the battle imagery is just that and nothing else, and that Krishna is indeed urging Arjuna to fight and kill the enemy. This is not glorification of war, nor even a resigned acceptance of its inevitability; it is a story about honor and duty—the duty of Arjuna as a member of the Kshatriya class to behave as a warrior should, courageously accepting the responsibility of war when it is destined to be. To do otherwise would be to shirk his duty, to upset the working of Dharma, and thus bring dishonor and evil to his family and to the entire social order.

It is difficult for many modern readers of the *Bhagavad Gita* to accept this point of view. A far more compelling interpretation is to see the *Gita* as metaphorical. But what is the metaphor? Eknath Easwaren puts it this way:

> Scholars can debate the point forever, but when the [teachings of the *Gita* are put into practice,] I think it becomes clear that the struggle the *Gita* is concerned with is the struggle for self-mastery. It was Vyasa's genius to take the whole great *Mahabharata* epic and see it as metaphor for the perennial war between the forces of light and the forces of darkness in every human heart.
>
> Arjuna and Krishna are then no longer merely characters in a literary masterpiece. Arjuna becomes Everyman, asking the Lord himself, Sri Krishna, the perennial questions about life and death—not as a philosopher, but as the quintessential man of action. Thus read, the *Gita* is not an external dialogue but an internal one: between the ordinary human personality, full of questions about the meaning of life, and our deepest Self, which is divine.[6]

Seen in this way, the real battlefield is right inside every man and woman ever born. It is the battlefield where the struggle between the higher nature and the lower nature is waged every day. To put it in the language of the Upanishads, the conflict is between *avidya* and *vidya*. Arjuna represents the ordinary, unenlightened man or woman. He is bound up in his ego attachments and the fear and suffering generated by that state of mind. Arjuna is the self with a small *s*; Krishna represents the *atman*, the Self with a capital *S*. Krishna represents our innermost Self. In terms of this metaphor, Krishna is lovingly urging Arjuna to do battle against his own infatuation with his ego attachments—to attack and "kill" them, as it were. His reluctance is perfectly understandable, but joining the battle is the only way that he can liberate himself from the grip of delusion and hope to awaken to knowledge of the Self. The way of liberation is yoga, and Krishna will teach Arjuna yoga.

Eknath Easwaren tells the personal story of his journey by train one time in northern India. The train stopped at Kurukshetra, the legendary site of the great battle, and everyone got off the train in excitement to see this dramatic place—everyone, that is, but Easwaren. He didn't have to get off the train to see the battlefield; it traveled with him wherever he went, and the same is true for everyone else. The battlefield of the *Bhagavad Gita* is to be found in our hearts and minds, not in the soil of northern India.

Seen in terms of this striking metaphor, the *Bhagavad Gita* becomes a personal message to all of mankind. It is universal, and it is relevant to everyone's life in every age and every culture. The metaphorical interpretation of the *Gita* elevates the entire *Mahabharata* to the level of sublime literature. It transforms the *Mahabharata* from a simple action-packed adventure story of one noble Indian family to the story of every person's odyssey from darkness to light.

The Awakened Person

At the end of Book One, we leave Arjuna, his will paralyzed, actually sitting down in his small war chariot, refusing to fight. To say the least, it's a dramatic moment. The spotlight, though, turns to Krishna. He'd better think of something to get Arjuna back into the fight, and he'd better do it fast! The battle is about to begin, and the leader of the Pandavas is out in the middle of the battlefield, sitting down on the floor of his chariot.

Krishna, not flustered in the least by the situation, smiles at Arjuna and speaks to him in a calm, friendly tone of voice: "This despair and weakness in a time of crisis are mean and unworthy of you, Arjuna. . . . It does not become you to yield to this weakness. Arise with a brave heart and destroy the enemy." Arjuna repeats his determination not to kill his kinsmen and former friends. It's a horrifying thought; he would rather be dead himself. Krishna responds by taking aim at the very heart of Arjuna's dilemma, the problem of death:

> You speak sincerely, but your sorrow has no cause. The wise grieve neither for the living nor for the dead. There has never been a time when you and I, and the kings gathered here have not existed, nor will there be a time when we will cease to exist. As the same person inhabits the body through childhood, youth, and old age, so too at the time of death he attains another body. The wise are not deluded by these changes.[7]

Clearly, the author of the *Gita* is using the character of Krishna to affirm the traditional, orthodox doctrines of *atman* and *samsara*. At the very beginning of the dialogue between Krishna and Arjuna, this all-important matter, the cornerstone of the Vedanta philosophy, is nailed down in a clear and distinct fashion. The author of the *Gita* wants no doubts to exist in the mind of the listener.

Why is it so important to affirm the reality of *atman* right at the beginning? We can only speculate. One possibility is that it was simply a reasonable place to begin. If the *Bhagavad Gita* is a summation of Upanishadic teaching and a practical guide for applying that teaching, then why not begin with the most fundamental principles? After all, Arjuna is grievously worried about the imminent death of many warriors, as if death were a real and final end of life. This is not an unreasonable interpretation. Another possibility exists, however. At the time the *Gita* was composed, the traditional teachings were being actively challenged by many reform movements. Some, such as the Buddhists, were even going so far as to deny the reality of *atman*, the spiritual bedrock of the whole orthodox tradition. It may well be that the *Bhagavad Gita* came into existence as an inspired counteroffensive against the self-styled reform movements. The author of the *Gita*, while accepting the need for some reforms, would not throw out the baby with the bathwater. In summing up the essential teachings of the Vedanta tradition, he would answer the reformers—especially the Buddhists—by revealing the great practical truths of the orthodox tradition, and he would begin by strongly proclaiming the fundamental correctness of the doctrine of *atman*.

Whatever the case may be, Krishna does indeed begin with a clear statement about the reality of *atman* and *samsara*. Proclaiming it, however, is one thing; knowing its truth is quite another, and Krishna's task is to lead Arjuna to an awakening in which he sees that truth. In so doing, Arjuna will see through the illusion that is responsible for his present state of confusion and suffering, and then he will be able and willing to stand up and fight. To achieve this end, Krishna declares that he will teach Arjuna yoga. "You have heard the intellectual explanation of Samkhya, Arjuna; now listen to the principles of yoga."[8] A little earlier, while expressing his feelings of despair, Arjuna had asked Krishna to accept him as a disciple. It was important for the author of the *Gita* to insert this piece of information, because in the Hindu tradition it is imperative that a person request the privilege of being another's disciple; a genuinely enlightened teacher never *recruits* disciples. Thus, it is now legitimate for Krishna to begin the teaching, and this is what the *Bhagavad Gita* is really all about. Above all else, it is a practical guide showing the listener (or reader) how to apply the teachings of the Upanishads in one's daily life. Krishna says that he will teach Arjuna yoga because, in its general sense, yoga refers to any path that can lead from ignorance to awakening.

One almost gets the feeling that Krishna is a little unsure about how to begin. His initial comments about yoga are lofty generalizations. He tells Arjuna that "Yoga is perfect evenness of mind" and that "Yoga is skill in action." Arjuna, however, is a man of action, a down-to-earth kind of person. He's not interested in theoretical discussions. Arjuna wants practical advice with concrete examples. After listening for a little while, Arjuna interrupts Krishna with a question. You can almost sense his frustration, but at the same time, his growing interest. Before getting into these more generalized matters, Arjuna wants to know, up front, what the person skilled in yoga is actually *like*; in other words, how does he recognize the real McCoy. Lots of people *claim* to be enlightened, but when you look closely, invariably it turns out to be only a pose. So, before getting into a discussion of principles, Arjuna wants Krishna to describe what the *really* awakened person is like. How does he walk? How does he talk? How does he behave in ordinary, everyday situations? Arjuna needs to know these things so that he will have something concrete in mind that he can relate Krishna's teaching to.

Krishna apparently sees the wisdom in Arjuna's question and responds in a short monologue at the end of Book Two that is one of the most beautiful sections of the entire *Bhagavad Gita*. Gandhi felt that if this eighteen-verse section were all that had survived of the *Gita*, we would still have all of its essential wisdom. Krishna answers Arjuna's question: He describes for him the essential features of the truly awakened man or woman. Before we get to that, though, this would be a good place to look briefly at Krishna's description of the kind of person who is *not* a genuinely awakened individual. This is a very important matter to Krishna, because the world is so obviously full of fakes. Many people are deluded by counterfeit wise men, and Krishna wants to be sure that Arjuna will not be one of them.

It seems that Krishna is most concerned about what he regards to be the false message of those who claim to be spiritually aware as a result of extremely ascetic lifestyles. Indian culture has always included a number of individuals who drop out of ordinary life to become itinerant monks—the "holy men," the sadhus. Generally speaking, they are respected by the common people, who believe that these monks have achieved a higher state of spiritual awareness as a result of their austerities. There have always been some who are willing to go to great extremes of asceticism. The thinking behind their actions, usually, is that a higher truth can be known only when the distractions of *maya* are *completely* transcended. The ultimate goal becomes total inaction, because all action is rooted in *maya*. Krishna declares this to be a false path. Both those who follow it and those who hold them in high respect are deluding themselves:

> He who shirks action does not attain freedom; no one can gain perfection by abstaining from work. Indeed, there is no one who rests for even an instant; every creature is driven to action by his own nature.[9]*

In a way, though, Krishna's strongest censure is for those more ordinary kinds of people who proclaim, through their lifestyle, that fulfillment is to be found in a selfish and materialistic pursuit of pleasure. That way of life is far more universal than the way of the ascetic monk and is therefore much more pernicious. Often dressed in a seductively appealing form, it is the false path that Arjuna and everyone else have to deal with

---

*It's quite possible that the author of the *Gita* was specifically fixing the Jains in his sights. Jainism was one of the reform movements that the *Gita* seems to be reacting to, and the Jains, especially in their early days, sought release from all worldly attachments through extreme ascetic practices.

all of the time. Krishna first turns on this erroneous way in the early part of his discourse:

> There are ignorant people who speak flowery words and take delight in the letter of the law, saying that there is nothing else. Their hearts are full of selfish desires, Arjuna. Their idea of heaven is their own enjoyment, and the aim of all their activities is pleasure and power. The fruit of their actions is continual rebirth.[10]

Krishna returns to this theme much later in the *Gita*. He makes his point in very strong words. The relevance of these words would be recognized by men and women from any age:

> "There is no God," they say, "no truth, no spiritual law, no moral order. The basis of life is sex; what else can it be?" Holding such distorted views, possessing scant discrimination, they become enemies of the world, causing suffering and destruction.
>
> Hypocritical, proud, and arrogant, living in delusion and clinging to deluded ideas, insatiable in their desires, they pursue their unclean ends. Although burdened with fears that end only with death, they still maintain with complete assurance, "Gratification of lust is the highest that life can offer."
>
> Bound on all sides by scheming and anxiety, driven by anger and greed, they amass by any means they can a hoard of money for the satisfaction of their cravings. . . . "I have destroyed my enemies. I shall destroy others too! Am I not like God? I enjoy what I want. I am successful. I am powerful. I am happy. I am rich and well-born. Who is equal to me? I will perform sacrifices and give gifts, and rejoice in my own generosity". . . . Self-important, obstinate, swept away by the pride of wealth, they ostentatiously perform sacrifices without any regard for their purpose. Egotistical, violent, arrogant, lustful, angry, envious of everyone, they abuse my presence within their own bodies and in the bodies of others.
>
> Life after life I cast those who are malicious, hateful, cruel, and degraded into the wombs of those with similar demonic natures. Degraded in this way, Arjuna, they fail to reach me and fall lower still.[11]

Now, having identified the principal enemies of the right path, we can return to Krishna's response to Arjuna's question. Arjuna had asked Krishna to describe for him, at least in general terms, the character of the person who is truly an awakened man or woman. "Tell me of those who live established in wisdom, ever aware of the Self, O Krishna. How do they talk? How sit? How move about"?[12]

Krishna begins his response to Arjuna's question in the section at the end of Book Two. It's a theme that he returns to often throughout the *Gita*. The essential points can be summed up as follows:

They live in wisdom who see themselves in all, and all in them; who have renounced every selfish desire and sense craving tormenting the heart. Neither agitated by grief, nor hankering after pleasure, they live free from lust and fear and anger.[13]

Free from self-will, aggressiveness, arrogance, anger, and the lust to possess people or things, he is at peace with himself and others and enters into the Unitive State. United with Brahman, ever joyful, beyond the reach of desire and sorrow, he has equal regard for every living creature and attains supreme devotion to me.[14]

In these beautiful passages, Krishna is emphasizing that the genuinely awakened person is one who has come to see the underlying unity of all being and who thus feels deep love and compassion for every being that exists. Such a person is a true "renunciate," not in the sense of renouncing the world, which Krishna insists is a false path, but rather in the sense of renouncing "every selfish desire and sense craving tormenting the heart." Thus, the genuinely awakened person does not denounce sense pleasure as such (a common misunderstanding), but only *attachment to* sense pleasure. It is the nature of life to often be pleasurable; this is natural and good. A problem develops only when the pleasures of life become objects of desire, the stuff of attachment. The awakened person is said to be free from attachment *and* its inevitable companion, aversion. The awakened person is kind, modest, and above all, reveals in his or her daily life a compassion for all other beings.

Krishna wants Arjuna to understand (and remember, Arjuna represents all men and women) that the awakened person is most definitely not some rare saintly being, far beyond the reach of ordinary mortals. The awakened person is the truly real, down-to-earth human being and dwells in the heart of every man and woman, waiting only to be "awakened" by that genuinely rich way of life that Krishna wants Arjuna to see as the right path: the path of yoga.

The remainder of the *Gita* amounts to a close examination of the way of yoga. Krishna will focus on three of the most prominent schools of yoga: Raja Yoga, Karma Yoga, and Bhakti Yoga. The author of the *Gita* chooses not to include Jnana Yoga, the way of special mystical and philosophical knowledge. Perhaps this is because it would obviously not be a suitable path for the not very philosophical Arjuna, as would be true for most people. Also, Hatha Yoga is never mentioned by name. Hatha, the yoga of highly specialized breathing and bodily exercises was seen as a way to condition and control the physical self. For the most part, Hatha was viewed as a companion of the yoga of meditation, and it was assumed that the student would learn its skills under the personal supervision of a master. It simply was not the sort of subject to be discussed in a work such as the *Gita*.

In the organization of the *Gita* as it has come down to us, the subject of Karma Yoga is taken up first; it is the theme of Book Three. Book Six deals specifically with Raja Yoga, the yoga of meditation. The remaining twelve books touch on many subjects, but are concerned largely with Bhakti Yoga, the yoga of devotion. The *Bhagavad*

Gita is not neatly organized, the way a modern text would likely be. To get the sense of the whole, it is necessary to read the entire work, slowly and thoughtfully, and that's exactly what I hope you will do. These pages are in no way a substitute for reading the *Gita* itself. Ideally, I hope that what you read here will inspire you to want to read the book itself and that you will be able to understand it a little better for having studied this first.

Karma Yoga

The word *karma* is derived from the Sanskrit word *kri* ("to do"), and in its most basic sense, karma simply means "action." This basic sense of the word, though, would come to have a variety of meanings in the evolution of Eastern thought. Speaking very broadly, karma is usually associated with the principle of cause and effect: Actions one performs will inevitably have consequences. It's best, though, to pin down the specific meaning of karma for each philosophical system individually. The word karma, along with so much else from the "mysterious East," became enormously popular with some in the West during the fifties and sixties. Not too surprisingly, its meaning suffered a bit in translation from ancient Hindu culture to the modern counterculture.*

Karma Yoga is the "path of right action." It deals with the kind of behavior—that is, lifestyle—that is appropriate for one who seeks to become a liberated man or woman. Having established that a life of action is natural and necessary, Krishna turns to the real question: What is *right* action? We are presented with two alternatives: action directed to the goal of personal profit and action directed to the welfare of all. It should come as no surprise that the author of the *Gita* chooses the welfare of all as the correct answer:

> Selfish action imprisons the world. Act selflessly, without any thought of personal profit.[15]

> The ignorant work for their own profit, Arjuna; the wise work for the welfare of the world, without thought for themselves.[16]

> You have the right to work, but never to the fruit of work. You should never engage in action for the sake of reward, nor should you long for inaction.[17]

Pretty startling suggestions, aren't they? Is Krishna really saying that I have no right to the fruit of my own work, that I should never engage in action for the sake of reward?

---

*A wonderful example of the modern misunderstanding of the word was provided by a memorable scene in an otherwise not very memorable film from the sixties. A hippie-looking young man is riding on a bus, and sitting next to him is his polar opposite, a yuppie-type insurance salesman, who is haranguing him about the virtues of life insurance. When he can't stand it any longer, the hippie type turns to the yuppie type and says, "Hey man, you're messin' up my karma!"

How can that be? Is he suggesting that I would be a better person if I refused my pay-check? These passages seem to fly in the face of common sense. Obviously, some careful interpretation is needed here.

In the view of the author of the *Gita*, the proper goal of life is to become an awakened person; everything takes its value in relation to that all-important goal. He would agree wholeheartedly with the spirit of the following line from the Gospel: "What does it profit a man if he gains the entire world, and suffers the loss of his immortal soul?"[18] If the essence of enlightenment is knowing the unity of all being, then the enemy of enlightenment is the private ego and its endless selfish cravings.

The path of Karma Yoga is directed at one thing: the obsessive attachment to the welfare of the private self. It seeks to overcome this attachment by redirecting the purpose of action to that which by its very nature is not ego-self—that is, the welfare of the larger community of which the individual is but a part. What it comes down to is a redefining of "self," a coming to see that the private ego-self is an illusion; the real self is the entire community, ultimately all of humankind. When one identifies with the whole community, he can be entirely "selfish," so to speak, and the welfare of all will be served. In this view, we have the very interesting contention that in the long run, one's personal interests are best served not by focusing on the desires of the private self, but rather by deliberately acting in what one perceives to be the best interests of the whole community. In other words, work for the good of the whole, and your own interests will be best served. That may sound a little crazy at first, but the *Gita* insists that it is true, and understanding it is the key to a genuinely successful life.

Karma Yoga is sometimes referred to as the yoga of Selfless Service. "Selfless Service" does not mean "good deeds"—helping someone across the street, for example, or picking up a hitchhiker. Good deeds are wonderful, of course, but that's not the point; "Selfless Service" means something else. The "service" in "Selfless Service" refers simply to action that in some way is of real value to the community. This could be just about anything. "Selfless" means simply that the action is not ego bound. We all know such "self-less" moments. In fact, anytime that one is totally absorbed in a task, ego consciousness is temporarily suspended. This is what happens naturally when you work at something you love to do. An artist absorbed in a painting, a scientist focused on a research project, even a farmer plowing a field—all of these are examples of potentially "self-less" action. The key point is that one forgets himself, temporarily transcends his ego-self, by becoming absorbed in a loved activity.

Now let's put things together. "Selfless Service" refers to any kind of action in which one loses oneself, so long as that action is beneficial to the community. Thus, the path of Karma Yoga is open to everyone! Anyone who works in a field that he or she loves and whose work is of value to the larger community is, in fact, a Karma yogi. The farmer, the scientist, the teacher, the homemaker, the sculptor, the student, the garbage collector (yes, definitely), the delivery person, and even that insurance salesman—almost every kind of worker can be a Karma yogi. The only requirement is that the work be of some genuine value to the community and that, all in all, the person love the work. This is essential, because it is only love that dissolves the grip of ego. If one does not love the work, then it becomes merely a means to an end. What this usually means is that the work becomes a means to making money, which can then be used to satisfy the desires of the ego. This separation between action and its reward is precisely what Karma Yoga seeks to overcome. So long as there is separation, the ego is in control. This is why Krishna wants Arjuna to see that it is essential that the reward be *in the doing*, not separated from it. If we work for the sake of "profit," we are separating the reward from the work itself, something which would never happen—could never happen—if the action was something loved in itself. Does a mother caring for her baby have to be paid for it? Of course not; the joy is in the doing, just as it is with the artist. It is truly said that there is no such thing as a poor artist. The bottom line is that *everyone* is an artist, potentially at least; everyone can be a Karma yogi. This is why Krishna says, "The ignorant work for their own profit, Arjuna; the wise work for the welfare of the world, without thought for themselves."

Karma Yoga is often misunderstood as meaning little more than that which is practiced by a giving sort of person, someone who does good deeds. Seen in its proper light, however, Karma Yoga amounts to a total reshaping of the goal of action in life. It is a renunciation of the belief that selfishly serving the desires of the ego is the way to fulfillment in life. Krishna sums it up well:

> True renunciation is giving up all desire for personal reward. Those who are attached to personal reward will reap the consequences of their actions; some pleasant, some unpleasant, some mixed. But those who renounce every desire for personal reward go beyond the reach of karma.[19]

Raja Yoga

In the still mind, in the depths of meditation, the Self reveals itself.

Book Six of the *Bhagavad Gita* focuses on Raja Yoga, the yoga of meditation. Raj means "royal" or "rule" in Sanskrit; thus, Raja Yoga is the "King of Yogas." Raja rules over the others in the sense that it is the most central; it is the interface between ordinary consciousness and knowledge of the absolute. Through the practice of meditation, the aspirant learns to control the mind, strip down the layers of ego, and, ultimately, achieve the state of consciousness known as *Samadhi*, the Unitive State. (We will have much more to say on this subject later.)

In the practice of Raja Yoga, one turns inward—deeply inward—shedding all of the layers of the private self and its restless mind. The goal is nothing less than getting in touch with the core of consciousness, in which state perfect peace reigns. Raja is thus the companion and the necessary obverse of Karma Yoga, whose nature is action. The out-going of Karma finds balance in the inward-turning of Raja. Together, they are a complementary whole.

These two great yogas, Karma and Raja, are found in all spiritual traditions, although, of course, they are known by many names. In Hinduism, they became highly developed traditions. Shakyamuni Buddha, for example, who was himself a Hindu sanyasin for many years, loved the practices of Raja Yoga. Whereas he would part company with many of the cherished beliefs of the Hindu tradition, he never abandoned the practice of meditation, which was to become the core practice of his teaching.

Up to this point in the discourse between Krishna and Arjuna, Krishna has wanted Arjuna to understand that, through the practice of Karma Yoga, he can refashion himself into the kind of unselfish man that is receptive to higher knowledge. Now, in Book Six, Krishna reveals that the actual awakening of higher knowledge is an interior experience born in the consciousness of one who has learned to control the restless mind—hence the need for Raja, as well as Karma, Yoga. But Arjuna, a normal human being, is dismayed by the thought of ever being able to control something so fitful as the thinking mind: "O Krishna, the stillness of divine union which you describe is beyond my comprehension. How can the mind, which is so restless, attain lasting peace? The mind is restless, turbulent, powerful, violent; trying to control it is like trying to tame the wind."[20]

How right Arjuna is! Controlling the thinking mind is like trying to tame the wind. In India, a land where monkeys abound, the ordinary mind is called the "monkey mind"; indeed, sometimes it is compared to a drunken monkey (quite an image, but not far off the mark). Nevertheless, the experience of countless men and women over the ages proves that controlling the mind is possible. With dedication and patience, the practices of Raja Yoga can lead one to a mastery of meditation, wherein "the mind is unwavering like the flame of a lamp in a windless place."[21]

In a much-loved section of the *Gita*, Krishna even gives Arjuna some practical advice about the way to practice meditation. These verses suggest that the author of the *Gita* must have assumed that his work would have a wide audience; ordinarily, this kind of teaching would be a private matter between guru and disciple. Krishna's suggestion about using a deerskin and "kusha" grass should not be taken literally; he was merely referring to what was traditional at the time among some sanyasins. He says,

> Select a clean spot, neither too high nor too low, and seat yourself firmly on a cloth, a deerskin, and kusha grass. Then, once seated, strive to still your thoughts. Make your mind one-pointed in meditation, and your heart will be purified. Hold your body, head, and neck firmly in a straight line, and keep your eyes from wandering. With all fears dissolved in the peace of the Self and all desires dedicated to Brahman, controlling the mind and fixing it on me, sit in meditation with me as your only goal. With senses and mind constantly controlled through meditation, united with the Self within, an aspirant attains *nirvana*, the state of abiding joy and peace in me.[22]

Bhakti Yoga

Fill your mind with me; love me; serve me; worship me always.
Seeking me in your heart, you will at last be united with me.

With these powerful words, Krishna gives expression to what is ultimately the great goal of the *Bhagavad Gita,* leading Arjuna from the ignorance of the separate self to awakening in union with the Divine. The *Gita* is an exposition of yoga. All paths of yoga are excellent and important, and they are clearly interrelated. But as the *Gita* develops, it becomes more and more apparent that its author, through the words of Sri Krishna, is proclaiming that Bhakti Yoga, the way of devotion, is the greatest yoga of all, greater even than Karma and kingly Raja. Loving devotion and service to a personal savior are what distinguishes Bhakti. Krishna—the incarnation of Vishnu, one with the Ultimate Ground of Being—presents himself to Arjuna as the personal, compassionate manifestation of the Godhead and, as such, a savior who can be worshipped as an approachable, loving friend of humanity.

Just to be sure that there is no misunderstanding in this matter, the author of the *Gita* has Krishna spell it out in lucid terms. Arjuna wants to know which is better, the way of the head or the way of the heart: "Of those steadfast devotees who love you and those who seek you as the eternal formless Reality, who are the more established in yoga"? Krishna's reply leaves no doubt as to where the author of the *Gita* stands: "Those who set their hearts on me and worship me with unfailing devotion and faith are more established in yoga."[23]

In no way is the preceding discussion meant to imply that there is some sort of fundamental conflict between the various paths of yoga. Nothing could be further from the truth. The various paths of yoga are complementary. Although a given individual may be disposed to emphasize this one or that one, *all* must be expressed in the life of a true aspirant, and, Krishna proclaims, the various aspects of living a life of yoga come together in the act of devotion, Bhakti Yoga. This is true not only for the less sophisticated person, for whom Bhakti means the customary forms of religious worship, but also for the philosophically minded person: "They worship me with a one-pointed mind, having realized that I am the eternal source of all. . . . Full of devotion, they sing of my divine glory."[24]

The opening up of unrestrained selfless love is what it all ultimately comes down to. That is the essence of Krishna's teaching. The various paths of yoga are ways of breaking down the love of an illusory ego-self and nourishing in its place a love of that which alone is real. Karma Yoga generates the love that transcends the private self, and Raja Yoga returns it to the source, nourishing love of the real Self. Finally, in the love of a personal representation of the Godhead, one achieves the perfection of yoga. Krishna sums it up beautifully:

> I am that supreme Self, praised by the scriptures as beyond the changing and the changeless. Those who see in me that supreme Self see truly. They have

found the source of all wisdom, Arjuna, and they worship me with all their heart.[25]

Lord Krishna, having given all of the teaching to his disciple Arjuna, brings the great discourse to a close. There is nothing more to say, and now Krishna wants to know if he has succeeded. Has Arjuna awakened to a higher truth? Will he now stand up and lead his men into battle? Krishna asks Arjuna if he has listened with understanding. Is he now free from doubt and confusion? Arjuna, a changed man now, answers with firmness: "You have dispelled my doubts and delusions, and I understand through your grace. My faith is firm now; I will do your will."[26]

Notes

1. Eknath Easwaren, The *Bhagavad Gita* (Petaluma, CA: Nilgiri, 1985), p. 54 (*BG*: 21–23).
2. *Ibid.*, pp. 56, 62 (*BG*: 1.45, 47; 2.9).
3. Quoted in George Feuerstein, *Introduction to the* Bhagavad Gita: *Philosophy and Cultural Setting* (Wheaton, IL: Quest, 1983), p. 47.
4. Easwaren, p. 52 (*BG*: 1.1).
5. *Ibid.*, pp. 54, 55 (*BG*: 1.28–30, 36–39).
6. *Ibid.*, p. 7.
7. *Ibid.*, p. 62 (*BG*: 2.11–13).
8. *Ibid.*, p. 65 (*BG*: 2.39).
9. *Ibid.*, p. 75 (*BG*: 3.4–5).
10. *Ibid.*, p. 65 (*BG*: 2.42–43).
11. *Ibid.*, pp. 191–192 (*BG*: 16.8–20).
12. *Ibid.*, p. 67 (*BG*: 2.54).
13. *Ibid.*, p. 67 (*BG*: 2.55–56).
14. *Ibid.*, p. 210 (*BG*: 18.53–54).
15. *Ibid.*, p. 76 (*BG*: 3.9).
16. *Ibid.*, p. 77 (*BG*: 3.25).
17. *Ibid.*, p. 66 (*BG*: 2.47).
18. Matthew 6: 26.
19. Easwaren, p. 206 (*BG*: 18.11–12).
20. *Ibid.*, pp. 107–8 (*BG*: 6.33–34).
21. *Ibid.*, p. 106 (*BG*: 6.19).
22. *Ibid.*, pp. 105–6 (*BG*: 6.11–15).
23. *Ibid.*, p. 162 (*BG*: 12.1–2).
24. *Ibid.*, p. 133 (*BG*: 9.13–14).
25. *Ibid.*, p. 186 (*BG*: 15.18–19).
26. *Ibid.*, p. 212 (*BG*: 18.73).

Study Questions

1. How did it happen that war became unavoidable between the Pandavas and the Kauravas?
2. Why is it stated, "There is profound symbolism in the fact that Krishna was a charioteer in the story"?
3. What does it mean to suggest that the *Bhagavad Gita* is metaphorical in character? What is your conclusion regarding this suggestion?
4. Why does Krishna begin his teaching with a strong affirmation of the doctrines of *atman* and *samsara*?
5. What are the essential features of an awakened person? How is such a person to be recognized?
6. What is the proper understanding of "Selfless Service"?
7. Correctly understood, what is the relationship between Karma Yoga and Raja Yoga? Can either one stand alone?

8.   The assertion is made that the author of the *Gita* regards Bhakti Yoga to be the greatest of all yoga paths. How do you feel about this? In what way could it be said to be true?

9.   How do the various paths of yoga come together to form a unitive whole?

10.   How do you interpret the teaching of the *Bhagavad Gita*? What is the quintessential message of the *Gita*?

5

An India Overview

We have been studying the unfolding of Veda, the body of sacred knowledge that took form in ancient India over a span of a thousand years. Veda is the foundation from which all else would grow, and over the course of time Indian thought became like an enormous tree with many spreading branches. In this chapter, we step back a little and attempt to see the big picture. We examine the many disparate parts that make up the tree of the Indian tradition and relate these individual parts to an organic whole.

Some would say that this organic whole is what is meant by the word "Hinduism." Others maintain that Hinduism more properly refers only to that part of the tradition which is based on the authority of the Vedas. In either case, nothing developed in isolation; there are interrelationships among all of the traditions that came into being over time. Our task, then, is to put all of these relationships together in the form of an overview, an "India Overview."

Originally, Veda was limited to the loose collection of ritual hymns that were known as the *Rig Veda*. In time, the *Rig Veda* was joined by three others—the *Sama*, the *Yajur*, and the *Atharva*—the four together making up the bedrock of Veda. Later, priestly commentaries known as the Brahmanas were appended to the Vedas. These were followed by the Aranyakas, the private Vedic studies of scholars who, for sheer love of Brahma, abandoned all creature comforts, making Aranya (that is, the forest) their home. The intellectual discussions of the Aranyakas opened the way for a wholly new surge of development: the Upanishads. In the Upanishads, the basic truths inherent in the Vedas were expanded into a fully developed mystical philosophy of life. Because the teaching of the Upanishads brought the unfolding of Veda to completion, it is known by the general term *Vedanta*, the completion of Veda. The essential wisdom of Veda was then magnificently summed up in the *Bhagavad Gita*.

It's difficult to be precise about dates in these matters. Speaking very broadly, we can say that the era in which the creation of Veda occurred spanned the time from approximately the middle of the second millennium B.C.E. to the middle of the first millennium B.C.E. (roughly 1500 B.C.E. to 500 B.C.E.). In the era that followed, the goals and methods of philosophy changed. The task was no longer to add to the body of Veda, but rather to *interpret* Veda. In particular, the mystical teaching of the Upanishads would be subjected to rational, philosophical interpretation. As a result of this approach, various distinct systems of thought, known as *darshanas*, took form. Those which accepted the infallible truths of Veda came to be known as "orthodox" darshanas. Those which rejected the infallibility of Veda, such as Buddhism and Jainism, are known as the "heterodox" darshanas. We will look at the principal darshanas in both the orthodox and the heterodox groups.

Over time, the Hindu tradition came to recognize six orthodox darshanas. By custom, these are arranged into three pairs: Vedanta and Purva Mimamsa, Samkhya and Yoga, and Niyaya and Vaisheshika. By far the most influential among these darshanas was, and continues to be, Vedanta. We will briefly examine the nature of each, beginning with Vedanta.

THE ORTHODOX DARSHANAS

Vedanta

The Vedanta darshana is intimately connected with the name of Shankara, a South Indian philosopher born in 788 C.E. Despite a short life of only thirty-two years, Shankara stands out as one of the giants of the Hindu tradition. It was Shankara who pulled together the diffuse, often mystical strands of the Upanishads and wove them into a coherent philosophical system—a darshana. Thanks in no small part to Shankara, Vedanta has consistently occupied the central place among the orthodox Hindu systems. Other darshanas are best understood in relation to Vedanta and, to a large degree, have been absorbed into it over time.

Shankara was an active, restless sort of person—a deep thinker, a prolific writer, and a much-traveled teacher. He was born into an upper-caste family in Kerala in South India, and, according to the story, astrologers predicted that he would become a great scholar. They prophesied that, in his destruction of false doctrine, he would be like a rampaging elephant let loose in a banana grove. Shankara was a very precocious child, and while still a boy, he wanted to become a Shaivite monk (one dedicated to Lord Shiva) so that he could devote all of his energies to study and the spiritual life. His widowed mother, though, refused to grant him her permission. One day, while bathing in a river, the young Shankara was attacked by a crocodile, or so we are told. It grabbed him by the leg and would soon have pulled him under. Shankara remembered the saying that if one vowed to become a monk when facing death, the gods might spare that person's life. He called out to his mother to give him permission, fast. Horrified by what she was watching, she shouted back, "Yes, yes; anything!" The struggling Shankara managed to raise his hands and call out, "Sanyasoham!" (Thus do I renounce.) Immediately, the crocodile let go of his leg, and a shaken, but still alive, Shankara climbed up on dry land. With tears flowing, his mother embraced him and confirmed her promise, saying that it was the will of the gods.

Thus the young Shankara received sanyas and entered upon the life of a celibate, itinerant monk. He was far more interested in scholarship than asceticism, though, and soon had become something of a guru in his own right. With his small band of disciples, Shankara traveled all over India, engaging in open debate with other religious scholars. Shankara's knowledge and his skill in debate were so impressive that, while still young, he came to be called *acharya* (great religious scholar). For this reason, he is often referred to as Shankaracharya.

A wonderful story is told about one of these debates. In the town of Mahismati, Shankara took on a famous scholar named Mandana Mishra. The fame of both men attracted a huge crowd. Bharati, Mishra's beautiful wife, was asked to be the judge. She placed a garland of fresh flowers around the neck of each man and announced to the crowd that at the end of the debate the one with the least withered flowers would be the winner. The loser must become a disciple of the winner. Shankara argued eloquently that the real purpose of the Vedas is to teach that Brahman alone is real. Mishra, who had never been defeated in debate, stuck with his main theme that the Vedas teach one how to accumulate merit through the correct performance of religious ritual. The debate wore on for eighteen days! When it was finally over, Bharati, sizing up the two garlands, was forced to admit that Shankara was the winner.

But Bharati wasn't about to lose her husband that easily; she had a trick up her sleeve. Announcing that, through marriage, a husband and wife become one, she declared that she was really a part of the life of Mishra and that therefore Shankara would have to defeat her, too, in debate. Until then, she said, his victory would not be complete. Surprised, but intrigued, Shankara said that he accepted her challenge. Turning then to the delighted crowd, she addressed them, saying, in effect, that she could not accept Shankara as a learned master until he had demonstrated that he had knowledge of *all* important matters. He must, she declared, prove that he had deep understanding of the arts of lovemaking. Could he prove that he was knowledgeable about the various forms of seduction, the ways of pleasing a woman in bed, the variety of sexual positions, and the relative merits of each? Could he speak intelligently about the sensual effects of different love potions and the influence of the full moon on the sexual urge of a woman? Turning back to Shankara, Bharati shouted, "Until you can answer these questions, you are not a master of all learning!"

Well, being that Shankara was a sixteen-year-old celibate monk, this could present something of a problem. But Shankara, too, was not without a trick up his sleeve. He asked for, and received, a forty-day delay, saying that he needed time to think the matter over. During this time, we are told, Shankara used his skill in yogic powers to leave his own body and enter instead into the body of a raja known for his extremely voluptuous lifestyle. For forty days (and nights), while his own body rested in a deep trance, Shankara used the virile king's body to explore every sexual experience the mind can imagine. There was *nothing* that he didn't know by the time the forty days were up. At the appointed time, he returned, in his own body, to continue the debate. To say the least, it was an astonished Bharati that soon confessed that Shankara was indeed a master of *all* learning and was the rightful winner.

In the course of his travels, Shankara established four *mathas*: one in the north of India, one in the south, one in the west, and one in the east. A matha is a monastery that, at the same time, is something like a college. In addition to offering the usual monastic disciplines a matha places a strong emphasis on scholarly pursuits. All of the mathas founded by Shankara are still functioning to this day and are living sources of his teaching.

Most of all, though, Shankara's philosophy is found in his writings, the most influential of which is the *Naishkarmya-siddhi*, a lengthy commentary on the *Brahma-Sutra* of Badarayana, composed several centuries earlier. In the *Naishkarmya-siddhi*, Shankara lays out the essential features of the Vedanta darshana. Brahman alone is Absolute Truth; Brahman alone is real. This uncompromising monism at the heart of Shankara's teaching is the reason for his system being labeled "Advaita Vedanta." *Advaita* means "non-dual" (*a-dvi*, not two). This is an important distinction, philosophically speaking, because some schools within the general Vedanta tradition taught the reality of a dualism in which both spirit and the world are separate, but real.

Drawing his inspiration directly from the Upanishads, Shankara held that the *atman* is Brahman and that the ultimate goal of life is the realization of the identity of the *atman* and Brahman. What stands in the way of attaining that goal is *maya*, the veil of illusion that seduces us into falsely believing that the world is real. The ego, itself a part of the world of *maya*, tumbles between pleasure and pain in a hopeless quest for self-centered happiness. This, of course, is the condition of *avidya*. The only hope for salvation is to accept the fact that the world of *maya* is a figment and to disengage oneself entirely from its enticing attachments. Only through renouncing *maya* can a person ascend to the knowledge of Brahman.

Shankara argued that through the disciplined pursuit of knowledge, a dedicated seeker can eventually transcend *ordinary* knowledge, rising to *perfect* knowledge. This is the path of *Jnana*. Shankara, though, was far from being purely intellectual. Although he was a highly rational man who could not accept any doctrine that was clearly in conflict with reason, he had a mystical side as well. Shankara taught that the path of knowledge was the one best suited to elevate a philosophically minded person to the state of *samadhi*, within which the *mystical experience* of knowledge of Brahman could occur.

Knowledge of Brahman, then, is in no way to be thought of as conceptual, or "philosophical," in the usual sense of the word. Knowledge of Brahman is a completely transcendental experience, which can be *approached* through philosophical knowledge. The Brahman of Shankara may not be a personal god—that is true—but neither did Shankara choose to describe Brahman as nothing more than an impersonal abstraction. In talking *about* Brahman, Shankara would wisely drop into the poetic style of Bhakti. He would even sometimes refer to Brahman as a "friend." Shankara composed a number of rather mystical verses dedicated to Govinda, one of the names of Krishna; these verses are thus known as the "Bhaja Govindam." It is fascinating to reflect on the fact that the words in the verses are being uttered by the man whose name is foremost among the rational philosophers of his time. Let me conclude this section with an excerpt from one verse:

> Worship Govinda. Worship Govinda.
> Oh you fools and rascals,
> Just worship Govinda.

Your rules of grammar and word jugglery
Will not help you at the time of death.
Just worship Govinda.

Purva Mimamsa

Perhaps the least well known of the darshanas, Purva Mimamsa (often referred to simply as Mimamsa) is in some ways the most fundamental of all. It is linked with Vedanta because both systems were originally known by the name "mimamsa," which refers to the solving of a problem—in this case, the liberation from *samsara*—by critically examining the nature of the problem. Purva (meaning "early") Mimamsa focused strictly on the Vedas and sought the solution there. Uttara Mimamsa (meaning "later" or, also, "higher"), which would come to be known as Vedanta, focused more on the Upanishads, as we have seen.

The Purva Mimamsa darshana is associated with Jaimini, the name of a little-known fourth-century Brahmin alleged to be the author of the *Mimamsa Sutra*. In this work, Jaimini sets forth an enormous code of rules for the correct interpretation and performance of Vedic rituals. It was his belief, as well as that of many others, that the right life—that is to say, the way of life that would lead to *moksha*—was the life that was lived in proper accord with Dharma. The nature of such a life could not possibly be determined infallibly through perception or reason; these frail human instruments are far too imperfect. The only sure path is to faithfully follow the injunctions contained in the sacred Vedas. And it became Jaimini's self-assigned task to interpret and clarify the ritual injunctions of the Vedas so that all could follow.

Clearly, this darshana is solidly fundamentalist. The words of the Vedas contain all truth. They are to be followed literally and without question. This is the one and only path to salvation.

Samkhya

The Samkhya and Yoga darshanas are closely associated with Vedanta, and over time many elements of both became integrated into the broader nature of Vedanta. The elucidation of the Samkhya darshana is attributed to Kapila, who authored the *Samkhya Karika* in the seventh century B.C.E. It was Kapila who enunciated the dual nature of *prakriti* and *purusha*. *Prakriti*, as we have seen, is said to be matter, the natural world, always changing and evolving through the operation of the three *gunas*. *Purusha*, on the other hand, is pure spirit, pure consciousness; it is the nature of Brahman or *atman*. According to Samkhya, *prakriti* acts; it is responsible for all of the forms of *maya* and all of the role-playing that goes on within *maya*. *Purusha* (pure consciousness) is a witness only; it does not act. The distinction is described well in the *Mundaka Upanishad*:

Like two golden birds perched on the selfsame tree,
Intimate friends, the ego and the Self dwell in the same body.
The former eats the sweet and sour fruits of the tree of life,
While the latter looks on in detachment.[1]

In the life of any given individual, *purusha* can become literally entranced by the play of *prakriti* and fall into the fatal error of identifying its being with *prakriti*. This, of course, is *avidya*, the illusion that the *prakriti*-self is the real self. Such ignorance is said to be responsible for all suffering and for the endless turning of the wheel of *samsara*. But there is hope: Difficult though it may be, it is at least possible for *purusha* to see through the illusion created by *prakriti* and come to the realization of its own distinct nature. This is *moksha*—perfect Self realization and the end of *samsara*.

It would be incorrect to conclude that Samkhya holds that the distinction between *prakriti* and *purusha* is the difference between good and evil. *Prakriti* is not evil in any sense at all. In fact, the evolution of *prakriti* is the necessary condition within which *purusha* works out its own rediscovery. Samkhya presents the philosophical explanation; how the work is actually accomplished is the field of Samkhya's companion darshana, Yoga.

Yoga

The nature of yoga is widely misunderstood in the West, where it is often thought of as dealing exclusively with unusual body postures and breathing exercises. These are the province of Hatha Yoga, an important aspect of yoga, but far from the whole story. Strictly speaking, the word *yoga* refers to any path of action that is intended to lead ultimately to enlightenment.

The roots of yoga are widely believed to reach far back into the pre-Vedic past. Artistic representations from Mohenjo-Daro and Harappa are strongly suggestive of yogic meditation practices. Undoubtedly, Dravidian practices greatly influenced the evolution of yoga. The word, though, is derived from *yuj*, an early Sanskrit word meaning "to join" or "yoke." Presumably, in early Aryan times, the "yogin" was the person whose daunting job it was to tame wild horses and harness them (yoke them) to the war chariot. The yogin was the battle charioteer. Metaphorically, this task came to symbolize the challenge of taming the wild impulses of the body and "yoking" mind and body for the purpose of self-discovery. It is no accident that Lord Krishna, the divine yogin, was presented as Arjuna's charioteer in the *Bhagavad Gita*.

By the time the *Bhagavad Gita* was composed, certain yoga paths had become pre-eminent in Indian society. The *Gita* examines three of these: Raja Yoga, the yoga of meditation; Karma Yoga, the yoga of compassionate service; and Bhakti Yoga, the path of devotion to a personal god. Jnana Yoga, the way of philosophical inquiry, is mentioned, but not discussed in the *Gita*, and Hatha Yoga is not mentioned by name at all.

The development of yoga into one of the classical darshanas was largely the work of a man named Patanjali, who lived in the second century B.C.E. Little is known about him personally, but he is the putative author of the *Yoga Sutras*, a work of major importance in the history of Hinduism. In this work, Patanjali draws together what he regards to be the essential elements of the yoga tradition and presents a program of action that the dedicated seeker can follow in the ascent from ignorance to the fullness of awakening.

The theme of the work is clearly presented in the first stanza of the *Yoga Sutras*: *Yoga nirodha chittam vritti*. Loosely translated, this reads, "Yoga is the cessation of the thought waves of the mind." What it means is that, in its most perfect sense, yoga is a state of consciousness, a state wherein all of the distractions of thought and ego have become quiet. The Self alone is all that remains, pure and simple. This state of consciousness is called *samadhi*. The attainment of *samadhi* is the ultimate goal of the practice of yoga. But *samadhi* is to be won only at the summit of a long and arduous climb, a journey that the truly dedicated alone can hope to complete.

In the *Yoga Sutras*, Patanjali presents a description of an eight-tiered ascent to the goal of *samadhi*. In modern translations, the tiers are often referred to as the "eight limbs" of yoga. Patanjali gives much attention to each limb; what follows is only the briefest of descriptions.

1. Yama   *Yama* is usually translated as "restraint." It refers to various practices aimed at replacing ego attachments with self-restraint and compassion. Among these practices are *Ahimsa* (nonviolence); *Sattva* (in this usage the word Sattva is taken to mean *non-lying*, that is, being truthful in all things); *Asteya* (non-stealing—i.e., refraining from stealing); *Aparigraha* (literally, nongrasping—i.e., overcoming the impulse of greed); and *Brahmacharya* (renouncing sexual lust; Patanjali expected the truly dedicated yogin to be totally celibate).

2. Niyama   Usually translated as "observances," the Niyama are habits of mind to be cultivated by the yogin. Both Yama and Niyama refer to habits of mind; the Yama emphasize removing impediments to growth, while the Niyama focus on building positive ones in their place. The Niyama include purity and cleanliness of mind and body, an attitude of contentment and acceptance, and the rigorous practice of ascetic disciplines, study, and devotion.

3. Asanas   The word *asana* refers to a bodily posture. By Patanjali's time, the tradition of yoga had worked out a large number of classical asanas, which, along with associated breathing exercises, were believed to constitute an excellent discipline for bringing the body under control and keeping it in the healthiest possible condition. Since mental states are greatly affected by the condition of the body, a strong and healthy body was seen to be essential to progress in the art of meditation.

4. Pranayama   Pranayama, referring to skillful breathing exercises, is closely linked to the practice of asanas. Whereas the asanas focus more directly on the condition of the body, pranayama builds on the asanas to increase one's vital energy, which can be turned inward for the task of building up the energy of consciousness. Pranayama is a conjunction of two Sanskrit words: *prana*, which refers to vital energy that is taken into the body through breathing (and without which there would be no life), and *ayama*, a word that means "to increase" or "build up," as in building up a fire. The Yogic practices of asanas and pranayama had become highly evolved by Patanjali's time. They were the jealously guarded province of ascetic communities. Only a true master was seen to be fit to initiate and teach another. The two practices together form the basis of Hatha Yoga. Important as Hatha Yoga may be unto itself, the tradition of yoga has always seen it as the servant of Raja Yoga, the yoga of meditation. Hatha prepares the individual for the richest possible experience in meditation. A popular image compares the two yogas to a tree. The crown of the tree, closest to the sun, is Raja Yoga. But the sturdy trunk, which holds up the crown, is Hatha. Without Hatha, there can be no Raja.

5. Pratyahara   Usually translated as "control of the senses," pratyahara is concerned with developing total mastery over the physical body and all of its desires and distractions. This is a matter of the higher nature coming to totally control the lower. *Pratyahara* does not mean "renunciation"; it means "control." There is an excellent description of pratyahara in Book Two of the *Bhagavad Gita*. "Even as a tortoise draws in its limbs, the wise can draw in their senses at will."

6. Dharana   Dharana is often simply called concentration. Perhaps this is too simple and thus misleading. Dharana is an ongoing condition of consciousness in which the restless activity of the thinking mind has been brought under control and the person is free to be totally aware of the present moment as it unfolds. Dharana is closely associated with *ekagrata*, which means "one-pointedness," a habit of focusing one's consciousness on the reality of the moment. Many practices were developed to help one become skilled in Dharana.

7. Dhyana   *Dhyana* is a supremely important word in the evolution of Eastern thought. We will see later in the text that it is the parent of the Chinese word "Chan," which in turn was the parent of the Japanese word "Zen." In itself, *dhyana* refers to the practice of meditation and to the state of mind of one who practices meditation. Patanjali described four stages of *Dhyana*, the fourth being synonymous with *Samadhi*.

8. Samadhi   In the state of *Samadhi*, consciousness has shed all traces of ego identification; the thinking mind is still, and consciousness is free to know its identification with the All. Such words may be accurate, technically speaking, but in truth no words are capable of describing the experience of *Samadhi*; it transcends all words, all thoughts. *Samadhi* is the ultimate goal of the practice of yoga.

Niyaya

Niyaya and its companion darshana, Vaisheshika, are the third of the three pairs of the so-called orthodox darshanas. Although prominent in their day, both have largely become absorbed within the broad umbrella of Vedanta over time.

The cornerstone of the orthodox view, so beautifully expressed in the Upanishads, is that the ultimate object of life is the attainment of *moksha*. But the Upanishads in no way attempt a carefully reasoned critique of what the experience of *moksha* is, or of how it is to be attained. Clearly, that was not the point of the Upanishads; for the most part they are poetic in style, emphasizing the importance of mystical intuition. Knowledge of Brahman is presented as intuitive knowledge that completely transcends ordinary knowledge. Put simply, the composers of the Upanishads had no interest in presenting critical philosophy. Their message was inspirational, intended for the ears of those who were already committed to the basic beliefs of the Upanishadic tradition and were in need only of encouragement and guidance along the path.

About the time that the Age of the Upanishads was reaching its maturity, which is to say around the middle of the first millenium B.C.E., various alternative philosophies began to develop into popular movements, often styled as "reform" movements. Buddhism and Jainism are two of the better known reform movements that developed during that time. The reform movements expressed a skeptical attitude toward the Upanishadic tradition. They criticized it for being too mystical, too dependent on intuitive knowledge. The philosophy of the Upanishads was criticized for lacking a foundation of reasonableness. However beautiful and inspiring it might be to some, it was argued, Vedanta was not a true philosophy, because it could not be rationally defended. The perception of its truth depended ultimately, not on reasoned argument, but on a highly personal mystical experience. Such an experience might be fine for the poet and the mystic, but it offered mighty slim pickings for the true philosopher.

It was largely in response to this criticism that Gautama, the second-century-B.C.E. architect of the Niyaya darshana, sought to establish the orthodox Upanishadic tradition on a solid, rational foundation. (Incidentally, he was no relation to Gautama Shakyamuni, better known as the historical Buddha.) His goal was not to prove the correctness of the assertions of the Upanishads; rather, his goal was to demonstrate that there was no inevitable conflict between reason and these teachings. One could be a person of intellectual curiosity and reason *and* be a follower of the teachings of the Upanishads. Rationality and the Upanishads were not necessarily mutually exclusive.

The problem that Gautama faced is similar to the situation that Thomas Aquinas found himself in. Aquinas lived in thirteenth-century Europe, a time when the traditional Christian faith was being assailed by a "new learning" which held that all religious belief is at best mystical intuition and often nothing more than childish nonsense. No intelligent, philosophically minded person would choose to waste his time on a pack of religious fairy tales. Aquinas, a Dominican monk and a brilliant thinker, rose to the challenge. His was a truly heroic response, resulting in a lifetime of writings that went far to establish the real possibility of being a man or a woman in tune with the new learning without having to abandon the traditional teachings of the Church. Aquinas is famous for his five "proofs" of the existence of God. Actually, these are not so much proofs as they are reasoned arguments which seek to demonstrate that there need be no conflict between reason and belief in the Christian concept of God.

What makes the example of Aquinas particularly interesting in our present context is that he leaned strongly on the rational philosophy of the Greek philosopher Aristotle. Aristotle was the first to work out the rules of logic and rational thinking in general. One can't help but wonder if Gautama, too, was influenced by the writings of Aristotle. There is no evidence for this, but the possibility cannot be ignored. During the century before Gautama's career, Aristotle's famous student, Alexander the Great, had, through conquest, carried Greek armies and culture as far as the region known as Gandhara, which is in the northwest part of the Indian subcontinent. Greek culture, including philosophical ideas, sank roots in Gandhara and, from there, influenced other parts of the Hindu world for a time.

Gautama based his defense of the Upanishadic tradition on a carefully reasoned epistemology. His goal was not to examine reality per se, but rather one's *knowledge of* reality. How does one know that his or her knowledge is accurate? How can one ever be certain? Perception can obviously mislead, as in the popular example of the snake in the road that turns out to be merely a coiled rope. Reason also, as we all know only too well, is not infallible. Gautama sought to show that reason *could* be reliable, so long as proper rules of thinking were followed. Much of his argument was presented in the form of syllogisms (a very Aristotelian method, incidentally). He then applied that rational process to an examination of the postulates of the Upanishadic teachings and proved to the satisfaction of many that the tradition was not in conflict with reason.

Gautama was not, however, denying the reality and the importance of mystical intuition; that was not his purpose. He, in fact, agreed that *moksha*, knowledge of Brahman, was intuitive knowledge of the highest order. But, he would argue, a reasoned "revelation" of the true nature of reality could lead to the mystical experience of *moksha*.

Vaisheshika

The Vaisheshika darshana was formulated by an unusual thinker named Kanada, a somewhat younger contemporary of Gautama, the founder of Niyaya. In the *Vaisheshika Sutras*, Kanada used the rational, realistic approach of Gautama to elucidate the underlying nature of reality. In other words, Gautama would clarify how it is that true knowledge is attained; Kanada would use that clarification to explain the true nature of the reality that right knowledge comprehends. Both schools of thought were in agreement that a true perception of reality, rationally attained, could open the door to the higher intuitive knowledge of Brahman.

Something of a mystic philosopher himself, Kanada practiced long hours of meditation by day and then went out searching for knowledge in the cool of the night. By examining experience in the light of Niyaya epistemology, Kanada reached an "atomic" interpretation of Nature. (Again, one has to wonder whether there might have been a Greek influence at work here.) Kanada concluded that reality is made up of certain irreducible substances. Like some of the Greek philosophers, he listed earth, water, air, and fire as basic substances. To these, he added ether, light, space, time, mind, and *atman*. The particular entries in the list are not what's most important; rather, it was the rational way in which Kanada went about determining the nature of reality that gives significance to his contribution. The Niyaya–Vaisheshika response was intellectually powerful in its time, but as we saw earlier, the impact of these darshanas gradually declined, and much of their contribution was absorbed into the evolving character of Vedanta.

THE HETERODOX DARSHANAS

As mentioned earlier, in addition to the six "orthodox" darshanas, the Hindu tradition recognizes various "heterodox" darshanas as well. The defining element of the heterodox schools is that they did not accept the infallibility of Veda. The three principal heterodox darshanas are Buddhism, Jainism, and Charvaka. In addition to these, the teachings of Tantra could be considered a heterodox darshana.

Buddhism

Buddhism is by far the best known and the most successful of the heterodox darshanas. Since the larger part of what remains in this text will be given over to a careful examination of the nature and evolution of Buddhism, I will only define it briefly at this point. Buddhism grew out of the teachings of Gautama Shakyamuni, who would later become known as the Buddha, "the Awakened One." Buddha was an itinerant guru of the sixth century B.C.E. who experienced a profound mystical intuition of truth (his "awakening") while in his thirties and dedicated the rest of his life to travelling about North India teaching his way of liberation to as many as would listen. What began as one of many reform movements within the body of Hinduism eventually became a heretical sect denying the validity of such traditional values as caste and the infallibility of the Vedas and questioning even the reality of *atman*. Buddhism would flourish for a while in India, but eventually it would all but die out in its homeland. The real success of Buddhism, though, was destined to be found in virtually all parts of eastern Asia outside of India to which Buddha's teaching migrated after his death. In its new homes, Buddhism would continue to grow and evolve into many widely differing forms. The history of Buddhism is a fabulous story and one that's still going strong today. We will take up the study of Buddhism in Part III.

Jaina

The story of the development of the Jain sect is an intriguing subject, much misunderstood in the West. Like Buddhism, Jaina developed as a reaction to what some perceived as intolerable flaws in traditional Hinduism. Also, Jaina appeared on the historical scene at about the same time as Buddhism, and it, too, began as a very small dissident sect. Jaina would not, however, experience anything like the explosive growth of Buddhism, but, unlike Buddhism, the Jain tradition has survived down to the present day in its homeland. It is estimated that there are about two million Jains living in modern-day India.

Historically speaking, the rise of Jainism is associated with the name of Mahavira, an ascetic monk who was born during the first half of the sixth century B.C.E., and lived to be about 70. It is believed that he was probably a contemporary of Buddha. Mahavira (whose birth name was Nat:aputta Vardhamana) was, to say the least, an ascetic's ascetic. During his years as a solitary sadhu, there were seemingly no austerities that were too extreme for him, and he went so far (we are told) as to pull his hair out by the roots and go about totally naked in all types of weather. He was determined to free himself from every vestige of attachment to worldly concerns. According to the story, Mahavira (like Buddha) eventually experienced enlightenment, a profound mystical insight into what he believed to be the nature of ultimate truth. Thereafter, Mahavira became guru to a small group of disciples who joined the master in his ascetic ways, also going about naked and hairless. (Presumably, though, they chose to simply shave their heads.) Mahavira called his disciples *jinas*—that is, "victors" in the battle against worldly attachments. The word "Jain" is derived from this name.*

Mahavira did not claim to be the originator of the Jain sect. Far from that, the sect had presumably been in existence for centuries by the time of Mahavira, but it had been only one of many small communities of ascetic monks, drawing little public attention. The leader of the Jains was known as the Tirthankara (literally, one who finds the way across the river). Mahavira claimed to be the twenty-fourth of this unbroken line. According to the Jain tradition, the first Tirthankara was a heroic figure named Rishaba, who was said to have lived for 8,400,000 years (one of his many great accomplishments). Whatever the case may be, Mahavira was the one who brought the Jains out into the open; the historical record really begins with him.

So, you may be wondering, what is the point of all this extreme asceticism? Why were Jain monks so dedicated to starving and otherwise mortifying their poor bodies? Well, it certainly wasn't an end in itself; they weren't masochists. It all makes perfectly good sense in the context of Jain philosophy. In accord with the Hindu world that it emerged from and lived within, Jaina accepted the reality of *moksha* and *samsara*. But that's about as far as the accord went. Jaina is a solidly dualist system of thought. Reality is twofold, consisting of *jiva* (spirit) and *ajiva* (nonspirit, or, in other words, the world). Jains reject the concept of *maya*; the world is not illusion, but is real. Both jiva and ajiva are real, irreducible, and eternal. Because they are eternal, there is no need for a creator god, and none is proposed, for which reason Jaina is sometimes said to be atheistic.

According to Jaina, the material world is in a state of constant change, but it is not meaningless, haphazard change. The change that we see is part of a vast, eternal cycling, with each individual cycle lasting for eons. Toward the end of a cycle, everything begins to deteriorate into chaos, but order will restore itself in the next turn of the wheel. The present age is a deteriorating stage, which explains the disorder and suffering that exist in the world. The reason for this is as follows: Ideally, jiva and ajiva are completely separate, as they should be. But in the deteriorating stage of a cycle, jiva comes into contact with ajiva (the material world), and therein lie trouble and suffering. Specifically, the individual jiva (spirit), already conjoined with a body, takes on a burden of karma as a result of worldly actions. In Jaina, karma is defined as a material substance, albeit an extremely rarified one. As a vapor sullies a mirror, all actions taint jiva with karma. It may be heavy karma, such as willfully selfish actions incur, or it may be relatively light karma,

---

*There is an attractive small park in New Delhi dedicated to the Enlightenment of Mahavira. It's an interesting irony that this park is located directly across the street from the opulent Maurya Sheraton Hotel. From their comfortable, air-conditioned rooms, guests can enjoy the view of a park honoring the memory of one of the most extreme ascetics of India's history.

such as results from selfless actions, but all actions result in furthering the burden of karma, necessitating rebirth (*samsara*). The character of the rebirth will be determined by the character of the karma at the time of death, but rebirth it will be: The wheel of *samsara* keeps turning over and over, dooming the individual jiva to successive rebirths into this world of endless suffering. Each individual person is jiva trapped in ajiva, and karma keeps the wheel turning.

But there's hope: *Moksha*, the ultimate goal, is attainable. It is possible for jiva to free itself from the wheel, free itself from all karma, and thus achieve the perfect bliss natural to it, but impossible so long as it remains bound up with ajiva. The perfected condition is known as *siddhashila*.

This is where the rationale for ascetic practices comes into the picture. Only a life of complete withdrawal and asceticism, the more extreme the better, will have any hope of success in burning out the burden of karma and avoiding the creation of new karma. Some went so far as to remain completely motionless for very long periods of time. A popular image in Jainism is a picture or statue of a standing monk with twining vines growing up his unmoving legs.

The Jain monk, especially in ancient times, was willing to abandon all of the pleasures and comforts of life and to take on the lifestyle of a naked ascetic because he was convinced that he was on the brink of *moksha*—that this lifetime would be the last, and when it finally ended, his jiva would at last be free to enter into the state of *siddhashila*. And speaking of the end of life, the perfect end would be religious suicide, the absolutely final and ultimate act of self-abnegation. It could not be a violent suicide, though; violence of all kinds was strictly forbidden. It would have to be a nonviolent end, such as fasting until one died. This is how Mahavira is said to have ended his own life. Other acceptable methods included walking out into the ocean until one's body was swept away, or, if an ocean was not available, walking out into the wilderness until one expired.

The lifestyle of the Jain monk, then, was structured in such a way as to completely eliminate the taint of karma. Ascetic practices played a large part, of course, but they were not the whole picture. Asceticism was something of an ongoing background. In order to minimize the effect of karma as much as possible, the affairs of daily life were shaped by the Five Great Vows that every Jain monk commited himself to. I'm sure that you'll recognize them; they are exactly the same five rules included in Yama, the first of Patanjali's five limbs of yoga. Actually, both Jaina and Patanjali's Yoga were drawing on the widely recognized vows of ascetic life that were already ancient in Indian culture: *Ahimsa* (nonviolence), *Satya* (truthfulness), *Asteya* (refraining from stealing), *Aparigraha* (abstinence from greed), and *Brahmacharya* (celibacy).

Ahimsa is an especially interesting vow in the context of Jaina. Apparently, in Mahavira's time, *ahimsa* did not yet include the meaning of compassion; it meant non-violence, pure and simple. Since all living beings were believed to be possessed of jiva, any violence toward a living being—especially killing—would result in a terrible burden of karma. For this reason, Jain monks went to great lengths to avoid killing anything, even accidentally killing a bug. It was not uncommon for a Jain to sweep the path before him so as not to step on a single insect, or to drink water through a piece of gauze so as to strain out any tiny critters that might be in the water. Naturally, all Jains were strict vegetarians. To some extent, these practices still exist among modern-day Jains. Jains are known for their benevolence to animals. They maintain animal hospitals, and, naturally, refuse to use or wear leather.

Over time, the Jain sect evolved and changed. For one thing, the order of monks split into two camps. One group adopted the practice of wearing a simple white robe; they were known as the Svetambaras (white clothed). Others continued to live by the strict rule of nakedness. They were the Digambaras (sky clothed). After all, if the monk was to disavow *all* ownership—even ownership of simple clothing—nakedness was unavoidable. Eventually the two groups merged, however, and almost all Jain monks became robed ascetics.

The biggest change was in the expansion of Jaina to include a large population of laymen and women. Although laypeople lived more normal lives than monks, the belief was (and is) that following some measure of the Jain lifestyle will bring a person (i.e., a particular jiva) closer to the time when, as a monk, he can make the final dedicated effort. Despite the fact that the greatest part of the Indian population has always been engaged in farming, a farmer could not really become a Jain, because the work of farming inevitably involves the killing of pests. Consequently, most lay Jains came from the merchant castes, and as a result, the Jains are relatively wealthier and better educated than is typically the case in India. Their wealthier status is evident in Jain temples, which tend to be elaborate and richly decorated. You won't find images of Hindu gods in Jain temples, though: Jains tolerate no idolatry! Instead, there are pictures of Mahavira and other of the legendary Tirthankaras. Temples play an important part in the life of Jains, but their use is almost exclusively for the lay population, not the monks.

Jaina is a puzzling phenomenon—at least to the outsider. On the one hand is the underlying philosophy, which seems so life negating. Jaina turned its back on the Vedas, which were so life affirming: Whereas the Vedas sought fulfillment in the human condition, Jaina seeks only release from it; whereas the Vedas encouraged ritual participation in the great events of life, Jaina chose instead the way of extreme asceticism and withdrawal. It would seem that Jaina holds human life in disdain, sees no value in it, and yearns only for complete escape from it. But on the other hand, we have before our eyes the lifestyle of modern-day Jain men and women. They are not in the least somber or withdrawn. The typical Jain is an attractive and engaging person: hardworking, peace loving, law abiding, and clean living. The ancient way of Jaina has survived through many ages and many persecutions. Perhaps this philosophy of life, so diametrically opposed to the way of modern materialism, will find a new surge of growth among those who seek a meaningful alternative.

Charvaka

Charvaka is the polar opposite of Jaina. Far from withdrawing from the world and embracing the privations of an ascetic life, the followers of Charvaka held that the present enjoyment of life is the only real value that exists. Charvaka is a thoroughgoing materialist philosophy of life. Nothing else exists; sense perception alone is real. The wise person is the one who knows this and devotes his or her energies to the pursuit of pleasurable situations and the avoidance of painful situations.

It's quite possible that Charvaka grew out of a growing skepticism concerning the infallibility of the Vedas, but it probably doesn't matter what the specific cause might be. It seems that every fully developed society includes a Charvaka, by one name or another. Among the Greeks, it was Epicureanism and hedonism. Certainly, no one can deny that the spirit of Charvaka is alive and well, perhaps even dominant, in the modern world. The "Playboy Philosophy" could be said to be Charvaka in modern dress.

The word *Charvaka* is derived from the name of the alleged author of the *Brahaspati Sutra*, a work composed around 600 B.C.E. No part of this work has survived to modern times, and next to nothing is known about its supposed author. Our only sources of knowledge about Charvaka come from Hindu, Buddhist and Jain writers, all of whom were deeply critical of the Charvaka school. It's hardly likely, therefore, that we're getting a fully objective view of this school, especially since followers of Charvaka openly attacked the others. They argued that religion was nothing but foolishness, or worse, a mental disease, and that so-called virtue is nothing but illusion. They aimed their strongest attacks at the Brahmin priests, whom they accused of being vipers, tricksters, and purveyors of superstition. It's no wonder that Charvaka was not exactly admired by the others. But because of this, it may be that Charvaka is getting a bad rap. Speaking about Charvaka, the modern Hindu scholar Radhakrishnan has taken the position that a philosophy professed seriously for centuries could not have been of the coarse nature that it is made out to be.

As best we can determine, the teachings of the *Bharaspati Sutra* held that only material reality exists and that the "soul," so central to the teachings of the Upanishads, is only an illusion. Consciousness is not evidence of an indwelling spirit; it is simply a product of the material structure of the body, and when the body dies, consciousness disintegrates with it. Moreover, the death of the body is final, so that, for any given person, the present life is the only one that will ever exist.

Given this state of affairs, what constitutes the "good life"? Charvaka held, very simply, that the good life is to be found in the pursuit of happiness and the avoidance of suffering. Presumably, this was not meant to be interpreted as pursuit of gluttonous self-indulgence; Charvaka was more Epicurean than hedonist. Good actions, born of compassion, conduce to happiness; bad actions, born of selfishness, result in unhappiness. In other words, learn from experience to do what works. Charvaka was very pragmatic.

Modern commentators often suggest that, apart from whatever value it might have unto itself, Charvaka may have played a valuable role within the evolution of Hindu society as a whole. The stinging attacks from the followers of Charvaka may have helped to awaken the Hindu tradition from its conservative, dogmatic slumber. The sixth century B.C.E. was, philosophically speaking, a restless and revolutionary time in the history of Hinduism, a time that saw the emergence of many active reform movements, Buddhism and Jainism being only two. Charvaka would have appeared on the scene at right about the beginning of this eventful century. Perhaps it did play a societal role.

Tantra

Tantra is a fascinating and much-misunderstood subject. Throughout its long history, opponents have condemned it as fraudulent, hedonistic, lewd, and even outright insane. Properly understood, though, it is none of these things. Tantra is a tradition that has enormously influenced the evolution of both Hinduism and Buddhism.

The beginnings of Tantra as a definable tradition can be traced to Buddhist communities of northern India in the sixth century C.E. This assertion conflicts with the long-held belief that Tantra began within the Hindu world and spread from there into Buddhism. Most scholars are now in agreement that, in fact, Tantra first appeared among the Buddhists and would coalesce into the school of Buddhism known as Vajrayana.

In any case, Tantra took form in both traditions at roughly the same time, historically speaking, and was heavily influenced by the orthodox doctrines and practices of both. But, influenced though it may have been, Tantra definitely was a radical counter-movement in both Hinduism and Buddhism. Tantra may have retained much of the old and may even show evidence of some roots that go back to pre-Vedic times, but what was new was such a departure from the orthodox, that Tantra was vigorously condemned by the traditionalists of both Hinduism and Buddhism.

The name "tantra" referred to the various texts that formed the scriptural base of the movement. This Sanskrit word, taken originally from the weaving craft, refers literally to the weft—the horizontal strands that weave the yarn into a unified whole, a fabric. Tantra texts did the same sort of thing: They wove the various strands of the tradition into a unified whole, a philosophical system. The reliance on texts would become far more important in Vajrayana than among Hindu Tantrists, whose approach was much more informal, emphasizing the relationship between guru and disciple, as well as spiritual practices tailored to meet the individual needs of each disciple, known as a *sadhaka*. It was these tantric practices that drew the condemnation of traditionalists, who denounced Tantra as being criminally lewd and misleading.

In Tantra, as in orthodox Hinduism (and Buddhism), the ultimate goal is the same: full awakening—freedom from the suffering of attachment. In more practical terms, we might say that the ultimate goal is the creation of that state of consciousness within which awakening can arise. In traditional Hinduism, this state of consciousness is known as *samadhi*. To the Tantarists this amounted to something much too passive—too body rejecting, too withdrawn from the fullness of human life.

Like orthodox Hindus, Tantrists, too, wanted to climb to the summit of Mount Meru (figuratively speaking, of course). But Tantra would offer a different means, a "fast track" to the summit. Tantric teaching took the position that if one is going to attempt to climb the mountain, he (or she) must start the climb from where he is, which means, of course, at the base of the mountain. You can't just spirit yourself to a higher level; you have to make the climb one step at a time, and square one (step one) starts at the base. Now, in the metaphor of Mount Meru, the base is associated with the animal roots of human nature. This is where happiness is equated with the pleasures of the flesh: eating, drinking, copulation, etc. There's nothing wrong with that; it's neither moral nor immoral. It's just the way things are at root. Where human consciousness is concerned, however, happiness is capable of ascending to much higher states, but the base is where it starts; ask any baby. (The point is illustrated graphically in the ground-level friezes of some tantric temples, which portray vividly sensuous scenes of orgies that include just about everything you can imagine—even bestiality.)

Tantra takes the position that as one attempts to ascend the mountain, it makes no sense to turn your back on the ground levels, rejecting and attempting to "transcend" one's physical nature. The mountain is all one piece; it's not made up of conflicting layers. The base of the mountain is the foundation of the entire (philosophical) edifice. Therefore, the sadhaka, instead of renouncing his bodily desires and pleasures, as is the case in traditional practice, embraces them totally. What gave Tantra its special character was its effort to involve the whole person in the adventure of spiritual growth. In place of the more traditional approach of self-discipline and transcendence of desire, Tantra developed a host of ritual practices that embraced the body, desires and all, and saw it as a wonderful vehicle that could be used to carry one to higher states of knowledge. Rather than regarding the pleasure-craving body as an impediment to growth, rather than renouncing desire, Tantra sought to harness the energy of desire and use it to generate higher states of awareness. Of course, such an unorthodox approach could hope to succeed only if it was directed by a highly skilled master. Consequently, in the spirit of the ashram tradition of India, Tantra originally took the form of small groups of disciples tightly bound to a guru.

The guru–sadhaka relationship is everything in Tantra. Almost always, it would take form within the context of an ashram. The guru trains the sadhaka, who, necessarily, is already a highly self-disciplined person and a dedicated master of Hatha Yoga. In no way at all is it reasonable to suspect that the disciple is actually a self-serving hedonist using the practices of Tantra as a front to disguise his or her appetite for sensual pleasure. Far from it! In an imperfect world, it may be true that a fraud slips through from time to time, but that would be very infrequent. For one thing, if a person was interested only in sensual pleasures, there would be far easier ways of satisfying those desires, even in India at any time in the past.

It's a rare person that fits the bill; definitely, Tantra is not for everyone. If an unsuitable person took up the tantric way of life, it would lead to disaster. And certainly an authentic guru would weed out the unfit early on. The guru is in control of the entire process; the disciple must be willing to surrender totally to the will of the guru. Without his (or her) guidance, the seeker would quickly become lost in the woods.

The long path to the summit begins with Diksha, the ancient ceremony of initiation that establishes an intimate, personal relationship between guru and sadhaka. The most important element of Diksha concerns the mantra. A mantra is a spiritually powerful word or syllable, or string of words or syllables, that a person repeats (often chants) in order to forge a strong psychic connection between himself and the force or deity that the mantra represents. The guru intuitively selects the appropriate mantra for his new disciple and gives it to him or her privately, perhaps by whispering it into the disciple's ear. The sadhaka repeats the mantra to make sure that it is being uttered correctly and then buries it in his or her heart, from where it will be repeated endlessly in the days and years to come. Disciples do not reveal their mantras to others, not because they're secret, but rather, because they are very personal. The importance of the mantra cannot be overstated: It is widely believed among adherents of Tantra that to reveal one's mantra would cause it to lose its power.

The actual work involved in climbing the mountain consists in a variety of psychoexperimental exercises collectively called *sadhanas*. It is through the execution of sadhanas that the guru steers the development of the sadhaka. Sadhanas come in many varieties, but all are grounded on traditional yogic exercises, especially Kundalini Yoga, and all are designed to prepare the sadhaka for the experience of powerful psychic states. The sadhaka is skillfully guided to discover the real nature of his or her mind by exploring all possible psychic states. Needless to say, nothing less than a fully enlightened guru is even thinkable in this kind of relationship. Does the guru employ the use of psychoactive drugs? Yes, sometimes drugs are used, but definitely not as a matter of course. As you might guess, this has always been one of the major objections to tantric practices, but it can be easily exaggerated. Much more common, and equally reprehensible to the traditionalists, is the presence of sexual intercourse in tantric sadhanas.

This needs to be explained. Like orthodox Hinduism and Buddhism, Tantra maintains that reality is One. The key to enlightenment is to see—to intuit—the unity behind the apparent polarities of life. Tantra uses a great deal of symbolism to express the unity of polarity—hence the myriad gods and demons. Chief among the symbols is that of male and female, representing the passive and the active principles of existence, respectively. The mating of these two principles, wonderfully symbolized in the act of sexual intercourse—or, more specifically, in the ecstasy of orgasm—became the central icon of Tantra. In Vajrayana (Tibetan Buddhism), this icon took the form of the yab–yum, a sculpture or painting depicting a male and his female consort joined sexually in the moment of ecstasy. That depiction did not become popular in Hindu Tantra, but the act itself did. Called the *maithuna*, it became the climax (so to speak) of a long and elaborate tantric meditation exercise known, appropriately, as the *Maithuna Meditation*.

Although intensely physical—involving the body, the emotions, and the mind—the maithuna was not at all meant to be an erotic experience in the sense that sex normally is, but rather, was seen as a powerful vehicle involving the whole person that, used properly, could transport the sadhaka into a transcendent state of consciousness in which he or she could experience—or better still, become—the unity, the oneness behind the illusion of polarities.

This viewpoint is best exemplified in the Maithuna Meditation exercise, which could easily take up the better part of a whole day. On the appointed day, the sadhaka would rise early to bathe and perform a variety of other ritual observances and offerings, including much chanting of prescribed verses. At the proper time, the sadhaka imbibed a liquid concoction of *Indicus cannabis* (a highly potent variety of hemp, which is to say, marijuana) known as *vijaya*. Following this, the sadhaka would use rice powder to trace a mandala on the ground, within which he would perform further offerings and chants. In the final part of the exercise, the sadhaka would ritually approach the "Five M's": madya (liquor), mamsa (meat), matsya (fish), mudra (roasted grain), and maithuna (sexual intercourse). The significance of these items is that they were specifically forbidden to the disciple in the orthodox Hindu tradition. So you might say that, by indulging in them, the sadhaka was flaunting his rejection of the traditional way. In another way, though, these things represent some of the most basic and natural elements of life. Why shouldn't they be celebrated? Also, it was believed that the three foods in the group, together with the liquor, were aphrodisiacs and would thus be very helpful to the sadhaka when he joined with his female partner (the shakti). The sexual finale might last for a very long time, during which it would be necessary for him to maintain an erection. It's interesting to the modern student of the subject that, with the possible exception of wine, the first four M's have no aphrodisiac properties at all. By contrast, the vijaya did indeed have that effect.

The grand finale of the Maithuna Meditation was the maithuna itself. Again, I want to emphasize that it was not intended to be erotic in the usual sense of the word. The prescribed posture for maithuna was the yogic position pictured in the yab–yum. The male sadhaka would sit, back upright with legs crossed, and the female, his shakti, would take her position in his lap, with her legs and arms folded around him. (See illustration on p. 293 and a somewhat similar image on p. 96.) Interestingly, in this position the male is capable of almost no movement at all, but the woman is capable of a great range of movements. It is she, in fact, who generates all of the action. This is in keeping with the symbolism, in which the male represents the passive principle and the female the active.

In the Hindu Tantric tradition, the discharge of semen was expected to occur. It was the ultimate perfection of the whole long procedure. In the Vajrayana tradition, however, discharge was most definitely *not* supposed to occur. (Avoiding it would obviously require great self-discipline on the part of the sadhaka.) It was believed that the discharge of semen would squander the vital energy of the sadhaka just at the time he needed every bit of it to break through to transcendental awareness. Retention of the semen (bija) thus became the *sine qua non* of perfection in the performance of this sadhana.

In the historical evolution of Tantra, two schools of practice developed. In one, called "right-handed Tantra," the sex act and other physical elements came to be represented only symbolically in sadhana exercises. This was especially true in Buddhist Tantra. The other school, the so-called "left-handed Tantra," continued to include actual physical experiences in sadhana. Whether one or the other is right, or more right, is, of course, a question that can never be answered definitively. In modern times, though, it would seem that right-handed Tantra pretty much has the field to itself—but not entirely.

THE DEVOTIONAL MOVEMENT

Focusing on the darshanas, as we have been doing, can result in a misleading impression. Those philosophical systems were, for the most part, of interest to specialized communities, generally drawn from the more privileged classes of Indian society. In other words, only a tiny minority of the people would have been personally involved as followers of a particular darshana. It would be going too far to say that these darshanas were of interest only to scholars, but it would definitely not be going too far to say that the great masses of the people were concerned with other things in their daily lives. As in all times and places, what mattered to most people were the *devotional* aspects of the spiritual life. Temples, idols, processions, prayers, bells, candles, gongs, incense, singing, and so on— this was the stuff of religious life for most. In others words, Bhakti, the passionate worship of a personal savior, was the chosen way for the huge majority of Hindu men and women.

The popular traditions of Bhakti grew from roots that reach far back into pre-Vedic times. These roots nourished, and continue to nourish, a strong and broadly based religious life among the common people, who always greatly outnumber the elite minority that favors a more philosophical approach to the mysteries of life.

At the same time that the principal darshanas were being formulated, a great surge of devotional movements took form among the common people. In part, the surge was fueled by the appearance of the *Puranas*, popular compositions that brought the teachings of the Vedas and Upanishads to the people at large in the form of mythical stories that often included the wondrous doings of the various Hindu gods. Also of importance in this regard were the great popular epics, the *Ramayana* and the *Mahabharata*. In the *Bhagavad Gita*, itself a part of the *Mahabharata*, Krishna proclaimed Bhakti to be the greatest of all Yogas.

Popular cults developed around all of the gods, but most of all for the worship of Vishnu and Shiva, the right and left hands of what would come to be known as the *Trimurti*. (Brahma, the central figure of the Trimurti, did not receive the same adoring

The Kandariya Mahadeva (Shiva Temple), Khajuraho. (P. Bresnan)

attention. In all of India, there are only a couple of temples dedicated to the worship of Brahma.) But the worship of Vishnu or Shiva (or both) spread throughout the land. Temples were going up everywhere. This vigorous devotional movement came to establish the general character of Indian life, and it would continue to define the broad nature of Hinduism down to the present time.

Vishnu Worship

Vishnu, the Preserver of the World, became enormously popular in all parts of India. Vishnu was pictured as an approachable, compassionate, loving god; someone you could pray to, and he would really *hear* your prayers—and care. To put it simply, Vishnu was a friend of humankind.

In some ways, Vishnu was like the Greek god Apollo. Better still, he was a Christ figure for the Hindu world: Not only was he a loving friend, but he was also a *savior*. As proclaimed in the *Bhagavad Gita*, the compassionate Vishnu would incarnate himself on Earth to rescue a troubled humankind in times of dire need:

> Whenever dharma declines and the purpose of life is forgotten, I manifest myself on earth. I am born in every age to protect the good, to destroy evil, and to re-establish dharma.[2]

Sculptured panel from the exterior of the Kandariya Mahadeva. (P. Bresnan)

These incarnations of Vishnu are called *avataras*, and according to traditional belief, Vishnu has played this all-important role ten times over the ages. Some of the incarnations were as animals; in fact, the very first one was as a fish. The most important avataras, though, were as men, and the most important of all was, of course, as Sri Krishna, Arjuna's charioteer in the *Bhagavad Gita*. Vishnu, as Krishna, became a highly popular deity in India (and still is). Indian spiritual literature reaches a great height in Book Eleven of the *Bhagavad Gita*, where Krishna allows Arjuna a brief glimpse of his sublime Vishnu-nature. It had to be brief: Without Krishna's help, a mortal would be completely overwhelmed by such a vision. Arjuna speaks:

> Just as you have described your infinite glory, O Lord, now I long to see it. I want to see you as the supreme ruler of creation. O Lord, master of yoga, if you think me strong enough to behold it, show me your immortal Self.[3]

Krishna responds to Arjuna's request.

> He [Vishnu] appeared with an infinite number of faces, ornamented by heavenly jewels, displaying unending miracles and the countless weapons of his power. Clothed in celestial garments and covered with garlands, sweet-smelling with heavenly fragrances, he showed himself as the infinite Lord, the source of all wonders, whose face is everywhere. If a thousand suns were to rise in the heavens at the same time, the blaze of their light would only resemble the splendor of that supreme spirit. There, within the body of the God of gods, Arjuna saw all the manifold forms of the universe united as one. Filled with amazement, his hair standing on end in ecstasy, he bowed before the Lord.[4]*

Strictly speaking, only nine of the ten avataras have thus far appeared among us. The tenth avatara, Kalki, is yet to come. He is pictured as a great warrior riding to humanity's rescue on a white horse (naturally). Many Hindus, however, believe that Vishnu is not limited only to these ten avataras, but that he has performed this loving service far more often. Many believe, for example, that Buddha was an avatara of Vishnu, and some would go so far as to include Jesus and Muhammed as well.

Shiva Worship

To enter the world of Shiva worship is to enter the world of India at its most awesomely mysterious and bewildering, at least for the non-Indian. In Shiva worship, the Indian creative imagination erupts in a never-ending multiplicity of gods and demons, occult

---

*Arjuna's vision of Vishnu has a most interesting parallel in the Christian tradition. Shortly before his death, Jesus took some of his disciples to a remote place in the mountains where he allowed them to see the sublime radiance of his divine nature. The experience was similarly overwhelming (Matthew 17:1).

rituals, and stunning sexual symbolism. The devotees of Shiva account for many of the odd stereotypes that exist in the Western mind regarding Indian spiritual life.

Like Vishnu, one of his partners in the Trimurti, Shiva, in various forms, came to represent all three aspects of the Trimurti: creator, preserver, and, ultimately, destroyer. In the enchanting role of Shiva Nataraja, a four-armed Shiva is pictured performing the Tandava Dance, the dance of the cosmic cycle. The beginning is slow, bringing the world into being; then it becomes a dance that maintains the cosmos. The wild finale, the dance of fire, represents the final destruction of the world. Then, after a time, it begins all over again.

Shiva as Destroyer is pictured as the archetype ascetic yogin, and as such, he became widely popular as the patron of India's myriad ascetic sadhus, who do the best they can to imitate the appearance of Shiva. This god of an untamed and brooding nature was said to spend most of his time in seclusion on Mount Kailash, far back among the Himalayan peaks in Tibet. He let his black hair grow wild and long, tying it in a top-knot from which he caused the mighty Ganges to rush forth. He practiced severe austerities, going about totally naked, but covering his body with ashes from the cremation grounds. He wore only a necklace of human skulls. As Destroyer, Shiva's symbol is the trident, which he carries everywhere.

Shaivite monks honor their patron by wearing a small trident on a string around the neck. Typically, they also wear little or nothing, let their hair grow long, and smear ashes

Shiva and Parvati: from an exterior panel of the Kandariya Mahadeva, Khajuraho, India. (P. Bresnan)

into it daily. The ashes come, not from the cremation grounds, but from the little sacred fire, the *dhuni*, which is lovingly set up and ringed by flowers every day. Ashes are also used to make three horizontal stripes on the forehead and on various parts of the body. This little ritual represents the three evils of ego, karma, and *maya*. Shaivite monks are wanderers, but not hermits. They participate in a loose organization, and from time to time they gather for religious festivals. Great numbers congregate at Allahabad on the Ganges for the Khumba Mela festival held at twelve-year intervals.

The itinerant, ascetic Shaivite monks are a fascinating part of Hindu culture, but they account for only a tiny proportion of Shiva's worshippers. Among the people at large, it is Shiva as Preserver that is most honored. In this role, Shiva is the patron deity of many temples throughout India. The symbol of Shiva the Preserver is the *linga*. A linga is a simple upright shaft, rounded at the top, that represents the erect phallus, the male sex organ. The linga is found and venerated *everywhere* within the world of Shiva worship! It is found in temples, shrines, and home altars; in earlier times, it was even worn around the neck by married women. Its voluptuous ubiquity was, to say the least, shocking to Westerners who first came into contact with Hindu culture.

The roots of linga veneration are very ancient in India, stretching far back, some think, into pre-Vedic times. There are some references to indigenous "phallus-worshippers" in the *Rig Veda*—and why not? The linga is a natural symbol for fertility, for procreative power, which is exactly what made Shiva the Preserver an all-important god. Ritual veneration of the linga was, and to some extent still is, the central act of worship in Shiva temples. Actually, the linga is usually found in association with a *yoni*, a round base, made of wood or stone, into whose center the linga is inserted. The yoni repre-

Linga and Yoni; South India.
(P. Bresnan)

sents the female sex organ; together, the two form a completeness symbolic of the dual male–female character of nature. The linga represents Shiva; the yoni represents his *shakti*—that is, his association with a female consort, the embodiment of the female nature.

The traditional manner of linga–yoni veneration can seem pretty startling to most Westerners. In a typical ritual, Shaivite priests pour milk, oil, and perfume onto the linga, which are then most gently kneaded into the surface of the sculpture. In some cases, a vessel is hung directly above the linga, onto which it continuously drips a sacred oil. Candles and garlands of fresh flowers decorate the scene. Clearly, this is a highly sensual form of worship, and to the devotees of Shiva, therein lies its special beauty.*

Linga–yoni veneration was not the whole of it. Sexual symbolism in general plays a huge role in Shiva worship: Some of the other sculpture associated with Shiva temples is very frankly sexual. Young women, known as devadasi, were commonly connected with Shiva temples, and participated in the rituals, sometimes only in a symbolic fashion, sometimes not. In a degraded form, the devadasi became nothing more than temple prostitutes. These extremes were more often to be found among the practitioners of Tantra, that enigmatic antithesis of conservative Hinduism that developed in northeastern India. Some Tantra temples became notorious for all kinds of extreme practices, including ritual rape and ritual murder. In Calcutta, the Temple of Durga (one of the forms of Shiva's shakti) held an annual festival at which many pigs, goats, sheep, fowl, and even water buffalo would be slaughtered and ritually burned before the statue of the goddess.

As mentioned, Shiva is often depicted in association with his shakti. The shakti represented female power, or the power of the female principle in nature. Shiva, in union with his shakti, forms a cosmic wholeness. The shakti is expressed in personal form in the nature of four goddesses, which could be seen as four separate individuals or as the four basic modes of the principle of shakti. In Shaivite art, they were understandably portrayed as the four individual consorts of Shiva: Parvati, Uma, Durga, and Kali. They are, to put it mildly, a foursome that would be hard to ignore.

Parvati, the subject of many mythic stories, is presented as Shiva's favorite. Maddeningly beautiful and intensely erotic, she and Shiva are often portrayed in passionate sexual intercourse. One time, to hide her nudity, Parvati playfully put her hands over Shiva's eyes. He immediately created a third eye at the center of the forehead, thus supposedly giving rise to the concept of the third eye in yoga. On another occasion, when Shiva had been away for a long time, she created a baby out of her

---

*Linga veneration is not something that existed only in the distant past. Nor is it limited only to exotic temples found in India. Devotees of Shiva see it as an entirely respectable form of religious worship, and it has traveled with them to many parts of the world. In Livermore, California, for example, right in the middle of a typically American tract of suburban homes, stands a Hindu temple dedicated to both Vishnu and Shiva. The temple maintains a staff of priests from India who perform traditional rituals daily. Far from being bizarre, it's really quite beautiful.

Ganesha. (P. Bresnan)

own skin and named him Ganesha. Then she put the child nearby to guard her privacy while she bathed outdoors. Not recognizing Shiva, Ganesha ordered his "father" away. Shiva wasn't exactly used to being so treated, and he promptly decapitated Ganesha. When Parvati discovered this, she was furious. To make a long story short, Shiva ordered his men to go out and bring back the first head they found. One of the men came upon a baby white elephant, cut off its head and brought it back to Shiva, who joined it to Ganesha's body. Thus was the origin of one of Hinduism's most popular gods, the fun-loving, snack-eating, good-luck-bringing, elephant-headed Ganesha.

Uma's roots probably go back to the time when she was a Dravidian mother-goddess. She is associated with domesticity and the abundance of the earth. Durga, too, probably evolved from a prehistoric mother-goddess, but unlike Uma, Durga could be fierce and bloodthirsty. Durga was the one who craved blood sacrifice, including human sacrifice. Kali is by far the most fearsome of the lot. She gives life, but she more often destroys it. Shaivite artists used a lot of imagination in portraying Kali. She is pictured as wild and hideously ugly, with fangs for teeth and a naked, withered body. She carries a severed head in one hand and a staff topped with a human skull in the other. There's much more, but you get the picture. Kali is associated with death and destruction, but out of that arises the potential for renewal.

The Trimurti

Trimurti is a Sanskrit word that means "threefold expression"—in other words, trinity. The Vedic Trimurti was the closley bound trinity of three gods—Brahma, Vishnu, and Shiva—that came to occupy the place of paramount importance in the Indian pantheon by the later part of the Vedic age.

The gods were brought forth in the first place to explain the forces of nature. Someone with rational intelligence and superhuman power, it was believed, was in control of the forces of nature and deliberately manipulated them in such a way as to account for the natural phenomena of daily life. The gods were created out of the imagination of men to play this role, and they personified the forces of nature that they controlled.

In early Vedic times, the gods were imagined, much like the Olympians of Greece, as a very humanlike family of individual characters, each possessed of enormous wealth and power, and stories of their adventures resembled a kind of celestial soap opera.

But from the very beginning, there was known to be more to the story than simply the ongoing exploits of the gods: Behind the doings of the individual gods lay a sense of the grand uniformity, the oneness, of Nature. The many had come out of the one and eventually would return to the one. Among the more thoughtful, a view emerged that over the long haul of time, worldly existence goes through enormously long cycles of generation, destruction, and regeneration. Existence alone endures forever, but the *things of existence*, gods as well as men, would emerge and eventually dissolve. Then the process of generation would begin all over again, and so on forever.

This more sophisticated view of reality called for a more sophisticated view of the gods. After all, the underlying purpose of the gods was not *really* to control the forces of nature, but rather to provide men with an intelligible symbol, or personification, of all those awesome aspects of nature that make up reality.

It would seem that, with the passage of time, what the forces of nature had in common became more important than how they differed. More and more, it was the unity of nature that interested thinking men and women. But the unity of nature expresses itself in grand dualities: male and female, light and dark, land and sea, youth and age, and so on. The most fundamental duality of all was seen to be the opposition between the process of generation and the process of dissolution—creation and destruction, growth and decay, and, life and death. The gods associated with these great processes gradually became more and more important.

All of the gods attracted cult followings. Devotion to the various deities, especially Vishnu and Shiva, has always been a major element of the Hindu tradition. Even the minor gods had cults dedicated to their worship. Vishnu was one such minor deity, mentioned only casually in the Vedas. But by late Vedic times, the cult of Vishnu had grown enormously, and Vishnu was clearly one of the most popular of all the gods.

Shiva is the god paired with Vishnu in a great duality; they are equal in importance if not everywhere equal in popularity. In no way should we think of Vishnu and Shiva as a Hindu version of Christ and Satan. Both Vishnu and Shiva were good and necessary. (There was no concept of Satan as such in the Hindu view.) Shiva was the destroyer, or "dissolver," in the sense that all things built up must eventually be dismantled. If it were not for the constant interplay of the forces of generation and dissolution, the processes of nature could not continue to unfold. Everything that grows, including our own bodies, must eventually decay, and out of that very decay new growth emerges. It is a never-ending interplay, like a dance, and in the end the whole world (i.e., the universe) will be consumed. Then the cycle begins again.

Like Vishnu, Shiva was not an important name in early Vedic times. In fact, the cult of Shiva was derived out of the cult of Rudra, with whom Shiva was closely associated. In a sense, the worship of Shiva came to replace the worship of Rudra. It is widely believed that a cult of Shiva or of Rudra–Shiva was well established among the Dravidian people in the distant pre-Vedic times. Among the Dravidians, Shiva was identified with the reproductive power, and, as we have seen, his sacred symbol was the linga, a stylized stone pedestal representing the erect phallus. When Shiva, like his alter ego Rudra, was adopted into the Hindu pantheon, veneration of the linga went with him, and it has remained to this day an essential part of all temples and shrines dedicated to Shiva.

The third member of the Trimurti, and in some subtle respects the most important of all, was Brahma. Brahma—derived from the Sanskrit root *brih*, which means "to grow"—was the designated god of creation. Nothing could be more important than the universal act of creation. Without it, nothing at all would exist. The creative power of Brahma is an ongoing reality that not only brought the world into existence in the first place, but also continues to act every day in the power of generation; the constant emergence of new life is the creative power of Brahma at work.

The nature of Brahma's creation also came to incorporate a strongly unifying theme. Creation was explained in mythological terms, but the character of the story reveals a profound sense of an underlying unity. The rishis believed that the world (the universe) evolved through a very long span of time called a kalpa, which was said to be 4 billion, 320 million years long (a span of time curiously close to the actual age of the Earth). At the end of this time, Vishnu would surrender his role as preserver, and Shiva, unopposed, would do the final "dance of death," initiating a great fire that would consume everything, returning existence to the empty void—the pure unified consciousness of Brahma—from which it had emerged in the first place. After an appropriate interval, a new kalpa would commence: A new universe would burst into existence, and the game would begin all over again. The kalpa was called "the day of Brahma"; the interval between kalpas was called "the night of Brahma." This great alternation was believed to go on forever.

Thus, we have Brahma who creates the world, Vishnu who preserves and protects that creation, and Shiva who eventually dismantles and dissolves the creation. Obviously, all three are necessary, and all three are closely related. That's why they are joined together into what was called the Trimurti.

In a fundamental sense, the Trimurti can account for everything. Little by little, the older gods lost the importance they had once enjoyed. What we see here is a gradual movement away from polytheism toward monotheism, a development common to the history of almost all cultures. The lesser gods could almost be seen as individualized aspects of the Trimurti. We can even go a step further, a step that would have been taken by only the most philosophically minded of the rishis. Brahma stood between Vishnu and Shiva in the Trimurti. He represented the state of equilibrium and balance between the opposing forces that they represented. Accordingly, one could conclude that Vishnu and Shiva, instead of being independent individuals, were best understood as fundamental *aspects of Brahma*. In this view, we have come all the way to monotheism. There is but one god. Seen face on, he is Brahma, the creator; the right side of his nature is Vishnu, the left side is Shiva. In fact, in the traditional art of India, Brahma is often represented in exactly this way.

Ramanuja

The devotional movement reached a summit in the person of Ramanuja, resident scholar (acharya) of the Sri Ranganathaswamy Temple at Srirangam in south India in the eleventh century C.E. Ramanuja was a brilliant thinker, fully rooted in the Bhakti tradition. His name is often linked with Shankara, whose abstract, intellectual philosophy he attacked. Ramanuja was a scholar, able to meet Sharkara on his own ground, and thus gave a respectable defense to Bhakti, all too often dismissed as naive and unphilosophical by educated Hindus. Ramanuja sought to establish Bhakti as a fully intelligent alternative to the intellectual philosophy of Shankara.

Ramanuja agreed with the Vedanta position of Shankara that reality is One, but strongly disagreed as to the real nature of the One. Ramanuja argued that the empirical world is real and is not the illusory *maya* of Shankara, but this does not amount to a dualistic interpretation because the world is not separate from Brahman; rather, it is the direct *manifestation* of Brahman. The One manifests itself in pluralities. He used the familiar analogy of the body to explain this point. Each part of the body is real and distinct unto itself, but altogether the parts form an organic whole, a "self," which is real, whose reality transcends that of the parts and is that upon which each of the parts is wholly dependent. You could say that the individual beings of the world are the manifested parts of the "body" of Brahman, but just as your own self is infinitely more than merely the sum of the parts, so, too, is Brahman, the ultimate "Self," the final one reality that defines everything.

The great importance of this interpretation is that it opens up the possibility of sin and redemption. If the individual self is real (even though that individuality is subsumed in the organic wholeness of Brahman), then it is capable of independent action, including sin. This is not the same as the *avidya* of the Brahman-*Atman* that results in suffering; Ramanuja is talking about real, free-will sin.

Human beings are capable of sin, but redemption is possible. Being that each of us is only a part of the organic wholeness of Brahman and that therefore none of us is in any way capable of independent existence, redemption consists in fully accepting the fact of our oneness with Brahman, loving Brahman with complete resignation. Loving Brahman is not loving some lifeless abstraction—the "absolute," for example. Since the whole is greater than the parts, and the parts (we, at least) are personally conscious beings, it must follow that Brahman, too, is at least as real and personal a being as we are. Ramanuja is encouraging men and women to love Bhahman in the form of a personal god, a compassionate savior, and for Ramanuja, none fit the bill better than

Vishnu, the much-loved deity who represented the Brahman nature. The way to exhibit that love, of course, is through Bhakti, the customary practices of which—worship at the temple, festivals, prayer, etc.—are the means *par excellence* for one to generate the saving grace (*prasada*) that brings redemption from sin—and the highest form of Bhakti, in Ramanuja's view, is the worshipful repetition of the name of God. Ramanuja urged his followers to pray constantly, lovingly repeating God's name. Thus did Ramanuja attempt to put the way of Bhakti on a par with the more intellectual darshanas.

THE MUSLIM ERA

The fortunes of civilization have risen and fallen for millennia in India. Empires have come and gone, and so, too, have invaders. Foreign invasion is as old as history in the Indian subcontinent. But always, it seems, the would-be conquerors became themselves the conquered as the great ocean of Hindu culture ultimately swallowed up the invaders, assimilating them into the multifaceted world of Indian peoples. The Muslim conquest of India was a different story: This time the invaders came, not only to stay, but to remain an aloof and unassimilated class of conquerors.

The Muslim conquest of India began a thousand years ago. Wave after wave of invaders poured in out of the Persian–Afghan west. Native Indian resistance was strong and fanatically determined, but all to no avail. Muslim armies ultimately succeeded in conquering and establishing rule over almost all of the subcontinent. Only parts of the far South escaped incorporation. Muslim rule would prevail in India until the nineteenth century, when it was finally replaced by another foreign power, the British. Muslim rule is finally over, but the bitter legacy is far from being a thing of the past: Modern democratic India continues to be wracked by problems born of ancient hatreds.

Actually, the very first Muslim incursion into the subcontinent occurred all the way back in 711 C.E. That was less than a century after the founding of Islam in far-off Arabia. After the death of Muhammed, crusading Islamic armies swept out of Arabia and in less than a generation had created an empire that stretched from Gibraltar to Persia. One of the principal centers of this empire was the Caliphate of Damascus, and it was from there that a small invading army was dispatched to India. The Muslim army succeeded in establishing control over a region in the lower Indus valley, but it really never went beyond there, and effective rule lasted for less than a century. It was a harbinger, though, of things to come.

The conquest began in earnest in the year 1001 C.E., when Mahmud of Ghazni, ruler of a small Afghan kingdom, launched the first of seventeen invasions into northwestern India. Between 1001 and 1026, Mahmud's fierce cavalries plundered and destroyed huge portions of northern India. His favorite targets were the temples, where so much of the wealth of the land was concentrated. So many temples were pillaged and desecrated that Mahmud is known in Indian history as the "Idol Breaker."

Mahmud's conquest might have been turned back at the start, and conceivably centuries of Muslim rule in India averted, had one particular day in history gone differently, or even if one little incident on that day had not happened. It was on a hot summer day in the year 1008 C.E.; the place was a broad, dusty field near Peshawar in northwest India. Mahmud's army, mainly an Afghan cavalry 15,000 strong, had been dug in for more than a month. They were facing the much larger army of Anandpal, the maharaja of the Punjab. Anandpal's father had lost an earlier battle with Mahmud, leaving 15,000 dead on the battlefield, and Anandpal vowed that that would never happen again.* Many of the *rajas* of north India had contributed forces to the army. The women had sold their jewels to raise funds. A force of several hundred war elephants had been gathered, and now the moment of truth was at hand. Anandpal ordered an attack. Perhaps that was the first mistake, although all went well at first. Mahmud was about to call for a retreat when, for some unexplainable reason, Anandpal's elephant panicked and charged away from the battle. In the confusion, the Indian army believed that their leaders were fleeing, and all began retreating in disarray. The battle turned into a rout: Mahmud's forces slaughtered thousands. Never again was he seriously challenged in India. Who can imagine how differently all of Indian history might have been if only Anandpal's elephant had stayed the course on that fateful day? But that's not the way it happened.

Following the invasions, vast quantities of loot were hauled back to Mahmud's Ghazni, originally the capital of a rather small and humble Afghan kingdom. But thanks to his conquests, both east into India and west into Persia, for a time Ghazni became a rich and splendid city, second only to Baghdad in the Islamic world. Mahmud's court attracted artists and thinkers from all over the Islamic world, and presumably, some of this cultural influence would be felt in India. But the people of the conquered regions were not yet thinking of that; they knew only death and devastation. Their people were slaughtered, their villages burned, and their beautiful temples broken and ransacked. Some of their finest "heathen" idols were hauled back to Ghazni, where they could be publicly desecrated and crushed under the hooves of the army's horses.

Successive waves of Muslim invaders followed Mahmud, extending Muslim rule throughout most of northern India. But it was a patchwork affair, not a unified state by any means. One of these invaders was to have special significance for the future. Timur, generally known in the West as Tamerlane, led his incredibly ferocious cavalry into northwestern India in the year 1398. Timur was in the process of forging a huge central Asian empire, and it was a process that knew no limit to violence and mayhem. It is said that his army competed with itself to see how large a pyramid of skulls could be built in the remains of devastated cities that lay in their path. North India felt his destructive violence, but fortunately for India, Timur had not come to stay. He did, however, lay claim to conquered regions in the northwest.

It was to claim Timur's legacy that another central Asian warlord entered India about a century after Timur had departed the scene. Babur, the founder of the Mughal Raj, invaded India out of his base in Afghanistan in 1525 C.E. Being descended from Timur on his father's side and from Ghengiz Khan on his mother's side, Babur certainly had the blood of conquerors in his veins. And conquest is what it was all about:

---

*Anandpal's father, incidentally, driven mad by his anguish over the defeat, is said to have committed suicide by throwing himself on a kinsman's funeral pyre.

Nominally, Babur, like Timur before him, was Muslim, but spreading the faith was not his real goal; his real goal was the creation of empire, and at that task he was very good. Babur welded together virtually all of the regions of northern India, creating a unified state ruled from the Sultanate of Delhi and Agra. This empire, known in history as the Mughal Raj, would endure for more than three centuries, until finally it would be absorbed into the growing British Empire during the nineteenth century.

It does not serve our purposes to go into detail about the political side of the story of India. Let us simply identify the principal successors of Babur so as to provide a temporal framework that we can refer to:

- Humayun (1530–1556). Babur's rather inept son and successor was an opium addict who lacked the zeal to extend the empire, but managed to hold on to most of Babur's conquests. His principal contribution was in being the father of Akbar.
- Akbar (1556–1605). Clearly the greatest of the Mughal line. Akbar made a contribution that could have changed the course of history, but his successors, unfortunately, did not choose to continue the work that he had begun.
- Jahangir (1605–1627). Something of a nonentity, Jahangir was in power during the time when the Europeans made their first important inroads into India.
- Shah Jahan (1627–1658). Shah Jahan is best remembered as the builder of the incredibly beautiful Taj Mahal. Constructed on the south bank of the Jamuna River in Agra, the Taj

Taj Mahal. (P. Bresnan)

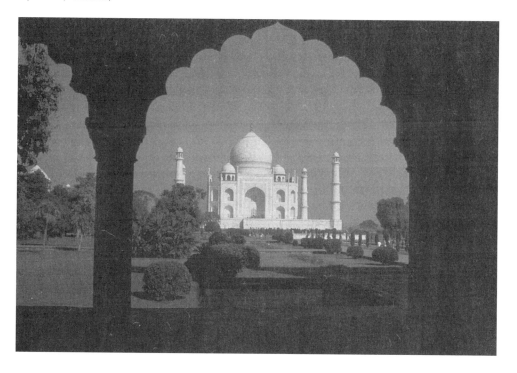

was finished in the year 1654 C.E. It is not a mosque; rather, it was built to be a mausoleum for Shah Jahan's much-loved wife, Queen Mumtaz, who died young. Workers began clearing a spot on the farther bank of the Jamuna, where an identical copy of the Taj was to be constructed, only this one would be all black marble instead of white. It was to be Shah Jahan's own final resting place, and the two were to be linked by an oval bridge of intermixed white-and-black marble. (Quite an awesome thought, isn't it!) Before building could begin, though, the Shah's sons, worried about the cost, declared their father to be mentally unwell and removed him from power. He spent the rest of his days confined to a splendid suite in the family palace a short distance upriver from the Taj, which he could gaze at from his window. His sarcophagus finally joined that of Mumtaz in the Taj.

- Aurangzeb (1658–1666). All of the great promise of Akbar's reign of tolerance was finally crushed out of existence by Aurangzeb. Apparently, he was a fundamentalist of an almost fanatical frame of mind who waged a nonstop holy war against his own Hindu subjects. Understandably, Aurangzeb was hated by the Hindus. All hopes of achieving Akbar's dream of some sort of cultural synthesis died on the vine. Aurangzeb's reign was the beginning of the end for the Mughal Raj. He was followed by a series of inept rulers who allowed the empire to fragment, making it much easier work for the Europeans (especially the British) to increase their influence until it reached the point of outright rule.

Of these successors of Babur, Akbar deserves more than passing mention. But first, we digress to discuss two non-Muslims who earlier had the same aim as Akbar.

Kabir

Akbar was not the first person in India who sought to find a bridge between the Muslim and Hindu cultures. Two other important names in this respect are Kabir and Nanak, both of whom were native Indians who made their mark decades before Akbar came to power. Before we learn more about the great Mughal, Akbar, and his dream of synthesis of religion and culture, we look briefly at the lives of these two ordinary men whose impact on Indian thought was great.

Kabir was a poet, a writer of religious verse. He was a deeply sensitive and compassionate man whom many regard as one of the finest thinkers in all of India's history. Kabir was born in 1440 C.E. into a family of weavers in Varanasi, the holiest of India's holy cities. He would live until 1518, which, as you may see, would make Kabir a close contemporary of two famous Italians: Christopher Columbus and Leonardo da Vinci. It is doubtful, though, that he would ever have heard of either of them. It is also doubtful that he ever heard of another famous European either: the Portuguese Vasco da Gama, who, of course, was the first European to reach the shores of India. That event, which was to have such far-reaching significance for all of India, occurred in the fall of 1498, at which time Kabir was fifty-eight years old. News of such a seemingly trivial event, happening far to the south, would not likely have reached the ears of Kabir, and anyway, he was not concerned with the Europeans—nor was anyone else at that time; his mind was totally absorbed in the problem of the great gulf that separated the Hindu and Muslim peoples.

Although Kabir's people were of the native stock, they were not Hindus. At an earlier time, the entire weavers' caste of Varanasi had converted to the Islamic faith. There were obvious advantages in doing this, and some of the other craft castes had done the same thing. As a result, Kabir was raised in a Muslim family and was educated in Muslim schools. Nonetheless, he did not become an ardent Muslim. He was, however, a lover of the Sufi way, that maverick sect within Islam which attaches so much importance to devotional practices and mystical intuition. But Kabir was also a lover of much that he found in the Hindu Bhakti tradition. He felt no love whatsoever, though, for the Brahmin priesthood, which he attacked as perpetrators of superstition:

> Kabir detested the fundamentalist spirit amongst the Brahmins and Ulemas alike. He opposed the superstitions perpetrated by them. He cast doubts on the authority of the Vedas, opposed idolatry and rejected the doctrine of incarnation. He also criticized asceticism, fasting, pilgrimage, ceremonial ablutions and denounced all forms of dogmatism.[5]

So what did Kabir *not* reject? On what would he anchor the bridge that he hoped to build? Kabir concluded that Islam and Hinduism—and, indeed, *all* religious philosophies attempt to accomplish the same thing: to break down the barrier that separates humanity from God. It is the *same God* that all are addressing, he believed, whatever the many different names that are used. All men and women are brothers and sisters, and whether they realize it or not, they are all striving to find union with the one God that is reflected in their many different religions. Muslims and Hindus must not quarrel; they should be united in love, knowing that they both seek the same God; they just use different words to address Him.

Much influenced by Muslim Sufi and Hindu Bhakti, and perhaps most powerfully of all by the teachings of Ramanuja, Kabir urged people of all faiths to find salvation in total surrender to God. That alone is the true path, and one walks the path by lovingly repeating the name of God. Any name will do; they all address the same loving God. Kabir's message is best expressed in his own emotional poetry:

> O servant, where dost thou seek me?
> Lo! I am beside thee.
> I am neither in temple nor in mosque.
> I am neither in Kaaba nor in Kailash.
> Neither am I in rites and ceremonies,
> Nor in yoga and renunciation.
> If thou art a true seeker,
> Thou shalt at once see me.
> Thou shalt meet me in a moment of time.
> Kabir says, "O Sadhu!
> God is the breath of all."[6]

Guru Nanak

Nanak was the founder of the Sikh religion, followers of which are those dignified, turbaned Indians one sees in seemingly all parts of the world. The Sikhs are known for a highly militant history, but it didn't start out that way.

Nanak was born in 1469 in a small village near Lahore, in what is today Pakistan. His family was Hindu, but his education was in Muslim schools, where he learned to read Persian and Arabic. As a result, he grew up with a foot in each world, and throughout his whole life he longed to find a way to bring harmony between the two cultures. Understandably, Kabir's poetry much influenced Nanak's thought and teaching. Nanak, too, composed religious poetry as a young man.

While still in his student years, Nanak became something of a leader of a group of philosophically minded young men who made a practice of bathing together every morning before dawn in a nearby river and gathering in the evening to discuss philosophy, often listening to the newly composed devotional poetry of Nanak. The group included both Muslims and Hindus, and it continued to meet for a number of years. One morning, when he was about thirty, Nanak went off to bathe alone, but he didn't return home at the usual time. His clothes were found near the river, and everyone was horribly afraid that he had drowned. Three days later Nanak reappeared, but he seemed as if he was in some kind of trance. He would not talk, except to repeat "There is neither a Hindu path nor a Muslim path. So how shall I know the right path? I will follow God's path, for God is neither a Muslim nor a Hindu."

Eventually, Nanak began to communicate again, and he told his friends about an experience he had had on the morning when he was at the river alone. According to the story, Nanak was all of a sudden overwhelmed by a powerful vision of God, who told Nanak that He wanted him to be His messenger. God told him, "Go, and repeat my name, and encourage others to repeat my name." Spiritually transformed by this mystical experience, Nanak vowed to become a guru and devote his life to spreading the true devotion to the One God. The very first thing he did was to express in writing the essence of what he had intuited in his vision:

> God is only One.
> His name is True.
> He is the Creator,
> He is without fear.
> He is inimical to none.
> He never dies.
> He is beyond births and deaths.
> He is self-illuminated.
> He is realized by the kindness of the True.
> Repeat His Name.[7]

This prayer became the opening words of the *Adi Granth*, a book composed of the collected teachings of Guru Nanak. Technically speaking, *Adi Granth* means "original book," but it is generally referred to as the "Holy Book." It is the "Bible" of the Sikh religion, and part of the prayers that make up the daily devotion of every Sikh. A beautifully bound copy of the *Adi Granth* is displayed in the central part of every Sikh temple.

The beauty of Nanak's spiritual philosophy is in its straightforward simplicity. In this regard the influence of Islam can be clearly seen. But Hindu influences are also evident. His overriding goal was to reveal an underlying harmony between the Muslim and

Hindu ways. He sought to get down to the roots by discarding all of the externals. Nanak rejected all dogma, *all* scriptures; he rejected the caste system and everything even suggestive of idolatry. After his thorough housecleaning of both traditions, there wasn't much left. But what *was* left was the all-important core.

Nanak declared that there is One God. ("Beside God there is no other.") Salvation consists in the soul's escape from *samsara*, the cycle of birth and death. This is accomplished by the total destruction of self-love, and *that* is accomplished through total submission to the will of God. The perfect, universally available way to achieve total submission is through *Nam Jaap*, the constant repetition of the Divine Name. Nam Jaap will slowly, but steadily, clear away all of the impurities of self-love. Nam Jaap, daily prayer, and service to the community—these three rules were the common core of worship that Nanak distilled from the teachings of Islam and Hinduism. Both groups respected the man and his work, and when Nanak died in 1539 at the age of seventy, both Hindu and Muslim groups claimed the body so as to honor it with their own ritual services.

Over time, a devoted group of disciples collected around Guru Nanak. He called his followers *sikhas*, a Hindi word meaning "disciples." The community remained small and peaceful during Nanak's lifetime. Before he died, however, Nanak appointed a successor, who would also bear the title of Guru. Thus did the Sikhs become a sect, one that would continue over time and preserve the teachings of the founder.

The history of the Sikhs was peaceful at first. The sect was supported by the tolerant Akbar, who even gave the community a grant of land in the city of Amritsar. This became the site of the splendid Golden Temple (the Harmandir Sahib), the earthly center of the Sikh faith. The Golden Temple, so named because of its golden dome, is situated at the center of a small artificial lake and is approached by a narrow causeway. Pilgrims can enter the temple through large doorways on each of its four sides. These doorways signify the four major divisions of the castes, which is to say, everyone is welcome.

The good times came to an abrupt end during the reign of Emperor Aurangzeb, the great-grandson of Akbar. Unlike his liberal-minded great-grandfather, Aurangzeb was a religious fundamentalist who launched a brutal persecution of all "nonbelievers." The Sikhs seemed especially to arouse his puritanical ire. He demanded that Guru Arjian remove some objectionable passages from the *Adi Granth*; when Guru Arjian, of course, refused, Aurangzeb ordered that he be tortured and put to death.

It was in direct response to Aurangzeb's persecution of the Sikhs that the tenth Guru, Gobind Singh, in 1606 established the *Khalsa*, a quasi-military group within the Sikh community whose function it was to protect the faith from persecution. The Khalsa was open only to men who were totally dedicated and fully willing to shed blood or even give their lives for the cause. Induction into the Khalsa followed an elaborate military-style ceremony that included the acceptance of the "Five K's": *kesh* (uncut hair), *kanga* (the hair comb), *kara* (an iron bangle), *kacha* (special knee-length trousers), and *kirpan* (a sword) or its substitute, *khanda* (a dagger). The long hair is typically tied in a top-knot and hidden under a turban.

Thanks to the ferocious resistance of the Khalsa, the Sikhs fought back effectively against their would-be persecutors, even going so far as to carve out an autonomous realm in the Punjab, which they hoped to make into an independent Sikh state. This was to have problematic consequences for the future, however. Fighting against the declining power of the Mughals was one thing, but taking on their well-armed British successors was quite another. After the British forcibly annexed the Sikh realm into their own growing Indian empire, the Sikhs perhaps saw the handwriting on the wall. From being violent opponents of the British, the Sikhs became loyal supporters. Many joined the British army, no small number of them serving in colonial security forces all over the Empire. Maybe they believed that, all things considered, that would be the most promising path toward eventual independence. Unfortunately, it was not to be. When independence came to India in 1947, the Punjab, to the bitter disappointment of the Sikhs, was divided between a Muslim Pakistan and a Hindu India. To escape horrible brutalities, the Sikh (and Hindu) families of the soon-to-be Pakistan had to uproot themselves and relocate to the eastern part of the Punjab included in Hindu-ruled India.

Even though the democratic constitution of India protected Sikhs fully, and many of them rose to the highest offices in India, including president of the republic, some of the more fundamentalist Sikhs continued to yearn for their own state. The Sikh independence movement continued in the new India, sometimes indulging in what the government labeled terrorist activities. Things came to a head in 1984, when Jarnail Singh Bhindranwale, the leader of a "rebel" group, and several hundred of his followers sought sanctuary inside the Golden Temple. After a brief siege, prime minister Indira Gandhi ordered her troops to storm the temple. It was a terrible scene: The sacred temple was partially destroyed, and hundreds of Sikh defenders were killed. Shortly after this bloody event, two Sikh members of Mrs. Gandhi's security guard assassinated her in the garden of her residence. And so it goes. What the future holds is impossible even to guess. There are approximately seventeen million Sikhs in the world today, many of them living outside of India. It is reasonable to assume that this large and vital population will contribute in as yet unimagined ways to the progress of Indian and world civilization.

Akbar

Akbar is known in history as Akbar "the Great"; he certainly deserves the name. Akbar was an enlightened ruler, a true visionary, in the same mold as Charlemagne, Frederick the Great, or, perhaps the best fit of all, that other great Indian ruler, Ashoka (whom we will meet in Chapter 11).

Akbar inherited an already large empire. Conquest was not the order of the day (although he did engage in some of that). Unification and consolidation were what was needed. Akbar took up the challenge with intelligence and passion. He wanted to be perceived as a just ruler of *all* the people. To achieve this aim, he instituted a policy of conciliation toward his formerly downtrodden Hindu subjects. The days of persecution were to be over forever. The special tax on the Hindu population, the *jizya*, was abolished (to the horror of his Muslim advisers). Hindu religious rights were respected, but the abhorrent practice of *sati* was outlawed. (*Sati* was the widely hated custom of requiring a widow to immolate herself on her husband's funeral pyre.) Akbar sought out famous Hindu holy men and listened respectfully to their teachings. Many high-ranking

Hindus were admitted to court, where they enjoyed the same opportunities as Muslim noblemen.

What began simply enough as a policy of conciliation, however, evolved into something bigger—much bigger. Akbar allowed himself to dream the impossible dream of genuine cultural synthesis between the two great religions. Why not use his power and influence to override the entrenched hostility between Muslim and Hindu? Indeed, the dream went even further than that: Why not add to this marriage the best of other great religions and cultures, too—the Christian, the Buddhist, the Jain, and the Zoroastrian? Akbar envisioned nothing less than a cultural synthesis that would bring together the finest elements of *all* of the world's great civilizations. And he got the ball rolling himself, shocking his traditionalist courtiers by marrying four wives: a Muslim, a Buddhist, a Christian, and a Hindu. In fact, it was the Hindu wife, a princess from nearby Jaipur, who bore him the son that was to become his heir and successor.

Under Akbar's leadership, the gentle war went well for a while. He built a splendid new palace and town at nearby Fatehpur-Sikri, a visible model of the policy of cultural fusion. At Fatehpur-Sikri, he created a wholly new architectural style, combining elements of both the Muslim and Hindu traditions. Akbar encouraged the arts and invited artists and learned men from all over the Eurasian world to come to his court and join in the great work. To Akbar, by far the most exciting part of his dream was what came to be called *Din-i-Ilahi*, known in English by the name "Divine Faith." Akbar hoped to create nothing less than a whole new religion, one that would incorporate the common elements and the best elements of all of the world's great religions. It was to be a religious syncretism of the highest order, and no doubt he dreamed that its obvious appeal would sweep the world and usher in a new and greater age. Akbar created a special forum for religious debate; Muslim theologians were there, and so were Buddhist scholars, Hindu Brahmins, and even Jesuits from Goa on the west coast of India, where the Portuguese had established a trading center.

Life was certainly exciting in those early days at Fatehpur-Sikri, but this little Golden Age of tolerance and cultural exchange was destined to be short lived. Perhaps Akbar was not sufficiently pragmatic; he failed to create a situation in which it would be to the personal advantage of his Muslim privileged class to want to continue the great policy of cultural synthesis. Human nature being what it is, it was thus only a matter of time before the tide would turn. When Akbar died at sixty three in the year 1605 C.E., the tide turned.*

Despite Akbar's heroic efforts, no real amalgamation ever occurred. There was a measure of artistic influence and, indeed, some resonance between Sufi mysticism and Hindu Bhakti, but the great goal of cultural fusion died. Perhaps it was doomed from the beginning, but the intolerant policies of those who came after Akbar guaranteed that his dream of uniting the two peoples and the two faiths would remain only that—a

---

*It was Akbar's dream that Fatehpur-Sikri would be the fountainhead of a great new culture for ages to come, but in little more than twenty years it was abandoned and forgotten. It is widely suspected that a shortage of water doomed the place. Today it is a popular tourist attraction—the exciting hope of the world when it was constructed, but now quiet and deserted.

dream. After Akbar, Hinduism in India seemed to turn in on itself, forsaking the often hostile world and stressing the devotional side of the spiritual life.

THE MODERN ERA

In 1858, Queen Victoria of England signed the bill that officially transferred political control of the Indian states from the British East India Company to the Crown. For almost another century, India would be the "Jewel in the Crown" of the British Empire. But Queen Victoria's signature was only the capstone to a process of British colonial involvement in India that had been developing since 1600, the very year in which Queen Elizabeth I granted a charter to eighty London merchants who had come together to form the British East India Company. What began as an opportunistic trading venture turned into a truly incredible adventure in which a private trading company, step by stumbling step, wrested control of an empire from the Mughal overlords. Muslim rulers had controlled the subcontinent of India since the invasions of Mahmud of Ghazni that began back in 1001 C.E.

The bottom line of this story is that Hindu India changed masters: The British Raj replaced the Mughal Raj. But there was far more to this transfer of power than simply a change of overlords: This time, the foreign power was really *foreign*. The British had absolutely no interest at all in invading India, taking up residence, and ruling as conquerors. Within the British Empire India was simply one jewel in the globe-circling necklace of colonial dependencies. History reveals that such empires have limited life expectancies, and therein lay the incredible possibility that after so many centuries of foreign rule, Hindu India might hope to once again become free and independent. British rule in India accomplished two great things: It served as a means for assimilating India into the modern world, and, despite itself, it provided a matrix within which Indian leadership could evolve the means for becoming a modern independent state. This is not in any way to excuse the abuses of colonialism; India suffered greatly under the exploitation that is an inevitable part of colonial rule. But, despite that, the nature of the British Raj included within it opportunities that were never available during the long centuries of the Mughal Raj.

Hindsight, of course, is 20/20. In the early days of European encroachment in India, no one could see what lay ahead in the distant future. The only thing apparent was that a new age was dawning in which the progressive civilization of the West had put the conservative Mughal rule on the defensive. To some thinkers, it became more and more apparent that a spirit of accommodation meant accommodation with the West, not accommodation with the Muslims. The first to tread out on this slippery new ground was Raja Ram Mohan Roy.

Raja Ram Mohan Roy

"The first modern man of India"—that is how Raja Ram Mohan Roy is often described. He was the first to see the wisdom of integrating India's ancient cultural tradition with modern currents of thought being generated by the West. Kabir and Nanak had sought integration with Muslim culture, and their efforts had ended in nearly total failure. That avenue was no longer open; it was time for something entirely new.

Roy was born into a Brahmin family of Bengal in 1772. As was generally the case in those days, Muslim schools offered the only opportunities for education, so, like Kabir and Nanak before him, Roy was educated in the classic curriculum of Persian and Arabic. But by the late eighteenth century, British influence had become strong in Bengal. Calcutta, a new city created by the British, was becoming a center of Western ideas and learning. The young Roy became captivated by Western ideas and chose to turn his back entirely on the Muslim alternative. He became a convert to Western ideology, but not a captive of it. To the mind of the young Raja Ram Mohan Roy, Western ideas could be *used* to rejuvenate a seemingly moribund Hindu culture. The seductive technology and philosophy of the West was just what the doctor ordered: Western ideas could *revive* the ancient Hindu tradition, not replace it.

In 1828, by which time Roy was fifty-six years old, he founded the Brahmo Samaj, the Society of the Devotees of Brahma. The program of the society was a blend of Upanishadic monotheism and liberal modern ideology. The essential heart of Hinduism was to be saved by cleaning out all of the accumulated evils that were now being denounced by Western critics. Roy condemned idolatry, sati, female infanticide, child marriage, and, of course, caste privilege. He argued that more than anything else, it was the caste system that kept Indian society disunited and thus unable to stand strong against foreign oppressors. What tied everything together was worship of Brahman, the one true God worshipped by all people, but called by many names.

In some ways, the Brahmo Samaj was like an early form of Unitarianism, a non-religious religion. The movement was popular with middle-class intellectuals in India, but never caught on with the masses of the people. The real significance of the Brahmo Samaj, though, was to be found outside the realm of the religious and philosophical: The society was an early voice in the Indian "national movement."

Swami Dayananda

Swami Dayananda, a puzzling religious figure from Gujarat, was the founder of another homegrown organization, the Arya Samaj. The name means "Aryan Society," but in this case the word *Aryan* is meant to refer to all native Indians; its use is meant to distinguish Indian from non-Indian. This distinction was very important to Dayananda, because he aimed at nothing less than cleansing India of *all* foreign influences, Muslim and European alike. He dreamed of returning India to its pure Hindu roots, namely the Vedas, which, in his very fundamentalist view, alone were the depository of truth and thus the only suitable foundation for life and culture. Dayananda's teachings are presented in his influential book, *Satyartha Prakash, The Light of Truth*, published in 1874, when he was fifty years old.

It might seem that the Arya Samaj was the direct antithesis of the Brahmo Samaj, and at the superficial level it was, but at a deeper level they shared much in common. Both helped to shape the early character and goals of the Indian national movement, and both were strongly influenced by Western ideals. Dayananda would never have admitted that; in fact, he would have argued that it was the other way around. He held that the Vedas contained all Truth and all knowledge, that *everything* of value in human history had grown from the teachings of the Vedas. In his convoluted logic, Dayananda could even "prove" that the principle of the steam engine, for example, had been known in Vedic times, and was only rediscovered by the modern West.

Dayananda taught, and personally believed, that a return to the wisdom of the Vedas would be the salvation of India. To the student of this subject, however, what is important and interesting is the character of the teachings that Dayananda inferred from his reading of the Vedas. His program has a familiar ring to it: It is very much in the spirit of all of the other reformers of relatively modern times. Dayananda proclaimed the existence of one God—one *personal* God—worshipped by many names. He condemned the hereditary caste system and, of course, "idolatry." Dayananda liked to tell the story about how, as a boy, he had come to see the light regarding the foolishness of stone idols. One time he had watched a mouse crawling around, disrespectfully, on the face of a stone god. It occurred to him that if the god lacked the power even to remove a little mouse from its face, how could it possibly be powerful enough to affect the affairs of people's lives? One other element of Dayananda's teaching also was significant: His was an early voice calling for the respectful treatment of women. This reform idea, certainly inspired in part by Western ideals, was perhaps the most important of all.

Both the Brahmo Samaj and the Arya Samaj enjoyed moderate success in their day, and in fact both still exist in India, although their membership is now not large. They, did however, play an important role in shaping the early character of the movement that would ultimately lead to the modernization and independence of India.

Ramakrishna Paramahansa (1836–1886)

If Mahavira was an ascetic's ascetic, Ramakrishna was a mystic's mystic. Another way of putting it is "If Raja Ram Mohan Roy was the mind, and Dayananda was the physical arms, Ramakrishna was the soul of the new India."[8]

Ramakrishna was born in 1836 and grew up in the vicinity of Calcutta. He spent most of his life associated with the Temple of Kali at nearby Dakshineshwar. Ramakrishna was totally devoted to Kali, the Divine Mother. This passionate relation began with an incident that occurred when he was a young man. His father had died, and the young Ramakrishna was so filled with grief that he was almost suicidal. He went to the temple of Kali and begged her to help him. In the awful silence that followed his prayer, he took a ceremonial sword from one of the statues, intending to kill himself. His own blood would be his offering to Kali. Just as he was about to do the deed, Ramakrishna tells us, a radiant vision of the goddess appeared before him. She embraced him lovingly, and he entered into a state of indescribable ecstasy. This experience transformed Ramakrishna; he became a teacher and devoted the rest of his life to promoting the worship of Kali.

Ramakrishna experienced many more ecstatic visions; his reputation spread, and he became widely known as a saintly mystic. Not all of his visions were of Kali; some, we are told, were of Jesus and Muhammed. These visions convinced Ramakrishna that all religions worship the same God. The God of the Hindus, the God of the Christians, the God of Islam—all are the same One Supreme Being. There are many paths—and that is good—but they all lead to discovery of the One God:

> Man is like a pillow-case. The color of one may be red, another blue, another black, but all contain the same cotton. So it is with man—one is beautiful, one is black, another is holy, a fourth wicked, but the Divine dwells in them all.[9]

Clearly, the teaching of Ramakrishna was not unique or revolutionary. What made him important was the saintly power of his person. He attracted people to him, and he inspired them. Perhaps what was most important of all about Ramakrishna was that he was responsible for the career of Vivekananda, his foremost disciple.

Vivekananda (1863–1902)

During the twentieth century, the Western world was visited by countless Eastern gurus, teachers, and seers, as well as more than a few charlatans. Many of them attracted huge followings in the West. This globalization of once remote Eastern philosophies is a major feature of modern culture. The dissemination of Hindu teachings began with Vivekananda, the great disciple of Ramakrishna.

At the urging of Ramakrishna, Vivekananda travelled to Chicago, Illinois, in September of 1893 to address the World Parliament of Religions, a rather unusual feature of that year's Chicago World's Fair. It was the first time that a Hindu had carried the message of Hinduism to the people of the world. Vivekananda's message, spoken so eloquently, stunned the gathering. One of the listeners summed it up beautifully: "That man; a heathen! And we send missionaries to his people. It would be more fitting that they should send missionaries to us!"

And send they did! Once Vivekananda opened the door, many would pass through. Yogananda, Satchidananda, Krishnamurti, Maharishi Mahesh Yogi, A. C. Bhaktivedanta, Eknath Easwaren, and Bhagwan Sri Rajneesh; these are only a few of the better known names from a long list. They range the gamut from exotic mystics, such as Yogananda, to the modern eclectics, such as Easwaren, and from the highly conservative, such as Krishnamurti, to the highly controversial, such as Rajneesh. It is a fabulous parade of ancient India's modern sons; the West has gained enormously from the experience.

Narendra Nath Datta, better known as Vivekananda, was born in Calcutta in 1863. Unlike Ramakrishna, Vivekananda's family was part of the English-educated elite of Calcutta. (By this time the sons of well-to-do Hindu families were being educated in English, not Persian.) Vivekananda met Ramakrishna in 1881, when he was only eighteen, and immediately became one of his disciples. Soon he was the most prominent disciple and was widely regarded as Ramakrishna's successor. From the beginning, Vivekananda was more concerned with the broad teachings of Vedanta than he was with Kali worship. He especially loved the spirit of compassion that he found in Vedanta, and he concluded that it offered the best possible philosophy of life for all people. Vivekananda ardently believed that a rejuvenated Vedanta could be the inspiration that would restore India to its former glory.

Following the explosive success of his talk in Chicago, Vivekananda launched a world mission, taking the message of Vedanta to many countries, where it was always warmly received. In 1892, he founded the Ramakrishna Mission, an organization dedicated to spreading the teaching of Ramakrishna in particular and the philosophy of Vedanta in general. Chapters of the Ramakrishna Mission can still be found in cities throughout the world.

Aurobindo Ghosh (1872–1950)

Like Vivekananda, Aurobindo hailed from Calcutta and received a Western education. He, too, loved the teachings of Vedanta, but whereas Vivekananda sought to carry the essential message of Vedanta to the world, Aurobindo sought to refashion that message in modern dress. In the process, Aurobindo constructed a truly fascinating body of teachings, presented in his work, *The Life Divine*. It is a wonder that Aurobindo is not more widely known and read in modern times.

Aurobindo anchored his teaching on the reality of Brahman, the absolute. The ultimate goal of all is identity with Brahman. The wheel of birth and death, *samsara*, whose seemingly endless turning is generated by karma, is the process through which reunion in Brahman is worked out. So far, so good; this is basic, traditional Vedanta. Aurobindo's contribution was to explain the working of *samsara* in the context of modern evolution theory. The dreary, ages-long turning became a whole new ball game when it was interpreted in the light of evolution.

Aurobindo argued that the entire universe is always in a state of evolution, struggling to change from a lower state to a higher state of perfection, which is to say, nearness to the Brahman nature. For any given part, the struggle is sometimes successful, sometimes not, but the general character of the whole is forward movement. Humanity is, of course, a part of this general evolution. Our challenge is to go beyond "mind," in the ordinary sense of the word, to "supermind," as Aurobindo called it. In other words, our challenge is to transcend ordinary, worldly based ego consciousness, achieving in its place knowledge of the pure spiritual nature that is the substratum of ego. Thus can we open the way to identity with the Absolute (Brahman). Aurobindo saw evolution as proceeding through stages. Humankind is a stage that is advanced over what came before, but it is the destiny of humanity (or at least some part of it) to ascend to the next stage of perfection, which Aurobindo called a Kingdom of Heaven on Earth. Aurobindo's philosophy may be summed up as follows:

> The evolution of the universe as a whole and of particular species within the universe is seen as the returning of the manifested powers of Brahman to their source. As these powers move toward their source, evolution moves to higher and higher forms of life and consciousness.[10]*

Individual men and women have some control over the direction of their own evolution. (After all, at root we *are* Brahman!) In *The Life Divine*, Aurobindo laid out the

---

*Doesn't this sound an awful lot like the evolutionary theory of Teilhard de Chardin, expressed in his book, *The Phenomenon of Man*? Chardin saw physical nature evolving through stages into spiritual nature, all directed toward an ultimate "omega point" at which time all would be reabsorbed back into the nature of the Creator.

program that could elevate personal existence to the point where it would become "life divine." He called it Integral Yoga, a program, or lifesytle, that "integrates" all of the aspects of traditional yoga in a way that is suited to the way of life of a modern lay man or woman. Aurobindo's teaching was to find its physical and spiritual center in the world-famous model ashram, Auroville, located near Pondicherry, not far from Chenai (formerly known as Madras) in southern India.

Mahatma Gandhi (1869–1948)

Mohandas Karamchand Gandhi is known to the world as Mahatma Gandhi, the "great souled" one. He was not a prolific writer—Gandhi wrote only one small book, his *Autobiography*. Nor was he a founder of a religious or philosophical sect or a political leader in the usual sense, but Mahatma Gandhi is universally regarded as one of the truly great figures in India's long and rich history. Albert Einstein put it well: "Generations to come, it may be, will scarcely believe that such a one as this in flesh and blood walked upon this earth."

Gandhi made his mark on history as the leader of the Indian National Congress, an organization that worked tirelessly to achieve India's independence. Struggling against incredible obstacles, Gandhi achieved his goal in 1947, only to be cut down at his moment of triumph by an assassin's bullets. With his dying breath, he whispered his life-long mantra: "Hare Rama; Hare Rama."

Gandhi's real greatness is to be found, not in the fact that he led India to independence, but in the way that he did it. His was not the way of violent confrontation; Gandhi's infinitely more powerful way was the way of love, compassion, patience, and humor. In the process, Gandhi became a living model for humankind.

So where did this great power in Gandhi come from? It certainly was not obvious at the beginning. His was a rather unremarkable youth. He grew up in Gujarat in a middle-class Hindu family that sent him to England to study law. Curiously, it was in England that he began to discover the richness of his roots in the Hindu tradition. After law school, he returned to India, but soon he was off to South Africa, where his personal experiences with racial discrimination set in motion a process that would change his life. Returning to India in 1914, Gandhi threw himself into the independence movement, summoning a great spiritual energy generated by his love for the teachings of the ancient Hindu scriptures. Founding his daily life on the teachings of the Upanishads and the *Bhagavad Gita*, Gandhi succeeded in transforming himself from a very ordinary man into a giant of spiritual strength and compassion. *That* is where Gandhi said his power came from.

Gandhi's philosophy is associated with two closely related key terms—*satyagraha* and *ahimsa*, usually translated as "passive resistance" and "nonviolence," respectively. As such, they do describe the visible character of Gandhi's struggle against British rule. His followers were unrelenting in their opposition, accepting physical brutality and imprisonment but never striking back in violence. Ultimately, they wore down the British and even won over some to the cause of independence for India. But at a deeper level, the two terms refer to something much greater than passive resistance and nonviolence. In fact, those are more an *effect* of what the words are really all about.

Satyagraha means "holding fast to the truth"—embracing it and not letting go for any reason. Gandhi used to say that "Truth is God." To know the truth is to know God; naturally, such knowledge cannot be compromised. But how does one know that what one believes is true? Doesn't everyone assume that his or her own beliefs are true? Gandhi was not interested in epistemology; he believed that truth was expressed clearly and distinctly in the Upanishads and the *Bhagavad Gita*. Therein one could find a beautiful expression of truth and could easily check it out in one's daily life. The teachings of the Upanishads and the *Gita*, brought to life in one's ordinary daily affairs, amounted to a clear affirmation of their truth. Gandhi had experienced this personally; he had transformed himself. The example of his life was all the evidence one needed.*

The cornerstone of Gandhi's personal life was summed up in the opening line of the Isha Upanishad: "The Lord is enshrined in the hearts of all." His special love, though, was the *Bhagavad Gita*, and most of all that sublime section of eighteen verses at the end of Book Two. In these verses, Arjuna wants to know what an awakened person is really like. How does he recognize the "real McCoy"? Krishna's reply beautifully sums up the essential spirit of what the *Gita* is trying to teach. He begins with the words, "They live in wisdom who see themselves in all, and all in them." Gandhi said that even if all of the *Gita* had been lost except those eighteen verses, we would still have, in essence, the entire truth of the *Bhagavad Gita*.

Ahimsa, a great word that we have encountered before, was for Gandhi the way of putting Truth into action. The two ideas are intimately related. *Ahimsa* may mean nonviolence in the literal sense, but *nonviolence* refers, not to controlling an urge to violence, but to the compassionate heart from which violence of any sort would be unthinkable. One who truly sees "the Lord enshrined in the hearts of all" is not capable of hatred or violence. For such a person, opposition to evil is to oppose the evil act, but love the evildoer. That is exactly what Gandhi did, and it explains the great power of his program of passive resistance. He proved that evil can be conquered by love.

In the long run, Gandhi's most important gift—and the basis for his greatness—is the way he showed by the example of his own life how every man and woman on Earth could transform themselves, as he did, and thus be able to solve the problem of evil in the world, not by the usual path of greater violence, but by the infinitely superior path of greater compassion.

---

*Gandhi acknowledged that his program of passive resistance was in part inspired by reading Thoreau's tract, *Civil Disobedience*. This admission is interesting, considering that Thoreau's personal philosophy was much influenced by his own reading of the Upanishads and the *Bhagavad Gita*.

Notes

1. Eknath Easwaren, *The Upanishads* (Petaluma, CA: Nilgiri, 1987), p. 115 (*Mundaka Upanishad*: III.1.1).
2. Eknath Easwaren, *The Bhagavad Gita* (Petaluma, CA: Nilgiri, 1985), p. 86 (*BG:* 4.7–8).
3. *Ibid.*, p. 150 (*BG:* 11.3–4).
4. *Ibid.*, p. 151 (*BG:* 11.10–14).
5. Hari N. Verma and Amrit Verma, *One Hundred Great Indians through the Ages* (Campbell, CA: GIP Books, 1992), p. 168.
6. Quoted in Verma and Verma, p. 167.
7. First ten lines of the *Adi Granth.*
8. John Spear, quoted in Verma and Verma, p. 236.
9. Ramakrishna, as quoted in Verma and Verma, p. 238.
10. John M. Koller, *Oriental Philosophies*, 2d ed., p. 127 (New York: Chas. Scribner's, 1985).

Study Questions

1. How would you sum up the essential teaching of Shankara? Why is his system referred to as "Adviata" Vedanta?

2. What are the "eight limbs" of yoga, as described in Patanjali's *Yoga Sutras?* Do the "limbs" form a hierarchy?

3. In what essential ways does the tradition of Jainism differ from Vedanta? In what ways are they similar?

4. Why was the Charvaka teaching attacked from all sides? What was the basic teaching of Charvaka? Is there an equivalent philosophy in the modern world?

5. Contrast the devotional worship of Vishnu with that of Shiva. In what essential ways did they differ?

6. Why is it suggested that the great importance of Ramanuja's teaching was that it opened up the possibility of sin and redemption? What does this mean?

7. What was significant about the reign of Akbar? How did he differ from other Muslim rulers? What did Akbar hope to achieve through the Divine Faith?

8. Both Kabir and Nanak hoped to build a bridge between the Muslim and Hindu cultures. How did each attempt to do this?

9. "So where did this great power in Gandhi come from?" So, where *did* it come from?

10. What role did *satyagraha* and *ahimsa* play in the personal philosophy of Mahatma Gandhi? How were these values expressed in his life?

Asia

PART II
Non-Buddhist Systems of China and Japan

Hinduism and Buddhism are both very broad umbrellas: Many distinct schools of thought are brought together under their names. Much of this book, then, is understandably given over to these two great traditions. There are other traditions of thought, though, that are not a part of Hinduism or Buddhism, but are equally important and also play a significant role in the history of Eastern thought. We have noted some Indian examples in Chapter 5. In Part II, we will examine three of the most important of these traditions that were to arise outside of India: Confucianism and Daoism, which developed in China, and Shinto, which developed in Japan. All three were well established in their homelands by the time Buddhism appeared on the scene. They would interact with Buddhism in various ways and significantly influence its development. Each of these traditions, however, has maintained its integrity over time and has survived into the modern era, showing signs of renewed vigor.

6

Confucius and Confucianism

Confucius gave Chinese civilization a grand ideal for the ordering of society. Followed perfectly, the Confucian system promised to fashion a society that would be harmonious, peaceful, prosperous, and governed by wise leaders dedicated to the welfare of all. Within this society, the individual would be a person of refinement and compassion. All of this was to be accomplished by reestablishing the harmony between human society and the natural order, which is continually threatened by unchecked selfish interests. More than other Chinese schools of thought, Confucius's vision of the right social order became a model that has inspired Chinese social thinking through the ages.

As best as we can tell, Confucius lived in eastern China from 551 B.C.E. to 479 B.C.E., a tumultuous, but undoubtedly exciting, time to be alive in that part of the world. Due to the incessant jockeying for power among the many feudal warlords, the time is known to historians as the Period of Warring States. It is also known as the Period of a Hundred Philosophers. The insecurity of the age spawned many (if not quite a hundred) competing philosophical systems, each claiming to have the cure for the ills of the time. Confucius was the founder of one of these schools, the one that was destined to become most famous and influential over time. His teaching, therefore, deserves our full attention. But to fully understand the teaching of Confucius, we must see it in its larger context, both with respect to the competing philosophical systems and in the broad historical context out of which the Age of Confucius evolved.

The formative period of Chinese civilization is known as the *Shang Period*, or the *Shang Dynasty*. Its time of birth was, of course, obscure and can't be dated precisely. Its end, though, was a different story; about that, we can be a little more precise. In the year 1054 B.C.E. (or close to it), the Shang Dynasty came to a violent end at the hands of its warlike neighbors (more about that later). Thus, Shang endured for some six or seven centuries, and during this formative time, Chinese civilization developed much of its basic character.

The people of Shang were conscious of their identity and distinguished their own small world from the surrounding sea of barbarian, "lesser" peoples. For one thing, they were an agricultural society, living in small settled villages and exercising some measure of control over their destiny. They were united under the rule of a hereditary king, and he maintained a royal court at a capital "city" that, in essentials at least, was an embryonic urban center. Finally, and most strongly felt of all, the men and women of Shang were united in a shared set of religious beliefs and practices.

The general animism of earlier times lived on in Shang, but became more refined. The world of spirits was presided over by a supreme being, known simply as Ti, who ruled over a heavenly realm, known as Ti Xian, that was an analogue of the earthly realm ruled by the Shang king. Generations might come and go like the leaves of the forest, but, unlike the leaves of the forest, departed ancestors were not mere dust to be lost and forgotten. Their spirits took up residence in Ti Xian and could remain an influential force in the world of living men and women. Thus, the people of Shang defined themselves, not only in terms of the space they occupied, but also as a society enduring over time. The past, the present, and the future were united as one great family in Ti Xian. It was therefore appropriate that ancestors should be respected and venerated. Indeed, eventually everyone would become an ancestor.

No hereditary priestly class took form in China, as it did in India. There were no Chinese "Brahmins," so to speak, but there were many who played the role of shaman and sorcerer. Religious ritual and sacrifice were a common part of life in the time of Shang and provide us with many of the artifacts that have survived from that distant time. Divination—the foretelling of future events through supernatural means—was apparently a widely practiced art that commonly took the form of heating animal bones (often the sternum of an ox) in a fire. The resulting cracks were believed to hold clues about the future, clues that could be interpreted by the skilled diviner. Large numbers of these so-called oracle bones have been found at Shang archeological sites. Sometimes the bones were inscribed with characters, which now give us valuable glimpses into the first stage in the evolution of Chinese writing. They also give us tidbits of information about life in the Shang Dynasty.

Of one thing we can be sure: The very success of Shang became its greatest problem. This was a difficulty shared by all early centers of civilization. The sedentary way of life, based on simple farming, made possible a growing wealth in agricultural land and valuable goods. Such a situation would, naturally, excite the interest of predatory neighbors. The resources of Shang must have been increasingly devoted to defense, but eventually the greater size and power of the outsiders proved to be too much. In the eleventh century B.C.E., the kingdom of Shang fell to an onslaught launched by the armies of their much larger and very warlike neighbors to the west, the people of Zhou. The story of the evolution of Chinese civilization would enter a new chapter: The Shang Dynasty was replaced by the Zhou Dynasty, which would hold the stage for eight centuries.

Zhou conquered Shang, but did not destroy it. The lands and resources of Shang were absorbed into the kingdom of Zhou, which extended over a vastly greater area of eastern China. In fact, the new Zhou kingdom was much too large to be ruled by a centralized authority. Instead, it was divided up into approximately seventy semiautonomous duchies, each presided over by locally powerful nobles who owed allegiance to the monarchy. Even some of the Shang nobles were allowed to continue to hold power, so long as they were willing to pledge their loyalty to their new king. The Zhou kingdom was, in other words, a solidly feudal state, similar in organization to the feudal states of Europe in the Middle Ages. The power of the king was directly proportional to the amount of control—and loyalty—he held over the regional princes. In the early days of Zhou this power was very strong, but it would slowly erode.

The ancient religious beliefs and practices were retained in Zhou, but evolved toward a somewhat more humanistic outlook. Man's proper relationship to nature became a matter of growing interest. The importance of this subject would remain central in Chinese thought throughout the ages. We can also detect a growing interest in the nature of right government. The concept of the "Mandate of Heaven" took form and became a major concern of Zhou. The *Mandate of Heaven* refers to the belief that the earthly king presides as something of a steward of the gods. His rule is legitimate only so long as he fulfills the will of heaven, which is to say, to govern wisely and well, in the interest of all. If he allows selfish interest to replace concern for the common good, he will lose the Mandate of Heaven and thus the right to rule. This principle became, retroactively, a rationalization for the Zhou conquest of Shang. After all, it was argued, they were just doing the work of heaven, dismantling a corrupt monarchy that had forfeited its right to govern and replacing it with legitimate rule.

In the course of time, the rulers of Zhou faced the same problem they themselves had caused for the rulers of Shang: aggressive incursions into the western parts of the kingdom launched by the more numerous tribal peoples from the lands beyond. Finally, in the year 771 B.C.E., the monarchy was forced to abandon the ancestral capital and move lock, stock, and barrel to a new headquarters farther east in the city of Luoyang (Lo-yang). The Zhou monarchs would hold on here, at least nominally, for another five hundred years, but the power of the king over his nobles gradually deteriorated to the point where the king of Zhou ultimately became nothing more than a figurehead. He was powerless to control the regional nobles, whose relationship degenerated more and more into a condition of constant feudal warfare.

The Zhou Dynasty would reach the end of its road in 255 B.C.E. The four centuries preceding its demise constitute a time of troubles known as the Period of Warring States. Feudal warfare, ravaging armies, brutal conquest, shifting boundaries, and ruined crops and villages—such was the general picture. Life for the peasantry was full of insecurity and suffering. Not only did they have to deal with the predations of unruly armies, but the men were forever being torn from their families to fill the battlefield-reduced ranks of those same armies. Death and privation were the order of the day.

Given the length and chaotic nature of the Period of Warring States, it should not be surprising that many thoughtful individuals felt inspired to try to find a better way, a way that would restore the much-yearned-for peace and security. "In disorderly times, men long for order," and, in fact, the time of the late Zhou did see the appearance of many new social philosophies, all of them seeking to be a blueprint for the right ordering of society and government. These philosophies were a natural response to the turmoil of the times, and there was quite a range of offerings to choose from. It is for this reason that the Warring States period is also known as the Period of a Hundred Philosophers. One of the great philosophies to emerge during that time was that which we know as Daoism (Taoism).* The tradition of Daoism deserves a full examination and, accordingly, is the subject of the next chapter. The earliest of the schools, though, and the one we examine in this chapter, was founded by the man we know as Confucius.

CONFUCIUS

Unfortunately, we don't have a great deal of verifiable information about the life of Confucius. The sources that do exist are pretty bare bones, and much of what is commonly reported about the man is based on legend and conjecture. The earliest known biography of Confucius is a short entry in the *Shiji*, a collection of biographies written in the first century B.C.E. by the Chinese historian Sima Qian (Ssu-ma Ch'ien). Four centuries had elapsed between the death of Confucius and the writing of this biography; Sima Qian had to rely on scanty and unreliable sources.

A much better source is the words of Confucius himself. Although he never wrote an autobiography (so far as we know), much of his teaching has been preserved. Confucius himself, though, was not moved to do a great deal of writing; most of what we believe to be his words are really nothing more than a collection of aphorisms written down and preserved by his disciples in the *Lun Yu*, which we know in English as the *Analects of Confucius*.

Perhaps the best source for reliable insight into the life and character of Confucius is the *Mencius* (*Meng Zi*), which is an exposition of the philosophy of Mencius, a devoted follower of Confucius. Mencius added much to the total picture of what we call "Confucianism." Though not a contemporary of Confucius—he lived about a century later—Mencius was close enough in time and association to have access to a great deal of reliable information about the man. The *Mencius* is full of little insights about Confucius.

These three works—the *Analects*, the *Mencius*, and the biography of Sima Qian—make up our basic sources of information about Confucius, his life, and his teaching. Other sources exist, but their accuracy is often questionable. From these various sources, taken as a whole, we can abstract a simple, but reasonably credible, account of the life of Confucius.

Let's begin with the name. Confucius, of course, was not his name; it is a Latinized version of the Chinese pronunciation, a practice popular in the West when Europeans first began to take scholarly interest in cultures other than their own. (It seems pretty quaint today. Imagine, for example, referring to Mao Zedong as Madocius.) The family

---

*There are two systems for spelling Chinese words in the Western alphabet: pinyin and Wade–Giles. Pinyin, the more recently developed of the two, attempts to overcome some of the phonetic and spelling problems of the Wade–Giles system. In Wade–Giles, for example, *Tao* is spelled with a "T" even though it is meant to be pronounced more like a "D," which is the correct spelling in pinyin. Pinyin is rapidly replacing Wade–Giles and is the system of choice in this book. In instances where it seems appropriate, I will include the Wade–Giles spelling in parentheses.

name was Kung, and he became known as Kung Fu Zi (K'ung Fu-tzu in the Wade-Giles system). *Kung Fu-tzu*, in the hands of nineteenth-century Europeans, became *Confucius*. So, should we now revert to the more properly Chinese pronunciation? Perhaps so, but the Western world has become so used to saying "Confucius" that there seems to be little inclination to do this. Even "K'ung Fu-tzu" is a far cry from the actual Chinese. Thus, for the time being anyway, Confucius he shall remain.

Confucius was born, according to the Western calendar, in 551 B.C.E. His home region was the state of Lu, which more or less corresponds to the modern Shandong Province. This is a very populous region in northeastern China that includes the large peninsula which forms the southern gateway to the Gulf of Po Dai. Then, as now, the area was very much at the center of Chinese life and culture. Not much is known about Confucius's early life. The family was not particularly well off, and the situation was made much worse by the death of his father when Confucius was only three years old. Confucius was raised by his widowed mother and claimed in later life to have known real poverty as a child. At nineteen he married, producing one son and two daughters. The family into which he married could claim some aristocratic ancestry, and this connection helped Confucius secure a government job around the time he married. He worked within the bureaucracy of the state of Lu, first as the manager of a state granary and later as the manager of some state-owned herds of cattle and sheep. Supposedly, he did very well at both posts, but his heart was set on other things.

Undoubtedly, Confucius had a brilliant mind and also a winning personality. From an early age, he had been interested in learning, especially the study of the already ancient history and culture of his people. While still quite young, Confucius made something of a name for himself as a scholar. At the amazingly young age of twenty-two, he gave up his bureaucratic post and opened his own school. This, of course, was not a school in the modern sense of the word; it was more a group of already educated young men from the better families who wished to associate closely with a master. It was probably much like the academies founded by such Greek philosophers as Plato and Aristotle. Confucius would draw on the traditional wisdom of China to teach his disciples about the principles of right living and right governing. He described himself as a transmitter, not an originator. Any sincere seeker, rich or poor, was welcome, but presumably, most of the disciples were from wealthy families, and Confucius was able to make a decent living doing what he loved most.

His career really took off when one of the leading nobles of Lu sent his own two sons to study with Confucius. This turn of events opened doors for him, and soon Confucius was associating with the movers and shakers of Lu. With his two noble students, Confucius visited the capital city and gained the respect of the Duke of Lu. What Confucius wanted most of all was to secure a government post that would make him the power behind the throne. Then he could put his ideas of right government into practice and transform Lu or any other place willing to give him the chance into a model of good government. "If any ruler would submit to me as his director for twelve months," he said, "I should accomplish something considerable; and in three years I should attain the realization of my hopes."

Unfortunately, Confucius never got the opportunity he longed for, largely because high posts in government went only to members of the top noble families. For a few years, Confucius did occupy the office we might today call Minister of Justice, and while serving in this post he instituted some social reforms that attracted a fair amount of attention. However, a feud in the ruling family forced Confucius to flee the state of Lu temporarily, and he never again had an opportunity to hold high office.

Confucius would not return to his home district of Lu for twelve long years. During this time of self-imposed exile, his was the life of an itinerant philosopher, accompanied by a small band of disciples. He was generally welcomed at the courts he visited, and shown high honor, but no one was willing to turn over the power of government to him. He yearned for the opportunity, though, and apparently felt rather bitter that no one recognized his genius. Commenting on the situation, he sometimes let his sense of frustration show: "Am I a bitter gourd, fit only to hang out of the way, not good enough to eat?"

Confucius's ideas on the right ordering of society remained basically in the realm of theory. But he had started a fire that would never go out: For all time to come, his name would be highly honored, and in time, his system of values would be integrated into the very essence of Chinese social and political life. Confucius died in 479 B.C.E. at the age of seventy-three. He was buried near his native town; a shrine at the grave site remains even to this day an important place of pilgrimage among the people of China.

The suffering of the common people was the central concern of Confucius. That point deserves to be emphasized. Confucius was a highly compassionate man, and the suffering that he saw everywhere among the common people moved him to action. Much like that of his great contemporary, Shakyamuni Buddha, Confucius's teaching amounted to a solution to a problem, and at the root of the problem was the ubiquitous suffering of ordinary men and women who were the victims of the turmoil of the age.

As pointed out before, Confucius lived during a highly stressful time in Chinese history. He was born into the later part of the Zhou Dynasty, the second of the great historical dynasties of Chinese civilization. The Zhou ruled during what was essentially a feudal era and would eventually give way to the Han Dynasty, which welded China into a great unified empire.

In Chinese history, the Han Dynasty plays a role similar to that of the Roman Empire in European history. But at the time Confucius was born, all of that was still three centuries in the future. In Confucius's time, the ruling Zhou no longer held the vast realm of China together as it had in former times. The tightly knit fabric of feudalism was unraveling. Petty wars, feuds, and class conflicts had become the order of the day. From our perspective, we can see that Chinese society was evolving away from feudalism toward something new, but the transition was difficult. People of the time, not being any better than we are at seeing into the future, looked backward instead. Life in the time of the ancestors had been peaceful and orderly, but now it had become chaotic. The social order was sick; it was in a state of decline; and the future would be even worse.

Confucius, too, looked back to a "golden age" when the feudal system had been strong, when everything had been in its appointed place and life was peaceful and prosperous. Undoubtedly, he exaggerated the positive side of the picture somewhat, but he did study the history of the early Zhou with great thoroughness. He identified certain prominent figures of the era—"sages," as he called them—to whom he attributed almost divinely inspired wisdom. By carefully studying the lives and the works of these men, Confucius believed that he could determine the essence of their wisdom and come to understand the essential elements of right governance. He would then be a teacher to his own troubled age, a transmitter of the wisdom of the ancients, and, hopefully, a reformer of the social order. He would reveal the truth of Dao, which, to Confucius, meant the right "way" for men to live.

A thoroughgoing reformation was obviously necessary. Leadership at all levels of society was in a sorry state. Government, which should be the leader and protector of the people, was often oppressive instead. Nothing was worse than living under an oppressive government. To emphasize this point, Confucius told the story of the woman he happened upon one day weeping beside a grave. She told him that her husband had been killed by a tiger at that spot, and before that, her husband's father had been killed at the same spot by the same tiger. "And now," she wept, "my only son has also been killed here by that tiger." Confucius asked her why she didn't go away from such a dangerous place. "Because," she answered, "in this place there is no oppressive government." "Remember," said Confucius, "that oppressive government is more terrible and more to be feared than a killer tiger."

To Confucius's mind, the overriding concern was order—that is, reestablishing order in society. But not just any kind of order would suffice; it must be a natural order. Confucius believed that there is a right ordering of society that is natural to it, in the same way that there is a right ordering to all of the things of nature. Human society had gotten out of harmony with the larger natural order of which it is a part. (Does all this sound familiar?) We are part of a natural world in which all of the myriad elements, from wildflowers to stars, fit together in a perfectly ordered harmony. Everything is an expression of the working of the whole. The ancients had understood this, but their descendants, pursuing selfish interests, had strayed from the path.

Nothing in nature ever sets itself apart and operates in conflict with the universal harmony—well, nothing, that is, until we come to the evolution of human society, and therein lies the problem. But it doesn't have to be that way: As the study of ancient society revealed to the mind of Confucius, properly led and properly ordered, human society can exist in perfect harmony within the natural order. Man is a part of nature, and therefore, human nature, in the judgment of Confucius, need not be in conflict with the natural order. Evil and selfish acts are a corruption of the innate tendency of man's nature to be in harmony with the universal order. Right leadership can reestablish that harmony.

So where does one begin? Confucius would begin with the institution of the family, which was seen as the basic unit of society; nothing was more important. In the Confucian system, the importance of the family cannot be exaggerated. Individual families are the living cells that together make up the organism of society. In other words, society is an extension of the family. In fact, the entire social order of China was regarded as being one great extended family. The ruler of the state was, in effect, the *paterfa-*

milias of this one great family, and he was expected to play the role and assume the duties appropriate to the father in that relationship.

In the Confucian system, though, the king "reigns," but he does not actually "rule." He is groomed from childhood to be a symbol—a father figure, a watchdog, in a sense—but the business of day-to-day governing is in the hands of carefully selected ministers, and these men, far from being the corrupt, self-serving nobles of Confucius's age, were to be a legion of "new men," chosen for their suitability and their dedication to the ideal of service. What a revolution that would be! Confucius would do nothing less than sweep away the entire predatory hereditary aristocracy and replace it with a new nonhereditary aristocracy, one based on talent, compassion, and commitment to serving the needs of the common people. The character of this "new man" that Confucius envisioned was called *junzi* (*chun-tzu*); the achievement of *junzi* was, and still is, the heart and soul of the Confucian system.

But where in the world was such a man to be found? Confucius could imagine that men of *junzi* were common in some idealized past age, but in his own troubled times such a one was as rare as a giant panda in the marketplace. Confucius was well aware of this dilemma; thus, his program of reform did not call for an overnight solution. Instead, in the Confucian program, a new system of government necessitated a new system of education. In fact, there was no real system of education at all at the time: The sons of noblemen were educated, if at all, by tutors and on-the-job training. Most of their time and energy went into mastering the arts of warfare. Confucius had no interest in this; he had a whole new plan in mind. He would institute an actual system of education, an organized program of development spread out over many years. This program, based largely on study of the classics of Chinese literature, was designed to produce the new man of *junzi*. Confucius would take the malleable child, and through the right kind of education, which included the teacher as role model, he would create a man of superior humanistic learning, of refined personal manners, and with the will to govern wisely and compassionately. Most important of all, this new system of education was to be open to all—at least, *potentially*. Anyone who showed promise would be accepted, no matter what his rank in society.

Considering all of this, isn't it amazing that Confucius is sometimes criticized as being a defender of feudalism? What could in fact be more revolutionary, more *non*feudal, than the system that he proposed? The charge grows out of a misunderstanding of Confucius's admiration for what he perceived to be the condition of society in the early days of the Zhou Dynasty. The social organization was undoubtedly very feudal in those days. What Confucius admired was the *stability* of society, the peace, the apparent respect for law and order, and the harmony with nature—all of the things, in other words, that were painfully lacking in his own age. He attributed the felicity of the former time to the wisdom of its rulers—"sages," as he called them. He saw his own role as being a *transmitter* of this ancient wisdom: He would be the bridge that would link his own troubled age with the wisdom of the past. But it was not so much the *form* of government that he wanted to emulate as it was the sagelike *character* of those entrusted with the actual task of governing. In other words, Confucius believed that he saw men of *junzi* in the past, and he wanted to bring that ideal back to life in his own time. Of course, despite his modest denial, Confucius was far more than simply a transmitter: His system may have owed a debt to traditional values, but nothing like it had existed before. Within the body of Confucius lived a creative mind of the first order.

To sum up, the perpetual suffering of the common people had persuaded Confucius that the existing social order, founded as it was on rule by a corrupt and predatory aristocracy, was untenable. In its place he would establish an orderly society governed by men chosen for their superior ability and dedication to service. His new system of education would mold the best from all ranks of society into men of *junzi*. They would become not only the governors, but the living models for all members of society, and in this way, health and order would be restored.

Confucius's vision of a healthy society is an inspiring creation. Let's now look more closely at the specific elements out of which this vision was constructed. Again, the place to begin is with the institution of the family.

For Confucius, as for virtually all Chinese, the family is the rock foundation of the social order, the beginning and end of all. Also, it is the model for the entire society—indeed, perhaps more than simply a model: Confucius viewed the whole society as being one great family. Values learned within one's own family were simply to be extended to the broader society as one matured. The family, in other words, was the learning ground where one (hopefully) developed the attitudes and behavior upon which the healthy social order depended. Chief among these social virtues was, and is still today, "filial piety."

The cultivation of filial piety could be said to be the cornerstone of Confucius's social philosophy. In its simplest sense, *filial piety* refers to the love and respect shared between father and son and between older brother and younger brother. The virtue of filial piety is first cultivated in these relationships, but by extension, it reaches out to embrace many other relationships that are part of the social order: ruler and subject, master and apprentice, and older person and younger person, for example. Filial piety, then, is the *proper* mode of behavior between individuals in situations in which a natural relationship of superior and inferior exists. In Confucius's day, society was organized hierarchically, and many such relationships were a part of daily life. Of course, modern society has its rankings, too, but not to the same degree.

Confucius's reform program, revolutionary though it was, did not aim to obliterate the hierarchical arrangement of the social order. His was not yet the "classless society." Confucius accepted class distinction as natural and therefore good. His goal was simply to carefully define the natural relationships that exist in a healthy society and to establish these relationships on a foundation of virtue and respect. It was Confucius's conviction that the proper ordering of society was the logical and necessary beginning place for his program of reform and that a clear definition of social relationships was at the heart of the proper ordering of society.

To be more precise, Confucius discerned five cardinal relationships within the social order: ruler and subject, husband and wife, father and son, elder brother and younger brother, and friend and friend. The first four of these—at least in his opinion and that of his contemporaries—carried a relationship between superior and inferior, which was expressed as rule and submission. Each party to the relationship had appropriate duties.

The responsibility of the "ruling" party was to govern with righteousness and benevolence; the responsibility of the "submitting" party was to obey with righteousness and sincerity. In the "friend and friend" relationship it was the responsibility of each to promote the growth of virtue in the other.

Note that this subject can take us onto some shaky ground. There is controversy among modern scholars regarding how deeply Confucius himself actually went into the matter. It's true that in the *Analects*, when Confucius was asked by a disciple what should be the first order of business, he answered, "the rectification of names." This is taken to mean defining the social order, identifying everything in its proper place, and *spelling out* the proper role of each. There is some evidence, however, that this part of the *Analects* was added at a later time by those who sought to use Confucius's authority to justify an authoritarian form of government. Making a virtue out of submission to the ruler would suit their purposes very well.

Confucius would never advocate blind submission to an unjust superior. But he obviously respected the role of submission, broadly speaking, in a natural relationship between superior and inferior, so long as that relationship was guided by the virtue of filial piety.

Now, what about the place of woman in the Confucian system? Well, it's also pretty obvious that Confucius did not believe in the equality of the sexes. We would have to search far in his age to find someone who did. Like ancient societies generally, the culture that produced Confucius believed that the female sex is innately inferior to the male sex, and therefore the natural and proper role of woman is submission. This is not to say, however, that the role of woman was not important; it was very important, but it was entirely bound up in the affairs of family life. (In fact, Confucius appears to have believed that it was not possible for a man to achieve real excellence of character without the help and support of the women in his life. Confucius was deeply attached to his mother and mourned her death with great passion, but not a word has come down to us about her, his wife, or either of his two daughters.)

We must keep in mind that Confucius believed that the discord of his age was to be explained by the fact that Chinese society had lost its moorings. What was needed was to reestablish the natural order of society, such as had existed in earlier times. This could be accomplished by studying the practices of the ancestral sages and applying that wisdom to the present situation. Above all, it was necessary to rectify the fundamental relationships in society and to reestablish respect for the duties appropriate to each of them. So far, so good, but stated in this way, the matter remains at the theoretical level. The working out of these relationships in daily life, though, is not theoretical at all; it is very real and very down to earth. Another way of putting this is to say that it's one thing to *design* a proper society and another to make it work. What is it that will regulate and maintain the proper harmony in the interrelationships among the members of society? This is where *li* enters the picture.

In its original meaning, the word *li* meant "sacrifice," but over time it came to refer more broadly to an elaborate set of procedures and protocol that governed the celebration of religious rituals, including the offering of sacrifice and the honoring of ancestors. *Li* was the operative procedure that regulated intercourse between the world of men and the world of spirits. As such, *li* was extremely important to the whole society. Gradually, the formal manners of *li* had expanded from this core religious position to embrace as well the formal manners that regulated social intercourse between members of the feudal nobility. By the time of Confucius, *li* had become something similar to the ceremonial code of chivalry that later evolved within the feudal nobility of medieval Europe. It was an elaborate system of customs and manners that specified the ways in which noblemen would relate to one another in formal situations; in other words, *li* was tantamount to court etiquette, including such things as what one said, how one said it, how one dressed, how one stood or bowed, whether one carried a sword—indeed, everything. There was never any guesswork, never any embarrassment or offense; everything was spelled out by the formal customs of *li*.

In effect, what Confucius proposed was to extend the scope of *li* to the entire social order. *Li* was not merely to regulate the relations of noblemen or of persons participating in religious celebrations; *li* was to become an external way of regulating *all* relations. All of the elements of social intercourse—for everyone—would be structured in certain ritualized manners. Many modern readers, particularly Westerners, probably find the whole concept of *li* somewhat repugnant; it seems to make daily life so formal, and it rigidly divides the social order into elitist ranks of authority and privilege. But remember that the world of Confucius was nothing like the world of today. He was not egalitarian in any sense of the word. People of his time accepted the ranking of the social order as natural and inevitable. The important thing was not to abolish ranking from society, but to bring harmony and peace to the complex interrelationships that ranking afforded. Confucius saw the customs of *li* as a marvellous way of achieving that end.

In the Confucian system, then, *li* became a refined set of manners designed to regulate the personal interactions arising out of the various social relationships. Most important, *li* supported and upheld this system of relationships, which Confucius believed to be the essence of a healthy social structure:

> [Confucius] believed that the proper observance of *li* was essential to the development of goodness in an individual as well as in a society. *Li* for him was the restraining and refining force, creating the sense of balance and harmony in a man. . . . The concept of *li* is "a kind of balance wheel of conduct," guiding a way of life that avoids extremes, and a state of mind in which human reasoning and feeling reach perfect harmony. This is exactly what Confucius said: "Among the functions of *li*, the most valuable is that it establishes harmony."[1]

Perhaps *li* is not as foreign to us as it might at first seem to be. To a certain extent, all societies have customs and manners that are deemed appropriate for certain relationships. Isn't one likely to act in a somewhat formal way with one's employer or with a judge in court? And in military society, these customs are not subtle at all. But the Confucian system went far beyond that sort of thing: *Li* was the superficial expression of a whole philosophy of social organization. However, Confucius would have been the first to insist that it was the *principle* of *li*—honor and respect for the dignity of the other person—that gave *li* its value. Practicing the external manifestations of *li* was worthless if it lacked a sincere heart. If it were only a matter of superficial display, Confucius had no use for it at all. "Does *li* mean no more than a display of jade and silk?" he asked.

To sum up, Confucius's vision of a healthy society was built on the foundation of order. The five cardinal relationships, which he believed to be inherent in the nature of human society, were the expression of that order. And *li*, the well-regulated system of relationships among the members of society, assured that the harmonious order of society would be maintained in daily life. Together, *li* and the five cardinal relationships provided the framework of a healthy social order. Separately, they were ineffectual, an orderly, but basically lifeless, arrangement. What breathed life into the system was *junzi*. It was Confucius's vision of *junzi*—the heart of his system—that evoked excitement in the hearts and minds of his disciples.

Loosely translated into English, *junzi* means "the Superior Man." Above all, what Confucius was after was the re-creation of the *kind of man* exemplified by the ancestral sages that he so much admired and loved. Such superior persons, men of *junzi*, occupying positions of leadership would be able to restore harmony and prosperity to Chinese society. Furthermore, such Superior Men, *by the power of their example*, would initiate a general spreading of the spirit of *junzi* throughout all of the parts that made up the great family of Chinese society.

So what actually is *junzi*? What is the "Superior Man"? To begin with, the Superior Man was created, not born. That is, the man of *junzi* was not some kind of inherently superior breed, such as people of noble birth liked to believe themselves to be; he could emerge from any rank of society. What made the Superior Man superior was that he had worked long and hard to cultivate within himself those virtues that distinguished the ancestral sages. Anyone willing to make the effort could make the grade. (We must again remember that traditional society excluded women from roles of public leadership. Although a woman might achieve great strength of character and be highly respected within the family, in the time of Confucius the term *junzi* could be applied only to men.)

Before all else, Confucius was a teacher by profession; he operated a school in the broad sense of the word. Understandably, he made education the foundation of the process of development that would lead to *junzi*. He was largely responsible for defining what education should consist of and for promulgating that it should be available to promising men from all ranks of society. The Superior Man would be knowledgeable in the entire legacy of the past. This was not simply book learning; it was total education for life. Confucius's Superior Man, rather like the Renaissance Man of European history, was to be a well-rounded human being, conversant and skilled in all areas of life. He was to be polished, dignified, self-confident, and very well mannered. He was to be the finest expression of his culture. The Superior Man was, in a word, a true *gentleman*. But there was much more to *junzi* than this.

The Superior Man did not seek to serve his own self-centered ends, no matter how refined they might be. His reason for being was to serve the common good. His goal was to make himself as fit as he could to best serve the needs of the community. If he held public office, service was the one and only reason for seeking it. After personal refinement, a deep-rooted spirit of altruism was the mark of the Superior Man—and there was more.

At the core of the Superior Man—in fact, the golden nugget at the absolute heart of the entire Confucian system—was *ren* (*jen*). This is a very difficult word to translate. Perhaps the best we can do in English is to call it "human-heartedness." It was not enough for a man to be refined and altruistic: Most important by far was that he be a man of *ren*; this was the real spirit of *junzi*. Indeed, the Superior Man was the *embodiment of ren*. *Ren* is sincere feeling and caring for others; *ren* is gladly putting others first; in a word, *ren* is compassion—human-heartedness.

How can such a thing be taught? Confucius would say that you can teach it to yourself; everyone can. There is nothing metaphysical about it, nothing supernatural: "*Ren* is a natural feeling that comes directly and spontaneously from the human heart."[2] Every normal person, Confucius would argue, has deep-seated warm and compassionate feelings about himself (or herself). By looking deeply inward, we can discover this core of love and learn to extend it gradually outward to embrace others—ultimately, all others. It begins with the immediate family and expands to include the greater family of the whole community.

But, you might ask, isn't this all rather naive? Loving your fellow man and practicing the Golden Rule are fine ideals, but most human beings are far too weak and selfish for such ideals to be dominant in real life. Not so, Confucius would respond: People are selfish and insensitive out of ignorance. They mistakenly believe that they will be the "winners" in life and achieve happiness. But all experience shows that that is not the case. Man is basically loving by nature; we see it clearly in our feelings about ourselves. If we fail to extend it to others it is because of fear and ignorance. We fail to perceive our underlying bonds with others. However, whenever we are moved to overcome this resistance, we experience great happiness—great joy—and that's because *it is our nature* to be loving. Confucius would never have asked anyone to take his word for this; it's something that each person can easily check out for him- or herself. The experience of dealing with others in a human-hearted way is its own reward and gives rise to the greatest happiness. One can see for oneself that the way of *ren* is *the human* way to live.

Confucius was a wise and practical man. However much he may have believed that *ren* was available to all, he was realistic enough to know that it wasn't simply a matter of pointing this out, and everyone would shout, "Why didn't we think of that before?" Then, suddenly, all society would become kind and loving. But there were undoubtedly some—those who were the true men of *junzi*—who would make the discovery. They would become the embodiment of *ren*. These Superior Men, out of a spirit of service, would become the leaders of society, *and they would be the models for society as a whole!*

Confucius firmly believed that the common people are profoundly influenced by the example set for them by the leaders of society. If the leaders are greedy, everyone is greedy. But if the leaders are selfless, that same quality of selflessness will flower among the common people. This is presumably what Confucius meant by his somewhat enigmatic statement, "Not more surely does the grass bend before the wind than the masses yield to the will of those above them." The sense of the statement is that bad government encourages bad habits in all, whereas good government promotes virtue in all. In an age in which the leaders are selfish and greedy, the people become cynical and think that that is the way it always was. But when a people establish procedures that allow Superior Men to become the leaders, that society will enjoy peace and harmony; indeed, it will enter a Golden Age.

And that, precisely, is what Confucius proposed to do for his own age. It is true that he never got the opportunity to implement his ideas on a grand scale, but his teaching touched the hearts of men, and for ages to come, Chinese society was profoundly shaped by the philosophy of Master Kung Fu Zi.

As we will see in the chapters that follow, there are many similarities between Confucius and Shakyamuni Buddha. Confucius, like Buddha, encouraged people to look inward. "Be a lamp unto yourself," as Buddha put it. Discover your true nature, and be free of ignorance and all of the human suffering that ignorance gives rise to. Surely, Buddha would have liked Confucius's core concept of *ren*. "The man of *ren* is always happy; a common man is always sad," Confucius declared. Buddha's invitation was to become an "awakened" person, a person of *prajna*. Confucius's invitation was to become a "superior" person, a person of *junzi*. Leaving feeble words aside, how different really are the two kinds of person?

MENCIUS

Confucius was survived by a community of disciples dedicated to preserving the teaching of the Master. As noted, this is how the *Lun Yu* (the *Analects of Confucius*) came into existence. The tradition flourished for a while, but might have become scattered and forgotten had it not been for the work of Mencius, who was born just about a century after the death of Confucius. Mencius (also a victim of the Latinizers—his Chinese name was Meng Zi) loved the teaching of Confucius. "There never has been another Confucius since man first appeared on Earth," he said. He also paid Confucius a high compliment by saying of him that "he had a child's heart." Broadly speaking, the evolving tradition that came to be known as Confucianism contains as much of the thought of Mencius as it does of Confucius himself. For this reason, Mencius is sometimes referred to as the "Second Sage."

Mencius was born in 372 B.C.E. (or close to it), and lived until 289 B.C.E., a generous life span of eighty-three years. Although not a contemporary of Confucius, his life, too, was situated squarely within the tumultuous Warring States period. If anything, things were even more tumultuous during Mencius's life. The warring among the Chinese states was building to a climax that would finally reach its bloody end only thirty-four years after his death.

Although Mencius was not an immediate disciple of Confucius, the two men were closely linked philosophically. One can't help but think of the relationship between Socrates and Plato. Confucius, like Socrates, was a relatively humble man with a passion for truth and devoted his whole life to an inquiry into the truth that men should live by. He wrote little, if at all, and were it not for his disciples, his teaching would have died with him. Mencius, on the other hand, was more like Plato; he was a rich man and took pleasure in elegant clothes and manners. He was far more doctrinaire than Confucius, though, seeming to want to preach the truth, rather than search for it. But he loved the teaching of Confucius deeply and was largely responsible for it becoming a permanent part of Chinese culture. Also, like Plato, Mencius built his philosophy on the teaching of the master, both developing what was implied in it and taking it further.

The work associated with Mencius is known by his name. (Sometimes it is referred to as the *Mencius*, sometimes as the *Meng Zi*.) As was the case with Confucius, and with many other philosophers of the time, it seems most likely that the *Mencius* was not written by Mencius himself, but rather was the master's collected teachings, put together by some of his disciples after his death. In many ways, the *Mencius* is similar to the *Analects*, but the *Mencius* offers us a much fuller development of the themes. Whereas the *Analects* is a rather brief collection of terse and pithy aphorisms, the *Mencius* is a collection of genuine stories, with far more detail and humor. The almost sardonic wit of the author comes through clearly. We don't have this kind of personal connection with the *Analects*. Reading the *Mencius*, though, throws much light on the *Analects*, because the *Mencius* takes up many of the same themes. The *Mencius* had similar themes, similar goals, and much the same spirit as the *Analects*, but by no means are the two works identical. If nothing else, times had changed too much between the lifetimes of their authors. The evolution of Chinese history was more than a century further downriver by the time of Mencius, and that shows clearly in his work. Metaphorically speaking, Mencius may have stood on the shoulders of Confucius, but doing so allowed him to see farther.

Before we focus on what Mencius contributed to the Confucian tradition, let's identify what the two men shared. Both Confucius and Mencius were from the same general region, the state of Lu. Both were products of the Period of Warring States. Both were itinerant philosophers who failed in their desire to hold powerful public office. Both founded schools, attracting large numbers of disciples; and, in both cases, it was the disciples who eventually put the teaching of the master into writing.

Of greatest importance was the basic agreement between them as to the truth of Dao, the right "way" of conducting one's life. Both men believed that right education could transform the wild infant into a man of *junzi*—a "Superior Man," a sage; and both believed that achieving sagehood was the only legitimate goal of life. Too, Mencius fully agreed with Confucius that the family is the basis of the social order and that the maturing of compassion begins within the family and then, through right education, can be directed to move outward, ultimately to encompass the universal family.

Perhaps the most salient point of difference between Mencius and Confucius concerns purpose. Confucius saw the Superior Man's reason for being in terms of government service. The sage would fashion men of *junzi* precisely so that they could enter the ranks of the governing class and dedicate their lives to serving wisely and being a model for all. Mencius, by contrast, focused on right living, not right governing, as the proper goal of the Superior Man. This is not to say that Mencius was indifferent to the need for wise rulers; far from it, but that was not the *focus* of his teaching. His interest was more basic, more individualized: Identify those who are capable, and help them achieve sagehood. A society that honors this ideal in its educational system will naturally incline toward good government.

Mencius believed that everyone is capable of becoming a sage, because he believed in the inherent "goodness" of human beings. This belief is often attributed to Confucius, but in fact, it was Mencius who added it to the teaching of Confucianism. Confucius had very little to say on the subject. This is not to say that Confucius denied that man is good by nature, but he focused more than Mencius did on the matter of "naturalness." Confucius believed that man is born in a state of harmony with the natural order and falls out of harmony only by choosing his own selfish interest that is in conflict with the common good. Mencius went beyond this notion to actually define human nature as being naturally inclined to that which is morally "good." Obviously, human nature can be corrupted, and it often is, but, Mencius would maintain, at its root human nature is good, and no matter how often it is wounded, the urge to goodness is always ready to grow back, like grass on the sunny side of a hill.

Anticipating the Daoists (or perhaps borrowing a metaphor from them), Mencius compared human nature to water: "Human nature is good just as water seeks low ground. There is no man who is not good; there is no water that does not flow downwards."[3] For all practical purposes, Mencius equated goodness with compassion. In accordance with his view, we could say that goodness is the latent disposition, and the action that flows from it is compassion. To support his contention that compassion (the inclination to goodness) is inherent in all men and women, Mencius offered the example of a person who suddenly comes upon a scene in which it appears that a small child is about to fall down a well. "My reason for saying that no man is devoid of a heart sensitive to the suffering of others is this. Suppose a man were, all of a sudden, to see a young child on the verge of falling into a well. He would certainly be moved to compassion, not because he wanted to get in the good graces of the parents, nor because he wished to win the praise of his fellow villagers or friends, nor yet because he disliked the cry of the child."[4]

In this example, Mencius is arguing that virtually any person would feel a spontaneous burst of compassion for the child. It's the universality and suddenness of the emotion that make the point. Given time to think the situation over, some might find selfish reasons to ignore the child or, on the other hand, find selfish reasons to go the child's rescue. But in so doing, they have allowed their natural disposition to be smothered by selfish desires and fears. What this all adds up to, at least for Mencius, is that the goal of right education must be to work with the natural inclination to goodness that lies at the heart of every person, to cultivate it from the time a person is very young, and not to allow self-centered fears to stunt its growth. On this path, any person can eventually become a sage.

In most respects, Mencius would agree with Confucius as to the definition of a sage. Confucius's Superior Man and Mencius's sage were similarly highly educated individuals in whom compassion ruled over selfish interest. Both admired the self-contained individual who freely chose to serve the needs of the community with no thought of reward. His reward is the abiding joy that comes from knowing that he is a contributory part of the whole. Mencius summed up his own view of the superior person in these words: "When he achieves his ambition he shares [it] with the people; when he fails to do so he practices the Way alone. He cannot be led into excesses when wealthy and honorced or deflected from his purpose when poor and obscure, nor can he be made to bow before superior force. This is what I would call a great man."[5]

But what *really* is a great man, a sage? Is it simply a matter of adding up all of these fine virtues, or is there something else, something most essential of all, that truly defines the sage? Mencius's answer would be far different from that of Confucius, and here it may well be that we come to that element of the teaching that most distinguishes Mencius from Confucius. In his heart of hearts, Mencius was a mystic; Confucius most definitely was not. For Mencius the ultimate reward for cultivating the self was to know the unspeakable bliss that arises only from the obliteration of that same self. The end of wisdom is to be achieved in becoming "one with Heaven," in which state all distinctions between the self and nonself are dissolved. "For a man to give full realization to his heart is for him to understand his own nature, and a man who knows his own nature will know Heaven."[6] Perhaps in this statement Mencius added a profundity to Confucianism that was something wholly new.

OTHER VOICES FROM THE PERIOD OF A HUNDRED PHILOSOPHERS

The teaching of Confucius inspired a host of alternative systems in the Period of a Hundred Philosophers. Some, like Mencius, loved Confucius's teaching and sought only to further develop its potential. Others disagreed fundamentally with the Confucian philosophy and sought to eclipse it with competing systems of their own. Among those who disagreed with Confucius, the Daoists would become paramount. We shall examine their contribution in the next chapter; here we will look briefly at three important figures from that restless time who reacted in various ways to the teaching of Confucius.

Xun Zi (Hsun-tzu)

Confucius's teaching occupied something of a central position; others ranged out from that center in all directions. If Mencius pondered the sage's teaching and concluded that man is by nature good, then it was almost predictable that another would ponder the teaching of Confucius and conclude that man is by nature evil. This, in a manner of speaking, was the conclusion of Xun Zi, and it became the cornerstone of his teaching in the same way that the goodness of man became the cornerstone of Mencius's teaching.

It may be going too far, though, to reduce their philosophies to such simple terms as "good" and "evil." Mencius focused more on the concept of compassion, arguing that man has a natural disposition to be compassionate, which, of course, results in behavior that we normally call good. Xun Zi, on the other hand, argued that man is selfish by nature, not compassionate. Goodness—that is, compassion—is an acquired virtue, which develops naturally as one's inherent selfishness is overcome. So, in a way, both compassion and selfishness are inherent in human nature, but selfishness is initially the stronger and crowds out nascent compassion unless the individual, through right education, learns to deny the impulse to selfishness. In that event, the individual is free to develop into a "Superior Man."

Like Confucius and Mencius, Xun Zi regarded self-cultivation leading to sagehood to be the most important goal of life, and he agreed that right education was essential if one were to follow the Dao, in the sense that Confucius used the term. Unlike Confucius and Mencius, however, Xun Zi believed that only a very few were capable of making the grade. Theoretically, his educational system might be open to all, but it was a foregone conclusion that the great masses of the common people would be excluded for lack of ability. Apparently Xun Zi thought of the common people as being little better than animals.

Perhaps, though, we're being a bit too hard on Xun Zi. Not much is known about him for sure, not even his birth and death dates: The best guess is that he lived from about 300 B.C.E. to 225 B.C.E., which would make him a much younger contemporary of Mencius. From what has survived of his teaching, we can see that he was a powerful thinker, very influential in his own day. Presumably, he was as popular as Mencius at the time. He certainly makes a nice foil to Mencius. If Mencius's relation to Confucius was like that of Plato to Socrates, then, in some ways, Xun Zi played the role of Aristotle in this triangle. Like Aristotle, Xun Zi was a brilliant thinker and totally rational; mystic insight seemed to have no place at all in his philosophy. In fact, he had no use for religion in any guise. To his way of thinking, religion was nothing more than a collection of ignorant superstitions, acceptable perhaps for keeping the common people in line, but not worthy of having any place whatsoever in the life of a Superior Man.

Although Xun Zi's creative mind carried the evolution of Confucian thought into rich new ground, his influence was short lived, and his name was eventually all but forgotten. Maybe this is due to the apparent dichotomy between the teaching of Xun Zi and Mencius; Mencius's insistence on the native goodness of human nature carried the day. Or maybe it was the result of his attitude regarding the common people; Xun Zi's contempt for the masses could have been the fatal flaw in his philosophy. H. R. Creel, the noted historian of Eastern thought, argues that Xun Zi simply lacked faith in humanity: "Hsun Tzu [Xun Zi] was, without qualification, one of the most brilliant philosophers the world has ever produced. But he lacked faith in humanity. This flaw, like the fatal weakness of the hero in a Greek tragedy, went far to nullify his best efforts."[7]

Mo Zi (Mo-tzu)

Mo Zi lived relatively close in time to Confucius, although we can't be sure exactly. We can say with some confidence that he lived at least most of his life in the fifth century B.C.E. and at an early age became an ardent Confucian. However, he soon became disgusted by what he perceived to be corruption of the master's teaching among many of those who claimed to be his followers. For example, there was a movement among some Confucianists to form themselves into a sort of elite class, a Confucian *literati*, distinguished by overly elegant manners and a special kind of elaborate clothing unique to themselves. Also, some Confucianists encouraged the practice of costly funerals, which they would manage at no small profit to themselves. These kinds of abuses sickened Mo Zi, and he finally abandoned his association with the Confucianists, going off to found his own school.

Apparently, the influence of Mo Zi's teaching was very strong even in his own time. It is presented in a short book of the same name, a collection of aphorisms compiled by his disciples. He completely agreed with Confucius with regard to some basic matters. Both men wanted above all to reform the corrupt social order of their time. They would accomplish this by persuading the rulers to turn over administrative power to virtuous men who were dedicated to serving the common good. Both men would fashion these new men through a process of education aimed at resurrecting the ways of the sage–rulers of ancient times. But that's where the similarity ended.

Mo Zi had no interest at all in the liberal humanities of the Confucian system. He felt that it simply did not get at the root of the common people's problem. Restoring order to society was the overarching need of the day. But not just any system of order would do; it had to be a system that would be in full harmony with the order of nature. Such a system, once achieved, would be perfectly stable. In Mo Zi's opinion, this called for a rigidly organized hierarchy of authority, which he believed was the way of nature. At the top of this pyramid of power would be the hereditary monarch, whom Mo Zi referred to as the "Son of Heaven." The government of the Son of Heaven would rule with an unchallenged authority and, interestingly enough, with the total support and loyalty of the people.

Why would the people be so supportive of an authoritarian regime? Because every man and woman would be imbued with a sense of what Mo Zi referred to as "universal love." He was not talking about love in the usual sense of the word; he had something far different in mind. In fact, that's exactly where this kind of love resided, in the mind. It was to be a philosophical kind of love, springing from the recognition of the natural interrelatedness of all of the parts of a society. When one grasped the organic unity of it all and saw one's own real identity in terms of that unity, a deep love and loyalty to the system would inevitably follow.

Mo Zi totally dismissed Confucius's emphasis on the family as being of fundamental importance. In Mo Zi's opinion, the family was a breeding ground of segregation and emotionalism; it was an obstacle, not a help, to the achievement of universal love. Everyone should love everyone, without distinction: "If everyone in the world would practice universal love . . . then the whole world would enjoy peace and good order." Education was the key: Every person must be educated to see, clearly and distinctly, that the way of universal love was in their own best interest. We might almost describe it as a love engendered by enlightened self-interest. The ruler–sages would be models, and their example would eventually be followed by everyone.

Mo Zi was willing to sacrifice anything and everything that might interfere with the success of his ideal society. His teaching was ruthlessly utilitarian: If it doesn't help, out it goes. One of the things to go was emotion. Strange as it may seem, Mo Zi held that emotionalism was the enemy of the state. It has no place in the natural order of things, because it serves no useful purpose. Emotion feeds individual desires and uncontrolled behavior. Therefore, in Mo Zi's ideal state, all expressions of emotion were to be purged. There was to be no art, no music—nothing at all that might excite the emotions of the people. It may seem hard to believe, but that is exactly what Mo Zi advocated.

In this highly Spartan state, absolutely everything was to be subordinated to the good of the whole. The love of all for all would arise when the people discovered that such a state was the natural way for human communities to be organized and that it was the only reasonable alternative to the chaos and corruption of the times. The smooth functioning of such a state depended on the unquestioned loyalty of the subjects. That loyalty would arise out of a sense of identity, and ultimately, all must identify with the supreme ruler, the Son of Heaven. He in turn identified with Heaven itself. When this state of total integration was achieved, the system would function perfectly.

But what if it didn't function perfectly? What if something went wrong? What if someone—even, conceivably, the Son of Heaven himself—were to do the unthinkable and choose selfish interest ahead of the good of the whole? Such disloyalty could be disastrous, but how would you know that such disloyalty had occurred? Mo Zi's answer to this was that wrongdoing (otherwise known as disloyalty) would be punished by Heaven; Mo Zi declared that natural calamities were the punishments of Heaven. "Heaven sends down immoderate cold and heat and unseasonable snow, frost, rain and dew. The five grains do not ripen, and the six domestic animals do not mature. There are diseases, epidemics, and pestilence. Hurricanes and torrential downpours occur repeatedly. These are Heaven's punishments, visited on men below because they fail to identify themselves with it."[8]

What would Confucius have said if he heard this? Confucius had sought to liberate the common people from their superstitious fears of the spirit world, but here was Mo Zi playing on these very fears, thus reviving what Confucius had attempted to purge.

Han Fei Zi and the Legalists

In the spring of 1974, a farmer was digging out a well near the modern city of Xian in central China. Not far from the surface, his shovel suddenly scraped against the head of a buried statue. It was a life-sized terra-cotta figure of a soldier, but not like any soldier seen in a very long time. The figure hauled out of the earth had not seen the light of day in more than two thousand years. It was, in fact, the startling first look at what was to become one of the greatest archeological finds in all of human history.

The farmer had stumbled upon the giant tumulus tomb of Shi Huang Di, the first emperor of China, founder of the Qin (Ch'in) Dynasty. His megalomania in life continued in death, and following his earlier orders, his body was laid to rest in a burial scene of incredible splendor and size. The whole world has become fascinated with the find and is eager to see it all uncovered, but the site is being most carefully excavated, and the work remains only partially completed. It is becoming clear, though, that a full-sized replica of the entire court accompanied Shi Huang Di to the grave in 210 B.C.E.

The original tumulus was over six hundred feet high, and that man-made hill was only the centerpiece. It was constructed to guard the court, little of which has yet been excavated. Surrounding the tumulus is an immense entourage of at least seven thousand full-sized terra-cotta soldiers and horses with chariots, all arranged in military formation. Each was originally painted and adorned with the appropriate provincial headdress.

All of this stupefying display of wealth and power was made possible by Shi Huang Di's successful conquests. But it hadn't always been that way. Before becoming the first emperor, Shi Huang Di had been simply the Duke of Qin, living in much humbler surroundings. However, things began to change one day when he read a philosophical tract authored by one Han Fei Zi.

Han Fei Zi was the principal spokesman for a group known collectively as the Legalists. The book that bears his name was presumably written by him, not compiled by his students, and lays out in chilling detail the essentials of the Legalist philosophy. They are called the Legalists, not because they valued law as a means of protecting the rights of the people, but rather because they saw written law as a powerful instrument by means of which the ruling authority could exercise control over the whole society. The Legalists were authoritarian in the extreme. A better word might be "totalitarian."

Like Confucius, Han Fei Zi aspired to reform the sick social order of his time, and he agreed with Confucius that that could not be accomplished unless hereditary rule was abolished. But he completely disagreed with Confucius about the power of virtue. To Han Fei Zi's way of thinking, virtuous, unselfish action was fleeting and unpredictable. In no way was it something to be counted on. To base the governance of a state on the presumed virtuous behavior of its ministers was, in his opinion, ridiculous.

Han Fei Zi was an advocate of strongly centralized rule and a thoroughly Spartan way of life. He went far beyond even Mo Zi in this regard. The entire society was to be regimented in the form of a military organization, always ready, and even eager, for war. The law, which would be publicized and clearly known by everyone, would be like military law. Terrible punishments would be meted out for even trivial offenses. For example, if Han Fei Zi had his way, one would lose a hand for merely throwing waste ashes into the street. Han Fei Zi believed that large crimes could be prevented by dealing severely with small crimes. Above all, law and order must prevail. On the other hand, extreme punishments were to be balanced by generous rewards. Reporting a crime, for example, would earn a handsome reward. A complete listing of rewards and punishments would be spelled out in the law. Indeed, *everything* would be spelled out in the law. But again, this was not to protect people's rights; the common people had no rights, as we understand the word. People exist for the state, whose will must be their will. Such a system, the Legalists argued, was a strong and healthy alternative to the chaos and corruption of the time.

This extreme philosophy of statecraft, so totally contrary to the spirit of the teaching of Confucius, might have remained only an academic curiosity had it not aroused the interest of our Shi Huang Di, the Duke of Qin, one of the independent regions of China during the Warring States period. After reading some of Han Fei Zi's writings, the duke wanted to meet the man behind the writing and learn more about his intriguing militaristic philosophy. Han Fei Zi accepted the invitation, traveling to the court of Qin in the year 233 B.C.E. Ironically, he died there in prison that same year, having been unjustly accused of spying. But the flame of interest was already lit, and it would soon grow to a bonfire in the state of Qin.

Inspired by the teachings of Han Fei Zi in particular and the Legalists generally, Qin made itself over into a one-hundred-percent military machine and then went on the warpath. The various states of China had been fighting among themselves for centuries, but no one of them had been able to overwhelm all of the others. That was about to change. In a series of unbelievably bloody conquests, the state of Qin finally brought the Period of Warring States to a close by conquering all the other states and welding all of China together into its first true empire. We know it as the Qin Dynasty. (Qin is spelled Ch'in in the formerly popular Wade–Giles system, and this, in fact, is why that land came to be known in the West as "China.")

The triumph of Qin was a violent affair. A bloodbath followed the completion of the conquest. Legend has it that 400,000 troops who had surrendered were summarily executed. Many similar incidents were reported. All critics of the new government—especially Confucian scholars—were executed. Han Fei Zi had written, "in the state of an intelligent ruler there are no books, but the laws serve as teachings." Consequently, a decree was issued ordering the burning of virtually all books; almost the only books to be spared were those dealing with military science and agriculture. The Spartan way of life of Qin was imposed on the whole land. The law came down with ferocity on even the smallest of offenses. It must have seemed that there was no way to avoid being labeled a criminal.

Given this general state of affairs, many gave up hope of being able to live peacefully in the new state. Great numbers of people, including many Confucians, fled into the hill country, where they organized themselves into guerrilla bands. As the rule grew more severe, the strength of the counterrevolution also grew. The government was completely unable to stamp it out. In the year 210 B.C.E., Shi Huang Di, the founding emperor of Qin, died. But he had done everything in his power to see that he would not be forgotten. The incredibly opulent burial scene discussed earlier was his parting shot, and it was certainly an appropriate send-off for the founding emperor of a dynasty that was decreed to see ten thousand more emperors. Well, not quite: Three years later, the whole Qin administration collapsed in the face of a general uprising led by a peasant soldier, Liu Bang, who would found a wholly new dynasty, the Han Dynasty, on the ashes of Qin.

The extreme totalitarianism of the Legalists moved from theory to practice in the administration of Shi Huang Di, but the downfall of Qin did not permanently put an end to this philosophy; it occupies a part of the spectrum of social philosophy that is ever present. The contribution of the Period of a Hundred Philosophers was to enunciate systems that represent virtually all of the various parts of that broad spectrum.

LATER DEVELOPMENTS IN THE EVOLUTION OF CONFUCIANISM

Confucianism in the Time of Han

Broadly speaking, the Han Empire was to eastern Eurasia what the Roman Empire was to western Eurasia. Both were universal states ruled by an authoritarian central power that had welded together the disparate parts of their respective cultures through military conquest. Broadly speaking, both empires existed at the same time in history. The Roman Empire came into being somewhat later than Han and would outlive it, but both endured for approximately four centuries. Both empires brought a long period of civil strife to an end, replacing it with an enforced peace upheld by uniform law and military power. Finally, the central authority of the Han Empire and the Roman Empire lost their vitality and eventually succumbed to the onslaught of barbarian peoples from beyond their frontiers.

The Qin Empire could conceivably have endured, and there never would have been a Han. Their own excesses of brutality and repression, however, provoked the uprising that resulted in the fall of Qin after less than half a century of rule. The founder of the new dynasty was, surprisingly, a peasant. His name was Liu Bang, but as the first emperor of Han he became known as Han Gaozu (Han Kao-tzu). He had been the leader of a resistance group whose original power base had been in the Han River valley, and it was in honor of that special place that the new dynasty took its name.

The Han Empire came into existence in 202 B.C.E. and would hold onto power for four centuries. Its boundaries would eventually include almost all of what we commonly think of as China today. To the east was the ocean, to the south and west great masses of mountains, and to the north the endless steppes of northern Asia. It was the northern frontier that was most worrisome. Here were to be found predatory tribal peoples in numbers beyond counting. Their mounted armies could sweep in like the wind. To hold them back, the Great Wall was begun in Qin times. During the Han Dynasty, the wall was greatly expanded and fortified. It worked well for a while, just as Hadrian's Wall worked well for the Romans—for a while. Eventually, both walls proved insufficient to their assigned task.

Of great importance in the history of Confucianism was the reign of Emperor Wu Di (140–87 B.C.E.). A strong ruler who did much to consolidate the power of the central authority, Wu Di became a champion of Confucianism, and during his reign the Confucian system of governmental administration became established as the orthodox system of the empire. With the usual ups and downs of fortune, it would remain a guiding influence in the government in China until modern times. We may question how deeply Emperor Wu Di understood or cared about the actual teaching of Confucius. Some feel that his adoption of Confucianism was a purely utilitarian move. Perhaps he simply liked what he heard about the Confucian respect for the rankings of authority. Here could be a philosophy, properly adjusted to fit the needs of the empire, that could both help to unify the state and provide a convenient disguise for his authoritarian rule. In any case, it was Wu Di who sponsored the implementation of the first Confucian system of governmental administration in China.

The real hero of the story, though, was a Confucian scholar by the name of Dong Zhong Shu. Dong was a man of great learning, widely respected and known to be a little unusual. For one thing, it was his habit to deliver his lectures from behind a curtain, so that the purity of his scholarship would not seem to be tainted by his personality. Unusual or not, it was to Dong Zhong Shu that Emperor Wu Di entrusted the daunting task of establishing a system which would produce the Confucian sages that would be needed to fill the ranks of administrative posts. It was Dong who created the famous

Confucian system of competitive examinations, designed to single out men of proven excellence and bestow upon them careers in government service. This became the established system not only in China, but in other East Asian countries as well.

The examination, however, was only the capstone of the process. Dong instituted an educational system, open to any young man who showed ability. The system was designed to be long and rigorous, focusing on what Dong identified as the essential five classics of Chinese culture (known as the Wu Jing): metaphysics, politics, poetry, the social graces, and history, with special emphasis on the classics of Confucian teaching. Far more students were accepted than would ever finish the course of study; their numbers were winnowed by a series of examinations leading up to the final great examination, conducted over a period of days by learned Confucian scholars. It was pretty formidable, to say the least, but those few who made the grade became highly honored members of society and were allowed to enter into careers in responsible government posts where they could spend their adult lives in service to the whole society.

The Confucian educational system, of course, took time to mature. When Dong Zhong Shu set up the first group at the court of Wu Di in 134 B.C.E., he employed only five teacher–scholars and had only a handful of students. Within ten years, though, the number of students had grown to fifty, and within a century there were more than three thousand. The initial establishment was something of an "imperial university" located at the emperor's court. In time, it became necessary to found branches in strategic locations. Eventually, the system created by Dong was responsible for more than a hundred men a year entering government service.

Great as the success of Confucianism was during the time of Han, by no means would it be true to say that the Confucians had the field all to themselves. By this time, the Daoists were a strong presence throughout Chinese society and in the imperial court as well. Confucians and Daoists engaged ceaselessly in a generally friendly competition for influence (much more about the Daoists in the next chapter), and the Buddhists, too, were slowly but steadily growing in influence, especially by the time of late Han. The Daoists, despite themselves, were intrigued by the philosophy of Buddhism and absorbed much of it into their own way. The Confucians, however, at least initially, were repulsed by what they perceived to be a foreign religion that sought to lure promising young men into the seclusion of the monastery instead of into a life of public service. They opposed the Buddhists and would have been happy to see the whole foreign "thing" extinguished. But that was not to be: They were destined, in fact, to work out an interesting accommodation.

Neo-Confucianism

Officially, the Han Dynasty came to an end in the year 220 C.E., but it had been unraveling for decades before that, due to a host of problems, internal and external. Chinese society would not be unified again until the establishment of the Sui Dynasty in 581 C.E., more than three-and-a-half centuries after the fall of Han. This long interregnum was marked by all kinds of civil strife, regional warfare, barbarian invasions, and a return to that troubling insecurity that was the hallmark of the Period of Warring States. The relative anarchy of the time was a boon to Buddhism, which flourished in China after the fall of Han, but the times were hard indeed for Confucianism, which had been so closely identified with the now-defunct Han establishment. By the time of the Sui reunification, Buddhism was triumphant. The Confucians had much work to do if they were to regain influence in the affairs of Chinese society.

The Sui Dynasty was short lived, existing for a total of only twenty-six years. Sui's contribution was simply the reunification of China. Tang and Song, however, the two dynasties that followed Sui, were long and brilliant. Together, they dominated the scene until 1236 C.E., a six-century span of time that many regard to be the golden age of Chinese civilization. It certainly was the golden age of Chinese Buddhism, which was ascendant in China during this historical period. Chan Buddhism (which would become Zen in Japan) matured in China during the Tang and Song dynasties. The relative stability of the times was the opportunity the Confucians had been waiting for. What resulted was a Confucian revival, but with a difference. Because of that difference, the Confucian revival of Tang and Song is generally known as "neo-Confucianism." This new breed of Confucianism would persist until the nineteenth century.

Oddly enough, neo-Confucianism resulted from what started out as an effort to reform Confucianism by going back to the purity of the original sources, Confucius himself and Mencius. But there was a problem with this approach; pure Confucianism, however admirable it might be as a system of social philosophy, would simply not be able to compete head to head with Buddhism, which had become a total philosophy of life, dealing with areas—metaphysics, for example—that had never been a part of Confucian thinking. If the Confucians were to restore the primacy of Confucianism, they would have to match what Buddhism offered. This they promised to do, and more.

If they were to meet the challenge of Buddhism, the Confucians would have to *read into* the Confucian classics much that simply wasn't there. The result, of course, was an interpretation of the classics that stretched their original meaning. It came down to an effort to make over Confucianism into something of a "secular religion." The net result was a hybrid of traditional Confucian teaching, some recast elements of Buddhism, and even bits of Religious Daoism. Taking parts from here and there, the Confucians produced what was really a brand-new creature—a revamped breed of Confucianism that would remain an important part of Chinese culture until the beginning of the twentieth century.

So, was neo-Confucianism a success? Did the Confucians reestablish their primacy? Did they succeed in matching what Buddhism had to offer, and more? Not really. Buddhism was entrenched among the masses of the common people, and that wasn't going to change one bit. Among the educated upper classes of Chinese society, though, Confucianism did reestablish a place of importance. Up to the time of the communist revolution, it was largely true to say that Buddhism was the way of the masses, but Confucianism was the way of the aristocracy.

Confucianism in the Modern Era

Following the Sui reunification in 581 C.E., China was ruled by an emperor until the collapse of the Jing Dynasty (popularly known as the Manchu Dynasty) in 1912. During this long span, Confucianism had reasserted itself, at least among the upper classes. It proved its durability, adapting well to the changing of dynasties, whether homegrown or imposed by foreign conquest. Jing, the last of the dynasties to rule China, came to power as a result of the Manchu conquest of 1644. From the beginning of Jing, Confucians played an important role in the government. The system of competitive examinations continued right up until the end. However, as time progressed, the upper classes became more and more conservative—indeed, *stagnant* might be a better word. This seems to be the destiny of all empires. The Confucian establishment was a part of the process of ossification. Far from being the reform-minded servants of the people envisaged by Confucius himself, the Confucian scholars had all too often become mere bookworms, deliberately distancing themselves from the people they were supposed to serve. They were frequently viewed as nothing more than "frail weaklings, laughed at by soldiers and farmers."

The winds of change began to blow, though, and they were blowing from the West. By the late nineteenth century, the windstorm had become a typhoon. The impact of the West had a powerful effect on the culture of China. While Chinese civilization was stagnating under the Manchu emperors, European civilization was plunging forward, creating the technological revolution that was totally changing the world. European influence—cultural, technological, and even religious—became very strong in China. While Manchu China had allowed itself to become mired in its conservative ways, the "Western barbarians" had become a force that imperial China could not control. The European powers arrogantly divided China into "spheres of influence" so as to better exploit its trade. The unthinkable had to be thought: China had become so weakened that it might lose its sovereignty altogether. What was to do be done?

What, indeed? Predictably, some wanted only to retreat into the shell of China's vastness and wait out the Westerners. Eventually, this time of troubles would pass; it always does. To many, that seemed to be the attitude of the imperial court. Others sought to deal with the challenge of the West by absorbing the enemy: Integrate the desirable elements of Western culture, and salvage the essence of traditional Chinese culture by making concessions where the nonessentials were concerned. Then it might be possible to stand up to the Western Powers without having to become one of them.

One such person was a reformer named Kang Youwei (Kang Yu-wei), who had become much impressed by the inspirational power of the Western religious groups that were aggressively proselytizing in China. Kang believed that all of the people of China could be aroused in a similar way by a new native religion based on the teachings of Confucius, which to his mind contained the essential germ of traditional Chinese culture. He would use the methods of Western religion to create a revolutionary movement that would unite all of the Chinese people in a crusade that would carry China back to independence and greatness. His vision of a new Confucian "religion" would go even beyond that. Under Chinese leadership, it would spread around the globe, initiating a New Age of world peace and progress:

> Kang argued that Confucius was not merely a transmitter of ancient teachings but a prophet who, ahead of his time, cast his message in subtle language full of hidden meanings. Confucius, according to Kang, saw history as a universal

progress through three stages, each with its appropriate form of government: the Age of Disorder (rule by an absolute monarch), the Age of Approaching Peace (rule by a constitutional monarch), and the Age of Great Peace (rule by the people). Kang's Confucius was thus a seer and prophet not only for China but for the entire world.[9]

Kang's interesting vision never materialized, but that of others did. The ultimate victors were, of course, the Marxists, who came to power in 1949. But it almost didn't turn out that way. Thirty-seven years before the communist triumph, in February of 1912, to be precise, six-year-old Pu Yi, the last of the Chinese emperors, abdicated the throne. A system of government that had ruled China for more than two thousand years had come to an end. It seemed at the time that China was destined to become a democratic republic on the Western model. Sun Yat-sen, the "Father of the Republic," and his successor, Chiang Kai-shek, labored hard to make that dream come true. But it was not to be. The stormy conditions of the time, both within China and globally, conspired to lead China down a different path. The leader of that different path was the peasant turned revolutionary turned national leader, Mao Zedong (Mao Tse-tung), founding father of the People's Republic of China.

From the very beginning, it had been a major goal of the communist movement in China to destroy all vestiges of Confucianism, and this has certainly been the policy of the Chinese Communist Party in modern times. The Confucian educational system, competitive examinations and all, was rooted out entirely. (It must be pointed out, though, that a start in this direction was made in the final years of the Jing Dynasty.) The official position of the People's Republic of China is that the teaching of Confucius is elitist and diametrically opposed to the goals of Marxist philosophy, particularly the goal of achieving a classless society.

Considering the state of Confucianism in China in recent centuries, it is easy to understand the bitterness that any self-respecting Marxist would feel. The Confucians in China had indeed become a privileged elite class, and they jealously guarded their special position. It could easily be argued that they had become parasitic and distanced from the common people. But would not Confucius himself condemn this situation just as vehemently as the communists did? I think so! The Confucianism condemned by the Chinese Communist Party was a corrupted version of the original teaching, a version that had grown largely out of neo-Confucian roots. The authentic teaching of Confucius has much to say to all who wish to establish a just social order in which those who govern are selected for their skill and compassion. Perhaps the time has come to reopen the door a bit, and rethink the teaching of Confucius:

> [T]he two areas of concern of Maoism [i.e., Chinese communism] are still very much like the Confucianism of the past. One concern is for values; the other for reality. For example, in Maoism, happiness means the relatively secure possession of the minimum necessities for decent life and the absence of suffering from deprivation, oppression, exploitation and neglect. These have also been the cardinal aims of Confucianism.[10]

No one knows what the future holds, both for China itself and for the human family as a whole. It seems plausible, though, that whatever the form of government may be, in the future China will move more in the direction of democracy. Should this be the case, the teaching of Confucius may be in for a resurrection: "Democracy values freedom and the individual, and denies unlimited authority to the state; so does Confucianism. The entire humanistic and liberal background out of which Western democracy grew has much in common with the best traditions of Chinese thought."[11]

Is a renaissance of Confucian humanism coming into view on the horizon? Or is it, perhaps, still just beyond the horizon?

Notes

1. Ch'u Chai and Winberg Chai, *Confucianism* (New York: Barron's, 1973), pp. 42–43.
2. *Ibid.*, p. 37.
3. D. C. Lau, trans., *Mencius* (London: Penguin Books, 1970), 6A: 2, p. 160.
4. *Ibid.*, 2A: 6, p. 82.
5. *Ibid.*, 3B: 2, p. 107.
6. *Ibid.*, 7A: 1, p. 182.
7. Herrlee G. Creel, *Chinese Thought from Confucius to Mao Tse-tung* (Chicago: University of Chicago Press, 1953), p. 115.
8. *Ibid.*, p. 59.
9. Conrad Schirokauer, *A Brief History of Chinese and Japanese Civilizations* (Fort Worth, TX: Harcourt Brace Jovanovich, 1989), p. 471.
10. Chai and Chai, p. 172.
11. Creel, p. 244.

Study Questions

1. The chapter begins with the statement, "Confucius gave to Chinese civilization a grand ideal for the ordering of society." In general terms, what was this grand ideal?

2. What did Confucius mean by saying that human society had gotten out of harmony with the larger natural order that it is a part of?

3. In what fundamental ways are Confucius and Mencius in agreement? In disagreement? What is your reaction to the suggestion that Mencius took the teaching further?

4. It is suggested that Mencius was a mystic at heart. What does this mean? What is the evidence for that claim?

5. What does it mean to say that Mo Zi revived what Confucius had purged?

6. What is neo-Confucianism? Why is it called *neo*-Confucianism?

7. How do you think Confucius himself would have reacted if it had been possible for him to examine the system that bore his name at the beginning of the modern era?

8. The chapter ends with the question, "Is a renaissance of Confucian humanism coming into view on the horizon? Or is it, perhaps, still just beyond the horizon?" What is your answer?

7

Daoism

We have already encountered the word *Dao* in the previous chapter. Confucius had made the intriguing assertion that "if a man hears about Dao in the morning, and dies in the evening, his life has not been wasted." For Confucius, though, the word *Dao* apparently referred only to the right *way* of conduct—the right *way* for a person to live. For the Daoists, it would mean much more.

"Way" or "road," was the original meaning of *Dao*. With such a broad possibility of applications, it's not surprising that use of the word became rather pervasive in Chinese culture. A very early derived meaning of *Dao* referred to the grand way in which the heavens revolve around the earth. The central pole of this revolution was seen to be the seat of the power of Dao, from which flowed continuously the creative force that ordered not only the movements of the heavenly bodies around itself, but all of the activities of nature. Over time, the concept of Dao became more and more abstract. Dao came to be regarded as the impersonal and infinite force, cosmic in scope, that stood behind the being and the unfolding of the natural order.

There is an interesting accord here between the Chinese concept of Dao, on the one hand, and the Indian concept of Dharma (Brahman-Dharma), on the other. In some ways, they appear to be quite similar. It would be a valuable exercise to mentally compare the two just to see to your own satisfaction how close a fit they really are. But that is just the beginning; many other tantalizing parallels are found between Chinese and Indian philosophical thought. This, as we shall see, is especially the case with regard to Buddhism. In the early days of Buddhism in China, many of its terms were translated using Daoist concepts.

The distinct philosophical system that we know as Daoism crystallized during the same historical era in which Confucius lived—that is to say, the tumultuous Warring States period. Daoism took form a little after the lifetime of Confucius and, to some extent, was undoubtedly a reaction to the teaching of Confucius. On the surface, at least, Daoism seems to be the very antithesis of Confucianism. You'll see what I mean by this as we go along.

Once established, the Daoist tradition, like the Confucian, would continue on to the present day. Both traditions, however, would evolve over the course of time. In neither case would it be true to say that what exists today is a faithful expression of the original teaching. In addition to that, the Daoist tradition is divided into two very different species: Philosophical Daoism and Religious Daoism. Our primary concern in this study will be with Philosophical Daoism, but some attention will be given to the nature of Religious Daoism as well.

The central teaching of Philosophical Daoism is to be found in two fascinating works: the *Dao De Jing* (*Tao Te Ching*) and the *Zhuang Zi* (*Chuang Tzu*). Both of these were produced during the Zhou period, and, as you might expect, there is a great deal of uncertainty regarding them. Modern research strongly suggests that the *Zhuang Zi* is the older of the two, but we will take up the *Dao De Jing* first. For one thing, it has become traditional to begin the study of Daoist with the *Dao De Jing*; it is a very succinct statement of Daoism thinking. Also, it would appear to be a more direct reaction to the teaching of Confucius.

THE *DAO DE JING* (*TAO TE CHING*)

The *Dao De Jing* is an awfully small work, considering the great size of its influence. The book consists of only five thousand Chinese characters, somewhat arbitrarily arranged into eighty-one short "chapters," perhaps better described as verses, many only a few lines long. The word *Jing* in the title refers to the fact that the work was regarded as a classic. *Dao* and *De* refer to what the work is all about. We will look into the meaning of these extremely ambiguous words shortly. The *Dao De Jing* is also commonly known as the *Lao Zi* (*Lao Tzu*), the name of its alleged author.

I say alleged because next to nothing is known about the man, not even whether he is fact or fiction. Therefore, as you might guess, a large body of legend has grown up around his name. *Lao Zi* is something of a nickname that means "the old master," possibly meant to be understood in the sense of "the old philosopher." Fortunately, the name *Lao Zi* escaped the attention of the Latinizers; otherwise we might know him as Laotius. There is an entry for Lao Zi in the *Shih Chi*, that collection of Chinese biographies compiled in the first century B.C.E., but the author, Sima Qian, admits that he is puzzled; there is so little to go on. That never stops the mythmakers, of course, and a life story was crafted that many mistakenly assume to be historically accurate.

According to the most popular version of the legend, Lao Zi (Lao Tzu) was an older contemporary of Confucius. He was born around 600 B.C.E. in the part of China that is today known as Honan Province, just to the west of Confucius's home region. It seems that he worked as a minor bureaucrat in the government of Zhou, possibly as a keeper of historical records in the royal library system. This would have given him a life-long access to the literary tradition of Chinese culture and would explain his deep knowledge of Chinese history. He was not an intellectual, though—far from it. It seems that Lao Zi felt only contempt for the *literati* of his age. He was a very humble man, living a simple life and avoiding public attention. His fame spread far, however, among those who loved the ancient traditions.

There is a wonderful story about a meeting between Lao Zi and Confucius. In the context of the legend, this would have happened when Confucius visited the capital city of Zhou when he was a young adult. At that time, Lao Zi would presumably have already been an old man. According to the story, Confucius sought out Lao Zi at his modest home and spent the better part of a day with him. A few disciples traveling with Confucius waited for him to return at the nearby village, and when Confucius finally did return to them, they were struck by his appearance. The young Confucius was exhausted and almost shaking. His visit with Lao Zi had been a profoundly moving experience, but he wouldn't talk about it except to say, "Don't have anything to do with that man. He is a very dangerous man!"

What in the world did he mean by that? We can only guess. Perhaps we are meant to imagine that the stark, uncompromising realism of Lao Zi had been too much for the young, intellectual mind of Confucius. Perhaps at that time in his life Confucius was full of a self-confidence that was deeply shaken by Lao Zi, who held Confucius's face to the edge of the abyss of nonconceptual reality and made him look. No one knows.

In the legend of Lao Zi's life, we are told that when he realized that he did not have much longer to live, he set off on foot to spend his final days in the wilderness. When he reached the frontier that led off into the barbarian lands, the warden of the gate tearfully begged him not to leave. How could they bear to live without him? His wisdom was too important to be lost forever. But Lao Zi was determined. Finally, out of compassion, he agreed to leave behind a brief written account of his understanding of the Daoist tradition. He stayed for a few days in the gatekeeper's hut, and there he wrote down the essential insights of his wisdom in eighty-one terse verses. The task completed, he said farewell and disappeared into the wild lands beyond the frontier of civilization. The work that he left behind is what we know as the *Dao De Jing*. The account is purely a story, of course—one of several about how this great work came to be composed—but something like that is not out of the question.

Legend aside, the facts about the author of the *Dao De Jing* present a much more prosaic picture. First of all, due to sharp and stylistic inconsistencies, it would seem likely that there was more than one author of the work. Most modern scholars agree that it is an anthology, a collection of aphorisms, some of which may have been popular for a long time before the *Dao De Jing* was committed to writing. There is general agreement that it was gathered together in the fourth century B.C.E. It is quite possible that there was one principal "gatherer," and it's not unreasonable that we should call this person Lao Zi, whatever his actual name might have been. In the pages that follow, the name *Lao Zi* will be understood to refer to the "author" of the *Dao De Jing*. In any case, he would probably have done his work after the time of *Zhuang Zi* and definitely could not have been a contemporary of Confucius.

Nevertheless, the *Dao De Jing* is to a large degree concerned with the same problem that Confucius addressed, namely, what sort of person is best suited to rule, and how should that person go about ruling his subjects. Like the *Analects*, the *Dao De Jing* is largely addressed to the ruler, offering him many sage, and often ambiguous, pieces of advice. "Ambiguous" is, of course, putting it mildly; translating the *Dao De Jing* into modern languages presents an enormous problem. The Chinese character, an ideogram, does not lend itself to a precise translation; many interpretations are possible. As a result, the various available translations differ from one another to a degree that can only be described as dismaying. Consider the following two examples.

From a recent popular translation by Stephen Mitchell, we have "The Tao is called the Great Mother; empty yet inexhaustible, it gives birth to infinite worlds."[1] In another popular translation, the same verse is rendered thus: "The valley spirit never dies; it is called the Mysterious Female. The entrance to the Mysterious Female is called the root of Heaven and Earth."[2] See what I mean? Here's one more: In the Mitchell translation, verse thirteen begins: "Success is as dangerous as failure. Hope is as hollow as fear." But in the Addis and Lombardo translation, we have "Favor and disgrace are like fear. Honor and distress are like the self." It's not that one is more correct than another. Each is the legitimate translation of its own author, but there is much latitude for individual interpretation (to say the least).

The best way to begin studying this intriguing subject that we call Daoism is to read carefully through the *Dao De Jing*. I strongly encourage you to do that. The rest of this section can serve as an introduction. In it, I give a brief overview of the essential components of the work, selecting some lines from it to illustrate the points being made. But again, this attempts to be nothing more than an introduction to the most enjoyable task of reading the entire work. Let's begin with the word itself, *Dao*.

To attempt to define the meaning of *Dao* is a daunting task because it is another of those concepts, like Brahman, which, *by its very nature*, cannot be put into words. The very first of Lao Zi's statements on the subject declares, "The Dao that can be spoken is not the eternal Dao." But we've been in this spot before, and a little matter like ineffability won't stop us. We must simply remember that "words are like fingers pointing at the moon." Words can be very helpful if we avoid confusing them with the reality of that which we seek to understand. Rather, we should allow words to nudge our consciousness toward the light of understanding. In that vein, consider the following passage from the *Dao De Jing*:

> There was something formless and perfect
> Before the universe was born.
> It is serene; empty; solitary; unchanging; infinite; eternally present.
> It is the mother of the universe.
> For lack of a better name, I call it the Tao.[3]

"For lack of a better name, I call it the Tao." (Sounds like he could have said, "For lack of a better name, I call it Brahman," doesn't it?)* Lao Zi is here alluding to the underlying reality that gives meaning to all that is. Never perceived directly, it is known

---

*Recall that there are two systems for rendering Chinese names and terms into the Roman alphabet. The newer system, the pinyin, is rapidly replacing the older system, the Wade–Giles. I have used pinyin throughout this book. However, since only recently published works are in pinyin, many of the quotations in the text include Wade–Giles spelling. Keep this in mind when you encounter a difference in spelling. (Quotations appear exactly as written.) For example, *Tao* in Wade–Giles becomes *Dao* in pinyin. And *Tao Te Ching* in Wade–Giles becomes *Dao De Jing* in pinyin. The spelling of individuals' names will also change. *Lao Tzu*, for example, becomes *Lao Zi*. This can be confusing, but it is the price we must pay to convert to a much more sensible system.

in its workings, and everything that happens is the working of Dao. Above all, though, the play of Dao is seen to be spontaneous and harmonious. To be in accord with Dao is to be one with it, like the wind and the waving of the wheat field. Now consider these verses:

> The great Tao flows everywhere.
> All things are born from it, yet it doesn't create them.
> It pours itself into its work, yet it makes no claim.
> It nourishes infinite worlds, yet it doesn't hold onto them.[4]

> If you open yourself to the Tao, you are at one with the Tao
> And you can embody it completely. . . .
> Open yourself to the Tao,
> Then trust your natural responses;
> And everything will fall into place.[5]

Daoism is founded on a deep love of nature, a love of the harmony and organic wholeness of nature. Mankind—that is, human society—is seen to be an integral part of the natural order, and as such, human life is potentially a perfect expression of the play of Dao. The currents of human life are one with the currents of the sea, the flight of birds, and the growth of grass and trees. From the movements of the stars to the movements of the tides, all is one awesome harmony—at least, potentially. Humans, unfortunately, have the ability to get out of synch with the harmony of Dao, and when they do, all hell breaks loose. All of the suffering and tribulations of human life are the consequence of human society straying from the "way," the Dao. To the Daoist, restoring humanity's proper harmony within the natural order thus, becomes the only matter of real importance. As with a person who has become gravely ill, restoring health is all that matters.

Thus, in the broad sense, Confucius was in agreement with the fundamental view of Daoism. He accepted without question that human society is one of the things that nature does, and that a healthy human society is one that lives in perfect harmony with the natural order of which it is a part. Confucius would create a system for the proper ordering of society, assuring that only enlightened, selfless men would come to power. In that way, he would reinstitute the harmony that had been lost.

The problem, in the eyes of the Daoists, was the nature of the remedy that Confucius proposed for reestablishing the harmony that had been lost. The Confucian "system" aroused the ire of the Daoists because, basically, they felt that not only did the system fail to restore man to his natural state, but it actually made things worse! The simple, natural life that the Daoists cherished was seen to be smothered in the complex, highly formalized way of the Confucian system.

As mentioned, the *Dao De Jing* opens with the cryptic statement, "The Dao that can be spoken is not the eternal Dao." The entire first verse reads thus:

> The Tao that can be spoken is not the eternal Tao.
> The name that can be named is not the eternal Name.

> The unnameable is the eternally real.
> Naming is the origin of all particular things.

Free from desire, you realize the mystery.
Caught in desire, you see only the manifestations.[6]

Dao is not a something in itself. Although its working is in everything, Dao can't be separated out and examined:

When you look for it, there is nothing to see.
When you listen for it, there is nothing to hear.
When you use it, it is inexhaustible.[7]

Dao, the beginning and the end of everything, is strikingly similar to the concept of Brahman. Consider these verses:

In the beginning was the Tao.
All things issue from it; all things return to it.[8]

All things end in the Tao, as rivers flow into the sea.[9]

The Tao is like a well: used but never used up.
It is like the eternal void: filled with infinite possibilities.[10]

Every being in the universe is an expression of the Tao.
It springs into existence, unconscious, perfect, free;
takes on a physical body, lets circumstances complete it.
That is why every being spontaneously honors the Tao.[11]

We can go on and on saying profound-sounding things about the Dao—it is the metaphysical first principle; it embodies and underlies all Being—but we can never say precisely what it is. The meaning of Dao lies beyond the power of language to describe; it is ineffable. We can only suggest, allude, imply. One must learn to sense the presence of Dao, to grasp it intuitively. Once we grasp the intuitive sense of Dao, we can spontaneously move in harmony with it. To a Daoist, this is what life is all about, moving in harmony with Dao, not in conflict with it.

Dao itself is the first principle. The ongoing *expression* of Dao is called *wu wei* (pronounced woo-way). This wonderful Daoist word refers to the way nature acts—perfectly, spontaneously, not forcing or trying to control anything. In the words of John Blofeld, *wu wei* is "The spontaneous, mindless activity with which nature succeeds most admirably in accomplishing her ends." The way grass grows is *wu wei*, and so is the flowing of a river, the blowing of the wind, and even the crying of a baby.

Literally, *wu wei* means "nonaction," in the sense, of "not forcing," but in the more everyday sense, it suggests flowing freely, going with the current. The natural patternings of nature, such as the grain in wood and the movement of clouds in the sky, are examples of *wu wei*. Note that *wu wei* is not a strictly passive concept; actually, it expresses a lively interplay. "Going with the flow" means far more than simply floating. Dead fish go with the flow; live fish swim against the flow, but they *use the current* to do it. *Wu wei is using the current* to get where you're going, whether this be in the river or in the marketplace.

Consider a person in a motorboat and a person in a sailboat. Each wishes to get from Point *A* to Point *B*. The motorboat roars its way to Point *B*, overpowering everything in its path, and probably gets there faster. But in the process, it has created a general disruption of noise and pollution. The sailboat also reaches Point *B*, but without disrupting anything. It is designed to fit into the natural order of the environment, *going with*, not *going against*, the forces of nature. By skillful handling, the sailor, like the fish, uses the natural currents to get where he wants to go. This example is an excellent metaphor for the basic difference between the modern lifestyle and the Daoist lifestyle. The Daoists would say that sometimes we should stop and ask ourselves if "getting there faster" is really all that important.

Wu wei is the way of living of a man or woman who is in harmony with the Dao—accepting, yielding, always flexible; *wu wei* is more like bamboo than an oak, more like water than a rock. The oak and the rock may *seem* to be much stronger, but in the long run, bamboo and water will win out every time; they can yield and spring back. It is like this:

> To describe this mindless, purposeless mode of life, Chuang Tzu [Zhuang Zi] turns most often to the analogy of the artist or craftsman. The skilled woodcarver, the skilled butcher, the skilled swimmer does not ponder or ratiocinate on the course of action he should take; his skill has become so much a part of him that he merely acts instinctively and spontaneously and, without knowing why, achieves success.[12]

The man or woman whose life is perfectly in harmony with Dao, whose life is an embodiment of *wu wei*, who cares nothing about fame and fortune—such is the one whom the Daoists consider to be a Superior Person. The word that describes such a person is *De*, the second word in the title *Dao De Jing*. *De* is a subtle word that refers to the *power of expression* of Dao. *Wu wei* has to do with the *flow* of Dao; *de* refers to what that flow *produces*. For example, the way grass grows, naturally and spontaneously, is a wonderful expression of *wu wei* in action, but the power of the earth and the seeds to germinate and grow *as grass* is *de*.

The meaning of *de* becomes especially important with regard to human activities. Certainly, the Daoist wishes to live in the spirit of *wu wei*, but how shall that be expressed in the work of daily life? So much that we humans do seems to be in stark conflict with *wu wei*, totally out of harmony with Dao. In Lao Zi's view, it is not technology and civilization *per se* that are at fault; it is their *exaggeration* that leads us astray. The simple life of the craftsperson can be an excellent expression of *de*. The special faculties of human intelligence are not an aberration of nature; human society doesn't have to be in conflict with Dao. The woodworker, the farmer, the child rearer—each working naturally and spontaneously at his or her craft—are fully in harmony with Dao, at least potentially. You might say that *de* is the "virtue" generated by the activity of *wu wei*.

Like the Confucians, the Daoists believed that the solution depended on the fashioning of a "new person," a person of *de*. But the Daoist new person was a far cry from the Superior Man of Confucius. The Daoists would fashion a new person whose lifestyle would be the embodiment of the Daoist philosophy of life. (The new person is really an old person, because Daoists believed that originally man lived in a state of nature in which human society was perfectly harmonious. This state had been lost in the progress of civilization and needed only to be restored.)

So how do we recognize the truly Daoist man or woman? In the *Dao De Jing*, Lao Zi offers many observations on the subject, but always stated in an oblique sort of way. The most foolish mistake of all would be to assume that such an important matter could be reduced to a few words on paper. In fact, it is Lao Zi himself who informs us that "Those who know, don't speak. Those who speak, don't know." That is to say, those who truly understand the Dao exhibit it in the way they live; such a person would never attempt to *explain* it. But, as we have noted many times, words can be useful if they act to stimulate thought and awaken insight. It is in this sense that Lao Zi's observations must be understood.

In the *Dao De Jing*, the truly Daoist person is often referred to as a master, not to be understood in the sense of master and servant, but rather as the master of an art. And the greatest art of all is the art of living. The true "life master," in the Daoist sense, is a very modest person—a modest, cheerful person living an absolutely simple lifestyle. That much seems to be fundamental to the Daoist view of right living:

> The Master has no possessions.
> The more he does for others, the happier he is.
> The more he gives to others, the wealthier he is.[13]

The master may in fact have some possessions—even Lao Zi had his small house and garden (or so we're told)—but they would be only the essentials of life, and most important, he would not be *attached* to material possessions. Attachment, of course, is the key, and like the Buddhist monk, the Daoist man or woman is free from that kind of bondage.

Simplicity in the form of one's lifestyle is fundamental, but so, too, is the way the Daoist master behaves in going about daily life. The Daoist master is completely natural, completely spontaneous; he goes with the flow of life without excessively trying to control it.

Lao Zi clearly preferred a society that was simple and that lived close to the earth. Only in that way could humans avoid the excesses of civilization. But even a very simple society needs some kind of governing leadership, however humble it may be. Government, too, is a craft, an especially important craft because of its broad influence. Only a true master, only a man or woman fully in harmony with Dao, is fit to be a leader. Many of the offerings in the *Dao De Jing* concern the subject of right government. This orientation may be in part a response to the teaching of Confucius; or perhaps more likely, both the teaching of Confucius and the teaching of Lao Zi arose mutually as a response to the discord of the age in which they lived.

Lao Zi was in total disagreement with the Confucian ideal in which the leaders of society constituted an elite class of "superior" men, highly educated and highly refined in their manners. He would have found Thomas Jefferson's views more to his liking. Both men seemed to think of government as, at best, a necessary evil. Both men would have agreed that "That government is best which governs least." Both idealized the agricultural and craft way of life based on small, largely self-sufficient communities. Jefferson strongly disliked and mistrusted the crowded city, the factory, and especially the machinations of high finance. No doubt, Lao Zi would have smiled and nodded in agreement.

Lao Zi's classic comment on the subject of government is found in Verse 60 of the *Dao De Jing*: "Governing a country is like frying a small fish." In other words, leave it alone as much as possible. Too much poking will wreck it. The Daoist leader helps, largely by example, to keep things in their natural channels. He or she does not attempt to control and shape events. The very last words of the *Dao De Jing* sum it up: "By not dominating, the Master leads." In other words,

> The Master doesn't try to be powerful;
> Thus he is truly powerful.
> The ordinary man keeps reaching for power;
> Thus he never has enough.
>
> The Master does nothing, yet he leaves nothing undone.
> The ordinary man is always doing things,
> Yet many more are left to be done.[14]

Lao Zi was well aware of the powerful temptation to use power to control people, but he was also aware of how disastrous that could be:

> When the will to power is in charge,
> the higher the ideals, the lower the results.
> Try to make people happy,
> and you lay the groundwork for misery.
> Try to make people moral,
> and you lay the groundwork for vice.[15]

The secret of success is self-restraint, yielding control, going with the Dao:

> If you want to be a great leader,
> you must learn to follow the Tao.
> Stop trying to control.
> Let go of fixed plans and concepts,
> and the world will govern itself.[16]

The true Daoist master "reigns," but does not "rule." He is a model of the virtue of *de*:

> The Master does his job
> and then stops.
> He understands that the universe
> is forever out of control,
> and that trying to dominate events
> goes against the current of the Tao.[17]

Lao Zi and the Daoists believed that the world could be restored to health and harmony, that the sickness of greed, violence, and human suffering could largely be healed. It all depended on returning to the simple life that is natural to mankind, and the role of the leader was to gently assist this process of reform:

> If powerful men and women could remain centered in the Tao,
> All things would be in harmony.
> The world would become a paradise.
> All people would be at peace,
> And the law would be written in their hearts.[18]

But what if the Daoists were to be successful? What would this Daoist "paradise" really be like? Surprisingly, in the next-to-last verse of the *Dao De Jing*, Lao Zi gives us a most interesting description of that ideal village community—the building block of a healthy social order.

> If a country is governed wisely,
> Its inhabitants will be content.
> They enjoy the labor of their hands,
> And don't waste time inventing labor-saving machines.
> Since they dearly love their homes,
> They aren't interested in travel.
> There may be a few wagons and boats,
> But these don't go anywhere.
> There may be an arsenal of weapons,
> But nobody ever uses them.
> People enjoy their food,
> Take pleasure in being with their families,
> Spend weekends working in their gardens,
> Delight in the doings of the neighborhood.
> And even though the next country is so close
> That people can hear its roosters crowing and its dogs barking,
> They are content to die of old age
> Without ever having gone to see it.[19]

Did Lao Zi really intend that his readers take this passage literally? Perhaps he did, but most likely he did not. It's difficult to believe that a man so profoundly wise and full of worldly experience would propose a social solution that, at least on the face of it, is so naive. He is asking nothing less than that mankind abandon practically everything that we consider to be the "advancements" of civilization and return to the elementary social life of the small agricultural community. The attractions are great, but the disadvantages are also great. Is there to be no light after dark, no books, no travel? One wonders whether Lao Zi didn't have a twinkle in his eye as he penned the line about never in one's life caring to travel even as far as the next village, even though "the people can hear its roosters crowing, and its dogs barking." (Actually, that's not a bad reason to stay home when you think about it.)

That line may provide the key to understanding the whole passage. Perhaps Lao Zi deliberately overstated it—in a way that his contemporaries would find amusing—in order to emphasize his point. The problem he was addressing results from the *overcomplexity* of civilized life. Lao Zi may be highlighting this insight in the reader's mind by dramatically *oversimplifying* the proposed solution. At least, it serves to emphasize how far civilized society has traveled from its original roots, at which time, no doubt, human society had much less difficulty living in harmony with Dao.

Leaving aside specific suggestions, the general tenor of the Daoist philosophy of life comes through loud and clear in the *Dao De Jing.* The "good life" for every man and woman is the perfectly natural life—that is to say, becoming one with the Dao. Such a person does not try to forcibly control his environment or to pile up worldly wealth and honor. These are ignorant delusions that lead inevitably to unhappiness and, all too often, to violence as well. Instead of trying to become great rocks, we are encouraged to become like water—accepting, yielding, moving spontaneously with the currents of nature, "seeking the lowest place." The *Dao De Jing* tells us in many ways that the simple life is the secret of happiness—the simpler, the better. To own nothing is to own everything.

The genuine Daoist man or woman is a very modest person, unrecognized by most people as anything special. He or she asks nothing of life and is content with what life offers. This kind of acceptance of life, this childlike spontaneity—frees the person from the customary anxiety that stifles cheerfulness. It's impossible to imagine Lao Zi, for example, as a somber sort of person. One gets the feeling from reading the *Dao De Jing* that he was often laughing (or at least chuckling). Confucius and Buddha might have been serious types, but Lao Zi?—not likely!

ZHUANG ZI (CHUANG TZU)

Zhuang Zi is a name that is linked closely with that of Lao Zi. It refers both to a man and to the work attributed to him. Historically speaking, we're on more solid ground with Zhuang Zi than with Lao Zi, but not much. The traditional view, which accepted both men as real, placed Zhuang Zi about a century later than Lao Zi, but it is now widely believed that the work we know as the *Zhuang Zi* was actually produced a little before the *Dao De Jing.* Both works, though, were probably produced in the fourth century B.C.E.

Unlike Lao Zi, about whom there is so much uncertainty, Zhuang Zi is presumed to have been a real live individual. As was the custom in his day, he was the founder of a school and had a following of disciples. It was probably some of these disciples who collected the teachings of the master into the book we know as the *Zhuang Zi.* As we have seen several times now, that was a common practice in those days.

Unlike the *Dao De Jing*, which is very terse and cryptic, the *Zhuang Zi* presents a much fuller exposition of Daoist themes. The book is composed in a down-to-earth prose style that reads like a conversation. The *Zhuang Zi* is enjoyable reading, often amusing and full of anecdotes. Zhuang Zi's focus is squarely on the nature of right living.

Unlike Lao Zi and Confucius, Zhuang Zi deals hardly at all with the matter of right government; it doesn't seem to interest him. The right way of living is his theme. Taken as a whole, the *Zhuang Zi* presents a fully developed philosophy of life.

Both Zhuang Zi and Confucius addressed the same question: How can a person find fulfillment and happiness in a world that is often meaningless, ugly, violent, and full of suffering? Zhuang Zi agreed with Confucius that the common response, which is to say, self-indulgence, will not succeed, not even if it is highly refined self-indulgence. To seek to create a little mini-universe of family and friends in which one can tastefully go about satisfying one's desires, safely out of view of the ugly realities of the larger world, is nothing more than a cultivated hedonism; it cannot succeed. Zhuang Zi disagreed, though, with the solution offered by Confucius—that is, the cultivation of *junzi*.

The idea of *junzi*, the "Superior Man," was at the heart of Zhuang Zi's complaint with Confucius. The Confucians envisioned a new ruling elite, based not on birth and wealth, but on demonstrated knowledge and compassion. These modest men would be the selfless leaders of society, cultivating by their example the native goodness that dwells in the hearts of all men and women. To the Daoists this vision was preposterous, and they held it up to ridicule. Man is by nature neither good nor evil, they would argue. If man is naturally good, then he must also be naturally evil; the two concepts are intimately bound together. You can't have one without the other; they are the two sides of one conceptual coin. To the Daoist, the very defining of a "good" man necessarily gives rise to the "evil" man; they arise mutually. "When people see some things as good, other things become bad."

This is a very subtle point, but it is an essential element of the Daoist philosophy of life. It strikes at the human tendency to conceptualize the realities that we encounter in daily life and then substitute the concept for the reality it represents. For example, happiness is a state of mind that we experience from time to time; it is an integral part of certain situations, such as being with a friend or eating a good dinner. To mentally abstract this condition of happiness, as if it were a something in itself, and then make it an object of desire is a fatal mistake. But that's what humans do all the time. "Happiness" thus becomes an external object, as it were; something to be attained, just as "unhappiness" is a *thing* to be avoided. The same can be said for "good" and "evil," and so on. In Zhuang Zi's view this was the problem with Confucius's concept of *junzi*; it was a *concept*! In other words, the problem with seeking to be a man of *junzi* was in the very seeking itself. Confucius, admittedly with the best of intentions, had mistakenly conceptualized the notion of a Superior Man, thus making it an external object that could never be realized. At best, Zhuang Zi would argue, the man of *junzi* would be only a well-behaved, intellectually cultivated person, but never a man of real fulfillment. He would see only the *effects* of Dao, but not its essence.

The central point of Zhuang Zi's teaching, and indeed of Daoism generally, is that fulfillment in life is not to be found by *seeking* it, which in everyday terms comes down to trying to *grasp* it. This inevitably results in an ongoing effort to *control* one's environment, an effort that is ultimately doomed to failure. The effort to grasp and control life creates both a kind of bondage to one's concept of what "the good" is and the desire to achieve it. Fulfillment, however, is to be found, not through seeking the good, but through *not seeking it*, through letting go of the self altogether! Only by letting go of our precious, but phony, conceptual world do we discover real freedom. Awakening to the nature of freedom is the key to understanding the teaching of Zhuang Zi.

All of us acquire a set of values as we grow up. Ordinarily, these are the "conventional values" of the society in which we live, values that were first taught to us when we were children. Having such values seems to be an important part of a successful life; our values shape our goals. But Zhuang Zi would have us unceremoniously discard the entire baggage of conventional values because they are concepts only; they have no corresponding reality in Nature. "Ills are only ills because we recognize them as such." In other words, something is "bad" and therefore makes us unhappy, not because it really is bad in some objective sense, but rather because we have *decided* that it is bad. If at some deep level we decide that having lots of money is good, then it must follow that having very little money is bad. Of course, neither one is objectively good or bad, but once the decision is made and the concept formed, it follows that we will seek to achieve the conceptual reality that we have defined as "the good" and thus, hopefully, be happy. Zhuang Zi maintains that freedom results from completely letting go of the struggle to *achieve* these conceptual goals:

> It is this baggage of conventional values that man must first of all discard before he can be free. Chuang Tzu [*Zhuang Zi*] saw the same human sufferings that Confucius, Mo Tzu, and Mencius saw. He saw the man-made ills of war, poverty, and injustice. He saw the natural ills of disease and death. But he believed that they were ills only because man recognized them as such. If man would once forsake his habit of labeling things good or bad, desirable or undesirable, then the man-made ills, which are the product of man's purposeful and value-ridden actions, would disappear and the natural ills that remain would no longer be seen as ills, but as an inevitable part of the course of life. Thus, in Chuang Tzu's eyes, man is the author of his own suffering and bondage, and all his fears spring from the web of values created by himself alone.[20]

The bottom line is simply this: When the struggle ceases, one is *free* to be in harmony with Dao—and not until then! This is the *natural* state of all things, including humans. When the struggle ceases, one is free to become an embodiment of *wu wei*, not intent on results, not calculating, not making value judgments about everything, not attempting to control one's little world; one can relax and allow him- or herself to be a free and spontaneous expression of the movement of the natural world. In doing this, one will intuitively come to see the magnificent unity of nature. All is one; all is equal. "Things," including myself, have no independent existence or meaning.

Very much at odds with the traditional Western attitude, Zhuang Zi saw no *special* relationship at all between man and nature, or, to be more precise, between the human mind and nature. But far from belittling human nature, the teaching of Zhuang Zi liberates humanity from the self-imposed isolation and loneliness of being some kind of godlike visitor in the universe, surrounded by the natural world, but essentially not a part of it. For Zhuang Zi, humankind is very much a part of the universe, wholly, integrally, voluptuously! It is for that very reason that nothing is to be gained by mentally setting ourselves apart. It's ridiculous to do so. The genuine Daoist does not have to prove to himself that he is a godlike being or that he can conquer nature; he does not have to prove *anything*. He is free to live simply and modestly. He has nothing more to prove than does the grass, and each is splendid just as it is.

Far from seeking to be at the center of things, controlling, governing—even governing righteously, as would the Confucian Superior Man—the genuine Daoist values solitude, sometimes to the point of being a recluse. Above all, the Daoist inclines to a lifestyle that permits the contemplation of nature—not just "woods and wildlife," but that grand order of nature that encompasses all, including the self. The joy derived from this awareness banishes all fear and suffering. Cosmic awareness reduces the trivial problems of life to the point of being meaningless. Even the once monstrous fear of death dissolves in the contemplation of the natural order. Like everything else, death is seen to be a perfectly natural event.

Zhuang Zi was clearly a mystic philosopher. In the *Zhuang Zi*, Daoism is elevated to the level of nature mysticism. John Blofeld, a modern Daoist philosopher, puts it nicely: "I do not see how anyone who has studied his works can doubt that he was well acquainted with states of mystical rapture lying well beyond the frontier of quietist accord with nature."[21] Perhaps this is what Zhuang Zi was referring to when he complained that Confucius did not go far enough—that he saw the *workings* of Dao, but never Dao *itself.*

Inspired by his vision of the unity of nature, the Daoist is thus free to live as a natural man—an embodiment of *wu wei*. This does not mean that the Daoist chooses a life of inaction, of torpor. That would be a misunderstanding of *wu wei*. He is like the grass or drifting clouds only in the sense that the energy of Dao *plays through* him naturally, without forcing or trying to control him. Nature is so beautifully regulated, that once in accord with it, one doesn't have to *do* anything, in the sense of pushing it around. Just go with it, the way the grass grows. Of course, the nature of grass is very different from the nature of man, and therefore, *wu wei* is expressed differently in a human being.

The true Daoist is a skilled artist. His or her instrument might be the keyboard of a piano or the keyboard of a computer, the brush of a painter or the knife of a butcher. It could be anything; the art is in the effortless way the person becomes one with the work; this is *wu wei*. Zhuang Zi tells the story of an old butcher who was so deft at slicing up a carcass, that even though he been doing it for years, he never needed to sharpen his knife. In a similar vein is the venerable old aikido master who looks so frail and never seems to expend any effort, but no attacker can ever lay a hand on him. This is *wu wei* in action. The ultimate art is life itself. When one's daily life becomes an expression of *wu wei*, the perfection of Daoism is achieved.

Like Lao Zi, Zhuang Zi loved the nature of water. Water is so all encompassing, so primal, so strong, yet yielding. The movement of water perfectly reveals the way of nature. Water is powerful; as a glacier or a tsunami, it can crush anything in its path. Yet it is also the most yielding thing in nature, and it always seeks the lowest place. Water is a wonderful example of *wu wei* in action and thus is a favorite metaphor for the Daoist lifestyle. Bamboo is another popular image in Daoism, for the same reason. Like water, bamboo is very strong, but it never tries to force itself; bamboo yields and then springs back.

Yielding is the key, not in the sense of surrendering, but rather in the sense of going with the flow. Bamboo yields to the wind and thus does not break. A sailboat, too, "yields" to the wind and thus reaches its destination. One of the great sailing crafts of modern times was the *Kon Tiki*, an embodiment of *wu wei* in action. In building the *Kon Tiki* and learning how to sail it, Thor Heyerdahl learned much about the meaning of *wu wei*. Commenting on his great adventure, he said, "Among primitive races the golden rule was: Don't resist nature, but yield to her command, and accommodate."

There is a popular story in the *Zhuang Zi* that makes the point beautifully. It's known as "Three in the Morning." A man acquired a small group of monkeys, and he planned to give them four measures of chestnuts in the morning and three in the evening. The monkeys, however, complained loudly when they heard about this, so he changed his plan and gave them three measures in the morning and four in the evening. Now everyone was satisfied. So, what's the moral of the story? It has nothing to do with the irrationality of the monkeys or the cleverness of their keeper. The point is that he was wise enough to see that stubbornly insisting that the monkeys were being unreasonable would solve nothing; he would only become unreasonable himself. Since his goal was to provide the monkeys with adequate nourishment, he was content to yield with regard to the means for achieving it. He became like water seeking the lowest place. So long as he reached the lowest place, he was perfectly willing to yield to the boulder in his path and go around it. The teaching of Zhuang Zi consistently follows the principle of "Three in the Morning."

RELIGIOUS DAOISM

To be human is to be able to think about the future, and thus to be able to worry about it, and thus to yearn for some measure of control over it. We humans have always done that; the evolution of technology, which gives us that measure of control, has been the result. In modern times, the "high priests" of society are the ones who understand and operate our amazing technology. But what about life in the early days? To whom did you turn in times of sickness, death, drought, and all those other worries that cause sleepless nights? Enter the shamans. By one name or another, all human cultures have produced men and women to play the role of the shamans. In early societies, the shamans were believed to have special powers that enabled them to make contact with the spirit world. Since it was customary to ascribe virtually all crises to the activities of spirits, the shaman held the power to influence the course of events. This was especially true with regard to illness, the most common and immediate of problems, but their powers could also be brought to bear in other important situations.

The tradition of shamanism evolved in China from the earliest times. We can assume that in China, as in other cultures, the roots of shamanism stretch far back before the beginnings of recorded history. Shamans would have served the general population in many ways: by contacting the spirit world, foretelling the will of the gods, interpreting omens, interpreting dreams, making rain, and, of course, healing the sick. It was probably as healers that shamans most often served the common people, but they served the aristocrats in other capacities. The aristocrats could afford to focus on other things besides their health; for example, they were especially interested in *divination*, by which is meant the foretelling of future events through the interpretation of omens and oracles. This became a highly refined art in early China. Archeological sites are rich in the tools of the craft, especially what are referred to as "oracle bones." Cracks formed in a heated bone would suggest a pattern that the diviner could allegedly interpret and thereby gain knowledge of a future course of events. The rationale for this practice rested on the belief that everything in the cosmos is interconnected. Everything that happens has an effect on everything else that happens, although that effect is usually too subtle to be seen. The special gift of the shaman enables him to detect its traces.

The other special interest of the aristocracy was longevity. Since, among other things, the shaman was a healer whose powers hopefully resulted in prolonging life temporarily, it was a reasonable step to want to extend those powers to prolong life indefinitely. In response to the longing for immortality that lives in all human hearts, a "science" of longevity developed. This included many elements that would seem pretty strange to us today and probably even seemed pretty strange to a great many in those days as well. There were special diets, potions, charms, breathing exercises, and even unusual sexual exercises. Only members of the privileged class had the necessary wealth and leisure time to pursue those sorts of things, and apparently, many did. By the time of the late Zhou dynasty a secret cult of immortality had developed.

The general picture, then, is of a large, complex society, mostly agricultural, that included a heterogeneous population of shamans. This was a perfectly normal situation; it was the responsibility of the shamans to deal with all those mysterious problems and worries that might somehow have a connection with the spirit world. In a way, the shamans served a religious function. This was an essential part of early Chinese society, and there are those who play such a role even to this day. Most of the things the shamans did were pretty mundane—healing, fortune-telling, etc.—but some of their arts, especially those dealing with the quest for immortality, were more specialized.

So what does all of this have to do with Daoism? Well, it's not exactly clear how it happened, but somehow the lexicon of Daoism was adopted by the shamanistic "religious" element within Chinese society, giving the impression that the two were really one tradition. Undoubtedly, there were some common points, but the Daoism of Lao Zi and Zhuang Zi was clearly distinct from the shamanistic tradition and the cult of immortality. Some would argue that Daoism was hijacked in order to lend respectability to the more decidedly religious tradition. In any case, during the time of the early Han dynasty, as the shamanistic tradition coalesced into something of a native Chinese religion, the terminology of Daoism became widely used. These new "Daoists"—referred to in modern times as Religious Daoists or Magical Daoists—even went so far as to claim spiritual descent from Lao Zi and Zhuang Zi, both of whom were deified. (What would Zhuang Zi have said about that!) Thus, the history of Daoism divides into two quite different traditions; Philosophical Daoism (*Dao Jia*), and Religious Daoism (*Dao Jiao*).

The Han emperors were strongly supportive of *Dao Jiao* (Religious Daoism), being especially interested in the possibilities of personal immortality. They turned their imperial backs on the old-fashioned court shamans, looking instead for guidance from a new group of itinerant "philosophers" known as the *Fang Shi*. These men were far more sophisticated than ordinary country shamans and were specialists in the more occult arts, particularly those associated with the quest for immortality. But they had a problem: In the opinion of many people, all those connected with the immortality cult were nothing but a bunch of charlatans. And it's not hard to see why. Some of their practices were, to say the least, bizarre. H. G. Creel reports, for example, that it was suggested by some that a man seeking immortality should have sexual intercourse with twelve hundred girls sixteen or seventeen years of age. (Seems like it would have the opposite effect, doesn't it?) The *Fang Shi*, above all, needed to bring a little respectability to their profession, and they were the ones most responsible for trying to cover themselves with the mantle of Philosophical Daoism.

Still, I don't want to leave the impression that these men were nothing more than a group of schemers who contrived to steal the name and reputation of others. It's quite possible that they honestly perceived some essential relationship between their teaching and that of Lao Zi and Zhuang Zi. Let's remember that the word *Dao* had wide application in Chinese culture; it was not coined by the Philosophical Daoists. In fact, it was Confucius who first focused on the use of the word. Those who objected to the Confucian system—Lao Zi and Zhuang Zi in particular—emphasized the word *Dao* in order to get it right. You might say that they regarded their teaching as *true* "Daoism," whereas other systems taught a *false* "Daoism." The Dao of the Religious Daoists was close in meaning to that of the Philosophical Daoists and was the foundation of their theoretical system. Dao is the ineffable ground of being and the source of all that is: "From the Tao all the myriad objects derive their being, their illusory separateness being wrought by the interplay of *yin* and *yang*."[22]

Many mistakenly believe that the concepts of *yin* and *yang* were a feature of Philosophical Daoism. The spirit of *yin* and *yang* is indeed implied in the writings of Lao Zi and Zhuang Zi, but the principle was actually enunciated in Religious Daoism, and let's give credit where it is deserved; the principle of *yin* and *yang* has profoundly influenced the development of Chinese philosophical thought and enjoys wide popularity in modern times.

All of nature exhibits a wonderful harmony that results from the interworking of the basic forces of nature, which the Daoists refer to as *yin* and *yang*. The movement of Dao is manifest in the interplay of *yin* and *yang*. Derived originally from the Chinese words for moon and sun, *yin* and *yang* stand symbolically for the dual forces of nature that are the most elementary of all. *Yin*, the passive force, associated with the feminine principle, is the force that maintains and regulates things and events. *Yang*, the active force, associated with the male principle, is the force that initiates action. A modern expression of *yin* and *yang* is energy and entropy. Radiant energy is *yang*; entropy is *yin*. One doesn't exist without the other, nor is anything ever purely an expression of one as opposed to the other. Even male and female are a mixture of the two, in which one is merely dominant. The play of *yin* and *yang* is *always* a mix—a dance, as it were. *Yang* thrusts a volcanic eruption out of the earth. At the same moment, *yin* goes to work, confining the explosion and giving definition to the new mountain that is formed. Over the course of time, patient *yin*, in the form of erosive forces, will gradually wear the mountain back to the level plain from whence it all began.

Everything is like that; you and I are like that. *Yang* keeps trying out new forms of being, and *yin* is always there to gradually dismantle them. Thus does the unfolding of nature progress through time. Eventually, we are told, the force of *yin* will return the entire universe to the state of amorphous dust from which it began. But this is not an ultimate victory of *yin* over *yang*, because *yang* is ever there, ready when the time is right, to start the game all over again with a new Big Bang. (I'm sure you see the similarity between the Daoist concept of *yin* and *yang* and the Hindu concept of the *gunas*. Some things are universal.)

Daoists do not see *yin* as being in *conflict* with *yang*; that is, it's not *yin versus yang*. It is very important to understand this. In the West, we're accustomed to seeing life in terms of great dichotomies—good versus evil, man against nature. The superior force must *win out* over the inferior. This is not the Daoist view at all. *Yin* and *yang complement* each other. They are more like positive and negative than good and evil. The goal is to achieve balance and harmony, not to have one force defeat the other. Thus, to the Daoist, the goal of human life is not to conquer the natural world and bend it to our purposes, but rather to *go with* the natural world, finding the "way" that achieves harmony with the whole. What a world of difference there is in these two attitudes!

The ceaseless play of *yin* and *yang* is the subject of the *Yi Jing* (*I Ching*), one of the most intriguing works to come down to us from the civilization of ancient China. The *Yi Jing* (literally, the "Book of Changes") probably evolved out of what was originally a manual of prophecy. It would develop into a guidebook that anyone could use to tap into the traditional wisdom of the culture and thereby acquire a kind of guidance for harmonizing one's life with the movement of *Dao*.

The *Yi Jing* consists of sixty-four sections, each of which has a name—such as "Following" or "Deliverance"—and a short commentary dealing with the subject denoted by that name. (It is traditional to ascribe many of the commentaries to Confucius, but it is almost certain that they were produced several centuries after his life.) The commentary is written in the form of (usually cryptic) personal advice and requires skillful interpretation. One approaches the *Yi Jing* as one would a sage or an oracle: to receive its guidance. The advice may be in the form of an answer to a specific question or, more likely, general guidance relevant to harmonizing one's life with Dao.

There is a precise, time-honored method for consulting the *Yi Jing*. A simplified method involves the use of three coins, but the classic method employs a bunch of fifty yarrow stalks—lightweight strawlike sticks. These are cast onto the ground, and from the random arrangement that forms, a precise pattern of lines can be derived. Lines are either solid or broken (— or – –). Solid lines represent *yang*, the male principle, broken lines *yin*, the female principle. Three lines, stacked one above the other, are called a trigram. A pair of trigrams forms a hexagram. Given the various combinations of broken and unbroken lines, sixty-four different hexagrams are possible. Thus it is that each hexagram corresponds to one of the sixty-four sections of the *Yi Jing*. It then remains only to look up the appropriate section and apply its commentary to the stated question. The process gets a bit more complicated than that, but in essence, that's all there is to it. The art, of course, is in the interpretation. *That* calls for real wisdom.

Defenders of the *Yi Jing* argue that it is in no way to be confused with fortune-telling or fortune cookies; it is not magic, not a Chinese version of the ouija board. The *Yi Jing*, they maintain, evolved out of the same worldview that produced the "oracle bones" in ancient times; it is a conviction that the entire cosmos is one interconnected whole. One part affects all parts. The human mind is an internal state that reflects the external state of the universe. The sagely advice of the *Yi Jing* prods the mind to bring forth solutions to the seeming dilemmas of daily life. The hexagram is something like a Rorschach blot; the individual's own struggle for meaning, together with the ancient wisdom contained in the text, creates the guidance. As one author puts it,

> Through studying the changing lines and developing ourselves accordingly, we are able to make our lives complete. The I Ching, therefore, is a lantern through the hidden world that underlies our everyday lives. In counseling us it does not take over our self-direction, it leaves us entirely on our own. It does not spell out right and wrong as a religion does; instead, it draws on our inner knowledge of what is good and reinforces this.[23]

In addition to Dao and *yin/yang*, there is a third fundamental element in the theoretical basis of Religious Daoism: the concept of *ji* (*chi*). The Daoist *ji* is similar to the Hindu concept of *prana*; both refer to a vital energy that permeates all of space and is responsible for life. As with *prana*, the amount, or fullness, of *ji* can vary in a given individual. The greater the fullness of *ji*, the stronger are the health and vitality of that person; the depletion of *ji* was believed to result in sickness and, ultimately, death. Given this belief, it's easy to see why followers of Religious Daoism gave much attention to practices that were designed to increase and retain healthy levels of *ji*. In the context of Religious Daoism, *ji* was believed to result from the interplay of *yin* and *yang*, at least under the right conditions. Therefore, a study of the operation of *yin* and *yang* could lead to an understanding of how to generate and control *ji*. Here, too, there is an interesting similarity to Hindu practices, particularly Hatha and Tantric Yoga.

This brings us back to that most important and fascinating aspect of Religious Daoism: the quest for immortality. Given that vital energy is identical to *ji*, and that *ji* could be controlled (or so they believed) through an application of perfect understanding of the operation of *yin* and *yang*, it was predictable, to say the least, that certain of the *Fang Shih* would seek to become experts in the art of extending life. What began as an interest in extending life became an all-out effort to find the secret of immortality.

There seemed to be no question about the real possibility of immortality. It was widely accepted that some humans did in fact achieve the state of immortality and that these lucky ones lived an Elysian sort of life, forever young and happy, in places distant from the hurly-burly of ordinary life in China. Some lived atop mountains far to the west, but the most fortunate of all dwelt in the "Isles of the Blessed," enchanting mountainous islands located somewhere in the eastern sea:

> During the reigns of Kings Wei and Hsuan of Ch'i, and King Chao of Yen, the practice began of sending men out to sea in search of the three sacred mountains, . . . reportedly not very far away from men. Unfortunately, just as the men are about to reach the shores, the boats are swept back and away by the wind. In earlier times, some people actually managed to reach them: there, the Blessed and the drug that prevents death can be found; there, all things, birds, and four-footed animals are white, and the palaces are made of gold and silver. When these people were just short of the mountains, they could see them from afar like a cloud. When they arrived, the three sacred mountains were washed away by the waves. In short, no one has ever been able to land there. There is not one of the rulers who would not like to have gone there.[24]

Three important elements are discussed in this passage. First, there is a matter-of-fact statement regarding the reality of these islands of the immortals. Second, several Chinese emperors sponsored searches for the islands. Third, there is a reference to "the drug that prevents death." Apparently, immortality could be had by ingesting a drug. What wonderful news that must have been! The only problem was, what drug? Was it a naturally growing plant, like soma? Was it common or rare? In that day—as would certainly be the case in this day too—the belief that immortality could be had through basically chemical means stimulated a passionate interest in identifying or creating the wonderful substance. The emperors may not have been any more passionate about it than anyone else, but they had the means to sponsor what promised to be difficult research. Thus was born the fascinating field of Chinese alchemy.

The pseudoscience of alchemy has a very interesting history, and there is much misinformation about the subject. It became a highly developed field in European civilization as well as in China. European alchemists are best remembered for their tireless effort to find the "philosopher's stone," the secret substance that would enable them to transmute common lead into gold. Chinese alchemists focused more on discovering the secret concoction that would forever banish the waning of *ji*.

Modern scholars divide the history of Chinese alchemy into two great parts: "external" alchemy and "internal" alchemy. Internal alchemy developed later and, in some ways, amounted to an almost metaphorical application of the procedures of external alchemy. (We will get to that in just a bit.) The original alchemists—the external alchemists—were so named because they put their faith in a substance, external to the body, which possessed properties that, when ingested, would confer immortality on the subject. The search for this elixir of life resulted in some pretty amazing concoctions, one of which led to the serendipitous discovery of gunpowder. An alchemist, having mixed some honey with saltpeter (potassium nitrate) and sulfur, accidentally touched a flame to the mixture. In the dazzling display that followed, the first example of fireworks was born. The result was even better when powdered charcoal was substituted for honey. For a long time, this amazing invention was used only for pyrotechnic displays. Later, particularly in the West, its potential for a much deadlier use was realized. Isn't it ironic that a recipe intended to confer immortality should end up conferring so much mayhem and death?

The principal alchemical text, the *Zandonji* (*Tsan-tung-chi*), listed a large number of substances that were thought to hold promise in the quest for immortality. Among these substances were lead, mercury, cinnabar (they especially loved cinnabar), sulfur, zinc, nickel, gold, and silver. These and other chemicals were carefully mixed and tried out on the eager subjects. One can only imagine the effect such a witch's brew would have on the poor victim. Needless to say, there were many deaths. Lacking a supply of laboratory rats, alchemists sometimes tested the various elixirs on condemned criminals. (There is no record of any having achieved immortality.)

The embarrassing paucity of success and the equally embarrassing ampleness of failure led to a growing lack of confidence in alchemy. By the time of the late Han, alchemy had all but died out. But it would experience a strong revival during the Tang dynasty, which followed the Han. A new development generated a lot of interest, especially among the Tang emperors, who were eager to fund a new program of research. What had them so excited was "the pill." It was believed that, under the right conditions, a small pellet would form naturally in certain rocks, and the pellet was in fact the long-sought-for "immortality pill." The only problem was that this natural process was extremely rare. It occurred only in stones that had absorbed *yin* and *yang* vapors in the form of exactly the right amounts of sunshine and moonlight. Worse, it was a process that took 4,320 years to complete. During this time there was a slow transformation of lead and mercury into cinnabar. The outcome was the crystallization of a tiny gold-colored nugget: the pill!

Understandably, given the complexity of the process and the time it required, Mother Nature wasn't likely to produce much in the way of immortality pills. But not to despair: Alchemy could rise to the challenge and synthesize the desired substance under "laboratory" conditions. All that would be necessary would be to simulate natural conditions in the laboratory and, of course, to speed up the process significantly. The heart of the procedure was a special cauldron, which had to be designed in such a way that it could function both as a furnace and a cooling chamber. It was necessary to duplicate the *yang* heat of the sun and the *yin* cooling of moonlight. Fire and water represent the activities of the sun and moon and so would be used alternately in a carefully balanced fashion. All of these machinations, of course, had to be timed precisely, in accordance with a very complex schedule that simulated the movements of the sun, moon, and stars. Further, it was essential that the ingredients be mixed with great precision. Even a tiny mistake could ruin the whole batch, to say nothing of what it did to the body of the hopeful imbiber. Mistakes did occur, but even if they didn't, the result was a poisonous elixir whose effects were far more likely to confer death than immortality on the poor subject. "Many poisonings did occur. People who swallowed the pills of immortality suffered slow poisoning that led to the failure of the liver and spleen. Other fatal effects included breakdown of the nervous system and various forms of mental disorder. After three hundred years of failure in research and experimentation, external alchemy declined."[25]

After many deaths, including those of some Tang emperors, and no successes at all, faith in the power of alchemy definitely began to wane. But the desire for long life, and possibly even immortality, did not wane at all. It merely looked for a new way to achieve its goals. During the Song dynasty, which followed the Tang, a whole new approach to alchemy began to take form. We call it "internal" alchemy to distinguish it from the older, discredited "external" kind. Instead of relying on something derived from outside the body—a pill, for example—internal alchemy worked with the naturally occurring *internal* condition of the body. Specifically, the new alchemists focused their interest on the body's store of *ji*: vital energy.

There was a range of opinion regarding a person's endowment of *ji*. Some believed that people are born with their full supply of *ji*, like a car starting out with a full tank of gasoline. Death results when the tank runs out, so the longer one can make *ji* last, the longer life will be. Those who followed this belief recommended "stillness" as the greatest of virtues. Since any kind of activity—even sensory activity—depleted *ji*, it was in the interest of long life to avoid all kinds of activity as much as possible. Some emperors went so far as to wear an unusual headdress with fringes of tiny pearls covering the ears and eyes. This practice reduced sensory involvement, and thus—or so they believed—added years to their lives.

More common was the belief that it was possible to actually replenish *ji*, although that was certainly not an easy thing to do. Activity did indeed reduce the original supply of *ji*, and some could simply leak away through bad mental and physical habits, but special steps could be taken to restore one's *ji* and thus achieve longer life, and maybe—just maybe—it was still possible for the really dedicated to achieve immortality. (The hope, at least, never dies.) Followers of this approach developed a body of practices designed not only to maximize the body's store of *ji*, but also to facilitate its optimum distribution and use by the body and mind. Religious Daoism's earlier interest in yogic techniques experienced a strong revival. Diet, for example, became a matter of prime importance, as did various breathing exercises. So, too, did a variety of Tantric-like exercises in sexual yoga. It was believed, for example, that sexual arousal increased *ji*, but, at least for the male, that increase was more than dissipated in the act of ejaculation. Therefore, as in Tantra, a veritable science developed around techniques for generating arousal, but retaining semen. Some practices, such as the last mentioned, would appear to be outlandish in the eyes of modern health science, but much of what these stalwarts practiced did undoubtedly contribute to better health and therefore to longer life.

The techniques of external alchemy were not entirely forgotten. Indeed, in a way, they were transposed metaphorically into the practices of internal alchemy. The body itself became the alchemist's cauldron. The *yin* and *yang* of fire and water became the interplay of body heat and perspiration. As in the cauldron, the process carefully burned away the impure dross, leaving only the "golden elixir" of pure *ji*.

The scope of Religious Daoism broadened over time as it evolved into something more like a genuine religion. The heavy emphasis on shamanistic practices continued, but there was room for other things as well. To some degree, the teachings of Philosophical Daoism, emphasizing man's relationship to the natural world, were integrated in fact as well as in name.

Religious Daoism borrowed heavily from Buddhism, its rival, but it gave as much as it took. Daoism was destined to exert a tremendous influence on the development of Buddhism in China. The easy naturalness of Daoism would help to bring Buddhism "down to earth," to ground Buddhism more deeply in a love of nature and, especially, in a love for the need of a healthy human society to live in harmony with the Natural Order. Daoism helped to soften some of the still-too-sacred and ritualistic edges of Indian Buddhism; in other words, it made Buddhism more "human." This would become especially obvious in the tradition we know as Chan Buddhism, the Chinese predecessor of Zen Buddhism.

Buddhism was not the only beneficiary of Daoist influence; practically everything in Chinese culture has been touched by it. We see the influence of Daoism strongly in the traditional art of China. Love of nature and the harmonious relationship between man and nature have been major themes in Chinese art over the ages, and that love and harmony have been extended to other cultures of East Asia.

The influence of Daoism can be seen in the modern world as well. The environmental movement has been strongly touched by the values of Philosophical Daoism (or Nature Daoism if you prefer), and there is more than a little of the programs of Religious Daoism to be found in the New Age movement, including the obsessive interest in exercises and elixirs that promise long and healthy life.

And what of the search for immortality? Did it finally just die out? Not really, but it is truly said that "The only thing immortal about the search for immortality is the search itself." That search finally tired of magical elixirs and pills. At least for some, immortality came to have more of a metaphysical meaning:

> An immortal is one who, by employing to the full all his endowments of body and mind, by shedding passion and eradicating all but the simplest and most harmless desires, has attained to free, spontaneous existence. . . . He has undergone a spiritual rebirth, broken free from the shackles of illusory selfhood and come face to face with his 'true self,' aware that it is not his personal possession, being no other than the sublime undifferentiated Dao! . . . Death, when it comes, will be for him no more than the casting off of a worn out robe. He has won to eternal life and is ready to plunge back into the limitless ocean of pure being![26]

The preceding words are from Zhuang Zi himself. It is interesting and fitting that he would have the final word on the meaning of immortality. In the final analysis, the true "immortal" turned out to be Zhuang Zi's sage.

Notes

1. Stephen Mitchell, trans., *Tao Te Ching* (New York: HarperCollins, 1988). Translation copyright © 1988 by Stephen Mitchell. Reprinted by permisssion of HarperCollins Publishers, Inc., TTC #6.
2. Stephen Addis and Stanley Lombardo, trans., *Tao Te Ching* (Indianapolis: Hackett, 1993), TTC #6.
3. Mitchell, *Tao Te Ching*, #25.
4. *Ibid.*, #34.
5. *Ibid.*, #23.
6. *Ibid.*, #1.
7. *Ibid.*, #35.
8. *Ibid.*, #52.
9. *Ibid.*, #32.
10. *Ibid.*, #4.
11. *Ibid.*, #51.
12. Burton Watson, trans., *Chuang Tzu* (New York: Columbia Univ. Press, 1964), p. 6.
13. Mitchell, *Tao Te Ching*, #81.
14. *Ibid.*, #38.
15. *Ibid.*, #58.
16. *Ibid.*, #57.
17. *Ibid.*, #30.
18. *Ibid.*, #32.
19. *Ibid.*, #80.
20. Watson, p. 4.
21. John Blofeld, *Taoism: The Road to Immortality* (Boston: Shambala, 1985), p. 46.
22. Quoted in Blofeld, p. 1.
23. Carol K. Anthony, *A Guide to the I Ching* (Stowe, MA: Anthony, 1988), p. xix.
24. Quoted in Max Kaltenmark, *Lao Tzu and Taoism* (trans. from French by Roger Greaves) (Stanford, CA: Stanford Univ. Press, 1965), p. 118.
25. Eva Wong, *The Shambala Guide to Taoism* (Boston: Shambala, 1997), p. 75.
26. Quoted in Blofeld, p. 16.

Study Questions

1. In what way is the Chinese concept of Dao similar to the Indian concept of Dharma?

2. The very first line of the *Dao De Jing* declares, "The Dao that can be spoken is not the eternal Dao." What does this mean?

3. What was it about the Confucian system that was attacked by the Daoists?

4. What do you suppose Lao Zi meant by saying that "Governing a country is like frying a small fish"?

5. What did Zhuang Zi mean by saying that the Confucians would see only the effects of Dao, but not its essence?

6. What is the point of the story known as "Three in the Morning"?

7. What is the relationship between Philosophical Daoism and Religious Daoism?

8. What role do the concepts of *yin* and *yang* play in Daoist thinking? Do you see a parallel here to any aspect of Hindu philosophy?

9. How would you describe the essential difference between external alchemy and internal alchemy?

10. In what important ways has the tradition of Daoism influenced Chinese culture, and in what ways does it continue to influence the modern world?

8

Shinto

A vast crescent of islands extends along the northern and western rim of the Pacific Ocean, stretching all the way from the Aleutians to Australia. The archipelago of Japan, a complex of more than three thousand islands, lies roughly in the central section of this crescent. Most of the islands of Japan are quite small; the four largest make up almost all of what we normally think of as Japan. By far the largest of the four main islands is Honshu. Tokyo, the modern capital of Japan, and Kyoto, the historic capital, are located on Honshu. South of Honshu lie the islands of Kyushu and Shikoku. Together with Honshu, they partially enclose an area of ocean known as the Inland Sea. Throughout much of Japan's history, the Inland Sea area has been a center of economic and cultural life.

Geologically speaking, Japan is new land. It and many of the other island groups exist because of the subduction of ocean plates in the western Pacific. The resultant volcanic activity slowly, but steadily, creates new real estate. For this reason, Japan is a very mountainous country, with many volcanic mountains, such as Mount Fuji, the symmetrically beautiful symbol of Japan. The tectonic movement is also the reason for Japan's being earthquake country. The mountains are relatively young and hence tend to be steep, with deeply cut valleys and fast-rushing streams. Such country can be very beautiful and can provide excellent locations for Zen monasteries that like to be tucked away in the wilderness, but it presents a real challenge to a farming population. Only about fifteen percent of Japan is flat enough to be good land for agriculture.

Long before our human ancestors became interested in agriculture, though, some of them were already living in the islands we know as Japan. Evidence of human occupation extends far back into prehistory. Perhaps the earliest migrants arrived in Japan on foot. From time to time in the geologic past, the ocean level has been low enough to expose dry land between Korea and southern Japan. For the most part, however, the modern Japanese are descended from a mainland people who migrated to the southern part of Japan in a series of waves beginning in the third century B.C.E. This sporadic migration continued for about four centuries. The newcomers had to do battle with a relatively primitive people already in possession of the land. We know these original dwellers as the Ainu. Little by little the Ainu were pushed back, but never entirely exterminated. Today, descendants of the Ainu can be found on the northern island of Hokkaido. The newcomers, though, took possession of all of the good land in the south, and by the beginning of the fourth century C.E., they had pretty much settled down to the task of building a new culture.

And build they did! The modern culture of Japan is the direct descendant of what was begun more than two millennia ago. All modern cultures have roots that extend back into ancient times, but unlike most others, Japanese culture still has a living link with that ancient past: the tradition known as Shinto.

Western travelers are often surprised to discover how strong a role Shinto plays in the life of modern Japan. Far from being a quaint old tradition, largely forgotten, the visible presence of Shinto is ubiquitous. Many thousands of Shinto shrines are scattered throughout Japan, and they play an ongoing role in the lives of the local communities that they serve. In addition, the Japanese people celebrate numerous annual festivals that are basically Shinto in nature. The imperial family, the absolute center of Japanese culture, derives its very meaning from the tradition of Shinto. The core of Japanese culture, Shinto unifies and defines the Japanese nation, but saying what it *actually is* is no easy task.

One of the first Europeans to write about Japan was the German traveler Engelbert Kaempfer, who visited the islands in the late seventeenth century and was greatly impressed by most of what he found there. Shinto, though, didn't interest him at all. He brushed it off as "the old religion of idol worship." Our knowledge of the Shinto tradition has come a long way since Engelbert's time. No one today would describe it as mere "idol worship," but most would agree that, broadly speaking, Shinto is a native Japanese religion. I say *broadly speaking*, though, because Shinto is far from being a perfect fit into our customary definition of "religion." Consider the following list of exceptions: Shinto has no distinct founder, no special scriptures, no revelation, and not even a special religious philosophy or moral code. Perhaps most important of all, in Shinto there is no worship of a supreme godhead.

So, on what basis can Shinto be defined as a religion? Let's begin with the word itself. The "shin" of *Shinto* is derived from an old word, *jin* (or its alternative form, *shin*), which carried the meaning of deity, or god. And the "to" of *Shinto* is a descendant of the Chinese *dao*, meaning "way." Thus, in its simplest form, Shinto means "way of the gods." This takes some explaining, though, because, among the Japanese people of ancient times, the concept of divinity was definitely not limited to celestial gods and goddesses with superhuman powers. Indeed, there were some of those—many, in fact—but a great many divine beings were not of humanlike form at all. Trees, mountains, and rivers could be divine beings, and so, too, could natural events, such as thunderstorms and earthquakes. Many animals were seen as divine. In fact, anything at all that held the power to inspire a sense of awe and mystery was easily seen as possessed of the divine nature. The spirits of such things, whether earthly objects or heavenly beings, were known as *kami*. "It may be said that 'kami' is essentially an expression used by early Japanese people to classify experiences that evoked sentiments of caution and mystery in the presence of the manifestation of the strange and marvelous."[1]

Note that it was not the *thing itself* that was the kami; *kami* refers to the *spirit* of the thing, that which gives it its awe-inspiring character. The kami, as spirit, resides within the place or thing, but is capable of moving about freely. Aspects of an earlier animism peek through clearly in developing Shinto. Veneration of the kami, through ritual and sacrifice, was an important part of life among the early people of Japan. Thus, we might more properly define Shinto as "the way of the kami," recognizing that "way" here refers to the proper observance of ritual veneration.

Due to the close association of kami with natural phenomena, Shinto is sometimes described as a "nature religion." There's more than a little truth to this suggestion. The Japanese have always felt a profound love for the beauty of nature, and it is no wonder; they inhabit an island world of magnificent natural beauty. That they would develop a sense of religious awe for the wonders of nature and a feeling of closeness to it all was perhaps inevitable.

THE SHINTO CREATION MYTH

But where did it all come from in the first place? Like people in all parts of the world, the Japanese of early times developed stories to explain the act of creation and the origins of their race. These mythic accounts are the foundation stones of Shinto; it is well worth our time to look at them closely. Naturally, there is frustratingly little in the way

The famous Torii Gate at Miajima on the Inland Sea, Japan. (P. Bresnan)

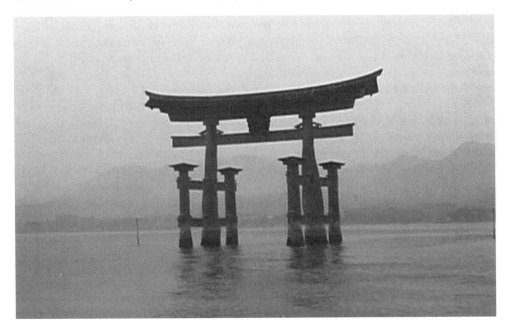

of dependable historical records about those early times, but we do have some records, and they are sufficient to give us a reasonably comprehensive picture.

Our earliest glimpses into Shinto come from excavations of third-century burial tumuli, in which we find some artifacts, but not much that is useful to the historian; indeed, there are no written records at all. The earliest written records derive from about the same time, but come from China, not Japan. The chronicler Wei Zhi made reference to the Land of Wa, an island kingdom located "in the middle of the ocean." He said that it was then ruled by a female shaman named Himiko, who occasionally sent tribute-bearing envoys to China. Further, he stated that the people of Wa engaged in the cultivation of rice and made fine linen and silk. It's not a lot of information, but it's a start. Much more helpful are the earliest Japanese sources, the *Kojiki*, written in 712 C.E., and the *Nihon Shoki*, from about 720 C.E Both of these were chronicles that recorded history beginning in the fifth century and also the important events of the mythic "history" before that time. From these sources, we can put together, in broad outline at least, the mythic foundation upon which Shinto was built.

The universe came into existence as a result of the mating of the kami representing the basic forces of nature, a sort of Japanese version of *yin* and *yang*. The mating also resulted in the creation of the twelve primary kami, who resided in a heavenly realm. The last to be created of this twelvesome were Izanagi, who would become the Sky Father, and Izanami, who was something of an Earth Mother. Before there was any land, the heavenly realm drifted serenely above a vast dark ocean. One day, Izanagi and Izanami strolled out from the heavens onto what is described as a "floating bridge," possibly a rainbow, from which they could peer down into the deep waters below. Izanagi plunged his bejeweled spear into the ocean, and each time he pulled it back, drops of brine would fall onto the water, where they would coalesce into beautiful islands. In this way, the islands of Japan were said to have formed. Enchanted by what they had done, Izanagi and Izanami descended to their new island creations, where, in the privacy of the forested mountains, they passionately made love. As a result of their lovemaking, more islands formed, and also more kami were born.

The last of the kami to be born was Fire. It was a terribly difficult and painful birth, and Izanami died as a result. Izanagi was overwhelmed with grief, and like Orpheus, he wandered off to the underworld in search of his lost love. He eventually found Izanami, but was ordered not to look at her, as by this time the decay of death had made her grotesque. Izanagi could not control his excitement; he disobeyed the order and was horrified by what he saw. In the next moment, furious kami drove him from the underworld. Izanagi fled to a nearby river, where he did two important things. First, he renounced his connection with Izanami, symbolically confirming the essential separation between the world of the living and that of the dead. Second, he washed himself thoroughly in the river water, symbolically purifying himself after being defiled in the underworld. This is regarded as the beginning of a rich tradition of purification rituals in Japanese culture. As Izanagi stood in the river, three more kami were created from his act of washing: the kami of the stars, of the moon, and of the sun.

The kami of the sun, the "sun goddess," was named Amaterasu and would become the most important of all the celestial deities in Japanese culture. Izanagi and Izanami played the role of the first parents, but it is Amaterasu that the Japanese people most revere. Ninigi-no-Mikoto, the grandson of Amaterasu, descended to Earth and introduced the all-important cultivation of rice, the physical foundation of Japanese civilization. Ninigi-no-Mikoto was also the direct ancestor of Jimmu Tenno, the legendary first emperor of Japan, thus establishing the imperial family's claim to divinity. The emperor is not the only divine offspring, though. We are told in the *Shinsen Shojiroku*, the Record of Surnames compiled in the eighth century, that the founders of 402 clans also trace their lineage to Ninigi. Thus could virtually all of the Japanese clans claim some measure of divine descent. In an interesting way, it is fundamental to Japanese belief that humanity (or at least the Japanese part of it) is *descended from* the gods, not *created by* them.

This origin myth provided the Japanese people with the story of their own beginning. It established a logical explanation for order coming out of the primeval chaos and also established a divine connection for the nation. That divine connection would continue forever in the special relationship between the people of Japan and the various kami of the land and sea. Shinto developed specifically to honor and perpetuate this tradition.

THE SHINTO SHRINE AND FESTIVAL

The most visible expression of Shinto is the shrine, *jinja* in Japanese. The shrine is the sacred place where the kami dwells. There, it can be directly approached and venerated. In the earliest days, the kami shrine was simplicity itself. Typically, it would be a natural place of some sort—a great tree, perhaps, or a waterfall—that the local people believed to be a source of spiritual power. Often, such kami places were located far back in the mountains; a remote spot was favored, mysterious and full of natural beauty. Those early shrines would be marked off with nothing more than a pile of rocks, or sometimes an ornamental rope to which strips of cloth would be tied. There, the community would gather from time to time in order to venerate the kami with ritual and sacrifice. Its goodwill was understandably a matter of high importance.

The spread of agriculture changed all that. Now, instead of the people going to the kami, the kami had to come to the people. More specifically, it was important for the kami to journey to the rice fields, especially at certain critical times, such as the time of the harvest. It thus became customary to build some sort of simple, temporary abode for the kami to dwell in while it was in attendance. This custom spread throughout all of Japan and is the background out of which the national system of Shinto shrines grew. Today, there are some 18,000 Shinto shrines in Japan, tended by approximately 22,000 Shinto priests. Most of these shrines are relatively modest affairs; only about 2,000 would be classified as major sites.

The most important of all is the great shrine at Ise, on the seacoast of southern Honshu. In an odd sort of way, Ise is both one of the oldest and one of the newest

Worshipper addressees a Kami at a Shinto Shrine. (P. Bresnan)

of Japan's many great shrines. It was constructed more than thirteen centuries ago, but it is completely torn down and rebuilt every twenty years. The plan, though, is meticulously copied each time, so that the Ise we see today is faithful in appearance to the original. The next rebuilding will be in the year 2013 C.E. Ise is the official shrine of the imperial family. By long-standing custom, the emperor announces important matters of state to the gods at Ise. New prime ministers are introduced to the gods at Ise, and even high-ranking sumo wrestlers dedicate themselves at the great shrine.

Although some evolution was inevitable, there has been a conscious effort through the ages to keep the nature of the shrine as much as possible as it was in the early days, and therein lies its special beauty. There is variety—sixteen subtly different styles of architecture are recognized—but the basics are common to all shrines, great and modest. For one thing, only natural materials may be used. For the wooden structures, this means cypress logs, shaped only with the use of hand tools. No metal parts or nails are used; they were not available in the early days. The carpentry is an amazing art: Complex joinings not only hold the parts together, but are able to slide against one another during an earthquake.

The fully developed Shinto shrine consists, first of all, of a fenced enclosure, usually rectangular, within which are one or more wooden buildings. This is a sacred precinct, and the visitor is reminded of that right at the entryway, which, not uncommonly, is flanked by two guardian stone lions. These fierce-looking beings, introduced from China in the ninth century, examine all who enter. Almost immediately, the path passes under the *torii*, the crossbar gateway that has almost become a symbol for Japanese culture. Often painted red, the two upright posts are joined by one or two crossbars. We are accustomed to seeing a gentle curve in the upper piece; this, too, is a Chinese introduction and would not have been found in the early days. As with so much else, we can only guess at the original intention. Quite possibly, the earliest torii were roosts for sacred birds and were meant to keep evil spirits away.

If means permit, the shrine will support two buildings: the *haiden* and the *honden*. In smaller shrines, the functions of the two are combined in one building. The haiden is the more public building. Referred to as the "worship sanctuary," it usually has an open front that the worshipper can approach for prayer and for making offerings. To get the attention of the kami, the worshipper will clap his or her hands and ring a bell by pulling on an ornate rope. He or she will then bow deeply and offer the prayer. The haiden is also the place where the Shinto priest conducts ordinary ceremonies.

The honden is more hidden from public view. It is the "holy of holies," the place where the kami dwells. Only priests are allowed inside the honden, and then only to tend the *shintai*—the *sanctum sanctorum*, the kernel at the center, the actual object within which the kami takes up residence. The shintai is a symbolic representation of a particular deity. It may be a stone, a scroll, or perhaps a sword. Bronze mirrors often serve the purpose. The shintai is always elaborately wrapped, usually in silk and linen. It is so sacred that not even the Shinto priest may gaze upon it. The shintai is the soul of the Shinto shrine.

There are other, less essential items that are likely to be found on the grounds of most shrines. One of these is the "sacred font," usually a natural stone basin filled with clear water intended for a simple purification ritual. The visitor uses a bamboo dipper to pour water over the hands and rinse the mouth before approaching the haiden. Purification is a major theme in Shinto. Another very popular feature of the Shinto shrine is the *ema-den*. An ema is a small wooden tablet on which the visitor writes out a short prayer, usually a request or a thank-you. The visitor then ties the ema to a standing wooden frame. In earlier times, members of the aristocracy often donated a horse to the shrine in thanks for an answer to a prayer. The common people, being unable to afford a horse, adopted the custom of donating instead an ema, a picture of a horse painted on wood. A large shrine may have hundreds of these on display at any given time. The sight is both picturesque and touching. Another common feature of the Shinto shrine is the *toro*, the familiar Japanese stone lantern resting on a stone pedestal. These may line pathways or be placed anywhere on the grounds. As a rule, the lanterns were acquired as gifts.

The Shinto shrine's most basic reason for being is simply to provide a sacred place for the kami to reside and thus a place where the local people can commune with the resident kami. The typical shrine, though, serves other important functions as well, including operating as a center for the performance of certain sacred rituals, such as festivals, rites honoring the major stages of life, and ritual purifications. This last is an extremely important function.

Oharai is the Japanese name for the ceremony whose purpose is to please and soothe the kami. Hopefully, a benign kami will extend its power to make things right. This is especially important in any situation in which there is danger of defilement, which results from contact with any kind of polluting influence, such as death and disease, or even plain old bad luck. Thus, "purification" is a good choice of words. It's not a matter of driving out evil; rather, it is the removal of *tsumi* ("impurity"). The priest beseeches the kami to correct the defilement, restoring natural order and harmony to the world.

There are myriad examples of situations that call for oharai—everything from the profound to the profane. Oharai may be performed at the shrine, or the priest may travel to the place where it is needed. In Japan, it is common to call in the Shinto priest to perform oharai before occupying a new home, an office building, a shop, or even a new car. On July 16, 1969, an oharai ceremony was conducted at the United Nations headquarters on behalf of the Apollo 11 mission when the first humans landed on the surface of the moon.

The ancient ceremony of oharai is conducted by the Shinto priest, dressed in his sacramental vestments. Typically, as he chants aloud, the priest waves the *onusa*, a wand made up of strips of paper, over the person or thing to be purified. The procedure will probably call for ritual washing as well. As anyone who has traveled in Japan knows well, the Japanese are a scrupulously clean people; everyone and everything gets scrubbed thoroughly and often. Undoubtedly, this national passion has roots in the purification ceremonies of Shinto.

Salt plays an important part in oharai. Salt is the symbol of purity. In ancient times, it was believed that salt water was a more efficacious purifier than drinking water. The Shinto priest will sprinkle salt over the thing to be purified, probably several times. Westerners may be familiar with this practice from watching sumo matches on television. Sumo has its roots in Shinto. The ring used in sumo is actually meant to be a replica of a Shinto shrine building. In modern times the uprights have been removed for the benefit of television cameras, but the roof is traditional Shinto and is suspended from above. When entering the ring, the sumo wrestler sprinkles some salt, a traditional Shinto purification gesture. He is, in effect, dedicating the match to the kami, just as Greek athletes in ancient times dedicated their games to their gods.

The traditional use of salt as a spiritual purifier has made its way into many aspects of Japanese life. People attending a funeral are customarily given a small bag of salt to sprinkle around the doorway of their home before entering, so as not to carry the defilement of death into the home. Restaurant owners, after diligently washing their section of sidewalk, often put little mounds of salt on either side of the entryway; thus, no defilement is carried inside. The Shinto scholar Stuart Picken even reports having seen salt sprinkled in the dugout of a Japanese baseball team that was in a prolonged slump.

The festival is another important feature of Shinto. Festivals are a big part of life in Japan. Some are huge productions and go on for several days. It seems that everyone gets involved. Feasting, partying, and endless decorations are the rule. The parade, or rather, the religious procession, is the big event. To the accompaniment of much drumming and cheering, the elaborately decorated floats are hauled down the crowded streets by throngs of boisterous young men. Since most of these festivals are Shinto in origin, one of the floats is special. It comes at the end and carries the kami. A delegation had gone to meet it at a designated spot and is now exuberantly escorting the deity to its home shrine. The kami rides in splendor, hidden deep within its lavishly decorated wagon. It's quite a spectacle! No wonder the traditions of Shinto occupy a special place in the Japanese heart.

The general word for festival is *matsuri* in Japanese. The tradition is deeply rooted in Shinto. Some matsuri are personal—family celebrations marking the important events in a person's life. The big ones, though, involve the whole community and celebrate the important events in the annual calendar. Most festivals have ancient roots and were originally related to the agricultural cycle, especially the spring planting of rice and the fall harvest. The imperial family has always played a major role in these festivals. Traditionally, the emperor plants the first rice seedlings and also harvests the first grains. These are then offered to Amaterasu at Ise.

The greatest festival of the year is *Niiname*, the autumn harvest festival. It is the central event of the Shinto annual cycle, much as Easter is in the Christian calendar. The Niiname festival is essentially a wedding feast, celebrating the marriage of heaven and Earth. The heavenly being represents the male, who descends to Earth to join with the female in order to renew the life that is now being celebrated in the harvest. A tremendous banquet precedes the wedding night "nuptials," for which a new wedding hut has been constructed. Typically, there is much singing, dancing, and drinking.

But things aren't intended to go entirely smoothly. In the traditional Niiname celebration, a "disruptive force" enters the picture. This intruding male, derived out of the Shinto myths, appears on the scene and tries to prevent the marriage from being consummated, obviously so that he can have the bride for himself. He, of course, is eventually defeated, but his intrusion provides all kinds of exciting opportunities for drama. Apparently, at least in ancient times, the village people were much more than mere spectators. The Shinto scholar Robert Ellwood gives us an interesting glimpse into early Niiname customs. He begins with a verse that was intended to be spoken by one of the participants:

> Though it be the night when I make
> Offerings of the early rice of Katsushika
> I will not keep you, darling,
> Standing outside the house.

> Away, you who rattle at my door,
> On this sacred night of new rice-offering.
> When I've sent my man out
> And worship in the house alone.

Ellwood goes on to say, "These poems suggest that on the night of Niiname, the husbands left the house and went out, leaving their wives within to make offerings of new rice. Later, 'mysterious visitors' arrived and banged violently on the doors. Of course these were the menfolk, perhaps disguised as gods and perhaps not at their proper home. No doubt in time they won admittance by proving they were gods, and renewed the seasons with feasting and orgy."[2] (Ellwood neglects to speculate on how these menfolk "proved that they were gods.")

HISTORICAL DEVELOPMENT OF SHINTO

The history of Shinto, like that of Japanese culture in general, is divided into three broad eras: ancient, medieval, and modern. The time that we call ancient was the formative period of Japanese culture. Our knowledge of that time must depend more on legend and myth than on solid history. During ancient times, Shinto was the religion of all the people; it had no rivals.

An enormous change came over the land in the eighth century. For one thing, the influence of Chinese civilization began to be felt strongly in Japan. In the year 710 C.E., an imperial capital, based on the Chinese model, was established at the new city of Nara. In 794 C.E., the court relocated to nearby Kyoto, where it would remain for more than a thousand years. This long period of time, characterized by a feudal organization of society, is known as the medieval period. During the medieval era, Shinto had to cope with a vigorous new rival, Buddhism, which arrived from China by way of Korea. It first appeared in Nara right at the beginning of the era and became very popular with the aristocracy. For a long time, interest in Buddhism was limited only to the feudal aristocracy; the religion of the common people continued to be traditional Shinto. Gradually, however, the influence of Buddhism spread to all classes of society. Interestingly, there was no war between the two ways, only a friendly rivalry. Buddhism in Japan absorbed much from Shinto. (One of Buddhism's great strengths has always been its adaptability.) For one thing, it was not uncommon for Shinto shrines to be included on the grounds of Buddhist temples. Shinto, however, was not greatly changed by its contact with Buddhism. It pretty much continued to go along as before, preserving the ancient ways. Buddhism gained a permanent place in Japanese society *alongside* Shinto; each has its own sphere of interest, and the two coexist peacefully.

Technically speaking, the modern era began with the promulgation of the Meiji Constitution in the year 1889. More realistically, though, the modern era could be said to have begun for Japan in the summer of 1853. In that year, the uninvited Commodore Matthew C. Perry of the United States Navy, in command of a small fleet of eleven warships, sailed into Tokyo Bay and demanded that the Japanese government grant certain trade concessions to his country. To be more precise, he "requested" these concessions and then departed, saying that he would be back in one year's time to receive a reply. Considering the fact that at that time the Japanese were hopelessly far behind the Western powers in military technology, Perry's not-so-subtle show of force was in effect "making them an offer they couldn't refuse." Nor did they. A small package of trade agreements was signed that was the initial wedge used to pry Japan out of its long self-imposed isolation. Commodore Perry's visit to the waters of Tokyo Bay opened an era in Japanese history that would not come to its end until another uninvited visitor from the American military appeared in the sky over Hiroshima slightly less than a century later.

Perry's visit was the catalyst that started the juices flowing again after centuries of relative stagnation in Japan. The entire society was seized with a passionate determination to remake the culture of Japan in the Western image, at least to the degree that was necessary in order to catch up and be able to compete as an equal with the highly aggressive Western powers of the nineteenth century. The rapid absorption of Western technology, and Western culture generally, was a truly amazing phenomenon. It can only be compared to the similarly ravenous appetite for all things Chinese that had occurred in Japan back in the Nara Period of the eighth century. The initial preoccupation understandably focused on military technology. Underdeveloped Japan was in a terribly precarious situation; the imperialist-minded Western powers, hungry for colonial possessions, had gobbled up nearly the entire globe. Other than Thailand, which was a special case, Japan was the only Asian nation to have escaped the colonial net of the Western powers. After Perry's rude interruption, it was obvious that time was running out.

The Japanese response to Perry's visit began only as an effort to modernize and acquire the means of national self-defense. But the Japanese industrial revolution proved to be so successful that, by the end of the nineteenth century, Japan had achieved parity with the Western powers and actually became one of their club, creating its own dream of imperial conquest in Asia. Shinto, like it or not, was destined to play an important role in this frightening adventure.

The Meiji Constitution officially brought an end to the long feudal age and established a constitutional monarch on the model of the German Empire. The emperor, in all his divine glory, would preside over this new government. The Meiji Constitution, though, did not emerge out of thin air; it was an outgrowth of what is called the Meiji Restoration of 1868, which itself was an outgrowth of the turmoil set loose by Perry's "opening of Japan" only fifteen years before. What was being restored in the Meiji Restoration was the authority of the emperor as the titular head of the government, as he had been in ancient times. For many centuries the Japanese emperor had been nothing more than a pampered figurehead, a symbol of the Japanese nation, holding court at his palace at Kyoto. The real power rested with the shogun, a military warlord who ruled over the feudal nobility from his own palace at Edo. One of the effects of the Meiji Restoration was to abolish the shogunate, installing the emperor in his place at Edo, which became the new national capital and was promptly renamed Tokyo.

The powerful clique responsible for the Meiji Restoration was concerned primarily with three goals: the total dismantling of feudalism, the rapid Westernization of the Japanese state, and the centralization of authority in the national government presided over by the emperor. The highly intoxicating spirit of nationalism swept over Japan. Those in power saw the ancient tradition of Shinto as a potentially useful tool for promoting the nationalist spirit and achieving strong national unity under the emperor. In fact, Shinto was a natural; it already was a source of national identity, and the central fact of Shinto was the divinity of the emperor. Thus it was that Shinto came to be pressed into the service of those who dreamed of transforming Japan into a strong and aggressive imperialist Asian power. The person of the emperor was to be at the center of it all, and his special importance was to be emphasized by stressing his divinity. The opening section of the Meiji Constitution says it all. Article One states, "The Empire of Japan shall be reigned over and governed by a line of Emperors unbroken for ages eternal," and Article Three continues with "The Emperor is sacred and inviolable." The sacredness of the emperor was stressed in every way possible, even getting into the schoolbooks of little children. A national reader for primary grades contained this verse:

> Great Japan! Great Japan
> Our seventy million citizens
> Look up to the Emperor even as to God
> And love and serve him as a parent.

This kind of thing was right up Shinto's alley, so to speak. But not just any old kind of Shinto would do. The government promoted a particular Shinto sect known as *Fukko Shinto,* referred to in the West as "pure Shinto." This highly nationalistic sect advocated a return to the "pure" roots of ancient Shinto. Followers would purge the religion of all foreign contaminations, such as Chinese influences in general and Buddhist influences in particular. The Fukko idealized a golden age in the past, before Japanese civilization had been vitiated by the cultural influences of "lesser" peoples, most of all the Chinese, but more recently the "Western barbarians." The Fukko would make Japan strong again by returning the country to its original source of strength, pure Shinto, centered on a divine emperor, the living voice of the will of Amaterasu, the goddess of the sun.

The most influential spokesman for Fukko Shinto was the nineteenth-century writer Motoori Norinaga. Reaching out from the central fact of the divinity of the emperor, he became unabashedly messianic:

> From the central truth that the Mikado [emperor] is the direct descendant of the gods, the tenet that Japan ranks far above all other countries is a natural consequence. No other nation is entitled to equality with her, and all are bound to do homage to the Japanese sovereign and pay tribute to him. . . . It relies on a rationalization of history in order to develop the two-fold thesis of a *jure divino* sovereign in an Imperial Line unbroken from divine ages and destined to rule Japan eternally and a divine Japanese race which, by virtue of the directness of its genealogical connections with the kami, is braver, more virtuous and more intelligent than all other races of mankind. The god-descended Japanese Emperor is divinely destined to extend his sway over the entire earth.[3]

The world watched with awe as the industrial and military strength of Japan mushroomed into greatness, but few outsiders could see that an also-mushrooming nationalism was a part of the same picture. When the warlords gained control of the government during the crisis of the Great Depression, it was only a matter of time before the Empire of Japan would attempt to make the dream come true. As the European colonial powers, newly intent on slaughtering one another in the second of the century's world wars, began to loosen their grip on their Asian possessions, Japanese leadership saw its chance and began to move into the power vacuum. Fulfilling what these leaders believed to be the obvious will of the gods, Japan would create its own imperialist empire in East Asia. It was an exciting vision, to say the least. There was only one problem. One of those Western powers, the United States of America, had similar designs—and, unlike the European nations, the United States was most definitely not a declining power. In one of the most horrendous miscalculations of all human history, the Empire of Japan made war on the United States in the vain hope of removing that country as a threat to their own imperialist designs. Four years later, a completely devastated and broken Japan was forced to face a very different future from the one that the warlords had dreamed about.

To begin with, in order to keep his throne, Emperor Hirohito was required to face the nation and publicly deny his claim to divinity. This dramatic disclaimer was to be the first step in a program aimed at dismantling the nationalistic infrastructure of prewar Japan. Under the direction of the occupying military government, a new constitution was promulgated in 1947, this time on the more liberal and democratic model of Britain and the United States. Included in the constitution was a clause specifically prohibiting public support of the Shinto religion. Never again could Shinto be the publicly funded tool of a nationalistic-minded government. The victorious allies naively expected that, forced to rely on local private funding, the institution of Shinto would simply dry up and blow away.

Well, not quite. Under the organizational leadership of the *Jinja Honcho* (the Association of Shinto Shrines), far from dying out, Shinto is now stronger than ever. Free from the shackles of government support and control, Shinto has become the inspiration for a healthy national unity in modern times. It's a truly amazing tradition. As before, Shinto shrugs off efforts to change it. In its time, Shinto has weathered the assaults of Chinese culture, Buddhism, Western influence, and totalitarianism. Shinto continues to live among the Japanese people, as it always has, preserving a living link with the ancient past.

Notes

1. D. C. Holtom, *The National Faith of Japan: A Study in Modern Shinto* (London: Kegan Paul, Trench, Trubner, 1938), p. 24.

2. Robert S. Ellwood, *The Feast of Kingship: Accession Ceremonies in Ancient Japan* (Tokyo: Sophia University Press, 1973), pp. 72–73.

3. Motoori, as quoted in Holtom, pp. 49 and 51.

Study Questions

1. On what basis can Shinto be defined as a religion? In what important ways does Shinto differ from the generally accepted definition of "religion"?
2. Describe the creation myth that Shinto employs to explain the beginnings of the Japanese people. What is the relationship of the imperial family to this myth?
3. Historically speaking, what has been the relationship between Shinto and Buddhism in Japan?
4. What was Fukko Shinto? What role did it play in the course of modern Japanese history?

ULAN BATOR

TOKYO

KYOTO

DUNHUANG

BEIJING

KASHGAR

XIAN

NANJING

LHASA

DELHI

HONG KONG

HANOI

Arctic Circle

Tropic of Cancer

Equator

40°

30°

20°

10°

0°

10°

East Asia

PART III
Buddhism

Buddhism is a subject that is vast in scope. It is compared to a wheel with many spokes, each one representing a distinct tradition. Taken altogether, the spokes represent a complete circle of possibilities. Buddhism can be highly religious or highly secular, very mystical or very philosophical. It can be comfortably at home with the supernatural and esoteric, as well as with the purely rational and scientific.

In Part III, we will follow the evolution of this great tradition, beginning with the life and teaching of its founder, Shakyamuni Buddha. We will then examine the major branchings of the tradition. The earliest of these was Theravada, which was followed by Mahayana, which radiated into many widely differing schools. Special attention will be given to Vajrayana, often referred to as "Tibetan Buddhism," and to Zen Buddhism, including the developmental years of that tradition in China, wherein it was more properly known as Chan Buddhism.

The evolutionary history of Buddhism has resulted in four major schools that are active in the modern world: Theravada, Vajrayana, Pure Land, and Zen. Each of these is making an impact on the present and will undoubtedly have a significant role to play in the future.

simple as human being. There is no super natural world

→ Opposite side of the theravada

9

The Life of Buddha

The man we know as Buddha (or, more properly, Shakyamuni Buddha) was not a mythic figure. He was a flesh-and-blood human being; of that we can be certain. He was born in North India sometime around 563 B.C.E. and presumably lived a long life, perhaps being about eighty years old when he died.

Buddha, of course, was not his name. The word *Buddha* is derived from the Sanskrit *budh*, which means "to wake up." Buddha was "the awakened one," one who had awakened to the ultimate truth of the nature of reality. Followers of this man, out of deep respect and love for him, conferred the title *Buddha* on him, and so he has been known ever since.

Unfortunately, very little is known about Shakyamuni Buddha that we could call historical fact. Historical record keeping was not much practiced in those days, and his followers were far more concerned about preserving his teaching than with the details of his life—and, of course, that's what really matters. Still, there has always been an inevitable curiosity about the life of this great man, and as a result, a body of legends has taken shape over time. I want to emphasize this point: Commonly repeated stories about the life of Buddha are the stuff of legend, not history. It is not unreasonable to believe that the seeds of such stories were originally founded on real events and circumstances, but over time they were richly embellished and given a mythic character. The legend was fashioned to fit the man.

Buddha was certainly one of the most influential persons ever to have walked the earth. His teaching blossomed into a tradition that has profoundly shaped the course of human history and continues to shape it to this day. Buddha gave us not so much a religion as a philosophy of life, and that philosophy is as vital today as it ever has been. The greatest impact of Buddha's teaching may still lie before us.

The critical event in Buddha's life—in fact, a critical event in the history of the human race—was the moment of his awakening. This occurred in his thirty-sixth year. The remainder of his life was devoted to teaching. In the company of a small band of disciples, Buddha wandered the northern plain of India, teaching as many as would hear his words how they, too, might awaken to the truth. The essence of that teaching is what most concerns us here, but the years that led up to his awakening are also of interest and relevance. Those years divide into two parts. The first part includes Buddha's youth and young-adult years. During that time, young Buddha was a prince being groomed to become a great king. Far from becoming a king, Buddha renounced this legacy and chose instead to become a forest dweller living the life of a spiritual renunciate. His six years as a renunciate form the second part of Buddha's preawakening life and led directly to his awakening.

Various ancient sources give us information about the life of Buddha. The oldest and most important document is the Pali Canon. Committed to writing in the first century B.C.E., the Pali Canon is a carefully assembled collection of the then-existing scriptural works and traditions regarding Buddha. (We will have much more to say about the document in Chapter 11.) The accounts in the Pali Canon, however, are really nothing more than two terse commentaries that deal with two different parts of Buddha's life. They give us only some basic facts. The first complete biography of the Buddha was written in the first century C.E. by the poet Ashvaghosha. This work, known as the Buddha-Charita, is unreservedly mythical; the author was not interested in historical veracity. Many of the legends about Shakyamuni Buddha's life are derived from the Buddha-Charita.

Again, the story of Buddha's life is much more the stuff of legends than of history. But it's well worth surveying, however briefly. As you might expect, there are numerous variations to the legends. My goal here is to present the story in its generally accepted form. The importance of the story of Buddha's life is simply to provide an understandable background for his teaching. The legend of Buddha's life is carefully structured, as you will see. It is an account of an evolution that leads dramatically and almost inevitably to the great moment of Buddha's awakening.

THE PALACE YOUTH

Before he became the stuff of legend, Buddha was known by his regular family name. Siddhartha was his proper name, and Gautama the family name. Even without becoming "the awakened one," Siddhartha Gautama was far from being a nobody. He was a prince, the only son of Shuddhodana Gautama, the leader (king, if you will) of the great Shakya clan, one of the many large clans that dominated the land of northern India. After Siddhartha gained fame as a great sage, a "muni," yet another part was added to his name; he became "Shakya-muni," the sage of the Shakya clan. Putting it all together, he was, Siddhartha Gautama Shakyamuni, the "Buddha." To distinguish him from other buddhas, recognized by some sects, he is often referred to simply as Shakyamuni Buddha.

The Shakya "kingdom" was an irregular-shaped patch of land in the far north, bordering on the foothills of the Himalayas. Its capital city was Kapilavastu; at a nearby place called Lumbini, young Siddhartha came into this world. His mother's name was Maya. To give you an idea of the kind of legend that has become woven into the story of Buddha's life, it is widely told that he selected his own mother before birth and entered into her womb. Ten months after this "immaculate conception," Siddhartha was born to the accompaniment of flowers blooming out of season and all the world knowing a brief period of peace and joy. Seven days later, *Maya* died peacefully, so as not to defile her sacred body by giving birth again.

The legend informs us that on the day of Siddhartha's birth a great sage named Asita learned of it from the gods, who told him that a person of exceptional spiritual power had assumed human form in the city of Kapilavastu. Asita went there immediately, and as he held the baby in his arms, he recognized the signs that foretold a glorious future. This boy, he prophesied, would grow up to be a great leader. But it wasn't clear which kind of leader he would be. Either he would be a great worldly leader, a king of kings, or he would be a great spiritual leader, a sage of sages. The stars left the question open; only the passage of time would reveal the answer. After announcing this news, Asita broke down in tears. He was an old man, and he wept because he knew in his heart that he could not possibly live long enough to know this little baby as a man, and to hear his teaching with his own ears.*

Shuddhodana could not be indifferent to this news. Spiritual leaders were fine and good, but this was his son, his *only* son, the heir to the throne and the future hope of his family and his people. In Shuddhodana's mind, Siddhartha was destined to be a great king. That's how the stars were to be read, and there was to be no doubt about it.

From the day of Siddhartha's birth, Shuddhodana put into play a carefully thought-out plan. The boy was to be groomed to be a lover of the things of this world. This is not to say that he would be allowed to become a self-centered hedonist serving only his sensual appetites. Far from it, he would learn discipline and self-restraint befitting a princely heir to the throne, but only to more perfectly refine his enjoyment of the good things of life. He would become a connoisseur of all things; a lover of fine music, food, poetry, and rhetoric. He would, in a phrase, become a first-rate man of the world. It was his father's hope that in this way Siddhartha would become so firmly attached to the worldly life that he would naturally seek his own happiness in the finest possibilities that a worldly life has to offer. In this manner, his destiny as a great king would be fulfilled.

Thus did Shuddhodana order that the young prince was to know nothing but the rich and beautiful possibilities of this world. During the character-forming years of childhood he was not to see, hear, or in any way experience the violent and ugly side of life. Within the confining walls of the palace grounds, all was to be perfect. Even the palace gardens were to be kept always in a state of perfection. Every evening, just after sunset, an army of servants would comb through the gardens, removing every leaf that had died, every petal that had wilted. Such was the world that the young Siddhartha would grow up in. Inside the walls of the palace, his gilded cage, he would know nothing of

---

*The story of Asita is amazingly similar to that of Simeon told in the Gospel of Luke. Indeed, many interesting comparisons are found in the accounts of the lives of Buddha and Jesus.

death and corruption, of ugliness and failure, or of imperfection. He would be a stranger to suffering. Years later, chatting with some of his disciples, Buddha commented on the extreme luxury of his youth:

> Monks, I was delicately nurtured, exceedingly delicately nurtured. For instance, in my father's house, lotus pools were made thus, one of blue lotuses, one of red, another of white lotuses, just for my benefit. No sandlewood powder did I use that was not of Kasi; of Kasi cloth was my turban made; of Kasi cloth was my jacket, my tunic, and my cloak. By night and day a white canopy was held over me.[1]

The legends of Buddha's life include many wondrous and supernatural happenings, appropriate, of course, for someone of his special importance. For example, we are told that when Siddhartha was still a little boy, he was taken by his family to the annual plowing festival. His father, the king, presided over the ceremonies and even plowed the first furrow. They made a comfortable spot for little Siddhartha in the shade of a large tree, thinking that he would fall asleep. Some hours later, they found him seated serenely upright in the posture of meditation, and though the shade of all the other trees had moved considerably, nature had bowed before the future Buddha, and the shade of his tree remained exactly in place.

As he grew older, Siddhartha was tutored by the finest teachers in all of the arts and sciences. He learned to ride like a champion, and his skill in archery was the talk of the kingdom. He became the model of a prince—handsome, gracious, refined, skilled in everything. He was a wonderfully happy young man, exuberantly enjoying the best that life has to offer. He lacked only an appropriate mate who would be his future queen and a befitting mother of the next heir to the throne. Here, too, the father's wishes were not to be foiled.

Yashodhara was to become the wife of Siddhartha, and as you might have guessed, she was the most beautiful young woman in all the kingdom. Her father, one of the most powerful nobles, arranged an archery contest to test the skill of her many suitors. Siddhartha's principal rival struck the target in the center of the bull's-eye, but the cool and steady Siddhartha did him one better, splitting that arrow down the center, thus winning the hand of Yashodhara. They were madly in love and soon produced the much-desired son. They named him Rahula, and he was, of course, everything parents could want in a child.

I'm sure you get the picture. The legend is carefully and deliberately setting up a situation in which everything is as perfect as it can be. If Siddhartha is going to turn his back on his princely life, as, of course, he will, it is important that there be nothing lacking at all. The life that he rejects must be the most perfect situation that a worldly life can offer. If the lifestyle of the young Siddhartha cannot deliver complete happiness, then it is the worldly lifestyle itself that is lacking in some fundamental way. This understanding is crucial to the development of the story.

Eventually, as one might have predicted, Siddhartha reached a time when he became aware that the pleasures of life had come to lose some of their former excitement. He was feeling restless without knowing why. For the first time in his life, he found himself bothered by age-old questions: Is this all there is? Is the good life simply a round of pleasures? Has life no purpose? The snake was in the garden now. The father's carefully laid plan, which had worked so beautifully, was in trouble. Siddhartha was no longer satisfied with his gilded cage. He was curious about the real world beyond his walls, and he made up his mind that he was going to go exploring.

At this point, the legend offers two major versions. One holds that Siddhartha went to his father and asked permission to visit the city beyond the palace walls. Shuddhodana felt a pang of anxiety as he recalled a prophesy that his son would renounce the world when he saw a sick man, an old man, and a corpse. However, he could not keep his son forever within the safety of the palace walls. Thus, Shuddhodana reluctantly gave Siddhartha his permission and then quietly ordered his son's driver to choose his route most carefully. Maybe, he thought, Siddhartha would see only "acceptable" sights.

In the other version, Siddhartha does not reveal his uneasiness to his father. Instead he goes to his old and much-loved charioteer (his "chauffeur," as it were), a man named Channa, and begs him to take him into the city. He will wear a disguise and no one will recognize him. Channa, feeling compassion for Siddhartha, finally relents. Late in the day they will slip out of the palace gate, and Siddhartha can see for himself what lies beyond his perfect little world. There were four gates in the palace walls, corresponding to the four points of the compass. On Siddhartha and Channa's first excursion, they would pass through the eastern gate.

Both variations come down to the same thing: Siddhartha breaks out of his artificial worldly paradise and comes face to face with the larger realities of life, most of all the reality of suffering. Siddhartha goes through the gate, actually and symbolically, and once through, he would certainly have experienced profound culture shock. The serene and perfect world of the palace grounds was suddenly replaced with all of the noise, disorder, and hubbub of the crowded city. Street vendors, animals, beggars, shouting people, shoving people, every imaginable smell and sight—what a scene it must have been to his eyes! They moved slowly through the crowded streets, Siddhartha taking it all in.

One thing in particular shocked him to the core, the sight of a badly diseased and crippled man. We can imagine it being a beggar horribly deformed by a disease like leprosy. Siddhartha had never seen a truly sick person before. He had never seen real suffering before. "What is that?" he would have shouted. "That is a very sick man, master," Channa would have answered. "Disease is a part of life, and it is no respecter of rank: You, too, could become like that someday."

It was a changed Siddhartha who returned to the palace that night. His uneasy curiosity had now become shock and dismay. The stark imperfections of life could no longer be hidden from him. His former pleasures no longer satisfied him. He yearned only to go back and see more. Again Channa wheeled him out into the city, this time by the northern gate. Again the wild scene greeted his eyes. This time his attention focused on a very old man, ancient and feeble, bald and toothless, bent far forward and able to hobble only slowly and painfully with the help of a stick. This, too, was a new sight for the pampered eyes of Siddhartha. He gazed in stunned silence, especially when Channa explained that Siddhartha, too, might become like that someday.

On the pair's third excursion they ventured into the city by way of the western gate, the direction of the setting sun. By now Siddhartha was becoming used to some of the sights, but nothing could prepare him for what he was about to see. It was a corpse, the stiff, dead body wrapped in funeral linens and being carried by weeping mourners to the place of cremation. When Channa explained what the procession was all about, Siddhartha was thunderstruck! This was his first encounter with the reality of death. His dread turned to horror when Channa said, "You may escape the agony of disease and of old age, but no person ever born escapes the fate of death. One day you, too, will become a corpse, and your loved ones, filled with suffering, will carry your body to the place of cremation."

Now Siddhartha could know no joy at all. His former happiness was gone. All he could think about was what he had seen in the world beyond the palace walls. How can anyone enjoy the present? It is only a fleeting moment, ready at any time to change into suffering and, eventually, into the awesome nightmare of death. Nothing of value endures; does anything matter? Siddhartha's awareness of the inevitability of death made all his temporal pleasures seem disturbingly imperfect. Siddhartha was brooding and depressed, but still there was one more gate to investigate. "What more could there be? Can anything be worse than death?"

It was a quiet and troubled Siddhartha that Channa drove into the city by way of the southern gate. For a long time, they pushed through the crowded streets. Siddhartha gazed without shock on the multitude. There were sick people and old people, beggars, and even more corpses. He had seen it all. They had gone all the way to the edge of the city, where the forest began. Darkness was setting in, and Channa was preparing to return to the palace. Just at that moment, Siddhartha caught sight of a man standing in a rigid posture at the edge of the forest. In the gloomy light Siddhartha could make out that the man was old and naked, his body covered with grime and his uncut, greasy hair hanging almost to his knees. The man's ribs stuck out from his emaciated body, and his eyes were gaunt and sunken.

"Well, this one seems to have it all, Channa," Siddhartha might have said. "He's old, he's sick, he's poor, and he's on the verge of becoming a corpse. Surely this man knows greater suffering than any of the others we have seen." "No, master," Channa would have answered. "This man is a sadhu. He is a forest dweller who has renounced worldly pleasures and has extinguished all desires. He has passed beyond suffering. He knows great joy; this man knows the bliss of perfect freedom."

Channa's answer stunned Siddhartha. It turned his world upside down. This naked recluse standing here appeared outwardly to be the ultimate of wretchedness. But he knows inner joy and freedom? And Siddhartha, who appeared outwardly to be the finest example of worldly success was inwardly miserable. Nothing made any sense.

In the days that followed, Siddhartha tried to shake off the gloom that his experiences with suffering had generated, but it only deepened. Shuddhodana began to worry when he saw that his much-loved son was brooding and withdrawing from the company of his friends. He decided that what Siddhartha needed was a party, a great feast to snap him out of it and remind him of the good things in life.

Well, according to the legend, it must have been the mother of all parties. Even the dancing girls were the most beautiful and the most friendly that Siddhartha had ever seen. To please his father, he gave it his best shot, but, of course, his heart was not in it. By the wee hours of the morning, the beautiful people weren't so beautiful anymore. Most were drunk and sleeping, their partially clothed bodies sprawled around in an assortment of indelicate poses. Some had been vomiting, and many were snoring loudly; it was quite a scene. As he surveyed the spectacle, deep disgust welled up within Siddhartha. He saw clearly that the life he was used to would never bring him true inner happiness. In that moment, Siddhartha made a fateful decision: He would abandon his princely life, turn his back on it forever, and become a sadhu.

A word of explanation is appropriate here. The legend of Buddha's life has a logical structure to it. His experience of awakening at the age of thirty-five is the great watershed of his life. From that experience will issue his teaching years, during which time he will establish the foundation of the Buddhist tradition. But the years before his awakening are significant, too; they carefully set the stage for the great event. As mentioned before, these years are divided into two parts, and the character of each part is deliberately described as being different from the other in the extreme. Until the age of twenty-nine, Buddha lives a life of luxury and ease in his father's palace. Then he does a complete reversal, and for the next six years he withdraws to the wilderness to live as a renunciate. He gives himself completely to both lifestyles and finds that neither path leads to the freedom he yearns for. His awakening emerges out of the desperation that follows. To better understand the nature of Buddha's awakening, we must look carefully at both parts of his life that led up to it.

What do we see when we stand back and look at the first part of his life, the palace years? We find Prince Siddhartha, a young man of intelligence and character, who wants passionately to make himself into the finest person he is capable of becoming. He wants to please his father, and he wants to fulfill his own destiny, which presumably means becoming a great king. In the process, he works out his father's plan, immersing himself in the life of worldly experiences, desiring only the best, and steadily increasing his sophistication. He becomes a connoisseur of the finest things in life.

Siddhartha finds great pleasure in this lifestyle, great self-satisfaction, but the perfect happiness that he yearns for always eludes him, and eventually his happiness is shattered completely when he comes face to face with the realization that happiness based on the satisfaction of desires inevitably includes the company of suffering. Try as his father may, he cannot keep the two separate, and, indeed, no one can. The greater the pleasure, the greater the pain—they go together like the two sides of a coin.

Why is it argued that pleasure and pain go together like the two sides of a coin? To begin with, we all seek to be happy, and we all seek to avoid suffering. To many, happiness can be defined simply as the pleasing state of mind that accompanies the enjoyment of pleasurable experiences, and suffering can be identified with the more or less unpleasant state of mind that is the companion of painful experiences. We desire to possess the one and to avoid the other. Therefore, according to this line of thinking, the good life—the happy life—is to be equated with satisfying our desires. To the degree that we are successful in satisfying our desires, we will be happy, and if we can succeed in satisfying our desires *perfectly* we will be *perfectly* happy. That's the theory. (Does it sound familiar?)

It *should* sound familiar, very familiar. It is a dominant theme of modern culture (and probably all others throughout time). This value is pitched at us in a million ways from cradle to grave. Look at the advertising that surrounds us. Do you want to be happy? Why aren't you? Is it because you desire a certain kind of car and you don't have it? Then get it, and you'll be happy. What about the right clothes, or house, or job promotion, or that beautiful eel-skin belt, and on and on and on? Of course, for a while, it does make us happy—even elated—to satisfy our desires. The problem is, as we all know, that it doesn't last. It is of the nature of desire that it can never be fully satisfied; desire always begets further desire.

At a deeper level, the problem with desire is that it begets attachment. The word *attachment* occupies a very important place in the philosophy of Buddha. *Attachment* means *craving*—the kind of desire that has grown so strong that one believes that he or she cannot possibly be happy without the object of desire. It could be a thing, another person, or even a way of life. Desires easily grow into attachments, and once they do, we are trapped, prisoners of our own desires. That, at least, is the argument, and that's why it is argued that pleasure and pain go together like the two sides of a coin.

Buddha—or should I say the young Siddhartha—had been totally absorbed in this way of life. He yearned passionately to know the joy of self-fulfillment. But as he stood surveying the ugly scene that was the aftermath of the party, he experienced a profound realization, the first in a series of realizations that led to his awakening. It can be stated simply: *There is no self-fulfillment through self-indulgence.*

The young Siddhartha had done the best job that anyone could ever hope to do of trying to achieve lasting inner happiness through indulging his desires, and he had discovered that taking that path simply doesn't work. In this he was a model for all humanity. But that would come later; his quest for the right path still had a long way to go. If the worldly way of self-indulgence was not the answer, then Siddhartha would reject it altogether. Compromise was out of the question; settling for a life that was only second best was equally out of the question.

Siddhartha had not been able to forget the sadhu that he had seen at the edge of the forest on his last venture out of the palace. The sight of the man haunted him, and so did Channa's words, "He knows the joy of perfect freedom." Was the wise and compassionate Channa right about this? Siddhartha had to know. To go on living the opulent life of the palace was out of the question. Why take any half measures? Why not go for broke and adopt the life of the sadhu, give it one hundred percent, just as he had given one hundred percent to his life up to now. He would find out for himself if that was the path to perfect happiness.

Channa was, of course, merely giving expression to what was widely accepted as true in the India of Buddha's time. Hindu society then, as in all times, held great respect for those rare few who were strong enough to give up everything and take on the harsh life of the renunciate, dedicating themselves to the search for a transcendent truth. Such a person, it was believed, paid a high price, but the reward was a perfect inner peace that passed beyond pleasure and pain. The sadhu escaped from the net of suffering and knew "the joy of perfect freedom."

Desire and its inevitable companion of suffering were believed to be the result of attachment to the ego role, and such attachment was the almost inevitable result of being human. It is the character of the role. According to traditional Vedanta teaching, the sole hope is to stop playing the role, completely. Only then can one discover the *atman* within. And the only way to stop playing the role is to drop out of ordinary life completely, practice ascetic disciplines that will slowly burn out every desire for worldly comforts, and peel back the layers of ego one by one until, ultimately, there is nothing left but the pure, undifferentiated consciousness of *atman*. Here, and here alone, can one come to knowledge of transcendent abiding happiness.

And so Siddhartha, at the age of twenty-nine, decided to go from one extreme to the other, from the luxurious life of the prince to the utter poverty of the sadhu. According to the legend, he acted on his decision immediately. In the middle of the night he summoned Channa, and after gently kissing his sleeping wife and baby son, he rode off to the edge of the forest where he had first seen the sadhu. Siddhartha scavenged some saffron-colored rags from the burial place of executed criminals. With these, he fashioned a simple robe; that and a humble begging bowl were all he would call his own. His former elegant clothes were folded and handed to Channa. Siddhartha also cut off his beautiful long hair and placed it atop the clothing. "Give these to my father," he is supposed to have said. "He will understand."

The bewildered Channa was stricken with sorrow. He begged Siddhartha to allow him to go with him. But this was a journey that Siddhartha intended to make alone. Channa returned to the palace in tears, and in the days that followed, his tears were joined by those of many others.

THE SADHU YEARS

Thus did Siddhartha embark upon the second great part of his life. For the next six years, he would live the life of a forest dweller, a sadhu. He would study with the finest gurus of his time, and he would become a master himself. His fame would spread far, and many other sadhus would seek him out to gain from his wisdom and the power of his example.

No one practiced the yoga of renunciation with greater zeal or with greater success. After long and hard ascetic practices, Siddhartha burned away every last vestige of desire for comfort and sensory pleasure. Cold or heat, wet or dry, a bed of soft grass or a bed of sharp thorns—it did not matter. He freed himself totally from the worldly attachments that had fettered him in his palace days. He fasted continuously, reducing his intake of food to but one grain of rice per day. Siddhartha's body came to look like a walking skeleton, and he rejoiced in this evidence of his progress. He practiced meditation for hours at a time and then for days at a time, without interruption. He became, indeed, a great master of the life of the renunciate.

Here again, the legend deliberately sets up an extreme situation. It is essential to the story that Siddhartha explore the path of the sadhu to its absolute fullest. He must be the perfect master; anything less won't do. If he is ultimately going to reject that way of life—and, of course, he will—it is necessary that he know that there is nothing in it that he did not personally experience.

Again, the goal of the sadhu's hard way of life is to slough off the ego—the role—layer by layer, until eventually, all that is left is *atman*. In the course of this quest, as his skills sharpened, Siddhartha had many a mind-boggling experience. His consciousness expanded, he saw things his mind had never imagined, and he transcended the earthly plane, but try as he might, he had to admit the awful truth; he never beheld the glory of the *atman*. Slowly, he was moving toward the terrible conclusion that this way of life, though capable of producing new and ecstatic experiences, was really no more capable of achieving true self-fulfillment than his old way of life was. The ego was just as strong as it had ever been. In fact, in insidious ways, it was stronger; he was proud of the self-discipline he maintained that separated him out from ordinary men. Siddhartha was on the verge of despair. He did not know what to do. Going back to his old life was out of the question, but continuing with the present way was coming to be equally unthinkable. What else was there?

While he was in this state of mind, Siddhartha reached his second great realization. The legends offer a variety of accounts of how it happened. In one of them, Siddhartha is walking alone beside a stream. He is deep in his inner quandary when he sees a young milkmaid. She has just milked a cow and is returning home with the warm milk in a wooden bowl. Without thinking, Siddhartha splashes across the stream and walks up to her, saying not a word. The milkmaid looks at his emaciated body, seeing that he is weak and sick at heart. Taking pity on him, or perhaps thinking that he is some sort of demigod, she offers him the bowl of milk, and he hungrily gulps it all down. As the fresh milk reaches his stomach, Siddhartha is transformed. He feels strength returning to his body and to his mind. In that instant he suddenly sees clearly the truth that he had not been willing to face: *There is no self-fulfillment through self-denial!*

Earlier, he had discovered that self-fulfillment is impossible through self-indulgence. So he had tried the opposite tack. There, too, he had ultimately come up against a dead end. There was no self-fulfillment through self-indulgence—and no self-fulfillment through self-denial either. What to do?

At this time, Siddhartha had been traveling with five companions who felt great respect and admiration for him. When they caught up with him and heard what he had done, they were horrified. Siddhartha had just broken two of the most basic rules of the life of the sadhu; he had taken milk, and he had consorted with a woman. They backed away from him in shock, but Siddhartha didn't care. His strength had returned, he could see clearly again, and he was through with this way of life. He continued on alone for a while, not knowing what to do.

Another variation of the legend holds that in a place where Siddhartha and his companions were temporarily staying, a pregnant young woman from a nearby village sought him out. She had heard of his great spiritual powers, and being somewhat superstitious, she thought he might be the incarnation of a god. The woman desperately wanted her baby to be a son and hoped that praying in Siddhartha's presence might produce the desired result.

The baby turned out to be a boy, and in thanksgiving the grateful mother prepared an assortment of delicacies, which she laid out before the ever-fasting Siddhartha. To the dismay of his companions, he accepted the offering, eating all of it. The nourishing food restored his strength and clarity of mind. The event triggered his realization that there can be no self-fulfillment through self-denial.

According to the story, Siddhartha then fashioned a makeshift oil lamp out of a large leaf, some oil from the food he had been given, and a piece of cloth from his robe that he made into a wick. He lit the wick and set the lamp afloat in the nearby stream. "If I am never to find the truth I seek, let this lamp drift downstream with the current," he said. With all eyes watching, the little lamp eddied around a bit at first and then moved slowly upstream, seeming to drift against the current.

THE AWAKENING

Siddhartha continued on alone for a while. He didn't know what to do. On the banks of the Niranjana River, near the town of Gaya, in a personal sense he reached the end of the line. There was no point in going on any farther. The one and only thing that mattered to Siddhartha was breaking through his own wall of ignorance, _avidya,_ and discovering the truth. What is the truth of the reality of life and death? Unless he could find his way to this truth, life itself was not worth living.

One element from the sadhu way of life was not to be discarded. All else might go, but Siddhartha held the deepest respect for the power of meditation. His last hope, meditation had become his real friend and teacher. Now he would ask everything of it; there was no other way.

Siddhartha found a roomy spot beneath the spreading branches of a large tree. He prepared a place on the ground for meditation, and taking his posture with the legs crossed and the spine straight, he turned inward. The legend would have him thinking something like this: "I have mastered the art of meditation. Now I will call upon that mastery to turn deep within myself, and I will not leave this spot, come what may, until I have uncovered the truth that I seek. The truth I seek is the ultimate truth of all things; I will find it within myself; I will be a lamp unto myself." Eknath Easwaren puts it nicely:

> Near the city of Gaya he found a tranquil spot under a sacred fig tree and carpeted a place with fresh, fragrant grass. Folding his legs beneath him, he drew himself straight for meditation and took a solemn vow: "Come what may—let my body rot, let my bones be reduced to ashes—I will not get up from here until I have found the way beyond decay and death." It was dusk, and the moon was rising, the first full moon of the first month of spring. Thus determined, full of peace, Siddhartha passed into deep meditation, when the senses close down and concentration flows undisturbed by awareness of the outside world.[2]

The time Siddhartha spent in meditation near the town of Gaya is the pivotal point in the story of the life of Buddha. Some accounts say it was for one full night, others say it was for seven days and seven nights; it doesn't matter. For Siddhartha, time stood still.

He withdrew completely from the world around him, and in the great depth of his own inner being, he worked through the layers of ignorance that had held him back from seeing the truth. When he returned from his withdrawal, he was a new man; he had found what he was looking for. He was awakened.

The legend tells us that, early on in his meditation, the Hindu god Mara came to visit Siddhartha. Mara, when he chooses to reveal himself completely, is described as the fearsome embodiment of death itself. No one had ever seen perfectly into the mystery of life and death before, and Mara was worried. Knowing the great strength and the great resolve of Siddhartha, Mara was worried that Siddhartha might discover the truth that could liberate humankind from suffering. He sat down beside Siddhartha and was silent for some time. When he finally spoke, in a soft and appealing fashion, it was to tempt Siddhartha. He was hoping to derail Siddhartha from his intended destination. Perhaps he could persuade Siddhartha to give up, to see his task as hopeless, and to choose instead some other path.

Of course, the presence of Mara need not be interpreted literally. It is a poetic way of telling the story. Mara can be seen as an aspect of Siddhartha himself. The demons that Mara sent against Siddhartha were the demons of his own inner struggle. There was a war going on within him. Siddhartha had to struggle against what remained of his own doubt, his own weakness, and his own worldly desires. In overcoming the temptations of Mara, Siddhartha's higher nature was victorious over his lower nature. This is the real meaning of his awakening: Siddhartha became Buddha by rising above all that was base and fearful in himself. Deep in meditation, he conquered his own fear and saw the truth.

The temptations of Mara resemble what we have seen in the hierarchy of Mount Meru or in the structure of a Hindu temple. There is a progression upward from the very simple to the very refined. After testing Siddhartha with visions of terrifying demons, Mara reversed the scene, attempting instead to tempt Siddhartha with his daughters, young women of maddening sexual beauty. "Give up this nonsense, Siddhartha, and enjoy the company of these women. Anything you want is yours. Enjoy yourself. You deserve it; you have denied yourself the pleasures of the senses for too long."

Sexual pleasure makes a good symbol for all kinds of pleasure. This is where happiness starts, close to the earth. Siddhartha was tempted, but his strong self-discipline made it relatively easy for him to get past that one. Before his eyes, the beauty turned into ugliness. Deeper he sank within himself. We can easily imagine Mara then moving on to a more subtle plane: "Siddhartha, the time has come to return home. Get up from this ridiculous quest, and return to the embrace of your wife and son. How happy your father will be; he will receive you with open arms. Do you not owe him that before he dies? You've seen both sides now. You can take your father's place when the time comes, and you can rule with wisdom and compassion. It is your destiny to be a king, not a 'holy man,' and the experience of your years as a sadhu will make you that much greater. Get on with it, Siddhartha, go back home, now."

Such thoughts must have arisen in Siddhartha's mind, and he would have been moved by them, but his resolve did not break. Calling upon great inner strength, he moved deeper into meditation. He would not allow himself to be swayed by temptation.

Shakyamuni Buddha with right hand in the posture of bhumishparsha (earth touching). (P. Bresnan)

Mara hurled his entire arsenal against Siddhartha; he tried everything available to him, but nothing would move Siddhartha. Finally, in anger, Mara appeared personally before Siddhartha; Mara, the undisguised, stark reality of death revealed himself to Siddhartha and demanded to know by what authority Siddhartha dared challenge this ultimate mystery of life. Siddhartha silently answered by touching the earth with his right hand. The earth itself, from which all came and to which all returned, would be his witness and his authority. At this, Mara retreated, leaving Siddhartha completely alone. He had weathered the storm of Mara's temptations. Now the farther shore was in view. Some say that when Siddhartha opened his eyes, the first thing he saw was Venus, the morning star, and the vision of it dissolved the last veil of ignorance. As Easwaren puts it,

> The dark waters of the unconscious closed over Siddhartha, and he slipped into that profound stillness in which thought stops and the distinctions of a separate personality dissolve. In this profound state he remained immersed throughout the night.
>
> When dawn came the tree under which he sat burst into bloom, and a fragrant spring breeze showered him with blossoms. He was no longer Siddhartha, the finite personality that had been born in Kapilavastu. He was the Buddha, "he who is awake." He had found the way to that realm of being which decay and death can never touch: *nirvana*.[3]

So what is this *nirvana* that Buddha experienced? Naturally, the experience is ineffable; that is, it cannot be expressed in words. Each person must experience it personally; no one can tell another what it is. The word *nirvana* literally means "to blow out," as to blow out the flame of a candle. What Buddha blew out was the last vestige of the ego illusion, and with it, the last remnant of ego craving. And in that moment, all illusions having gone, he saw perfectly the truth of his own nature: that his being was one with all Being. He saw the truth of life and death. He saw that human fear arises from a nightmare of illusion. But he was now awake, and the nightmare was gone forever.

According to the story, Buddha was overwhelmed by the rapture of his vision of truth. He remained in meditation for a long time, absorbed in the joy of it. Once again, Mara came to him. Now Mara had good reason to be worried. Again he sat down beside Buddha and remained silent for a long time. At last he spoke: "Well Buddha, you have done what no other person has done. You have seen what no other person has seen. You are free even from the tyranny of the fear of death. Congratulations, Buddha; I salute you. What is there left for you? Surely you can no longer expect to keep the company of other men. No one could understand or share your experience. You would be treated as a fool if you tried to talk about that which no one else can fathom. What is there for you now but to withdraw to a private place for the remainder of your mortal days, there to enjoy the perfect bliss of your enlightenment?"

Mara was in fact putting Buddha to a test; in a way, it was the "last temptation of Buddha." If Buddha had agreed with this eminently sensible suggestion, Mara would have known that Buddha's awakening was not perfect awakening. But Buddha's awakening was perfect awakening, and he did not take the bait. However tempting it might be to go off alone and enjoy the bliss of his discovery in splendid solitude, Buddha would not even consider such a thing. The greatest thing about Buddha was his compassion, compassion for all of the suffering men and women of the world. He had discovered a path that led to the release from suffering, and all that he cared about was sharing this discovery with others. He himself could not be perfectly happy until all others were, too. This act of total compassion is taken to be conclusive evidence of the fact that Buddha's enlightenment was perfect.

To Mara's objection that no one would be able to comprehend his message, Buddha answered with the analogy of the lotus pond, a familiar sight to the people of Buddha's time. Then, as now, the lotus pond was a part of the natural landscape in many places in India. The lotus plant begins as a seed buried deep in the muck at the dark bottom of the pond. From there, the stalk grows to the surface of the pond, where, in the full light of the sun, the tightly wrapped flower bud opens up into a beautiful symmetrical blossom. Few things in nature seem more fully open than does a lotus blossom in full bloom. The whole process, from seed to flower, makes a wonderful symbol for the path that leads to awakening.

Buddha said that everyone can be compared to some stage in the growth of the lotus plant. Many people are still at the seed stage, immersed in darkness. Others have begun to sprout and are making their way toward the light. Some have broken through the surface, but are still holding back; their buds are well formed, but still tightly wrapped. And there are those few who are already beginning to open up and simply need the full light of the sun to blossom completely. Buddha's teaching would be like the sunlight. "Everyone," he said, "can benefit from it to some degree. No matter where he or she may be, every person can make some progress toward the light. And some can be moved to awaken completely." For this reason, Buddha concluded, his mission was to bring the light of his teaching to as many as could hear his words. He would dedicate the rest of his life to spreading the good word of his awakening.

THE TEACHING YEARS

And that's exactly what he did. Buddha was in his mid-thirties at the time of his awakening. He lived for about another forty-five years. For all of this time, he lived as an itinerant teacher, walking the length and breadth of the great Ganges plain, spreading his message to the crowds that would gather wherever he stopped. He became famous in his own time. Buddha treated all people with equal compassion and respect; there was no caste system of privilege in his eyes. He accepted equally the hospitality of kings and poor farmers.

According to the story of Buddha's life, his first discourse after awakening occurred at a place called the Deer Park, near the town of Sarnath, which is not far from the holy city of Varanasi. The spot would naturally become a place of pilgrimage for followers of Buddha, and today it still attracts great numbers of visitors. In time, a large shrine was erected there to commemorate the event.*

When Siddhartha went off alone to meditate, his dismayed companions lost track of him. But soon they missed him deeply and went looking for him. They caught up with him at Sarnath, and it was to this small group of companions that Buddha delivered his first discourse. They were shocked at the sight of their friend and at the great change that had come over him. When Siddhartha, now properly referred to as Buddha, told them that he had seen through to the truth of life and death, they begged him to share his vision with them, and thus did the teaching career of Buddha begin. We will examine the substance of this discourse in the next chapter.

The original group of five companions eventually grew to ten. Buddha referred to them as the *sangha*. The sangha would become a permanent and basic element of Buddhist life. The communal group, living closely together under the direction of a spiritual leader and helping one another along the path, was seen from the earliest times to be a powerful help in the quest for awakening. The sangha was very much like an ashram. The word *sangha* referred to a representative body of nobles that consulted with a king. There was something of a democratic element in a sangha. Perhaps Buddha chose the word because he encouraged a more individual, democratic spirit in his group and thus wanted to distinguish his ashram from the more traditional type. Although Buddha retained much of the Hindu tradition, in a fundamental way he was making a break with the past.

---

*There are four "holy sites" associated with the life of Buddha: Lumbini, where he was born; Bodh Gaya, where he experienced his awakening; Sarnath, the site of his first discourse; and Kusinara, where, according to traditional belief, Buddha died.

In addition to the small group of close companions who traveled with Buddha, many others who heard his words were deeply moved and wished to dedicate themselves completely to this new way of life. Thus did communities of monks, to use the common English term, take form in many places. Buddha referred to these men as the Order. For a time, he resisted the suggestion that women be allowed to join the Order; he feared that the distractions and temptations would be too great for human nature in a community of men and women living closely together. Eventually, though, he relented and organized a separate Order of women.* This is not to suggest that ordinary householders were left out of the picture; the sunlight of Buddha's teaching was to fall on everyone. But some felt the heat more intensely and were eager to dedicate themselves wholeheartedly to the quest. For these zealous ones, the communal life of the Order was the logical path.

Buddha and his immediate group of disciples lived the itinerant lifestyle, calling no place home. It is said, though, that in the later years he accepted a small piece of land near the town of Sarvatti that the group could use as a home base. The land was a gift from a wealthy landowner and would have been a real benefit during the rainy season. Most of the time, though, the small band would have been out on the dusty road. Buddha wanted to share his teaching with as many as possible. In this, Buddha was far from being a unique figure; the itinerant guru has always been a part of life in India, and in the turbulent time of Buddha's life there must have been more than the usual number. Undoubtedly, Buddha and his teaching attracted especially great attention. Still, he was only one of many teachers, and we might never have heard of him had it not been for the work of his disciples. Buddha never wrote any books; all that we know of his teaching was preserved in memory by his disciples and handed down for several centuries in the oral tradition.

There were many disciples in Buddha's sangha; tradition has it that ten of these were especially close to him. Tradition also has it that one of these ten was his own son, Rahula. There is a legendary story about Buddha returning to his home city, Kapilavastu. By this time, he was a famous man. During his stay in Kapilavastu, Buddha made peace with his father and with his wife, Yashodhara, who joined the Order of women. It was at that time, according to the story, that Rahula became one of the Ten.

---

*Buddha's commitment to equality, including gender equality, was undoubtedly very far ahead of the general attitude of his time. Nonetheless, his stand regarding the place of woman has drawn criticism in modern times. Kate Wheeler, herself a practicing Buddhist for seventeen years, takes up the matter in an article she wrote for the Buddhist periodical, *Tricycle*. She points out that Buddha was actually very reluctant to organize a women's order and agreed to it only on the condition that the women accept many additional rules, the total effect of which was to assure that the women would live in subjugation to men. The very first of these rules concerned bowing. Male monks bowed to all senior male monks, but Buddha decreed that a woman monk, "even of a hundred years standing," bow before all male monks, even those who had been monks for only one day. Wheeler concludes her article with the interesting and intentionally provocative challenge, "In the case of women, the Buddha was wrong—and we have to have the courage to say so."

This account is clearly one of the later embellishments, and whether anything like it ever actually happened is impossible to say.

In any case, even if Rahula did become a disciple, he is not described as Buddha's favorite. The "one that Buddha loved most," according to the legend, was the young Ananda (whose name means "bliss" in Sanskrit). Ananda probably joined the group as a boy. He is described as youthful, charming, and something of an innocent. We can imagine him being totally devoted to Buddha, always ready to help him out with any chore. He is often pictured sitting close to Buddha. (How similar this is to the story of Jesus's relationship with his young disciple, John.)

Almost the opposite of Ananda in personality was the disciple named Malunkyaputra. Here was a man who dearly loved to think deeply and rationally about the problems of life. In a way, it's odd that he became a disciple at all; Buddha was nothing like that. In no way at all were Buddha's "discourses" rational expositions. He taught by example and by parable. In Buddha's opinion, metaphysical questions were a waste of time; they did not get at real truth. Such discussions come down to nothing more than intellectual game playing. When metaphysical questions were raised, Buddha's typical response was to remain silent. This must have been very perplexing to Malunkyaputra. Apparently, he tried endlessly to draw Buddha into a discussion of metaphysical matters, especially the nature of *nirvana*, but Buddha always deflected the discussion to other subjects. Finally, in desperation, Malunkyaputra went to Buddha and put the matter right on the line. His mind was in turmoil regarding certain vexing questions, and if Buddha refused to answer them, he had decided that he was going to leave the Order and go back to his home:

> Blessed One, there are theories which you have left unexplained and set aside unanswered: whether the world is eternal or not eternal; whether it is finite or infinite; whether the soul and body are the same or different; whether a person who has attained *nirvana* exists after death or does not, or whether perhaps he both exists and does not exist, or neither exists nor does not. The fact that the Blessed One has not explained these matters neither pleases me nor suits me. If the Blessed One will not explain this to me, I will give up spiritual disciplines and return to the life of a layman.[4]

It's easy to picture Buddha sighing deeply when Malunkyaputra had finished. "Malunkyaputra," he might have said, "when you took up the spiritual life, did I ever promise you I would answer these questions?" Poor Malunkyaputra; he must have known then that he wasn't going to get his answers—not in the way he wanted, anyway. But Buddha did give him a reply. He asked Malunkyaputra to imagine a man being wounded in the leg by a poison-tipped arrow. The wound was severe, and the man was in imminent danger of death. What he needed *above everything else* was to have that arrow removed, immediately! Would he tell the surgeon to wait until he knew more about the man who shot him? Before having the arrow removed, would he demand to know the archer's caste, his family background, the kind of wood his bow was made from, the name of the fletcher who made the arrow? Of course not! Malunkyaputra had to agree that only a fool would raise such questions; he'd be dead long before they were answered. "Well, Malunkyaputra," Buddha would have said, "I don't teach whether the world is finite or eternal. I teach how to remove the arrow."

The disciple named Kasyapa fell somewhere between the extremes of Ananda and Malunkyaputra. He was devoted, loyal, compassionate, and very intelligent. One gets the feeling that if the group had been the crew of a ship, Kasyapa would have been the first mate. It was to Kasyapa, we are told, that the Buddha entrusted his only possessions—his robe and begging bowl—when he knew that the end was near. These two items would later be interpreted as the "insignia" of the rightful claim to be the spiritual successor of Shakyamuni Buddha.

Buddha was about eighty years old when he died. He had spent the last forty-five years of his life traveling through much of north India, and his teaching had an enormous impact wherever he had gone. But like all things in life, the teaching career of Buddha must finally reach its end. The Pali Canon gives us a fairly detailed record of Buddha's last days. The final three months are summed up in a short work known as the "Discourse on the Great Decease." It was fitting that death would come to Buddha while he and his closest disciples were on the road. They were on their way to the city of Kusinara (also spelled Kushinagara; modern Kasia) when the end came.

It was the custom of the sangha to spend the night wherever they happened to be at nightfall. They would gratefully accept whatever hospitality might be offered to them. Buddha had become famous and much loved; it was a great honor to give him and his disciples shelter for the night. At one place where they stopped, a humble village on the road to Kusinara, the excited owner of a blacksmith shop did his best to make them comfortable. The smith, a man named Cunda, prepared a dinner for Buddha and his companions. It would be Buddha's last meal. As the story goes,

> The Master and his group were invited to a meal for the following day by the smith Cunda. In order to put something special before the venerable guest, Cunda had, among other dishes, prepared *sukara-maddava* [literally, the "soft food of pigs"]. What exactly this was still remains uncertain. Some writers think it was pork, others think of tender bamboo-shoots such as grow near a pigsty, others again some kind of fungus, possibly truffles. But, whatever it may have been, the Buddha viewed this food with suspicion, and asked Cunda not to offer it to the other monks. He himself, however, partook of it, in order not to disappoint the well-meaning smith.[5]

Buddha became very sick and suffered extreme pain. Nevertheless, the next day the group moved on. They stopped to rest in a fruit orchard near the town of Kusinara. It was springtime and the trees were in bloom. Buddha's disciples made a comfortable place for him to rest, but it was soon clear to everyone that the end was near.

That which they dreaded was now close at hand. What would happen to them without their beloved leader? Who would lead the sangha? Indeed, who *would* lead the sangha? This has been an important question in the history of Buddhism. Did Buddha appoint a successor, and if he did, what would have been the basis for making such a profoundly important choice? The tradition of Zen Buddhism teaches that Buddha chose the brilliant monk, Kasyapa, to be his successor, and he in time chose another, and so on in a long unbroken succession down to the time of the founding of Zen.

From the writings of the Pali Canon we get a different view. When the disciple Ananda, whom Buddha loved greatly, approached the master and tried to discreetly raise the subject of a succession, Buddha gave him this answer:

> Ananda, you should live as islands unto yourselves, being your own refuge, seeking no other refuge; with the Dharma as an island, with the Dharma as your refuge, seeking no other refuge. . . . Those monks who in my time or afterwards live thus, seeking an island and a refuge in themselves and in the Dharma and nowhere else, these zealous ones are truly my monks and will overcome the darkness.[6]

In other words, at least according to this version, Buddha chose not to name a particular person to stand in his place. His teaching (the Dharma) would be their leader, and the Dharma would stand on its own as the guide for all time to come. Buddha made a strong point of insisting that followers of his teaching be "islands unto yourselves." Elsewhere, he had declared, "Be ye lamps unto yourselves. Be ye a refuge to yourselves." This is not to say that the sangha, the community of monks helping one another, was not important; it was seen to be very important. Ultimately, though, each person must discover the truth within himself. There is to be no blind dependence on an outside authority.

On the afternoon of his last day, Buddha wanted to be sure that there were no strings left untied. He gathered his disciples around him and asked whether anyone had any last questions. Was there anything at all that they had perhaps been reluctant to ask? "It may be that one of you has doubts or uncertainty about the Buddha, the Dharma, or the sangha, or about the practice. Ask, if you do, lest afterward you feel remorse." Everyone was silent. A short time later, Buddha uttered his last words: "Now, monks, I declare to you: all things that come into being are subject to decay. Strive on untiringly!" After saying this, Buddha slipped into a coma, and during the night he died.

To say the least, his disciples were stricken with grief. They were now orphans. But Buddha had been with them a long time and had instructed them carefully. They would take the time to lovingly perform the rites of cremation and then get on with the work. Buddha had entrusted them and all who would come after them with the task of spreading the word of his teaching, of not ceasing to work with compassion until every man and woman on earth had achieved the freedom of awakening. It is to an examination of this wonderful philosophy of life, the teaching of Buddha, that we turn in the next chapter.

Notes

1. Kenneth Ch'en, *Buddhism* (New York: Barrons, 1968), p. 19.
2. Eknath Easwaren, The *Dhammapada* (Petaluma, CA: Nilgiri, 1986), p. 26.
3. *Ibid.*, p. 27.
4. *Ibid.*, p. 40.
5. H.W. Schumann, *The Historical Buddha* (London: Arkana, 1989), English translation copyright © M. O'C. Walshe, 1989. Reproduced by permission of Penguin Books, Ltd., p. 247.
6. Digha-Nikaya, as quoted in Schumann, p. 246.

Study Questions

1. How did Sakyamuni come to be called "the Buddha"?
2. Why is it important to the story of Buddha's life that both his youth in the palace and his years as a sadhu be perfect examples of those two kinds of lifestyle?
3. What did Siddhartha encounter when he left the palace by each of the four gates, and what is the symbolic significance of each gate?
4. What led Siddhartha to conclude that self-fulfillment cannot be attained through either self-indulgence or self-denial?
5. What was the essential character of Buddha's "awakening"?
6. What was the role of the god Mara in Buddha's struggle to become awakened? How is Mara's role to be interpreted?
7. What is the meaning of the "analogy of the lotus pond"?
8. In responding to Malunkyaputra's effort to lure him into a discussion of metaphysical questions, Buddha tells a story about a man wounded by a poison-tipped arrow. What point is Buddha trying to make?

10

The Basic Teaching of Buddha

Buddha taught by word of mouth and by personal example. So far as we are aware, he didn't commit anything to writing. Thus, all that we know of Buddha's teaching has come down to us from others. From the very beginning, though, both an oral tradition and a written tradition developed. Approximately four centuries after Buddha's death, the first great effort was made to gather together the existing sources and determine, insofar as was possible, the true record of Buddha's life and teaching. This scholarly and thoroughgoing work came to be known as the Pali Canon. We shall examine it in detail in the next chapter. The Pali Canon is the scriptural core of Theravada, the first great organized movement in the evolution of Buddhism.

Historically speaking, there are two great traditions in the evolution of Buddhism. The earlier of these is what is referred to here as Theravada, the "doctrine of the elders." Strictly speaking, the name *Theravada* (pronounced tair-a-VAH-da) refers to only one school—the dominant school—within the closely related parts of the early development of Buddhism. In the course of time, Theravada Buddhism would be joined, and even overshadowed, by the second of the great traditions. For the most part, these later developments are united under the name *Mahayana Buddhism.* The Mahayanists referred to the older, orthodox tradition as "Hinayana," which was something of a derogatory term, and implied that it had a lesser status. Due to the great influence of Mahayana, the terms *Mahayana* and *Hinayana* are used by many even to this day to distinguish between the two great Buddhist traditions. In modern times, however, there is a growing preference for the term *Theravada* in place of *Hinayana*. For one thing, Theravada is the only part of the original tradition to survive into modern times. For all practical purposes, *Theravada* and *Hinayana* mean the same thing. In this work, I shall use the term *Theravada*.

We shall thoroughly examine both Theravada and Mahayana in the appropriate place. Naturally, the presentation of Buddha's teaching, and the emphasis given to various themes, would evolve over time. Mahayana differs from Theravada in many important respects. Fundamentally, though, all of Buddhism emerges from the same original core. In this chapter, we shall consider the initial core teaching, essentially as it is given in the Pali Canon. This is the logical place to start. The far-flung evolution of the teaching, as we find it in the history of Mahayana, will be presented as we examine the historical development of Buddhism.

It is a common mistake to think of Buddha as a spiritual leader, the deliberate founder of one of the world's great religions. He, however, did not see himself as a religious leader at all. Buddha was a teacher. Following his awakening, he dedicated his life to teaching others how to do what he had done—that is, how to find the way to freedom from fear and suffering.

It has long been popular to compare Buddha to a doctor; his "patients" were all of the suffering men and women of the world. Buddha's task was to help them get well again. That's what awakening is: getting well. Buddha would help people to heal themselves. He would show them the path by which they could find the way to their own awakening.

Buddha was not interested in dogma. He did not wish to tell people what is right and what is wrong. He made no appeal to a higher authority of any kind, What Buddha taught was a philosophy of life, a way of living. This way of life could lead to freedom— that is, to awakening—for any man or woman willing to follow it. Neither sex, nor age, nor wealth, nor rank in society would make any difference at all. Any person, in any place or time, willing to take on the way of life and follow the path, was assured of making progress toward liberation. Throughout the ages countless men and women have taken up the challenge and have found their own lives revolutionized by the teaching of this man who lived so long ago.

The various Buddhist traditions that have evolved over the past two-and-a-half millennia range from the very secular to the decidedly religious. Each, of course, claims to be faithful to the original spirit of Buddha's teaching. Our task is to attempt to determine the essential teaching that is fundamental to all of Buddhism, Buddha's own foundation from which so much has grown.

The place to begin is Buddha's awakening. It is because of the awakening that we call him *Buddha*. Recall that the name is derived from the Sanskrit *budh*, which means "to wake up." In a moment of supreme insight, Buddha "awakened" to a clear vision of the truth of his real nature. There was no way that he, or anyone else, could describe his experience in words. Buddha couldn't share this great experience with others simply by telling them what it was, but through his teaching, he could show others how to achieve the same experience of awakening in their own lives.

In talking about Buddha's awakening, we tend to fall back on metaphor. The word "awakening" is itself a metaphor. Buddha compared our ordinary state of consciousness to a dream state. While sleeping, we don't know that we're dreaming; at the time, it all seems very real and often very frightening. But when we wake up, we know instantly that we were dreaming—that our experience was an illusion and there was really nothing to be afraid of. Buddha would say that, even when we wake up from what we ordinarily call dreams, we remain in something of a dream state. Of course, we don't recognize that; we assume that our everyday state of consciousness is a state in which we are fully awake. But is it? Buddha would say that it is not—that we remain prisoners of our illusions and fears. It is possible, though, to awaken from this state in the same way that we awaken from dreams.

Buddha's awakening is sometimes referred to as his "Enlightenment" or "Liberation." Whatever word we use, we are talking about an experience that was the great watershed of his life. When Buddha (or rather, Siddhartha) withdrew into meditation, it was as though he died, and then in the moment of awakening he came forth reborn, a "new man." He "awakened" to a sudden and clear vision of the truth of his real nature. But what does that mean? Is metaphor the only way we can approach this tantalizing subject?

Granted, the subject of Buddha's awakening is not something that can be neatly captured in words. Words can go only so far, but they can help to point the way to understanding truth. It is of the essence of Buddha's awakening that he experienced clearly and perfectly the truth of the underlying unity of all being. It's one thing to say that one believes it to be true, but it's quite another thing to *see* the indisputable truth of it. Our commonsense perception is that reality is not one at all, but rather is made up of myriad separate and discrete things, "myself" being one of them. Buddha saw beyond this illusory sense of separation and beheld the more fundamental, universal reality of which all the seemingly separate realities are but manifestations. Thus it is that by seeing into the essential reality of his own nature, he beheld the fundamental reality of *all* nature. Penetrating to the core of *any* expression of reality is penetrating to the core of *all* reality.

Vedanta philosophy had, of course, taught that All is One, and the One is Brahman. For Buddha to penetrate to a deep vision of this truth would not put him in conflict with the Hindu tradition of his time. In fact, his awakening would be a dramatic affirmation of the Vedanta tradition. It is argued by some that this is the correct way to interpret the awakening of Buddha. His great insight was not fundamentally in conflict with the traditional teaching of Hindu spirituality. Buddha did not use the term *Brahman* in his teaching, but in a section of the Pali Canon known as the Udana, he is said to have referred to "the unborn, the unformed, the unbecome." Some would see this as carrying essentially the same meaning as the concept of Brahman. Interpreted in this way, Buddha's awakening was a reaffirmation of the essential truth of the Hindu tradition; he simply saw more deeply and clearly and thus was able to give new life and meaning to the age-old wisdom. He was not so much a revolutionary as he was a reformer.

There is another, quite different interpretation. Some maintain that what Buddha discovered in that moment of perfect insight was in stark contradiction to the fundamentals of the traditional teaching. It was a new departure, and it was the moment of birth of a revolution in human thought. This interpretation can be summed up in what is generally referred to as the *Doctrine of Anatman*. (Writers on this subject often use the Pali word *anatta*, but we shall stay with the Sanskrit term, *anatman*.)

Buddhism is not a dogmatic system of thought. There is no such thing as a Buddhist "pope" to make final decisions about the truth. Ultimately, each person must make these decisions for himself or herself. Buddha set the tone for this attitude in his famous words, "Be ye a lamp unto yourself." The matter of *anatman* is no exception; the student must evaluate it personally. It is a fascinating subject and well worth our time to examine carefully. What follows is an exposition of the Doctrine of *Anatman*. Bear in mind that this is not an attempt to present the truth in a convenient package; it is simply an effort to clarify what is meant by the doctrine, and its possible implications for the teaching of Buddha. The Doctrine of *Anatman* is the philosophical centerpiece of several closely related principles that concern the nature of reality. We shall focus on *anatman*, but bring into the discussion other matters as they become appropriate.

THE DOCTRINE OF ANATMAN

In Sanskrit, the prefix *a* or *an* is a negative; it negates the noun. Therefore, the word *anatman* technically means "no *atman*," "no Self." Before we go into this idea, it would be helpful to briefly review the meaning of *atman*. Belief in *atman* was the cornerstone of traditional Vedanta teaching.

According to that teaching, all is Brahman, the creator and upholder of the universe. Brahman, as *atman*, is the core, the soul, of every sentient being. The Brahman-Atman is the core consciousness; ego is the role. Our own role-playing enthralls us and blinds us to the deeper truth. The ignorance (*avidya*) of ego identitfication, and the hopeless effort to satisfy the cravings of ego burden us with all of life's suffering.

The Vedanta tradition taught that the way to freedom from suffering is to break out of the cage of ego delusion and discover the real Self, the *atman*. Such discovery was called *moksha*. It might take many lifetimes, but eventually all would climb to the summit of the mountain, and Brahman would rediscover itself perfectly.

During his sadhu years, Buddha (then Siddhartha) gave himself over completely to freeing himself from the shackles of ego and to discovering the pure vision of *atman* in the depths of meditation. He put forth as fine an effort as any human being possibly could, but, as we know, it didn't happen. Thus came about what we may call his second great realization: There is no self-fulfillment through self-denial. The second great realization goes hand in hand with the first. Seemingly, they are the two sides of one coin. First Buddha discovered that he couldn't find self-fulfillment in self-indulgence; then he found that its opposite, self-denial, didn't work either. What else is there?

In desperation, Buddha withdrew into deep meditation, determined not to leave the spot until he penetrated through his ignorance and discovered the true nature of his Self. What set the stage for the great moment of his awakening was what we might refer to as a third and final insight regarding self-fulfillment. Buddha saw that his first two insights, though truthful in themselves, were founded on a fundamental error that we may put in the following way:

In his first great realization, Buddha concluded that *there is no self-fulfillment through self-indulgence*. In the second great realization, he concluded that *there is no self-fulfillment through self-denial*. His third great realization was the sudden awareness that there is no self-fulfillment at all—*no self-fulfillment, period!* There can *be* no self-fulfillment because *there is no self to be fulfilled!*

His heroic quest had been an impossible one from the beginning because there is no *atman* to be discovered (*anatman*; no *atman*). It's a shocking thought; let me repeat it. His quest had been an impossible one from the beginning because *there is no atman to be discovered!* There is no *atman*-Self to be fulfilled. The whole notion of *atman*, the cornerstone of Vedanta philosophy, was simply a fantastic error. However appealing, however enticing, however reasonable, however enshrined in tradition, Buddha saw in a flash of insight that it was all a construction of the human mind, without any objective reality at all.

The concept of *atman* had developed as a logical necessity. I am a conscious being. What I am conscious of (aware of) are my own experiences. I am aware of what I see, what I taste, what I think. In other words, I am the conscious subject of my own experiences; that seems self-evident and undeniable. My sight cannot be aware of itself; "I" am aware of what I see! According to the Vedanta view, the "I" that is aware is *atman*, the conscious core, the subject of all conscious experiences, the hearer of sounds, the see-er of sights, the feeler of feelings, the thinker of thoughts. The ego role is part of the world of *maya*; it "dances" before *atman*, so entrancing it that *atman* is hypnotized into falsely identifying with it. Thus evolved yoga, whose goal it became to shed the layers of ego until one discovered the *atman*, the seed at the core of one's being. In the words of the *Bhagavad Gita*;

> The body is mortal, but he who dwells in the body is immortal and immeasurable.[1]
>
> As a man abandons worn-out clothes and acquires new ones, so when the body is worn out a new one is acquired by the Self, who lives within.[2]

A similar line of thinking developed in modern Western philosophy. The British empiricist John Locke introduced the concepts of what he called primary qualities and secondary qualities. Secondary qualities are the things that we perceive with the senses: color, texture, smell, etc. We never directly perceive the primary qualities, such things as extension in space, but they are what "hold," or express, the secondary qualities, which we do perceive. Someone once asked Locke how he could be sure that the primary qualities really did exist if we never perceive them. His answer was classic: "My God, man, they have to!"

Well, given Locke's system of reasoning, they do have to exist. But that doesn't mean they really do. The same could be said with regard to the concepts of *atman*. Buddha, like virtually everyone else of his culture, had accepted the reality of *atman* without question because it seemed so reasonable and necessary. The only problem was that it was nowhere to be found. Buddha (as Siddhartha) had become a master of all the disciplines of yoga, yet try as he might, he never experienced any state of consciousness that he could honestly identify as the *atman*. Buddha concluded that there is no such thing as *atman*. There is no subject of the role; there is only the role. That insight finally freed him from all ignorance. Suddenly, the dreamlike state that is ordinary consciousness dissolved, and Buddha saw clearly the true nature of his being. He was awake.

Buddha saw that there is no "substanding" self of any kind—that is to say, no substantive enduring reality "standing beneath" and supporting the changing appearances.

There is movement; there is change; there is development over time. But there is nothing that is *doing* all of this. There is just the process itself, no do-er thereof. Reality, you might say, is a constant flow of patterns of energy. But there is nothing that is *doing* it; there is just the flow. All underlying "things," including the notion of *atman*, are simply illusions of the imagination. Buddha is supposed to have said, "There is liberation, but no *one* who is liberated."

According to the Doctrine of *Anatman*, Buddha was saying, in effect, that not only does the concept of self lack substantial reality, but *everything* lacks substantial reality. Anything you can think of is, at bottom, a fleeting process of change. Nothing can really stand on its own as a permanent, self-explaining entity. This teaching is expressed in two principles: the Doctrine of Anitya, which holds that impermanence is a characteristic of all existence, and the Doctrine of Dependent Origination, which explains that the intelligibility of anything is dependent on a variety of causes and conditions outside itself. In other words, nothing can explain itself. The existence of every single thing a house, a star, or whatever—can be understood only in terms of other things that define it and cause it to be. These two matters, then—impermanence and dependency—are said to be of the fundamental character of existence. They explain the insubstantiality of everything, including, of course, the concept of *atman*.

The concept of *anatman* can sometimes seem to stand common sense on its head. And it does! But sometimes common sense can mislead us. The discoveries of modern physics make that abundantly clear. Let's examine this subject in an orderly way, and I think that most (if not all) of the confusion will disappear. Remember, the most important thing is that you *understand* the concept of *anatman*, not necessarily that you agree or disagree with it. What follows is an attempt to explain how the all-important sense of a separate substanding self develops. The Doctrine of *Anatman* holds that this error— virtually universal among humans—is the root cause of suffering.

Virtually every normal person has a strong sense of "myself"—a strong sense of "I am." And the "I" here refers to a purportedly substantive entity with which the person identifies. It is the conscious "me" that is the subject of all personal experience, of all memories; it is the feeler of feelings and the thinker of thoughts. It is the underlying "me" that remains constant through time from birth to death and perhaps beyond death as well. It is the ego, the "me," that makes decisions and hence gives me a sense of control and direction in life. When I make a fist, "I" make a fist; when I walk across the room, "I" walk across the room.

We are conditioned from infancy to see ourselves in this way. A baby receives a distinct name right on his or her birth certificate and is encouraged in myriad ways to identify with it. One of the first words a child learns to say, usually loudly, is "mine." The language is full of such subtle conditionings: "Let yourself go." "Be yourself!" "Collect yourself!" And then there's always "self-esteem," "self-pity," and even "self-loathing."

Everywhere we turn, the culture supports our unquestioned conviction that the sense of self—a substantive, enduring self—is real and beyond question; it is self-evident. This fixed belief was given the seal of authority by the French philosopher René Descartes, who laid the cornerstone of modern Western philosophy with his famous dictum, *Cogito, ergo sum*: "I think, therefore I am."

Personal experience also comes into play in support of the reality of the ego-self. It has to do with the experience that we call "self-consciousness." Rather than attempting to merely talk about it, let me ask you to take a few minutes to perform a simple meditation exercise. It won't matter whether you do or do not have experience in the practice of meditation. Just sit quietly in a comfortable position, and turn your attention inward. Become aware of the chatter that's going on in your thinking mind. Try to let the thoughts drop away so that, as far as possible, you're not *doing* anything mentally; you're simply aware of the fact of your existence, your act of being.

This exercise in self-consciousness can lead to a dramatic experience, and the deeper you're able to go, the more dramatic it will become. As the activity, the play of the mind settles down, you will become aware of yourself as a watcher, an observer, of what it is that you do. This subtle sense of self, usually lost in the background of our active daily life, can become very profound when the activity is turned off and the awareness is turned inward. It is as though the real me, down at the core, is some silent, unblinking, wise being from which emanates all this ego role-playing that I endlessly engage in. Thus, the sense of the underlying, enduring self is supported not only conceptually, but experientially as well.

Buddha was a master of meditation. He plumbed the depths of his own inner being, convinced originally that the silent self at the center was *atman*, and he would not rest until he saw it perfectly, until he was one with it. But as we know, all his efforts came to nothing. In this, the most important goal of life, he came up empty. Buddha concluded that the whole concept of *atman* was only that: a concept. He didn't find the *atman* because there was no *atman* to be found. Those who claimed otherwise were simply deluding themselves. *Atman* is just another trick of the thinking human mind. It is nothing more than a subtle way of conceptualizing the self-image, the ego.

Ego is at the heart of the problem. Buddha believed that the attachment to ego is what human suffering is all about. It is the core attachment; all others relate to it because, ultimately, all cravings seek to satisfy the wants of the ego. Awakening depends on liberating oneself from the bondage of attachments. Most of all, this means liberation from the prison that is the delusion of the ego-self. There is no substantive underlying "me" at all. We are urged to awaken from the dreamlike delusion that we take to be real and cling to desperately.

Of course, the authors of the Upanishads had also taught that liberation means liberation from the delusion of the ego role. Both Buddha and the Upanishads taught that the road to ruin lay in man's hunger to identify with the ego. Attachment to ego is fundamental *avidya* for the Upanishads and for Buddha. The great difference, though, is to be found in the matter of *atman*. The Upanishads proclaimed that one broke through the illusion of ego by discovering the real Self, the conscious subject, the *atman*, Buddha proclaimed that this was an impossible dream. There is no *atman*! Faith in its existence only perpetuates the delusion of a substanding self. Faith in the existence of *atman* tragically *increases* one's attachment to ego. In smashing the idol of *atman*, Buddha was breaking with the most cherished belief of the past and stepping out onto entirely new ground. This matter of the revolutionary nature of the Doctrine of *Anatman* is summed up very nicely by the Buddhist scholar Walpola Rahula:

> What in general is suggested by Soul, Self, Ego, or to use the Sanskrit expression *atman*, is that in man there is a permanent, everlasting and absolute entity, which is the unchanging substance behind the changing phenomenal world. According to some religions, each individual has such a separate soul which is created by God, and which, finally after death, lives eternally either in hell or heaven, its destiny depending on the judgment of its creator. According to others, it goes through many lives till it is completely purified and becomes finally united with God or Brahman, Universal Soul or *atman*, from which it originally emanated. This soul or self in man is the thinker of thoughts, feeler of sensations, and receiver of rewards and punishments for all its actions good and bad. Such a conception is called the idea of self.
>
> Buddhism stands unique in the history of human thought in denying the existence of such a Soul, Self, or *atman*. According to the teaching of Buddha, the idea of self is an imaginary, false belief which has no corresponding reality, and it produces harmful thoughts of 'me' and 'mine', selfish desire, craving, attachment, hatred, ill-will, conceit, pride, egoism, and other defilements, impurities and problems. It is the source of all the troubles in the world from personal conflicts to wars between nations. In short, to this false view can be traced all the evil in the world.[3]

"To this *false view* can be traced all the evil in the world." That's quite a statement! It certainly emphasizes why the Doctrine of *Anatman* is regarded by many as a key to understanding the teaching of Buddha. He urges us, as did those before him, to seek liberation through discovering the truth about our real nature. And the first order of business is to proclaim that the traditional path is a false path: There is no *atman*; it is just an idea created by the human imagination.

There was a wonderful line in the movie *Total Recall*. A very bewildered Arnold Schwarzenegger asks, "If I'm not me, then who the hell am I?" That question expresses the frustration that one often feels at first in trying to comprehend this whole matter of *anatman*. You may well be asking the same sort of question: If there is no *me*, then who am *I*? If I am being asked to believe that I am deluding myself by believing that I, at the core, am a substantive being, then *who* is it that is doing the deluding? And who is it that is being deluded? Who is it that decides to walk across the room? Who is it that remembers events from the past and makes plans for the future? Who or what am I really? If I'm not *me*, then who the hell am I? Is Buddha saying that I don't *really* exist?

Certainly not. It's not that you don't exist; obviously, you do exist. It's that you *as a substantive entity* do not exist. According to this interpretation, you are the "doing" itself, not someone doing-the-doing. Another way of putting it is to say that there is no you; there is a "you-ing." Words at best are awkward in trying to capture the meaning of this. One needs to get a feeling for it, as well as an intellectual definition.

Consider the word "drift." It's a noun, a fixed idea. We speak, for example, of gla-cial drift. But when we look closely at it, we see that there really is no such *thing* as drift; it's always a drift-*ing*. In fact, there is really no such thing as a glacier that *is drifting*; the drifting *is* the glacier. Everything is like that, including you and I. According to this interpretation, all of the "things" of experience are patterns of movement (or should I say pattern-ings). Patternings often give the illusion of substantiality, as, for example, when a wave crosses a wheat field on a breezy day. It is obvious that the wave is not a *thing* that crosses the field; the wave is really a wave-ing.

This is also obvious in such perceptions as a whirlpool, or a circle of flame made by a fast-spinning torch. It's just as true, though perhaps not as immediately obvious, in the case of your own being. The real you is a pattern of energy flowing through the "wheat field" of time. The concept of self-identity is rooted in the continuity of the movement of the pattern, exactly as we perceive continuity in the wave that the breeze creates in the wheat field or the sustained spiral form that the wind creates in a hurricane.

As mentioned earlier, Buddha is said to have proclaimed, "There is liberation, but no *one* who is liberated." He might also have said, "There is birth, but no *one* who is born. There is death, but no *one* who dies." Buddha wanted to wake us up to the illu-sory nature of the separate self that we cling to. He probably would have smiled at Descartes's dictum, *I think, therefore I am.* What a preposterous unquestioned assump-tion is inherent in that statement! How would Buddha have finished Descartes's decla-ration? "I think, therefore. . . . [therefore what?]" Buddha would probably have said, "I think, therefore there is thinking."

Still, that unquestioned assumption, the belief that your *idea of self* realistically rep-resents a substanding being that is the real you, doesn't easily roll over and die. This feel-ing is unquestionably very strong. But, as Buddha would surely point out, it never actually goes beyond feeling, never goes beyond an *idea* of self. Ultimately, it comes down to being only an inference, a mental image. We never, *never* directly confront the reality of this being whom we tenaciously assert to be the *real me*, the thinker of my thoughts, the controller of my actions. What we do experience—and *all* that we ever experience—is a never-ending succession of discrete mental and sensory events. From these events, we *infer* the existence of a substantive me that is the *subject* of these events. But again, that is only an inference.

In reflecting on this succession of discrete mental and sensory events, Buddha described them collectively as the Five Skandhas, or, as it is often put in English, the Five Aggregates. Put simply, the Five Aggregates are sensations, perceptions, feelings, mem-ories, and volitions. They are the ever-fleeting bits and pieces of consciousness, and they are all that we ever know and experience directly:

> [Buddha said that he] found only a conglomeration of the five *skandhas* or
> aggregates, material body, feelings, perception, predispositions, and conscious-
> ness. At any one moment, according to him, we are but a temporary compo-
> sition of the five aggregates, and as these change every moment, so does the
> composition. Therefore all that we are is but a continuous living entity which
> does not remain the same for any two consecutive moments, but which comes

into being and disappears as soon as it arises. Why then should we attach so much importance to this transitory entity, in which there is no permanent self or soul? Once we accept this truth of the nonexistence of a permanent self, when we see that what we call the self is nothing but a stream of perishing physical and psychical phenomena, then we destroy our selfish desires and self-interests, and instead of suffering from anxieties and disappointments, we will enjoy peace of mind and tranquillity.[4]

The Doctrine of *Anatman* is not simply a theoretical curiosity, something merely to amuse scholars, but not really concerned with matters of practical importance. The implications of *anatman* are profound and important. Perhaps the most important implication of all concerns the matter of the reality of spirit. Some (but definitely not all) maintain that, by denying the reality of *atman*, Buddha was implicitly denying the fundamental reality of spirit. This is a matter of tremendous significance, both in Buddha's time and in all times. Men and women of virtually all human societies in all times of history have been terribly burdened by their belief in, and fear of, the world of spirits. Typically, the spirit world has been believed to be more real, and much more powerful, than the perceived world of everyday experience.

By denying the reality of *atman*, it is argued, Buddha pulled the rug out from under the rationale for belief in spirits. To believe that I am, at the core, a spirit gives credence to the proposition that reality comes in two kinds, matter and spirit. The Brahmin scholars may have limited spiritual reality to the concept of Brahman, but to the masses of the people, as you would expect, spiritual reality meant a vast and dazzling population of gods, demons, and departed souls. By sweeping this multitude away like the goblins of a nightmare, Buddha, in his great compassion, sought to set his people free from the tyranny of fear.

An extremely important liberation was involved in this attitude regarding the reality of spirits. The caste system was posited on the reality of *atman* and, more specifically, belief in reincarnation (*samsara*). It was accepted belief that a person was born into a given caste because his *atman*, due to past karma, had ascended (or descended) to that particular level and no other. For any individual to attempt to defy his destiny was a grievous sin and would generate a devastating burden of negative karma. The rigid hierarchy of the caste system was governed by this dogma. Buddha saw the caste system as a great evil. The elite few took advantage of this belief to suppress and exploit the suffering masses. In Buddha's eyes, there were no caste distinctions. Every man and woman was equally a glorious part of the one seamless whole of humanity. He yearned to liberate his people from the evil of caste, but so long as the hypnotic spell of *atman* endured, there would be no hope for change.

According to this interpretation, then, the Doctrine of *Anatman* denies the reality of a substantive self and, by implication, denies also the reality of spirit. And there is more: In sweeping away the reality of a spirit world, the Doctrine of *Anatman* has special significance with regard to the awesome matter of death. Death, the frightening mystery, the great nightmare—what's it all about? What a horrible thought—that I, this infinitely wonderful being, this personal center of the universe, could eventually just stop existing. Reflecting on it leads to a feeling of despair. How hopeless and meaning-less it all ultimately is if at some point I simply go out of existence forever. Shakespeare's *Macbeth* captures the feeling so perfectly:

> Life is but a walking shadow, a poor player who struts and frets his hour upon the stage, and then is heard no more. It's a tale told by an idiot, full of sound and fury, signifying nothing.[5]

Vedanta had stood up to the challenge of death and denied its reality. The real you is *atman*, and *atman* is Brahman; it never dies. Krishna expresses it succinctly in the *Bhagavad Gita*: "There has never been a time when you and I and the kings gathered here have not existed, nor will there be a time when we will cease to exist. As the same person inhabits the body through childhood, youth, and old age, so too at the time of death he attains another body. The wise are not deluded by these changes."[6] The *atman*, unfolding through the path of *samsara*, is reborn over and over, until it finally achieves perfect reabsorbtion in Brahman. The ego "dies," but that is only a role. *Atman*, the real you, never dies.

What, then, if there is no *atman*? Has our victory over the horror of death been only another dream? Buddha would answer that our fear has no basis; death has no real meaning. There is nothing to die—no *thing* that can come to an end and be annihilated. "There is death, but no *one* who dies." Worry about death is based on attachment to our idea of the substantive self, the "me" that exists for a time and then may be annihi-lated in death. But to those who have seen through the illusion of the separate self, death is nothing more than the cessation of a particular flowing pattern of energy. The wave across the wheat field comes to an end, but nothing has "died"; nothing has been destroyed.

The concept of *anatman* places the unreality of death on a new plane. No one dies, not really, because there is no one to die. Death is the cessation of a doing, not the anni-hilation of a being. It is the running out of a pattern of energy, as when we say the music "died" out.

At this point, we must take note that many people in this world who call themselves Buddhists do not personally accept the Doctrine of *Anatman* as explained here. Instead, they consider reincarnation to be real and consequently accept the reality of an individ-ual spirit that is reincarnated. Others, including some who do accept the Doctrine of *Anatman*, choose to see a real and continuing presence in the succession of generations. Death can be interpreted as a sort of transfer of karmic energy. A personal, individual soul may not migrate from one life to the next, but the great pattern of energy that is any given personal life endures in one way or another and continues to influence the condition of succeeding lives. There is thus a sense in which "rebirth" is real (much more about this later).

Thus do we have the Doctrine of *Anatman*. Again, let me point out that this par-ticular interpretation of Buddha's teaching is speculative. Indeed, there are those who contend that it does not accurately represent his thinking. There are also those who argue that we do not know enough to have any idea what Buddha's stand would be on this subject. But in the long tradition of Buddhist scholarship, there have always been many who take the position that the Doctrine of *Anatman* provides the conceptual key to making sense of the teaching of Buddha. Hence, if for no other reason, it is essential that the student of Buddhist philosophy have a clear understanding of this matter of "no self" and its profound implications.

What it comes down to is simply this: Either Buddha was an exponent of traditional Upanishadic philosophy, in fundamental agreement with its teaching, or he was a revolutionary, a man who parted with the past and struck out on a new path. It all comes down to the character of his awakening. If his awakening was a powerful reaffirmation of what was traditionally regarded to be truth, the life and teaching of Buddha can be seen as the flowering of the Hindu tradition. On the other hand, if the essence of Buddha's awakening is that he saw a whole new meaning in the ultimate truth of self, then his life and teaching can be seen as the beginning of a new path to liberation.*

Did Buddha affirm *atman* or did he deny *atman*? Or is there another possibility? An interpretation that has gained favor in recent times is that he neither affirmed nor denied *atman*. Rather, Buddha took the position that it is all completely irrelevant. One could never know *atman* even if it were to exist, no more than your eye can see itself. Since *atman* would be completely unknowable, even if it were to be real, the only sensible thing for us to do is to ignore the whole subject and get on with our lives.

Wouldn't it be wonderful if Buddha himself could enter the room and sit down among us? What would he say if we could ask him about these things? Very probably, he would say nothing at all; he would just smile and remain silent. We are told that this was his customary response to metaphysical questions. Buddha was concerned with teaching a way of living that would lead men and women to liberation from suffering. But we are students of the teaching of Buddha, and we seek a meaningful philosophical interpretation of it. The nature of Buddha's awakening is the proper place to begin, and that's what we have done. That was the seed from which all else would grow. Let us now turn to that growing.

THE FOUR NOBLE TRUTHS

Shortly after Buddha's awakening, his five sadhu companions caught up with him and were startled by the change that had come over him. They begged their friend to share with them what he had discovered. So, according to the story, the freshly awakened Buddha delivered his first discourse. This great event occurred at a place called the Deer Grove, not far from the town of Sarnath, which itself is near the holy city of Varanasi. To his five companions, Buddha laid out what would become the essence of his teaching.

Arya-satya is the Sanskrit term that identifies this foundation piece of Buddha's teaching. Literally, the term translates into English as "noble truth," and since there are

---

*Both views are alive and well: The Hindu world eventually made a place for Buddha, declaring him to be one of the incarnations of Vishnu.

four facets to its presentation, it has come to be known as the Four Noble Truths. Perhaps you recognize the Sanskrit word *arya* in there. This was the Aryans' name for themselves, the "noble ones." Hence, it is technically accurate to say the Four "Noble" Truths. Some find the word *noble* misleading in modern English, believing that it wrongly implies a kind of aristocratic meaning. These individuals prefer to say "the Four Great Truths." There is some logic in this interpretation, but in the present work I will stay with the traditional usage, the Four Noble Truths.

In the Four Noble Truths, Buddha succinctly lays out the problem of human life and what can be done about it. He goes right to the heart of the problem: human suffering. If it weren't for suffering, there would be no problem; everything would be perfect. Suffering, as everyone ever born knows, is the spoiler of life, and yet, Buddha assures us, suffering is totally unnecessary. Suffering is not inevitable; it is not inherent in the nature of life. Suffering can be overcome and left behind forever. This is the promise of awakening: freedom from suffering.

The First Noble Truth deals with the reality of suffering. It is universal, and it is the essence of the human problem. In the Second Noble Truth, Buddha identifies the cause of suffering. He then goes on in the Third Noble Truth to assure us that release from suffering is possible, that every man and woman is capable of awakening to the truth that brings freedom from suffering. The Fourth Noble Truth lays out the way of life that can lead one to awakening. This way of life is referred to as the Noble Eightfold Path.

The character of the Four Noble Truths reveals why it has been popular through the ages to compare Buddha to a doctor. (There is no evidence, however, that Buddha used that analogy himself.) He has a patient: humanity. The patient is suffering. He examines the patient and determines the nature of the illness and its cause. Then he makes a prognosis: A cure is possible, even though it may not be certain. Finally, he prescribes a course of treatment, which, if followed faithfully, has a very good chance of resulting in a full recovery. Like a genuinely good and compassionate doctor, Buddha does not depend on drugs; his treatment encourages the working of the patient's own natural healing power. Buddha can't *make* us get well, but the medicine of his teaching can certainly help us to heal ourselves.

Maybe it all sounds too simple when reduced to these terse everyday words. But simple it's not: The correct understanding of these concepts calls for much pondering. It is important that we enter into this subject carefully. The Four Noble Truths are separate, but closely related, facets of one subject: suffering. For this reason, it would be best—before going into the Four Noble Truths separately—to examine this topic as a whole—that is, to present a general exposition of the whole matter of suffering. Following that, we can examine suffering in terms of the Four Truths separately. As our inquiry unfolds, I hope you will see why we first took the time to analyze the meaning of *Anatman*. Many believe that understanding the Doctrine of *Anatman* is the key to understanding the Four Noble Truths.

Let me begin with a riddle: What is it that everyone wants to avoid at all costs—in fact, will do virtually anything to avoid—and yet wants to be able to say that he or she has experienced more of it than anyone else? The answer is, of course, suffering.

There's more than a little truth in that suggestion. Some, indeed, may wish to claim that they have known suffering in the past, in the odd belief that it somehow builds character. But no one looks forward to the likelihood of suffering in the future. As a matter of fact, we will do almost anything to avoid it. If it were not for suffering, life would be paradise. But life, of course, is a mixed bag. There are bound to be both good times and bad times. Not *all* of life is suffering—at least, not in the usual sense of the word. Certainly, life can have its bitter times, but it can also be sweet. We all sometimes—maybe even most of the time—know the joy of living.

Nevertheless, misery and suffering never fail to claim their share. A survey of human society at any time and place reveals the same dreary story of widespread violence and agony. We humans have a long history of exploiting, and torturing, and slaughtering one another. Suffering—indeed, just the threat of it—is a very real and disturbing fact of life. We even devastate the natural environment on which we depend. In the present age, human society has managed to totally dislocate itself from its original harmony within the natural order. Incredible though it may seem, we are actually in danger not only of destroying ourselves, but of taking the entire natural order of life on Earth with us. Something has gone terribly wrong!

Buddha was very sensitive to the problem of human nature. He was passionately aware of the ubiquity of suffering in human life. Indeed, it was personal suffering that propelled him, step by step, to his own awakening, and once he realized that liberation was possible, it was the suffering of others that moved Buddha in a spirit of compassion to return to the world of everyday life. He would devote his life to trying to help others find their own path to liberation. Buddha would show us how to win freedom from suffering.

But is that really possible? Each of us has personal knowledge of suffering; we experience it in our own lives. If that is what Buddha is referring to, how can he truthfully speak of eliminating it? Is not suffering an inevitable part of the great duality of nature, like youth and age, winter and summer, night and day—joy and suffering? Is freedom from suffering really possible?

To answer this question, let's examine the way in which the problem develops. As we know all too well by now, the human mind—and, presumably, *only* the human mind—is very good at creating an idea of itself, the ego, with which it identifies tenaciously. In doing this, I have separated "myself" out from everything else, and once I have fashioned this "myself"—this ego—and placed it upon its throne at the center of the universe, I naturally yearn for it to be happy—in fact, to be *perfectly* happy. Memories of past experiences record that when I wanted something, I was happy (temporarily, at least) if I satisfied that desire. It might be a desire to *get* something, like food or sex, or it might be a desire to *avoid* something, like hunger or loneliness. If satisfying *some* of my desires makes me *partially* happy, then isn't it reasonable to conclude that satisfying *all* of my desires will make me *perfectly* happy? It seems logical enough: The way to banish suffering from my life is simply to satisfy all of my desires and to do that consistently. Thus do I embark on the quest of the perfectly "good life" by attempting to satisfy all of the desires of the ego.

There's only one problem: It's impossible to be completely successful in such a quest. In order to be successful, I need control. But it is painfully obvious that, to a large degree, I lack control over that world out there. In order to satisfy the desires of the ego, I need control, and if I am a reasonably normal human being, I will work hard at fashioning a mini-universe over which I do have imperial control. But even the most successful effort is doomed to fall far short of perfection. I want to control everything, but I can't even come close.

Desire creates a dislocation in the human mind. On the one hand, we have the world as it is perceived to be—reality the-way-it-is, in other words. On the other hand, we have an imaginary view of the world the-way-it-is-desired-to-be. The desired world and the real world are not the same world; there is a gap between them. The driving power of desire seeks ceaselessly to close that gap, but it can never be done. One can become a control freak, but no matter how much control one succeeds in acquiring, it will never be perfect control. Some things—such as freedom from old age and death—are beyond our power to control. Therefore, so long as desire rules, the gap will persist, and it is in this gap that the problem of human suffering is to be found. To close the gap, I need control. I want to control everything, but I can't even come close. So what happens?

What happens can be nicely summed up in the term "a sense of insecurity." Once we have created the ego-self and identified with it, a deeply felt sense of insecurity is inevitable. This is at the core of the human problem: a pervasive sense of insecurity. Sometimes it is felt very strongly, sometimes it lurks in the background, but it is always present in human thought. At least, it is always present in the mental states of humans who are held in the grip of ego. I hope you see why it is true to say that a sense of insecurity is inevitable. The ego perceives certain needs in order to be happy. The gap between the desired world and the real world opens up. The ego tries to gain control over its own little universe in order to close that gap and ensure that the ego's needs are satisfied. But it is at the mercy of forces that it can't possibly control. Life is threatening. A sense of insecurity is the result.

The sense of insecurity breeds fear. The ego yearns for lasting happiness, but happiness is conditional, its continuation uncertain. Thus, the anxiety of insecurity expresses itself in the feeling of fear. It may be very great, as in the fear of death or the loss of a loved one, or it may be less dramatic, as in the fear of loneliness or failure. It may even be relatively insignificant, as in the fear that dinner will be overcooked. But the common element throughout is a disquieting anxiety born of the fear that what we want in order to satisfy the ego might not be attained. The gap may never be closed.

I think it's important in this discussion to distinguish between the words *fear* and *fright*. Fright is a kind of fear, but it has to do with the perception of a clear and present danger, as, for instance, when one suddenly sees a snake in the path. This is a natural and good thing; it moves one to take appropriate defensive action. Fear, on the other hand, is born out of the act of *thinking about* a perceived threat, brooding over it, and worrying about it. Fear, then, is a form of thought, and the word *fear* is indeed synonymous with the more common word, *worry*.

Fear—or call it worry if you prefer—is at the heart of suffering. Look at it closely. Examine your own experiences with suffering. I think you will find that by far the greatest part of the anguish is the mental state of fear, worry. Thinking about that which we fear is what worry is, and the continuing fear—the continuing worry—is that I, this ego-person, will not achieve and preserve what is thought to be necessary for happiness.

Fear is what suffering is all about. Fear rises inevitably out of our sense of insecurity, which itself is the inevitable companion of ego identification. Fear pervades all of our mental states, even, to some degree, our most joyful ones, because all is flux and nothing will last. The working of fear, conscious or unconscious, generates a host of unhappy states of mind that we ordinarily call suffering.

The key point here is that fear (as distinct from fright) is a form of thought, a creation of the thinking mind. It arises from the deeply felt concern that the desires of the ego will not be satisfied—that the gap between desire and reality will not be closed. And of course, satisfying the desires of the ego is what is perceived to be essential for the state of mind called happiness. But the concept of ego is also a product of the thinking mind. My sense of self and my worry about it are both but *forms of thought*! In seeing this, the way to a solution of the problem should reveal itself.

It is of the essence of Buddha's awakening that he saw through the illusory nature of the separated self. He proved that it is possible for human consciousness to transcend the order of the thinking mind and to see clearly a higher truth, expressed as the underlying unity of all being. In the Hindu tradition that Buddhism grew out of, this cosmic awareness is referred to as the "unitive state"; it is the state of consciousness in which one perceives the seamless unity of all being clearly and directly. In the unitive state, one is free from the chains of fear. The Buddhist tradition, although denying that any substantial being (such as Brahman) is responsible for the underlying unity, would continue at its heart to hold to the indivisible oneness of reality. This would come to be called the Buddha-nature (much more about this in the discussion of *Dharmakaya* in Chapter 12). To be fully aware of the Buddha-nature is, in fact, to be in the "unitive state." The illusory character of the separate ego is clearly beheld. It is like waking from a dream—a nightmare—and the terrors of the dream melt away in the sun of this higher knowledge. How can one worry about satisfying the needs of an ego that has no real existence?

Buddha freed himself, but how does someone who is not Buddha do that? To begin with, it is inherent in the meaning of the Buddha-nature that we are all One; at the deepest level, we *are* Buddha. The Buddha-nature is universal. We have only to clear away the cobwebs of ignorance to see what already exists. This is precisely what Shakyamuni did, and he then dedicated all of his vital energy to showing all others how to do it, too.

Siddhartha Gautama Shakyamuni, the Buddha, had already fully explored the two extreme paths—the path of self-indulgence and the path of self-denial—and found them to be dead ends. We do not need to repeat that experience; he has done it for us. Buddha proposes instead a path between the extremes, a "middle path." In Sanskrit, it is known as *madhyamarga*. Walking this path will not lead to a dead end; it will take one all the way to liberation. But it is not an easy path to follow: In the words of Buddha, the middle path is "the razor's edge."

To guide the dedicated seeker, Buddha laid down certain rules of behavior. These rules came to be known as the Noble Eightfold Path. Taken together, the elements of the Noble Eightfold Path constitute a total lifestyle—a lifestyle crafted and designed by Buddha to carry a man or woman safely across the river from the bank of ignorance to the bank of enlightenment.

Let us now turn to a more specific exposition of the Four Noble Truths, examining each one in its turn. I think you will see why it is said that these four are really but separate aspects of one great truth.

The First Noble Truth: *Sarvam Duhkha*

Sarvam Duhkha is a Sanskrit term that is generally translated as "All is suffering." This is square one in Buddha's philosophy of life, the recognition of the fact of human suffering. Suffering is a universal reality, pervasive throughout life and the spoiler of human existence. Liberation from suffering is the endless quest of all human beings.

Because of this fundamental emphasis on the universality of suffering, Buddhism is sometimes said to be a pessimistic philosophy, as if Buddha had taught that life is *nothing but* suffering and pain. Nothing could be further from the truth. Such an accusation rests on a misunderstanding of Buddha's characterization of suffering. Buddha's teaching is in fact *realistic*, not *pessimistic*, with regard to suffering. It is an undeniable fact that suffering plays, and always has played, a major role in the lives of human beings. But it is also an obvious fact that not *all* of life is suffering, not in the usual sense of the word, anyway. Life is a mixed bag, an interplay of the sweet and the bitter. Buddha, of course, did not say, "All is suffering"; he didn't speak English. What he said was that all is "*duhkha.*"*

Sarvam carries the meaning of universality, but *duhkha* is not quite so precise. In addition to meaning "suffering," *duhkha* can also imply incompleteness, impermanence, and dissatisfaction. It is the antonym of the Sanskrit word *suhkha* which means "happiness" in the sense of sweetness or pleasure. In his very first discourse, the famous "Turning of the Wheel of Dharma," Buddha had this to say about the nature of *duhkha*: "Birth is *duhkha*; aging is *duhkha*; sickness is *duhkha*; dying is *duhkha*; care, distress, pain, affliction, and despair are *duhkha*; the nonattainment of what one desires is *duhkha*."

This statement reveals that Buddha was getting at something far more profound than simply the states of anguish that we customarily call suffering. *Duhkha* certainly refers to states of terrible pain and grief, but it refers as well to other kinds of experiences, *including* ones that we ordinarily call happy. In other words, *duhkha* is a feature of human consciousness that pervades *all* of our experiences, not simply the painful ones that we want to escape from.

---

*Actually, Buddha didn't speak Sanskrit either, so he wouldn't have used the term *duhkha*, but it was close. We don't know for sure what language Buddha spoke, but many scholars believe that it was the Sanskrit derivative, Pali, or something close to it. The Pali word is almost the same as the Sanskrit; we spell it *dukkha*.

The final statement in the foregoing quote of Buddha's provides the key: "*Duhkha* [suffering] is the non-attainment of what one desires." Let me refer back to the concept of the "gap" discussed earlier. There is always a *gap* between the world as we want it to be and the world as it actually is. In our yearning for happiness, we wish for the world to be a certain way *and to remain that way*. Nothing less than perfect happiness will fully satisfy us, but perfect happiness must be beyond all that threatens it. This, of course, is impossible in the real world. Even if we were somehow able to arrange all of the things of life exactly as we wanted them, it would still be imperfect because they simply would-n't stay put for very long. All things are impermanent; all of life is in a constant state of flux. No state of life can be held permanently; *life itself* is transient. Thus, the gap can *never* be closed. The gap itself is *duhkha*. When it is manifest as some terrible pain, such as the death of a loved one, *duhkha* is clearly suffering in the usual sense of the word. But even when it is manifest as a happy experience, such as pleasure in the company of a loved one, it is still *duhkha*, because rumbling underneath the temporary experience of pleasure is the disquieting knowledge that it *is* temporary; its continuation is always uncertain, and its loss—over which I have ultimately no control—would be devastating.

At the deepest level, *duhkha* is the inescapable awareness that *everything* is transitory and always in flux. This applies even to the perception of my own being. I yearn for real-ity—especially my own reality—to be permanent and perfect, but the undisguised fact of impermanence stares me in the face. This is *duhkha*, and in the attempt to flee from it, I try to find happiness (*suhkha*) in myriad distractions. Talking, including thinking, becomes a wonderful form of escape. Music, partying, and television can work well for a while. When all else fails, there are always drugs and alcohol. But ultimately nothing can work perfectly: The unblinking fact of impermanence swallows even the happiest moments.

Thus, at root, *duhkha* permeates all of ego life. It is the irrepressible dissatisfaction that arises from the ever-present gap that exists between the world as it is and the world as we wish it to be. It is a worrisome fear that I will not acquire—or, if I do, will not sustain—what it is that I deem necessary for my happiness. *Duhkha* is a mental condi-tioning, and it is present in all of our experiences, from the most sorrowful to the most joyful.

The Second Noble Truth: *Trishna*

In its original Sanskrit usage, *trishna* (*tanha* in Pali) meant "thirst." By Buddha's time, though, it had come to have the derived meaning of "desire." *Trishna* does not mean desire in the everyday sense, such as a desire for world peace. Rather, *trishna* refers to strong selfish desire. "Craving" would be the best English equivalent. It is craving—self-ish craving—that is the cause of suffering.

Ordinary desire can grow to become craving, but the difference is profound; it's not simply a matter of degree. I might, for example, desire to spend my vacation in Hawaii. That's a simple desire, and I can remain happy even if it is not fulfilled (well, maybe). Craving, on the other hand, guarantees suffering. Craving breeds attachment, which can be defined as a state of mind in which a particular craving has grown so strong that one is convinced that he or she cannot be happy unless that which is desired is also possessed. For example, let's say that I have experienced pleasure in some of the expensive things of life and can easily imagine that a rich lifestyle would make me wonderfully happy all of the time (a common enough example). I desire wealth with which to live this rich lifestyle. Even if I am largely successful in this pursuit, it will never be enough. Desire begets desire and grows to craving. Craving breeds attachment, which, once again, is nothing less than the conviction that I cannot be happy unless I am in possession of what it is that is desired. The desire for more and the desire for permanence are doomed to be something less than perfectly satisfied (to say the least). And in that frustration of desire is suffering, *duhkha*. It may be very great—especially if I should lose my wealth and know the agony of the desire to recover it—or it may be relatively less dramatic. But so long as attachment is present, the anguish of unsatisfied craving is inevitable.

There are many species of attachment; attachment to wealth is only one of the most visible. There can also be attachment to youth, for example, or to one's home or job; one can become attached to comfort, to drugs, to a loved one, to fame, or even to some object, such as a beautiful eel-skin belt. The greatest attachment of all, though, is attachment to oneself—to one's *self*—that is to say, attachment to the much-beloved ego identity. Whatever form it takes, attachment guarantees suffering, and selfish desire that grows to craving guarantees that attachment will follow.

We have seen that our normal human obsession with ego results in a split, a gap, between the world as it is and the world as we wish it to be. We *desire* to close that gap in myriad ways. Some of these desires will become obsessive; that is to say, they will become *bona fide* attachments. To the extent that we are successful in satisfying our desires, a state of partial and temporary happiness will result. It will never be perfect, though, because the gap between desire and reality can never be perfectly closed. Thus does Buddha say that *trishna*, selfish craving, is the cause of suffering.

The Third Noble Truth: *Nirvana*

The Third Noble Truth concerns the cessation of suffering, the total liberation from suffering. Buddha's awakening was the prototype of such liberation, and the whole point of his teaching was to show others how to duplicate his experience in their own lives. His choice of term was *nirvana* (*nibbana* in Pali). Literally, *nirvana* means "extinction" or "extinguishment," as in the extinguishing or blowing out the flame of a candle. In *nirvana*, what is to be "blown out" is the last trace of the illusion of the separate self, the lordly ego that holds us in its grip.

Buddha would not attempt to describe the nature of *nirvana*. It is a reality that is inexpressible, beyond the power of thought and words. *Nirvana* cannot be captured by the imagination. Nevertheless, although we cannot describe the nature of *nirvana*, we can say some meaningful things about the subject by way of indirect abstraction. To begin with, we can say that *nirvana* is perfect Reality, perfect Truth. (Of course, the absolute truth is that there is nothing absolute; everything is conditioned and impermanent.) Absolute Truth, in which all illusion of fundamental separateness is overcome, is what we mean by the unitive state. *Nirvana*, the final and perfect expression of that state, can be apprehended only by the awakening of an intuitive wisdom that transcends ordinary human consciousness. Such intuitive wisdom is known as *prajna*. The power of *prajna* is latent in everyone, but only when it is awakened is the truth of *nirvana* revealed.

In Buddhism, the full realization of the Buddha-nature is likened to a river returning to the sea. There are many individual rivers, but their separateness is something of an illusion: They are really all expressions of one great system that begins in the sea and is destined ultimately to return to the sea. Perhaps for this reason, many in the West have wrongly assumed that *nirvana* refers to the extinguishment or annihilation of the person altogether, a sort of melting away into nothingness. This is certainly a false view. Once again, what ceases to exist is ignorance (*avidya*)—the attachment to the separate self born of ignorance that fuels the arising of *duhkha*.

So long as the grip of the ego illusion persists, one will necessarily center his or her quest for happiness on satisfying the cravings of the ego. But as we have seen, this will inevitably create a gap that no amount of manipulation can close. The self, though—the sense of a separate, enduring self—is an illusion. Buddha saw the truth of this perfectly at the time of his awakening. There is no enduring self—no ego, no ego player, no *atman*— of any kind. Thus, there is no *objective self* to be satisfied. The attempt to satisfy the cravings of the ego can never be successful because, fundamentally, *there is no ego-self to be satisfied*. It's all a great hoax that we perpetrate on ourselves. Once this illusion is unmasked—which is essentially what *nirvana* entails—the cravings associated with attachment must necessarily melt away as dream images do upon one's waking from sleep. The flame of selfish desire is "blown out" with the extinction of the ego illusion.

But if an objective self does not exist—and is ultimately seen to be an illusion—who is it then that does the seeing? Who is it that *experiences nirvana*? This is a very good question. It might seem that the concept of *nirvana* affirms the ultimate reality of the individual self. Such a conclusion, however, is a complete misunderstanding of the Buddhist view. Strictly speaking, *nirvana* is not an *experience*; there is, indeed, no one to experience it. *Nirvana* is simply the final and natural expression of the *process* that, in its developmental stages, is manifest as what we call individual life. Like the river returning to the sea, the process we call a person is not complete—and thus will continue to cycle on—so long as ego-based desire continues to generate unresolved effects.

Referring to the process "continuing to cycle on" brings up a matter that is worth considering briefly at this point. You sometimes read that *nirvana* is defined as the cessation of *samsara*, which is to say, the cycle of rebirth, but—at least according to the Doctrine of *Anatman*—didn't Buddha deny the reality of *atman*? How can there be rebirth if there is no permanent self to be reborn? It all comes down to how you define "rebirth." Unlike Hinduism, Buddhism does indeed deny the reality of a permanent self, but the process of change that we identify with individual life does nonetheless generate karma, both positive and negative, as a result of all volitional acts. The effects of this karma will be played out over time, affecting the character of successive "rebirths." What is reborn is not, for example, an *atman* that endures through time, but the *process itself*. Life is "reborn" every moment. Each of us is "reborn," in a sense, every morning when we wake up. Shakespeare referred to sleep as a "little death." Looked at another way, one life process is "reborn" in another through the continuation of the karmic influence one person's life has on another. It is like the flame of one candle lighting that of another. In the case of human beings, desire creates karma, and karma keeps the "*wheel of samsara*" turning. Only with the end of desire—*nirvana*, in other words—does the wheel come to a stop, and we can speak of the "cessation of *samsara*."

To sum up, *nirvana* is the realization of perfect freedom, perfect unending joy. *Nirvana* is the "blowing out" of the ego illusion and hence the "blowing out" of desire (craving). With the end of desire comes the end of suffering. How that is to be achieved is the subject of the Fourth Noble Truth.

The Fourth Noble Truth: *Madhyamarga*

In the First Noble Truth, Buddha nailed down the universality of suffering. In the Second Noble Truth, he identified selfish craving as the cause of suffering. Then, in the Third Noble Truth, Buddha affirmed that liberation from suffering is possible. Liberation does not depend on a power outside oneself; it arises from the personal realization of *nirvana*. *Nirvana* is rare, and the way to it is difficult, but liberation is available to every man and woman. Buddha's teaching, the Dharma, will show the way; it is known as *Madhyamarga*, the "Middle Way." The well-known "Eightfold Path" is how one walks the Middle Way. The name does not refer to eight "steps," so to speak, but rather to the eight fundamental elements of the lifestyle of one who seeks to walk the Middle Way.

Buddha said that the true Middle Way is a "razor's edge" between the false ways of self-indulgence and self-denial. Certainly, he should know, having devoted many years of his life to a full exploration of both extremes. It is important to see that the life of self-indulgence can never lead to lasting happiness. It is important for the simple reason that the vast majority of men and women fool themselves into believing that really will work—if only it's done right. This is clearly the prevailing philosophy of our own age and probably all other ages, too. But Buddha would insist that, so long as the quest for happiness is founded on the satisfaction of desires, it is ultimately a hopeless quest.

In like manner, the quest for transcendent happiness through a life of self-denial is also doomed to failure. The very *effort* to expunge the self by ascetic self-disciplines only increases its psychological strength. Here, too, the basic problem lies in the cultivation of self-centered desires. In an interesting way, the desire to *destroy* the self is every bit as much an ego-centered desire as the desire to *please* the self. So what's left?

It must be remembered that Buddha taught that, at root, the sense of separation is only that—a "sense," a concept. The sense of separation—*all* separation—is an illusion born of ignorance. *Nirvana* does not depend on changing what we fundamentally already are; all that is necessary is for us to get out of our own way—to allow the arising of our own natural endowment of intuitive wisdom, called *prajna* in Sanskrit. It is *prajna* that sees through the clouds of ignorance and beholds the Buddha-nature. To guide us along the Middle Path to the place where *prajna* may open, Buddha gives us the guidelines of the Noble Eightfold Path.

THE NOBLE EIGHTFOLD PATH

In Sanskrit, it is *arya-astangika-marga*; we know it as the Noble Eightfold Path. It constitutes the basic elements of the total way of life of one who seeks to follow Buddha's Middle Way to enlightenment. When we consider the Noble Eightfold path, we must not think that it consists of eight separate activities, eight steps to be followed consecutively. Rather, the path comprises the interwoven aspects of the daily life of one who seeks to awaken intuitive wisdom.

Students new to the subject of Buddhism are often surprised—even disappointed—by their first reading of the Noble Eightfold Path. One might expect that Buddha's own core teaching regarding the path to liberation would be highly dramatic and exciting. But in reading over the Noble Eightfold Path, as it is customarily presented, one can't help but ask what all the fuss is about. *As usually presented*, the Noble Eightfold Path seems to be surprisingly mundane stuff, more like a list of common platitudes than great spiritual insights. This is due partly to the fact that the elements of the Noble Eightfold Path actually *are* concerned with rather common, down-to-earth behaviors. Perfecting these behaviors, though—fully integrating them into one's life—is not common at all. Also, it is important to see the eight elements in the context of the whole—a viewpoint that is often overlooked. They are the facets of one reality, one total life, which is greater than the sum of its parts. Seeing the Eightfold Path in relation to the larger reality gives meaning to the individual parts.

Let me first present the breakdown of the Noble Eightfold Path in the way that one usually encounters it. The eight principles are as follows:*

1. Right Understanding
2. Right Resolve
3. Right Speech
4. Right Action
5. Right Livelihood
6. Right Effort
7. Right Mindfulness
8. Right Concentration

Perhaps you, too, find it difficult to see how these principles can be the basic elements of a revolutionary lifestyle, one that can transform an ordinary man or woman into an awakened buddha. Once again, please remember that this is not a secret recipe for enlightenment; it is merely a group of words that identify behavioral categories of the lifestyle of a person who is working to transform himself or herself into one who is

---

*The Sanskrit word for each of these is *samyak* (*samma* in Pali). Translating this term as "right" can be misleading, because it suggests the duality of right and wrong. An alternative translation is "perfect," in the sense of complete. Various writers, including the well-known Buddhist scholar Lama Govinda, prefer this translation. However, because the word "right" has come to be so widely used and recognized, I will continue to employ it in this text.

free from the attachments of ego. The greatness is to be found in the *doing*, not in the words. Let's look at the eight principles separately.

Right Understanding (often referred to as Right Views) is square one. It means seeing things as they are, understanding reality as it really is. Clearly, Buddha's awakening was not a rational sort of experience, an "understanding" in the usual sense of the word. Rational understanding by itself could never result in awakening; it is, in fact, the rational mind that must be transcended. Nevertheless, it is an appropriate place from which to begin. Right Understanding is square one in the Eightfold Path because, if a person is going to address the problem of human suffering, he or she must address the *real* problem, not some imaginary problem. Thus, "seeing things as they really are" is what is meant by Right Understanding.

In Buddha's age, as in all ages, human suffering was typically blamed on a host of external causes. It could be due to the working of demons, for example, or to a cruel fate, or even to divine punishment. Buddha would say that efforts to solve the problem based on these views are doomed to failure. Buddha wanted men and women to see—to *understand*—that we ourselves are the cause of the problem. The root cause of suffering (*duhkha*) originates in our own minds, not somewhere outside of us, as we tend to believe. Therefore, the solution to the problem also lies inside of us.

What it boils down to is this: Buddha wants us to see reality as it *really* is—that is, as a unified process of constant change, constant flux, in which there simply are no separate, permanent essences of any kind. The mind's yearning to see reality as made up of separate, permanent essences is a self-generated illusion born of ignorance and insecurity. This illusory view of reality—particularly as it applies to the concept of the separate self, the ego—is what gives life to the web of desire and hence to the inevitable companion of desire, suffering. To see this relationship is to have "right understanding." To see it perfectly is, in fact, to be liberated.

It should be pointed out that the fullness of this understanding is not some sort of prerequisite to living a genuinely Buddhist lifestyle. All of the elements that make up the Eightfold Path are interrelated; they can mature together. But the development of Right Understanding is fundamental, and that's why it is presented first.

In Sanskrit, the second principle is known as *samyak-samkalpa* (*samma-samkappa* in Pali). *Samkalpa* allows for many different translations in English. Consequently—unlike the situation with the other members of the Eightfold Path, for which there is broad agreement on their translation—you will encounter a variety of terms that identify this principle. In addition to "Resolve," authors on the subject use such terms as "Resolution," "Intention," "Purpose," "Motive," "Mental Attitude," and "Thought." What do all of these terms have in common?

We may say that *samyak-samkalpa* deals with a particular kind of thought or mental attitude, one that could be described as a firm resolution to live in a certain way. Generally, that way is described as a sincere renunciation of the mental patterns that, through right understanding, one has come to see as being the underlying source of the problem of suffering. Prime among such negative mental patterns are selfish desire, hatred, and violence. Not only does one resolve to renounce negative mental attitudes, but (of course) to nourish positive ones in their place. A follower of Buddha's teaching resolves that mental attitudes of compassion, goodwill, and nonviolence—qualities, in other words, that promote growth toward the unitive state—will replace mental attitudes that serve to strengthen the illusion of the separate self.

The mental attitude that one seeks to develop can be summed up in the word *ahimsa*, one of the most important words in the Sanskrit lexicon. Gandhi loved the term and seemed to feel that it summed up the essence of all virtuous action. "Nonviolence" is the customary English translation of *ahimsa*, but it is something of a weak choice, because *ahimsa* means far more than merely refraining from violent behavior. Also, *ahimsa* is a positive concept, not a negative one. What should not be *violated* are the rights—the natural rights—of all beings. This is accomplished, not by the negative process of avoidance, but by the positive effort to love and identify with all other beings. Consequently, *ahimsa* is compassion in action. Seen in this way, *ahimsa* identifies the very essence of the spirit of action that Buddha is promoting in the Eightfold Path.

Right Resolve must be understood as a total dedication to the task of changing one's mental attitude. It calls for a kind of rebirth; nothing short of total dedication is sufficient. Following the path of Buddha must be the most important thing in one's life. In fact, if it is truly *right* or *perfect* resolve, one must be willing to completely renounce his or her previous way of living in whatever way is judged necessary to do so. Right Resolve is the attitude of a man or woman who is like a starving person who will do *anything* to find food. In this case, the food of life is the Dharma, the teaching of Buddha.

"Right Speech" simply means applying the principle of *ahimsa* to all the utterances of the mind, whether spoken aloud to another or quietly to oneself (which is what we ordinarily call "thinking"). Unflagging honesty and goodwill are the defining characteristics of Right Speech. Buddha specifically warned his followers to be on guard against the temptation to lie, to speak ill of others, and to engage in idle gossip.

Right Action (often referred to as Right Conduct) is also a matter of applying the principle of *ahimsa* to what one does. The scope is broader than speech, though, extending out to embrace one's relationships with all other beings. In the way we relate to other beings, we can either break down or build up the existing sense of separation. Action that breaks down the sense of separation, such as behavior that is respectful and compassionate, is in the spirit of *ahimsa*. Contrary action, including such obvious examples as stealing, wounding, and killing, are clearly to be renounced. Some things are not quite so obvious, however: Buddha denounced "immoral sexual activity," a subject that probably needs to be defined anew by the men and women of each new age.

Right Action applies not only to a person's dealings with other people and not only to his or her dealings with other sentient beings; it concerns a person's relations to the entire universe of being. *Ahimsa* means respect and compassion for *all* of the environment. The unity of being is seamless; an enlightened person knows his or her identity with *all* of existence.

Right Livelihood is also an application of the principle of *ahimsa*. If one is to follow the path of Buddha with total dedication, it's pretty clear that he or she will have to structure the ongoing work of daily life in a way that is in harmony with the spirit of Buddha's teaching, specifically with the Noble Eightfold Path. Any kind of work that is in conflict with the spirit of goodwill toward the environment and other sentient beings will obviously not do at all. Buddha pointedly denounced such professions as trading in weapons, drugs, or poisons; or procuring others for prostitution; and working in a field that involves the killing of animals. These, of course, are only a few of a myriad possible examples, the point being that *any* kind of work that potentially hurts others or deliberately causes suffering is in conflict with the teaching of Buddha and will sidetrack one from the path that leads to liberation.

In Buddha's time, the work that a person did was largely a family matter and was tied up with one's birth and place in society. It was the defining centerpiece of a whole way of life. Clearly, that's not the case in today's world. Therefore, it might make more sense for us to speak of "Right Lifestyle" instead of the narrower term "Right Livelihood." What's really at stake here is a person's entire way of life, which certainly includes one's profession, but involves much more than just that. In an important way, the choices one makes about a home, a neighborhood, and even the car one drives, are all tied together with the work one does; it's all one package. And, of course, work is not necessarily limited to a job. For many, work may mean being a student, for many others, it may mean being a homemaker, and for some, it may mean nothing more than being merely an interested observer of the unfolding drama of life. In other words, "livelihood" has a richer meaning within the context of Buddha's teaching if we broaden it to include all of those elements that go into making up a total "lifestyle."

Many of those who chose to follow the path of Buddha, especially in the early centuries, gave up everything in order to become Buddhist monks. It was widely believed that only total dedication to the disciplines of the monastic life was sufficient to the challenge of achieving *nirvana*. Is, therefore, the really "right" livelihood, the "right" lifestyle, that of the Buddhist monk? Not necessarily. For some, it may undoubtedly be the right choice, but clearly, Buddha did not feel that becoming a monk was essential. If he did feel that way, he would have said so. The fact that he denounced certain specific kinds of livelihoods implies that he accepted others as appropriate. Without question, the way of the monk is a powerful lifestyle for one who wishes to live the Dharma, but liberation is not the exclusive prize of the monk: Anyone of sincere heart and dedication can make the grade.

The sixth principle is called *samyak-vyayama* in Sanskrit. This term is usually translated as "Right Effort." Buddha's meaning of the term, however, is not easy to pin down neatly. The Buddhist scholar Walpola Rahula (and others who have followed his lead) explains Right Effort as the will to get rid of existing habits of thought that give rise to evil and unwholesome states of mind, and to prevent new ones from forming. Also, Right Effort involves developing existing states of mind that are good and wholesome, as well as encouraging new states of mind that will be good and wholesome. But what does this mean?

Right Effort is associated with the principle of *karma*, a concept that weaves through the evolution of Buddhist thought from the very beginning. Karma is the continuing influence that ethical decisions have on the course of subsequent events. Karma is not the effect itself, as many mistakenly believe; it is the *influence*, or *disposition*, that leads to certain kinds of effects. Karma greatly influences the character of a person's life at any given time. Most simply put, Right Effort refers to the determined will of a man or woman to replace existing negative karma with positive karma. This is accomplished by a consistent act of the will which determines that all of one's behavior—in thought, word, and deed—will be motivated by a spirit of selfless compassion. (That, at least, is the ideal.) In this way, a person can more easily escape from the bondage of selfish attachment and thus become receptive to the experience of awakening.

The seventh principle is Right Mindfulness, or, as it is sometimes called, Right Attentiveness. This is a wonderful quality of mind, much emphasized in Buddhist teaching. Right Mindfulness concerns the cultivation of the habit of mind of being consciously one with the present experience, being aware of thoughts, feelings, and sensations as they occur—in other words, *being here now*. Living with one's awareness rooted in the present is not as easy as it may seem. Despite the fact that one never lives anywhere *other than* in the present moment, the typical human mind seems determined to give as little attention to it as possible. We substitute instead a fantasy world of imaginings about the past and future. This thought-based fantasy world, the home and support of the ego illusion, becomes more real than reality itself, which is to say, the continuing reality of the present moment. To locate oneself in the reality of the experience of the present moment, just as it is, is to begin to free oneself from the ignorance of the separate self.

Right Mindfulness is the companion of the final principle, which is nearly always referred to as Right Concentration. It is somewhat baffling that this has come to be the widely accepted word. The Sanskrit term is *samyak-samadhi. Samadhi* refers, not to concentration in the usual sense of the word, but to that meditative state of consciousness which has risen to the unitive state. As there is no word in the English language that carries this meaning, perhaps it would be best simply to say "Right *Dhyana*," or Right Meditation. Nevertheless, it has become customary to refer to the eighth principle as Right Concentration. What is to be concentrated on is growth in the practice of *dhyana*, which involves what we ordinarily call the practice of meditation. Buddhist teaching identifies four stages in the growth of *dhyana*, the final one leading to, and becoming one with, *nirvana. Dhyana* is thus the culmination of the Eightfold Path; it is the way in which a dedicated Buddhist lifestyle ultimately transcends itself in *nirvana*.

When one looks over these eight separate principles and views them as a group, the mind seeks to see relationships among them. One traditional way of doing this is to divide the eight principles into three groups known as Mental Discipline, Moral Conduct, and Intuitive Wisdom. Through Mental Discipline—which includes Right Effort, Right Mindfulness, and Right Concentration—one becomes free of bondage to attachments. In Moral Conduct—which includes Right Speech, Right Action, and Right Livelihood—one develops compassion, which has the effect of breaking down the sense of the separate self. Finally, in Intuitive Wisdom—which includes Right Resolve and Right Understanding—one engenders *prajna* (the intuitive wisdom itself), which ultimately issues in *nirvana*.

There is no one necessary way of interpreting the Noble Eightfold Path. Each person is free to be personally creative in making sense of it. Let me suggest a way of looking at it in which it is seen not so much as a list of behavioral *guidelines*, but rather as a simple *description* of the overall way of life that leads to awakening. The path begins and ends in Right Understanding, seeing reality as it really is. Initially, this seeing is of a rational sort—seeing that selfish attachment is the cause of suffering—but ultimately, rational understanding will transcend itself in the perfect understanding of *prajna*.

Once one has Right Understanding of the problem, Right Resolve enters the picture. A true follower of Buddha must dedicate himself or herself to walking the path. Buddha's teaching involves a transformation of consciousness; Right Resolve means dedicating oneself to replacing the mental attitude of separation with the mental attitude of compassion.

Understanding the problem and resolving to do something about it are preliminary matters, in a way: The actual doing begins in Right Lifestyle, the reconstitution of the elements of one's way of living so that it serves rather than hinders the goal of living in harmony with the teaching of Buddha. Right Effort involves putting that chosen lifestyle into execution on an ongoing daily basis. It is the actualization of *ahimsa* in all that one does—in thought, in word, and in deed. Right Speech and Right Action simply focus on the working of Right Effort in these two major aspects of human behavior.

These six principles in themselves, if lived to the full, describe a rather remarkable person. But the goal is to go beyond this, to work a transformation of consciousness through the enkindling of intuitive wisdom—to break down completely the illusion of the separate self and achieve the unitive state. Meditation is the key to this. Right Mindfulness trains the mind to live in the present reality and prepares the ground for the planting of the seeds of Right Meditation. The practice of meditation leads one through the stages of *dhyana* to the point where the ripening of intuitive wisdom (*prajna*) "sees reality as it really is." Thus does consciousness become *nirvana*.

An even more fundamental way of analyzing the Noble Eightfold Path is to boil it down to the two essential qualities that define the character of the Buddhist lifestyle: *prajna* (wisdom) and *karuna* (compassion). These are the two sides of the one coin that is the Dharma, the teaching of Buddha. Ultimately, they amount to one and the same thing, but in the ongoing affairs of daily life we speak of them separately. Compassion is the outgoing, behavioral side of life. It seeks to "feel with," to be one with all other beings. *Prajna* is the inner side of life. It is the intuitive state of consciousness—influenced by compassion—in which one comes to see the unity of all being. The two go together; one nourishes the other. Seen in its most fundamental sense, the Noble Eightfold Path is simply a description of the way of life that is ideally suited to the engendering of wisdom and compassion.

As mentioned earlier, the elucidation of the Four Noble Truths and the Noble Eightfold Path was central to the teaching of the first great organized movement in the history of Buddhism. This movement is known as *Theravada Buddhism*. In time, Theravada would be largely overshadowed, though not replaced, by another great movement known as *Mahayana*. We will examine each of these traditions fully. In Mahayana Buddhism, the teaching of the Noble Eightfold Path would become somewhat transformed, though never renounced. The place to begin, however, is at the beginning, and that is what we have done in this chapter. The Four Noble Truths and the Noble Eightfold Path, as presented here, constitute the core of the first great presentation of Buddha's teaching. Let us now turn to a broader consideration of the Theravada tradition from which that teaching emerged.

Notes

1. Eknath Easwaren, The *Bhagavad Gita* (Petaluma, CA: Nilgiri, 1985), p. 18.
2. *Ibid.*, p. 22.
3. Walpola Rahula, *What the Buddha Taught* (New York: Grove Press, 1983), p. 51.
4. Kenneth Ch'en, *Buddhism* (New York: Barrons, 1968), pp. 44–45.
5. William Shakespeare, *Macbeth*, Act 5, Scence 5.
6. Easwaren, *BG*: 2.12–13 (p. 62).

Study Questions

1. In what way is it true to say that the word "awakening" is itself a metaphor?
2. Buddha is said to have referred to "the unborn, the unformed, the unbecome." Some would argue that this amounts to a reaffirmation of the essential truth of the Hindu tradition. Why is this?
3. Siddhartha was longing for self-fulfillment. As Buddha, he came to realize (or so it is claimed by some) that self-fulfillment is impossible. Why is this?
4. "These two matters then—impermanency and dependency—are said to be the fundamental character of existence." What does this mean?
5. "Some maintain that, by denying the reality of *atman*, Buddha was implicitly denying the fundamental reality of spirit." How so?
6. "So long as desire rules, the gap will persist." What is this "gap" referred to here? How does it operate?
7. Sarvam *Duhkha* is usually translated "All is suffering." Why is this an imperfect translation?

11

Theravada Buddhism

In 80 B.C.E., virtually all of the leading Buddhist monks and scholars of the time gathered at Anuradhapura, the capital city of the island kingdom of Sri Lanka. In addition to nourishing their own practice, they were there for the purpose of formally establishing an authentic body of Buddhist scripture. They worked long at the task, debating issues and weeding out what they believed to be questionable sources. It was their hope that they could come to agreement on a fundamental corpus of documents that faithfully preserved Buddha's teaching and Buddha's views on the proper organization and discipline of the sangha. After many months of work, the members of this great council put their seal of approval on a collection of writings that has come to be known as the Pali Canon.

The Pali Canon constitutes the definitive core of Theravada Buddhism. As mentioned earlier, the history of Buddhism is broadly divided between two great traditions: Theravada (also known as Hinayana) and Mahayana. Over time, Mahayana would become the larger and historically more influential movement. Actually, the roots of both Theravada and Mahayana can be traced back to the earliest days, but Theravada preceded Mahayana in becoming a well-defined and organized movement, and for this reason we shall examine it first. It was the Pali Canon that established the character of Theravada.

The Pali Canon is known by that name because scholars within the council reproduced all of the agreed-upon works in the written language of Pali. Although not the spoken language of the common people of Sri Lanka, Pali had come to the island with invaders from North India. Pali was a derivative of Sanskrit in much the same way that Italian is a derivative of Latin, and it was widely believed by the members of the council that Pali was the language that Buddha himself had spoken.

The Pali Canon is of enormous value to the student of Buddhism. It is where the documentary history of Buddhism really begins. Almost everything before that time is speculation, but with the Pali Canon, the fundamental teachings and practices of Buddhism were written down and preserved for all time. Since they were written in Pali, that language became a sort of quasi-official language of Theravada Buddhism. This creates something of a problem, because the original writings of Mahayana were typically in Sanskrit. Thus, both Pali and Sanskrit terms will often appear in the study of Buddhism. Usually, they are quite similar: *Dharma* in Sanskrit becomes *dhamma* in Pali, for instance, and *nirvana* in Sanskrit becomes *nibhana* in Pali.

Note that 80 B.C.E. is a long time after the death of Shakyamuni Buddha—four hundred years, to be exact. So how can we be sure that the writings of the Pali Canon do in fact faithfully preserve the teaching of Buddha as Buddha meant it to be understood? We can't, of course, but there is broad consensus among modern scholars that the tradition was carefully preserved in the centuries following Buddha's life and that the scholars at the Anuradhapura council used great care in their research and textual criticism. We can be reasonably confident that the Pali Canon does indeed give us an accurate presentation of Buddha's teaching, true to the intentions of the founder.

But what had happened during those four long centuries between the death of Buddha and the establishment of the Pali Canon? During that time, the acorn had grown into a spreading oak. To understand the mature character of Theravada, it is helpful to have a general knowledge of its background. Let's pick up the story, as best we can determine it, at the time of Buddha's death and see how the tradition developed. Some of our evidence for what went on in those centuries comes from the Pali Canon itself; other parts of the story, such as the reign of the emperor Ashoka, are from research in the broader fields of history and archaeology. We will look more closely at the Pali Canon in its appropriate place in the development of the story.

THE EARLY CENTURIES

During his lifetime, Buddha himself was the strong unifying influence among his followers. But what would happen after he was gone? Would the sangha that he had worked so hard to create be able to preserve itself without him? After all, Buddha had not founded a religious organization with a priesthood and a fixed body of dogma. Instead, the followers of Buddha were a diverse lot, and they were spread over a vast area of northern India. Many were so-called forest dwellers, individuals who pretty much went their own way, like the sadhus of the broader Hindu tradition. Others, the members of the Orders, were collected into communities, but they were widely scattered and had only limited contacts. There was a real danger that things might come apart or at least go off in a multitude of different directions.

Aware of these problems, the leaders of the movement came together in council within a year after Buddha's death. This was the first great council of Buddhism, and the place they chose was the city of Rajagriha, the capital of the Magadha kingdom, which at that time was the dominant state of North India. Buddha had spent much of his teaching career in that part of India. We are told that five hundred *arhats* (awakened ones) attended the council and that it stayed in session for seven months. They had a twofold purpose: to compile a body of doctrine and to develop a monastic code that would be an authentic expression of the teaching of the master.

The First Council established the tradition on a firm foundation and prevented a kind of doctrinal centrifugal force from developing that would have splintered the movement. But after the passage of a century, the leading Buddhists were back in council again. This Second Great Council met at Vaisali, and it would seem that its purpose was to deal with a split that was opening up within the ranks.

The controversy concerned the fundamental nature of Buddhahood. The argument came down to a simple issue: Was enlightenment something that one *acquired*, or was it *uncovered*? In other words, did one become a buddha by working hard to change oneself fundamentally, or was everyone born a buddha, but simply ignorant of the fact until awakening? It might seem like an unimportant distinction, but it had far-reaching implications. At the council, the argument was settled in favor of the "acquired" faction, but the seeds of a permanent division were already in the ground.

Our source of information for both of these councils is the Pali Canon, and some have wondered whether the councils ever really occurred. Perhaps they were invented by the creators of the Pali Canon in order to give the impression that their research grew out of a solid tradition. Their own work would thus seem more credible. This is possible, but most agree that if it were the case, the Pali Canon would not have reported the deep doctrinal disagreements at the councils. Almost surely the councils did occur, and they reveal to us that the tradition of Buddhism was growing and flourishing in its early centuries, struggling to preserve an integrity of doctrine.

In tracing the evolution of this tradition we have to remind ourselves that, strictly speaking, there was really no such thing as "Buddhism." This is a subtle point, but one well worth reflecting on. The three letters *i–s–m* effect a profound influence on the meaning of a word, and the use of "ism" is a modern innovation that reflects a modern way of thinking. As soon as we make a word into an "ism"—be it Marxism, capitalism, fascism, or Buddhism—we have mentally organized it into a distinct *system* of thought. We have put it in a mental box, distinct from other mental boxes. There is sometimes value in this, but there is also danger.

When we use the term "Buddh-*ism*" we tend to picture a precisely defined movement with its own internal organization. Such a movement would stand beside, and perhaps be in conflict with, other precisely defined movements, such as Jain*ism*, or Hindu*ism*. This was surely not the case. The followers of Buddha's teaching never encountered the concept of Buddhism. They were integrally a part of the rich and varied culture of India at that time, and Buddha was one of many great leaders who had attracted a following. As the tradition developed, there was much interplay, much give-and-take between the Buddhists and others. It was a very fluid situation that might have lived and flourished for a while and then merged back into the broader culture that it was a part of. It's even possible that the modern world might never have heard of Shakyamuni Buddha had it not been for one person. That person, to say the least, played a pivotal role in the development of the Buddhist tradition. His name was Ashoka.

ASHOKA

Ashoka (pronounced Ah-SHO-ka) was a very powerful conqueror who hammered all of North India into a strong empire during the third century B.C.E. He then sought to unify that empire internally on the basis of Buddhist teachings. Under his patronage,

Buddhism flourished and began its migration to the world outside India. Ashoka was the grandson of Chandragupta Maurya, the founder of the Mauryan dynasty.

During the time of Shakyamuni Buddha, North India was divided into a number of relatively small competing kingdoms. But just beyond the mountains to the west, the process of making big kingdoms out of small ones had produced a huge and powerful neighbor—the Persian Empire. Then, in the fourth century B.C.E., Alexander the Great appeared on the scene. After consolidating all of Greece, he turned on the Persians, totally defeating them in one of history's most spectacular upsets. Alexander then reorganized the Persian Empire as his own. His campaigning in the conquered lands brought his army all the way to the fringes of the Indian world in 326 B.C.E. There were some test raids, not really an invasion, in the northwestern part of the subcontinent. Then peace returned temporarily as Alexander focused on consolidating what he had already won.

But would the insatiable Alexander return, intent on devouring all of North India? Who could possibly stop him if he did return? Well, an early death stopped Alexander and caught his whole world by surprise. But the warlords who inherited the pieces of Alexander's empire were no less of a threat. The handwriting was on the wall. It seemed that India was destined to be unified, if not from within, then from without.

It was in this climate that a powerful north Indian king, Chandragupta Maurya, began a successful series of conquests. Only five years after the departure of Alexander, Chandragupta's armies were forcibly annexing the very territories Alexander had claimed. Chandragupta created an empire of great military strength that included much, if not all, of north India. Feeling the need for a buffer zone to the west, he even annexed territory in the region of the Hindu Kush mountains that had technically been part of the Persian Empire. Alexander's successor in the region, Seleucus Nicator, sensing the great power of Chandragupta, chose to make peace instead of war. Chandragupta sent Seleucus five hundred elephants, and Seleucus in return sent one of his daughters to be a wife of Chandragupta. (In the climate of the times, she must have been quite a prize to be the equal of five hundred elephants!)

Chandragupta created what history calls the Mauryan Dynasty. For a while, India would be safe from outside invaders. After a reign of twenty-three years, Chandragupta was succeeded by his son, Bindusara, who also reigned for twenty-three years, during which time India enjoyed relative peace. Bindusara was a consolidator, not a conqueror. He preferred to use his great wealth on things like building up the splendor of the royal court. The story is told that Bindusara, hearing about the fame of Greek philosophy, sought to purchase a Greek philosopher. He was told that their philosophers were not for sale. "What a strange people," he is supposed to have said. "These philosophers that they brag about cannot really be worth much."

The most important thing about Bindusara is that he was the father of Ashoka. Ashoka came to the throne in 274 B.C.E. and would reign for twenty-eight years. There is a popular story that Bindusara had sixteen wives and one hundred sons. Ashoka, in order to secure the throne for himself, arranged the slaughter of all ninety-nine of his brothers. There is no historical evidence for this event, but some kind of palace civil war is easy to imagine. During his youth, Ashoka apparently had no scruples about being ruthless.

Once he had the crown on his head, Ashoka lost no time in returning to the warpath. During the first part of his reign, he carried out an incredibly bloody series of campaigns, seeking to complete the total conquest of north India begun by his grandfather. Much of the warring was in the eastern part of India, in the region known as Orissa. Success finally came to Ashoka; all of the Indian subcontinent except the most southern part was welded into one great empire. But India had paid a terrible price. In Orissa alone, over 100,000 men had been slain, and countless more had been uprooted and driven into slavery. The burden of suffering was enormous.

Then, supposedly, something remarkable happened that truly sets Ashoka apart from the other great empire builders of history: He had a change of heart. We are told that Ashoka, surveying the devastation and suffering that he had caused, was deeply moved by a spirit of remorse. Compassion replaced greed, and he vowed to dedicate the remainder of his years to healing the wounds that he had inflicted. He would transform the empire of gloom into the peaceable kingdom, and he would do it by promoting the Buddhist way of life in every way possible. Ashoka had been won over to Buddhism; he had seen the light, and now all of his energy would go into the conquest of the spirit, not of the sword.

Ashoka is sometimes compared to Saint Paul. What Paul did for Jesus, Ashoka did for Buddha. Perhaps a better way of looking at it is Heinrich Zimmer's comparison of Ashoka to the Roman emperor Constantine. Constantine was a practical man. Instead of persecuting the Christians, who had become numerous, he adopted Christianity and made it the official religion of the empire. In this way, he unified the state and gave it greatly renewed strength. Then, under his own authority, Constantine convened a great council of all the Christian bishops at the city of Nicaea, which was close to his own new capital, Constantinople. Apparently, there was much greater advantage in *using* the Christian Church than in opposing it. In like manner, Ashoka called for a great council of Buddhist leaders. It met, under Ashoka's sponsorship, at his capital city, Pataliputra (modern Patna). Like Constantine, Ashoka understood the value of controlling a powerful spiritual organization.

This is not to say that Ashoka's conversion to Buddhism was not sincere. Perhaps it was. According to the story, Ashoka, feeling deeply distressed as he reflected on the suffering he had caused, summoned a famous and much respected Buddhist monk to his court. The monk's retreat was a great distance from the court, but he and a few companions obligingly made the long trek on foot. When Ashoka heard about the teaching of Buddha, his heart was won over. He and the entire court were consecrated to the Buddhist way of life, and the same day he set out on a pilgrimage to Lumbini, Buddha's birthplace.

At Lumbini, Ashoka had a memorial stone pillar erected. Inscribed on the pillar were quotes from the Buddhist sutras (discourses said to have been delivered by Buddha himself). This seemed like such a good idea that Ashoka repeated it hundreds of times all over the empire. A vast number of these rock pillars were commissioned, thirty-five of which still exist today. They were placed along the roadways and in the towns. On the pillars, and sometimes simply on large natural rocks, were inscribed the Imperial Rock Edicts, Buddhist ethical principles intended to shape the lives of Ashoka's subjects.

In addition to establishing the Rock Edicts, we are told that Ashoka funded count-less Buddhist monasteries, which supported 64,000 monks. He paid for the creation of 80,000 stupas, shrines that honored the memory and teaching of Buddha. Ashoka trav-eled extensively throughout his vast empire, checking personally on the progress of his many programs. He built a first-rate system of roads, with drinking-water wells at regu-lar distances and, along with them, a series of comfortable inns for both human travel-ers and their animals. True to Buddhist teaching, Ashoka insisted on respectful treatment toward all living beings. He outlawed the sport of hunting and the use of ani-mals for sacrifice. He encouraged all to adopt vegetarianism (though he himself came to it only gradually). Ashoka was the benefactor of many hospitals, and they were to treat needful animals as well as human patients. In a way, Ashoka is the first important name in veterinary medicine.

So what are we to make of all this? Was Ashoka's conversion to Buddhism really sin-cere, or should one adopt the cynical view that Buddhism was merely a convenient device that he could use to consolidate and pacify the empire that he had won by vio-lence? Once there was nothing left to conquer, perhaps it had become expedient to switch horses. Or should I say, change gloves? Replace the iron-gloved fist with one of velvet; seek to pacify his potentially rebellious subjects by giving them peace, an improved standard of living, and, above all, an inspiring ethical system that would jus-tify his rule. Seen in this light, Ashoka's conversion to Buddhism could be very conven-ient, indeed.

It can be argued that it wasn't even Buddhism that Ashoka was promoting—at least, not exclusively. Buddha's name does not appear anywhere on any of the Rock Edicts that have survived the ravages of time. Although the inscriptions are Buddhist in spirit, some have speculated that Ashoka was not promoting Buddhism specifically, but rather a sort of "universal wisdom" distilled from many sources, Buddhism being only one of them. Indeed, Ashoka is quoted as saying, "The faiths of others all deserve to be hon-ored for one reason or another. By honoring them, one exalts one's own faith and at the same time performs a service to the faith of others. . . . If a man extols his own faith and disparages another because of devotion to his own and because he wants to glorify it, he seriously injures his own faith."

Perhaps Ashoka—like another great Indian emperor, Akbar, who ruled almost two thousand years later—was hoping to create a kind of religious and philosophical syn-cretism, a new philosophy of life that would bring together the best of many religious and philosophical systems. Drawn from many sources, the new philosophy would be the most powerful tool of all for pacifying and controlling his subjects. Ashoka's own words give us another reason for wondering just how dedicated a Buddhist he had become. He inad-vertently tips his hand while praising himself for being available at any time to someone with a problem. He is quoted as saying that he is available "whether I am dining, or in the ladies' apartments [the harem], or in my bedroom, or in my closet, or in my carriage, or in the palace gardens." This simple description of his lifestyle is hardly that of some-one—even a king—who has sincerely dedicated himself to following the Eightfold Path.

Nevertheless, after all is said and done, the weight of the evidence seems definitely to fall in favor of the argument that Ashoka did indeed sincerely embrace Buddhism and worked hard to spread it throughout the empire. It's possible that his motives were largely pragmatic at the beginning, but over time he became more genuinely committed to the Buddhist lifestyle. For one thing, he gradually phased out the serving of meat at court dinners, eventually adopting the strict vegetarian rule of Buddhism. One is not likely to go that far merely for show.

By far the most significant piece of evidence that Ashoka's Buddhism was genuine was his sponsorship of missionary activity. Not only did he promote Buddhism within the empire, but he was responsible for sending Buddhist missionaries to many other parts of the world. Ashoka was broadcasting the seeds of Buddhism, hoping they would fall on fertile ground. It is even recorded that Buddhist emissaries from the court of Ashoka traveled all the way to the Mediterranean world, visiting such centers of Hellenistic culture as Alexandria in Egypt and Ephesus in Syria. These seeds did not fall on fertile ground, but closer to home it was a different story; neighboring Burma (now known as Myanmar) received the teaching, and Buddhism began to sink roots there.

Of all the foreign contacts, it was in the island kingdom of Sri Lanka that Ashoka had the greatest success. In fact, it can be argued that Ashoka's claim to greatness rests on the single act of transplanting Buddhism to Sri Lanka. Considered from the long view of history, all of his other accomplishments fade into insignificance when compared with this one success. Under Ashoka's sponsorship, Buddhism in India flourished and enjoyed a brief golden age. But Buddhism was destined to decline in its homeland. However, outside of India, most notably in Sri Lanka, Buddhism would not decline, but rather would continue to grow and spread. We can thank Ashoka for that.

At the time of Ashoka, the ruler of Sri Lanka was King Tissa. There is a legendary story that Tissa, wanting to be on friendly terms with the superpower to the north, sent a valuable gift to Emperor Ashoka. It was a large, perfectly formed black pearl that had been found in the waters off Sri Lanka. "This is the most perfect thing that I know of in the whole world," Tissa is reported to have said. Ashoka graciously accepted the pearl and responded with a gift of his own to Tissa. "This is the most perfect thing that *I* know of in the whole world, the teaching of Buddha." He sent his own son, Prince Mahinda, to carry the message of Buddhism to Sri Lanka.

King Tissa and the whole court were won over by Mahinda and were consecrated to the Buddhist way. Mahinda lost no time in forming an order of monks, and he summoned his sister, the Princess Sanghamitta, to come to Sri Lanka and form a women's order. Sanghamitta is said to have brought with her a cutting from the Bodhi Tree, the tree that sheltered Buddha at the time of his awakening. It is claimed to this day that a pipal tree in Anuradhapura is the direct descendant of that cutting. It is also claimed that a relic in the stupa at nearby Kandy is a tooth from the mouth of Buddha himself!

The important thing, of course, is that Buddhism established strong, healthy roots in Sri Lanka. It was the first place outside of India proper where that would happen, and a century and a half later Sri Lanka would be the site of the great council that would lay the scriptural foundation of Buddhism—which brings us back to the Pali Canon. I hope that this diversion into the historical background of Buddhism helps you to better understand the big picture. The Pali Canon did not emerge out of thin air; it was the end result of a long line of development, and there were good reasons that Sri Lanka was the place where it happened.

After Ashoka's death in 232 B.C.E., the Mauryan line fell into decline, and so, too, did royal sponsorship of Buddhism. It's a complicated story and certainly an overstatement to say simply that Buddhism entered into a period of decline. It's likely, though, that Buddhists looked upon the time of Ashoka as the good old days. The old Hindu ways were making a strong comeback, challenging Buddhism, and the Buddhists themselves were separating into different schools of teaching, quarreling among themselves. In other words, it was a time of troubles for the Buddhists. Undoubtedly, there was a yearning in the hearts of many to reestablish order and orthodoxy. This was the climate out of which grew the call for the Great Council that would meet at the serenely distant site, Anuradhapura, in Sri Lanka.

THERAVADA BUDDHISM

The Great Council convened in 80 B.C.E., during the reign of King Vattagamani, and as we know, the outcome of its work was the Pali Canon. The intention was to set the practice of Buddhism on a solid scriptural foundation, one that would permanently provide a reliable link with the life and words of Buddha himself. The council would give a specific character to the tradition of Buddhism in its time. This tradition, the first great organized movement within Buddhism, is known by the name *Theravada*. (As mentioned earlier, Theravada is often referred to as Hinayana. We will take up this subject in the next chapter.)

Literally, *Theravada* means "the doctrine of the elders," but in more everyday language we could translate it simply as "the orthodox tradition." The Theravada tradition, given form in the Pali Canon, is spelled out in the scriptural writings that make up the canon. These writings are divided into three groups that together are known as the *Tripitaka*, which literally means "three baskets." The various books were written on palm leaf sheets, which were carefully bound and stored in separate collections, one for each of the three great categories.

The first of the categories is the *sutras*—sayings and discourses believed to have been handed down directly from the lips of Buddha. The sutras constitute an extensive collection of writings. Included among the sutras is the well-known *Dhammapada*. The second category is the *vinaya*, the rules of organization and everyday life for the members of the sangha. These, too, were believed, at least essentially, to have come from Buddha. The third "basket" held the *abhidharma*, works of a more speculative and philosophical nature that were held in high respect. Such writings were later than Buddha, but were important interpretations of the tradition and added to its full development.

Through his teaching, Buddha had shown humanity how to liberate itself from suffering. Theravada's reason for being was to preserve and promote that teaching. The goal of Theravada, therefore, was to provide a nourishing context within which any person who wished to make the effort could strive to become an *arhat*—that is, a fully awakened man or woman. The *vinaya* was the way this was worked out in daily life.

Vinaya, therefore, was the matter of most immediate practical concern. Although all men and women—indeed, all living beings—were considered to be within the embrace of the Buddhist way of living, it was clearly the underlying conviction of Theravada that only the person willing to dedicate his or her life totally to following the Middle Way (in other words a Buddhist monk) had any realistic hope of achieving *nirvana*. The Theravadin monk, free from family entanglements and worldly concerns, was thus able to devote his life to the way of poverty, celibacy, study, and discipline.

Laypeople were not left entirely out of the picture. They, too, could generate karma that would affect their own lives in positive ways. This was done by observing certain moral rules and engaging in devotional practices. Most of all, though, laypeople gained merit by helping the Order through the giving of alms. The laity, therefore, could play a supporting role and would benefit enormously from this in their personal lives, but realistically speaking, only the monk stood a reasonable chance of reaching the farther shore. More than that, the farther shore was attainable only to the monk who lived scrupulously by the rules of *vinaya*. We must not think of these rules as some kind of moral code handed down from a divine authority. Instead, they were very practical, time-tested guidelines derived from the teaching of Buddha and centuries of experience.

Buddha taught that it is ignorance that is at the root of human suffering. Ignorance (*avidya*) leads us down the path to the bondage of attachment. The path that leads to freedom from attachment is long and difficult; it is, indeed, the razor's edge. Only by living every day in perfect accord with the Dharma—that is to say, with the ideals of the Eightfold Path—can one hold his balance on the razor's edge and avoid falling into the fatally self-destructive impulses of "lust and hatred and confusion." (Interestingly, these appear similar to the terrible triad that Krishna introduces in the second book of the *Bhagavad Gita*, "lust and fear and anger.") Thus, all of the rules of the Buddhist monastic orders were directed at helping each member do the best job he or she could in becoming a living expression of the Eightfold Path. The rules of *vinaya* were designed to keep the traveler narrowly on that path.

The essence of the Theravadin rules of *vinaya* are summed up in the "Five Dedications": no killing, no stealing, no lying, no unlawful sex, and no alcohol. This is not as arbitrary a list as it might at first seem. Although expressed in the negative, it pretty well sums up the Theravadin monk's way of life. The rules were meant to guide the life of anyone who wished to follow the way of Buddha, but it was primarily the monk who was expected to adopt them with dedication. Let's look at each rule briefly.

1. **No Killing:** Buddha taught compassion and respect for all living beings. Life is one; there are no real separations. How could anyone dedicated to living according to the Dharma even *think* of deliberately taking the life of another living being? For this reason, Buddhists strove to develop a love not only for all men and women, but for all life—for all of Nature.

Understandably, Theravadin monks lived according to a strictly vegetarian diet. But aren't plants living beings, too? Yes, but most would follow the traditional Hindu interpretation and take living beings to mean only "sentient beings," in other words, animals. But there was really no need to *kill* plants anyway. Monks lived on an extremely simple diet. It was possible to take from the plant world what some plants naturally produce to be food, such as fruits and the fleshy part of seeds. The important thing, though, was to show love and respect for all living beings. Like Jain monks, one of the few simple possessions of a Theravadin monk was a small piece of gauze, which he would use to strain liquids before drinking. After all, there might be some tiny living beings in the liquid. (It probably resulted in a longer life for the monk, too.)

2. **No Stealing:** This might seem like a rather odd rule for a Buddhist monk. Can't we take it for granted that a monk will not be a thief? Not necessarily: Stealing can take many forms. Greed is a form of stealing. Even envious thoughts are a kind of mental stealing. Hoarding something may be legitimate from the legal point of view, but from the moral point of view it's really stealing if someone else is in need. In fact, do I have a right to *anything* more than I need if someone else is lacking what he or she needs?

Living in accord with the Dharma is living in a spirit of love and compassion for all others. We are all brothers and sisters of one family. This is the love that matters; the love of wealth and material possessions is in direct conflict with it. When one puts the love of possessions before compassion for one's suffering fellow man and woman, it ultimately comes down to what is essentially stealing.

The only solution to this dilemma is to simply give up worldly wealth altogether; become totally poor and thus drop out of the acquisitive game completely. Stealing, in thought and deed, will then have no meaning. Buddhist monks, following the example of Buddha himself, were to own nothing except the absolute basic necessities, and strictly speaking, in most cases such necessities were really "owned" by the monastic order to which the monk belonged. A Buddhist monk was allowed two robes, a pair of sandals, and a begging bowl—that's all. There were two robes so that one could be worn while the other was being cleaned. In modern times, in countries where the Theravadin tradition continues, one other item has become common: an umbrella (a practical necessity in tropical climes). By reducing his possessions to the absolute basic necessities of life, the monk was totally freed from the prison of acquiring, managing, protecting, worrying about—and lusting for—material possessions. He or she could give full time and energy to practicing the Dharma.

3. **No Lying:** Obviously, this rule involves more than what we ordinarily mean by lying. Lying in speech is preceded by lying in thought, and that's what this precept is directed at. The Buddhist monk was expected to make every effort to be completely truthful, not only in dealings with others, but in dealing with himself as well.

4. **No Unlawful Sex:** To the Theravadin Buddhist of old, *unlawful* did not refer to the civil law of the state; it referred to what was understood to be the moral law of Dharma. If the great power of sexual desire was not to hurl one off the path, it must be controlled. For the householder or the parent, this meant one thing, but for the Theravadin monk, it meant simply that there was no legitimate place whatsoever for sexual thoughts or sexual deeds. So long as one was a monk, one was to be entirely celibate.

This outlook is not new. In the Hindu tradition, the person who left his family home and took up the life of yoga was expected to commit himself to *brahmacharya,* which meant total abstinence from sexual behavior in thought and deed. And, of course, celibacy has always played an important part of the religious life in the Western tradition. The reason for this is fairly obvious: It's not necessarily that sex has been seen as evil or corrupting; it's just that if one is to have any hope of reaching the goal of freedom from attachment, sexual desire must be controlled, and all experience shows that, particularly among the young, the only realistic way of controlling sexual desire is to eliminate it from one's life altogether. Not to do so would be like trying daily to thread a needle in the middle of a raging forest fire. You may well be thinking that this expectation is ridiculous. Certainly, it's not for everyone, but for those who are willing and able to make the sacrifice, the promised reward will be infinitely great (or so we're told). The incredible energy of the sex drive can be channeled into the all-consuming effort to walk the path of Dharma.

5. **No Alcohol:** Like the other Theravadin rules, this simple dictate is really something of a symbolic way of getting at a much larger concern. This is not to say that alcohol was not forbidden, it was strictly forbidden, but the rule went much further than that: *Any* intoxicating influence was forbidden. The purpose was not to prevent the monks from partying; it was to help each monk avoid the kinds of powerful enticements that could lure him off the path and ensnare him (or her) in the fatal briar patch of attachment. Freeing oneself from attachments was (and is) the *sine qua non* of the Buddhist way.

And there is a more subtle aspect to the rule about alcohol as well. The practice of meditation is at the core of the Eightfold Path. A community of Buddhist monks would spend a good part of each day meditating together. Meditation looks so calm from the outside, but internally it can sometimes be a ferocious struggle. To succeed in meditation, one must concentrate tremendous energy into the act of consciousness. That's why all other forms of energy use are temporarily shut down. Anything that lessens the available energy is to be avoided. Long experience shows that alcohol and drugs, without necessarily being bad things in themselves, rob the body of energy to some degree, thereby compromising the meditation experience. For this very practical reason, they can have no place in the life of one who loves meditation and is dedicated to exploring its possibilities.

These Five Dedications, taken as a whole, constitute a broad program of guidelines intended to help the monk stay true to the spirit of the Eightfold Path throughout the routine of daily life, which began early for the Theravadin monk. We can observe that routine today in the daily life of Buddhist monks, particularly in southeast Asian countries such as Burma (Myanmar) and Thailand, where the underlying influence of Theravada has endured over the centuries.

The monks leave the monastery grounds shortly before dawn and go into the neighboring towns or cities to practice mendicancy—that is to say, to beg for food. The word *beg* needs to be explained. In no way does it refer to begging in the sense of panhandling or pleading. Rather, it is a highly dignified, almost ritualistic matter. Carrying their bowls in both hands, the monks in their saffron robes walk slowly about the dawn-lighted streets of the town. In many places they will find one or two people waiting for them with a large bowl of food, usually rice. They bow silently to each other, and the layperson will scoop some rice or vegetables into the monk's bowl. They bow again and the monk moves on. This practice is not seen as charity; it is considered an honor to share one's food with the monks, and it is a way of increasing one's store of positive karma.

When the bowls are full, the monks return to the monastery and share their food with each other. They eat in silence and consume all of the food or use it in some other way; nothing is wasted. Then the utensils are carefully cleaned and put away. In many monasteries, all of the day's food is taken before noon, so that the rest of the day can be devoted completely to the practice of Dharma. This means that the remainder of the day is given over to work, study, teaching, and meditation. Monks will spend several hours of each day in communal meditation. At certain times of the year, the time spent in meditation is increased to almost the entire day for several days in a row.

Becoming a Buddhist monk is not necessarily a lifetime commitment, as is generally the case with monks of the religious orders in the West. In Thailand, for example, the custom that every man is expected to spend some part of his life as an active member of a Buddhist monastic order has continued down to the present day. It may be for only six months or it may be for several years, but joining an order is commonly done in early adulthood, before entering upon a lifetime career. While serving as a monk, the person follows the rules of the order completely. It makes no difference what rank in society he comes from: All are treated exactly the same in the order. Even the king of Thailand is expected to serve. It's a wonderful custom. One can't help but wonder how different the world would be if all countries followed that custom.

Theravada Buddhism, as it originally took form, was not a religion. It was a powerful secular movement, based on the very practical teachings of Buddha, which aimed solely at helping a person become an arhat, a fully awakened man or woman. As such, it is one of the truly sublime achievements of the human spirit.

Theravada Buddhism emerged out of the common beliefs and practices of the early centuries of Buddhism and was given solid, enduring expression in the Pali Canon. By

All young men in Thailand are expected to serve some time as a monastic. (P. Bresnan)

the time of the Pali Canon, Buddhism had been growing and evolving for four centuries, and its influence had spread far beyond the Indian homeland. Sri Lanka had become a bastion of Theravada Buddhism, and it became a new fountainhead of missionary activity, particularly in southeast Asia, where it has endured through the ages and evolved into one of the major schools of Buddhism in the world today. As recently as 1955, a great council of Theravadin scholars was held in Burma (Myanmar). The council remained in session for two years.

Meanwhile, back in north India, the homeland of Buddhism, conditions were changing rather dramatically. As mentioned before, in India Buddhism was not seen as a totally separate and distinct philosophy, a revolutionary alternative to Hinduism. Rather, it was seen as a somewhat radical movement, but still well within the vast umbrella of Hinduism. The teachings of Buddha certainly were in conflict with some of the mainline traditional views of Hinduism, but that was true of many sects. Buddha himself was a Hindu. He probably saw himself as a reformer, not a rebel, and he had incorporated much of the Hindu tradition into his teaching. In this respect, Buddha is understandably compared to Jesus, who was a part of the Jewish culture of his age and is quoted as saying, "I have come not to overthrow the Law, but to fulfill it."

Hinduism was not a religion in the Western sense of the word. There was no precisely defined doctrine in Hinduism and no Hindu pope to enforce conformity of belief. One of the great strengths of Hinduism was, and is, its tolerance of differences, a natural consequence of which its great variety of sects. At the time of the Pali Canon, Buddhism in India would undoubtedly have appeared to most observers to be one of the sects of Hinduism, albeit a radical one. Over time, various sects would rise and take form like the waves of the ocean and then eventually decline and merge back into the sea. There was danger that this would happen to Buddhism in India.

During the time of Ashoka, Buddhism had enjoyed a splendid period of support and expansion, but its growing popularity reversed in the years after Ashoka. By the time of the Pali Canon, the future of Buddhism in India was in trouble. By far the greatest part of the Indian population was poor and lived in the numberless rural villages. These villagers went about life in ways that hadn't changed much over the ages. The traditional ways of Hinduism lived in the villages then as now. Buddhism had not advanced much into this part of the population. Even though Buddha intended that his teaching be for everyone, in fact most of the Buddhists were from the better educated upper classes. The hardworking rural people were not much attracted to a philosophy that must have seemed lofty and esoteric to them, that appeared to demand total commitment to a different way of life, and, worst of all, that turned its back on traditional beliefs and ceremonies—all at a time in history when a reinvigorated Hinduism was giving new life to the traditional ways and beliefs.

All these circumstances conspired to invigorate a revolutionary movement within the Buddhist community of India. A growing number of Buddhists were moved to reject the general spirit of Theravada. They were ready and eager to embrace a new interpretation of Buddhism. They called it "Mahayana," and it would drastically change the character of Buddhism forever.

Study Questions

1. What does it mean to say that in the centuries immediately following Buddha's death there was no such thing as "Buddhism"?
2. Why is it argued that the spread of Buddhism to Sri Lanka is Ashoka's single greatest contribution to the progress of Buddhism?
3. The writings of the Pali Canon are divided into three major groups, known as the Tripitaka. How would you describe each of these three groups?
4. What was happening to Theravada Buddhism that opened the way for a revolutionary new movement, ultimately to be known as Mahayana?

12

Mahayana Buddhism

To preserve and spread his teaching, Buddha formed the sangha, and in the centuries following his death it grew into a strong, unified tradition. Countless men and women came together in Buddhist communities to help one another along the path that leads to liberation. The tradition that we know as Theravada brought it all together and established a solid orthodoxy based on the scriptural foundation of the Pali Canon.

Theravada Buddhism was not a religious institution; it was a secular movement based on Shakyamuni Buddha's teaching, within which men and women could devote their lives to the great quest for personal liberation. The sangha was preserved in the form of the monastic order, a community of monks, each of whom was totally dedicated to becoming an arhat—an enlightened person. It was the commonly shared belief that the great goal of awakening could only be achieved by one who worked constantly at realizing the aims of the Noble Eightfold Path in his or her daily life. Because awakening was all that really mattered in the long run, it followed that only the select few who joined the orders and gave their lives to the discipline of the *vinaya* were really Buddhists in a truly meaningful sense of the word.

The doctrinal system that came to be known as Theravada represented the views of the majority in the early centuries of Buddhism. However, from the earliest times, there had been a minority—an "opposition party," so to speak—whose views did not neatly conform with those of the majority. These were the Buddhists of a more spiritual, more mystical frame of mind. We may speculate that this minority group wished to see Buddhism become more influenced by traditional Hindu beliefs and practices. The writings of the Pali Canon do not give us much information about these "dissenters," but there are allusions to their existence in references to protesting groups who "walked out" of various councils. This dissenting minority, in existence from the very beginning, provided the background out of which the Mahayana movement would grow. Although there were occasional clashes, it would appear that the two groups generally coexisted in harmony during the early centuries:

It is clear that Mahayana developed in organic connection with the whole of Buddhism, that is, that it originated directly from the early schools of Buddhism as a result of internal division. We know from the sources that the followers of both vehicles lived peacefully for a long time side by side in the same monasteries, observing the same *Vinaya* discipline.[1]

The nascent Mahayana movement began to gather momentum in the century following the Great Council that produced the Pali Canon. Very likely, it was a response to what had happened at the Council. Although all of northern India was affected by the stirrings of Mahayana, it was in the northwestern part of the subcontinent that the greatest activity was focused. In a way, it is true to say that the real homeland of Mahayana Buddhism was the upper Indus Valley in what is today parts of Kashmir and northern Pakistan. This is a hilly region rich in fertile valleys. A look at the map will show that the area, called Gandhara in ancient times, is tucked into a large bulge in the great mountain systems of the north. Alexander the Great had claimed Gandhara for a time, and as a result, it became something of a distant outpost of Hellenic culture. Greek artistic styles became established in Gandhara and from there would spread their influence as far as China. Gandhara was a crossroads of trade routes and hence a place where foreign ideas and religions could mix freely. It was in this climate that Mahayana, the great alternative to Theravada, would begin to mature into an entirely new tradition in Buddhism. Not all Buddhists of India were part of the Mahayana reform movement; many remained true to the traditional way. But the Mahayana was going to carry the day.

What initially fueled the rise of Mahayana was a deep dissatisfaction on the part of some with the traditional interpretation of Buddha's teaching by the dominant majority, the Theravadins. An attitude was developing among some Buddhists that the Theravada tradition had become too conservative, too rule bound, too elitist, and too narrow in scope. It seemed that the only genuine Buddhists were the members of the monastic orders; the laity played hardly any part at all. Buddha, though, had directed his teaching at everyone, not just a select few, and within the orders, which seemed to attract members almost exclusively from the upper classes, each monk directed virtually all of his attention to his own personal goal of achieving *nirvana*. In other words, Theravada had become far too self-centered—an ironic turn of events, considering that the whole thrust of Buddha's teaching had been directed at overcoming the prison of self. Yes, it seemed to a growing number that the Theravadins had become too concerned with discipline and had lost sight of Buddha's real concern, the nurturing of compassion.

Mahayana, however, was far from being *only* an opposition party, only a protest movement. It was a positive revolutionary movement in its own right. Mahayana would reinterpret the meaning of the Dharma. During the first century C.E., the movement, somewhat diffuse up to that time, began to coalesce around a powerful new body of writings known as the *Prajnaparamita* (Prahg-na-pahr-a-MEE-ta). A collection of about forty separate works, the *Prajnaparamita* was declared to be a sutra by its votaries. In essence, the *Prajnaparamita* purports to be a series of discourses between Shakyamuni Buddha and some of his closest disciples. The philosophical foundation of

Mahayana is laid out in these discourses. In fact, the name *Mahayana* itself is derived from the *Prajnaparamita*. Subhuti, one of Buddha's disciples, asks Buddha, "O Lord Buddha, what is this Great Vehicle, the Mahayana? What is its point of departure? Its destination? Through what realm does it move? How can one who travels in the Great Vehicle be recognized? Who is the person courageous enough to travel this way?" Buddha begins his reply by saying that, "Mahayana is synonymous with immeasurability." He then expands on this theme for the remainder of the dialogue, spelling out what the adherents of Mahayana regard to be a new and deeper interpretation of the meaning of his teaching.

Mahayana is a Sanskrit word; literally, it means "great vehicle," as noted in the previous paragraph. One popular interpretation of "great vehicle" is that it refers to the kind of vehicle that serves as a ferryboat, in this case a "large ferryboat." Buddha compared his teaching to a raft (a *yana*) that could ferry a person across the river of ignorance. It was an apt metaphor to use; India is a land of many rivers and few bridges. The traveler, especially in ancient times, often needed the services of the ferryman. Ordinarily, ferryboats are small, just a simple raft or dugout that carries only a few people. Such a craft was known as a "hina-yana," a small ferryboat. The adherents of the new wave of Buddhism, the self-styled "Mahayana," labeled the traditional school of Theravada the "Hinayana." They themselves would pilot the large ferryboat, the "mahayana," which had room enough for everyone, while the conservative Theravadins would make do with the little ferryboat that had room only for an elite few. It was logical to use symbols that the people were familiar with. If the movement were occurring today, we might instead refer to minivans and city buses.

There is undoubtedly some appeal in this metaphorical understanding of the words *Mahayana* and *Hinayana*, seeing them as referring to larger and smaller vessels, respectively. The Hinayana has room only for the elite few, while there is room on board the Mahayana for the whole population. Perhaps, though, it is more accurate to understand Mahayana as simply meaning "greater vehicle," in the sense that the doctrine and teaching of Mahayana, expressing the profound and true meaning of the Dharma, constitute a greater vehicle than what came before them. In this sense, Hinayana is simply a lesser, and therefore inferior, vehicle (at least in the opinion of the Mahayanists). As one source puts it,

> The focus of the change to the Mahayana within India can best be represented as a modification of the ideal of enlightenment. Those Buddhists who did not go along with the new Mahayana changes were labeled the Hinayana or Smaller Vehicle by their opponents. It was a pejorative term and was intended to suggest that the ideals of this more conservative group were more confined and more limited. The Mahayanists asserted that the others had become too easily satisfied with merely becoming arhats, persons whose whole goal was defined in terms of their own private and individual enlightenment. They charged that the Hinayanists were relatively unconcerned about the fate of others and what would today be called a "social conscience." The Mahayanists claimed that any enlightenment or *nirvana* enjoyed by an indi-

vidual in and by himself would not really be enjoyable at all. In their more acerbic comments, they castigated the Hinayanist group as being, at bottom, self-absorbed and even selfish. How, they asked, can the adherents of a philosophy that states that there is no permanent "self" allow themselves to become so concerned only for their own spiritual well-being?[2]

The Theravadins—insensitively referred to as Hinayanists by the self-styled Mahayanists—complained that the *Prajnaparamita* and other so-called sutras that soon followed it were not sutras at all. By definition, a sutra is a record of the words of Buddha himself, the teaching of the master directly from his own lips. The Pali Canon, they would argue, was a careful compilation of sutras that had been composed shortly after the death of Buddha and lovingly preserved over the centuries. But these Mahayana "sutras" were brand-new productions. How could they be the authentic words of Buddha? They were, in fact, nothing more than the heretical imaginings of contemporary authors. Now it was the turn for outraged Theravadins to walk out of meetings in which Mahayanists insisted on recitation from the new works.

Mahayanists responded to attacks on the veracity of their sutras by arguing that the *Prajnaparamita* and other sutras were not new at all. They had been passed directly from Buddha to some specially chosen disciples, but deliberately not committed to writing. Instead, they had been most carefully preserved in memory and passed along from generation to generation in the grand oral tradition. The reason for this, the Mahayanists argued, was that they preserved the deep and esoteric heart of Buddha's teaching. At the time of Buddha's death, most of the world simply was not ready to receive that teaching. Hence, sutras of an important, but less profound, nature were promulgated first. This "lesser vehicle," the Hinayana, was what one found in the Pali Canon. But now, the Mahayanists would say, after five centuries of evolution, the Buddhist world was ready to hear the deeper truth; it was time to commit the secret teaching to writing and make this "greater vehicle," the Mahayana, available to all.

One may be forgiven for being a little cynical about this Mahayana explanation. It sounds like an all-too-convenient way of getting around the Theravadin objection. The majority of modern scholars agree that the Mahayana sutras were in fact composed by anonymous authors at the time of their appearance in the first and second centuries C.E. Nevertheless, there is probably more than a grain of truth in the Mahayana argument. In premodern times, it was not all that unusual for scriptural works to be memorized and preserved orally. After all, the Upanishads were passed along for centuries in the oral tradition before being written down. Many of the themes that appear in the Mahayana sutras very likely were passed along orally, a sort of secret tradition, before being finally incorporated into the *Prajnaparamita* and other sutras. But on the whole, these compositions, however faithful they may have been to the spirit of Buddha's teaching, were essentially the product of the genius of the time when they were written.

The Mahayana sutras made their appearance in the first and, at the latest, the second century C.E. All originated in India and were written in Sanskrit. Some, however, have survived only in Chinese and Japanese translations. Taken together, they constitute a Mahayana canon that established the spiritual and philosophical foundation of the new tradition. The Mahayana sutras build upon and overshadow—but do not replace—the Theravada sutras of the Pali Canon. Let me identify by name the basic Mahayana sutras and then discuss some of the general features of Mahayana that derive from the influence of these sutras.

First, in both time and importance, is the great *Prajnaparamita*. *Prajna* refers to "intuitive wisdom," the wisdom that sees into the deepest truth of reality. Paramita literally means "attaining the farther shore." The derived meaning is "perfected," "transcendent," or "supreme." Put them together, and *Prajnaparamita* becomes "the Sutra of Transcendent Wisdom." As mentioned earlier, the *Prajnaparamita* purports to be a series of discourses between Buddha and certain of his disciples. These conversations are not exercises in discursive reasoning, such as we find in the dialogues of Plato. Rather, they are discussions that provoke intuitive responses. The *Prajnaparamita* is revelation, not exposition.

With all the later additions included, the *Prajnaparamita* became vast in size, running to more than 100,000 verses. Reference to the *Prajnaparamita*, though, generally means only what many consider to be the oldest part, known simply as "The *Prajnaparamita* in 8,000 Verses." Two sections that are excerpted from the *Prajnaparamita* are known as sutras in their own right and have been immensely popular over the ages: the *Diamond Sutra* and the very short *Heart Sutra*.

Probably second in the order of time was the *Avatamsaka Sutra* (short for *Buddhavatamsaka Sutra*, which translates as the "Garland of Buddha Sutra"). This sutra, focusing on the oneness of all being, was traditionally believed to have been delivered by Buddha only a short time after his awakening; it dealt with matters too deep for most of his followers to understand at the time.

Another sutra of major importance is the *Lankavatara Sutra*. The dialogue of this sutra takes place at an imagined assembly of notables convened by the king of Sri Lanka (as the name implies). In response to various questions, Buddha enunciates the doctrine of *Tathagata-garbha*, which holds that the Buddha-nature dwells in all sentient beings. It remains only to be uncovered. This is accomplished purely by removing the ignorance that hides its realization. As we shall see, this highly psychological sutra, along with the *Diamond Sutra*, would later have a profound influence on the development of Zen Buddhism.

Finally, there is the much-loved *Saddharma-pundarika Sutra*, popularly known as the *Lotus Sutra* (or, to be more precise, the "Sutra of the Lotus of the Good Dharma"). Among the last of the sutras to be written down, the *Lotus Sutra* is something of a summary or compendium of the essential teachings of Mahayana Buddhism. The setting here is also an assembly of notables, both worldly and supernatural, gathered at Vulture Peak, a highly dramatic setting at Mount Gridhrakuta near the Indian city of Rajagriha. The *Lotus Sutra* would exert a powerful influence over the development of Buddhism in China and Japan. Among its many notable features, the *Lotus Sutra* emphasizes the dignity of woman and teaches that enlightenment is open to women as well as men.

These four sutras—the *Prajnaparamita*, the *Avatamsaka*, the *Lankavatara*, and the *Saddharma-pundarika* (six if we include the *Diamond Sutra* and the *Heart Sutra*) constitute the core group of Mahayana scripture. Many other important writings are peripheral to the core four (or six); two in particular deserve to be mentioned: the *Vimalakirti Sutra* and the *Sukhavati-vyuha Sutra*. These two sutras deal extensively with the way in which a layperson can achieve enlightenment, a subject almost totally ignored in the Theravada tradition. *Vimalakirti* was in fact the name of a householder, not a monk. The sutra that bears his name lays out a picture of the ideal way of life of a layperson who is devoted to following the path of Buddha and confirms very clearly that one does not have to be a monk to seek enlightenment. The *Sukhavati Sutra* is the cornerstone of Pure Land Buddhism, which is by far the most "religious" of all Buddhist sects. The *Sukhavati Sutra* proclaims the way in which all men and women, whatever their status, can achieve Buddhahood. Over the ages, Pure Land Buddhism has been enormously popular with the population at large in Buddhist countries. In modern times, it is fair to say that the great majority of people who call themselves Buddhists are members of the Pure Land sect. We will have more to say about this interesting school of Buddhism in Chapter 14.

The sutras provided the spiritual and philosophical underpinning of Mahayana. From this base, the evolution of Mahayana radiated in many directions. Different though the various sects became over time, all of the schools that make up the Mahayana share certain essential elements. In the remainder of the chapter, we will examine five of these most fundamental aspects:

1. Diversity and Religious Elements in Mahayana
2. The Nature of Buddha
3. The Doctrine of *Shunyata*
4. The Bodhisattva
5. Artistic Expression in Early Mahayana

DIVERSITY AND RELIGIOUS ELEMENTS IN MAHAYANA

Diversity is the most immediately apparent feature of Mahayana. Unlike Theravada, in which there was general uniformity of doctrine and practice, Mahayana opened its arms to embrace a huge variety of *upaya* (ways of practicing the Dharma). In Mahayana, there is something for everyone. Included within this new openness was the appearance of decidedly religious practices. It is in the development of Mahayana that Buddhism begins to take on a distinctly *religious* character.

Not only were elements of Hinduism generously incorporated into Mahayana, but also, its development was influenced by systems of thought that were completely non-Indian. This was especially true in the Gandhara region, where so much of the early growth occurred. Out of this intermixture emerged a broad spectrum of "schools," each proclaiming its own version of Buddhist doctrine. On the one hand, we have Theravada: conservative, traditional, and orthodox; on the other hand, we have Mahayana, a new and revolutionary movement proliferating into a broad variety of sects, all of which identified themselves as Buddhists. Something very fundamental was holding them all together.

The popular British Buddhologist Christmas Humphreys (so named because he was born on Christmas Day) gives us the image of a wheel to indicate the fundamental relationships within the family of Buddhism. Theravada is the hub of the wheel: solid, essential, at the core. Mahayana is represented by the many spokes of the wheel, a full circle of variations, but all having their source in the hub. The essential teaching of Buddha was common to both Theravada and Mahayana. But the interpretation and application of Buddha's teaching allowed for some very dramatic differences. The scriptural writings of Theravada may have remained at the hub of the wheel—they were never renounced by Mahayana—but their importance was eclipsed by the new Mahayana sutras.

In the history of the growth of Mahayana, it is an obvious fact that what we ordinarily think of as "religious" elements—that is to say, devotional practices—came to have an important place in the total picture; indeed, devotional practices became one of the essential elements of Mahayana Buddhism. Undoubtedly, that was largely the result of assimilating into the Buddhist family great masses of people from the humbler classes of society to whom the relatively nonreligious character of traditional Theravada must have seemed barren and uninspiring. In its original Indian homeland, Mahayana Buddhism was responding to a resurgent Hinduism; it had to meet this challenge on its own ground. To a certain extent, the Dharma was reinterpreted in terms of the myths and religious customs of the common people.

Among the common people of the Hindu world, the practice of Bhakti Yoga—so much celebrated in the *Bhagavad Gita*—had become an important part of daily life. Bhakti focuses on devotion to a loving and compassionate deity, with all the attendant *puja* (forms of service) and paraphernalia. Flowers, incense, bells, gongs, statues, mandalas, chants, processions, pilgrimages, prostrations, icons, etc., etc.—all were part of the daily fare of Bhakti. Bhakti would have an enormous influence on the development of Mahayana, which was being shaped as well by both Hinduism and the traditional beliefs and practices of non-Indian cultures. It seems that in the numerous Buddhist cults that germinated, everything could find a place somewhere.

And why not? Was not the teaching of Buddha supposed to be open to all? Had not Buddha compared the human family to a lotus pond? Everyone could benefit from the Buddhist way of life, but each person would have to "plug into" that way of life at his or her own level. If, for some, this meant belief in deities and the trappings of religion, so be it:

> During this prolonged period of expansion, Buddhism infiltrated many cultures and absorbed unfamiliar influences. It should, therefore, come as no surprise to encounter, in the permissive, far-wandering Mahayana, types of worship that seem unrelated to early Buddhist teaching. In various sects and schools of the Mahayana, one finds proliferation not only of Buddhas and Bodhisattvas of varying significance and with different attributes but also complicated pantheons of such minor deities as Guardians of the Four Directions, Serpent Kings, wrathful demons, assorted nature spirits and so on, each "manifestation" accompanied by the inevitable altars, rosaries, gongs,

bells, incense, prayer wheels, mantras, thankas, mudras, and asanas representative of the ritual-loving and mythmaking proclivities of mankind and the resultant art of religious expression.[3]

THE NATURE OF BUDDHA

The most striking of the religious features to be found in Mahayana is the near deification of Shakyamuni Buddha himself. Whereas in the Theravada tradition Shakyamuni was a man of flesh and blood, with his feet very much on the ground, in the Mahayana Sutras he is transmuted into a godlike being whose feet are far removed from the dusty earth. The superhuman characterization of Buddha, which runs through all of the sutras, is established at the very beginning of the *Prajnaparamita*:

> The Lord dwelt on the Vulture Peak at Rajagriha with a large gathering. He sat down cross-legged on His lion throne and entered the King *Samadhi*. . . . His whole body became radiant. The thousand-spoked wheels on the soles of his feet shone forth sixty hundred thousand trillions of billions of light rays, as did every other part of his superhuman body. These light rays illumined and lit up our vast billion-world universe. . . . And all the beings lit up and illuminated by these dazzling light rays became focused upon the unexcelled, true and perfect enlightenment.[4]

Further on in the *Prajnaparamita*, in another typical scene, six thousand monks kneel reverently before Buddha. Bowing their heads, the monks begin to bring their hands together at the level of the heart. At that moment, Buddha miraculously causes their hands to fill with flowers. Then, "With surprise and jubilation, the practitioners reverently scatter the brilliant and fragrant blossoms over the golden body of the Awakened One." Buddha (of the golden body, no less) responds with a smile, "variously colored rays of light sparkle like rainbows from the parted Buddha lips and pearl-like Buddha teeth, assuming delicate and harmonious shades of blue, yellow, red, white, crimson, crystal, silver and gold. . . . This smile of light ascends to the highest paradise realm, returns again across vast distances to the shining body of the Buddha, swirls thrice around it, and vanishes, just as the beautifully formed lips meet once more."[5]

As if that's not impressive enough, the scene becomes even more awesome in the *Lotus Sutra*. Here the vast assembly includes every kind of sentient being, not only monks, sages, and kings, but even dragons and gods. After the enthroned Buddha had delivered a discourse, the multitude was "filled with joy and, pressing their palms together, gazed at Buddha with a single mind." Buddha then "emitted a ray of light from the tuft of white hair between his eyebrows, one of his characteristic features, lighting up eighteen thousand worlds in the eastern direction. There was no place that the light did not penetrate, reaching downward as far as the Avichi hell and upward to the Akanishtha heaven." Going beyond this, he later "extended his long broad tongue upward till it reached the Brahma heaven, and from all his pores he emitted immeasurable, countless beams of light that illuminated all the worlds in the ten directions."[6]

We could go on and on with examples like this. The Mahayana sutras are full of such marvelous doings. Over and over, Buddha is portrayed as a being of godlike power and majesty, far removed from the humble daily life of the man who trekked the dusty roads of North India preaching to crowds of very ordinary people.

So what's going on here? Were the authors of the Mahayana sutras in fact attempting to deify Buddha? Did they really intend that their listeners imagine Shakyamuni Buddha to be a divine being and that the scenes pictured in the sutras be taken as literally accurate descriptions? Not exactly: No doubt, the literary style of the sutras involves a good deal of poetic license; the depiction of Buddha in heavenly splendor was deliberate and unrestrained hyperbole. But there was a purpose to all of it. Each of the sutras was a vehicle for the presentation of a new interpretation of the teaching of Buddha, and the transcendent character of the setting—even if not meant to be taken as a factually accurate description—was a very important element in the literary presentation of that new interpretation. The mind-boggling descriptions were intended to overwhelm the imagination and jolt us out of our customary ways of thinking. This is most pointedly the case with regard to the new—that is, the Mahayana—understanding of the nature of Buddha.

The Buddha of the Theravada tradition was very much a flesh-and-blood human being. He was a compassionate and much-honored teacher of mankind. The Buddha of the Mahayana tradition remains the human teacher, but he comes to represent much, much more as well. The nub of the difference comes down to this: In Theravada, Buddha was seen to be a mortal; in Mahayana, Buddha comes to be seen as an eternal being.

Mahayana teaching regarding the nature of Buddha is summed up in the Doctrine of Trikaya, which translates literally as "three bodies." The flesh-and-blood body is referred to as the *nirmanakaya* ("body of transformation"). This was the "body" known as Shakyamuni, the man who lived and taught in north India. Just like any other man, Shakyamuni was born, grew old, and died. But Shakyamuni was not just an ordinary human being, albeit one with extraordinary gifts. Rather, Shakyamuni was the incarnation—the temporary, human incarnation—of "Buddha," who, on a higher plane of understanding, is seen to be a transcendent being, the embodiment of wisdom and compassion.

This higher order of being is *sambhogakaya* ("body of joy"). This is the aspect of Buddha that is pictured in the Mahayana sutras and consequently, explains the use of superhuman descriptions by the authors of the *Prajnaparamita*. When Shakyamuni died, his *nirmanakaya* ceased, but *sambhogakaya* transcends earthly time. In *sambhogakaya*, Buddha is seen as a transcendent, godlike being—the embodiment of enlightenment—who does not die, but exists throughout time in a paradise (known as a "Buddha-realm" or "Buddha-field") over which he presides. *And*, there is not just one such Buddha, but a countless number of them, all presiding over their respective Buddha-realms, which are populated by vast numbers of their devoted followers, including some who are on the path to becoming future Buddhas. (In Pure Land Buddhism, the word "Buddha" does not refer to Shakyamuni Buddha at all, but rather to Amitabha Buddha, a completely different Buddha, into whose Buddha-field, the "Pure Land," his devotees yearn to be reborn.)

According to this view, from time to time over the ages, a Buddha will be moved by compassion for the suffering of mortals and choose to be born among them in the form of *nirmanakaya*. By means of this selfless act, he can bring the liberating truth of Dharma directly to the people in a time of special need. According to Mahayana teaching, this is how Shakyamuni came to be. It should be pointed out that Mahayanists believe that the world we live in is only one of a great many worlds. Since the beginning of time, incarnate Buddhas have been arising in this and myriad other worlds. Shakyamuni was only the most recent occurrence in this world—and, we are told, Shakyamuni will not be the last. The next Buddha—who will appear when the time is right—will be known by the name Maitreya.

Mahayana teaching holds that Buddha chose to incarnate himself as Shakyamuni purely out of a spirit of love and compassion for suffering humanity. Clearly, this is a theme of broad scope in human history. Can we doubt that Mahayana Buddhism, heavily influenced as it was by the traditions and beliefs of Hinduism, is here reflecting the Hindu teaching regarding Vishnu, who became incarnate on several occasions in order to be of help to a world in trouble? In fact, Hinduism's final accommodation with Buddhism was to declare that Shakyamuni himself was one of Vishnu's incarnations. Another obvious parallel is to be found in the Christian story of the incarnation of Jesus, who became man for the express purpose of bringing "salvation" to a wayward humanity. Jesus could be described as the *nirmanakaya* of God "the Father." The Mahayana interpretation of the incarnation of Shakyamuni Buddha is very much in this spirit.

To sum up, the *nirmanakaya*, then, is the manifestation of a *sambhogakaya* Buddha. This manifestation, or incarnation, appears in the world as a flesh-and-blood man for the purpose of teaching the Dharma in a time of need. The historical Shakyamuni was the *nirmanakaya*, who, as a *sambhogakaya* Buddha, is a transcendent being of supernatural powers that is the embodiment of the Dharma and, like myriad other Buddhas, presides over a divine domain known as a Buddha-realm. It is Buddha in the *sambhogakaya* mode that is presented in the Mahayana sutras.

The apex of the Doctrine of Trikaya is *dharmakaya* (the "universal body"). *Dharmakaya* is one of the truly sublime terms in the lexicon of Mahayana. It is where everything—literally *everything*—comes together. *Dharmakaya* refers to the ultimate metaphysical nature of all being. The ultimate nature of being—the essence of the universe—is oneness; ultimately, All is One. This universal oneness is identified with Buddha, the Buddha-nature. *Dharmakaya*, then, refers to the essential nature of Buddha, which is identical with the indwelling oneness of all Reality. Thus, all Buddhas, all mortals—indeed, all of the universe—is joined in *dharmakaya*. In the most final sense that we can imagine, *dharmakaya* is the unity of Buddha within all that exists.

I'm sure you will agree that this description of *dharmakaya* can become very abstract, very metaphysical. The nature of the subject makes that inevitable. It's true today, and it was just as true in the formative days of Mahayana. Largely as a result of this abstract nature, the concept of *dharmakaya* came to be represented by a symbol that the human mind could more easily take hold of. One of the more important Buddhas—Vairochana by name—came to *symbolize* the *dharmakaya*. This was especially helpful in artistic representations. The *dharmakaya*, of course, transcends all individual entities, including Buddhas, so it is important to remember that Vairochana was not *identified* with the *dharmakaya*; rather, Vairochana *represents* the *dharmakaya* (in much the same way that a statue depicting Brahma might be intended to represent the principle of Brahman).

Speaking of Brahman, this description of the trikaya may bring to mind a similar teaching in Hinduism. Certain similarities do indeed exist. The *dharmakaya* can be likened to Brahman and the *sambhogakaya* to various Hindu deities—Vishnu, for example. The *nirmanakaya* suggests the kind of incarnation we find in Vishnu becoming Krishna. The most important difference, though, concerns the *dharmakaya*. Buddha as *dharmakaya* is not a *being* that *does* the universe, such as Brahman was conceived to be. That is, there is no "Buddha-*Atman*;" *dharmakaya* is the process itself, seen in its simplest, most universal essence.

It is this universality of the Buddha-nature that is at the heart of the Mahayana revolution. This is the Buddha of the Mahayana sutras, so different from the very human teacher of the Theravada sutras:

> [Buddha] is now conceived as a being who transcends all boundaries of time and space, an ever-abiding principle of truth and compassion that exists everywhere and within all beings.[7]

"An ever-abiding principle of truth and compassion that exists everywhere and within all beings"—this theme, the universal Buddhahood of all reality, is especially stressed in the *Avatamsaka Sutra*, in which we are encouraged over and over to see the Buddha-nature in everyone and everything. A love of Buddha and a love of the harmony of Nature are one and the same thing. The harmony of Nature is the larger context within which human life takes its meaning. Thus, the natural order has a certain sanctity about it and is deserving of reverence. Even the smallest thing contains the mystery of the entire universe. The author of the *Avatamsaka Sutra* uses many humble analogies to illustrate the universal indwelling of the Buddha-nature. We are assured that we can know the entire ocean in a drop of water and see all of the universe reflected in one grain of sand. This same great theme was given expression in the Chandogya Upanishad and also brings to mind the famous lines of William Blake:

> To know the world in a grain of sand,
> And a heaven in a wild flower;
> Hold infinity in the palm of your hand,
> And eternity in an hour.[8]

The teaching of *dharmakaya* has profound implications. It grew out of Buddha's view regarding the unity of being. The Mahayanists believed that everything and everyone possesses the Buddha-nature; or to put it more precisely, everything and everyone is an expression of the Buddha-nature. Differences and separations are only superficial.

Given this view of truth, each person's underlying reality is, *by its very nature,* complete and perfect. It remains only for one to sweep away the cloud of ignorance (*avidya*) to see that reality. The illusion of ego and its fierce attachments are what stand in the way of our seeing the real truth of our nature. Buddhahood is not something separate from us, to be *acquired* through long, hard work; it is our very nature and remains only to be *uncovered*.

Another way of putting this is to say that everyone is "Buddha" by nature, but, through ignorance and fear, our true nature—our "Buddhahood"—is hidden from us, and we falsely identify with ego. The goal is to see through the stifling illusion of ego and to wake up to what we really are. Buddhahood is uncovered, not acquired. This difference of opinion had already had a long history in Buddhism. It was, as you may recall, the major issue that divided the members of the second Great Council held only a century after Buddha's death. The Buddhologist Nancy Wilson Ross makes the following interesting comment on the matter:

> A modern Zen roshi has suggested a further point of comparison between the two great divisions which also warrants careful consideration. In his view, Theravada emphasizes the humanity of the Buddha; Mahayana emphasizes the Buddha-nature of humanity. Whereas Theravada stresses the following of a moral life and high-principled behavior as the road to eventual Buddhahood, Mahayana inclines more toward tapping an intuitive wisdom to achieve the realization that one already possesses the Buddha-nature; it has simply to be "recovered" or uncovered, so to speak.[9]

The reason I maintain that this difference is of great significance is that it focuses on a very basic question: Is the human problem of suffering due to a real imperfection in our nature, albeit one that can be healed, or is it the result of a self-created illusion about what we really are? There's a great difference in these two alternatives. Mahayana takes the position that all beings possess the Buddha-nature, and that it is only ignorance which stands in the way of realizing it. Overcoming this ignorance— uncovering one's Buddhahood—is what the Buddhist way of life is all about, and the Buddhist way of life, thanks to the Mahayana Doctrine of Trikaya, was free to find almost limitless forms of expression. Trikaya was open to every imaginable kind of interpretation, everything from cult veneration to highly sophisticated philosophy—and all of it was brought together in *dharmakaya*.

THE DOCTRINE OF SHUNYATA

Like Theravada, Mahayana is a part of the evolution of Buddhism; at the deepest level they share a common core. But Mahayana doctrine moved far from the original teaching of Theravada. The foregoing discussion of the nature of Buddha should make that very clear. The changes that we find are not to be explained simply by arguing that Mahayana was allowing itself to fall back into the Hindu world out of which Buddhism had emerged in the first place. Nor, in similar fashion, can it be argued that Mahayana Buddhism was nothing more than a religious and philosophical syncretism in which a spirit of "anything goes" became dominant. There is, in fact, a solid philosophical foundation to Mahayana; it is what unites and gives common substance to the many different spokes that make up the wheel. This philosophical foundation, known as the Doctrine of *Shunyata*, does not stand in opposition to Theravada; rather, it transcends it.

Often translated as the "Doctrine of Emptiness," *Shunyata* is truly fundamental to the teaching of Mahayana; everything turns on it. *Shunyata* is derived from the word *shunya* (pronounced shoon-ya), which, in Sanskrit, means "zero." What an important word that is! Allow me to digress for a moment. In ancient times, Indian civilization was the source of many great discoveries in the arts and sciences, but perhaps none has had more far reaching significance than the "discovery" of the zero. Indian thinkers were the first to develop a notation for the mathematical concept of zero. Without it, the evolution of modern mathematics and science would have been impossible. (The Central American Mayans were the only other culture to independently devise a notation for zero.) In medieval Europe the arithmetically clumsy Roman numerals were replaced by what we call "Arabic" numerals. But they were Arabic only in the sense that Arabic-speaking traders and scholars introduced them to Europe through Spain. The homeland of the numbers that all of the modern world uses, including zero, was India.

Less well known, but equally significant, was the role that the humble word *shunya* would play in the development of the philosophical system known as *shunyata*. The *Doctrine of Shunyata* is a philosophical examination of the nature of reality—and, of course, the whole Buddhist way of life is directed at helping one to wake up to a true knowledge of reality. The Theravada tradition identified awakening with seeing through the illusion of the separate, substanding self; the process is what we might call a validation of the *Doctrine of Anatman*. Without actually contradicting this notion, Mahayana takes a quantum step beyond it in the *Doctrine of Shunyata*. In a most subtle way, this move opens the door to the rich variety of paths that characterize the Mahayana philosophy.

When the *Doctrine of Shunyata* is correctly understood, the word "emptiness" is seen to be a perfectly suitable term. (Sometimes the word "void" is used instead of "emptiness.") Some in the West, though, lacking understanding of *shunyata*, have misconstrued the use of the word "emptiness," concluding that *shunyata* (and by association, all of Mahayana Buddhism) is fundamentally a nihilistic philosophy of life. *Shunyata* is not nihilistic; indeed, it is not negative at all. Properly understood, *shunyata* is a positive approach to seeing the ultimate truth of reality.

The body of teachings known as *shunyata* is given expression in the Mahayana sutras, most of all in the *Prajnaparamita*. The teachings of *shunyata*, though, are diffused throughout the sutras, where they are never presented in a concise form. It remained for the Indian philosopher Nagarjuna to pull the various ideas together. Nagarjuna (pronounced na-GHAR-joo-na), one of the most important names in the history of Buddhism, was the founder of the philosophical school known as *Madhyamika* (mah-dya-MEE-ka), the "middle way" to the truth of reality—that is, middle between all dualities, including being and nonbeing. All of this is laid out in his seminal work, the *Madhyamika-karika*.

Not a whole lot is known about Nagarjuna. Some say that he was raised by serpents (nagas) in an undersea palace where he was initiated into the ways of the occult. While exploring some underwater caves, he discovered a collection of Buddhist scriptures that had been hidden there. Overwhelmed by their message, he left the nagas and became a passionately devoted Buddhist. Well, anything's possible, but a more humdrum version of his life presents Nagarjuna as a Brahmin priest living in North India during the century from 150 C.E. to 250 C.E. In the course of his studies, he discovered the *Prajnaparamita* and was won over to Buddhism by it. He devoted the rest of his life to elucidating the inner meaning of this great work. In the process, he gave lasting definition to what we know as the Doctrine of *Shunyata*.

Nagarjuna took as his starting point the position that suffering is the result of ignorance (*avidya*)—that is, a fundamentally false view of reality. Ordinarily, though, one does not perceive his own view of reality to be false; normally, one clings to his ignorance and believes it to be truth. But liberation from *avidya* is possible. Buddha did it and urged all men and women to follow him. Buddha gave us his teaching, the Dharma, as a path to follow. But how does it work? (This may seem more like a modern than an early Buddhist sort of question, but in essence, that's what Nagarjuna was asking.) Granted that the ordinary state of human consciousness is a condition of ignorance, and granted that following the way of life recommended by Buddha may result in an awakening from that ignorance, what actually *happens* that brings about the awakening?

In exploring this question, Nagarjuna carefully observed human consciousness and concluded that there are two kinds of knowledge, two fundamentally different ways of knowing. First, there is ordinary knowledge, which is conceptual and rational and which sees the relationships among things. This kind of knowledge is very practical and is good at discerning relative truth, but because, by its nature, it is always bound up in relative truth, it is completely incapable of knowing the deeper essential truth of reality. Second, there is transcendent knowledge, known by its Sanskrit name, *prajna*—an intuitive, direct seeing into the nature of reality. *Prajna* is different in kind from ordinary knowledge; it is not simply a matter of degree that separates the two. The action of *prajna* is the only way of knowing absolute truth. Although the rising of *prajna* is rare—so rare that few even know of its existence— its potential is inherent in human nature and lies dormant in the consciousness of every person, waiting only for the right conditions to bring it to life. Truly seeing for oneself the insufficiency of ordinary knowledge is a right condition that can clear the way for the rising of *prajna*.

Thus did Nagarjuna attempt a critique of ordinary knowledge. He was not offering a new theory of knowledge; in fact, Nagarjuna wanted to reveal the ultimate absurdity of *all* theories of knowledge, insofar as none is capable of uncovering absolute truth— at least, not at the level of ordinary knowledge. His method, referred to as a "dialectic," consisted of a critical examination of all opposing positions and, through a process of *reductio ad absurdum*, revealing that no imaginable position can stand by itself as a revelation of absolute truth. Once again, Nagarjuna was not dismantling existing theories of knowledge so as to offer a new and better way of arriving at the truth. Instead, he was attempting to demonstrate that no method at the level of ordinary knowledge is capable of revealing more than the relative truth of ordinary experience. Let's clarify this claim by looking at the general conclusions that Nagarjuna reached.

Ordinary knowledge is conceptual. We don't often think about it—and in the practical affairs of daily life it's better that we don't—but when we sit back and reflect on the nature of our knowledge, it becomes clear that all that we know is a body of concepts. Concepts are ideas—interior, subjective states. These, of course, include such things as sensations and feelings. The important point is that everything we experience, everything we know, ultimately comes down to a subjective state of consciousness. Putting it very loosely, all we ever know are our own ideas. (Or, as a modern-day biologist might put it, "All that one ever knows is the constantly changing electrochemical conditions of his central nervous system.") Naturally, we wish to believe that our internal ideas faithfully represent the reality of external existences in the phenomenal world, and the seeming reliability of our way of experiencing things reinforces this belief strongly. Nevertheless, it is undeniably true that when I "know" something, I know it (if I know it at all) indirectly, not directly. Take that tree over there, for example. I may say that by observing it, I know that it exists, and although this is certainly true at the practical level of everyday experience, it remains nonetheless a fact that what I *know* is not the tree itself, but only my idea *of* the tree. Whether or not my idea presents accurate information about the tree is not the point; the point is that what I know—and all that I ever know at the level of ordinary knowledge—is my own collection of ideas, my own concepts. This is true of all concepts, including those that seek to interpret reality.

To come to see that all of our knowledge is conceptual is a tremendously important understanding, because concepts are a product of the way the mind works. In other words, what we call ordinary knowledge is determined not by objective existential reality, but rather by the character of the human mind. Mental processes have evolved to be practical, not to be instruments of philosophical speculation. In forming concepts, the human mind *by its very nature* seeks to find meaning in relationships. A concept has meaning *in relation to* other concepts. This is quite obvious in some cases, such as night and day, and hot and cold. But it is equally true for all concepts, although often the relationship is more subtle. Take the concept of "house," for example. "House" doesn't stand in clear opposition to something else the way night and day do, but "house" does stand in opposition to "all that is not a house." It may seem a little far fetched at first to suggest that we understand the concept of a house by contrasting it with all that is not a house, but when you think about it, I'm sure you will see why Nagarjuna would argue that this is exactly how the human mind works. We get so good at contrasting things in this manner that we don't even think about it. And if we break "house" down into the elements that make it up—doorknobs, nails, windows, etc.—the same mental process continues to apply. No matter how far we go, any element of existence that can be conceptualized cannot be known, except in terms of the conditions that caused it and that relate it to other elements. This, as mentioned earlier, is given expression in the Doctrine of Dependent Origination: Nothing can explain itself; everything is intelligible only in relation to the causes and conditions that bring it about.

The important thing to understand here is that conceptual knowledge is always *relational* knowledge. No matter what we think we know, we know it only in relation to other things. Nothing can stand entirely by itself. In this world of ceaseless flux—and the knowing mind is itself an integral part of that flux—things have meaning only in relation to other things. That is to say, concepts have meaning only in relation to other concepts. Even our concept of the entire universe—call it "being"—has meaning only in relation to the concept of nonbeing.

All of this reasoning led Nagarjuna to what is summed up in the wonderful Sanskrit word *svabavata*, which means "empty of self-existence." *Svabavata* is at the heart of *shunyata*, the "Doctrine of Emptiness." If the reality of any given thing (at least conceptually) is conditionally dependent upon its relationship to other things, then nothing can stand by itself. Everything is "empty" of self-existence. Any given "thing" is the result of the causes and conditions that define it. Take these causes and conditions away, and the "thing" ceases to exist:

> The world perceived through the senses, the phenomenal world as we know it, was described in early Buddhism as "empty" because it was taught that all such phenomena arise from causes and conditions, are in a constant state of flux, and are destined to change and pass away in time. They are also held to be "empty" in the sense that they have no inherent or permanent characteristics by which they can be described, changing as they do from instant to instant.[10]

Everything—everything that we can imagine—is bound up in the conceptual relationships that give it meaning. Thus, nothing is fundamentally real *unto itself*. There is no such *thing* as night; "night" is a concept only, and it has meaning solely in relation to other concepts, such as "day." This notion poses no problem with such concepts as night and day, but the heat gets turned up when we direct Nagarjuna's spotlight on such concepts as the Doctrine of *Anatman*. Nagarjuna would insist that, no less than any other concept, that of *Anatman* must be seen as ultimately empty of self-standing reality. *Anatman* has meaning only in relation to *atman*; both are aspects of one conceptually relative reality. Is this to say, then, that *atman* is real after all, or at least as real as *anatman*? In fact, is not to say that *atman* is real or unreal. *Atman* is what it is, a concept—and the same goes for *anatman*. Both are empty of substantive reality; neither represents absolute truth. Thus did *shunyata* clear the way for Mahayana to break free of the narrow orthodoxy of Theravada and be able to follow many different paths—even seemingly contradictory paths.

Because nothing imaginable is exempt from conditional existence, ultimately all of being is reduced to a state of "emptiness." Thus, what we hold to be reality is actually emptiness, or, as is often stated, "Emptiness is form; form is emptiness." Emptiness, though, definitely does not mean nonexistence: To say that reality is empty of permanent self-standing forms is not to say that reality does not exist. In no way was Nagarjuna denying the existence of reality (a common misunderstanding of his teaching); instead, he was simply denying the ability of the conceptualizing mind to know reality in itself. With regard to ordinary knowledge,*

> voidness does not mean nothingness, but rather that all things lack intrinsic reality, intrinsic objectivity, intrinsic identity or intrinsic referentiality. Lacking such static essence or substance does not make them not exist—it makes them thoroughly relative.[11]

Discovering the emptiness of the phenomenal world does not necessarily lead to negativity and nihilism. Instead, it can open the way for an altogether different order of knowing—and that brings us back to Nagarjuna's other way of knowing: the way of *prajna*. *Prajna*—intuitive wisdom—*sees through* emptiness and beholds the positive truth of reality. When the thinking mind is reduced ultimately to emptiness, it can at last be gently persuaded to stop and get out of its own way. When this happens, the eye of *prajna* is allowed to open. *Prajna* transcends the ordinary mind; it is a breakthrough to a higher hidden truth. *Prajna* sees reality as it is. Since absolute reality transcends all categories of existence that can be conceptualized, the ultimate nature of reality cannot be described in words:

> The reality to which all names refer is utterly ungraspable and inconceivable, possessing absolutely no physical or metaphysical self-existence. . . . Given this irreducible fact of unthinkability—not as a frustrating limit to our understanding, but as a beautiful, blissful openness and freedom from all limits—we know that no authentic expression of Perfect Wisdom will permit us to picture or conceptualize What Is.[12]

In effect, we cannot conceptualize what is; we can only experience it. Doing so is the experience of awakening.

Prajna is *completely* different from the working of ordinary knowledge. No amount of discursive reasoning will ever open consciousness to the inner truth of reality. So then, what is the point of all this philosophizing, all this dialectic? Isn't it just a grand example of the very thing it criticizes? If the exercise were an intellectual end in itself, that would surely be true, but the real objective of the dialectic is to help free the mind from its attachment to concepts. By loosening the grip of the thinking mind a little at a time and coming to accept the seamless unity of Being that *shunyata* proclaims, one is moving closer to the place and time when the great light of awakening can occur. The dialectic then becomes a form of *upaya* (skillful means):

> There comes a moment when this consciousness of the inescapable trap in which we are at once the trapper and the trapped reaches a breaking point. One might almost say that it "matures" or "ripens," and suddenly there is what the *Lankavatara Sutra* calls a "turning about in the deepest seat of con-

---

*Doesn't this discussion of *shunyata* remind you of the Vedantic concept of Brahman and *lila*? It also brings to mind the notion of the *quantum vacuum* in modern physics. Physicists no longer think of "empty" space as really empty. Space, at least at the micorcosmic level, is thought of as a state of being infinitely full of potentiality that is constantly being realized in the spontaneous emergence and dissolution of virtual particles.

sciousness." In this moment all sense of constraint drops away, and the cocoon which the silkworm spun around himself opens to let him go forth winged as a moth. The peculiar anxiety which Kierkegaard has rightly seen to lie at the very roots of the ordinary man's soul is no longer there. Contrivances, ideals, ambitions, and self-propitiations are no longer necessary, since it is now possible to live spontaneously without trying to be spontaneous. Indeed, there is no alternative, since it is now seen that there never was any self to bring the self under its control. Reduced to the bare essentials, such is the inner process which the Sunyavada [that is, the application of the doctrine of *shunyata*] is trying to set in motion with its philosophy of total negation. . . . The positive and creative content of the Sunyavada is not in the philosophy itself, but in the new vision of reality which is revealed when its work is done, and Nagarjuna does not spoil this vision by trying to describe it.[13]

The Doctrine of *Shunyata* recast the philosophy of Buddhism in a very fundamental manner. In varying ways it would shape the character of the many disparate "schools" of Buddhism that make up the Mahayana. We will see later that *shunyata* was a powerful shaping influence in Zen Buddhism; in different ways, though, it is equally influential in sects far removed from the spirit of Zen. Turning again to the image of a wheel, we may say that Theravada and the Pali Canon are the hub of the wheel and the various expressions of Mahayana are the spokes. It might be helpful in this metaphor to picture *shunyata* as a circle that surrounds the hub. *Shunyata* is physically separate from the hub, but is closely associated with it, and, like the hub, it joins the spokes together.

It is important to keep reminding ourselves that awakening is what the teaching of Buddha is all about. Be it Theravada or Mahayana, Buddhism is given meaning by the achievement of awakening. Mahayana, influenced by the Doctrine of *Shunyata*, gave a new meaning in turn to the quest for awakening. Freed from the strict interpretation of Theravada—indeed, freed from *all* conceptual interpretations—Mahayana Buddhism could follow any and every path that led to the opening of *prajna*. These paths might even seem contradictory in some ways, but that would be of no consequence.

The value of the Doctrine of *Shunyata* is simply this: It established the fact that awakening consists in the opening of *prajna*. That's the bottom line. *Shunyata* clears the ego's thinking mind out of the way and focuses on the rising of *prajna*. This is the teaching of Buddha; the *Prajnaparamita* and Nagarjuna are simply expounding on it. But *prajna* by itself is not the whole story. You may recall that Buddha linked *prajna* with *karuna* (compassion). They are the two elementary facets of one reality. In seeking the opening of *prajna*, seeing the insufficiency of ordinary knowledge may be helpful, but the cultivation of compassion is essential—and that brings us to the subject of the Bodhisattva.

THE BODHISATTVA

As has been repeatedly stressed, one of the distinguishing features of Mahayana is that it offers a Buddhist way of life for the whole community, not just for the elite dedicated few. Mahayana is Buddhism for the entire lotus pond; there's something in it for everyone. In Theravada, it seems that the principal function of the laity was simply to provide support for the sangha. Mahayana goes much, much further than that. Reflecting the broad scope of Hinduism, Mahayana Buddhism, too, came to include an endless variety of popular rituals, ceremonies, and cults. The lay man and woman had access to a lifestyle that was thoroughly Buddhist and, as the *Lankavatara Sutra* proclaimed, they too could achieve enlightenment.

However rich the life of the laity might become, though, it was clear from the beginning that the order of monks remained central in importance. The monk would continue to lead the way. The Mahayana Buddhist monk was, and remains, the embodiment of the philosophy of Mahayana.

The goal of the Theravadin monk was to become an arhat—that is, a fully enlightened person. He sought to achieve enlightenment by following the Eightfold Path with total dedication. Mahayanists criticized the Theravadins for being self-centered; the enlightenment of an arhat was simply for himself. The goal of a Mahayana monk, on the other hand, was to become a bodhisattva.* A bodhisattva is also an enlightened person, but the meaning of the term embraces far more than what the arhat stood for. For one thing, it is the intention of a bodhisattva to achieve enlightenment not for his own good alone, but for the good of all beings.

Strictly speaking, a bodhisattva is one who has achieved awakening, but the word is sometimes used to include as well those who have not yet become fully awakened, but have made great progress and are destined ultimately to achieve it. Whereas a Theravadin monk is dedicated to the Eightfold Path, a Mahayana monk works on the "Six Perfections" (eventually increased to ten in some Mahayana sects). There is much similarity between the two. The "perfections," also known as *paramitas*, are to be fully mastered by the bodhisattva-to-be in the course of his or her development. In brief, the Six Perfections are as follows:

1. *Dana-paramita* (becoming a giving, other-directed person)
2. *Shila-paramita* (developing correct moral discipline)
3. *Kshanti-paramita* (cultivating patience and tolerance)
4. *Virga-paramita* (striving for determination and perseverance)
5. *Dhyana-paramita* (developing skill in meditation)
6. *Prajna-paramita* (seeking supreme wisdom that sees Reality as it is)

Each of these *paramitas* nourishes all of the others, but the apex, of course, is *Prajnaparamita*, mastery of which makes the person a fully realized bodhisattva—an "awakened one." In the Mahayana tradition, it was widely understood that achieving mastery of the Six Perfections could take a very long time—many lifetimes, in fact. Consequently, a fully realized bodhisattva was believed to be one who had lived through many previous lives.

---

*Bodhisattva is a Sanskrit word that simply means "one who has achieved the goal" (the goal being enlightenment).

The preceding statement may come as something of a shock. "*Many previous lives*"? Is this not a bold reassertion of the idea of *atman*, the very heart of *avidya* that Buddha had sought to liberate humankind from? Not really: For one thing, Buddha never had a defined doctrine; he assiduously avoided answers to metaphysical questions. He was much more interested in the right way to live. Much of what we hold to be the philosophical character of Buddha's teaching is what has been inferred by various traditions, beginning with the Theravada. The Doctrine of *Shunyata* had undermined the either–or approach to truth. It was no longer a question of whether *atman* did or did not exist; *all* conclusions based on conceptual thinking were ultimately irrelevant. They could go either way. Mahayana simply opened the door to a much wider spectrum of interpretations. If there are to be many paths—something for everyone—then it should come as no surprise that humanity's infatuation with the idea of reincarnation would find some place for expression in Mahayana Buddhism.

I don't want to give the impression, though, that Mahayana was philosophically indifferent on the subject of reincarnation. It may be true that the absence of a defined orthodoxy has resulted over the ages in many taking up a belief in personal reincarnation, but, *philosophically speaking*, the Mahayana tradition has always been steadfast in denying the existence of any permanent, self-standing essence that endures through time. If, however, there is no "self" (in the sense of *atman*) to be reborn, then how does one explain the "many previous lives" of a bodhisattva?

Here is one way of responding to this question: In Mahayana, the word *samsara* refers to the cycling of existence—a great cycling *process* that is a continuous flow of energy. What we call human life is a part of that process, but a human "life" in its totality is a process that extends over many "lifetimes." Rebirth, then, is an aspect of a process that is going on all the time—every moment, in fact. The word does not refer to the rebirth of an *atman*; rather, it refers to the repetition of an identifiable and enduring *pattern* within the process. In this way, a particular process of energy (like a wave, which can seem to have an individual identity) can roll on, continuing to express the same pattern over several "lifetimes." But again, it is not some *one* who is being reborn; it is the process itself that is reborn—that is continuously regenerating itself. The term "mindstream" is often used in this connection. A given bodhisattva (or anyone else, for that matter) is the inheritor of an evolving mindstream—or, to be more precise, the bodhisattva *is* the mindstream. The rationale for a bodhisattva having many "lives" is that the process of development that leads to mastery of the Six Perfecions takes a very long time. Over time, positive karma that influences subsequent development is generated. Eventually, karma sufficient to the genesis of awakening is accumulated.

The life of compassion (*karuna*) generates the karma that leads to awakening. The importance of compassion cannot be exaggerated; it is a truly distinguishing feature of Mahayana. Compassion, however, cannot be separated from *prajna*; indeed, perfect compassion *is prajna*. *Prajna* is the wisdom that sees reality as it is, which is to say, that opens in awakening. But the ultimate victory of *prajna* over the entrenched power of *avidya* does not come easily. It is growth in compassion, not discipline, that, little by little, loosens the grip of *avidya*. Thus, in seeking to extend compassion until it has no limits, the bodhisattva is dissolving all illusions of separation and is daily moving closer to the point at which *karuna* and *prajna* merge in awakening.

A bodhisattva is, in fact, *defined* by the ultimate and perfect act of compassion. He or she, just like Buddha, willingly postpones entry into the perfect and permanent reality of *nirvana*. In fact, the Mahayana monk takes a vow *not* to accept the final perfection of *nirvana* until all other beings may also enter into it. This is done out of a spirit of pure and unlimited compassion; it would be unthinkably selfish to accept the fullness of *nirvana* until all other beings can do so too. The decision reflects Buddha's decision to put off the perfect solitary enjoyment of his awakening, choosing instead to return to the everyday world and dedicate his life to helping others along the path to freedom. Also, the decision to postpone *nirvana* is evidence that one has fully awakened to the truth that there is no self apart from the whole; there really can be no other course for a genuinely awakened man or woman. We can express the difference by saying that in the Theravada tradition, one seeks to become totally enlightened, whereas in the Mahayana tradition one seeks to become totally compassionate.

To sum up, a fully realized bodhisattva is a man or woman who, through dedication to the spirit of the Dharma, has seen through the illusion of the separate ego. The bodhisattva is a liberated person, free from fear and attachment, one who genuinely sees the underlying truth in the unity of being. Such a one could, to put it in the clumsy way of words, go on to extinguish his or her ego individuality completely, dissolving perfectly—at least at the time called death—into the universal emptiness that is the underlying reality of all that is. But to allow this would be to put the interests of the self first, which is unthinkable (and impossible) to one who has truly come to realize that the separate self is an illusion. The whole is all that matters—all that is. Only the wholeness of being can enter into perfect *nirvana*; nothing else really exists. So, out of boundless compassion for all beings who have not yet made the discovery, the bodhisattva must choose to wait at the brink, being of service to others, until *nirvana* is available to all. Heinrich Zimmer describes the bodhisattva thus:

> In the Mahayana tradition the term designates those sublimely indifferent, compassionate beings who remain at the threshold of *nirvana* for the comfort and salvation of the world. Out of perfect indifference (egolessness) and perfect compassion (which is also egolessness) the Mahayana Bodhisattva does not experience the "real or true enlightenment" (*samyak-sambodhi*) of the Buddha and then pass to final extinction (*parinirvana*), but stops at the brink—the brink of time and eternity—and thus transcends that pair of opposites: for the world will never end; the round of the cosmic eons will go on and on without ceasing. The vow of the Bodhisattva, to remain at the brink till all shall go in before him, amounts to a vow to remain as he is forever.[14]

"... to remain at the brink till all shall go in before him, amounts to a vow to remain as he is forever." The concept of a bodhisattva as an enlightened person of infinite compassion who lovingly puts off the completed perfection of *nirvana* so long as any other being needs help is, I'm sure you will agree, a magnificent ideal. It would be a mistake, though, to picture the bodhisattva as a lofty being, distantly removed from the humdrum affairs of daily life. The true bodhisattva is a very down-to-earth person, a friendly, caring, compassionate man or woman. And the bodhisattva's caring extends not only to other people, but to everything in nature. The true bodhisattva is the finest example of a human being that we can imagine.

Another important matter concerning the compassion of a bodhisattva has to do with the huge store of positive karma that he or she accumulates. According to popular belief, that karma is available to be shared with less enlightened folks and thus help them along the path to their own liberation. (In a sense, this parallels the Christian concept of "grace," which can be dispensed among the faithful.) As a predictable result of the potential sharing of karma, certain eminent bodhisattvas have become cult figures, attracting large and devoted followings among the laity. Such revered bodhisattvas play the role of "saints" within Mahayana Buddhism. Many bodhisattvas have risen to this role in the history of Mahayana. Three of the most beloved are Avalokiteshvara (Kannon in Japanese), the embodiment of compassion; Manjushri (Monju in Japanese), the embodiment of wisdom; and Maitreya (Miroku in Japanese), who is believed to be a bodhisattva who will eventually achieve Buddhahood and become the next and last earthly Buddha. Representations of these bodhisattvas (and others) have always been highly popular in the art of Buddhism.

ARTISTIC EXPRESSION IN EARLY MAHAYANA

The rise of Mahahyana was accompanied by a great flowering of Buddhist art, in both the Indian homeland and every other place that Mahayana Buddhism migrated to. In sculpture, painting, architecture, and many other forms, much of the finest art produced in Asian cultures throughout the centuries has been inspired by Buddhist ideals. It's probably true to say that familiarity with Buddhist art is the only experience that most people in the West have with Buddhism. That, however, is bound to change as Buddhist influences continue to sink roots and grow in the West.

Perhaps in the not-too-distant future the Western world will experience a whole new flowering of Buddhist art, a modern renaissance, this time inspired by a marriage of Buddhist ideals and the Western artistic tradition. It's interesting to note that this actually did happen once, back in the early days of Mahayana development. Recall that Alexander the Great had extended not only his conquering armies, but Greek culture as well, across the world of the Persian Empire as far as the region in northwest India known at that time as Gandhara. This Hellenistic cultural influence, profoundly affected the artistic styles of early Mahayana Buddhism, especially with regard to sculpture. Such influences can be seen clearly in some of the finest Buddhist sculpture of the early period in north India and central Asia. The early affair with the West was, unfortunately, destined to be short lived. Nonetheless, some of those early renderings of Buddha and various bodhisattvas make them look positively Greek.

The Theravada tradition deliberately abstained from honoring the memory of Buddha with artistic likenesses; statues and paintings could all too easily become idols. Undoubtedly, this abstention was in part a reaction to the voluptuous religious art of

A bodhisattva from third-century Ghandara shows strong Hellenistic influences. (P. Bresnan)

Hinduism. The Theravadins were not entirely iconoclastic, though; some symbolic works of art were tolerated, such as a carved or painted footprint representing the path of Buddha's teaching. And of course, that perennial trademark of Buddhism, the stupa, was widely distributed in the lands of Theravada Buddhism.

A stupa is a structure that looks like an inverted bell and is generally made of masonry covered with painted plaster. It can be any size, but not even the largest ones are meant to be entered. The original stupas, derived from Hindu sources, were simply ceremonial monuments erected over the remains of the dead. In Buddhist hands, the stupa became a shrine to house a relic of Buddha or sometimes of a bodhisattva. As such, the stupa provided an attractive focus around which a Buddhist community could gather for the purpose of honoring the memory of Buddha and renewing their commitment to the Dharma. In no way was the stupa a sacred object meant to be a place of worship.

(At least, that was the intention.) Some Theravadin stupas were modestly ornate, but on the whole, the artistic side of Theravada was noticeably less than exuberant.

What Theravada shunned, Mahayana welcomed with open arms. The stupa, a relatively small and humble affair in Theravada, became a splendid memorial in Mahayana Buddhism. Each land that Mahayana migrated to evolved its own style. Although most stupas remained small, some were built on a colossal scale. The Tibetan Buddhist stupa at Bodhnath near Kathmandu, for example, is a full square block at its base and several stories tall. Festooned with prayer flags and large painted eyes at the summit, it is one of the most striking examples of Buddhist art to be found anywhere in the world. Some of the greater stupas became Mahayana pilgrimage sites. At Bodhnath, there is a never-ending flow of pilgrims circumambulating the great stupa, endlessly turning the many prayer wheels built into all four sides of the base. It's an entrancing spectacle, full of beauty and spiritual power.

Sculpture, too, evolved in many directions as Mahayana migrated to new lands. Like the stupa, sculpture also found expression on the grand scale. In India and China, Buddhist statuary of incredible size was carved right out of the virgin rock in some places. At Kamakura, Japan, an immense seated Buddha was until recently the largest bronze statue in the world. On a more modest scale, but no less spectacular, the Wat Trimitr temple in Bangkok is home to a larger-than-life Buddha cast in solid gold. These are just a very few examples; I could go on and on. The point is that wherever it went, Mahayana Buddhism inspired a tremendously rich and varied output in the arts.

Oddly enough, with all this wealth of imagery, a great many people in the West continue to cling to the notion that Shakyamuni Buddha was a jolly fat man with a big belly. Nothing could be further from the truth. This mistaken idea stems from a confusion of Buddha with certain mythical characters. In fact, one of the most popular themes for images of Buddha represents him at the time of his awakening. At that time in his life Buddha had been practicing extreme ascetic disciplines, including fasting. Such statues often show him looking almost like a skeleton, the only thing protruding being his ribs.

But far and away the favorite theme, found in all Buddhist cultures, is the seated Buddha in the posture of meditation. Serene, peaceful, blissful—that is what it's all about. What an interesting contrast this makes between the central icons of Christianity and Buddhism. The figure of Jesus is shown on the cross, writhing in the agony of a terrible death. Buddha, on the other hand, is shown as a man perfectly composed and totally at peace with himself and the universe.

So what are we to make of this "great vehicle," the self-styled Mahayana? One thing should be clear: Mahayana was a part of the same broad development that had earlier produced Theravada. Mahayana is not a system that stands in opposition to Theravada. Just as the open lotus is the symbol of Buddha's awakening, some have compared all of Buddhism to a lotus plant; Theravada is the roots and stalk, and Mahayana is the flowering. It certainly was an opening up of Buddhism. Everyone now had access to it. It's almost as if Buddhism turned the tables on Hinduism. Early Buddhism, in danger of being swallowed up in the vastness of Hinduism, transformed itself into something of a likeness of Hinduism. All of the various Yogas found new expression in Buddhism,

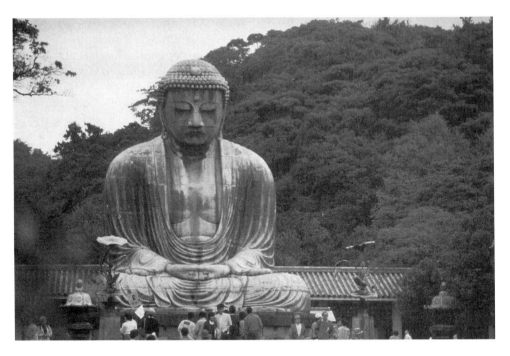

Great bronze statue of Amida Buddha at Kamakura, Japan. (P. Bresnan)

including Bhakti, the devotional Yoga that promotes love and veneration of a personal savior. In this way Buddhism transcended itself, invigorating its practice with great new life and launching out on a new age of expansion that is still continuing today.

The Doctrine of *Shunyata*, implications of which can be traced back to Buddha himself, was a logical new foundation for Mahayana. It cleared away dependence on philosophical systems of all kinds, opening the way to every conceivable kind of expression of the Dharma. *Shunyata* allowed the focus to be solely where it should be, on the development of wisdom and compassion. More and more, Buddha came to be referred to as "the compassionate Buddha." Compassion, not arhatship, became the guiding principle of the Buddhist monk.

An important question in this study concerns the matter of religion. Did Mahayana, as it grew to overshadow Theravada, transform Buddhism from a fundamentally secular way of life into a fundamentally religious way of life? Many believe that it did and that therein lies its glory. Quite obviously, that is the opinion of the Russian Buddhologist T. Stcherbatsky. Consider this florid comment of his on the subject (and all in one sentence at that):

> When we see an atheistic, soul-denying philosophic teaching of a path to personal Final Deliverance consisting in an absolute extinction of life, and a simple worship of the memory of its human founder, when we see it superseded

by a magnificent High Church with a Supreme God, surrounded by a numerous pantheon, and a host of Saints, a religion highly devotional, highly ceremonial and clerical, with an ideal of Universal Salvation of all living creatures,
a Salvation not in annihilation, but in eternal life, we are fully justified in
maintaining that the history of religions has scarcely witnessed such a break
between new and old within the pale of what nevertheless continued to claim
common descent from the same religious founder.[15]

Stcherbatsky nicely states the prevailing opinion of the nineteenth and early twentieth centuries. Theravada was seen as a purely secular, nontheistic system, limited in
scope, that was replaced—and transcended—by the magnificent new spiritual system,
Mahayana, which rapidly grew to become one of the world's great religions. The modern view is much less polarized. Modern study of the history of Buddhism is more interested in the common roots and shared interests of Theravada and Mahayana. Mahayana
is seen not so much as a system in conflict with Theravada as it is a new direction, an
opening up, in the evolution of Buddhism. Obviously, Mahayana, in its willingness to
offer a meaningful interpretation of Buddha's teaching to all sectors of society, absorbed
into itself some elements of practice that we ordinarily think of as religious in nature.
And some of the "spokes" of the wheel of Mahayana went much more deeply into that
sort of thing than did others. But we must keep in mind that part of the greatness of
Buddhism is the freedom that ultimately resides with every individual man and woman
to follow the Dharma in the way that he or she personally judges to be right. Religious
elements? Definitely, for many. But a religious institution? That's a different story.
Unlike the evolution, for example, of Christianity, there has never developed within
Buddhism an overarching institutional framework; there has never been a Buddhist
"establishment" to define and enforce orthodoxy.

Undoubtedly, some within the Buddhist fold did transform the Dharma into what
can generally be regarded as religion. Buddhist "churches" flourish throughout the
world even today. In this, Buddhism was reflecting the general character of the world
that it grew up within. Some of the spokes of the wheel, such as Pure Land Buddhism,
became highly religious. Others, such as Zen Buddhism, much less so. Speaking of that
metaphor of the wheel—Theravada at the hub and Mahayana being the spokes—I suggest that the outer rim of the wheel, where the rubber meets the road, represents the
actual practice of the Dharma. That's what keeps the whole thing rolling.

And roll it did. Mahayana Buddhism would make its way north to central Asia and
China and then on to Vietnam, Korea, and Japan. A look at the map might suggest that
the route to China would go through Tibet, but the geography of the region worked
against that. Actually, Buddhist ideas entered China by way of the great trade route
known as the Silk Road, named for that much-desired trade item that originated in
China. It was an overland route that wound for over two thousand miles through the
wilds of central Eurasia, connecting the civilized centers of the East and the West. The
Indian subcontinent was connected to the Silk Road by way of a subsidiary route that
wound up through the mountain passes of the northwest. Goods—and ideas—were
thus passed back and forth between India and China. The teaching of Buddha entered

China during the time of the Han Dynasty and eventually found a welcoming new home there. Other than Marxism in the present century, Buddhism is the only significant foreign philosophical system ever to be integrated into Chinese culture.

The Chinese part of the story is very rich, but before we turn to that, we will detour slightly into the high plateau of Tibet, where Mahayana would evolve into one of the most fascinating species of Buddhism to be found anywhere on Earth. In the isolation of their Himalayan world, the people of Tibet created Tibetan Buddhism, otherwise known as Vajrayana.

Notes

1. Heinrich Dumoulin, *Zen Buddhism: A History,* 2 vols., trans. James W. Hesig and Paul Knitter, (New York: Macmillan, 1988), Vol. 1, p. 28.
2. William LaFleur, *Buddhism* (Englewood Cliffs, NJ: Prentice-Hall, 1988), p. 23.
3. Nancy Wilson Ross, *Buddhism; A Way of Life and Thought* (New York: Vintage Books, 1981). Copyright © 1980 by Nancy Wilson Ross. Reprinted by permission of Alfred A. Knopf, Inc., p. 49.
4. Lex Hixon, *Mother of the Buddhas* (Wheaton, IL. Quest Books, 1993), p. ix.
5. *Ibid.,* pp. 187–188.
6. Burton Watson, trans., *The* Lotus Sutra (New York: Columbia Univ. Press, 1993), reprinted with permission of the publisher, pp. 6, 273.
7. *Ibid.,* p. xix.
8. William Blake, "Auguries of Innocence," 1863.
9. Ross, p. 44.
10. Watson, p. xv.
11. Hixon, p. xvii.
12. *Ibid.,* p. 14, 35.
13. Alan W. Watts, *The Way of Zen* (New York: Vintage Books, 1957). Copyright © 1957 by Pantheon Books, A Division of Random House, pp. 66–67.
14. Heinrich Zimmer, *Philosophies of India* (Princeton, NJ: Princeton University Press, 1951), p. 535.
15. T. Stcherbatsky, quoted in T. R. V. Murti, *The Central Philosophy of Buddhism: A Study of the* Madhyamika *System* (London: George Allen and Unwin, 1955), p. 6.

Study Questions

1. What was it about the character of the Theravadin tradition that opened the way for the rise of Mahayana?
2. Why did Mahayanists refer to the Theravada tradition as "Hinayana"?
3. What is the *Prajanaparamita*? Why does it occupy the central place in the canon of Mahayana scripture?
4. How does the nature of Shakyamuni Buddha change from Theravada to Mahayana?
5. Explain the Doctrine of Trikaya. Why was trikaya a logical development in the growth of Mahayana?
6. What is the Doctrine of *Shunyata*? Why is it sometimes referred to as the "Doctrine of Emptiness"?
7. What does *svabavata* mean? How does it relate to the Doctrine of *Shunyata*?

8. What is a bodhisattva? How does the Mahayanist bodhisattva differ from the Theravadin arhat?

9. In general terms, what was the difference in the role of the arts between the Mahayana tradition and the Theravada tradition?

10. What do you make of the quote from the Russian Buddhologist T. Stcherbatsky? How has the general attitude changed since his time?

13

Buddhism in Tibet

California is a land of many unusual things. Few, though, are more unusual than one that is to be found in a secluded spot along the northern coast. Its brilliant copper roof gleams golden in the sunlight and is often used as a reference location by passing ships. This amazing place, tucked away in the coastal redwood forest, is in fact a Tibetan Buddhist monastery known as Odiyan.

Named after the region in India that was the home of the founder of Tibet's first Buddhist monastery, Odiyan defies description. Surrounded by two hundred acres of rolling wooded hills, the monastery is a vision of rare beauty. On its main structure, a great copper roof surmounts a temple constructed in the style of a pagoda. The edifice rises eighty feet above the central courtyard of a large square complex that is the heart of the monastery and that houses, among other things, the library and residence hall. Each of the four sides is pierced at the center by an entry that is itself overarched by a large pagoda-style roof. Surrounding the whole is a broad moat whose still water reflects the beauty of the pagoda within.

From any perspective, it is an enchanting sight. Bridges span the moat at the center of each of the four sides. From the bridges, pathways lead into the grounds of the monastery, on which stands a variety of shrines and other structures. More than a hundred stupas of varying sizes are to be found at Odiyan. The largest, dedicated to the quest of enlightenment, is located just to the east of the central temple complex. On the western side is the Vajra Temple, within which is a ninety-six-foot-tall pyramidlike structure holding a hundred thousand small statues of Padmasambhava, the eighth-century founder of the monastery after which Odiyan is fashioned. A thousand prayer wheels turn endlessly at Odiyan. Despite all this size and splendor, not many people even know of Odiyan's existence; publicity is shunned, and except for rare public events, the grounds are closed to all would-be visitors. The community at Odiyan goes about its work in peaceful seclusion.

Odiyan was founded by Tarthang Tulku, a refugee Tibetan lama of the Nyingma sect, the most ancient of the Tibetan Buddhist sects. In addition to being a potential haven for other refugee scholar–monks, the Odiyan community has assimilated a number of Western men and women into its midst. Working together, all are dedicated to creating a safe refuge for the living tradition of Tibetan Buddhism, which they believe faces the real possibility of extinction in its homeland. Above all, the residents at Odiyan are laboring to translate and preserve the vast literary corpus of Tibetan Buddhist works.

But much more is at stake here than merely preserving those scriptures, important though that may be. Just as the founder, Tarthang Tulku, is regarded as being a reincarnate lama, Odiyan itself may be seen as the reincarnation of the spiritual essence of Samye Gompa, the very first Buddhist monastery of Tibet. (*Gompa* is the Tibetan word for "monastery.") Samye Gompa was founded in the eighth century and remained a fountainhead of Tibetan Buddhist culture until the late 1960s, when the monastery system of Tibet was violently undermined by anti-Buddhist zealots, commonly known as Red Guards. Just a decade later, Odiyan was founded. With its consecration in 1979, Odiyan became a genuine Tibetan Buddhist monastery, a "reincarnation," in a sense, of the spirit of Samye Gompa.* The ancient tradition, though threatened with annihilation in its homeland, has sunk roots in new places and is determined to cling to life and even to flourish.

Odiyan is not the only Tibetan Buddhist monastery outside the Himalayan world. Since the scattering of refugee monks following the Chinese assimilation of Tibet in 1959, Tibetan Buddhist communities have taken form in many parts of the world. But in some ways Odiyan is the most remarkable, and its ties are closest to the ancient core of the tradition. How Odiyan happens to be there, peeking out from among the redwood trees of northern California, is a complex and fascinating story. It begins "a long, long time ago in a faraway land across the sea."

Tibet is the high ground of Eurasia—*very* high ground. A look at the map of Eurasia shows the great oval plateau of Tibet dominating the geography of the eastern part of the continent. Everything seems to flow from it in all directions. But it wasn't always that way. Many millions of years ago, what we know as the plateau of Tibet was basically a low coastal plain occupying the southern flank of the Eurasian continent. It probably looked much like the Gulf Coast of the United States. Approximately sixty million years ago, this all began to change, slowly, but dramatically. The Indian plate collided with the southern boundary of the Eurasian plate and was subducted beneath it. Over eons of time, this had the effect of driving the southern portion of the Eurasian continental mass upward. Higher and higher it rose, creating the great plateau of Tibet and its many associated mountain ranges and river systems. We find a similar geographic phenomenon in western North America; the high, mountainous plateau of Nevada and Utah is much like Tibet, but significantly smaller in scale. The Tibetan plateau is five times the size of the Nevada plateau and averages twice the altitude.

The entire complex of the plateau of Tibet forms a huge oval, approximately fifteen hundred miles from west to east and seven hundred miles from north to south at the widest part. The southern flank of the plateau is enclosed by the mighty Himalayas, the

---

*Since there is not yet an actual population of ordained monks at Odiyan, in a strictly technical sense it is not yet a monastery. Presumably, this will change in the future.

greatest mountain chain on Earth. Many Himalayan peaks are over 24,000 feet; Everest, the greatest mountain on Earth, tops off at just under 30,000 feet. The northern boundary of the oval is formed in large part by another great mountain system, the Kunlun Shan. North of this range the plateau descends steeply into the vast desert of the Takla Makan. (This unlikely region was temporarily to play an important part in the evolution of Buddhism; that story is taken up in Chapter 14.) Between the Himalayas and the Kunlun Shan lies a high and arid world of alternating ranges and valleys. Many of these valleys support icy blue lakes of varying sizes. It is a stark and beautiful landscape, appearing much like the semidesert geography of Nevada, though much higher. The average altitude of the plateau is around 15,000 feet; few of the valleys are below 10,000 feet. The valley that is home to Lhasa, the capital of Tibet, is 12,000 feet above sea level. (Compare that with Denver, the "mile high city," which is a mere 5,300 feet. Even thin-aired Mexico City does not quite reach 8,000 feet. Imagine the Olympic Games being held at Lhasa!)

The high ground of Tibet is in the western part of the plateau. The mass of mountains in the western region is home to the sources of some of the world's greatest rivers. Here, the Indus begins its way westward, creating a maze of deep valleys that connect Tibet with Kashmir and other parts of northwestern India. Flowing southward are the tributaries that will join to form the great Ganges River, and traveling in an eastward direction is Tibet's own great river, called the Tsangpo in Tibet and China, but known by its Indian name, the Brahmaputra, in most of the world. The Tsangpo travels from west to east across the whole breadth of the Tibetan plateau. It parallels the Himalayan range, running approximately a hundred miles north of the crest line. The Tsangpo forms the main artery of Tibet's geography; most of the country's population is to be found along its course and in the valleys of the tributaries that feed into it.

In the east, the plateau falls off sharply, forming a massive tangle of ranges and very deep river valleys. The appearance of this region on a relief map suggests that the gods once removed a huge cork from the corner of Tibet, and a great cascade of mountains plunged down into the adjoining lands of China and southeast Asia. Here, too, are the beginnings of many great river systems, the Yangzi (Yangtse) and the Mekong among them. The Tsangpo, rushing down through some of the wildest geography on Earth, cuts a sharp U-turn to the southwest and then flows out to the sea through the northeastern section of the Indian subcontinent. After a journey of nearly 2,000 miles from its source in the mountains of western Tibet, the Tsangpo (Brahmaputra) joins the delta of the Ganges and mixes its waters into the Bay of Bengal.

All in all, the geography of the Tibetan plateau is truly awesome: great snowcapped mountains, high passes, roaring rivers, high desert plains, cold mountain lakes, and vast distances of unspoiled natural beauty. Taken together, they conjure an image of a very special place.

"Tibet" is a Mongol word; in Chinese the country is known as Xi Dang (Hsi-tang). To the people of Tibet, though, their mountain world is often referred to as *Khang Yul*, the "land of snow." The ancestors of the Tibetans were a Mongol people who, long before the beginning of recorded history, had already infiltrated the high country from the trackless lands to the north. Their migrations gradually carried them southward, eventually to the region of the Tsangpo and its tributaries' valleys, where most of the population would ultimately become concentrated. Over the generations, the Tibetans became a sturdy people, physically well adapted to living at very high altitudes. Understandably, their economy also centered around what was suited to their high-altitude way of life. For the most part, this has meant herding, especially yaks and sheep, and simple farming. The raising of barley was, and still is, the mainstay of Tibetan agriculture.

The staple of the Tibetan diet is *tsampa*, a coarse flour made from roasted barley. Typically, this is simply mixed in a bowl with a little yak butter and salt.* Tsampa is consumed with prodigious amounts of tea. The Tibetans are world-class tea-drinkers; forty cups a day is not uncommon. Tibetan tea, brewed from hard cakes of compressed tea leaves, is liberally mixed with butter and salt. Butter made from yak's milk plays an important role in Tibetan life. Among its many uses, butter sometimes serves as a substitute for money. It is also used in place of clay for sculpting small religious statues, which are then painted.

The original settlers of Tibet were loosely tied together along tribal lines, and this pretty much remained the bond that defined them as a people. Over time, though, they developed a distinct "Tibetan" culture. The core around which early Tibetan culture developed was a shared set of religious beliefs. In common with folk cultures in virtually all parts of the world, the Tibetan people developed a highly animistic system of religious beliefs and practices in which the power of myriad good and evil spirits influenced every aspect of human life. This original religious tradition of Tibet, known as Bon, would never die out completely. Over time, Buddhism assimilated much from Bon and became the unique tradition of Buddhism peculiar to Tibet.

Although Tibet has been richly influenced by the neighboring civilizations of India, Nepal, and, especially, China, it is nonetheless accurate to say that the Himalayan culture of Tibet developed in relative isolation from the rest of the world. Beyond their great mountain fortresses, the people of Tibet created and preserved a distinct culture and an autonomous feudal way of life that remained very little changed until modern times.

The Western world became aware of Tibet in the nineteenth century. Its mysterious and isolated character appealed greatly to the romantic spirit of the time. The most unknown parts of the globe were being "discovered" by intrepid European adventurers, and Tibet, in its unapproachable Himalayan remoteness, was among the most unknown of all. Tibet took on a "Shangri-la" image in the mind of Westerners. It was a land of enchantment about which very little was known; imagination filled in where factual knowledge was scarce.

Factual knowledge about Tibet, though, began to accumulate gradually. One of the first to write knowledgeably about the landlocked country was L. Austine Waddell, a British military officer stationed on the Himalayan frontier of India. Drawing from his

---

*Strictly speaking, the word *yak* (Tibetan *gyag*) refers to the bull of the Himalayan cattle species *Bos gruniens*. Thus, "yak butter" is an impossibility. However, the word has come to refer to both males and females of the species.

personal research—much of it controversial today—Waddell published a detailed account of the religion and history of Tibet, although he himself spent very little time within Tibet proper, which in the late nineteenth century was closed to Europeans. On his brief excursions into Tibet he had to travel in disguise.

More widely read were the fascinating journals of the Frenchwoman Alexandra David-Neel, who, in the company of a Tibetan monk from Sikkim, made five extensive journeys through Tibet in the early twentieth century. Like Waddell, she put her life at risk by entering the country, and she sometimes found it prudent to travel disguised as a monk. An "adventurer" of the highest order and basically objective, David-Neel nonetheless was clearly enchanted by the more mystical side of Tibetan Buddhism and offered her readers many accounts of supranormal powers supposed to be had by those who had mastered the arcane arts. Her books remain very popular.

Of a more erudite nature were the studies of the Oxford scholar W. Y. Evans-Wentz, who translated some of the principal Tibetan scriptural works into the English language, including the famous *Bardo Thödol*, to which he gave the name "Tibetan Book of the Dead." Also of significance was Lama Govinda, a German Tibetologist who became a *bona fide* Tibetan Buddhist monk, and authored many books that introduce the Western reader to the inner meaning of Tibetan Buddhism. These are only a few of the better known names; as the twentieth century progressed, many others became active in the field of Tibetan studies, and gradually the fund of knowledge was growing. Still, the Shangri-la image of Tibet prevailed in the West, a happy illusion that was finally and abruptly shattered in 1959.

In the summer of 1959, army units of the People's Republic of China carried out an aggressive military operation within Tibet for the manifest purpose of suppressing a popular uprising and decisively establishing China's claim to sovereignty over Tibet. This military action was the outcome of an enormously complex situation, and its roots go far back in history. Suffice it to say—at least for the time being—that the leaders of the People's Republic of China did not see their action as a ruthless land grab; in their eyes, it was a rightful action—a liberation of a sort—and was supported by *some* of the Tibetan population. Some, perhaps, but certainly not all; many Tibetans believed that Tibet was an independent nation and had been throughout its history. The Chinese "invasion" precipitated a mass exodus. As many as one hundred thousand Tibetan refugees fled over the mountain passes to neighboring Nepal and India. Among them were approximately ten thousand Buddhist monks, including the Dalai Lama, the spiritual (and formerly political) leader of Tibet. The Dalai Lama set up a headquarters in exile at the town of Dharamsala in the mountainous northwestern region of India. Operating from this base, he has traveled the world, enlightening people in all nations about the tradition of Tibetan Buddhism and the desperate plight of the Tibetan refugees who are struggling to keep alive the ancient tradition, though faced with poverty and all the other problems of life in exile.

In the decade following 1959, the "The Great Proletarian Cultural Revolution" raged through China and swept into Tibet as well. What had started fundamentally as a political annexation became temporarily a fanatic crusade to wipe out the old ways altogether and transform Tibet into a collectivized Marxist utopia. Units of young Chinese

Red Guards systematically destroyed many Buddhist temples and monasteries. Eventually, this "Cultural Revolution" was to be repudiated, and more tolerant times would return to Tibet. But before that happened, many more refugees fled in despair, adding to the already swollen numbers in India and elsewhere.

The result of all of this was a Tibetan diaspora. Refugee Tibetans, including Tibetan Buddhist monks, began to find new homes in places very different and very distant from the Himalayan world they had grown up in. Like a bursting seedpod, Tibet scattered its seeds to the four winds. Some fell on fertile ground in new and strange places. The ancient and intriguing Buddhist culture of Tibet, preserved and largely hidden in its remote Himalayan sanctuary, was suddenly out in the world, making itself known and offering its potential enrichment to all who might be interested. Thus, we are brought back to Odiyan, which, together with the numerous other Tibetan centers that have come into being around the world, plays an important part in the new life of Tibetan Buddhism—a new life thrust upon the ancient tradition by the tumultuous happenings of the twentieth century.

Our goal is to try to gain a general understanding of the very complex and mysterious subject of Tibetan Buddhism. In a work of this scope it is possible only to make a start in that direction; a full understanding of Tibetan Buddhism is the work of a lifetime. But a good start is a thing of much value. The place to begin, naturally, is at the beginning, the way in which Buddhism was first introduced into Tibet. We will then take a closer look at the doctrine and practices of Tibetan Buddhism. Following that, we examine the broad historical evolution of Buddhism in Tibet. That will bring us up to the present day, which I hope you will see is pregnant with exciting possibilities. Tibetan Buddhism is one of the major branches of Buddhism that is alive and well in the modern world. After many somnolent centuries, the ancient tradition is fully awake and ready to make its impression on the future.

THE ESTABLISHMENT OF BUDDHISM IN TIBET

The first person to impose political unity on the Tibetan people was King Songtsen Gampo, who reigned from approximately 617 C.E. to 650 C.E. He was a feudal warlord who succeeded in uniting the clans of the south through a series of bloody conquests. His home turf was the Yarlung Valley, a tributary of the Tsangpo southeast of Lhasa; hence, the "empire" that he created is known as the Yarlung Empire. Songtsen Gampo's domain, however, extended far beyond the Yarlung Valley proper; virtually all of southern Tibet came under his feudal rule. He established a new headquarters at a more centrally located place that would come to be known as Lhasa, and from that time to the present, Lhasa has remained the political capital and the spiritual center of Tibet.

Songtsen Gampo cemented his ties with some of the more powerful feudal barons of Tibet by the time-honored practice of marrying their daughters. Three Tibetan "princesses" became his wives. But Songtsen Gampo was looking farther afield than just the high country of Tibet. In addition to the three Tibetan wives, he married a Nepalese princess and—an impressive accomplishment for a "barbarian" warlord—a Chinese princess as well. According to the story, more legend than history, we can thank these two ladies for the introduction of Buddhism into Tibet.

We are told that the Nepalese princess—known in Tibet as Tritsun, the "Royal Lady"—brought her Buddhist faith with her to Lhasa. Buddhism was strong in Nepal by this time, and Tritsun did not intend to leave it behind when she journeyed off to the wild lands of Lhasa. She continued to practice her faith and took a variety of Buddhist art objects and writings with her to Tibet. These caught the attention of her new husband, who, wishing to be like his more sophisticated neighbors to the south, was persuaded to commission the building of a Buddhist temple in his new capital city. Nepalese craftsmen and artists were hired to carry out the project, and the result was the construction of the Jokhang, Tibet's first Buddhist temple.

The Jokhang was established right in the heart of Lhasa and has always been regarded as the spiritual center of Tibetan life; it is the navel of Tibet, the point around which the life of the entire nation revolves. In fact, the name *Lhasa* means "Place of the gods" and was derived from the fact that it was the city that embraced the Jokhang. Over the centuries, the Jokhang has been much modified and added to, but some remnants of the original structure are still to be seen (or so they say). Amazingly, the Jokhang escaped destruction during the troubled days of the 1960s. Today, with its brilliant golden roof, the Jokhang is one of the most impressive sights in Lhasa. It attracts a never-ending stream of devout pilgrims who are ever circumambulating the temple, euphoric in the knowledge that they are at the exact center of Tibet's spiritual geography and the very spot where it all began long ago.

The Chinese princess was named Wenzheng. She, too, was Buddhist, and, like Tritsun who had preceded her, Wencheng had her own Buddhist possessions in her baggage. In addition, as a gift for her new husband, Wencheng brought with her a large, bronze statue of Shakyamuni Buddha as a young prince. (This may actually have arrived later, after Wencheng wrote home to say, "They have no religion here.") The much-admired statue was housed in the new Jokhang. It must have given the temple a sort of official legitimacy; both the Nepalese and the Chinese had contributed to its completion.

The construction of the Jokhang marks the beginning of Buddhism in Tibet, but it must have remained only a novelty among the upper echelon of Lhasa during the time of Songtsen Gampo. The entrenched priesthood of the old Bon religion remained firmly in the ascendant for some time to come. Nevertheless, Buddhism had made its initial appearance in Tibet, and from this beginning, it would steadily grow. Whether or not the two princesses really had anything to do with it will probably always remain uncertain.

What is not uncertain, though, is that Songtsen Gampo sent a handpicked group on a mission to Kashmir. They headed off on the long and difficult trip in 632 C.E. and were gone for four years. Ostensibly, their charge was to study the Kashmiri alphabet and modify it as needed for their own language, so that Tibet, too, could join the civilized nations in the arts of writing. Although this was accomplished, it is probable that they brought back far more than just a workable alphabet. These receptive Tibetans may very well have felt the influence of the dynamic Buddhism of the Gandhara region and initiated the kind of connection that would have allowed Buddhist ideas to flow after them into Tibet. Perhaps this kind of influence, more than the machinations of exotic princesses, accounts for the germination of Buddhism in Tibet. Or perhaps it is some combination of all of these. In any case, by the end of the seventh century, Buddhism was in Tibet to stay.

The next important name in this story is that of King Trisong Detsen, who was born in 742 C.E. and is said to have lived to the age of fifty-five. He was an even greater warlord than Songtsen Gampo, extending his conquests throughout Tibet and, indeed, beyond its borders. Trisong Detsen's feudal war machine was so powerful that he even temporarily occupied the Chinese capital, Changan. But for all his successes on the warpath, Trisong Detsen was totally powerless to prevent a series of natural calamities that occurred in Tibet during his reign. In addition to a terrible plague, a series of floods repeatedly wiped out the harvest, and on top of that, the royal residence was struck by lightning, undoubtedly the work of an angry demon. In fact, it was assumed that all of these disasters were the work of angry demons. But why were the demons angry? Well, according to the leaders of the Bon priesthood, it was because Trisong Detsen, himself a devout Buddhist, had taken the extreme step of inviting a renowned Indian Buddhist scholar named Shantarakshita to Tibet and given him a free hand to travel about the country, teaching the Dharma.

The spirits of the ancient Bon were visiting havoc on the land because they were displeased by the growing interest of its people in Buddhism—and things promised to get worse, not better. Many Tibetans, including some powerful nobles, were eager to uproot the new growth and exterminate it altogether. This presented King Trisong Detsen with a dilemma. He personally favored Buddhism and wanted to see it prosper in Tibet, but under the circumstances, he could not openly oppose the hostile nobles. With great reluctance, Trisong Detsen was forced to ask Shantarakshita to give up his mission and depart from Tibet, at least temporarily. Shantarakshita agreed, but before he left he suggested to the king that he invite in his place the much respected Vajrayana master, Padmasambhava (pronounced Pahd-ma-sahm-BAH-va). This luminary was known to be not only a very learned man, but a master of the arts of sorcery as well. If there was anyone with the power to control the demons, it was Padmasambhava, and if successful, he would greatly advance the cause of Buddhism in Tibet.

It was a wonderful solution, and it turned out to be a total success. According to some chronicles, the venerable Padmasambhava arrived in Lhasa in the year 747 C.E., having made the long and difficult journey through the mountain passes of the west. Padmasambhava was his Sanskrit name, meaning "lotus-born one"; among the Tibetans he is generally referred to as Guru Rinpoche, which means "very highly respected teacher." According to legend, Padmasambhava was a native of the Indian country of Oddiyana (from whence the name *Odiyan*). His birth was rather spectacular; a large golden lotus bud rose miraculously from the center of a sacred lake. When the lotus opened, there stood Padmasambhava, already having the appearance of an eight-year-old boy and holding in his hands a vajra and a lotus.

In many important ways, the arrival of Padmasambhava (or Guru Rinpoche if you prefer) marks the *real* beginning of Buddhism in Tibet; what came before amounts to something of a prelude. Before Padmasambhava, Buddhism was a small and disorganized movement; the traditional Bon was everywhere dominant. After Padmasambhava, Buddhism rapidly became dominant and assimilated much of Bon into itself.

Padmasambhava stayed in Tibet for about two years (although some legendary accounts put the figure at fifty). The first thing he did was to confront the angry demons. His power proved to be superior to theirs, and to everyone's great relief he subdued them. The natural disasters ceased. The outcome, however, was more of a compromise than an unconditional surrender. Padmasambhava made a deal with the demons. They would desist from causing calamities and accept the superior position of the Buddhist powers, in return for being incorporated into the system and permanently cared for with appropriate offerings and sacrificial rites. As a result of this arrangement, Bon was not vanquished, but was assimilated; the ancient spirits of Bon, good and evil, would remain real to the common people of Tibet, and right down to modern times they would demand and receive their share of religious attention.*

The most important thing that Padmasambhava did during his stay was to found the first of Tibet's Buddhist monasteries. It was officially consecrated about two years after his arrival in Tibet and was named Samye Gompa (Samye Monastery, after which California's Odiyan is fashioned). Padmasambhava—with the help of Shantarakshita, whose return to Tibet he had artfully managed—established Samye in a valley on the north bank of the Tsangpo, about sixty miles southeast of Lhasa. The monastery was built in the form of a great mandala, intended to replicate the Buddhist cosmological order of the universe. At the center of the mandala was the Utse, a pagoda-style temple that incorporated the architectural styles of Tibet, India, and China. It seems that King Trisong Detsen wanted the size of the monastery to be really impressive. With a kingly lack of practical self-limitation, he declared that each of the four sides of the monastery grounds should be equal to the distance he could shoot an arrow. Fortunately, some of his more realistic advisers smuggled some heavy mercury into the hollow shaft of the arrow he used. But Samye Monastery still turned out to be a huge—and wonderfully beautiful—new center for Buddhism in Tibet. Samye was home to the very first order of Buddhist monks established in the country, but it would be far from the last. What Padmasambhava started on a modest scale would become enormous in scope and, far more than anything else, would come to define the character of Tibetan civilization.

THE GENERAL CHARACTER OF BUDDHISM IN TIBET

Padmasambhava was a Vajrayana Buddhist, and it was this great school of Mahayana Buddhism that became established in Tibet.** Vajrayana is derived from the Sanskrit word *vajra* (*dorje* in the Tibetan language). *Vajra* was originally an Indian term refer-

---

*Bon was not entirely *assimilated* into Tibetan Buddhism; to some extent, it continued to exist side by side with it. Bon priests continued to exercise their shamanic work in the villages. In fact, even in the twentieth century, a number of large Bon monasteries were found in some parts of Tibet.

**In general, Tibetan Buddhists feel that Vajrayana is far more than merely one of the divisions of Mahayana Buddhism—that it is, in fact, a third great branch of Buddhism, the other two being Theravada and Mahayana.

ring to the personal "weapon" associated with the god Indra. The vajra, a short shaft with a stylized trident head at each end, became the symbol that identified Indra. It is often described as a "thunderbolt," but this is most likely a mistaken notion arising from the western association of the Hindu god Indra with the Greek god Zeus, whose personal weapon was indeed a thunderbolt.

Indian Buddhists adopted the symbol of the vajra, but it took on a whole new meaning. The vajra became the symbol of Enlightenment. The word *vajra*, which literally means "diamond," came to be associated with the indestructible (that is, "diamondlike") union of wisdom and compassion. The Buddhist vajra, generally made of metal or bone and small enough to be held in the hand, is a highly stylized art object. At the center of the short shaft is a simple circular ball that, like the hub of a mandala, represents the emptiness from which all things emerge. At each end, the shaft blossoms into a lotuslike form from which five prongs emerge—a straight central one and four curved prongs, all of which close back together at the tips. There is great beauty in the simplicity and symmetry of the vajra.

Vajrayana developed out of the Tantra movement that was growing strong in north India in the sixth century, and from there it was carried to the highlands of Tibet. In large measure, Tantra grew out of the movement to incorporate the rich variety of esoteric folk beliefs and rituals into Mahayana Buddhism. This went so far as to include a great deal of what were frankly magical and superstitious elements.

What gave Tantra its special character was its effort to involve the whole person in the adventure of spiritual growth. In place of the more traditional approach of self-discipline and transcendence of desire, Tantra developed a host of ritual practices that embraced the body, desires and all, and saw it as a wonderful *vehicle* that could be used to carry one to higher states of knowledge. Rather than regarding the pleasure-craving body as an impediment to growth, rather than renouncing desire, Tantra sought to harness the energy of desire and use it to generate higher states of awareness. Of course, such an unorthodox approach could hope to succeed only if it was directed by a highly skilled master. Consequently, in the spirit of the ashram tradition of India, Tantra originally took the form of small groups of disciples tightly bound to a guru. The name

Dorje (P. Bresnan)

'tantra' referred to the various texts that formed the scriptural base of the movement. This Sanskrit word, taken originally from the weaving craft, refers literally to the weft, the horizontal strands that weave the yarn into a unified whole—a fabric. Tantric texts did the same sort of thing; they wove the various strands of the tradition into a unified whole—a philosophical system.

Exponents of the Tantric movement claimed that most of these texts had been delivered by Shakyamuni Buddha and had been preserved in a secret oral tradition for a thousand years before finally being written down. For all practical purposes, the tantras amounted to a further addition to the body of Buddhist sutras, but the followers of Tantrayana regarded the traditional sutras to be inferior to the tantras. Not so, however, with regard to the great *Prajnaparamita*, which was much loved and became the very centerpiece of the Vajrayana system. Because of the central importance of the *Prajnaparamita*, the Doctrine of *Shunyata*, as enunciated by Nagarjuna, became the philosophical foundation of Vajrayana Buddhism. Awakening was (and still is) seen as the opening of consciousness to the ultimate reality of "emptiness."

In Vajrayana, as in Mahayana Buddhism generally, the place of Shakyamuni Buddha was overshadowed by the various transcendent Buddhas, among whom Vairochana Buddha occupied the place of greatest importance. Each of the principal Buddhas was associated with various bodhisattvas, as well as with a specific female consort. All were properly venerated. A special affection was felt, though, for Amitabha, the Buddha of Sukhavati, the "western paradise." The great goal of awakening was commonly described as "rebirth" in Amitabha's realm, where enlightenment was assured. Whether this was interpreted literally or metaphorically depended, then as now, on the particular mind-set of the individual.

The metaphorical interpretation of Mahayana teaching became profoundly important in the development of Vajrayana. It led to the creation of a very rich symbology, much of it frankly sexual in nature. This is an aspect of Vajrayana that has puzzled and even shocked many Westerners. Some have even grossly misinterpreted Vajrayana, confusing sexual symbolism with sexual practice. The widespread use of sexual symbolism results from the tradition of associating wisdom (*prajna*) with the female principle and compassion (*karuna*) with the male principle. Because enlightenment is synonymous with the union of perfect wisdom and compassion, it follows that the ecstatic sexual union of man and woman provides a wonderfully rich field of symbolic possibilities. Sexual union is something that most men and women are familiar with, and this most earthly of acts can thus be used metaphorically to represent knowledge of the perfect unity of all being.

The vajra itself, the symbol of Enlightenment, includes sexual symbolism. In a highly stylized way, the arrangement at each end of the vajra represents the union of male and female sexual organs, the central prong being the male enclosed within the lotus form, which is often employed to represent the female organ. Note, however, that although this may be highly erotic in its essential meaning, it was not intended to arouse erotic feelings, at least not in the usual sense of the word. In both Vajrayana and the Tantric tradition that produced it, the sexual theme was seen to be an excellent metaphor for the unity of being in which all dualitiy is dissolved. To the puritanical

A beautiful sculptured example of a Yab/Yum; perhaps ninth-century Tibet. (P. Bresnan)

mind, this might seem shocking, but clearly, the creators of Vajrayana were not troubled by that problem at all.

The most widely recognized employment of sexual symbolism in Vajrayana is found in the Yab-Yum. Whereas the symbolism may be subtle in the vajra, it's not in the least subtle in the Yab-Yum (which literally means "father and mother"), a depiction of a man and woman joined together in the ecstasy of sexual union. Typically, the couple represented are a Buddha, or bodhisattva, and his female consort. They sit face-to-face in a yoga posture, their bodies intertwined. The theme of the Yab-Yum is very highly regarded; it appears over and over in sculpture and painting. Properly understood, it is an extremely powerful theme that represents the state of perfect union.

Awakening to knowledge of the perfect unity of being is, of course, what it's all about. This is enlightenment, which, in the Tibetan language, is called *tharpa.** The ultimate goal of all practice is *tharpa*, but in accordance with Vajrayana, this great goal was not to be ascended to slowly, by denying the flesh-and-blood realities of human life. In contrast to other schools of Buddhism, Vajrayana offered a dynamic path, an active "fast track" to enlightenment. Awakening was to be had by grappling with life—all of it—and bursting through the illusions and restraints created by the self-loving ego. As in all Buddhist traditions, meditation was seen as a most important part of the path, but in Vajrayana, meditation would become active and dynamic, involving the whole person. Consequently, a vast body of meditation techniques and ritual practices developed in Vajrayana.

Generally speaking, the various meditation practices of Vajrayana are derived from what are known as the sadhanas. These are lengthy and involved sections from the Tantric texts that the guru uses to initiate the student into successively higher states of meditative consciousness. The principal element of the practice of sadhana is what is called "visualization." In a visualization exercise, the meditator concentrates on visualizing, and identifying with, a particular Buddha or bodhisattva. In this way, the meditator seeks to instill within himself (or herself) the particular qualities of the one being visualized. The very popular bodhisattva Avalokiteshvara (pronounced Ahv-a-loh-keet-esh-VAR-a), for example, is identified with perfect compassion. Skill in visualizing Avalokiteshvara, it is believed, will increase the quality of compassion in the person practicing this exercise. Note that, in performing the exercise, the student does not believe that he has created an actual vision of Avalokiteshvara. Not at all; the visualization is accepted as a purely psychic experience, but an extremely powerful one.

Associated with the visualization exercise, and nurturing it, are many other elements of meditation practice. Chief among them is the recitation of *mantras.* The mantra plays a big part in the life of Vajrayana Buddhism—so much so, in fact, that Vajrayana is sometimes referred to as *Mantrayana*, the "way of the mantra." A mantra is a spiritually powerful syllable or string of syllables that a person repeats (often chants) in order to forge a strong psychic connection between himself and the force or deity that the mantra represents. *Om* ("Aum"), for example, is the fundamental mantra of the Hindu tradition and was transported into Buddhism, whereupon it evolved into new forms. By far the most popular mantra of Tibetan Buddhism is *Om mani padme hum.* This mantra, an invocation to Avalokiteshvara, is repeated endlessly by all Tibetan Buddhists. It is ubiquitous in Tibet, inscribed everywhere in the arts, as well as in the minds and hearts of all Tibetans. *Om mani padme hum* is printed on prayer flags, amulets, and long chains of paper that fill the ever-turning prayer wheels. The mantra translates literally as "Om—the jewel in the lotus—hum." The lotus can

---

*To be precise, the Tibetan word for enlightenment is *chang-chub*. *Tharpa* literally means liberation, but it is commonly used by Western writers to denote enlightenment.

be seen as referring to human consciousness, and the jewel is the enlightened mind that is embraced within the lotus. Of course, there is the possibility of sexual symbolism here, too. The verbal meaning, though, is not terribly important; the power of a mantra transcends its verbal meaning.

The recitation of a mantra is often accompanied by its appropriate *mudra*, which is a particular posture or symbolic hand gesture. The practice of mudra has evolved into a highly complex and refined art. There are specific mudras associated with virtually every important emotion and state of consciousness. Typically, in the art of Vajrayana, every figure is represented in the form of a mudra appropriate to his or her role. This matter is often very subtle to the eye, but it is of essential importance to the meaning of the work. Each Buddha and bodhisattva is generally depicted in one of the mudras associated with him. Shakyamuni Buddha, for example, is often shown seated in meditation with crossed hands in his lap, in the position of the *dhyana mudra*. Sometimes Shakyamuni Buddha is shown in the *bhumisparsha mudra*, which was the posture he assumed when, tempted by Mara, he summoned the Earth to be his witness and authority. In this mudra, the left hand remains in the lap, while the right hand, palm inward, is extended over the knee and points at or touches the ground. Vairochana is often shown with his hands in the mudra of supreme wisdom. It is believed that skill in mudra, just as skill in mantra, will greatly intensify the effect of a meditation exercise, especially a visualization exercise.

Yet another highly important element in the performance of sadhanas in general and the visualization exercise in particular is the *mandala* (*kyilkor* in Tibetan). The creation and use of mandalas are major features of Tibetan Buddhism; it is doubtful that any other tradition in human history has put so much emphasis on the value of the mandala. Its use goes well beyond the specific practices of meditation, but in sadhana practice the mandala plays a very powerful role.

In Tibetan Buddhism, the mandala that is designed to be an aid to meditation is often painted on a wall hanging known as a *thangka*, a symbolic representation, in mandala form, of a theme that is meaningful in the context of Tibetan Buddhism. The thangka may be something as simple as a pictorial arrangement of scenes from the life of an important Buddha or bodhisattva. Often, wrathful demons and mythological characters are depicted, each of them representing some particular psychic aspect of life. The "Wheel of Life" is a popular thangka theme. Another very common theme is the "palace" of a celestial Buddha. The mandala architecture of the palace, together will all of the beings that inhabit it, is a way of symbolically portraying the Buddha-realm of the particular Buddha, presented in the appropriate mudra at the center of the mandala. The use of a thangka such as this can profoundly influence a sadhana visualization exercise. The depiction, of course, is not meant to be interpreted literally; rather, the symbols and images are used to represent an enlightened state of mind. Through creative visualizations, the meditator unites psychically with the mandala, becoming one with the state of consciousness that it represents:

> Practitioners are regularly reminded, however, that the figures in the mandala have no real ontological status; they are symbols of the mental qualities

A fine example of a modern thangka, painted in the traditional style. (P. Bresnan)

toward which tantric adepts aspire and are intended to provide templates for mental transformation, but they are empty of inherent existence. This is also true of demons and wrathful deities, which represent factors of human consciousness that are transmuted through meditation into virtuous qualities.[1]

The production of thangkas has always been a highly skilled, busy profession within the monasteries of Tibet. The thangkas come in a great variety of sizes and types, some entirely abstract and highly complex. Usually, they are painted or inked on linen cloth, but sometimes on paper, silk, or wood. Some of the most elaborate are made entirely with sand of various colors. Only the most skilled (and patient) artists work on the sand mandalas, which are typically quite large, up to ten feet in diameter. The sand mandala originated as part of a sadhana ritual at the conclusion of which the mandala would be swept up and seen no more (which is true of *all* things eventually).

A dramatic event concerning a sand mandala occurred in San Francisco in 1993. Two Tibetan monks were constructing the highly complex *Kalichakra* sand mandala at the Asian Art Museum located in Golden Gate Park. It takes many days to complete a big mandala, and a large number of people would gather around the platform to watch its progress. All of a sudden, a woman, apparently mentally disturbed, jumped up on the platform shouting angrily about witchcraft. Before the guards could seize her, she kicked the sand in all directions. Everyone was stunned—everyone, that is, except the two monks. The most interesting part of this little drama was their reaction. Without being flustered in the least, they both bowed deeply to the woman, who was by this time being held tightly by the guards, and began calmly to sweep up the remaining sand. Then, as if nothing had happened at all, they patiently began work on the mandala again, starting at square one. (That's unflappability!)

Vajras, mantras, mudras, thangkas, chanting, dancing, prayer flags, prayer wheels, rosaries, bells, candles, incense, stupas, and on and on—Tibetan Buddhism is packed full of wonderful and intriguing elements. And it all serves a lofty purpose in association with the performance of sadhana, the royal road to *tharpa*, the experience of awakening. But *tharpa* may lie at the end of a very long road, so how does one know that he or she is making progress? Are there signs or experiences that indicate progress? In the tradition of Tibetan Buddhism, it is widely held that a person who is dedicated to the life of Vajrayana and who has acquired skill in its ritual practices will come to exhibit certain supernormal powers and that this is evidence of spiritual progress. Such powers are said to be super*normal*, not super*natural*—that is, not miraculous—a fine distinction, perhaps, but an important one. Tibetans believe that all powers, even the most amazing ones, are based on perfectly natural principles, even if they are not always understood.

Vajrayana powers can take many forms. Telepathy and clairvoyance are said to be fairly common, especially between a disciple and his guru. *Tumo* is another widely reported power. A master of tumo can sit outdoors for hours in the freezing Himalayan cold, wearing little or nothing, and through only the power of concentration generate sufficient body heat to dry linen sheets that have been dipped in icy water and draped around his shoulders. *Lung-gompa* is yet another power said to be mastered by many Tibetan monks. One skilled in lung-gompa has mastered a specialized gait that permits him to walk at a truly incredible speed, covering (or so it is said) more than a hundred miles a day. In a country where the pilgrimage is a common part of life, this could indeed be a valuable power. Needless to say, many people outside the fold of Tibetan Buddhism are understandably skeptical about such assertions, and obviously, it is a field that could lend itself to exaggeration or even self-deception. Perhaps the true meaning and use of such "powers" can be understood only within the monastic community that cherishes their existence.

By far the most important evidence of progress, though, is an entirely personal experience, one that cannot possibly be described in words. The real reward of adopting the monk's life is to be found in those rare and unexpected moments in which a vision of great truth and great beauty takes form in one's consciousness. Such an experience—a moment of inexpressible joy—clarifies the meaning of the quest, and in a highly personal way, it is all one needs to be reassured that life is unfolding as it should.

But what if a monk (or a devout layperson), despite various profound experiences, dies before ever actually achieving the fullness of awakening? Tibetan Buddhism teaches—at least at the ordinary, literal level—that when a person dies, the spirit of that person will be reborn after a passage of time that can last up to forty-nine days. Ideally, the person will be reborn in Sukhavati, Buddha Amitabha's "western paradise," where the realization of perfect enlightenment is assured; this is what most Tibetans yearn for. If it is not possible, the individual will be reborn in human or animal form, depending on the condition of his or her karma at the time of death.

Naturally, in a discussion of this sort, the question "How literally is all of this to be understood?" will keep arising in the reader's mind. All the talk about reincarnation seems to contradict the basic teaching of Buddhism. Is it not a fundamental tenet of Buddhist philosophy that all is change, no *thing* exists, there is no substantive enduring entity—including "spirit"—*that can be reincarnated*? Indeed, it is: Vajrayana Buddhism, solidly grounded as it is on the teaching of *Madhyamika*, definitely does not contradict the basic teaching of Buddhism. But it must be remembered that Vajrayana is part of the evolution of Mahayana Buddhism, and in casting out its net to include everyone, Mahayana has no problem with a full spectrum of personal interpretations. Perhaps a better analogy would be Buddha's own—the lotus pond. There are many different levels of growth, and Mahayana wants to provide a meaningful interpretation that is appropriate to the level of understanding of all of them.

From the very beginning of the Mahayana tradition, it has been the custom to use rich metaphor and poetic license in attempting to express philosophical truths that simply cannot be stated objectively in words. We saw this clearly in the sutras, the scriptural foundation of Mahayana. The practice of using familiar imagery to suggest the meaning of that which is not familiar was well developed in Hinduism and was carried over into Mahayana Buddhism. Whatever may have been the intention of the creators of the sutras, though, it is nonetheless true that a great many people in every age have chosen to accept such expressions as literally accurate, and so far as Mahayana Buddhism is concerned, that's just fine; everyone is welcome to plug in at the level where he or she feels most comfortable. If one wishes to conceive of Avalokiteshvara as a distinct being—a distinct *spiritual* being—who, in the company of Buddha Amitabha presides over the Pure Land of Sukhavati, a genuine paradise into which one's spirit may be reborn, then Mahayana Buddhism has not the slightest problem with that. If such a belief and the practices that go with it help one to grow in Buddha's lotus pond, where is the problem? Isn't this what it's all about?

But there are some in that lotus pond who are receptive to the light of a different understanding. For them, the literal interpretation is not the best way. For these more philosophically minded ones, spiritual growth is nourished by following the path of metaphorical understanding. After all, the underlying oneness of being is fundamental to the teaching of Buddhism. If one understands this perfectly, then all talk of separate beings, including spiritual beings that can be reincarnated, must *necessarily* be metaphorical. To such a person, the Five Celestial Buddhas (including Buddha Amitabha) are not to be seen as distinct beings presiding over objectively real Buddha-realms; rather, they are metaphorical ways of depicting the fundamental aspects of enlightenment, and the Buddha-realm is the interior *state of consciousness* that the disciple aspires to. Admittedly, this is the approach of a minority of the population; the common understanding is much more likely to be the literal one. Within the monastic tradition of Tibet, though, there have always been many who have risen to the metaphorical understanding of Vajrayana teaching. The great Tibetan wonderland of myths, spirits, and rituals can be seen to be a wonderfully rich way of expressing—and exploring—the complex psychology of the human mind, particularly one that is searching for ultimate truth.

Again, though, the literal expression of the teaching holds that a person's "spirit" will be reborn following the death of the body. How it all turns out depends to a very large degree on how the person responds to a series of perceptions he or she will experience in the hours and days immediately after death. It is believed that the person, whose body is now dead, will nonetheless pass through several distinct planes of consciousness (called *bardos* in Tibetan). Some are alluring and some are terrifying, but all call for some kind of response, and, as mentioned, the quality of the rebirth is the direct result of how successful (or unsuccessful) the response is.

In this matter, the help of a trained spiritual assistant can be immensely valuable. Consequently, it has long been the custom in Tibet that many monks are trained to be expert guides whose task it is to help the dying prepare for death and, after death, to help the disembodied spirit successfully navigate the *bardos* and be reborn in the finest possible condition.* In the case of a layperson, the monks go to the home of the dying and conduct an elaborate ritual that may go on for days. The spirit is talked to and given instructions, even though the body may be dead and cold. Eventually, the body is disposed of, also according to ritual. In the high country of Tibet, where firewood for cremation is scarce, the body is customarily taken to a place where it is cut up and offered to hungry vultures. Tibetans see nothing morbid or repulsive in this at all.

The character of the *bardo* experiences and instructions for dealing with them are discussed in an ancient Tibetan work known as the *Bardo Thödol*. It is widely believed that Padmasambhava himself was the author of this work. The Buddhologist W. Y. Evans-Wentz translated the work into English, giving it the imaginative title, *The Tibetan Book of the Dead*. It's an intriguing work and has become very popular in the West. Perhaps the most intriguing thing of all about the *Bardo Thödol* is the suggestion that, at the deepest level of meaning, it is an esoteric work that is really directed at the living, not the dead. In this interpretation, death, as it is ordinarily understood, is a metaphor for death of another kind—death of the ego. The *Bardo Thödol*, then, becomes a powerful guidebook in the hands of a spiritual master to help the initiate "die" to his ego-self, pass successfully through the stages of psychic resistance (the *bardos*), and be reborn (i.e., "awakened") in the new life of enlightened consciousness:

> For all who are familiar with Buddhist philosophy, it is clear that birth and death are not phenomena that happen only once in a human life, but something that happens uninterruptedly within us. At every moment something within us dies and something is reborn. The different *bardos*, therefore, are nothing other than the different states of consciousness of our life. . . . The *Bardo Thödol* is addressed not only to those who see the end of their life approaching, or who are very near death, but equally to those who are in the

---

*Literally, the word *bardo* refers simply to the state between death and rebirth. It has become customary, though, to use the word in the plural, referring to the various stages that can be identified.

prime of life and who for the first time realize the full meaning of their existence as human beings. . . . Under the guise of death it [the *Bardo Thödol*] reveals to the initiate the secret of life. He must go through the experience of death, in order to gain liberation within himself.[2]

Seen in this light, the *Bardo Thödol* provides the student of Tibetan Buddhism with a glimpse into the fabulous insights that this tradition has produced with regard to the nature of consciousness and the ways in which a person may overcome his own psychic fears. The *Bardo Thödol* becomes a guidebook for passing from ordinary ignorance to the freedom of perfect understanding.

While it is true to say that Tibetan Buddhism—Vajrayana—became the defining spirit of the entire culture of Tibet and deeply affected the daily lives of all the people, it is also true that the wellspring of this culture, as well as the place where it all comes together, is the monastery—the *gompa*. Since Padmasambhava founded Samye Gompa in 747 C.E., the monastery has been the matrix of Vajrayana Buddhism in Tibet.

This is an appropriate place to take a brief look at the character of the Tibetan Buddhist monastery. Such a picturesque structure is the only image that many people have of the Himalayan world. Unlike the early gompas, which were built after the fashion of Indian and Chinese monasteries, the ones we see today are more representative of a native Tibetan style of architecture. Typically, one pictures an attractive-looking jumble of multistoried buildings arranged in tiers on a hillside, the whitewashed walls sloping gently inward as they rise. The gleaming white of the walls is offset by dark wood trim and narrow balconies on the upper stories. The rooftops, sometimes gilt, are likely to be festooned in colorful pennants and prayer flags. It's a highly attractive sight, and—at least until recent times—it was a sight to be found with great frequency in the Himalayan world. Over the course of time, thousands of monasteries came into existence in all parts of Tibet and the neighboring Himalayan lands. At the beginning of the twentieth century more than three thousand monasteries were functioning. Many, of course, were very small and local, but some were huge, counting thousands of monks in their membership.

Perhaps "monastery" is a misleading translation of *gompa*. Alexandra David-Neel commented, "Though for lack of another word in the English language we are compelled to refer to the gompas as monasteries, they do not in the least resemble a Christian monastery." This is undoubtedly true with respect to modern times. Western monasteries in this day and age tend to be purely religious communities that have withdrawn from the world in order to focus on the spiritual way of life. But it wasn't always that way. Western monasteries of an earlier time, especially during Europe's feudal age, took on many of the worldly functions of life that would later gravitate to the more secular part of society. At that time in history, Christian monasteries shared many features with the typical Tibetan Buddhist monastery.

Indeed, some of Tibet's monasteries became enormous, more like full-fledged towns than religious hermitages. Perhaps the best comparison of all would be to a university. In many important ways, the traditional *gompa* is like a university, albeit one that is solidly organized around a religious core. In addition to the pursuit of the spiritual life, all of the members of the community are involved to some extent in other fields of learning as well. Over time, several areas of study became standard, scriptural study being only one of them. Philosophy was another, and so was medicine. In Tibet, one of the most important fields of study—and to the Western mind the strangest one of all— is the field of ritual magic. Only the most prestigious monasteries have offered advanced study in the occult sciences. The masters of these mysterious arts became the ones charged with the crucial responsibility for controlling the wrathful spirits and attending to the needs of the Bon demons. Beyond these rather lofty offices, they also served the general population as sorcerers, exorcists, astrologers, diviners, and prophesiers—whatever was needed in the daily lives of a population obsessively concerned with the machinations of a potentially threatening spirit world. In traditional Tibet few undertakings were begun without first consulting an experienced sorcerer. For some Tibetan monks, mastery of ritual magic would become a full-time profession.

The *gompa* became the source of virtually *all* of the "professions" in traditional Tibet. It had to be; just as in feudal Europe, in Tibet there was not yet any other social structure that could provide training and employment in the professions. Some members of the *gompa* specialized in the study of medicine, for example, although this, too, was heavily interfused with magical and occult elements. Those who showed promise were steered into the path of artistic studies, eventually becoming full-time professionals. Thangka production alone has always supported a multitude of artists.

It might seem surprising, but some monks were even trained in the worldly arts of business. This was necessary because, except for the smallest and humblest, the monasteries could not support themselves solely on the donations of the laity, no matter how generous. Not only did the bigger monasteries become very wealthy in land and serfs, but they also became active centers of a rough-and-ready capitalism, engaging in trade, simple banking, and moneylending (changing interest, of course). Waddell criticized the monasteries for growing rich on trade and lending money at usurious rates. He referred to the monks as "the chief traders and capitalists of the country." (Predictably, this state of affairs would attract the attention of Marxist reformers in the twentieth century.)

Undoubtedly, abuses did sometimes occur, and it is also true that many monasteries became extremely powerful and wealthy. But that was inevitable in a feudal society in which the monastery was the only institution that was capable of taking on the multifarious social and economic functions that, in a more complex society, would be spread out among many specialized sectors. In more recent times, Western monasteries have been able to focus exclusively on the core spiritual function, but only because other institutions have arisen to relieve them of their former, more secular, responsibilities.

One explanation for the great diversity within the monastery is to be found in the broad spectrum of the population from which the membership was drawn. In a modern Western monastery, most of the monks are recruited from the young-adult population, and only those sincerely willing to commit themselves to the spiritual life are accepted. The traditional Tibetan monastery, on the other hand, accepted its novices from virtually all families in its area, and boys were admitted at a very young age, often as young as eight. It was a common practice for the firstborn son in every family to enter the monastic life; many families would give more than one son. As a result, a significantly large proportion of the Tibetan population came to be concentrated in the monasteries. Not uncommonly in Tibetan history, a full quarter of the population consisted of Buddhist monks. Given this situation, it should come as no surprise that many monks were more concerned with worldly professions than with the spiritual life. It's fair to say that in a modern society many of these young men would have chosen to follow a more secular path, but in traditional Tibet these opportunities simply did not exist; hence, in a way, the monastery filled the void by attempting to be all things to all people.

Let's not lose sight of the fact, though, that the monastery was, at its foundation, a *monastery*, a *gompa*—a community of men and, in some cases, women—manifestly dedicated to following the path of Buddha in order to achieve awakening. The great goal of *tharpa* was unquestionably enshrined at the heart of every *gompa*. No matter how many secular activities the monastery might be involved in, no matter how many monks might be more interested in worldly pursuits than spiritual pursuits, it is nonetheless true that the secular activities were, and still remain, peripheral matters. The heart and soul of the Tibetan Buddhist *gompa* has always been the preservation of the country's unique tradition of Buddhist teachings and practices that lead to *tharpa*.

To at least some degree, *all* monks who have been accepted as members of a Tibetan *gompa* participate in the religious life of the community. Such life involves a large measure of communal ritual, often including the music and chanting that Tibetan monks are famous for in the West. This can be quite a joyous spectacle: pounding drums, blaring horns, clashing cymbals, and deep droning voices. In the Vajrayana tradition, however, the individual monk has a great deal of personal freedom with regard to how much and in what way he will participate. Indeed, his participation may range from the bare minimum to total dedication to spiritual disciplines. In their zeal for spiritual growth, some few choose to become lonely anchorites living the solitary life in a tiny hermitage, dedicating all of their time to meditation and ascetic disciplines. The hermit monk is a part of every religious tradition, but in Tibet this exceptional life seems to have taken on an especially alluring value. The solitary hermit searching for wisdom in the lonely isolation of his Himalayan cave has become a veritable icon of the world's image of Tibet.

There is a hierarchy of rank in the *gompa*. Properly speaking, only the highest-ranking monks are known as *lamas*. The name *lama* originated at Samye, the very first Buddhist monastery of Tibet. In founding Samye, Padmasambhava referred to the community as the "order of lamas." Literally, the term means "the superior ones," but it should be understood in the sense of those who have chosen the "superior" path of Buddhist discipline. Within the Tibetan world, the word *lama* is used out of respect for all elderly and learned monks, regardless of rank, but outside of Tibet it has become customary to refer to *all* Vajrayana monks as lamas. From this word also comes the term *lamaism*, which is yet another popular name for Tibetan Buddhism.

In the Tibetan language, the fully ordained monk is known as a *gelong*. This is the full-time professional monk whose life's work is bound up in the affairs of his monastery. He has studied and trained for a minimum of twelve years before becoming a gelong, at which time he publicly affirms the 253 vows that spell out the monastic rules of Vajrayana. The novice monks—those studying to become gelongs—are known as *tra-*

pas. Generally, these are young men under the age of twenty, but many trapas become entangled in a particular line of work and never go on to become ordained gelongs. Monks from poor families often fall into this category, because the family is expected to pay a sizable part of the tutoring cost that a student monk necessarily incurs.

Bear in mind that these comments about the Tibetan monastery are very general and refer to an institution that grew and evolved over many centuries. The early gompas were very simple affairs compared to the huge and complex monastery–towns of later times. But from the beginning, the essential core of *every* monastery has been the tradition of Vajrayana Buddhist teaching.

Indeed, the monasteries have always been the wellsprings of Tibetan culture, and the entire land has been richly watered by their potent influence. Prayer flags flutter picturesquely around every village, and also to be found are the ubiquitous chortens, shrines, prayer wheels, and myriad other implements of a living Buddhism. (This, of course, is the picture of *traditional* Tibet; much has changed since the Chinese annexation, but by no means has it all been eliminated.)

It must be remembered, though, that Tibetan Buddhism is an amalgam of Vajrayana Buddhism and the ancient tradition of Bon. The beliefs and practices of Bon were never exterminated. Rather, the outlook of Bon came to be something of a "ground" upon which Tibetan Buddhism was built. At a deep level, the belief system of Bon continued to live on, especially among the common people. Fundamental to that system is the acceptance of a world of spirits. More than anything else, this acceptance defines the basic worldview of the ordinary Tibetan:

> Their importance to ordinary people should not be underestimated, since in the consciousness of most Tibetans the world is full of multitudes of powers and spirits, and the welfare of humans requires that they be propitiated and sometimes subdued. Every part of the natural environment is believed to be alive with various types of sentient forces, who live in mountains, trees, rivers and lakes, rocks, fields, the sky, and the earth. Every region has its own native supernatural beings, and people living in these areas are strongly aware of their presence. In order to stay in their good graces, Tibetans give them offerings, perform rituals to propitiate them, and sometimes refrain from going to particular places so as to avoid the more dangerous forces.[3]

Nature spirits, demons, gods, ghosts, departed ancestors—the unsophisticated Tibetan has always earnestly believed that he lives his life surrounded by a vast number of spiritual beings, some benign and some malicious, and that they influence every aspect of daily life. The spirits must be dealt with; there is no question about that. The only question is, how best to deal with them. It is in this area, dealing with the spirit world, that the most significant contribution of the Buddhist tradition is to be found, at least among the common people.

The Buddhist establishment embraced the role of dealing with the spirits from the earliest times, taking over (but never entirely replacing) the functions of the Bon priesthood. In a land where superstition pervades everything, perhaps it was only natural that some Buddhist monks would become specialists in astrology, necromancy, sorcery, and all of the occult arts. Propitiating the spirits while holding the dangerous ones at bay has always been an obsession with the people of Tibet. For this purpose, specialized charms are to be seen virtually everywhere:

> Their inveterate craving for material protection against those malignant gods and demons has caused them to pin their faith on charms and amulets, which are to be seen everywhere dangling from the dress of every man, woman, and child.[4]

The dependence on Buddhist rituals and objects as protective charms is an interesting aspect of grassroots Tibetan Buddhism. In addition to the ubiquitous rosaries and handheld prayer wheels, printed thangkas are found everywhere among the common people. Certain ones are widely believed to have healing power and are actually eaten to ward off illness.

Like every other kind of affliction, illness is believed to be caused by demons. The greatest affliction of all, naturally, is death, and here, too, the specialist monk stands ready to perform the proper ritual which will hold off the terrifying demons that await the deceased and guide his or her spirit through the awesome *bardos* to a satisfying rebirth. The most satisfying of all would be rebirth in Sukhavati, the last and greatest hope of all Tibetans.

When I say "all Tibetans," I do not mean to imply that every Tibetan understands rebirth in Sukhavati in a literal sense; indeed, some interpret this metaphorically. Quite obviously, there is a huge difference between the understanding of the learned, philosophically minded Buddhist monk on the one hand, and the common uneducated, unsophisticated Tibetan layperson on the other. To some, it is true to say that "Gods, demons, the whole universe are but a mirage which exists in the mind, springs from it, and sinks into it," and perhaps a great many Buddhists of Tibet would assent to that truth, at least verbally. But realistically speaking, the great majority of common people, including many of the monks, accept as undeniably true the assertion that spirits do in fact exist, that they affect the affairs of daily life in powerful ways, and that, fundamentally, each individual is a spirit capable of a series of rebirths.

What it all comes down to is simply this: Each person will relate to the Dharma in the way that is appropriate for him or her. The teaching of Mahayana, in the spirit of Buddha's lotus pond, offers something for everyone.

A HISTORICAL OVERVIEW OF BUDDHISM IN TIBET

Buddhism in Tibet cannot be understood apart from its history; it has been an evolving story, and it is continuing to evolve in modern times. The purpose of this section is to present a broad overview of this history, a big picture, as it were. The fourteen centuries of the history of Tibetan Buddhism can be divided into three great eras. Each of these eras constitutes a cycle that begins with a stage of growth, is succeeded by a time of flourishing, and then concludes in a period of decline.

The earliest era, during which time Buddhism was introduced into Tibet, is referred to as the Era of the Yarlung Empire. It spans the time from the beginnings of Tibetan Buddhism in the seventh century to the end of the tenth century. The second era, which may be called the Sakya Era, lasted from the early eleventh century to the end of the fourteenth century. The final of the three, the Era of the Dalai Lama, began in the fifteenth century and has continued down to the present time. It can well be argued that we are presently in the final stages of the third great era (though, of course, no one really knows for sure). We will briefly examine each era with an eye toward understanding how the historical development of Tibetan Buddhism has shaped its special character.

The First Period: The Era of the Yarlung Empire

As we have already seen, Buddhism was introduced into Tibet during the reign of Songtsen Gampo, the king who married the Chinese and Nepalese princesses and who also sent the mission to Kashmir to acquire that region's alphabet. It was Songtsen Gampo who was responsible for establishing the Jokhang, Tibet's first Buddhist temple. During the next century, King Trisong Detsen invited Padmasambhava to Tibet, and that's where the story of Tibetan Buddhism really takes off. Padmasambhava, as you will remember, founded Samye *Gompa*, the first of Tibet's Buddhist monasteries.

After the founding of Samye *Gompa* in 747 C.E., Buddhism grew rapidly in Tibet. Monasteries sprouted in many places and were receiving the warm support of the royal court (a warmth not necessarily shared by all of the noble families). Many Indian Buddhist gurus were active in Tibet in those early days. For the most part, they were exponents of Vajrayana, the Tantric school of Indian Buddhism, and this became solidly and permanently established as the essential character of Tibetan Buddhism. As you might expect, these early years saw an intense interest in translating the corpus of Buddhist scripture into the Tibetan language. Those most treasured works were meticulously written out by hand on thin, narrow sheets of parchment that were bound in stacks and lovingly preserved. Many exist even to this day.

The new tradition of Buddhism grew rapidly, but not without opposition. In fact, these two countervailing forces grew apace; the stronger Buddhism became, the stronger became the opposition. The principal opposition to Buddhism came, as one might expect, from the traditional Bon priesthood. They were allied with some of the old nobility, and together they waited for their chance.

That opportunity came in 838 C.E. In that year, the king, a friend of Buddhism, was assassinated by his brother, a man most definitely not a friend of Buddhism. The brother assumed the throne and is known in history as King Lang Darma. What is most remembered about his brief four-year reign is that he launched an all-out war against the Buddhist establishment. Clearly, his intention was to wipe out Buddhism altogether in Tibet, to use any means to end forever what he and others saw as a mortal threat to the ancient Bon tradition of the Tibetan people. He very nearly succeeded. There was a wholesale destruction of Buddhist temples, monasteries, and art objects, and Buddhist monks were slaughtered or forced to return to their families. It might well have been the end of Buddhism in Tibet had not Lang Darma himself been murdered in 842 C.E. The assassin was a dagger-wielding Buddhist monk, and he claimed that his deed was actually an act of great kindness to Lang Darma, who was thus spared the effects of further accumulation of negative karma generated by his brutal and ignorant persecution of the Buddhists.

Regardless of whether one sees Lang Darma's assassination as an act of kindness, it certainly had the effect of saving Tibetan Buddhism from extinction. The new king quickly ended the persecution and began the long, slow process of repairing the damage. One very interesting and significant sidelight to the story of the persecution of Buddhists at the hands of Lang Darma is that the very same kind of persecution was occurring in China at just about the same time. (We will look at that part of the story in Chapter 15.) In both realms the persecution was intense, but short lived, and in both cases the Buddhist establishment was badly damaged, but not exterminated. The road back to health, though, was to be long and difficult.

In Tibet, a period of deterioration followed the persecution of Buddhists by Lang Darma. During the ninth and tenth centuries, the once-strong unity of the Yarlung Empire broke down. Tibet sank into a fragmented patchwork of small feuding principalities. It was something of a Dark Age in the history of Tibet. (European civilization was going through a similar era at the same time.) The fire of Tibetan Buddhism, formerly so strong, was now languishing and in danger of flickering out altogether. To a large degree, it was kept alive during this difficult time by the nurturing influence of Buddhist monasteries to the north of Tibet in the wild lands of the Takla Makan. (That too is a story to be taken up later.) But all things must change eventually, and the depression of the ninth and tenth centuries was no exception. With the coming of the eleventh century, a new day was about to dawn, but for Tibet it would dawn in the west, not the east.

The Second Period: The Sakya Era

The middle period in the unfolding history of Tibetan Buddhism takes its name from the great monastery of Sakya in southern Tibet. The abbots of Sakya dominated the religious and political life of Tibet for much of the twelfth, thirteenth, and fourteenth centuries. The revival, though, did not begin with Sakya, which was not founded until 1073. The revival began in the mountainous west of Tibet, in the region called Guge, which, because of its location, had close ties with the northwest Indian regions of Ladach and Kashmir.

Wishing to reinvigorate the Buddhism of their realm, the royal family of Guge sent delegations of students to Kashmir. Not only were they to study at the ancient centers of Buddhism, but hopefully, they might attract learned Buddhist missionaries to Tibet as well. The most notable result of this effort was the arrival in Guge of the great Atisha in the year 1038 C.E. Atisha (pronounced Ah-TEESH-a) was a scholar–monk from northern India who launched a reform movement sometimes referred to as the "second spreading" of Buddhism in Tibet. Already nearly sixty years old when he arrived in Guge, Atisha spent the last twelve years of his life spreading the good word in Tibet, first in Guge and then on to the central parts, including the former capital, Lhasa. With the help of his devoted nephew, Dromton, Atisha founded many new monasteries in Tibet.

There is a wonderful legend concerning how it happened that Atisha accepted the invitation to restore the Dharma in Tibet. He was, after all, no young man when he made the journey, one that was by no means easy or lacking in danger. When he was first approached by the agents of Yeshe, the king of Guge, Atisha was offered a large amount of gold as an inducement. He politely declined, though, saying that he was needed in his Indian homeland. Informed of this, Yeshe concluded that he had not sent enough gold, so he personally scoured the kingdom, trying to raise more from his nobles. In the process, he was captured by a rival king and held for ransom, which was to be nothing less than Yeshe's own weight in gold. If the ransom was not paid, Yeshe would be put to death. Yeshe frantically got word back to his court: Forget the ransom; send the gold to Atisha. This is what the courtiers did, and poor Yeshe died in prison. When Atisha heard about Yeshe's demise, he was deeply moved by his act of self-sacrifice and so decided to go to Tibet after all.[5]

The reform movement spearheaded by Atisha and the monasteries he established coalesced into what was in effect a new sect of Tibetan Buddhism. It would come to be called *Kadam-pa*. The emphasis in Kadam-pa was placed on the correct transmission and interpretation of the sacred texts. Before this time, there were no significant divisions within the world of Tibetan Buddhism; it was all one. But now the formerly seamless fabric was rent. A distinct new reform sect had come into existence, and others would soon follow. "They arose in revolt against the depraved Lamaism then prevalent, which was little else than a priestly mixture of demonolatry and witchcraft. Abandoning the grosser charlatanism, the new sects returned to celibacy and many of the purer Mahayana rules."[6]

Eventually, four major Buddhist sects would take form in Tibet. By default, the traditional orthodox, pre-Atisha school of Buddhism would also be seen as a sect in its own right. This sect came to be called the *Nyingma-pa,* the "school of the ancients." Padmasambhava (Guru Rinpoche) is regarded as being the founder of Nyingma; thus, Samye, the first of all Buddhist monasteries in Tibet, is a Nyingma monastery. (California's Odiyan, the spiritual heir of Samye, is therefore also a Nyingma monastery.)

The third of the sects is known as *Kagyu-pa*. This, too, was a reform sect and was distinguished by its special emphasis on the personal transmission of spiritual awakening from teacher to disciple. The Kagyu-pa was founded by Marpa and his disciple, Milarepa, one of the most loved and revered figures in all of Tibet's history. The story of Milarepa's life is well known to all Tibetans; it is a classic example of the journey from youthful ignorance and hardship to the ultimate perfection of enlightenment. Milarepa was inspired as a young man by Marpa, a scholarly layman who made several trips to India, where he studied with Naropa, the abbot of the renowned monastery at Nalanda. In the process, Marpa acquired a wealth of sacred texts and devoted himself to translating them into the Tibetan language. These texts were the vehicle for introducing the *Mahamudra* system of Tantric practices into Tibet.* For that, Marpa is held in very high respect and is referred to simply as "The Translator."

*Each of the sects cherishes its own highly refined method for realizing the true nature of mind. In the Kagyu sect, it is *Mahamudra*. In the Nyingma, the method is known as *Dzogchen*.

Marpa must have been an interesting character. He was much respected as a sorcerer. In fact, that's what originally attracted the young Milarepa to him. (At that time in his life, Milarepa was seething with desire for revenge against an uncle who had cheated his poor mother.) Marpa was said to be totally unattached to worldly wealth—an odd assertion, considering that he charged wealthy "clients" as much as ten ounces of gold for protection against demons.

As a guru, Marpa was a harsh taskmaster who placed truly Herculean challenges before the young Milarepa, who would rather die than fail. Eventually, the highest success was Milarepa's, and he withdrew into the remoteness of the Himalayas, where he could find perfect serenity and devote his remaining years to expressing his wisdom in verse. These "songs" of Milarepa are some of the greatest treasures of Tibetan Buddhism. Milarepa became the epitome of the cave-dwelling hermit, blissfully happy in his solitude, but not really cut off from the world. By sharing his wisdom with others who sought him out, he made a mighty contribution to the development of the tradition of Tibetan Buddhism. Marpa and Milarepa were giants, deserving of much more attention than can be provided in a work of this scope. Unfortunately, their names can hardly more than be mentioned, and we must move on. The student of Tibetan Buddhism, though, is well advised to search them out.

Marpa and Milarepa were the inspiration behind the founding of the Kagyu-pa sect, but the actual labor of establishing the monasteries of Kagyu-pa was the work of disciples. The various sects, of course, differed from one another with respect to the emphasis they placed on certain interpretations and practices, but this was not the whole story. There was a political dimension as well. Each sect—and, in fact, each monastery within a given sect—was the "protectorate" of a specific group of noble families, generally based on geographic location. The nobles gave their monastery the support it needed—financial, political, and, when necessary, even military. And too, as you might expect, sons of these families would by and large fill the higher posts within the monasteries.

The fourth great sect in Buddhist history, the *Sakya-pa*, came into existence in the late eleventh century in south central Tibet in the region of the ancient city of Gyantze, which lay along a tributary of the Tsangpo about one hundred miles southwest of Lhasa. The Sakya tradition, too, traces its roots to India, specifically to the legendary Tantric master, Virupa. He also was a most interesting character; at least, that's the way the stories describe him. Supposedly, he first attracted attention as an infant when he would scratch holy Sanskrit words in the sand and then refuse to crawl over them. He was said to have lived for seven hundred years, eventually achieving perfect enlightenment just before he died. Along the way, he mastered all the magical skills of a Tantric wizard. At one point, in order to increase his mastery, he dedicated twelve years to repeating an especially effective mantra twenty million times! (But, when you live to be 700, twelve years doesn't seem like all that much.)

Virupa was no ascetic. The most popular story about him concerns a time when he stopped at an inn and promptly washed down flagon after flagon of wine. When the innkeeper became nervous about the bill, Virupa stuck his dagger in the table and said that he would pay up as soon as the sunlight coming in the window reached the dagger. Well, Virupa thereupon used his magical powers to hold the sun still *for several days*, meanwhile putting away countless more flagons of wine. With everyone getting understandably frightened and the unmoving sun scorching the nearby crops, the local king finally paid the bill just to get Virupa to move on.

The first temple of what would be the great Sakya monastery was erected on the outskirts of Gyantze in 1073 C.E. Situated in the striking scenery of the northern foothills of the Himalayas only about fifty miles from Everest, Gyantze is described as gray-earth country. (*Sakya* means "gray earth.") A powerful aristocratic family named Khon was largely responsible for establishing Gyantze, and members of that family have been the abbots of Sakya right down to modern times. Sakya would definitely have been a powerful monastery and very influential in the affairs of Tibetan life, but not necessarily the most powerful. The rise of Sakya to preeminence resulted from the Khon's unique connection with a dramatic new element in the isolated world of Tibet, the Mongols.

The northern parts of the Eurasian continent form a vast rolling ocean of grasslands trailing off to the tundra and ice of the far north. Since time immemorial, this land has been the homeland of immeasurable numbers of nomadic peoples. In the west it was the Aryans, in the east the Mongols. The horse gave them wings, and when they gathered as a fighting force, their power was awesome; it seemed that nothing could stop them. Aryan hordes invaded many regions of western Eurasia, and a similar force overwhelmed Han China in the third century C.E. Now it was happening again.

In the early thirteenth century, the great Mongol conqueror Genghiz Khan welded together an army of nomadic horsemen that burst out of the wildlands of the north, devastating and subduing everything in their path. It was the beginning of what history knows as the Mongol Empire. At its height, the Mongol Empire was one of the largest ever to be created. Under Genghiz's grandson, Kublai Khan, China would become the home of the central authority, and from his capital at Khan-Baluc (the site of modern Beijing), Kublai ruled an empire that stretched all the way to Russia and included as well parts of the Islamic Middle East. Tibet, too, was included for a time in the Mongol Empire, but Tibet enjoyed something of a special status; after all, the Tibetan people were themselves descended from ancient Mongol clans.

Genghiz's son Godan Khan (father of Kublai Khan) was assigned the task of subduing Tibet. In 1239, his army began a series of sorties into the high country, throwing the feudal nobles of Tibet into an understandable fit of anxiety. Fearing that they lacked the strength to halt an all-out invasion, they prevailed on one of their own—Sakya Pandita, abbot of Sakya monastery—to meet with the Mongols in order to see whether negotiations were possible. In the year 1247, Pandita traveled on horseback to the northern frontier town of Lanzhou to meet with Godan Khan. It must have been quite a scene! Apparently, the Mongol warlord was quite impressed by the learned spiritual leader of the great monastery. He offered Pandita a deal: If the warrior nobility of Tibet would accept the suzerainty of the Mongols, there would be no invasion. The abbot of Sakya monastery would become, in effect, the viceroy of the Great Khan, who would rule Tibet through him. For all practical purposes, Tibet would become an autonomous state within the Mongol Empire; the khan would be recognized as overlord, but within Tibet, supreme religious *and* political power would be united in the person of the khan's viceroy, the abbot of Sakya Monastery.

When Pandita returned, he gathered together the other nobles and made a little speech, ticking off the practical advantages to the proposed arrangement. He is supposed to have ended with a statement that might have begun, "Oh, by the way, the number of their horsemen is beyond counting." To say the least, this was the most practical consideration of all. Despite resistance on the part of many of the noble families, the plan was accepted, and Sakya Pandita became something of a "Sakya pope." For almost a full century, his successors would hold, at least nominally, supreme temporal and religious authority within Tibet. Still, the Sakya authority was hotly challenged by many of the Tibetan nobles, so that it never really enjoyed anything close to absolute power.

Pandita was succeeded by his nephew, Sakya Phagpa, a young man of great intelligence and charm. His position of "Imperial Perceptor" of Tibet was reconfirmed by Kublai Khan, who by this time was the emperor of a freshly conquered China (a significant precedent in light of modern history). For the investiture ceremony, Phagpa journeyed to Kublai's fabulous capital. Kublai was deeply impressed by Phagpa and wanted to hear all about his Tibetan religion. It is said that at that time Kublai was hunting around for a suitable religious philosophy that could be used to spiritually unite his vast and checkered empire (shades of Ashoka). There's a wonderful story—maybe even true—that he invited learned representatives of the major religions of the empire to engage in a debate about the merits of their respective systems. Kublai himself would judge which one was best. There were Moslems, Christians, Daoists, and, of course, Buddhists. Phagpa himself argued on behalf of "Lamaism." Apparently, Kublai was more impressed by miracles than philosophical subtleties. According to the story, Phagpa was able to persuade a silver wine goblet, without a hand touching it, to rise from the table to the lips of the emperor. That settled it. Kublai decreed that henceforth Lamaism was to be promulgated as the "official" religion of the empire. At least among the Mongol people (if not the rest of the empire), Tibetan Buddhism did begin to spread its influence. [Incidentally, the losers in the great debate called foul, but they didn't accuse Phagpa of sleight of hand; rather they said he summoned the help of devils (definitely unfair).]

Mighty though it was at its inception, the Mongol Empire did not last for a long time. Hardly were the conquests complete than the whole thing began to fall apart. In China, Mongol rule, known in history as the Yuan Dynasty, lasted for less than a century, and in Tibet, the authority of the Sakya abbots weakened apace with the decline of Mongol power. The Tibetan nobility once again splintered into warring factions. Sakya leadership came to be largely rejected by the others, and during the latter half of the fourteenth century Tibet degenerated as it had before into near feudal anarchy. Naturally, the vigor of Tibetan Buddhism suffered along with all else. But the dark of the later fourteenth century was again the dark before the dawn. The great wheel of history was about to begin yet another turn.

The Third Period: The Era of the Dalai Lama

Once again, a great man came to the rescue; his name was Tsong Khapa. Unlike Padmasambhava and Atisha, who both came to Tibet from India, Tsong Khapa was a fully homegrown Tibetan. (His name literally means "man from the region of Tsong-kha.") According to a popular legend, in a previous life Tsong Khapa had known Shakyamuni Buddha, who predicted that one day his would be a powerful voice in the spreading of the Dharma. To say the least, a powerful voice was much needed in the early fifteenth century. Feeling that the existing sects were hopelessly mired in depravity and superstition, Tsong Khapa focused his reform effort on the establishment of an altogether new sect that would embody correct and rigorous principles of Buddhist monasticism, including the vow of celibacy. The new sect was called *Gelug-pa*, the "virtuous ones."

The traditional monk's robe in Tibet was reddish brown in color, but to distinguish themselves from these others, the Gelug-pa adopted a robe and hat that were somewhat yellowish. Since a conical hat was their most identifiable part, this difference led to the Gelug-pa being known as the "yellow hat" sect as opposed to the "red hats." Among the "red hats" were the men of Kadam-pa, the sect begun by Atisha three centuries before. As the Gelug-pa reform movement grew, the Kadam-pa was effectively absorbed into it; thus, the number of major sects remained at four.

Tsong Khapa founded several new Gelug-pa monasteries, the first of these being Ganden, which was begun in 1409 C.E. in the mountainous country about twenty-five miles east of Lhasa. Ganden became the preeminent Gelug-pa monastery and thus the place where the mortal remains of the founder were interred when he died ten years later. Before his death, though, Tsong Khapa created several other monasteries, among them Sera and Drepung, which were both close to Lhasa. Drepung grew to an incredible size. In the seventeenth century, it was home to more than ten thousand monks, making it by far the largest monastic community ever to have existed anywhere.

Tsong Khapa also turned the first spade at what would become the large and beautiful monastery of Tashi Lhunpo. This famous center of Tibetan Buddhism was established on the south bank of the Tsangpo, near the city of Xigaze (Shigatze), about one hundred and thirty miles southwest of Lhasa. The Grand Lama of Tashi Lhunpo would later be known as the Panchen Lama and would rival the Dalai Lama in spiritual authority (much more about that later). All of these historically important monasteries have survived into the modern day, although some were greatly damaged by Red Guards during the 1960s. (For political reasons, beautiful Tashi Lhunpo was left totally undamaged.)

Like Atisha, Tsong Khapa had a devoted nephew who was his right-hand man during the years of hard work. When Tsong Khapa died, the nephew, Gendun Grubpa, was given the title Grand Lama of Gelug-pa. (He became the *first* Grand Lama of Gelug-pa; Tsong Khapa, although he was the founder, had never been invested with the title.) When Gendun Grubpa died, the title was passed on to the second Grand Lama, Gendun Gyatso. Something else was passed on, too, something that would have immense significance in the future. It seems that Gendun Gyatso was very young when he was chosen to be the Grand Lama. He was born shortly after the death of Gendun Grubpa, and the leaders of Gelug-pa decreed that the "spirit" of the first Grand Lama had been reincarnated in the infant Gyatso. Gendun Gyatso was thus a *tulku*, a reincarnated lama. This fascinating custom was to become widespread within the monastic orders of Tibet. (We will have more to say about the process of selecting lamas shortly.)

The third Grand Lama of Gelug-pa was Sonam Gyatso. He, too, was said to be the tulku of his predecessor, and he was something more as well; Sonam Gyatso was the first to be named Dalai Lama. This is how it happened: The great growth of Gelug-pa had understandably aroused some anxiety in the other sects. Recall that the monasteries were intrinsically part of the feudal system of Tibet. Factions were constantly forming and reforming; small-scale feudal warfare was a part of the way of life of the nobility. Gelug-pa faced growing opposition from some of the others, particularly from groups within the Kagyu-pa sect, which was supported by some of the most powerful nobles of the land. All-out civil war was by no means out of the question. In looking around for ways to build up their base of support, leaders of Gelug-pa went so far as to sound out the Mongol warlord Altan Khan, chief of the Tumed Mongols. Even though Mongol power had declined substantially from what it had been at its height—they were no longer the emperors of China—the Mongol homeland to the north, "Mongolia" as we know it, was still a vast and powerful realm, and the Mongol horsemen were still very much a fighting force to be taken seriously.

As a result of these meetings, an alliance was concluded. In return for the promise of military help if needed, Sonam Gyatso officially recognized Altan Khan as "Ruler of Gods and King of the Dharma." Altan Khan then bestowed upon Gyatso the brand new title "Dalai Lama." The Tibean word *dalai* translates into English as "vast ocean"; thus, the term *Dalai Lama* means, more or less, the Grand Lama whose greatness is as "vast as the ocean." Sonam Gyatso, the third Grand Lama of Gelug-pa, was the one to receive the title, but he liked it so much that he wanted it to be more than merely his personal possession; he wanted it to become synonymous with being the Grand Lama of Gelug-pa. Consequently, he made the title retroactive to his two predecessors, and he, at least officially, became not the first Dalai Lama, but the third.

Meanwhile, Altan Khan was so pleased with the Tibetan connection that he and all of his subjects became Tibetan Buddhists of the Gelug-pa ("yellow") sect. This was no half-hearted adoption; the Mongols became wildly zealous followers of their new way. They even made it clear to their Tibetan Gelug-pa allies that they would be profoundly happy should the reincarnated spirit of the next Dalai Lama be discovered residing in the body of a young Mongol lad—and, wonder of wonders, that's exactly what happened. Shortly after the death of Sonam Gyatso in 1589, those entrusted with the search for his reincarnated tulku claimed that they had found him. Not only was the boy a Mongol, but amazingly, he was the great grandson of Altan Khan himself. He took the name *Yontan Gyatso* and became the fourth Dalai Lama, the Grand Lama of Gelug-pa.

This matter of the search for the reincarnated spirit of the Dalai Lama would become one of the most intriguing aspects of Tibetan Buddhism. Now would be a good time to look at how it's done. Tibetan men and women, just like everyone else, face the inevitability of death. As mentioned before, the common Tibetan yearns, though, to be reborn after death in Sukhavati, the "western paradise" of Buddha Amitabha. If this can't be, then the next best thing is to be reborn in human form, but in the best possible human form—that is, the one that is most likely to achieve rebirth in Sukhavati next time around. In this regard, it may be necessary to try again and again. One of the most important services of the Buddhist priest, as we have seen, is to assist a person at the time of death so that his or her spirit will achieve either Sukhavati or the most favorable rebirth that can be had. In any case, the possibility of reincarnation is a common belief among the Tibetan people. It is an accepted fact that virtually everyone is a reincarnated being.

Some few, however, are very special reincarnations. They are already enlightened beings who, out of deep compassion, *choose* to be reincarnated in human form in order to be of help to their still-unenlightened brothers and sisters. Such a person, generally a lama, is called a *tulku*. A tulku, then, is a reincarnated lama who is reborn in order to help lead others to enlightenment. A tulku gives signs that others can use to identify the specific person in which the spirit has been reborn. In this way, a lineage can be established. The faithful can feel confident, for example, that over many generations the Grand Lama of a particular monastery has been one great spirit, reincarnated over and over, each time successfully identified by the leading lamas of that monastery. For the past five centuries, the most important lineage in Tibet has been that of the Dalai Lama. There have been fourteen historical Dalai Lamas. To the faithful, however, there has really been only *one* Dalai Lama, incarnated and re-incarnated fourteen times, and not merely the reincarnation of a highly enlightened lama, but of Avalokiteshvara himself, the bodhisattva of infinite compassion.

Here again, we confront the dichotomy between the basic Buddhist teaching that ultimately there is no "one" to be reborn and the custom of behaving as if reincarnation is real, indeed. However one might choose to interpret the traditional teachings, the stated view is that when a Dalai Lama dies, his "spirit" is shortly afterward reincarnated in the body of a newborn baby. It thus becomes a matter of prime importance to locate that child and see to it that he is properly groomed for the life that is his destiny. To this end, the leading lamas of Gelug-pa gather at the time of the death of a Dalai Lama. The very first order of business is to conduct an investigation into the deceased's words and activities in the days just preceding death. Perhaps the words hold some clues that will help in the search—some repeated utterance, for example. Or perhaps the dying lama has exhibited some unusual behavior. The leading lamas will also examine the embalmed corpse carefully. In one case, we are told, the embalmed body kept realigning its position as if by magic. It was laid out each night so that the head was pointing to the north, but in the morning the position of the body had changed so that the head was pointing east. This was interpreted as a clear sign that the search should be made to the east of Lhasa.

The search committee also consults with the official oracle of Tibet, located at Nechung Monastery in Lhasa, and by long-standing tradition visits the sacred lake of Hlamo Latso, approximately ninety miles southeast of Lhasa. Committee members might spend several days at the lakeside, contemplating its surface with almost trance-like attention. It is believed that apparitions produced by mists rising from the lake can provide powerful clues. One might see a vision of particular kind of house, for instance, or a tree in bloom, or a geographic landmark. Finally, when all of the preliminary information has been gathered and studied, the real search is ready to begin. This might take many months or even years. Advance units of the search group are likely to travel in disguise, dressed as ordinary pilgrims. At last, a promising candidate is identified. This, of course, will be a little boy, often about two years old by the time he is found. Now he is put to the test.

The highest lamas conduct the examination of the child. They watch with the keenest interest to see if he exhibits any of the knowledge or personal traits of the recently deceased Dalai Lama. Part of the procedure is to place before the child various objects that belonged to the deceased—things such as rosaries, scarves, prayer wheels, and perhaps a walking stick. Mixed in with these will be exact replicas. If the boy is truly the tulku they are looking for, he will, it is presumed, recognize his own things and pick up the right ones. The whole examination is quite elaborate, and the modern reader can't help but wonder how much unconscious prodding goes into it. In any case, when the little boy succeeds in convincing these visiting dignitaries that he is indeed the reincarnation of the Dalai Lama, it is a cause for great rejoicing.

When all is ready, an entourage of notables will escort the young tulku to Lhasa, where, during a lengthy ceremony of investiture, he will be officially presented as the new Dalai Lama. (His family, by the way, will most likely accompany him and take up comfortable residence nearby.) Now begins the long process of grooming the child so that by the time he is a man he will be fully able to take his place as the leader of the country. He will be thoroughly educated in all of the traditional disciplines, including philosophy and theology. Eventually, he must pass grueling oral examinations in order to win his scholarly degrees. In addition, he will be trained in all of the monastic disciplines. The Dalai Lama is a full-fledged ordained monk of the Gelug-pa order; it is *expected* that he will observe all of the vows, including celibacy. The young Dalai Lama grows up in a highly controlled environment, and if all goes well, by the time he is a young adult he will have been molded into a man of exceptional abilities. As Dalai Lama, he will be able to play the role of priest–king with wisdom and virtue.

Defenders of this unique way of producing a national leader argue that it is the best of all possible ways. To begin with, the risky problems of hereditary rule are totally avoided. From out of the rich variety of the general population, a child of sound mind and body is selected and then most carefully educated for the role of leadership. He is tutored by the best in every field and is raised in an environment of Buddhist monastic discipline. From the time he is a little boy he is encouraged to identify with the highest ideals of Buddhist teaching. Not only are the risks of hereditary rule avoided, but so also the risks of the elective system. There are no rival cliques promoting their candidates—no cliques, no political parties, no feuding aristocratic families—all of this is avoided. The entire system gets a fresh start each time. (It doesn't really matter whether one interprets the selection procedure literally or metaphorically; in either case, it can be reasoned that it is an excellent way to select and groom one for supreme leadership.)

One potential problem with the system, though, is that the new Dalai Lama must necessarily be a young child. Hence, for many years the tasks of leadership will have to be in the hands of others. These others are called *regents*, and although every effort may be made to appoint dedicated and selfless men to the post of regent, there remains nonetheless the real possibility that self-serving individuals may come to occupy these powerful positions. Throughout much of the past five centuries, the regents, not the Dalai Lama, have been in control of Tibet's government, and their rule has not been entirely innocent of palace intrigues and feuding factions. Still, for the most part, this very unusual system has worked well and has enjoyed the passionate support of the Tibetan people. Incidentally, the obvious advantages of the tulku system were not lost on the other sects. Before long, the leading lamas of virtually all monasteries were proclaimed to be tulkus. The Dalai Lama, however—the reincarnation of Avalokiteshvara—has remained the paramount tulku of the land down to modern times.

The fourth Dalai Lama died in 1617, and the search began immediately for his successor. The fifth Dalai Lama was named Nagwan Losang Gyatso, but his reign was so tremendously important in the history of Tibetan Buddhism that he is generally referred to simply as the "Great Fifth." It was largely the work of his reign that established the character of Tibetan Buddhism that has come down to the present. He was born in 1617 C.E., and took over full personal responsibility of rule in 1640 at the age of twenty-three. The first order of business was to deal with the growing opposition of the other sects and their client noble families. The threat of civil war was again in the air. Losang dealt with this danger by taking the dramatic step of calling upon his Mongol allies for help. The Mongol response was an all-out invasion of Tibet. Under the warlord Gursi Khan, Tibetan resistance was crushed and the entire land was subjugated. But this was not a Mongol conquest; it was a military operation for the purpose of establishing the uncontested authority of their friend and ally, the Dalai Lama, who now became the undisputed all-powerful ruler of Tibet. Temporal power and spiritual authority were united in the office of the Dalai Lama. In 1650, the Chinese emperor confirmed the supreme political and religious authority of the Dalai Lama within Tibet.

But the Great Fifth wanted even more. It was already accepted that, as the Grand Lama of Gelug-pa, he was a tulku, the reincarnation of his predecessor. What Losang added to this was the assertion that the spirit being reincarnated in the line of Dalai Lamas was none other than that of Avalokiteshvara, the great bodhisattva companion of Buddha Amitabha, the presiding Buddha of Sukhavati, the Western Paradise. In effect, Losang was saying that he was the flesh-and-blood incarnation of Avalokiteshvara, and so was every other Dalai Lama, past and future. This was quite a declaration, and it was received with enthusiastic acceptance. And it didn't stop there. Having declared himself to be the incarnation of Avalokiteshvara, Losang then went on to magnanimously declare the Panchen Lama, the Grand Lama of Tashi Lhunpo, to be the incarnation of Amitabha Buddha! This might seem to suggest that the Dalai Lama, as the incarnation of Avalokiteshvara, was actually inferior in status to the Panchen Lama. In the convoluted doctrinal logic of Tibetan Buddhism, however, that was not the case—at least, not so far as worldly affairs were concerned. Thus could the people of Tibet celebrate the wonderful news that the spirits of Amitabha and Avalokiteshvara were dwelling with them and leading them, not simply in a mystical, religious sense, but in the flesh-and-blood persons of the Dalai Lama and the Panchen Lama.

The Potala; Lhasa, Tibet. (P. Bresnan)

It was a golden day for Tibetan Buddhism in general and for Gelug-pa in particular—and the Great Fifth used it to full advantage. He used his power and prestige to greatly expand the Gelug-pa establishment throughout Tibet. Fences were mended with his former opponents, and Tibetan Buddhism entered upon a new day of prosperity and growth. The symbol of the new age was the construction of that most fabulous symbol of Tibet, the Potala.

Rising in lofty tiers from its Lhasa hilltop, the huge thirteen-story Potala is surely one of the architectural wonders of the world. Its magnificent white-and-red facade, crowned by golden rooftops, is synonymous with the charm and mystery of Tibet. It seems more like a beautiful dream than a real place. It is believed that the name *Potala* was derived from the name of the mystical south Indian hermitage of the Hindu deity Shiva. Tibetans regard Shiva to be closely related to Avalokiteshvara. From the beginning, the Potala was intended to be much more than just a residence for the Dalai Lama; it housed as well a small monastery, a museum and archives of Tibetan Buddhist history, and a meeting hall for the Tibetan National Assembly. Don't let this last name mislead you. The National Assembly was in no way a democratic congress; it was a feudal assembly drawn from the great aristocratic families of Tibet whose only purpose was to advise the Dalai Lama.

Beginning with Nagwan Losang, the Great Fifth, every Dalai Lama down to the present time has, at least officially, occupied the splendid residence located at the top of the central section of the Potala. The current Dalai Lama, the fourteenth, fled to India in 1959 and since that time has occupied a considerably more modest residence in exile.

The Potala today, stripped of its former sacredness, has become a national museum. Common footsteps now tred daily in places formerly forbidden to all but the gods and those close to the gods.

The Great Fifth died in 1670, but oddly enough, the news of his death was not made public until 1682. At the time of his death, the Potala was still unfinished, and supposedly the death was concealed so as to avoid any chance that the Potala might not be completed. During the twelve years after Nagwan Losang's death, Tibet was governed by the regent Sangye Gyatso, a most unusual man. It is widely believed that he was actually the son of the Great Fifth, and he used his influential position in the palace to create a political clique that supported his own control of power. Eventually, a search for the new Dalai Lama was launched. We may assume that Sangye was fully in control of the procedure, and if keeping real power in his own hands was what Sangye yearned for, he couldn't have been happier with the outcome.

The new Dalai Lama, Tsangyang Gyatso, installed in 1697, grew up with no interest whatsoever in the responsibilities of rule. In fact, he was said to be a libertine who spent much of his time carousing and drinking to excess. He and his drinking buddies were well known in the brothels and seamier establishments of Lhasa. Tsangyang Gyatso was not even a fully ordained monk of the Gelug-pa sect. He refused to take the final vows, preferring instead the life of wine, women, and song. Nevertheless, he was the Dalai Lama, and, we are told, he was accepted by the Tibetan people, who rationalized his earthy lifestyle as being but a chimera. Others, however, were not in a mood to be so generous. In 1706 a Mongol force invaded Tibet, specifically to depose (and later murder) the completely intolerable Tsangyang Gyatso. The regent, Sangye, was also put to death.

At this point, the story takes an interesting and fateful turn. The rulership of China was again in foreign hands, this time the Manchus and a people related to the Mongols and whose vast homeland lay to the north and northeast of China. The Manchu emperors believed they had rights—and responsibilities—where Tibet was concerned. In 1720 the Manchu emperor, Kang Xi (K'ang Hsi), intervened in a big way—and, of course, he possessed potentially sufficient military strength to fully back up his action. The first thing Kang Xi did was to brush aside the man that the Mongols had put in Tsangyang Gyatso's place, installing instead Kalzan Gyatso, who officially became the seventh Dalai Lama.

In name, Kalzan Gyatso was an independent ruler, but in reality, he was a puppet of the Chinese emperor, and this is essentially the way the relationship would remain until the fall of the Manchu Dynasty in 1912. Kang Xi declared Tibet to be a Protectorate of the Chinese Empire, dispatching "ambans" to Lhasa—official Chinese representatives whose task it was to oversee the administration of Tibetan affairs and report back to the emperor's government. It was the beginning of a two-century-long period of Chinese control over the internal affairs of Tibet.

Insofar as Tibetan Buddhism was concerned, matters did not change substantially as a result of the closer Chinese connection. The Gelug-pa sect remained paramount, and the Dalai Lama continued—at least so far as outward appearances were concerned—to exercise kingly rule over Tibet in both the worldly and the spiritual realms. The office of the Panchen Lama, however, grew steadily more powerful. The Chinese developed strong ties to both the Dalai Lama and the Panchen Lama and were not altogether averse to playing one against the other.

With the installation of Kalzan Gyatso, the seventh Dalai Lama, Tibet entered into a long and rather stagnant period characterized by strong ties to the Manchu government of China. In 1912, however, the aging Manchu regime finally collapsed. For a time, China became a democratic republic under the leadership of Sun Yat-sen and, later, under Chiang Kai-shek. But the republic was destined to know only a brief life. In 1949, Mao Zedong (Mao Tse-tung), leader of the People's Revolutionary Army, overthrew the democratic government, establishing in its place the People's Republic of China. A thoroughgoing Marxist system was established in China, and once again the ages-old connection with Tibet was restored by military force. Things might still have worked out reasonably well; after all, Tibet had existed for centuries under Chinese suzerainty. So long as that arrangement was accepted, the old ways had been allowed to continue without much interference. Initially, the Marxist government seemed inclined to continue the policy. But all that was about to change—dramatically.

Fearing that the aging party leaders were straying far from the righteous path of Marxist revolution, Mao Zedong sought to inspire the youth of China with a new communist fervor; then, filled with revolutionary zeal, they were to be unleashed on the country. Their energy, he hoped, would reinvigorate the revolution. Their energy, however, gave birth to a monster totally out of control. By the millions, they formed into paramilitary brigades known as Red Guards whose sole purpose was to cleanse China of every taint of "imperialist" corruption and to erect a thoroughgoing Marxist utopia. Beginning in October of 1966, the fire raged for a decade. During that time, China was convulsed in a revolutionary terror determined to destroy the old and create the new. Universities were closed, and "intellectuals" were killed off or forced to go into the country and work on farms, most of which were collectivized according to the communist model. All traces of religious life were mercilessly persecuted. (It was a time in Chinese history suggestive of the years known as "The Terror" during the dark days of the French Revolution.)

Tibet felt the full brunt of the Cultural Revolution. Red Guards sought to totally destroy what they saw as a corrupt feudal system in which the elite privileged class ruthlessly exploited the peasant masses, who were deliberately held in a degraded state of ignorance and poverty. The Red Guards saw the monastery system as the principal upholder of this depraved order. They would root it out altogether. Thousands of monasteries were destroyed, often systematically blown up with dynamite. Monks were slaughtered or forced to return to their families. Uncountable numbers of Buddhist art objects were demolished. Their destructive zeal was fierce; it's a wonder that anything is left! (If it weren't for all that dynamite, doesn't this seem like a *déjà vu* experience? Remember Lang Darma and the Great Persecution of the mid-ninth century?)

With the death of Mao in 1976 the Cultural Revolution quickly collapsed. More responsible figures within the Communist Party regained control of the People's Republic of China. The excesses were repudiated, and the leaders of the Cultural Revolution (including Mao's wife) were jailed or executed. A new policy of tolerance replaced the hysteria. But the damage had been done—a *great deal* of damage. Nonetheless, the slow process of rebuilding began immediately. However, nothing would ever be the same again. Tibet was now wholly annexed to the People's Republic of China, and a full-scale policy of integration was put into action. The once-isolated and independent culture of Tibet, it would seem, had become a thing of the past. Like it or not, the days of the ancient culture were over.

So where does that leave us? Now that the dust has settled (or at least is settling), we can see that Tibetan Buddhism faces a whole new situation. Tibet itself is now a part of the People's Republic of China, which exercises tight control over the Buddhist establishment. Revolutionary changes have destroyed or swept away much of the traditional order. The monastery system has been enormously reduced in size, wealth, and power. In effect, the feudal establishment that the monastery system was a part of has been abolished. The old aristocracy, both temporal and spiritual, has been largely killed off or driven out of the country. The Dalai Lama, along with thousands of others, is in exile, and the Potala has been converted into a people's museum.

But not all of the news is grim; there is a bright side to this picture, too. Most important of all, Tibetan Buddhism is far from annihilated. However diminished, it is at least recovering to some degree within Tibet. Recall, too, that Tibet is not the only home of "Tibetan" Buddhism; we might more properly speak of Himalayan Buddhism or of the Vajrayana Buddhism of the Himalayan lands. Regions adjoining Tibet, such as Nepal, Sikkim, Bhutan, Mustang, and Ladach, were not affected at all by the Chinese action, and there the old traditions still survive to some extent. Most significant, though, is the work of the Tibetan refugees who have taken up residence in many places around the globe. This Tibetan diaspora has sown the seeds of new growth that may well usher in a new age in the long tradition of Tibetan Buddhism.

Perhaps that's what it's all about. When we step back and look at the big picture, it has all the earmarks of the beginning of a whole new era. The Rip Van Winkle of traditional Tibetan Buddhism was violently awakened in the mid-twentieth century, but it has come through the ordeal lean, reformed, and ready to take on the future. No one can say what that future will be. Perhaps someday the Dalai Lama will be welcomed back to Tibet. Or perhaps the Gelug-pa sect has run out its allotted time in history. The fourteenth Dalai Lama has let it be known that he is seriously considering the possibility of not being reincarnated again. It could be that the Nyingma-pa is poised to close the circle, restoring its own ancient lineage to preeminence. As mentioned before, California's Odiyan may be the symbol of a reincarnate Samye, and Tibetan Buddhism may be about to take on a new life stemming from a resuscitated version of its own original beginning. Or it may be that the time is ripe for the founding of an altogether new sect. Perhaps a modern Tsong Khapa is waiting to make his (or her) entry onto the stage of history.

We can speculate on and on; many directions are possible. But one thing seems certain: Tibetan Buddhism will remain firmly grounded in the teachings of Mahayana Buddhism in general and Vajrayana Buddhism in particular. The ancient tradition of Tibetan Buddhism is alive and well, and whatever form it takes in the years ahead, it will have much of value to offer the world of the twenty-first century.

Notes

1. John Powers, *Introduction to Tibetan Buddhism* (Ithaca, NY: Snow Lion Pubs., 1995), p. 228.
2. Lama Anagarika Govinda, *Fundamentals of Tibetan Mysticism* (New York: Samuel Weisner, 1960), pp. 123–124.
3. Powers, p. 432.
4. L. Austine Waddell, *Tibetan Buddhism* (New York: Dover, 1972), p. 570.
5. After an account in Powers, p. 137.
6. Waddell, p. 74.

Study Questions

1. How did it happen that Padmasambhava was invited to Tibet? Why do some say that he was the real founder of Tibetan Buddhism?

2. What is Vajrayana? How does it fit into the general picture of Mahayana Buddhism? In what ways does Vajrayana reveal its Tantric origins?

3. What is the place of Shakyamuni Buddha in Vajrayana?

4. What is the place of sadhana practice in Vajrayana? How do all of the various possible elements fit together?

5. How does Tibetan Buddhism deal with the matter of reincarnation? Are there various approaches to the interpretation of this matter?

6. How did the title *Dalai Lama* come into existence? What is the relationship of the Dalai Lama to the Panchen Lama?

7. What was so great about the "Great Fifth"?

8. On what does China base its claim to rightful suzerainty over Tibet?

9. How do you assess the state of affairs of Tibetan Buddhism in the present day? What does the future hold?

14.

Early Buddhism in China

The source of the Mahayana revolution was that now-familiar region in the northwestern part of the Indian subcontinent. In the early centuries of the common era, Mahayana Buddhism radiated out from there, ultimately traveling great distances. (In fact, it's still traveling.) Much of north India was influenced by Mahayana, but Buddhism's days were numbered in its Indian homeland. Over the next several centuries, Buddhism in India would slowly fade into insignificance. In some ways, it would become almost indistinguishable from Hinduism. Those Buddhist communities which did endure were ultimately all but destroyed by foreign invaders, first the Huns in the second century C.E. and finally the Turkish Mughals, whose brutal conquest of India began in the eleventh century. By this time, though, Buddhism—especially Mahayana Buddhism—was alive and well in many places outside of India.

Geographically close to India is Tibet, and as we have seen, Mahayana, or more specifically, Vajrayana, Buddhism traveled up into the high country, where it became solidly established. To travel farther afield, Mahayana had to hitch a ride on that fascinating highway of trade that we know as the Silk Road. As noted earlier, the Silk Road was an extremely long caravan route that connected China with the other parts of the Eurasian continent. Much more than silk was traded, though; everything imaginable made its way back and forth between East and West and, thanks to a subsidiary route, south into India as well. Buddhist ideas, Buddhist books, and even Buddhist monks entered the flow and moved with it wherever the Silk Road might take them. The lands to the west were not particularly receptive, however. During late Roman times the institutional monolith of the Christian Church presented a bulwark of resistance, and beginning in the late seventh century, the Church was superseded by the even more intransigent resistance posed by the rise of Islam.

Toward the east, though, it was a different story. Mahayana Buddhism would eventually make its way into China and become thoroughly integrated into that culture. But there was an intermediate step that most people in the modern world have never heard about.

Near the center of the map of Eurasia is a well-defined oval depression named the Takla Makan. Today one of the world's most formidable deserts, the Takla Makan ranks with the Sahara in heat and lifeless aridity. It is a nearly thousand-mile-wide sea of scub grasses and shifting sand dunes. But it wasn't always that way. Tens of thousands of years ago, a large part of the Takla Makan was a lake. That was when much of the northern hemisphere was covered with ice. Then, about ten thousand years ago, the ice began to retreat. By the time Mahayana appeared on the scene, the lake was gone and the desert was well established. But there was still a good deal of residual glaciation in the higher elevations of the mountains that surround the Takla Makan. Continual glacial melt fed numerous rivers that plunged out of the mountains and into the desert, where they eventually petered out and disappeared. But along the fringes of the desert, at the base of the mountains, there was a margin of well-watered and fertile land. Here were to be found many towns, some of them quite large, that grew rich on the trade passing through the Takla Makan region.

When it reached the desert of the Takla Makan, the Silk Road necessarily split into a northern route and a southern route. In the extreme west, caravans traveling westward stopped at the cosmopolitan city of Kashgar just before heading into the treacherous passes of the Pamir Range. Kashgar is still there, but today's city is only a tiny hint of what it used to be. Kashgar was a major stopping place, and transfer place, for the caravans traveling the Silk Road. At its height, the exotic bazaars of Kashgar rivaled those of Istanbul. Everything in the world was available in Kashgar, for the right price.

Kashgar was not a Chinese city, but at the eastern end of the Takla Makan the routes converged on Dunhuang (Tun-huang), the farthest western outpost of Chinese civilization. Dunhuang was a lot like Kashgar, but it was decidedly Chinese. A section of the Great Wall—the farthest west it would go—was constructed to the area of Dunhuang. From there, it was another thousand-mile journey to the great city of Changan, the imperial capital of China in those days.

Changan, now known as Xian,* is a capital city no longer, and the original character of Dunhuang has disappeared entirely. So, too, have the glaciers and the rich life of the towns and cities they nourished around the perimeter of the Takla Makan. But in the days when water poured from the mountains and goods moved on the caravan routes, Buddhism became established in the area and flourished for several centuries. It was a mini-"golden age" that history has largely forgotten. Numerous Buddhist monasteries were established in the area, some actually out in parts of the desert where water was still available at that time. These monasteries were surprisingly rich treasure-houses of Buddhist art and scholarship. Some of them were home to hundreds of monks. Then—as is the fate of all things eventually—this happy age came to an end. The drying up of the highlands was only a part of the story, though undoubtedly a big part. Nature was assisted by a series of invasions; Mongol tribesmen from the north and, later, the conquest of the area by Islam. One by one the monasteries were destroyed or aban-

---

*It was near Xian that the amazing army of full-size terra cotta figures was discovered in 1974. The site is still being excavated.

doned. In time, the sands covered their remains and they were forgotten. By the end of the eighth century, nothing much was left of the region's once-great Buddhist culture.

Thus did the remains of this great historical legacy lie unnoticed beneath the desert sands for more than a millennium. Interest in the area was revived in nineteenth-century Europe as the study of history and archaeology began to take its modern form. Unfortunately, it wasn't quite modern enough yet. With no strong government to control research in the area, freebooting self-styled "archaeologists" ransacked the region in the late nineteenth and early twentieth centuries, plundering everything they could find. Their "excavations" more often looked like battlefields than careful research sites. Monastery libraries were looted of their manuscripts, well preserved in the dry desert conditions. Much artwork, too, was stolen, some of it chiseled directly from the walls of monastery rooms and shipped back to museums in Europe and America that were willing to pay top dollar for these treasures. Finally, in 1920, the Chinese government moved to halt the plunder, and today what is left is being properly studied and exhibited. Enough remains to dazzle the eye and convince the world of Buddhist studies that in the region of the now desolate Takla Makan Buddhism once flourished. It was from there that Buddhism launched the beginning of its gentle conquest of China.

The earliest Chinese Buddhist document that is widely accepted as being historically verifiable comes to us from the middle of the second century C.E. It is a fragment of the Pali Canon translated into Chinese by a scholar named An Shigao (An Shih-kao). There is reason to believe, however, that Buddhist monks had been spreading the good word in China for a full century before that. Thus, Buddhism first encountered Chinese culture during the time of the Han Empire, a time when China was unified and the governing class was strong. The Han Empire was to the far eastern parts of Eurasia what the Roman Empire was to the far western parts. They coexisted during the first and second centuries C.E.

During the time of Han, there was some resistance to Buddhism from Confucians, who, as a group, held virtually all important government posts. Buddhist roots grew slowly at first. But the Han Empire, like the Roman, was destined to fall. The Great Wall had kept the barbarous hordes of the north at bay for five centuries, but in the third century C.E. they finally broke through, overwhelming China and plunging much of the land into an era of tumult and division. (It's a fascinating story; two centuries later, descendants of these invaders, known to history as the Huns, would wreak the same kind of havoc on Roman Europe.) In the aftermath of the fall of Han, Buddhism grew rapidly in China. So, in sum, we can say that Buddhism entered China during the first century C.E., grew relatively slowly for its first couple of centuries, and then began to spread rapidly.

Like so many other countries, the land of China is divided into a "north" and a "south." Speaking very broadly, northern China centers on the basin of the Yellow River (the Huang Ho), and the south centers on the great Yangtse, one of the longest and mightiest rivers in all of Eurasia. The invaders overran only the northern parts of China. Many people, especially from the upper classes, fled to the south, where the traditional culture, if not the empire form of government, was preserved. Life was far from peaceful, though; for three centuries all parts of China would be convulsed by constant warfare and shifting borders. Slowly, very slowly, the Chinese people would win back the land of the north, but it would not be until the year 589 C.E. that all of China would be reunited. In that year, the Sui Dynasty was established, and the bad old days were over, at least for a while.

Buddhism became solidly established in China during the turbulent three centuries that separate the fall of Han and the rise of Sui. There were a number of reasons for this, the most obvious being that Confucian officials lost their position of power with the fall of Han and thus were not able to offer effective resistance to this "foreign" influence. In northern China, the very foreignness of Buddhism worked to its advantage; the conquering warlords of the north were attracted to the fact that Buddhism was not a native Chinese system. In the south, though, where Confucian and Daoist scholarship continued to flourish, Buddhism succeeded *despite* its still-evident foreign character.

Little by little, the original hostility changed to curiosity and, finally, to warmth. But why? Why did Buddhism eventually experience a friendly reception in China? What was the appeal? What did this exotic philosophy have to offer to a people who already possessed a rich and ancient civilization? This is a very interesting question, especially when one stops to consider that, with the exception of Marxism, Buddhism is the *only* foreign philosophy of life ever to be integrated into the culture of China (and the jury is still out with regard to the enduring effect of Marxism).

For one thing, the essentials of Buddhism did not really stand in conflict with the teachings of Daoism and Confucius. There was a resonance among them, especially between the philosophies of Buddhism and Daoism. Apparently, Buddhism's emphasis on disciplined meditation was a strong part of its initial appeal. Meditation in the broad sense of the word was a part of the Daoist way of life, but it was ill defined. Buddhist meditation would give a new and dynamic form to this latent potential of Daoism. One cannot help but think of a similar situation that exists in the modern Western world, where we have seen a succession of Indian gurus promoting various schools of meditation. Huge numbers of Westerners have been excited by this "new blood" from old India. Perhaps something like that was part of Buddhism's early days in China.

This "resonance," though, went much deeper than simply a shared interest in meditation. Buddhism did not work a *revolution* in China; rather, it helped to bring out and give clearer form to attitudes that were already inherent in Chinese philosophy. This was true even at the deepest levels. For example, the Daoist belief that all things have non-being as their origin was in harmony with the Buddhist teaching that all things by nature are empty. As Heinrich Dumoulin points out, "Buddhists were especially impressed by the Chinese rejection of the duality between being and non-being, and by their emphasis on the ineffability of reality."[1]

Before long, the entire vast world of Buddhist scripture was being translated into Chinese. What an undertaking that must have been! In some places, government-sponsored "Translation Bureaus" were established. The languages, like the cultures, were very different. Finding appropriate words in Chinese was no easy task. Since Daoism seemed to have the closest philosophical affinity to Buddhism, Daoist terms were widely used in the work of translation. Just as Christians are sometimes accused of "baptizing" Aristotle in translating his works into Latin, the Chinese to some extent "Daoicized"

Buddha. It was the beginning of a process of development that would eventually result in a thoroughly Chinese Buddhism.

We can't overstate the scope or the importance of the work of translating the vast literature, especially the Buddhist sutras, into Chinese. In this connection, one name stands out with singular greatness. We know him as Kumarajiva. Born in 344 C.E., Kumarajiva studied for many years at a Theravadin monastery in Kashmir, that fertile ground of Buddhism up in the northwestern part of India. He started out as a Theravadin, but the exciting new ways of Mahayana were in the air and, in time, got into his blood. Finally, he relocated from Kashmir over the mountains to Kashgar, where before long he began to make a name for himself in the work of translation. His fame spread to China, and at long last he took up residence in the great city of Changan. Kumarajiva headed a large Translation Bureau in Changan, focusing mainly on translating the Mahayana sutras into Chinese. His most important work was the meticulous translation of the *Prajnaparamita* and the related works of Nagarjuna into Chinese. These works had a tremendous impact on the developing character of Chinese Buddhism. Given the fundamental importance of the *Prajnaparamita* in Chinese Buddhism, it's no exaggeration to say that Kumarajiva was largely responsible for the ultimate ascendancy of Mahayana in China. "That the Chinese showed a preference for Mahayana over Hinayana is due principally to the wisdom teachings of the *Prajnaparamita* sutras, which they found to resonate deeply with their own spiritual heritage."[2]

Kumarajiva died at the age of sixty-three in 409 C.E. By this time, Buddhism—in particular, Mahayana Buddhism—was well on the way to becoming an established part of the culture in all parts of China. The Mahayana sutras, newly translated from Sanskrit into the Chinese language, provided a base from which many different "schools" of Buddhism would grow. Not all of these schools emerged immediately—some would not take final form until the sixth or even the seventh century—but the net effect was a broad proliferation of Buddhist sects in China. All, however, shared common roots in the Mahayana sutras. Let me mention just a few of the better known ones; they are representative of the wide variety of possibilities.

TIANTAI BUDDHISM (T'IEN-T'AI)

Tiantai takes its name from Mount Tiantai, where, in the sixth century, a monk named Zhiyi (Chih-i) founded a monastery and initiated this new school of teaching. It would be transplanted to Japan in the ninth century, where it would become known as Tendai Buddhism. Although Zhiyi is recognized as the founder of Tiantai, he was (as is so often the case) largely responsible for pulling together and giving a coherent form to currents that had been developing for centuries before his time. Zhiyi played the role of a peacemaker, a compromise maker, who brought together the disparate and often feuding members of the family of Buddhist teaching in China. Tiantai Buddhism became something of a syncretistic school in which all of the elements of Buddhist teaching could live in harmony.

As the vast storehouse of Buddhist scripture was translated into Chinese, many were puzzled by its seeming inconsistencies and even contradictions. How could Buddha have been so inconsistent in his teaching? This was especially problematic with regard to the doctrinal disputes between Mahayana and Theravada. How was one to ferret out the true teaching from all of this?

Tiantai solved the problem by proclaiming that *all* of it was true teaching. Differences were to be explained not as contradictions, but as having originated in different *levels* or *periods* in Buddha's teaching career. According to Tiantai, the total message of Buddha's teaching unfolded in five distinct periods following his awakening. The first of these lasted for only three weeks. This was the time, immediately after his awakening, when Buddha gave the teachings that subsequenty found their way into the *Avatamsaka Sutra*. To his surprise, Buddha discovered that this teaching was too deep for his disciples; they were not yet ready to understand its message. He therefore changed gears and for twelve years taught the very fundamental doctrine to be found in the Theravada sutras. In this, the second period, he introduced such matters as the Four Noble Truths and the Noble Eightfold Path. In the third period, which lasted for eight years, he gave his disciples the elementary Mahayana sutras, stressing the superior worth of the bodhisattva over that of the arhat. Then, for a full twenty-two years, he gave the "wisdom teachings" that were to appear in the *Prajnaparamita* Sutra It took this long time to fully work out the Doctrine of Emptiness and its implications. Finally, in the fifth period, the final eight years of his life, Buddha proclaimed the teachings of the *Lotus Sutra*, which brought everything together, resolving all dichotomies and revealing the absolute identity of all contrasts.

It's a wonderful approach. Tiantai dissolves all conflicts within the Buddhist fold, most notably that between Theravada and Mahayana. Theravadins might not have appreciated being relegated to the most immature ground floor, but there weren't really many Theravadins in China anyway; Mahayana had succeeded in claiming the field almost entirely for itself. The problem was not one of resolving difficulties with Theravadin *groups*, but with Theravadin *sutras*, the basic sutras of the Pali Canon. The Tiantai approach was an excellent solution to this problem. *All* of the sutras had an important place, but in the most cherished place of all was the lordly *Lotus Sutra*. This became the bible of Tiantai Buddhism.

According to the teaching of Tiantai, the most significant dichotomy resolved by the correct understanding of the *Lotus Sutra* concerned the philosophical problem regarding the reality of the phenomenal world. In revealing the innermost meaning of the *Prajnaparamita*, the great Nagarjuna had established the ultimate and absolute reality of emptiness. What, then, of the phenomenal world, the world of everyday experience? In the minds of many, there existed an uncomfortable feeling that the implications of the Doctrine of Emptiness undermined any *real* value in the stuff of ordinary daily life. After all, how can there be value in what is fundamentally ignorance and illusion?

Without getting into complicated details, suffice it to say that Tiantai had a solution for this problem, too. Zhiyi and his followers taught what was called the Threefold Truth. In its simplest terms, the Threefold Truth holds that, fundamentally, all indeed is emptiness; this is the ultimate truth of reality. But the phenomenal world—which emerges from emptiness—has a *temporary* reality. The appearance of permanence may indeed be illusory, but the phenomenal world is not chimera; it truly exists, at least in some form, in order to be the material of our experiences. Thus, both worlds are real. Absolute emptiness is the ultimate nature of reality, but all phenomena are *expressions* of the absolute, albeit in a temporary sense. The synthesis of emptiness and temporary existence—the fact that something can be both empty and temporary at the same time—is a "middle" truth, the all-important Third Truth of the Tiantai system. Ultimately, the absolute and the phenomenal are one. In this way, everyday life is affirmed as an expression of the absolute. Everyday life is the Buddha-nature.

HUAYAN BUDDHISM (HUA-YEN)

Like Tiantai, Huayan Buddhism began to take on a coherent form in sixth-century China. Huayan Buddhism had much in common with Tiantai Buddhism. Both held that Buddha's teaching unfolded in five distinct periods, although the two schools differed somewhat with regard to the particulars of the periods. Also, the doctrine of both schools centered on one of the sutras. But whereas Tiantai focused on the *Lotus Sutra*, alleged to be the last of Buddha's sutras, Huayan based its teaching on the *Avatamsaka Sutra*, regarded by most in Mahayana to be the *first* of Buddha's sutras. The name *Huayan*, in fact, is the Chinese translation of the Sanskrit *Avatamsaka*. In both languages, it has the literal meaning of "flower garland."

Like Tiantai, Huayan was concerned with the nature of absolute reality, but unlike Tiantai, the focus of Huayan was much more directed toward relationships within the world of phenomenal reality. The message of the *Avatamsaka*, and hence the thrust of the teaching of Huayan, is the inherent mutual interrelationship of all things. Everything is related *inherently* to everything else. The Buddha-nature is universal, and everything is an expression of it; that is to say, *everything* is a perfect manifestation of the absolute. Reality is one seamless unity, but it manifests itself as the many. All "particulars" are thus equal and interdependent. Everything—even a grain of sand—manifests the perfection of the Absolute. "To see the universe in a grain of sand" is to discover the Buddha-nature in all things.

The Buddhologist Kenneth Ch'en tells the story of a Huayan master who illustrated the principle of universal interpenetration in an interesting way. He assembled ten large mirrors in such a way that eight of them formed the walls of an octagon. He then placed one mirror above the octagon and one below it. Finally, he used strings to hang a small statue of Buddha right in the center of this arrangement. When he illuminated the whole thing with torchlight, the effect was enchanting. Not only was the Buddha image directly reflected in the ten mirrors, but each reflection was rereflected *ad infinitum* in all of the other mirrors. Well, it was supposed to make the point that every single thing in the universe reflects the being of all other things. The unity of being is absolute; all is the Buddha-nature.

PURE LAND BUDDHISM

Pure Land Buddhism warrants our special attention. Pure Land, also referred to as Amitabha Buddhism, grew directly out of the broader world of Mahayana, but its doctrine is arguably the farthest removed from the original teaching. Despite this, in sheer numbers alone, Pure Land has consistently been the largest of all Buddhist sects.

We have seen that in the broad system of Mahayana belief, Shakyamuni Buddha is regarded as only one of many Buddhas, each presiding over his own celestial Buddha-realm. A Buddha-realm is also known as a "Pure Land" (*Jingtu* in Chinese, *Jodo* in Japanese). The Pure Lands are identified with the directions of the compass. In the south, for example, is the Pure Land of Buddha Ratnaketu, in the north Buddha Dundubhishvara, and in the east Buddha Akshobhya. Most popular by far, though, was (and is) the Pure Land of the west, presided over by Buddha Amitabha (*Amida* in Japanese). This "western paradise," an unimaginably great distance from Earth, is known as Sukhavati.

Philosophically minded Buddhists have in all ages interpreted the matter of Pure Lands in a metaphorical way. The different Pure Lands represent the various aspects of enlightenment. This approach has been popular in Buddhist art, particularly in the use of mandalas to represent the totality of the Dharma. The mandala becomes like a great compass, with the many Buddhas appropriately located. Often, the central position is occupied by Buddha Vairochana, who represents the *dharmakaya*. Less sophisticated folks, however, have tended to interpret the concept of Pure Land, and the possibility of personal rebirth in a Pure Land, in a literal way. This range of interpretations is characteristic of Mahayana; everyone plugs in at their own level. Buddha's teaching is for the *whole* lotus pond. It was in response to the active role of the common people in Mahayana and their interest in the possibility of rebirth in a Buddhist paradise that Pure Land Buddhism took form.

The deepest roots of Pure Land Buddhism are lost in the obscurity of the early centuries of Mahayana. No such school ever took definite form in India, but it is quite possible that the tradition germinated in the spiritually fertile region of northwest India that was the original source of Mahayana. One of the many non-Indian religious systems active in that region was Zoroastrianism which originated among the Persians. Some scholars feel that Pure Land Buddhism exhibits some parallels with Zoroastrianism and was influenced by it. In any case, the first systematic organization of Pure Land doctrine was accomplished by a Chinese monk named Hui Yuan, who founded a Buddhist organization named the White Lotus Society in the year 402 C.E. The purpose of this organization was to form a community of people—monks and laypersons—who were dedicated to being reborn in Sukhavati, the western Pure Land of Buddha Amitabha. The doctrine of the White Lotus Society was based on the teaching of various sutras, the most important of which was the *Sukhavati-vyuha*. (Actually, it is two sutras, a larger and a smaller.)

All Buddhist sutras address the matter of enlightenment; achieving enlightenment is the bottom line in Buddhism. The *Sukhavati-vyuha* also deals with the path to enlightenment, but in a very special way. It holds out the possibility of awakening for *everyone*, not in some distant future after many rebirths as a monk, but *here and now*, at the end of this lifetime, and it matters not in the least how great a sinner a person may have been. The prevailing view was that the road to enlightenment is long and difficult; one has to slowly overcome the enormous burden of negative karma that has accumulated over time. But Hui Yuan and those who followed him taught that there is another way, a faster and easier way. Incredible though it may seem, it is possible, even for the worst of sinners, to be rescued from the ignorance and depravity of this life and at the time of death be reborn in the Pure Land of Buddha Amitabha, where the fullness of enlightenment is assured. Thus did reverence of Buddha Amitabha become the central concern of Pure Land Buddhism. Note that in Pure Land the word "Buddha" by itself refers not to Shakyamuni Buddha, but to Buddha Amitabha. Shakyamuni's importance is limited to his role as deliverer of the sutras upon which the Pure Land doctrine is based.

According to the teaching of the sutras, Amitabha began his career toward Buddhahood immeasurable ages ago when he lived on Earth as a king. He lived during the time of an earlier Buddha, Lokesvara-raja, and after hearing one of this Buddha's sermons, he gave up everything and became a monk, taking the name Dharmakara. Dharmakara became a genuine bodhisattva and was reborn countless times before finally achieving perfect enlightenment, at which time he became more properly known as Buddha Amitabha (the Buddha of "infinite light"). Amitabha's Buddha-realm is Sukhavati, the Pure Land of the West, where he has presided over a vast number of followers ever since.

The story gets interesting when it is revealed that Dharmakara had taken a special vow. Every bodhisattva declares many vows, and Dharmakara was no exception. One of these vows, though (the eighteenth, to be exact), stated that he would not become enlightened unless he were to make good on a promise to welcome into his Buddha-realm all beings who trusted themselves to him with sincere devotion: "If all beings in the ten quarters, when I have attained Buddhahood, should believe in me with all sincerity of heart, desiring to be born in my country, and should, say ten times, think of me, and if they should not be reborn there, may I not obtain enlightenment."

But how is such enlightenment to be accomplished? How in the world could an ordinary human being, full of greed and anger and depravity, possibly make himself deserving of rebirth in the Pure Land of Sukhavati? The answer was simple; he couldn't. No one could do such a thing on his own—but Buddha Amitabha could! By compassionately sharing his infinite store of merit, built up over eons of time, Buddha Amitabha could wipe out the negative karma of anyone and transform that person into a being suitable for entry into his Buddha-realm, where enlightenment was assured. Indeed, he had vowed to do exactly that for any person who came to him with a sincere heart. It's a can't-lose situation. No wonder this school of Buddhism grew rapidly among the common folk!

This approach to enlightenment might seem to involve a very basic change in the teaching of Buddhism, perhaps even a contradiction. From the beginning, Buddhism had taught that one is capable of transforming himself or herself on the road to enlightenment; no outside supernatural help is necessary. Shakyamuni himself had said, "Be ye lamps unto yourselves; be ye a refuge to yourselves; betake yourselves to no external refuge!" But now, advocates of Pure Land Buddhism were proclaiming that no amount of self-directed effort can ever be sufficient. There will always be an inescapable taint of ego in everything we do. Many people continue for a long time to have confidence that they can achive enlightenment on their own. But they are fooling themselves. Eventually, each person will reach the point, like someone who is drowning, where he or she will realize that one's own efforts are simply not enough. When that point is reached, the person will finally be willing to give up the struggle and appeal to the compassionate Buddha for help. Buddha—and Buddha alone—can save us. Buddha can, and will, pluck us out of the water—but we have to ask for help. We have to have *faith* in Buddha.

It's no wonder that Pure Land Buddhism has often been compared to the teaching of the early Protestants in the history of Christianity. Martin Luther was proclaiming very much the same sort of thing. Luther concluded that man is by nature sinful, and therefore, no amount of "good works" can ever *earn* salvation. The finite can never add up to the infinite. Salvation cannot be earned, but it can be had nonetheless as a loving gift of God. Luther taught that the infinite merit (grace) created by Jesus in his death on the cross is available to everyone. All that is required is *faith*—a loving faith in God.

How similar this is to the teaching of Pure Land Buddhism. One cannot achieve "salvation"—that is, awakening—through self-power, but one can achieve salvation through "other-power." All that is required is *faith*—a loving faith in the goodness and infinite compassion of Buddha Amitabha. He has vowed to bring salvation to every person who is sincerely devoted to him.

Devotion to Buddha Amitabha is demonstrated in many ways, but one is of crucial importance. It is generally identified by its Japanese name, *nembutsu* (*nienfo* in Chinese). Nembutsu is the distinguishing feature of Pure Land Buddhism, so much so, in fact, that some simply refer to Pure Land as Nembutsu Buddhism. Nembutsu involves the repetition of the name of Amitabha (*Amida* in Japanese). Nembutsu, the repeated invocation of the name of Amitabha, is the operative agent in bringing about salvation in the Pure Land. Here is how the modern Japanese Buddhist scholar D. T. Suzuki puts it:

> When Amida [Amitabha] attained the Supreme Enlightenment, he compressed all the merit he had acquired through the spiritual discipline of innumerable kalpas into this one phrase, *na–mu–a–mi–da–bu–tsu* (Namu Amida Butsu). For this reason when this one phrase . . . is recited with singleness of purpose and with all the intensity of feeling, all the merit contained in it is miraculously transferred into the soul of the devotee, and he is at once embraced into the light of Amida. The miraculous power thus lying latent in the name of Amida belongs to the unfathomability of the Buddha-wisdom, and the only thing we ignorant mortals can do or have to do for our own salvation is to believe the wisdom and invoke the name just for once; for the "other-power" achieves the rest for us. In one sense, "Amida" is a kind of mystic "Om," a spiritual "sesame," or a mantra which unlocks the secrets of life.[3]

It would be inaccurate to think of nembutsu as some sort of magical device; it's not *really* a spiritual "sesame." Nembutsu is an external manifestation of what comes from within, the power of *faith*. A sincere, loving faith is what it's all about. But nembutsu, the external expression of that faith, plays an important role. Another valuable external in Pure Land is "visualization." It is believed by the faithful that the practice of nembutsu becomes especially powerful if one is trying to visualize Buddha Amitabha or his Pure Land. Visualization helps to deepen one's devotion and thus the bond between oneself and Buddha Amitabha. If a person experiences a spontaneous vision of Amitabha, it is taken as evidence that that person is certain to be free of terror at the time of death and will be reborn in Sukhavati. According to traditional belief, when death occurs, Amitabha's companion, the much-loved bodhisattva Avalokiteshvara, will come to ward off fear and guide the spirit of the deceased to its splendid rebirth in the Pure Land.

And what of this Pure Land? What's it like to be reborn there? As you might suspect, the wishful thinking of the folks has greatly influenced the traditional picture. In general terms, the Pure Land is a place of blissful happiness; there is no suffering of any kind. It's basically a paradise and therefore an ever-popular subject in the temple art of Buddhism. Perhaps the designation "paradise" would depend on whom you're talking to. This may come as a surprise, but there are *no women* in the Pure Land! This doesn't mean that women are barred from entry; what it means is that an earthly female is reborn as a male. Well, strictly speaking, that's not entirely true. In the Pure Land, all beings are transcendent beings (referred to as "golden bodied"). They have risen above the practical considerations of gender; there is no need for sexual difference. Everyone is a *perfected* being in every way, including the physical. Given the prevailing attitude of that day, a perfected being would naturally exhibit male characteristics if there's a choice between male and female. This probably seemed perfectly reasonable in the early days of Pure Land, but it has caused problems through the ages, and you can imagine the problem it causes today! (This preference for the male appears in many spiritual traditions throughout history.)

It must be remembered that the overriding value of being reborn in the Pure Land is that, in that way, one can achieve enlightenment. The object of being reborn in the Pure Land is to be brought to enlightenment; that's ultimately what it's all about. When a person admits that he cannot do it on his or her own, that person surrenders voluntarily to the infinite power of the compassionate Buddha Amitabha, who has *vowed* to share his enlightenment with all those who have faith in him. Not only would a person be brought to enlightenment in the Pure Land, but then he or she might expect to return to Earth as a compassionate bodhisattva in order to help others. This being the case, the "heavenly body" that transcends gender makes perfectly good sense. However accurate this interpretation of the Pure Land may be, though, it must be admitted that in the minds of most people, achieving enlightenment has not necessarily been their prime concern. Throughout the ages, most have seen this "western paradise" as a permanent abode, a sort of heaven where one will be reunited with ancestors and deceased family members and live together blissfully until the end of time in the loving company of Buddha Amitabha.

So, is Pure Land Buddhism nothing more than another variation on the theme of "die and go to heaven"? Do the followers of this school believe in the literal truth of these teachings? Some do; indeed, a great many do—that's the nature of Mahayana. But there is another way of interpreting all of this that needs to be recognized. The great popularity of Pure Land may indeed have been anchored in the common folk from the beginning, but there are also followers of Pure Land who in no way would be described as naive or gullible. In a somewhat surprising way, Pure Land has always had strong appeal to some of the most sophisticated among Buddhists. Pure Land is not likely to attract the strongly rational and philosophically minded, but it is pure enchantment for the person of a more mystical frame of mind. Pure Land represents the more emotional, artistic, "spiritual" side of Buddhism. More than any other sect, Pure Land is the *bhakti* of Buddhism.

The teachings of Pure Land Buddhism can be seen as a grand metaphor for that which can never be reduced to understandable words and concepts. Suzuki expresses this point of view very well:

> Those who are told . . . to seek rebirth in Amida's kingdom are not really seeking after a Western world lying so many thousands of kotis of miles from this earth of ours, but an inner illumination which has a miraculous power to transform or rather transfigure every object it touches into that of the Pure Land. . . . Wherever its historical development may be traced, the Pure Land is not a world existing in space-time but an idealistic world of enlightenment, or, to use the phraseology of the Pure Land sutras, a world illumined by the eternal light of Amida and subsisting in it. In one sense, it has nothing to do with this world of dualistic limitations and defilements, but in another sense it is right here with us and has reality as we read in the *Vimalakirtinirdesa Sutra* that "Wherever your hearts are pure there is a Pure Land."[4]

Of the many Buddhist sects that flourished in China, two were destined to dominate the scene in the long run. One of these was Pure Land Buddhism. The other, which developed under the name *Chan Buddhism*, is known to most people in the modern world as Zen Buddhism. The word *Zen* is simply the Japanese rendering of *Chan*. Zen is the product of a tradition that matured in China and then continued to develop in Japan. In modern times it has spread out of Japan and taken root in many parts of the world. The evolution of the Chan–Zen tradition is an interesting and very important part of the total history of Buddhism. That story will be the subject of Chapters 15 and 16.

The spread of Buddhism in China was a great success story in the centuries following the fall of Han. Buddhism gained acceptance with all classes of society and prospered in both the north and the south. A variety of sects flourished, and by the mid-fifth century Buddhist monasteries had proliferated throughout many parts of China. The monasteries were often well endowed and attracted large numbers of men (and women) to the monastic way of life. More than a few of these monastic communities became quite wealthy, especially in land. In general, it was quite a rosy picture for Buddhism. However, there was a dark side, too, and this would become painfully evident in the year 445 C.E.

To say the least, not everyone was delighted with the growth of Buddhism in China. There were those among the Confucians and Daoists who feared and hated the intrusion of this powerful new institution. In their eyes, Buddhist monasteries were responsible for the disharmony of the age. They saw the monasteries as seditious institutions that were undermining the stability of the society. Buddhist monastic communities even went so far as to set themselves up as independent entities, refusing to recognize the overlordship of imperial governments. They paid no taxes, they offered no military service, and they even adopted their own insignia and calendar. Worst of all, Buddhist monasteries threatened the stability of the Chinese family, luring away increasing numbers of sons and daughters to the parasitic and celibate life of the monk.

Things came to a head in the state of Northern Wei, which had grown to include almost all of northern China. In 445 C.E., the emperor of Northern Wei was persuaded to order an attack on the monasteries that was clearly intended to culminate in their total annihilation. All monks were to be slaughtered and all traces of Buddhism erased from the soil of Wei. Hopefully, the movement would spread from there to the rest of China. Thus commenced the first great persecution of Buddhism in China. There would be others, and as we know only too well, the modern era has not been exempt.

The extremely violent nature of the program provoked revulsion in all classes of society, and as a result, the persecution was short lived. After only three years, a change of leadership not only put an end to the persecution, but did a complete about-face. For the time being, the enemies of Buddhism were defeated. The friends of Buddhism wished to repair the damage that had been done and sought to reestablish Buddhism in China on a new and higher level than ever before. In the state of Northern Wei the imperial government, far from being an adversary of Buddhism, would now be its protector and benefactor. New monasteries were sponsored, new translation bureaus were established, interchange between China and India was encouraged, and Buddhist works of art were commissioned to be displayed in public places.

Among the art projects, one was especially impressive. In a hilly region, at sites known as Longmen (Lung-men) and Yungang (Yun-kang), work began in the late fifth century on a series of rock carvings, many of them inside natural caves, that over time would become truly unbelievable in scope. Altogether, the statues of various Buddhas would grow to number more than a hundred thousand! Five of the Buddhas are gigantic, the tallest reaching seventy feet. There are more than two thousand caves in this complex, all of them filled with artwork. Outside the caves are forty pagodas chiseled from the native rock. Only sites like Dunhuang in the far west of China and Ellora in India can boast of anything close to the colossal scope of Longmen and Yungang. Surviving inscriptions show that, in addition to generous contributions from the imperial family, works were commissioned by people from all ranks of society. Why had this interest in Buddhist sculpture become so strong? Undoubtedly, the persecution of 445 C.E. had something to do with it. It was seen that books and bodies can be destroyed rather easily but enormous stonework is likely to endure. Longmen was a statement that Buddhism was here to stay.*

---

*As recent events in Afghanistan sadly reveal, even very large works of sculpture can be destroyed when extremist passions run high. The standing Buddha at Bamiyan was not, however, the world's largest. Topping out at 233 feet, that honor continues to belong to the rock carving of Shakyamuni Buddha at Le Shan in western China. It was created in the eigth century C.E. and would seem to be secure in its title for many more centuries.

In 589 C.E., China was finally reunited in the Sui Dynasty. Shortly after, an interesting event occurred that gives further evidence of the triumph of Buddhism. The event is known as the "Enshrinement of the Relics of Buddha." The new emperor wished to symbolize the unity of the country, not only politically, but spiritually as well. In his possession in the imperial treasury were thirty relics of Shakyamuni Buddha (or at least that's what they were said to be). Step One of the plan was to order the construction of stupas in thirty different regional capitals. Step Two was to commission thirty separate Buddhist delegations to carry the relics to these cities. Then, on the same day—in fact, on the fifteenth day of the tenth month of the year 601 C.E.—with great ceremony, the relics were enshrined in the waiting stupas. At the exact same time, a similar ceremony was being conducted at the imperial palace. By royal edict, the day was declared a national holiday; everyone could take part in the celebration. Thus, with the full support of the imperial government, Buddhism would be the ideological system that gave unity to the people of China.

The official actions of the new government of Sui more or less put the capstone on a process of Buddhist growth that had been developing all through the previous three centuries. As mentioned earlier, one of the elements of the new policy of openness that followed the persecution of 445 C.E. was the encouragement of Buddhist contacts between China and India. In those days, Indian and Central Asian Buddhists of all kinds were traveling and teaching in various parts of China. Of these Indian meditation masters, one in particular was going to have an especially significant impact. His visit would initiate a new and profoundly important tradition in the history of Mahayana Buddhism. His name was Bodhidharma.

Notes

1. Heinrich Dumoulin, *Zen Buddhism: A History*, trans. James W. Hesig and Paul Knitter (New York: Macmillan, 1988), vol. 1, p. 66.
2. *Ibid.*, p. 66.
3. D. T. Suzuki, "The Development of the Pure Land Doctrine in Buddhism," in *Collected Writings on Shin Buddhism* (Kyoto: Shinshu Otanika, 1973), p. 4.
4. *Ibid.*, p. 5.

Study Questions

1. When was the Takla Makan basin the scene of a flourishing Buddhist culture, and what effect did this have on the development of Buddhism in China?

2. Given the original hostility, why was it that Buddhism eventually experienced a friendly reception in China?

3. Who was Kumarajiva? What was special about his role in the historical development of Buddhism in China?

4. How did Tiantai Buddhism attempt to solve the seeming inconsistencies of the early Buddhist tradition?

5. Who is Amitabha Buddha? What is his relation to Shakyamuni Buddha?
6. Pure Land Buddhism's approach to enlightenment "might seem to involve a very basic change in the teaching of Buddhism, perhaps even a contradiction." What does this mean?
7. "The teaching of Pure Land Buddhism can be seen as a grand metaphor for that which can never be reduced to understandable words and concepts." What does this mean?

15

Chan: The Origins of Zen Buddhism in China

Chan is the name of a school of Buddhism that developed in China. The word is derived from the Sanskrit *dhyana*, a term that refers to the practice of meditation. "Chan" is simply the Chinese version of the Sanskrit word. An emphasis on *dhyana* practice was introduced into China from India in the fifth century. The school of Chan Buddhism was the result; it flourished for several centuries before declining and all but dying out in its Chinese homeland.

In the twelfth century the school of Chan Buddhism was transplanted from China to Japan, where it also took root and flourished. In Japan, the tradition is known as Zen Buddhism. Just as *Chan* is the Chinese pronunciation of the Sanskrit *dhyana*, Zen is the Japanese pronunciation of the Chinese word *Chan*. Thus, *Chan* and *Zen* are fundamentally the same word; both are variants of the root word *dhyana*.

In essence, the Zen tradition is a continuation of the Chan tradition; there is a seamless flow between them. Because of the decline of the Chan tradition in China, though, the modern world is far more familiar with the tradition in its Japanese form. For this reason, many modern writers choose to avoid confusion by simply referring to the entire tradition—the Chinese part as well as the Japanese—by the name *Zen*. There is logic in doing this. After all, it is one continuous tradition, and the names *Chan* and *Zen* both refer equally to that tradition. *Zen* has, in fact, become something of a universal word in modern times.

In this and the next chapter, the aim is to understand the tradition as a whole, viewed from the perspective of modern times. The two chapters are closely linked. For this reason, and to avoid confusion, in this chapter it is appropriate to use the term *Zen* when referring to the tradition in general and to use the term *Chan* only where specific historical references within China are concerned.

Both *Chan* and *Zen*, derived from the Sanskrit *dhyana*, refer to the practice of meditation. Considering the central place of meditation in the development of Eastern traditions—especially Zen Buddhism—it is appropriate to begin this chapter with a closer look at the nature of this often mysterious and elusive subject.

The practice of meditation was well established in Hindu culture by the time of Buddha, and although he rejected much of the Hindu tradition, Buddha loved and cherished meditation. Meditation was his last hope when, in the hour of his desperation, he sat down beneath the bodhi tree, resolved not to move until he found the truth he sought. Buddha stressed the importance of meditation in his teaching, and this emphasis is reflected in the high position that *dhyana* occupies in both the Eightfold Path of Theravada and the Six *Paramitas* of Mahayana. Meditation (*dhyana*) was seen as being the royal road to liberation. So, what precisely does the word mean? What is the proper place of meditation in the life of one who would follow in the footsteps of Buddha?

Let us state at the outset that there is no single answer to this question. There are many different traditions, all of which have developed their own particular "schools" of meditation. Still, despite the differences, it is possible to perceive some common elements in the various traditions—a sort of fundamental core that is shared by all.

To begin with, we must make a distinction between the *state* of meditation and the *practice* of meditation. By itself, the word *meditation* refers to a particular state of mind, a state of consciousness. Meditation as a practice, however, refers to various techniques and disciplines that are designed to help one enter into the meditative state of mind. The many different "schools" of meditation—Zen, yoga, "transcendental" and so on—are concerned primarily with differences in technique. They offer different ways of arriving at the center, but the center—the state of the mind in meditation—is essentially the same for all.

The mind in meditation is the state of "no-mind"; that is, the customary thought-based processes that we associate with mental activity are temporarily suspended. When the thinking mind and its close association with the ego-identity are allowed to become quiet, consciousness becomes very clear and absorbed in the reality of the present moment. Background dualities of thought evaporate, and one enters into state of consciousness that is generally described as the "Unitive State." This simply means that the consciousness of one who is in a true state of meditation is freed from the usual human split between self and other. The underlying unity of being is perceived, not intellectually, of course, but directly, experientially, in the present moment. The experience of the Unitive State can be more or less perfect. Perfect meditation is the perfect expression of the Unitive State.

It is a common mistake to imagine that the mind in meditation is in some sort of trance. Ideally, the meditative state of mind—even if far less than perfect—would be our normal state of consciousness, our ordinary state of mind. Many speculate that the consciousness of nonhuman beings is always essentially a meditative state. And that would be true of human infants too; all of us started out in life as perfect little meditation masters. But the development of the human thinking process—especially its great production, the ego identity—has the effect of dislocating us far from our natural beginnings. In a sense, meditation disciplines are really nothing more than devices designed to loosen the grip of the ego habit and help restore us to the natural state.

The *practice* of meditation—as opposed to the *state* of meditation—is the practice of various techniques designed (hopefully) to help one achieve the state of mind-in-meditation. That state, however, is by no means necessarily limited to those times set aside for "practicing" meditation techniques. Ideally, it becomes the background condition of one's normal state of consciousness. Specific times for the practice of meditation are valuable in that the state of mind experienced at such times may expand to become more or less one's continuous state of mind. A master of meditation is a person who lives his or her ongoing daily life in a state of consciousness that can be accurately described as the meditative state. It is important to note that this is not an altered state of consciousness, nor is it something transcendent, something lofty that only a rare person can aspire to. It is actually the natural way to live.

Once again, meditation techniques are aids that one employs during a session of meditation practice. Myriad techniques have become popular over the centuries, many of them borrowed from the tradition of yoga. Probably the most widely recognized technique employed in the *practice* of meditation is what is called "sitting meditation." Typically, this involves the form of the cross-legged sitting posture that has become virtually an icon in the art of Buddhism. The advantage of this posture, pure and simple, is that, once mastered, it permits the meditator to remain comfortable, though sitting very still for long periods of time. One does not have to sit, however, to practice meditation. Many postures are possible. (Some people even claim to be able to make a meditation practice out of jogging or swimming.)

To sum up, the *practice* of meditation is the deliberate practice of certain disciplines, often including the sitting posture, whose aim is to encourage the meditative *state of mind*, the Unitive State. Perfect meditation is the perfect expression of the Unitive State. This is what the word *dhyana* refers to, and it is why *dhyana* occupies the summit position in Buddha's teaching. The word *dhyana*, like its English counterpart, "meditation," refers to both the state and the practice. The Buddhist tradition holds that in the mastery of *dhyana* one ascends through four stages of growth, the fourth being the opening of *prajna* and thus the experience of awakening. To be in a state of perfect *dhyana* is to *be* an awakened person.

From the earliest days, many followers of Buddha found it reasonable to conclude that diligent practice of the disciplines—especially the practice of meditation—would lead slowly, but inexorably, to awakening. Given the amount of resistance normal in human beings, the process would most likely be long and slow, and of course, some would never make it at all. We could metaphorically compare the process to the fashioning of a mirror for a great telescope. We start out with a large, rough lump of glass, which is like the ordinary person before embarking on a life's work of Buddhist discipline. The perfect mirror is already there; it is inherent within the rough glass, remaining only to be brought out. If all goes well, years of grinding and polishing will bring out the mirror that is latent in the glass from the beginning. The improvement takes form gradually; no one can say at what moment perfection is achieved, but eventually, the mirror does become perfect. (In a similar vein, Michelangelo was once asked to explain the genius that made it possible for him to transform a block of rough stone into a lifelike replica of a horse. "It's easy," he said; "I just chip away everything that doesn't look like a horse.")

The aspirant himself is the large rough lump of glass. Years of grinding and polishing (spiritual disciplines and meditation) will bring out the mirror (the Buddha-nature) and will eventually make it perfect. It's a gradual approach to the attainment of Enlightenment. In some ways, the approach appeals to something basic in human nature. Perhaps it's because people want to feel that they are in control of their lives. Ironically, this is the very ego-centered problem that Buddhism seeks to solve, but there it sits nonetheless. If I can imagine that "awakening" (whatever that may be) is the pay-off at the end of a clearly defined program of work, then I can apply myself to the disciplines involved and feel reasonably confident that the prize will ultimately be mine; I'm in control. Again, it's like polishing that telescope mirror. If I work hard at it, eventually I will see the truth of the universe. It's up to me.

This gradual approach to the goal of awakening pretty much sums up the general character of Buddhist meditation practice in China around 500 C.E. A thousand years had passed since Shakyamuni Buddha had started the ball rolling. Men and women were as passionate as ever in their determination to follow him into the awakened state. Buddha had taught mankind how to do that, but his teaching needed to be interpreted. The prevalent interpretation emphasized a life organized around the disciplines of the *vinaya*, centered on attaining mastery in meditation practice. In that way—that *gradual* way—the obstacles would be removed, and the Buddha-nature would eventually be uncovered. This general state of affairs might not have changed much for a long time had it not been for one thing. A Buddhist revolutionary named Bodhidharma appeared on the scene. Bodhidharma is a semilegendary figure whose name is associated with a very different approach to the role of meditation. Bodhidharma was destined to be the founder—at least, the titular founder—of a powerful new movement that would coalesce into one of the major historical branches of Buddhism.

From the earliest times, those who favored the *gradual* approach to awakening were opposed by those who argued that awakening, *by its very nature*, must be a *sudden experience*. No amount of gradual "polishing" would ever *produce* awakening. It happened—if it happened at all—suddenly, all at once. This did not mean that the "sudden" school rejected the practice of meditation—not at all. What they rejected was the notion that one could *achieve* awakening gradually, through dedication to the discipline of meditation practice. In their eyes, the value of meditation was that it helped to foster the right state of consciousness—a fertile ground, you might say—*out of which* the sudden experience of awakening might be more likely to occur. Meditation practice was thus seen as a powerful help to the dedicated seeker, but by no means was it a necessity. The crucial difference between the "gradual" school and the "sudden" school was that the former regarded meditation practice as a *means* to awakening, whereas the latter regarded it as a *help*. Both, however, following the lead of Shakyamuni Buddha himself, held the practice of meditation in high regard.

Even though both schools, the gradual and the sudden, could trace their roots back to the beginnings of Buddhism, the gradual school had clearly dominated the Buddhist scene during its first millennium of development. Evidence of the existence of a minority sudden school continued to appear, however. Recall that the First Great Council of Buddhism divided over this very issue. Although seemingly suppressed in the Theravada tradition, those who favored the sudden approach would find new life in Mahayana. Some pointed references to sudden awakening are to be found in the Mahayana sutras.

While evidence exists that some exponents of the sudden school were active in China as early as the third century, it remains apparent that the way of the gradual school was clearly the dominant approach. Its days of dominance were numbered, though, and beginning in the early fifth century a new opposition movement began to come together. As mentioned before, the tradition holds that this movement became organized around the person of Bodhidharma, a Buddhist meditation master from India. The school of Buddhism associated with the name of Bodhidharma was known simply by the Sanskrit term *dhyana*. In Chinese, this became *Chan-a*, ultimately shortened to *Chan*. Thus began Chan Buddhism, a wonderfully rich tradition within the great wheel of Mahayana. Chan Buddhism would flourish for many centuries in China, but eventually it would decline and nearly die out in its homeland, just as the original Buddhism had declined in India. But like Indian Buddhism, which had migrated to foreign lands, so, too, would Chan Buddhism find its way to new places—Vietnam and Korea, for example, and eventually Japan, where the tradition would continue under the name *Zen*.

BODHIDHARMA

The story of Chan and Zen Buddhism first began to take on a coherent form around the teaching of a man named Bodhidharma. He was a semilegendary meditation master from India who spread the good word of Buddhism in China during the early sixth century. Note, however, that Bodhidharma is the *legendary* founder of Zen; virtually all

Bodhidharma. (P. Bresnan)

modern historians of Buddhism agree that the roots of the Zen tradition were in existence in China a full century or more before Bodhidharma.

In the Zen tradition, Bodhidharma is referred to as the first patriarch of Zen in China. Let me explain what this means. Shakyamuni Buddha freed himself forever from the prison ground of human misery. He selflessly gave the rest of his life to teaching others how to follow him to freedom. But how was his teaching to be preserved? Its essence went far beyond anything that could be captured in mere words. If words could do it, Buddha would have simply written down the formula, and that would be that. But words can't do it, formulas can't do it, and practicing certain disciplines can't do it. Then what can do it?

According to the tradition of Zen Buddhism, the reality of Buddha's enlightenment was transmitted *personally and directly* by him to his disciples. All other things might be helpful in clearing the way so that the experience could happen, but the experience itself is initiated in the disciple as the result of a sensed personal connection between disciple and master. This connection is commonly referred to as a "transmission," but it is not meant to be understood as a spiritual something that is *given* from one person to another. The awakening is personal; it arises within each individual, but it can be initiated by a "transmission," a deeply felt sense of shared consciousness, between an enlightened master and a disciple. The intimacy of the master–disciple relationship in Buddhism clearly has its roots in the Hindu tradition out of which Buddhism developed.

In the Zen tradition, the way that the purity of Buddha's enlightenment was to be preserved through the ages would be by direct, personal transmission between teacher and student, master and disciple. Through his personal influence, Shakyamuni Buddha undoubtedly nudged many into that state of being wherein they were at last willing to let go completely and become awakened. But according to the tradition, when his life was nearing its end, Buddha made a point of identifying one of his disciples whose enlightenment was perfect. That disciple, Kasyapa by name, was chosen to be Buddha's personal successor; he would be the leader and unifying center of the sangha, the community of monks, after Buddha was gone. In time, he would name his own successor, choosing the person whom he deemed to be perfectly enlightened and best suited to become the custodian of the tradition.

Kasyapa was a loyal and much-loved disciple of Buddha. One day, Buddha called all of his close disciples together, something he did often in order to share his teaching with them. When they were all assembled, Buddha took his usual place before them. Ordinarily, he would talk for a while and engage them in dialogue. But on this occasion he just sat there saying nothing. At last, raising his eyes to the group, he drew out from under the folds of his robe a beautiful flower, perhaps a lotus in full bloom, and simply held it before the group. That's all; he just held out the flower, remaining silent and gazing peacefully at his disciples. There was some general uneasiness. Only one, Kasyapa, understood. His eyes joined with Buddha's, and Kasyapa smiled; it was the smile of perfect recognition. Buddha knew beyond any doubt that this was the man he would entrust with the leadership of the sangha.

In selecting Kasyapa, Buddha was implicitly verifying the purity of Kasyapa's enlightenment. Kasyapa would take the place of Buddha in the sangha, so that even death could not break the continuity. In a way, it was a device for preserving the presence of Buddha among them. In time, Kasyapa chose his own successor, who happened to be Ananda, the young disciple that Buddha had loved with great affection. Apparently, Ananda was not yet ready for the role of successor during Buddha's lifetime; he achieved perfect enlightenment after the death of Buddha. When Kasyapa was chosen, Buddha gave him his own robe and begging bowl as a symbol of Kasyapa's right to the succession. When he selected Ananda, Kasyapa passed on to him these treasured personal items of Buddha. Ananda in turn would pass them on to his own chosen successor, and so it would go for generations to come.

In the Zen tradition, the designated successors of Buddha are called "patriarchs." Kasyapa, Buddha's immediate successor, was the first patriarch, Ananda the second patriarch, and so on. Altogether, the patriarchs formed an unbroken line of continuity, beginning with Buddha and preserving over time the authenticity of Buddha's awakening. After all, that's what it's all about.

Although historical verifiability has to be stretched a little, the Zen tradition accounts for a line, a "lineage," of twenty-eight patriarchs from Buddha to Bodhidharma. Bodhidharma was the twenty-eighth patriarch of India, and when he began his mission in China, he became the first patriarch of China. The line does not continue down to the present day; the numbering system came to an end with the sixth patriarch of China. Each of the twenty-eight patriarchs of India is listed by name in the archives of Zen history. The great second-century Indian philosopher, Nagarjuna, is designated the fourteenth partriarch.* Thus did Bodhidharma come to be known as the first patriarch of Zen. Although the living roots of Zen go directly back to Buddha himself, the distinct Buddhist tradition that bears the name *Zen* by common agreement is said to begin with Bodhidharma. Zen was an outgrowth of Mahayana, but the Zen tradition maintains that it alone has preserved the essential purity of Buddha's teaching.

As you might have guessed, not a whole lot is known for sure about Bodhidharma. The scant historical record we have comes from two brief accounts that were included in chronicles of Buddhist masters written about a century after his death. These documents give us some very basic facts, but most of the traditional story of Bodhidharma's life is based on conjecture and legend.

We can say with a fair degree of certainty that he was born in India, quite possibly to a noble or Brahmin family from the south of India. He was said to have died in 532 C.E. "at a ripe old age" (although presumably not quite so ripe as the 150 years often cited). He may have been around eighty or ninety at the time of his death, which would put his birth sometime in the mid-fifth century. Bodhidharma's life coincided with the final collapse of the mighty Roman Empire in the far-off Mediterranean world, but in those days that drama might as well have been happening on another planet.

---

*This matter of the lineage will strike a familiar note with anyone who is knowledgeable about the Roman Catholic Church. The "apostolic succession" of the popes seems to be very much the same sort of thing.

Like Shakyamuni Buddha before him, Bodhidharma parted company with his family, choosing instead the spiritual path. Eventually, he became a disciple of the Buddhist master Prajnadhara, known in the Zen tradition as the twenty-seventh patriarch. There are some grounds for speculating that Prajnadhara was a woman, certainly an interesting element in the story if true. In any case, Prajnadhara selected Bodhidharma to be the successor and conferred on him the insignia of Buddha's robe and bowl. Prajnadhara also, according to the story, charged Bodhidharma with the mission of carrying the truth of Buddhism to China. Buddhist monks had been active in China for a long time, but that distant land had not yet been visited by one with the perfect enlightenment of Bodhidharma.

We don't know for certain how Bodhidharma traveled from India to China; some think it was by sea, but in those days an overland route was far more likely. Bodhidharma must already have been along in years when he began the arduous trek. Don't let the appearance of the map deceive you. In those days there was no direct route from India to China; the mass of the great mountains of the north prevented that. A traveler would have to follow the passes of the northwest deep into the deserts of central Eurasia and then follow the winding Silk Road east into the land of China. It took Bodhidharma at least three years to reach his destination; presumably, he stayed for periods of time at monasteries along the route. It would seem that he made his way slowly across southern China from west to east and attracted a lot of attention. He was not just another Buddhist monk; he was a powerful and impressive figure. He was an Indian master of meditation, and he was teaching a new way and a new meaning for the practice of meditation.

The chronicles tell us that in 520 C.E. Bodhidharma finally reached the region of modern Guangzhou (formerly known as Canton, about twenty miles upriver from Hong Kong). His fame preceded him, and the Emperor Wu, wanting to meet this exotic foreigner, summoned him to the court at Nanjing. Emperor Wu was a pretty interesting character in his own right. He reminds one of Emperor Ashoka. Both were powerful monarchs who ruled vast empires, and both experienced a profound change of heart in adult life, which resulted in their embracing Buddhism. Wu had been a dedicated Confucian, but he gave that up when he discovered Buddhism; he even, we are told, became a monk himself for a short time. He lavished his kingly largesse on the Buddhist sects, supporting many temples and monasteries. He sponsored translations of Buddhist scriptures, paid for the upkeep of innumerable monks and nuns, and, like Ashoka, earnestly encouraged a policy of nonviolence toward all animals. Emperor Wu was, to put it mildly, actively involved in promoting the Buddhist way of life in China even before the arrival of Bodhidharma.

No doubt, Emperor Wu derived great personal satisfaction from his efforts on behalf of the Buddhist cause, but clearly, he had another reason as well. Some of the Mahayana Buddhist sects (as discussed earlier in this work) held to a belief in personal reincarnation, including belief in the possibility of rebirth among the gods in a sort of paradise. Emperor Wu had been won over to this school of thought. He believed that his impressive list of "good works" was piling up a mountain of positive karma that would guarantee him an excellent place among the gods in the next life. In his own mind it was certainly no accident that he was a great king in this life; it was the working of karma, and it was his karmic destiny to be an even greater figure in the next life. Undoubtedly, a man of his wealth and power would have had no trouble finding others, including Buddhist monks, to reassure him in this belief. And now the great Bodhidharma himself was coming to visit the court. Confirmation from the lips of Bodhidharma would really gladden the emperor's heart. This was the setting into which Bodhidharma entered.

We can't say for sure what Bodhidharma looked like, but he is traditionally pictured as having a ferocious appearance: tall, dark, with deep-set penetrating eyes and bushy eyebrows, a gruff exterior, but a soft heart inside. He approached Emperor Wu, probably fixing his gaze on him instead of looking modestly downward. Bodhidharma said nothing, but Emperor Wu wanted to do the talking anyway. We can imagine him leaning back and ticking off the long list of his many charitable ventures. The litany was meant to impress Bodhidharma. What a noble and generous man! Finally, he turned to Bodhidharma and asked, rhetorically, "So what do you think my reward will be for all of this?" That was supposed to be Bodhidharma's cue to start unctuously heaping flattery on the king, assuring him that he would be numbered among the gods in the next life. Then, of course, Wu would add another notch to his record by magnanimously bestowing some further gift on the monastery of Bodhidharma's choosing. Emperor Wu must have sat up straight when he heard Bodhidharma's reply.

"No merit at all," Bodhidharma said (probably in a gruff tone of voice).

"No merit?" the astonished Wu responded. "How can you say that? Why?"

We don't know precisely what Bodhidharma answered, but it's easy to guess what the gist of it would have been. If I may be permitted to paraphrase, "If you believe that all these so-called good works are going to earn you some great reward, you totally fail to understand the basic principles of Buddha's teaching. Those who work for profit only intensify the stifling delusion of ego. The reward you speak of is in the doing, not separated from it. Not only do you deceive yourself about some future reward, but you risk falling into a hell of your own making right here in this life."

"Then what," Wu asked, "*is* the merit of these generous acts of mine? Surely, there is some kind of merit associated with the good things we do in life!"

Bodhidharma's response was cryptic. Wu wants to know what Bodhidharma regards to be the kind of action that is right action, the kind that is truly meritorious. The Buddhologist Heinrich Dumoulin puts Bodhidharma's response in these words: "It is pure knowing, wonderful and perfect. Its essence is emptiness. One cannot gain such merit by worldly means."

We can easily imagine that Emperor Wu was feeling somewhat tense at this point in the conversation, but that wouldn't faze Bodhidharma in the slightest. Having only muddied the water by going directly to his question about merit, Wu apparently decided that it might be a better course to drop that for the moment and start with first things first. "What is the first principle of this holy doctrine?" he asked.

"Vast emptiness," Bodhidharma answered bluntly, "and there is nothing holy about it."

"And who then is it who stands before me now?" Wu asked.

"I don't know."

With that, the conversation ended and Bodhidharma left the palace. It hadn't turned out quite the way that Wu expected. The chronicles tell us that the emperor did not experience enlightenment as a result of this meeting.

Bodhidharma withdrew to the monastery of Shaolinsi (Shao-lin-ssu), where he was a welcome guest, and he remained there for the next nine years of his life. During these years he spent a great deal of time practicing *piguan* (*pi-kuan*), which translates roughly as "wall gazing." It is likely that Bodhidharma introduced a new technique into meditation practice. Traditional meditation exercises in India were generally practiced with the eyes closed and often included chanting or other kinds of yogic techniques to still and center the mind. Bodhidharma's method was to sit before a blank wall with the eyes at least partly open and to empty the mind of thought by concentrating on the simple nonverbal reality of the moment. One's ordinary mind—in perfect harmony with the oneness of the moment—is the mind that is truly in meditation.*

Bodhidharma spent long hours in meditation, but even this great *dhyana* master could not prevent himself from occasionally nodding off to sleep (a universally annoying problem for those who practice meditation). This infuriated Bodhidharma, and according to one quaint little story, one day he got so upset that he tore off his eyelids and flung them on the ground. The sleepy eyes can't close if the eyelids are gone. The eyelids were nourished by the soil, and from them grew the first tea plants. Tea became the drink of choice among Buddhist meditators; it tastes great, and it helps to keep sleepiness at bay. In a less gruesome version of the story, Bodhidharma plucked out his eyebrows, and it was from these that the first tea bushes grew. Regardless of whether Bodhidharma's eye parts had anything to do with it, the careful brewing and drinking of tea did in fact become almost synonymous with the practice of Zen. Strong green tea is said to exude "the flavor of Zen."

Certain of the monks at the monastery wished to become disciples of Bodhidharma, but the master seemed to be unapproachable. One of them, though, wouldn't take no for an answer. His name was Hui Ko (pronounced Wee-koh), and he was destined to become Bodhidharma's successor. Hui Ko was *very* persistent. He would sit patiently for hours, even days, in the presence of the master, waiting to be granted the opportunity to learn directly from him. But always he was rebuffed; Bhodidharma acted as if Hui Ko didn't even exist. The story gets really dramatic one cold and stormy winter night. The snow is swirling and the wind is howling at the monastery windows. Only a small oil lamp lights the room in which Bodhidharma sits; as usual, he is quiet and immobile

---

*The modern Buddhist scholar D. T. Suzuki has argued that a literal translation of *pi-kuan* is incorrect. How could mere wall gazing start a revolutionary movement in the Buddhist world? Rather, Suzuki maintains, the term refers to the character of the state of consciousness of one who is practicing meditation in the proper way. In support of this interpretation, Suzuki cites to documentary sources that made reference to the manner in which Bodhidharma instructed his chief disciple in meditation: "Externally keep yourself away from all relationships, and internally, have no hankerings in your heart; when your mind is like unto a straight-standing wall you may enter into the Path" (from *Zen Buddhism*, p. 63).

before the bare stone wall. Hui Ko can't bear it any longer. In desperation, he takes a large knife or a cleaver and actually cuts off his left arm at the elbow. Blood dripping from the ragged stump, he interrupts Bodhidharma's meditation, presenting the severed arm. This, he shouts, is evidence of his determination. He'll do anything to receive instruction from the master. "If cutting off my arm doesn't move you, I will take this knife and cut off my head!" Now maybe Bodhidharma would pay attention to him.

At last, Bodhidharma did pay attention to Hui Ko. (Thank god!) He turned to Hui Ko, surveying the bloody scene, and asked almost in exasperation, "What is it you want from me?"

"I want to know the truth of my own nature," Hui Ko answered. "I know no peace of mind."

"Alright," said Bodhidharma, "bring your mind out here, and I'll pacify it for you."

"That's just the problem. My mind troubles me endlessly, but no matter how hard I search for it, I can never lay hold of it."

"There!" said Bodhidharma. "Your mind is pacified."

With those words, we are told, Hui Ko saw into the nature of the problem he had created and was instantly enlightened.

This is indeed a dramatic story. Unfortunately (at least for the sake of drama), it is undoubtedly fictitious. It's not that Hui Ko is fictitious or that he did not achieve enlightenment as a disciple of Bodhidharma. But the part about cutting off his arm is unlikely, to say the least. The brief account in the chronicles gives a far more prosaic story. Hui Ko may have lost an arm, but a violent encounter with bandits is probably how it happened. Nevertheless, the story makes a couple of valuable points about Zen and uses sensational elements to emphasize them. It has long been a part of the tradition of Zen that one who seeks to be a disciple of a master can often expect to be ignored or brusquely turned away at first. This is not really a lack of interest; rather, the seeker must prove—must demonstrate—his genuine determination before being accepted. It may not be necessary to cut off one's arm, but some show of total sincerity is necessary. The second point concerns the abruptness of Hui Ko's enlightenment. It happened in a sudden flash of insight.

After Hui Ko, Bodhidharma accepted a few other monks as his disciples. When the ninth year was drawing to a close, Bodhidharma announced that he had become an old man, and he wished to return to his homeland while he still could make the journey. It was time to designate a successor. He gathered his four disciples together and posed a question: "What have you learned from me? What is the meaning of Buddha's teaching?"

The first person to answer was Dao Fu: "The ultimate truth of reality cannot be expressed in words. Words are concerned with dualities, but truth is beyond duality. Truth is Dao."

Bodhidharma listened carefully and then said, "You speak well, but your understanding is not perfect. You shall inherit my skin."

The next disciple to speak was a woman named Zongji (Tsung-ch'ih). Her rather mysterious offering concerned a reference to a passage in the *Prajnaparamita*: "As I understand it, the truth can be likened to the time when Ananda experienced a glimpse of the Buddha-field of Akshobhya. It is perceived once and then never again."

Bodhidhharma took it all in intently and then responded, "You too speak well, but your understanding lacks perfection. You shall inherit my flesh."

Dao Yu was the third to speak: "The four elements are empty. The five skandas don't really exist. In truth, nothing can be said about the truth."

Bodhidharma probably smiled. "Your words are clever and well chosen," he said, "but you contradict yourself. You say that nothing can be said about the truth, but in so doing you try to say something about it. Your understanding, too, lacks perfection. You shall inherit my bones."

The last of the four was Hui Ko. He approached the master, bowed deeply, and spoke not a single word. Bodhidharma embraced Hui Ko and whispered to him, "You shall inherit my marrow."

Hui Ko also inherited the robe and bowl of Buddha. He was to become the second patriarch of Zen (Chan) in China. Bodhidharma, feeling secure about the future of what he had begun, set off on the long journey home and was seen no more.

So what are we to make of Bodhidharma? Why, within the broad umbrella of Buddhism, is his teaching said to be the foundation stone of that distinct sect we know as Zen? The place to begin is with the following terse statement:

> A special transmission outside of scriptures;
> No dependence on words or letters;
> Direct pointing at the mind of man;
> Seeing into one's nature, and the attainment of Buddhahood.

This verse (called a *gatha* in Japanese) is widely regarded as being the fundamental statement or definition of Zen Buddhism. This basic gatha says it all, and according to tradition, Bodhidharma is credited with being its author. Modern Buddhist scholars almost unanimously agree that the precise wording of the gatha came later, but the spirit of its meaning derives from the time of Bodhidharma.

"Direct pointing at the mind of man; seeing into one's nature and the attainment of Buddhahood." The gatha is saying that true awakening is a sudden and direct experience; it is not simply the end result of a long process of mental cleansing. This point is all important. The tradition of Zen teaches that the basic gatha gives expression to the central matter of Bodhidharma's revolutionary teaching. The function of Zen is to preserve and re-create the genuine experience of Buddha's awakening. Awakening is the great flash of insight in which one suddenly "sees into one's nature." Absolute Being is perfectly simple, one, indivisible. It can be understood only in its totality, all at once. Therefore, it makes no sense to talk about *gradual* enlightenment; rather, "The fruit drops when it is ripe."

If it's the real thing, it happens all at once—sudden enlightenment. In Chinese, "sudden enlightenment" is called *wu men*. Most people in the Western world are more familiar with the Japanese term, *satori*. The central and essential importance of satori is what the teaching of Bodhidharma was all about. As D. T. Suzuki bluntly puts it, "The coming of Bodhidharma to China in the early sixth century was simply to introduce this satori element into the body of Buddhism."

It is not possible to exaggerate the importance of satori. Unfortunately, it is very possible to miscast the precise meaning of the term, since, once again, we are attempting to talk about that which by definition cannot be expressed in words or thoughts. The best policy is to keep things simple and allow the intuitional faculty an opportunity to sense the meaning of the word.

Suzuki calls satori "an intuitive looking into the nature of things" and, more poetically, "the opening of the mind flower." In this sense, any sudden, powerful insight is a kind of satori. Everyone has had this sort of experience at one time or another. Even insights that relate to the meaning of life can be "great satoris" or "small satoris," but the experience that gives Zen its meaning is, of course, the ultimate insight that banishes all the clouds of unknowing: perfect awakening. This is perfect, unlimited satori and is usually what is being referred to when the word is used.

In focusing on the essential place of sudden enlightenment, Bodhidharma set the course of this new Buddhist teaching on a track different from the rest. As discussed at the beginning of the chapter, Buddhist teaching in China had emphasized the gradual approach to Buddhahood. The idea of sudden enlightenment, though, did not exactly originate with Bodhidharma. In fact, we find both the sudden and the gradual approach discussed in the sutras. The gradual approach, though, had been dominant in the tradition of Buddhism, at least up to the time of Bodhidharma.

What made Bodhidharma something of a revolutionary and the founder of a new way of Buddhism, is that he flatly disagreed with the traditionalist approach. This is not to say that Bodhidharma condemned the practice of the traditional disciplines. Far from it: He himself was an ardent practitioner of sitting meditation. All of the disciplines, he would argue, are good and helpful, but by themselves they are empty of value. They lack the central, essential element without which true awakening cannot occur.

Studying the sutras is a fine thing to do; such study brings great joy and enrichment. But by itself, all of the intellectual knowledge of the human race is like but "a tiny hair dropped into the vastness of space." Not even kingly meditation, by itself, can transform consciousness into *prajna*. That would be like lifting yourself by your own bootstraps:

> The experience of enlightenment is not dependent on meditation; there is no causal connection between the two. Meditational practice is neither the cause nor the condition for coming to a realization. Once awakened to wisdom, the mind sees nature, its own nature, which is identical with the Buddha nature.[1]

The practice of meditation is an excellent thing to do, but it is not by itself the means to awakening. Then what is? The answer to that question is given in the first two lines of the basic gatha: "A special transmission outside of scripture; no dependence on words or letters."

The gatha proclaims that the *living experience* of enlightenment can be awakened in one only by a direct, personal *transmission* from an already awakened man or woman. In sharing his or her state of consciousness with the disciple, the master arouses awakening in that person. In other words, the influence of the master excites the satori experience in the disciple. The satori experience is the opening of the "mind flower" to the awakened state of consciousness. Bodhidharma, we may assume, would have taken the position that the "transmission" between master and student is the *only* reasonable way in which a genuinely perfect satori experience can be aroused. The master need not be physically present at the moment, though; it is the character of the relationship that matters, and that relationship will bear fruit when the person is ready—that is to say, when the person is finally willing to let go completely.

"The fruit drops when it is ripe." In other words, satori is not something that can be *achieved*, not something that can be *won* by diligent effort. It occurs when it occurs, if it occurs at all, just as the fruit drops when it is ripe. No amount of effort can have any effect at all. You can no more force yourself to "wake up" than you can force yourself to remember something. But when one is ready—just as when Buddha was ready—almost anything may trigger the dropping of the fruit. The simple sound of someone stepping on a dry leaf can do it, a long-forgotten aroma can do it, or, as was the case for Buddha, it can be triggered by the sight of the morning star (Venus) in the predawn sky.

At this point, you may well be wondering whether Bodhidharma, and the Zen tradition in general, would insist that personal transmission is really the one and only way that true awakening can occur. Buddhism in general is not dogmatic; ultimately, each individual must decide such matters for himself. Buddha, of course, driven to the state of desperation, discovered the truth of his nature entirely on his own. But that's why Buddha is so loved and honored, almost to the point of being regarded as a "savior" by some. Conceivably, others can, and have had, the same experience, but at the very least, the Zen tradition would say that such a thing is exceptional. However, there is no law preventing the transmission from taking many paths over time. Zen masters are not necessarily confined to the grounds of Zen monasteries.

It is important to understand that Bodhidharma was not attacking the practice of meditation *per se*. Bodhidharma loved meditation; his awakening by no means put an end to it. He made an important place for it in his daily life, and so have innumerable men and women down through the history of Buddhism to the present day. Bodhidharma—or, more precisely, the tradition associated with his name—was attacking only what was seen to be a wrong view—that is, that the discipline of meditation *by itself* can work as a means to the achievement of awakening.

What, then, might Bodhidharma say is the *proper* role of meditation in one's life? If the practice of meditation does not in itself constitute an effective means for achieving awakening, what value *is* there in the practice? Bodhidharma might begin by pointing out that the practice of meditation, in conjunction with the other disciplines, helps prepare the person to become receptive to the influence of the master. It's not essential, but it certainly might be of help, in which case it would be a wonderful value. But this is still looking at meditation as a means to an end. The *real* value of meditation is, like that of dancing or singing, that it is an end unto itself. The practice of meditation has the capacity to greatly increase the joy of living.

It's a very modern question to ask: What good is it? Why deliberately give time to doing *nothing* when you could be doing *something*? This is like asking what's so good about sleep. One could argue that we squander a third of our lives sleeping. Of course, we know that in the total view of life, sleep not only is enjoyable in itself, but is necessary to good health. And so are eating and exercising. Meditation is like sleeping, eating, and exercising in that it is part of the natural balance of right living. It's healthy to pull the plug on the conceptualizing mind from time to time and give it a rest. Still, I don't want to give the impression that the value of meditation is because "it's good for you." Undoubtedly, meditation *is* "good for you," especially if you are a reasonably normal modern man or woman (that is to say, a tightly wrapped storage chest of tensions and anxieties), but that's beside the point; that's simply an attractive bonus.

In the final analysis, meditation is its own reward. It may be good for you in a practical sense, but that's not why one does it. Sex is undeniably good for you; it's a fine aerobic exercise. But who in their right mind would engage in lovemaking simply because it's good for you? Does that make the point? The same can be said for dancing, or having dinner with friends, or hiking in the mountains. What's so good about the practice of meditation? It helps to relax the tyranny of the thinking mind and restore a more natural state of consciousness that is in harmony with the larger reality. In so doing, the practice of meditation increases the joy of living. In fact, meditation practice may well make the difference between the *joy* of living and the *agony* of living.

Let's end this section where we began, with the basic gatha of Zen Buddhism:

> A special transmission outside of scriptures;
> No dependence on words or letters;
> Direct pointing at the mind of man;
> Seeing into one's nature, and the attainment of Buddhahood.

I hope that you see now that this is a beautifully terse statement of the essential character of Zen Buddhism. By declaring the two basic positions, the gatha sets the foundation for all that will come later. We are told that "a direct pointing at the mind of man" (satori) is the sudden way in which awakening shall happen. We are also told that satori is aroused by "a special transmission outside of scripture." This has been the guiding light of the tradition of Zen Buddhism from the time of Bodhidharma to the present day.

HUINENG (HUI-NENG)

Two great masters shaped the development of Zen in its early days: Bodhidharma and Huineng. Bodhidharma is honored as the first patriarch of Zen (Chan) in China. He brought the teaching from India, Buddha's homeland, and planted it in the soil of China. Huineng, the sixth patriarch, in a sense completed the work begun by Bodhidharma. Whereas Bodhidharma was something of a foreign missionary, Huineng was thoroughly Chinese. In the teaching of Huineng, we reach the mature expression of Zen Buddhism, which by now had become a decidedly Chinese creation. After Huineng, Zen Buddhism would continue to grow and evolve, but the essential philosophy would not change. Indeed,

> The figure of the sixth patriarch came to embody a comprehensive and inspiring image of the perfection of Zen—what disciples came to call the "Zen of the Patriarchs." . . . It is the figure of Hui-neng that Zen has elevated to the

stature of the Zen master par excellence. His teachings stand at the source of all the widely diverse currents of Zen Buddhism.[2]

The teachings of Huineng are to be found in a long discourse known as *The Sutra of the Sixth Patriarch* (more popularly known as "The Platform Sutra"). This work was lovingly copied and preserved through the early centuries of Zen history and has come down to us in a reasonably complete form. The fact that it is called a sutra is significant. Technically speaking, "sutra" refers to words of Buddha that have been preserved in writing. To identify Huineng's discourse as a sutra is to imply a belief that his teaching is perfectly in accord with the teaching of Buddha.

Presumably, Bodhidharma departed from China around 530 C.E., turning over the role of patriarch to his chosen successor, Hui Ko. Huineng does not appear on the stage of Zen history until the year 662 C.E., at which time he was accepted as a young novice in the monastery of Hongren (Hung-jen), the fifth patriarch. In the intervening hundred thirty or so years, Zen had been growing and establishing its place, but there had been no dramatic changes. The time was ripe for the work of a great leader.

Bodhidharma got the ball rolling in a new direction; he initiated a process of development that would continue through the sixth and seventh centuries, finally reaching completion in the time of the sixth patriarch, Huineng. The traditional way of gradual enlightenment had great appeal, however, and would remain strong well after the time of Bodhidharma. The brotherhood of Zen (Chan) was divided on the issue of gradual versus sudden enlightenment. The seventh century progressed toward a showdown on the matter. It came to a head in the conflict between Shenxiu (Shen-hsiu) and Huineng. Both men were nominally disciples of Hongren, the fifth patriarch. It's possible that their chroniclers have exaggerated the men's personal roles in this conflict, in order that they may stand as dramatic symbols of the two sides. In any case, the future of Zen was to be fundamentally shaped by the outcome of this controversy.

It must have looked as if the future belonged to Shenxiu (pronounced Shen-shoo), a brilliant scholar and a dedicated Buddhist monk. He was the leader of a broadly popular movement within Zen known as the "Northern School." Essentially, the Northern School was a refitting of the gradual approach to enlightenment.

Shenxiu accepted without question that at the core of one's being is the Buddha-nature, pure and undefiled. He compared the Buddha-nature to an absolutely perfect mirror, so pure, in fact, that you don't even know it's there. (This mirror simile, by the way, was originally introduced by the Chinese philosopher Zhuang Zi, a great Daoist master who followed Lao Zi.) The purity of the Buddha-nature becomes clouded over with the accumulating "dust" of the thinking mind's attachments, especially the passions of ego. The path to enlightenment is to clean the mind-mirror by long practice of the disciplines, especially meditation. Then, once cleaned, the mind-mirror must be watched and recleaned constantly through the continuous practice of meditation. Thus, meditation becomes the all-important discipline, gradually removing the obstacles—the "dust"—that prevent us from looking within and knowing the Buddha-nature (in other words, from achieving enlightenment). It's an appealing doctrine, especially to those who had chosen the way of life of the Buddhist monk. Shenxiu's doctrine doesn't exactly negate the teaching of Bodhidharma; it leaves the door open, but clearly, the emphasis is on the more traditional Buddhist approach of the gradual way to enlighten-ment through uncovering the obstacles to it.

The traditional way reached its finest expression in the teaching of Shenxiu. It was taken for granted by his admirers that Shenxiu would become the sixth patriarch; it was only a matter of time. Then, one day, modest little Huineng arrived at the monastery gate. No one would have paid much attention to him at the time. They should have, though; he was destined to win the struggle with the great Shenxiu. It was Huineng who would become the sixth, and last, of the patriarchs and who would set the charac-ter of Zen Buddhism for all time to come—but not without a struggle.

Like Confucius, Huineng experienced poverty as a child. Both lost their fathers at the age of three, and because his mother was too poor to afford schooling, Huineng remained illiterate. They lived in a small rural village in the south of China, where Huineng helped out by gathering firewood which he sold in the village market. One day when he was about twenty-four years old, he overheard someone in the marketplace reciting passages from the *Diamond Sutra* (part of the *Prajnaparamita*). One line in particular made a deep impression on him: "Let your mind rise freely, without attach-ing it to anything." We are told that these words had a profound effect on Huineng. Suddenly, the only thing that mattered in life was pursuing the deeper wisdom of the Buddhist scriptures. After seeing to it that his mother was cared for, Huineng set out on the long journey north to the monastery of the Zen Master Hongren, known in Zen history as the fifth patriarch. The monastery, known as *Paolinsi*, was located in a region of the north known as the Yellow Plum Mountain.

Hongren was a famous man. His monastery was home to five hundred monks; some say a thousand. When the humble-looking Huineng arrived and asked to be admitted, he was rebuffed by Hongren. They had no room for an illiterate "barbarian" from the south. Indeed, could *anything* good come from the south? Hongren, of course, was following a common procedure in Zen by brusquely turning away someone seeking to become a disciple. It was up to Huineng to persuade the master that he was genuinely sincere. This he did by commenting that north and south constitute the kind of duality that Buddha taught has no real meaning. In Buddha's teaching, all people are the same. Hongren was immediately impressed by the young man before him and allowed him to join the com-munity. He would not become a monk right away; typically, a novice remained a layper-son for several years before being initiated into the brotherhood of monks.

Compared to the others, Huineng was a very humble sort. He was poor, he was uneducated, he couldn't even read or write, and as if that weren't bad enough, he was from the rural south, a region regarded as "hillbilly country" by the more sophisticated northerners. Presumably, Huineng was treated poorly by the monks, who held him in contempt. He was put to work as a rice pounder, the most menial task in the monastery. This was a job often done by animals, stomping on the dried rice kernels to separate the husks from the grain. Huineng was so small and light that he had to tie a heavy stone weight around his waist when he worked.

On the one hand, this picture of Huineng—the humble, illiterate farm boy despised by his betters—may be entirely accurate. On the other hand, it may be contrived to some extent. Zen has always set itself against the way of the intellectual, favoring instead the way of the innocent and natural person. Heinrich Dumoulin, a modern-day historian of Zen, suggests that the character of the young Huineng may be a carefully fashioned composite of desired elements: "All the particular features of the story, whether factual or idealized, are fashioned into a composite whole. First we are shown the strong farm boy whose care for his aged mother manifests the filial piety that is so distinctive of the humanity of his people; then there is the image of the illiterate youth, untouched by book learning, a pure child of nature and at the same time a 'seeker of Tao.'"

After Huineng had been working as a rice pounder for about eight months, an event occurred that was to change the course of Zen. Hongren invited each of the monks to write out a gatha that would summarize that monk's understanding of Zen. If one of the gathas revealed that the writer had achieved enlightenment, that person would be named Hongren's successor and would inherit the much-treasured robe and bowl of Buddha. At the time, the senior monk was Shenxiu. As mentioned before, he was brilliant, dedicated, and much admired by the other monks. Shenxiu was a true scholar, and apparently, it was almost taken for granted that he would be Hongren's successor. Shenxiu was a star. None of the other monks even considered writing out a gatha; this was clearly the time for Shenxiu to demonstrate his brilliance and claim the prize that he so rightly deserved.

Shenxiu, however, may not have been quite so confident. According to one popular version of the story, he composed his gatha during the night and wrote it out with chalk on a monastery wall, but left it unsigned. Perhaps he wanted to see what the reaction would be before claiming it as his own. Here's what he wrote:

> The body is the Bodhi tree,
> The mind is like a clear mirror.
> At all times we must strive to polish it,
> And must not let the dust collect.

The following day, everyone was awed by the gatha. There was no doubt who the author was, and praise of Shenxiu's wisdom was on everyone's lips. Hongren also praised Shenxiu, even going so far as to burn incense and conduct a brief ceremony before the gatha. That was for public display; privately, he invited Shenxiu to his room for a little talk. Hongren said that the gatha was very good, but it revealed to him that Shenxiu had not yet really attained enlightenment. It was as if he was at the gate, but had not yet entered. He encouraged Shenxiu to keep striving and to try writing another gatha.

Why do you suppose that Hongren felt that Shenxiu's gatha revealed something less than real enlightenment? Clearly, the theme of the gatha was in line with widely held beliefs at the time. Many of the other monks must have been experienced and knowledgeable, yet the general feeling was that Shenxiu had done a remarkable job of capturing the essence of Zen Buddhism.

There was one person, though, who did not agree with Shenxiu's statement at all. Huineng could not have read the gatha himself, but it was the talk of the monastery, and he overheard others repeating it aloud. In his mind, he had been thinking about the assignment, and after hearing what Shenxiu had written, he couldn't restrain himself. It was a bold move for a rice pounder, one who wasn't even a monk, but it was one of those things that just had to be done. Huineng talked one of the monks into writing out his gatha for him in the middle of the night. The next morning, the community discovered a new gatha, right there on the wall beside Shenxiu's gatha. It was a response to the statement of Shenxiu. This is what it said:

> Originally there is no tree of enlightenment,
> Nor is there a stand with a clear mirror.
> From the beginning not one thing exists;
> Where, then, is a grain of dust to cling?

The monks were more than a little shocked to discover that Huineng was the author of the gatha. This time there was no ceremony, no burning of incense, no expressions of praise—but there was a little talk in Hongren's room. Hongren saw at once that modest little Huineng was a genuinely enlightened man. Illiterate rice pounder though he was, he towered over all of the others in the perfection of his wisdom. And this could cause problems. Given the social politics of the monastery, it would be unthinkable for Hongren to openly declare that Huineng was to be his successor; such an announcement would provoke an uprising. It was almost as if Shenxiu was the leader of a party; his followers would never tolerate his being set aside in favor of this uneducated "barbarian" from the South.

On the other hand, Hongren couldn't deny the succession to the one truly enlightened man in the community, humble though he might be. To keep the peace, he devised a plan. There in his tiny room in the middle of the night, Hongren invested Huineng with the legitimacy of the succession; Huineng was named the sixth patriarch. He was given the robe and bowl of Buddha, which Hongren had carefully preserved, and then Hongren told Huineng to leave the monastery at once, to go back to the South and stay there out of harm's way until things had cooled off. In time, Hongren hoped, he could persuade the others to accept his choice. Things would work out; Huineng was, after all, the rightful heir of the patriarchate.

Predictably, there was an uproar when the others discovered what Hongren had done. Certain monks, led by one Huiming (Hui-ming), took off immediately after Huineng, hoping to overtake him on the road south. Apparently, some of the followers of Shenxiu felt bold enough to openly defy the master of the monastery. Undoubtedly, there is much to this story that we will never know, but we can assume that the followers of Shenxiu were not willing to tolerate the idea of someone else inheriting the succession. Perhaps they perceived some sort of conflict between Hongren and Shenxiu. Maybe they thought that Hongren was envious of Shenxiu's popularity and had joined some sort of conspiracy to deprive him of what was rightfully his. Why else would he have sent the precious robe of Buddha off with that ignorant rice pounder in the middle of the night? The insignia of the robe and the bowl were the all-important symbols of the right to preside as patriarch. They must be retrieved at all costs.

Huiming and his companions succeeded in catching up with Huineng. It was in a high pass of the Mount Da Yu region that the meeting took place. Huiming demanded that Huineng return the robe. Presumably, the robe was no longer worn; it was a sacred relic, probably folded and wrapped in protective layers. Was it actually Buddha's robe? Who can say? It might have been, but it's doubtful that much would have been left of a simple cloth garment more than a thousand years old. Any old robe would have served the purpose just as well. Huineng remained calm. He placed the robe on a large rock and said in so many words, "This robe is a symbol of our sacred tradition. It must not be an object of violence. It was given to me, and it's wrong for you to take it, but it would be worse still for us to fight over it. Take it, if you must, and go on your way."

According to the legendary story of this encounter, Huiming walked over to the robe and took hold of it, but he couldn't lift it. Try as he might, he was unable to budge it from the rock. At last, shaking with fear, he turned to Huineng, saying, "The robe is a symbol of the Truth. It's the Truth I want, not the robe. I thought I came here for the robe, but I see now that I came here for the Truth. Please, show me what it is that I seek."

Huineng's response to this dramatic turnabout was original. He didn't quote from the sutras or anything like that. Instead, he posed a question to Huiming that brought him up short. He asked Huiming a simple question that had the effect of turning his thinking inside out. It was the beginning of a technique that was to become very popular in the evolution of Zen. Huineng approached Huiming and said something like this: "If you wish to see the truth of your own nature, forget about these value judgments of who's right and who's wrong. Instead, look deep inside yourself and tell me, what does your original face look like, before you were ever born?"

It's not important that these words do not seem to make sense literally. It was not Huineng's intention to be speaking rationally at that moment. Indeed, the question was not *meant* to be answered rationally; its purpose was to provoke a certain kind of consciousness in Huiming, which could then open into a higher understanding. And that's exactly what happened. We are told that Huiming experienced enlightenment on the spot. Huineng, the simple man unfettered by scholarly learning, had devised a new and direct way of communicating. Zen would never be the same again.

Huiming returned without the robe, and Huineng continued on to a monastery at Cao Qi (T'sao-ch'i), which would be his new home for the next five years. (Some say it was closer to sixteen years.) During this time, Huineng received full monastic ordination and began to attract a following. Huineng had a new way of getting at the truth of Buddha's teaching. He didn't depend on the sutras or on long hours of meditation practice. He focused on loosening the mental straightjacket of our customary way of thinking. A famous example of this occurred one time when Huineng was visiting the monastery of Zhi Zhi (Chih-chih). He encountered three young monks embroiled in a passionate argument concerning the true nature of a pennant above the roof of one of the buildings. The first monk argued that it was the pennant itself that was flapping. The second monk claimed that it was the wind that was waving. The third monk argued that both were inanimate objects and that neither was flapping. Huineng interrupted them, saying, "It is not the wind that flaps, nor is it the pennant that flaps. It is your mind that is flapping."

Eventually, Huineng would return in triumph to the monastery of Paolinsi (Pao-lin-ssu; known in Japanese as the monastery of Horin-*ji*). Hongren had died in the meantime, and Huineng became the master of the monastery. It was during this time that Huineng delivered his famous discourse known as the Sutra of the Sixth Patriarch. Some say that he returned again to the south to spend his last days at Cao Qi. In any case, his body was buried there in a splendid shrine. Huineng died, we are told, in 713 C.E. at about the age of seventy-five. His death was mourned by thousands; he had become a legend in his time. Huineng was the epitome of what a Zen Master should be. As mentioned earlier, "It is the figure of Huineng that Zen has elevated to the stature of the Zen Master par excellence. His teaching stands at the source of all the widely diverse currents of Zen Buddhism."

Huineng did not designate a successor; the line of patriarchs came to an end with him. The character of Zen was now fully formed; there was no longer seen to be a need for preserving a distinct line of development.* We may also speculate that Huineng was personally sensitive to the problems that the succession could cause. For example, it could result in political divisions within the brotherhood, and that could lead to violent quarrels between the factions. Also, the robe of Buddha, meant to be an inspiring symbol of the tradition, could all too easily become a fetish in the minds of many. It had become something to be fought over, and venerated almost as if it possessed magical powers. Add to this the difficulty of caring for it—and the likelihood that it wasn't really Buddha's robe anyway—and the best course of action became clear to Huineng: Honor the traditions of the past, but allow a new way to open for the future of Zen. Put to rest the elements that could be divisive and misleading, and encourage instead that which united the brotherhood, the way of Buddha as preserved in the teaching of Zen.

Hongren was once asked why he made the seemingly unlikely choice of Huineng as his successor. His answer was wonderful: "Of my five hundred disciples, four hundred ninety-nine possessed a remarkable understanding of Zen. Only Huineng did not understand Zen. That's why I chose him." Clearly a facetious reply, but not entirely. Hongren was distinguishing between rational understanding and intuitive understanding. The four hundred ninety-nine had crafted an impressive intellectual understanding based on knowledge *about* Zen. They knew all about the history and the doctrine, and they were skillful in the disciplines. In other words, as Zen monks, they made an excellent appearance. Huineng, on the other hand, would never be mistaken for a great intellectual. But his understanding transcended the rational and the discursive; it was of the intuitive sort that spontaneously grasped the real nature of Zen consciousness.

It would be a mistake, though, to characterize Zen as antirational or antiintellectual. Far from it; Zen has a rich tradition of historical and philosophical literature. In fact, it's ironic that in modern times Zen—with its "no dependence on words or letters"—enjoys almost an embarrassment of riches in this respect. It's very important to understand that point: The tradition of Zen Buddhism does not in any way damn the rational, thinking

---

*Each of Huineng's five principal disciples was said to be the founder of a distinct school of Zen derived from the teaching of the master. Out of respect for their contribution, these men are often referred to as patriarchs in the history of Zen Buddhism.

mind. The mind is an excellent human faculty. In its proper sphere, the reasoning ability has much to contribute to life. But the rational thinking mind has its limitations.

The object of thought is always "things," including ideas. The thinking mind can thus amass great conceptual knowledge concerning everything that may be an object of thought. But that which thinks can never be an object of its own thought, anymore than the eye can see itself. Real self-knowledge, therefore—not conceptual knowledge *about* the self—depends on a mode of knowing that transcends the limitations of the thinking mind. In the Zen tradition, as in Mahayana generally, this power is known as *prajna*, the highest wisdom—the intuitive, experiential knowing of one's act of being. As mentioned before, the eye of *prajna* opens only when we are willing to let go of our fixation on the activity of the thinking mind.

The main thrust of Zen training is to help the student break free of the normal human attachment to discursive thinking. Zen teaches that one will never discover the truth of one's own nature (the Buddha-nature) through the thought processes of the reasoning mind. Awakening is an intuitive leap of insight that completely transcends thought; in fact, it can't occur until one is willing to let go of the grip of the thinking mind. Only when one does that is the eye of *prajna* free to see the truth. *Prajna* is intuitive wisdom. We might say that the opening of the eye of *prajna* is what satori is all about.

Establishing the central importance of the satori experience was the combined work of Bodhidharma and Huineng. Bodhidharma, the first patriarch of Zen, began the formative process. Huineng completed the work begun by Bodhidharma. By the time of Huineng's death in 713 C.E., the fundamental nature of Zen was established. Zen (Chan) had become a unique expression of Buddhism within the broad umbrella of Mahayana. Zen would continue to grow and evolve, and it is evolving even today, but the original character laid down during the time of Bodhidharma and Huineng has remained a solid and unchanging foundation. This is known as the Zen of the Patriarchs.

Whereas Bodhidharma introduced the concept of satori, sudden enlightenment, into China and taught that that was the correct understanding of how awakening occurs, Huineng went on to clarify, in a sense, the nature of an authentic satori experience. One could conceivably be fooled by the dramatic impact of a powerful insight. Genuine awakening, genuine satori, has about it a particular character. Huineng said it best in his famous wall gatha:

> Originally there is no tree of enlightenment,
> Nor is there a stand with a clear mirror.
> From the beginning not one thing exists;
> Where, then, is a grain of dust to cling?

"From the beginning not one thing exists." Here we have a concise statement of *shunyata*, the "Doctrine of Emptiness." Huineng, in opposition to the point of view expressed by Shenxiu, was declaring that *emptiness* is the ultimate ground of all being. In doing this, he was reviving a current of philosophical interpretation that the Zen tradition believes can be traced back to Buddha himself. We find elements of this interpretation in the *Prajnaparamita*, from which Nagarjuna developed the teaching of *shunyata*. If I may paraphrase an earlier section of the book dealing with the thought of

Nagarjuna, "As the familiar perceptions of reality are stripped away, there remains ultimately nothing but a great void, an emptiness, but a hugely pregnant emptiness. This infinite emptiness (*shunyata*) is reality. It is the eternal womb from which issues all that is. To know the reality of *shunyata* is to experience awakening."

Bodhidharma, too, was clearly in the spirit of *shunyata*, though we have only fragments of his words to base this assessment on. One such fragment derives from his conversation with Emperor Wu. Perhaps you will recall his seemingly mysterious answer to Wu's question, "What is the first principle of this holy doctrine?" "Vast emptiness," was Bodhidharma's reply (and, he went on to say, there is nothing holy about it).

Zen Buddhism maintains that *emptiness* is ultimate reality. Conceptually, this may seem negative. Actually, it is not negative at all; it seems negative only because the thinking mind cannot form a concept of emptiness; we must mentally *negate* every possible "thing," every possible form that can be an object of thought. What's left is the emptiness *out of which* the forms of reality are forever becoming. The matter of central importance in the teaching of emptiness (*shunyata*) is that nothing—*no thing*—is real in any substantive sense. Everything is a *doing* out of emptiness, from whence it comes and shall return. (Does this remind you of the Vedanta interpretation of *maya*?) No thing—*nothing*!—is real unto itself. Yet the thinking mind greedily conceptualizes a reality for all that it fastens upon. The thinking mind creates its own personal reality and then creates an attachment to it. (No wonder we have troubles!)

The idea of "mind" is itself one of the *things* that the thinking mind conceptualizes. In an insidious way, this is the strongest of all mental illusions. After all, this is home base. Mind ("my" mind) is what one ordinarily identifies as self and clings to with a psychological death grip. To deny the substanding reality of mind is to pull the rug—indeed, the rug *and* the floor—out from under one. There is nothing for the ego to stand on. But that is exactly what the Doctrine of Emptiness does. It flatly denies the substantive reality of mind, thus removing this illusory psychological foundation. True, there is nothing left to stand on, but this is seen as the necessary condition for the awakening of true knowledge.

Huineng came to represent what would become the fundamental position of Zen with regard to the nature and attainment of satori. His wall gatha makes the point beautifully. Perhaps this whole matter of Huineng's doctrine of emptiness will make better sense if we look at both gathas side by side.

Shenxiu	**Huineng**
The body is the Bodhi tree,	Originally there is no tree of enlightenment,
The mind is like a clear mirror.	Nor is there a stand with a clear mirror.
At all times we must strive to polish it,	From the beginning not one thing exists;
And must not let the dust collect.	Where, then, is a grain of dust to cling?

In his gatha, Shenxiu clearly treats the mind as a thing; it is an unquestioned assumption. The goal is to see the mind in its original purity and then continually clean it (wipe away the dust) so that it retains its original purity. In his gatha, Shenxiu was expressing the dominant belief prevailing up to his time:

> The position of the Northern school is clearly expressed in Shen-hsiu's [Shenxiu's] metaphor. The mirror of the mind must be wiped clean continually lest the dust of erroneous notions collect on it. This is why one meditates. In such meditation an ongoing process of cleansing takes place until enlightenment is attained.[3]

Huineng's gatha was a response to Shenxiu's. As you can see, he flatly rejects the fundamental assumption of Shenxiu's position. One can practice meditation for a thousand years, but one will never uncover the "clear mirror" of the mind, for the simple reason that mind—as a something in itself—simply does not exist. It is only an idea, and so long as one clings to that illusory idea, true awakening will remain forever elusive:

> In the dust-wiping type of meditation it is not easy to go further than the tranquilization of the mind; it is so apt to stop short at the stage of quiet contemplation, which is designated by Huineng "the practice of keeping watch over purity." At best it ends in ecstasy, self-absorption, a temporary suspension of consciousness. There is no "seeing" in it, no knowing of itself, no active grasping of self-nature, no spontaneous functioning of it, no *chen-hsing* ("Seeing into Nature") whatever. The dust-wiping type is therefore the art of binding oneself with a self-created rope, an artificial construction which obstructs the way to emancipation. No wonder that Huineng and his followers attacked the Purity school.[4]

Plainly, Huineng asserts that there is no causal connection whatsoever between meditation and awakening. Shenxiu and his followers in the Northern School are mistaken; the experience of awakening is not dependent on meditation. Awakening happens—if it happens—when, and only when, the person is ripe for the experience. One can no more work to achieve awakening than can a sleeping person deliberately work at *achieving* the event of awakening in the morning. It simply happens spontaneously.

Huineng dismissed the attitude of the Northern School regarding the practice of meditation, but he did not condemn meditation altogether. Presumably, Huineng did not personally find satisfaction in long hours of sitting meditation—certainly, not to the extent that Bodhidharma did—but he and the Southern School generally were open to the possibility that under the right conditions the practice of meditation could be very valuable. In fact, that practice (zazen) has always been a highly important part of Zen practice. Even today, members of Zen communities spend a significant part of each day meditating.

The lifestyle of a Zen Buddhist, in accord with the general principles laid down by Shakyamuni Buddha himself, is geared to freeing oneself from bondage to the ego attachments and aversions generated by the thinking mind. The whole Zen Buddhist way of life works to achieve this transformation of consciousness. Properly understood, *everything* becomes a meditation exercise: working, eating, walking, studying, sweeping—*everything*! Little by little, one is loosening the grip of the ego-centered thinking mind and thus creating a more receptive condition for the occasion of satori. This may or may not occur; one has no control over that, but one does have a measure of control with regard to a lifestyle that is more or less receptive to it. I would compare it to the matter of love. There is nothing in the world that you can do to *make* love happen. It springs into being, or it doesn't; it's not under your control. But there are many things you can do to influence the environment (so to speak), to improve the conditions for it.

Practicing meditation must be seen in this light. Again, *everything* becomes a meditation practice. But sometimes—not all the time, but some of the time—it is appropriate, and profoundly enjoyable, to just sit quietly for a while doing nothing, allowing your consciousness to turn deeply inward. Not everyone responds in the same way to this, but most people, once they get used to it, find the daily practice of sitting meditation to be a wonderful part of the total lifestyle of Zen Buddhism. The goal, of course, is not to find that "mind-mirror" down there beneath all the rubble of the thinking mind; Huineng took care of that misconception long ago. In fact, there is no goal; meditation is an experience that can be a boundless joy unto itself. Perhaps more than any other activity, sitting meditation provides the opportunity to turn inward and peer into the emptiness—the awesome emptiness—that is the fountainhead at the center of all that is.

"The fruit drops when it is ripe." The entire way of life of Zen Buddhism, including the practice of meditation, has the effect of nourishing the soil and thus the tree—and thus the fruit.

AFTER HUINENG

This is a good place to step back for a moment and take in the broad view—the big picture—that shows the relationship of Zen Buddhism to the larger story of which it is a part. The map of Eurasia will be helpful in that regard.

Over many centuries, the people of China had developed the arts of civilization to a high level and had evolved a society that was culturally and politically united. Chinese civilization had spread out to establish its homeland throughout the great river valleys of the far eastern part of the Eurasian continent. The land area of China was vast, but it was nonetheless defined rather clearly by geography. In all directions, the land of China ultimately gave way to the mountains of the south, the forests and deserts of the west, the high plains of the north, and, of course, the ocean to the east. So far as the people of China were concerned, these frontiers marked the limits of the civilized world. Beyond the pale were the "barbarian" lands. These neighboring people, however, borrowed much from Chinese civilization, which was the cultural fountainhead whose waters nourished everyone. Thus, the Chinese came to regard their own land as the "Central Kingdom." Chinese civilization could go about its way of life, serene, superior, and securely situated at the center of the universe—well, not entirely secure: One of those "barbarian" frontiers refused to remain obligingly peaceful and subordinate.

To the north of China were the vast steppes of north-central and northeastern Eurasia. This was the trackless homeland of the people known to history as the

Mongols. They were a conglomerate of nomadic tribal peoples, and their numbers were beyond counting. The Mongols' way of life was much like that of the nomadic Aryans, with whom this story began many pages ago. From time to time, mounting pressures would unleash migrating waves of these nomadic people onto the lands of their agricultural neighbors. Whereas Aryan predations were directed toward India and the western parts of Eurasia, the Mongols' land of opportunity was southward into the great civilization of China. The Huns had been a Mongol people, and the Great Wall of China was constructed to hold them back. It helped the Han emperors keep the peace for more than five hundred years before finally being overwhelmed. Eventually, peace and order returned to China, and the northern defenses were reconstructed. But the pressure began to build again, and in the twelfth century Mongol horsemen swept down from the north once more. Within about a century, they had extended their rule over much of China, bringing down the curtain on a particular era of Chinese history. It was during this era before the mongol conquest, known as the Tang and the Song dynasties, that the great story of the early development of Zen Buddhism in China had been played out.

The historical dates of the Tang (T'ang) Dynasty are 618 C.E. to 907 C.E. Bodhidharma had set the course of Zen (Chan) in the century preceding the formation of Tang, but for the most part, the initial developmental stage of Zen, the "Age of the Patriarchs," was in the time of Tang. This was a wonderfully creative period; some regard it as the high-water mark of Chinese civilization. The late Tang was the "golden age" of Zen Buddhism (Chan Buddhism) as well. After a brief time of internal disorder in the early tenth century, the more military-oriented Song (Sung) Dynasty became established in 960 C.E. Among other things, the Song emperors had the job of holding back the Mongol hordes, which they succeeded in doing until 1129 C.E., at which time the dam broke and the entire northern part of the empire was lost to the invaders. The court retreated to the south, where the dynasty, known as the "Southern Song," continued to rule for another century and a half. The Mongols, though, under the leadership of such warlords as Ghengiz Khan, eventually conquered the south as well, creating a new Chinese–Mongol empire known in history as the Yuan Dynasty.

Yuan came into existence in 1280 C.E. and would rule China for a century. The first of the Yuan emperors was that intriguing character we know as Kublai Khan. Being essentially a foreign conqueror, Kublai Khan found it expedient to employ many non-Chinese in high government posts. Perhaps he felt more secure that way. One of his highly placed foreigners, incidentally, was a young traveler named Marco Polo from a very, very faraway place named Venice. Marco Polo was one of the first Europeans to visit the empire of China, and when he finally returned to Venice, his countrymen found it hard to believe his stories about the dazzling refinements of Chinese civilization. Only two centuries later, however, another of his countrymen, Christopher Columbus, took Polo's stories seriously and risked everything on a daring sea voyage that, hopefully, would find a direct route to the rich land of China. In addition to Polo's book, Columbus carried with him a letter from the Queen of Spain introducing him to the emperor of China. It's a wonderful story; all the strands are woven together like a tapestry. But now let's get back to that part of this history which we call Zen Buddhism.

Once again, Zen as a distinct school of Buddhism took form in China during the six centuries prior to the Mongol conquest—that is to say, during the time of the Tang and Song Dynasties. During the first part of this period, the time of the six patriarchs, the basic character of Zen was established. (Recall that the Zen tradition was known as Chan during its developmental years in China.) By the time of the death of Huineng in 713 C.E., the various factions within Zen had come together. The controversies that had formerly divided the Zen movement into a Northern School and a Southern School had been resolved, and what came to be called the "Zen of the Patriarchs" gave a unity of doctrine and practice to all men and women who followed the way of Zen.

Several features of Zen gave it its distinct character within the broad umbrella of Buddhism. Most fundamental of all was the Zen emphasis on satori, sudden awakening. Various Buddhist disciplines, including meditation, might have a role to play, but no practice can *achieve* awakening. Through the guidance of an already awakened teacher, an individual can be urged to the state wherein he or she may be willing to let go of attachment-to-self and suddenly and spontaneously see the real truth of one's nature. The real truth is, of course, the Buddha-nature, which is the common essence of all beings, hidden from us only by our ignorance and the fear born of that ignorance.

The time following the death of Huineng was a time of consolidation and enrichment for Zen Buddhism. Daoist influences, always strong within the culture of China, were richly woven into the fabric of Zen during that time. Zen experienced near-explosive growth during the late Tang and Song periods. Zen was far from being the only Buddhist sect in China, though. Buddhist groups were so numerous and diverse as to be likened to the trees of a forest. Zen was only one part of the forest—an important part, to be sure—but just one part nonetheless.

Not all Buddhists, of course, were monks. One of the great attractions of Mahayana Buddhism was that it offered something for everyone. Lay men and women could also enjoy a rich Buddhist way of life. But those few who were willing to give up everything and dedicate their lives one hundred percent to practicing the Buddhist disciplines—in other words, the monks—would remain at the core of the movement.

From the very beginning of Buddhism in China, dedicated men and women formed themselves into monastic communities.* We have encountered references to monasteries often in the story of Buddhism's evolution in China. Bodhidharma, for example, stayed for nine years at the "monastery" of Shaolinsi. But the early monasteries were little more than loosely organized communities of men (or, in some cases, women) who shared a common interest in following the Buddhist way of life as best they understood it. As in the ashram, the role of the leader was all important. Undoubtedly, there was a large amount of personal freedom in such communities. During the late Tang and especially during the Song period, there was a great proliferation of Buddhist monasteries throughout China. Hilltops were favored sites, as often as not to leave the more fertile low regions available for agriculture. Hilltops throughout China were blossoming forth

---

*By the way, the word "monk" can refer to either a man or a woman, but it has become customary to use the more familiar word "nun" in referring to a woman. This, too, to say the least, can carry some unfortunately misleading connotations.

in Buddhist monasteries. With this increase in the number of monasteries came, for better or for worse, a general tightening of monastic discipline.

Zen monastic discipline underwent a transformation at this time, too. In the late eighth century, a Zen Master named Paijing (Pai-Jing) formulated a discipline for his own monastery that was soon being adopted by virtually all Zen monasteries. It was known as the "Pure Rule of Paijing," and it did for Zen Buddhism in China what the "Rule of Saint Benedict," the founder of the Benedictine Order, did for Christian monasticism in far-off Europe. (There is an interesting similarity between these monastic rules, but it is due only to coincidence. The likelihood that at that time they could have influenced one another is virtually zero.) The Rule of Paijing adapted the traditional Buddhist *vinaya* to a fully worked-out regimen for daily life in the monastery. It was the beginning of the monastic system that is still followed today in most Zen monasteries. Paijing gave special emphasis to the importance of manual labor. The Zen community must be fully self-supporting. Mendicancy would cease to have a necessary place in the life of a Zen Buddhist monk, although a purely ritualized mendicancy would continue to be practiced by most Zen monasteries. Paijing is credited with laying down the maxim "A day without working is a day without eating." But it wasn't just the practical need for labor that Paijing emphasized; he made work an important and dignified part of a monk's normal daily life. Instead of being something to be despised, manual labor of all kinds became an excellent form of active meditation. From that day to this, physical work became an essential part of the daily organization of every Zen monastic community; it is looked upon as honorable and joyful.

During this time of expansion, the "forest" of Buddhism not only spread throughout China, but began to encroach into some of the lands beyond China as well. To the south Chinese Buddhism spread into Vietnam, and in the northwest into Korea. It was from Korea that Chinese-style Buddhism would first begin to influence the world of Japan which, at that time in its history, was hungrily absorbing all that it could from the civilization of China. The Japanese cultural appetite was insatiable, and Buddhist ideas became an important part of the feast. In the year 801 C.E., a Japanese Buddhist named Saicho arrived in China for a four-year stay. He visited many monasteries, studying the teachings of different schools of Buddhism. His focus of study, though, was Tiantai, and when he returned to Japan, he founded what came to be known as Tendai Buddhism. This was something of a syncretism of Chinese Buddhism with a strong emphasis on the more "religious" and supernatural aspects than was common in some schools of Chinese Buddhism. With its strong mass appeal, Tendai laid the foundation of the Buddhist tradition in Japan; Zen would later have to compete with it. Japan was home to many Tendai monasteries when Zen first began to sink roots in that country in the twelfth century. But that's getting ahead of the story.

The Zen emphasis on self-sufficiency turned out to be a lifesaver. In the middle of the ninth century, something unexpected and horrible happened to Buddhism in China. The Tang emperor Wu Zung ascended to the throne in 841 C.E., and he immediately launched what Buddhists refer to as the Great Persecution. (Very much the same sort of thing had happened almost exactly four hundred years before, and at that very time as well, the persecution of Lang Darma was raging in Tibet. Perhaps the Tibetan persecution helped to evoke its companion in China.)

It seems that Wu Zung was determined to wipe out Buddhism altogether in the land that he ruled. His reign, mercifully, lasted for only five years, and his successor quickly put an end to the persecution, but in those few years Wu Zung clear-cut the forest of Buddhism in China, and many Buddhist organizations never recovered from the devastation. He forced more than two hundred thousand monks to give up the monastic way of life and return to their families. More than four thousand monasteries were closed, most of the land being confiscated and sold. These are staggering numbers! However, much as Wu Zung was determined to stamp out Buddhism, there was at least some civilized touch in his method. For one thing, the monks were not slaughtered this time; they were simply required to go back to their family homes. And monks who were too old or too sick to work were allowed to live out their final years in a few special monasteries that were spared for this purpose. So it would seem that real hatred was not the motivating force behind the persecution.

Why, then, did Wu Zung so fervently wish to expunge Buddhism from China? We can only guess, but some things seem pretty clear. To begin with, Wu Zung was not acting entirely alone in this matter; he was the leader of an anti-Buddhist movement made up of some Daoists, some Confucians, and probably a fair percentage of the common people as well. This group within the Chinese population perceived Buddhism as a threat, to themselves personally and to the much-loved traditions of Chinese culture. When one of their own became emperor, the time to act was at hand.

As we have seen, from the very beginning there had been tension between the Buddhists on the one hand and the Chinese Daoists and Confucians on the other. Despite the strong cross-fertilizing influences between Buddhism and Daoism and even between Buddhism and Confucianism, many Daoists and Confucians still harbored negative feelings toward the "foreign" philosophy of Buddhism. This was especially so among Confucian scholars, who enjoyed a virtual monopoly of government positions. As long as the Buddhist movement remained relatively small in China, the conflict could be contained. But during the Tang period, Buddhism began to grow very rapidly in China.

More specifically, Buddhist *monasticism* was growing rapidly. Confucians in government and leaders of Daoist organizations probably felt threatened, not by the philosophy of Buddhism in general, but rather by the "institutional" power of the Buddhist monasteries, which were specifically defined centers of Buddhist influence and potential political power. At least that's how non-Buddhists might well have seen them, and they were increasing in numbers at an alarming rate. In the eyes of the anti-Buddhists the Buddhist monastery system threatened to overwhelm the traditional institutions of Chinese culture. The movement must be halted before it was too late. Wu Zung and company looked upon Buddhist monasticism as if it were an unhealthy foreign weed that had invaded the soil of China. Exterminate it, and the soil could once again nourish the native plants (Confucianism and Daoism, for example) that were age-old products of Chinese culture and were thus much better suited to meet the needs of society. Better work fast, though; exterminate Buddhist monasticism quickly, before its defenders could mount a counterattack, as had happened in the fifth century.

This was the setting in which the Great Persecution occurred. All that was needed was a rationale that would find broad support among the common people. To justify the closings of the monasteries, Wu Zung focused on the alleged threat they posed to the social order. (As we have seen in recent history, this was an argument that would prove useful again in the twentieth century.) This is not to say that the rationale was insincere. Ardent Daoist that he was, Wu Zung was presumably fully sincere in arguing that the Buddhist movement posed a threat to the social order. How reasonable that point of view was, though, is another matter altogether.

Wu Zung's argument, something of a replay of 445 C.E., would have gone something like this: Above all else, the Buddhist monastery system posed a dire threat to the institution of the family. Absolutely nothing in Chinese civilization (then as now) is of greater fundamental importance than the family. It is the bedrock foundation of the culture. The birth of children is what maintains a family over the generations. They are lovingly raised and nourished in the culture, and the expectation is that they will play a role for life in the support and maintenance of the family. Also, the family is what gives the individual identity. This is especially important in an agricultural economy, in which the loss of a son through war or illness is a severe blow.

Then, another sort of sinister influence entered the scene. Sons in many families were being lured away by the appeal of the monastic life. (The reason for such appeal is not easily defined; it resides deep in the heart of each individual who answers the call.) The Buddhist monk gives up the ties to his family completely; he becomes literally a homeless person. He voluntarily departs, depriving his loved ones not only of the warmth of his company, but also of his contribution to the work of the family. Off he goes to join another "family," a community of monks. Their life of celibacy assures that they won't even replace themselves, but will forever drain away a percentage of the productive young men from the families and villages of China.

And what of the monasteries themselves? These were not productive centers, viable alternatives to the agricultural villages they drew their membership from. With few exceptions (such as Zen monasteries), the monastic communities were actually parasitic. They depended largely on the generosity of others for their sustenance. And what did they give in return? Many were exempt even from paying taxes. Their members, arguing that they had "left society," claimed that they were thus exempt from rendering homage to the ruler and also that they were exempt from levies for providing military or social services. To the cold eye of an outsider, a typical Buddhist monastery might appear to be a totally unproductive institution made up only of individuals who wished to escape from reality and the work of human life. The seeming preoccupation with meditation practice would only reinforce this prejudice. There was just one thing to do: Strike it out. And Wu Zung struck.

When the dust finally settled after Wu Zung's death in 846 C.E., Buddhist monasticism in China had been dealt a devastating blow. Perhaps his crusade went too far too fast. There was a countermove when Wu Zung died, and, as mentioned before, his successor quickly clamped the lid on the campaign against the monasteries. But it was too late for many; their membership was scattered, their property confiscated or destroyed. Zen, however, came through the ordeal without being badly injured at all. Only Zen

Buddhism and Pure Land Buddhism, the two extremes of the Buddhist movement, escaped devastation during the Great Persecution.

Zen monasteries had been able to keep a low profile, partly because they preferred very remote locations and also because the Zen discipline emphasized self-sufficiency. Since Zen monasteries were accustomed to providing all of their own needs, they could more or less pull into their shells and wait out bad times. We can also speculate that Zen monasteries were well respected by the general population in the areas where they were located.

In any case, Chinese Buddhism in general experienced a major die-off as a result of the Great Persecution and thus went through something of an "evolutionary bottle-neck" in the mid-ninth century. The survivors—again, Pure Land Buddhism and Zen Buddhism—did the natural thing and began to expand rapidly to fill the void. This scenario helps to explain why Zen played such an important role in Chinese Buddhism by the time of the late Tang period. In the early Tang, Zen was only one small part of the forest, but by late Tang, much of the forest consisted of the various "schools" of Zen.

It is not within the scope of this work to go into detail regarding the various divisions that evolved within Zen Buddhism in the Tang and Song periods. Suffice it to say, for the record, that five major "schools" of Zen emerged. All were derived from the teaching of Huineng. The five were not in conflict; they got along together quite well, but each emphasized a somewhat different philosophical approach. The five would ultimately be reduced to two, and these two would flourish and come to dominate the world of Zen Buddhism up to the present time. This twofold division seems mysteriously to represent something basic in nature; it keeps reemerging. It seems that whenever one side manages to conquer the other and absorb it—as the Southern School did to the Northern School—before long, the resultant unity splits itself into a new two-some. Perhaps such dualism accords with some fundamental duality in the nature of the human psyche.

The split in Zen was expressed in the formation of Soto Zen and Rinzai Zen. Soto and Rinzai are the Japanese names, which are more familiar to the modern reader. The development of Soto and Rinzai, though, began during the late Tang period in China, where they were, of course, known by their original Chinese names. (In Chinese, *Soto* becomes *Caodao* in the pinyin system, *Ts'ao-tao* in the Wade–Giles system. *Rinzai* becomes *Linji* in pinyin; *Lin-chi* in Wade–Giles.)

The split between Soto and Rinzai is suggestive of the earlier division between the Northern School and the Southern School. In this comparison, Soto would be more akin to the Northern School, Rinzai to the Southern School. The resemblance, though, is only superficial; Soto and Rinzai have always been in fundamental agreement as to the nature of enlightenment. The differences between the two are almost entirely concerned with what are seen to be appropriate disciplines, especially with regard to the place of meditation practice.

Soto's resemblance to the Northern School is due largely to the great importance placed on sitting meditation, zazen, in daily life. But Soto did not revert to the "dust-wiping" interpretation of meditation practice that we found in the Northern School. Rather, Soto emphasized what was called "quiet illumination," meaning simply that long practice of zazen could create the perfectly "quiet" state of consciousness most conducive to the arising of satori. The rival (if I may call it that) Rinzai school took very strong exception to this position, contending that a preoccupation with zazen did not encourage illumination, "quiet" or otherwise; it produced only a state of peaceful tranquilization:

> Recently a type of heterodox Zen has grown up in the forest of Zen. By confusing the sickness with the remedy, they have denied the experience of enlightenment. . . . Because they have not experienced enlightenment, they think others have not either. Stubbornly they contend that an empty silence and a musty state of unconsciousness is the original realm of the absolute. To eat their rice twice a day and to sit without thoughts in meditation is what they call complete peace.[5]

And so the argument continues: to sit or not to sit. Perhaps, as mentioned before, the controversy ultimately boils down to a basic difference in human personalities. One type, which benefits tremendously from the more conservative and introverted approach, will incline toward Soto. Another, which prefers a more active approach, will choose Rinzai. Both Soto and Rinzai, though, respect the elementary power of zazen; it's a matter of emphasis. The debate is as much alive today as it ever was. By coincidence, two modern Japanese Zen Masters who have had much to do with transplanting Zen to the West were both named Suzuki. Daisetz T. Suzuki, of the Rinzai school, was a Zen scholar whose writings have greatly influenced Western students of Zen. He was personally much opposed to the practice of sitting meditation and may have inadvertently created a somewhat mistaken impression regarding the attitude of Zen in general on this matter. Shunryu Suzuki Roshi, a modern Soto Zen Master and founder of the Zen Center of San Francisco, put the whole matter of zazen very nicely in perspective:

> If you think you will get something from practicing zazen, already you are involved in impure practice. . . . When you practice zazen, just practice zazen. If enlightenment comes, it just comes. We should not attach to the attainment. The true quality of zazen is always there, even if you are not aware of it. Just do it.[6]

Soto and Rinzai are the right and left hands of Zen Buddhism. It would be seriously missing the point to think of one as better or more correct than the other. It comes down to a matter of where a given individual fits best. We will have more to say about Soto Zen later on; for now, let's turn to the development of the Rinzai tradition, which played a more dynamic role in the story of Zen's evolution in China.

The putative founder of the Rinzai school was one of the truly great characters in the history of Zen Buddhism. His name was Linji (Lin-chi). (To be more technically accurate, his name was Yi Xuan; Linji was the name of the monastery he headed, but he is universally referred to by the name Linji. "Rinzai" is simply our spelling for the way in which the Chinese name *Linji* was pronounced in Japanese.) Linji was also a product of the ninth century, that final and most splendid time of the Tang period. He died, probably in his mid-fifties, in 867 C.E. Most of what we know about his teachings are preserved in the *Rinzairoku*, the Japanese name for a collection of Linji's discourses.

Linji was interested in nothing less than creating a new kind of person, a genuine man or woman of Zen. He used the term "true human." Linji borrowed this term from Daoism, which philosophy heavily influenced his thinking. In a way Linji brought to fruition the long Buddhist affair with Daoism. Zen Buddhism, as a way of daily life, was seen to be an excellent vehicle for becoming a true human, a man or woman of Dao.

According to the teaching of Linji, the true human is first and foremost an *ordinary* person. Linji insisted that "in no way is the true human anything special," meaning that he or she is not interested in such artificial things as wealth or rank in society. The true human is free of attachments, is natural and simple in lifestyle, moving through daily life in a relaxed, cheerful manner. Linji further described such a person as "without root, without source, and without any dwelling place, yet brisk and lively." Linji's true human is a natural man or a natural woman at peace with the ultimate emptiness of reality and thus free to wander cheerfully through the mysterious adventure of human life.

Linji's true human was the beginning of that characteristically Zen type that gives a special and refreshing kind of charm to Zen Buddhism even to this day. (More than anything else, it was the ideal of this "Zen hobo" that inspired an interest in Zen among the younger generation of the West in the mid-twentieth century.) This Zen bikkhu was a very different kind of person from the more traditional monk, who, by comparison, was something of a monastic recluse withdrawn into an interior world of meditation. The character of the traditional Buddhist monk, including Zen monks, may well have played a part in the negative attitude that allowed Wu Zung's persecution to occur, and that very attitude may have influenced Linji's eagerness to fashion a "new man," a Buddhist monk who *really was* an embodiment of the Daoist ideal. Linji's dates would certainly support this speculation.

The way of the true human (the "Zen person") was, of course, opened up through awakening to the truth of one's nature—through seeing experientially that one's personal being is one with the universal Buddha-nature. Linji played down the use of such terms as "enlightenment" and "satori." Awakening, however, whether talked about or not, was naturally a matter of prime concern to him. Where his own students were concerned, however, he would employ a very different approach. Linji felt only scorn for those schools of Zen (including the newly forming Soto) which emphasized long hours of meditation: "Having stuffed themselves with food, [they] sit down to meditate and practice contemplation; arresting the flow of thought they don't let it rise; they hate noise and seek stillness. This is the method of the heretics!"[7]

Well, "heretics" may be overstating it, but it certainly wasn't overstating the intensity of Linji's personal feelings on the subject. He wanted a dynamic approach to Zen, as opposed to what he saw as quietism in others. Linji kept urging his disciples to believe in themselves, to give up running around searching for truth outside of themselves. His way of encouraging his students was also new and was the beginning of a tradition in Zen instruction that is often rather shocking to a person new to Zen study. Linji was not at all reluctant to strike his students with his staff, and strike them hard. Or he would come up close and shout at them, so loudly that one student complained that he couldn't hear anything but a ringing in his ears for three days. Linji really loved the technique of shouting. Consider this passage from the *Rinzairoku*:

> Sometimes a shout is like the jeweled sword of the Vajra King; sometimes a shout is like the golden-haired lion crouching on the ground; sometimes a shout is like a weed-tipped fishing pole; sometimes a shout doesn't function as a shout.

A shout "doesn't function as a shout," presumably, when it's intended that it function as something else. The real purpose of the blows and the shouts was to jolt the student out of his state of ego self-hypnosis. Naturally, this had to be artfully timed and delivered. Only a Zen Master like Linji could work such a technique effectively. Actually, Linji learned to use the rough stuff from his own guru, Ma Zi (Ma-tsu), another interesting personality who was said to be able to stick out his tongue so far that he could cover his nose. (If you're not impressed, try doing it yourself.) In addition to kicks and shouts, Ma Zi would sometimes grab a student's nose and twist it so hard that the person would cry out in pain.

I'm sure you're wondering whether all this violence is really necessary. The answer, of course, is no, but it was a specialized technique that became enormously popular as Linji's reputation spread. It was a dramatic way of emphasizing the new active approach to Zen, as opposed to the more traditional passive approach. There is something intriguing about it all. Direct physical involvement can break through in a way that mere words never will. Sometimes a student can be on the verge of awakening, but somehow be unable to go the final step. The discomfort of a blow from the master's staff is a trifling matter if it succeeds in breaking the mental knot of ego frustration. Let's face it; nothing jolts one into the here and now more abruptly than a sudden kick or a blow on the head. This technique remained popular, particularly in Rinzai monasteries, when Zen spread to Japan, but the modern Western world would seem to want no part of it.

Beginning in the time of Linji, the Rinzai tradition was grounded solidly on the basic Zen premise of satori: sudden enlightenment. Thus, Rinzai teachers were interested in methods that would get at satori in a more direct way than the path of meditation would. They preferred techniques that would jolt the mind out of its customary fixation on discursive thought. Blows and shouts could be helpful, but there was another method which was seen to be far more effective in the long run. In time, it would become the very trademark of the Rinzai approach. We can most simply describe this method as the "Zen paradox." By skillfully employing paradoxical statements and questions, the Zen Master attempts to jolt the mind of the student out of its normal rational mode of thinking and open it to an insight of a higher truth. This can be a progressive process, culminating ultimately in the opening of *prajna*, perfect satori.

The finest form of the "Zen paradox" is the *koan* (*gongan* in Chinese), a particular kind of question or riddle that cannot be solved rationally. In the hands of a skillful master, the koan becomes a razor-sharp knife for cutting through the knots of the thinking mind. The "Zen paradox," though, includes much more than the koan. There is a great wealth of Zen stories and one-liners out of which most of the popular koan have evolved. ("Koan," pronounced "koh-ahn," is the preferred form for both singular and plural.) Before examining this matter of the koan, let's look at a few representative Zen stories. Again, these are popular tales, drawn from the long tradition of Zen, that are paradoxical in nature. They might seem ridiculous in the everyday rational sense, but it is that very nonsensical feature which attempts to open the mind to a meaning *outside* the rational. It is truly said that the essence of Zen is condensed in the Zen story.

Huineng's encounter with the three students who were arguing about the waving pennant is an excellent example of a Zen story. In another story involving three students, a Zen Master approached the monks to test their understanding of Zen. He picked up a rice cake and, holding it out to the first monk, said, "What is this?" The flustered monk replied, "It's a rice cake, sir." The master shouted, "You fool!" and cracked him on the head with his staff. Then he asked the second monk, "What's this?" The second monk didn't say anything. He simply picked up the rice cake and took a big bite out of it. "Not bad; not bad," the master muttered. Then he turned to the third monk, who, without waiting to be asked, took the rice cake and, placing it on the top of his head, walked out of the room like a duck. "Now that man understands Zen," the master said.

Don't feel dismayed if you don't "get it." Zen stories are not jokes with punch lines (although that's another genre in itself). These stories are *meant* to be illogical. In each case, the Zen Master is looking for an expression, a *demonstration*, of the other person's understanding of Zen. Seemingly strange behavior or words can be that demonstration. In a way, we are eavesdropping on the Zen Master's conversation.

Zen Master Nanchuan (Nan-ch'uan), a contemporary of Linji, called his disciples together in order to test their understanding of Zen. Nanchuan was sitting in front of the group, holding one of the monastery cats in his lap. Suddenly he stood up, holding the cat high in one hand and a large knife in the other. "Anyone: Give me a true expression of Zen, or I will kill the cat!" The startled group of disciples remained silent. After a long moment, the master sliced the cat in two. That evening Nanchuan was telling the story of the cat to Zhao Zhou, one of his more advanced disciples, who had been away for the day. Without saying anything, Zhao Zhou took off his sandals and, putting them on top of his head, walked out of the room. "Oh, if only you had been there this afternoon," Nanchuan sighed. "That cat would still be alive."

I don't mean to give the impression that the "right" thing to do is to put something on your head and walk out of the room. These two stories just happen to end that way. Nor do I mean to suggest that Nanchuan really killed a cat to make his point. Maybe he did, but it's not likely that a Zen Master would do a thing like that. It makes a good story, though.

Zen Master Zhu Zhi (Chu-chih) was a quiet sort of person. When a student would ask him a question, he would often answer by simply smiling and raising his index finger—that's all, raising the finger just slightly. One day he caught one of his disciples imitating him. Zhu Zhi grabbed a kitchen knife and cut off the offending finger. In shock and pain, the disciple howled, "Why did you do that?" Zhu Zhi's answer was simply to smile and raise his finger. In that instant, the disciple achieved awakening.

Zen Master Bozhang (Po-chang) was very popular. His monastery grew so large that he decided to split the group in two, opening a new monastery not far away. He called his disciples together in order to select a master for the new monastery. He placed a large water pitcher on the floor in front of the group. "What is this?" he asked. The head monk was the first to speak. "Well, it's definitely not a piece of wood." The master was not impressed. The monastery cook, who had been standing at the back of the group, walked up to the pitcher and kicked it over; then he left the room. Bozhang made him the master of the new monastery.[8]

Many Zen stories include humor. In fact, the love of laughter is one of the most significant characteristics of Zen, as well as one of the most unusual. As R. H. Blythe points out, "It is possible to read the Bible without a smile and the Koran without a chuckle; no one has died laughing while reading Buddhist sutras. But Zen abounds in anecdotes that stimulate the diaphragm. Enlightenment is frequently accompanied by laughter of a transcendental kind which may further be described as a laughter of surprised approval." Throughout the ages, one of the best authentic demonstrations of Zen has been simply to break out in a genuine hard laugh (better even than putting your shoes on your head and walking out of the room). A very popular pair in the Zen tradition are the two monks Kanzen and Jittoku. These two "happy lunatics" would bum around together, laughing uproariously at everything they encountered: falling leaves, birds, broken chairs, even the full moon. No, they did not have the help of drugs; it was just their nature to see the humor in everything. This attitude is much admired in Zen.

Do you remember Ma Zi, the one who could cover his nose with his tongue? One of his monks asked him for help with the koan he had been working on. Ma Zi reminded him that he was supposed to bow deeply before addressing the master. The monk immediately bowed very deeply, and Ma Zi snuck around behind him and gave him a hard kick in the pants. The kick did the trick; the monk attained immediate enlightenment. It was the humor of it, though, that made the kick effective. "Since I received that kick from Ma Zi," the monk told everyone, "I haven't been able to stop laughing."

In their search for ways to jolt the student into satori, no device served Rinzai masters better than the koan. This is the most unusual and intriguing aspect of Rinzai Zen Buddhism. As mentioned earlier, the word *koan* is the Japanese form of the Chinese term *gongan*, which originally referred to a public announcement. In the Zen tradition, though, the word came to refer to a sort of riddle that was designed to defeat the dominance of the discursive intellect and thus allow the student to open up to an insight into the greater nonrational nature of reality. A koan exercise is given to a student by a Zen teacher. In "solving" the koan, the student, in effect, comes to share the state of mind of the teacher. The koan, therefore, is a dynamic tool that the skilled teacher uses to bring the student to satori.

To a large degree, the Rinzai tradition developed out of an effort to put new life—new direction—into the Zen movement and prevent it from slipping into the "quietism" that could lead to stagnation. Masters such as Linji scoured the accumulated lore of the Zen tradition, looking for stories and insightful sayings that could be used as *pointers* in the guidance of Zen disciples. Items that emphasized the "Zen paradox" were particularly favored, and out of this, the way of the Zen koan was born.

A koan can be a simple question, such as the one that has become a veritable cliche: "What is the sound of one hand clapping?" One of Huineng's questions became a very popular koan, often assigned to beginning students in Rinzai monasteries. "What is your original face, even before your parents were born?" Much more often, though, a koan is a combination of a question and the response. The question may be quite reasonable, but the response is what makes it a koan. For example, Zhao Zhou (Chao-chou) was asked, "What is the Buddha-nature?" His reply, "Three pounds of flax." Another koan, even more obscure, begins, "In what way do my feet resemble the feet of a donkey?" The answer is, "When the heron stands in the snow, its color is not the same."

A vast number of "official" koan have been collected in the Rinzai tradition—perhaps more than two thousand. The ones noted are just a few representative samples. They illustrate, though, the essential feature of all koan: There is absolutely no way that the rational mind can "make sense" of them, and a serious effort to do so will drive the rational mind into a fit of anxiety. Dumoulin refers to the koan as a "perplexing puzzle":

> One becomes confused, and the more one tries to come up with an answer and search for a solution, the more confused one gets. The essence of the koan is to be rationally unresolvable and thus to point to what is irrational. The koan urges us to abandon our rational thought structures and step beyond our usual state of consciousness in order to press into new and unknown dimensions. This is the common purpose of all koan, no matter how much they may differ in content or literary form.[9]

The koan exercise may seem harmless, but it's not meant to be fun and games at all. The appropriate place for it is within the monastic community, where the master can personally monitor the student's progress. In the routine of the monastery each student meets privately from time to time with the master. This practice is called *dokusan* in Japanese. The master may choose a koan exercise for the student, one that he judges to be appropriate to that particular student's state of mind. The student is then expected to give *all* of his time and energy to trying to understand the meaning of the koan. The master will check the student's progress during dokusan. It can be a terribly frustrating and exhausting ordeal for the student. For days, or even weeks, the rational mind tries to "figure out" a solution. No amount of cleverness, though, will ever fool the master, who insists that the student *demonstrate* in some fashion his understanding of the koan. Eventually, the discursive mind may give up and collapse in despair. And then— eureka!—the thing is had (maybe).

The whole point of the koan exercise rests on the premise that the rational thinking mind is capable, at best, of giving us a very imperfect knowledge of true reality. This is not to say that the rational thought process does not have an important role to play in the practical affairs of daily life—of course, it does—but it *is* to say that when we allow ourselves to become transfixed on thought, believing that the world of thought encompasses the whole of reality, we are very, very much self-deluded. As one author puts it,

> Zen holds that the so-called rational mind is incapable of solving an individual's deepest problem: his meaning to himself and to life. There is no way, in the Zen view, that conclusive answers to existential questions can be found by discussion, dialectic, or even ordinary thought. Final awareness, lasting freedom, and true psychological equilibrium come only when the deepest intuitional faculties of the human being have been tapped. It follows that, in Zen, reason is never permitted the unquestioned place of rulership it has occupied for centuries in Western philosophy. Zen holds that the reasoning process's function is separation, discrimination and the division of "this" from "that," thus making it impossible ever to see life's *wholeness* and oneself in relation to it. In Zen, since All-is-One, knowledge of one's own true nature predicates knowledge of all nature, or the universe itself.[10]

The role of the koan exercise, then, is to grapple with the rational mind, wrestle it to the floor, and pin it there. Only then can consciousness break free from its self-imposed prison.

Perhaps the most famous and best-loved of all the koan is the one that is offered first in the *Momunkan*, a prominent collection of Zen koan. In the *Momunkan*, it is titled "Zhao Zhou's dog," but usually it is simply referred to as the koan on *Mu*. A monk once asked Zhao-Zhou, "Does a dog have Buddha-nature?" Zhao-Zhou replied, "Mu!" Actually, he replied, "Wu!" which is the Chinese equivalent of the Japanese "Mu." Both words literally mean "nothing," or "zero," but the literal meaning is not necessarily important (though, of course, it *could* be). Countless Zen students have struggled with Mu over the ages. Wu Men, the compiler of the *Momunkan*, called "Mu" the "gateless barrier of the Zen school":

> The character *mu* is, as he explains, "the gateless barrier of the Zen school." "Do you not wish to pass through this barrier?" If so, "then concentrate yourself into this Mu, with your 360 bones and 84,000 pores, making your whole body one great inquiry. Day and night work intently at it. Do not attempt nihilistic or dualistic interpretations. It is like having bolted a red hot iron ball. You try to vomit it but cannot. . . . Now how should one strive? With might and main work at this Mu and be Mu. If you do not stop or waver in your striving, then behold, when the Dharma candle is lighted, darkness is at once enlightened."[11]

Well, this is only a tantalizing glimpse into the mysterious world of the koan. We will have more to say about the subject later. But all of the words in the world wouldn't begin to really *explain* it. That's the way it is with koan. We must not underestimate its importance, though, in the evolution of Zen Buddhism. D. T. Suzuki maintained that the koan exercise was critical to the success of Zen Buddhism. "To my mind it was the technique of the koan exercise that saved Zen as a unique heritage of Far Eastern culture."

We've come a long way from the time when Bodhidharma stood before Emperor Wu and answered, "I don't know" to the question, "Who are you?" It's quite a journey from Bodhidharma to Linji, four long centuries of development and refinement. Out of this development, though, emerged a mature Zen Buddhism, one of the finest creations of the human spirit in all of history.

The essential character of Zen Buddhism was established during the Age of the Patriarchs. In the period following the death of Huineng, the essential character was filled out; flesh was added to the bones. By the time of the death of Linji in 867 C.E., a mature Zen Buddhism had been achieved. Zen (Chan) would continue to flourish in China for another three centuries before it would enter upon a slow, but permanent, decline in the land of its birth. There is something of a life cycle to any great cultural movement, and Buddhism is no exception. Constant renewal is the secret of life. Buddhism began in India, where it grew and flourished for a time, and like a flower, it spread its seeds before beginning to decline. Some of the seeds took root in China, where a new Buddhism grew and blossomed, also spreading its seeds before going into decline. Some of these seeds took root in Japan, where yet another flowering occurred. Today, perhaps, we are witnessing the same process once again. The seeds of Japanese Zen Buddhism have been cast throughout the globe and are sinking healthy roots in places that are very new to Buddhism.

I hope you now see that the development of Zen Buddhism in Japan began with the importation of an already mature form of Zen from China. Zen Buddhism—or more properly speaking, Chan Buddhism—was originally a creation of the civilization of China. The next stage of the story, though, will be worked out in Japan, and to say the very least, it is a great story in itself.

I shall end this chapter with a very beautiful quote from the Chinese Zen Master, Ching Yuan. It captures perfectly the essential spirit of the experience of Zen Buddhism:

> Before I had studied Zen for thirty years, I saw mountains as mountains, and waters as waters. When I arrived at a more intimate knowledge, I came to the point where I saw that mountains are not mountains, and waters are not waters. But now that I have got its very substance I am at rest. For it's just that I see mountains once again as mountains, and waters once again as waters.

Notes

1. Heinrich Dumoulin, *Zen Buddhism: A History*, trans. James W. Hesig and Paul Knitter (New York: Macmillan, 1988), vol. 1, p. 140.
2. *Ibid.*, pp. 123, 137.
3. *Ibid.*, p. 139.
4. D. T. Suzuki. *Zen Buddhism: Selected Writings of D.T. Suzuki* (Garden City, New York: Doubleday, 1956), p. 176.
5. Ta-hui, quoted in Dumoulin, p. 257.
6. Shunryu Suzuki, *Zen Mind, Beginner's Mind* (New York and Tokyo: Weatherhill, 1970), p. 155.
7. Linji (Lin-Chi), quoted in Dumoulin, p. 194.
8. Told in Watts, *The Way of Zen* (New York: Vintage, 1957), p. 129.
9. Dumoulin, p. 246.
10. Nancy Wilson Ross, *Buddhism; a Way of Life and Thought* (New York: Vintage Books, 1981), p. 144.
11. Wu Men, quoted in Dumoulin, p. 259.

Study Questions

1. "The mind in meditation is a state of 'no-mind.'" What does this mean?

2. What is the reasoning behind the metaphor in which the gradual way to enlightenment is compared to the making of a perfect telescope mirror?

3. How do you interpret Bodhidharma's responses to the questions of Emperor Wu? In particular, what did he mean by answering, "I don't know" to Wu's question, "Who then is it who stands before me now?"

4. When Bodhidharma chose Hui Ko to be his successor, he whispered to him, "You shall inherit my marrow." What do you think he meant?

5. The basic gatha of Zen (attributed to Bodhidharma) is said to sum up the special character of the Zen way. How so? What is it that makes Zen different from other schools of Buddhism?

6. Why did the monastery's master, Hongren, privately reject Shenxiu's gatha and tell him that he had not yet entered into real awakening?

7. What is the essential difference in meaning between the wall gathas of Shenxiu and Huineng?

8. Explain Hongren's comment, "Of my five hundred disciples, four hundred ninety-nine possessed a remarkable understanding of Zen. Only Huineng did not understand Zen. That's why I chose him."

9. In what way is it correct to say that Huineng completed the work of Bodhidharma?

10. What did Linji, the founder of Rinzai Zen, mean by the term "true human"? Why is it significant that his approach might have been in part a reaction to the terrible experience of the Great Persecution?

11. What is a koan? How does a skilled teacher use a koan to help bring a student to satori?

12. How would you sum up the essential character of the evolution of Zen Buddhism from the time of Bodhidharma to the time of Linji?

16

Zen in Japan

JAPAN BEFORE ZEN

Early Japanese society was organized by clans. Eventually, one of the clans succeeded in creating a measure of unity among them all by conquering and welding together a part of Honshu at the eastern end of the Inland Sea. This region, including one of Japan's few arable river valleys, came to be called Yamato. The chief of Yamato became Japan's first "emperor." (The Japanese have always preferred "emperor" to "king.") According to legend the first emperor of Japan was named Jimmu Tenno, and we are even given a very precise date for his accession to the throne: February 11, 660 B.C.E. As we have seen in Chapter 8, he was believed to be descended from the sun goddess, Amaterasu. One account holds that, with the help of his many wives, he produced seventy-seven sons, who became the chiefs of the various clans. Thus could all of the Japanese nobility claim some measure of divine descent.

Legend aside, the reality is much more mundane (as always seems to be the case). We don't know the name of that first clan chief who established unified rule in the region of Yamato; moreover, it was probably a process that took several generations to complete. That process, though, would have been worked out during the fourth century C.E., a full thousand years after the legendary date of 660 B.C.E. The clans were unified within a sort of confederacy, and all accepted the legitimacy of the "emperor" at Yamato. Recall that "Yamato" refers to a region, not a city; during the early centuries, there was no capital city. The entire court, such as it was, moved to a new location and constructed a new palace each time one emperor died and was succeeded by a new one. This practice was probably derived from traditional religious rites of purification. But as the size of the court grew, creating a new home could get expensive. At last, in the year 710 C.E., a permanent capital was established. The site selected was the place we know as Nara. It was a beautiful location, a hilly, sparsely wooded area about twenty miles up from the head of Osaka Bay at the eastern end of the Inland Sea.

Nara, was patterned after Changan, the splendid capital of Tang Dynasty China, but on a somewhat humbler scale. The Chinese-style grid pattern of streets was only the beginning. The Japanese ruling class hungrily borrowed all that they could from Chinese civilization. Among other things, the Japanese adopted the Chinese system of writing, as they had none of their own. With the adoption of a system of writing and, hence, the keeping of written records, the true history of Japan begins.

Perhaps China's most important contribution to nascent Japanese civilization was Buddhism. Actually, the very first recorded incident regarding Buddhism in Japan dates back to 538 C.E. At that time, one of the regional "kings" of Korea sent a small gilt statue of Buddha as a gift to Emperor Kinmei of Japan. The emperor, not quite sure what to do with the statue, entrusted it to the care of an important noble family, the Soga, who preserved it and began to develop an interest in the religious teachings it represented.

Buddhism did not enter into a religious void in Japan. As we have seen, from very early times the Japanese people had followed a rather loosely organized religious system known as Shinto. The word "Shinto," however, did not come into use until after the rise of Buddhism. It then became necessary to distinguish between the two. *Shinto* referred to the "way of the gods"; *Bukkyo* referred to the "way of Buddha."

Shinto began as a primitive animistic collection of beliefs and practices, focusing on reverence for the spirits (kami) of natural phenomena, such as mountains, and also the spirits of departed ancestors. The practices tied the Japanese clans together, encouraging a belief that they were a unique and superior people ruled by an emperor of divine descent. The fundamental character of Shinto has survived even to the present day. The foreign traveler in Japan is often surprised to discover how ubiquitous the shrines and temples of Shinto are. It seems that almost everyone is connected, however casually, with a local Shinto shrine. For many, the shrines and temples have an important association with the ritual events of life and are important for honoring the spirits of departed family members.

No real conflict developed between Buddhism and Shinto when Buddhism entered on the scene. You might expect that there would have been some conflict, but Buddhism and Shinto have coexisted peacefully right from the beginning. In fact, early Buddhism in Japan absorbed many Shinto beliefs and practices into itself. Thus, it is quite possible for a Japanese man or woman to be both a Buddhist and an active member of a Shinto organization.

During the Nara Period, which occupied almost all of the eighth century, Buddhism continued to grow in southern Japan, especially at the capital itself. Still, despite frequent visits and exchanges between Japan and Tang China, there was no effort to fashion a native Buddhism; what Japanese Buddhists followed was strictly Chinese Buddhism transplanted to Japanese soil. (This suggests a modern parallel: Buddhism in the West is still in its infancy; Zen Buddhist monasteries in America, for example, are to a large degree careful replicas of the Japanese model.) It's a somewhat amazing fact that we can still see with our own eyes the evidence of the early Chinese influence in Japan. Some of the earliest Buddhist temples *still exist* in the city of Nara. They have been carefully maintained and appear today much as they did in the eighth century. They show clearly the Chinese architectural style that inspired them, although their counterparts from Tang China have disappeared centuries ago. One temple, the "Golden Hall" from the monastery Horyu-ji is said to be by far the oldest extant all-wood structure in the world. Not only do we have the oldest, but also the largest wooden building under one roof: the "Buddha Hall" of the monastery Todai-ji. This building houses an enormous, fifty-three-foot-high bronze and gilt statue of a seated Buddha. The gilt alone is said to weigh in at more than half a ton.

In 784 C.E., the imperial court abandoned Nara and moved about thirty miles north to the brand new imperial capital, which we know as Kyoto (pronounced as two syllables, "Kyoh-toh").This magnificent city was also laid out according the the Chinese grid system and quickly became the greatest city in Japan. It would remain the seat of the imperial residence until 1868, at which time the first of the Meiji emperors would move the imperial residence to Tokyo (which word, by the way, is simply the reverse of *Kyoto*). The emperor, although honored as a divine being by the people, gradually lost the real power of rule. He became something of a grand, but powerless, figurehead, while real power was exercised by the *shogun*, a hereditary post that controlled military power. It was an unusual arrangement, almost suggestive of the relationship between the papacy and the Holy Roman Empire in medieval Europe.

It was at Kyoto that we find the beginnings of a truly Japanese Buddhism.* In the year 805 C.E., a Japanese monk named Saicho was received at court in the still new imperial palace at Kyoto. Saicho had just returned from a four-year visit to China (as mentioned in Chapter 14) during which time he had studied the ways of several different Buddhist sects. He was now ready to weave together various strands of Buddhist practice and some aspects of Shinto as well, to fashion a new, distinctively Japanese school of Buddhism. It would be called *Tendai*, the Japanese rendering of the name of the Chinese monastery, Tiantai, which had been the major base of Saicho's study abroad. Tendai, with its emphasis on the magical and the supernatural, was a far cry from Zen, but it appealed to the needs of the people of the time.

With the help of the imperial court, Saicho established the first Tendai monastery, Enryakou-ji, on Mount Hiei just to the northeast of Kyoto. In those days, it was popularly believed that evil spirits controlled the northeasterly direction, and a Buddhist monastery on Mount Hiei could protect the city from their demonic influence. The power and prestige of Tendai Buddhism grew rapidly. Before long, the numerous monks of Mount Hiei became a political force—and even, oddly enough, something of a paramilitary force—to be reckoned with in Kyoto. Tendai monasteries began to proliferate, especially in the south and west of Japan. It was the first truly native Japanese school of Buddhism. A rival school, known as *Shingon Buddhism*, was founded by the monk Kukai only a year after Saicho began work on his monastery. Kukai, too, had studied in China

---

*Kegon Buddhism—essentially Chinese Huayen transplanted to Japan—flourished in eighth-century Nara, but it was an unmodified Chinese school of Buddhism. A native Japanese Buddhism first developed at Kyoto. Incidentally, the Nara monastery of Todai-ji was a kegon monastery, and its great gilt Buddha is a representation of Vairochana Buddha, not Shakyamuni Buddha.

and had established his monastery on Mount Koya in the southwestern sector of the Kyoto area. Like Tendai, Shingon spread beyond the Kyoto area, but never enjoyed anything near the growth experienced by Tendai.

Buddhism in Japan, especially Tendai Buddhism, developed slowly, but steadily, in the centuries following the founding of the imperial capital of Kyoto. As mentioned before, the emperor became more and more a figurehead, while real power was exercised by the military dictator, the shogun, who presided over a class of warrior nobles known as the *samurai*. Endless divisions among the samurai led to civil war on many occasions. The shogunate, a hereditary office, passed from one dynasty to another as a result of these civil wars. In 1185 C.E., when Minamoto Yoritomo, the first to hold the title of shogun, succeeded in defeating his rivals in an especially bloody civil war, he abandoned Kyoto, leaving its opulent imperial court, and moved the seat of his own military government to Kamakura, a small coastal city just south of modern Tokyo. The "Kamakura Shogunate" would rule Japan until 1338 C.E., when the shogun would again return to Kyoto.

It was during the time of the Kamakura Shogunate that Japan was nearly invaded and conquered by the huge Mongol armies of Kubali Khan. Not content with the conquest of China only, Kublai Khan sent enormous invasion forces against Japan on two occasions (1274 C.E. and 1281 C.E.), landing both times on the shore of the island of Kyushu. The Japanese beat back the first invasion, but would surely have been overwhelmed by the second had it not been for the fortuitous help of a typhoon. Of more than 4,000 ships in the Mongol force, only 200 returned, and only 30,000 men survived out of an invasion force of 140,000. Naturally, the Japanese interpreted the typhoon as a heaven-sent answer to their prayers; it was a *kami-kaze*, a "divine wind."*

What all this adds up to is that the relatively simple life of Japanese society in its earlier days had given way to times that were more complex and unstable. At the end of the twelfth century, Tendai Buddhism, which had the field pretty much to itself for four centuries, was being challenged by new Buddhist sects that were more in tune with the needs of the Japanese people. During the thirteenth century, three new schools of Buddhism would become firmly established in Japan: Nichiren Buddhism, Pure Land Buddhism, and Zen Buddhism.

Closest to traditional Tendai was Nichiren Buddhism, named after the monk who began the movement in the thirteenth century. He was a fiery, messianic sort of person who was determined to save Japanese society from what he perceived to be the corrupt state it had fallen into. He gave Nichiren Buddhism a highly nationalistic spirit, which had great appeal among the common people. About the only doctrinal innovation that he introduced was an intense emphasis on the recitation of the sutras, especially the

---

*In 1945, threatened with another great invasion, the Japanese military leaders revived the idea of *kamikaze*. The spirits of the ancient gods were to work through the minds and bodies of aviators, who would form a "divine wind" of suicide planes that would destroy the American warships by deliberately crashing into them, thus saving Japan once again from imminent invasion. This time, though, the fleet was not destroyed. However, the threatened invasion never did take place.

Lotus Sutra. At odds with the usually tolerant attitude of Buddhism, Nichiren argued that all other Buddhist sects were heretical; he alone held the key to the truth of Buddha's teaching.

Unlike Nichiren, which was a homegrown sect, Pure Land Buddhism (known as *Jodo* in Japanese) was an import from China. In the long run it would prove to be vastly more popular with the common people, and it is still a very popular sect within the umbrella of Buddhism. In modern times, about half of the Japanese people classify themselves as Buddhists, and well more than half of these identify with the Pure Land sect.

Pure Land Buddhism was founded in Japan in the late twelfth century by the monk Honen, who preached a simple, unsophisticated doctrine that quickly became enormously popular with the common people. As we have seen, Pure Land Buddhism is the most "religious" of Buddhist sects in the ordinary sense of the word. Following the tradition of Chinese Pure Land Buddhism, Honen taught that one can achieve salvation simply through the ceaseless invocation of the name of the loving and compassionate Buddha Amida (from the Sanskrit and Chinese Amitabha). Called nembutsu, this continual chanting of the name was said to result in a spiritually meditative state of mind that would lead to one's being reborn after death in the western paradise of the "Pure Land" of Buddha Amida. Much like the early Protestant reformers, Honen taught that all that is required is faith—faith in the compassionate Buddha and the consequent ritual practice of nembutsu.

RINZAI AND SOTO ZEN

The seeds of Zen would fall on extremely fertile ground in Japan and would reproduce the two great schools already existing in China. In Japan, they would come to be known as Rinzai and Soto. We will examine them by looking at the contributions of three historically great figures: Eisai, Dogen, and Hakuin.

Eisai

A Tendai scholar–monk named Myoan Eisai (pronounced "Ay-sigh") is credited with introducing Zen Buddhism into Japan. Troubled by what he perceived to be a decline in the vigor of Japanese Buddhism, Eisai concocted a wonderful plan. His dream was to trace the development of Buddhism backward in time from his own age in Japan, through the stages of evolution in China, all the way to its roots in India. And he would do this not through books, but *on foot*. Eisai would travel through China all the way to India, leisurely studying the developmental stages of Buddhism at important sites along the route. In this way, he hoped to gain a deep, personal understanding of the true nature of the Dharma practice. Ultimately, he would drink from the very wellspring of the tradition. Finally, he would return to Japan, prepared to reinvigorate the Buddhism of his native land.

Well, Eisai never got as far as India, sad to say, but he did make two trips to China, and in the process he fell deeply in love with the teaching and practice of Zen Buddhism—

specifically, the Linji school of Zen (which would come to be known as Rinzai in Japan). During his second Chinese trip, a four-year sojourn from 1187 to 1191, he studied "Rinzai" extensively, finally receiving the Dharma seal at the monastery of Tiandong. When Eisai returned to Japan in 1191, he was determined to recast the character of Buddhist practice. His goal was to reinvigorate Japanese Buddhism by emphasizing the strict adherence to the precepts that he had observed among Chinese Buddhists.

Eisai, as the legitimate Dharma heir of a recognized Zen Master, was in effect introducing a new Buddhist sect into Japan, but it seems that he wanted to play down that fact. Eisai did not seek to replace Tendai; what he wanted most of all was to launch a genuine reform movement that would reinvigorate all of Buddhism in Japan. Perhaps he naively believed that Tendai could be absorbed into the reform movement and integrated into a new Zen-oriented Buddhism. In any case, he avoided using the term "Zen," speaking instead of the "school of the Buddha mind." Also, he remained technically a Tendai monk. None of this, however, could long hide the fact that something new was in the air. Zen Buddhism had at long last arrived in Japan.

Eisai's reform movement caught fire immediately, and he lost no time in organizing Buddhist monasteries on the new model. The honor of being the first Zen monastery in Japan goes to Shofuku-ji, established in 1195 at Hakata (now known as Fukuoka), on the north shore of the island of Kyushu. Before long, though, Eisai was back at Kyoto; the center of the nation was to be the center of the Zen movement. With the help of the royal family, he established Kennin-ji, the first Zen monastery at Kyoto. (Kennin-ji still stands and, like almost all of the many famous Zen monasteries of the Kyoto area, is open to the public.)

To mollify worried Tendai leaders, Kennin-ji was "officially" designated a Tendai monastery, and Eisai even agreed to include both Tendai and Shingon shrines on the grounds. Another little addition to the grounds of Kennin-ji was to have far-reaching effects. It was a tea garden, presumably the first to be planted in the soil of Japan. Eisai had acquired a taste for tea while studying in China, and he brought that taste home with him. Not only did he find tea an excellent aid to Zen practice, but he was also impressed by its general medicinal qualities. Technically speaking, the monk Kukai, the founder of Shingon Buddhism, introduced tea into Japan, but nothing much came of his efforts. The real credit belongs to Eisai; his little tea garden launched a thirst that soon engulfed Japan.

It did not take long for Zen Buddhism to usurp Tendai's favored position at Kyoto. Both the emperor's court and the shogun's government sought close ties with Zen, especially the Rinzai school. Rinzai Zen and Soto Zen would be transplanted to Japan, and both would flourish there, but it was Rinzai Zen that developed a close association with the government. In fact, the association was so close that Rinzai Zen, in a sense, could be said to have become an operative organ *of* the government. Skilled Rinzai monks were often enlisted by the government to perform some of its diplomatic tasks. To give just one example, in 1342 a Zen monk led a delegation to China seeking financial help for a planned memorial to the recently deceased emperor, Go-Daigo. He succeeded not only in raising the funds, but also in negotiating a rich and complicated trade agreement with China.

Many Rinzai monasteries were generously underwritten by government funding. Kyoto continued to be the headquarters of Rinzai activity, and several impressive Zen monasteries began to take form in the countryside ringing the city. During the time that the shogun governed at Kamakura, important Rinzai monasteries were founded there as well. The various Zen monasteries of Japan were organized by rank into a system that resembled a mountain or a pyramid. Altogether, it was known as the "Gozan System." The entire complex included even the *rinka*, small, semiindependent monasteries in rural areas. Ranking at the top of the system were the "Five Mountains," the leading Rinzai monasteries of Kyoto. (In Japanese, *go* means five, and *zan* is the word for mountain.) Presiding at the very peak of the pyramid was the great Nanzen-ji, constructed in the countryside just southeast of the city in the late thirteenth century. Kennin-ji continued to be important, but its place at the top was taken over by the much larger Nanzen-ji.*

It might seem somewhat puzzling to the modern reader that these Zen monasteries were so closely connected with the government. We must remember that "government" is not being used in anything like the modern sense of the word. In those days, Japan was a feudal society with only two great classes. The common people made up the vast majority of the population and were engaged, for the most part, in a farming way of life. The feudal ruling class, relatively small in numbers, was a warrior nobility, the samurai. The noble families of the samurai controlled virtually all of the land and all of the power.

The life of a samurai nobleman was the life of a warrior, and true to the spirit of all feudal societies, the samurai were often on the field of battle. Endless interclan quarrels were the order of the day, sometimes very large in scale, usually small and local. Whatever the case, the samurai must always be ready to fight and to fight well. Out of this way of life arose the tradition of *bushido*, the "way of the warrior," an uncompromising code of conduct that defined the character of the samurai.

Bushido has caught the imagination of modern society, especially with respect to skill in the martial arts. According to the code of bushido, a samurai was to give absolute, unswerving loyalty to his feudal lord and his peers and was also to show reverence to the divinity of the emperor. This loyalty could not be compromised for any reason. To do so would be to bring dishonor on himself and his family, and such a thing was unthinkable. A samurai warrior was expected always to accept death before dishonor, even if it meant taking his own life, the highly dramatic act of *seppuku*. When it came to a fight, the samurai was expected to be both brave and highly skilled. Typically, the samurai fought with a sword that was a masterpiece of the steelmaker's craft. About three feet long (approximately one meter), slightly curved, and sharp as a razor, it was

*As mentioned before, many of these great monasteries, as well as the former imperial palace, still exist and are open to the public. Kyoto and its environs were off limits to saturation bombing during the Second World War, and for this reason there were some who pushed hard to make Kyoto a target of one of the atomic bombs. Nothing would be left if they had had their way. The world can be eternally thankful that they were overruled.

a deadly weapon in the hands of a skilled fighter. Supposedly, the samurai sword was capable of taking off the head of an opponent with a single lightning blow.

The sword was the symbol of the samurai, but so was the cherry blossom. The two make an interesting contrast. The code of bushido maintained that great gentleness is evidence of great strength. When challenged, the samurai would fight like a tiger, but in the ordinary course of life he was to be a model of modesty and simplicity. In addition to its concern with the martial arts, the code of bushido emphasized the basic virtues of honesty, directness, protection of the weak, and respect for traditional institutions. (In many ways, the Japanese samurai was a kindred spirit to the Spartan warrior of ancient Greece.)

Zen Buddhism, with its emphasis on simple virtues, self-discipline, and self-reliance, was speaking right to the heart of the samurai. This helps to explain the close association that developed between the ruling class—that is, the warrior class—and Zen Buddhism. Rinzai Zen monasteries became, among other things, the training grounds of the samurai. This is certainly not to say that that was the only function they served, but it definitely was an important one. Samurai families were typically associated with a particular Rinzai monastery, at which they trained from time to time in the disciplines of Zen, especially when young. Zen discipline was seen to provide an excellent foundation for training in, and mastery of, all the skills that made up the samurai way of life. For this reason Rinzai Zen monasteries were generously supported by the ruling class.

Rinzai Zen became the Buddhism of the aristocracy, whereas Pure Land became the Buddhism of the common people. To say that the Gozan System became a network of "military academies" for the samurai is overstating things, but there is a measure of truth in it. Our use of the word *monastery* is a little misleading. The Zen monastery was not a "religious" institution in the present-day sense of the word; it was a specialized community dedicated to a highly disciplined manner of living aimed at perfection of the human character. It is easy to see why such an institution would have great appeal to the samurai class.

Dogen

One of the great figures in the history of Japanese Zen Buddhism is Dogen Kigen, the founder of Soto Zen in Japan. Dogen was a disciple of Eisai. Whereas Eisai is something of a shadowy figure, Dogen stands out as a strong personality, and we know a good deal more about him. Much of our knowledge about Dogen and his thinking comes from his extensive writings, collectively known as the Shobogenzo, a ninety-two book compendium of his thoughts on a great variety of subjects. A brilliant philosopher, Dogen has often been compared to the great Western philosopher Martin Heidegger.*

Dogen was born in the year 1200 C.E. His father, a nobleman, died when Dogen was only two, and he lost his mother when he was just seven. The mother's deathbed

---

*For an excellent examination of this linkage, see Steven Heine, *Existential and Ontological Dimensions of Time in Heidegger and Dogen* (Albany, NY: State University of New York Press, 1985).

wish was that the young Dogen should become a Buddhist monk, and after her death the family made arrangements for her wish to be honored. While still just a boy, Dogen was admitted to the community of Tendai monks at the monastery on Mount Hiei near Kyoto.

New things were in the air. The reform movement launched by Eisai excited the interest of the young Dogen, and while still in his teens he abandoned the old-fashioned ways of Mount Hiei, becoming instead a disciple of Eisai, whose approach to Buddhism was far more to Dogen's liking. He loved the spirit of Zen, but his hunger to know more could only be partially satisfied at this brand-new little outpost of the tradition. As a result, he planned a trip to China, the seemingly indispensable journey that every ardent seeker had to experience in those days. He wanted to study the tradition of Zen in its homeland and seek enlightenment in the company of a certified master.

Dogen departed for China in 1223 and remained there for four years. During this time, he visited many Zen monasteries, but finally settled down at the monastery at Mount Tiantong (T'ien-t'ung), presided over by the elderly Zen Master Rujing (Ju-Jing), a man very much established in the school of Cao Dong (Ts'ao-tao) (from which name is derived the Japanese word "Soto"). In Rujing, Dogen found exactly the kind of master his heart craved. Rujing was totally committed to the practice of zazen, sitting meditation. He and the monks under his supervision would sit until eleven o'clock in the evening, and then he'd be back at it again at three in the morning. Sitting meditation was the dedicated work of Rujing's monks. He wanted no one to be able to say that they worked less hard at their vocation than did the farmer, the soldier, or anyone else outside the monastery.

Dogen fell in love with this total dedication to zazen, and he believed that it finally resolved his struggle for enlightenment. It happened one evening when one of the monks in the meditation hall fell asleep. Rujing gently chastised him, saying (in a rather koan-like way), "If your mind and body are sloughed off in meditation, how can it be that you sleep?" These words, according to Dogen, jarred him out of his ego illusion, and he became instantly enlightened. This was later verified by Rujing, who gave Dogen a document "certifying" his enlightenment and naming him a Dharma heir in the house of Caodao. The followers of Dogen regard this event as the official beginning of the school of Japanese Soto Zen.

While in China, Dogen learned a very important lesson, and the unlikely teacher was an old cook at one of the monasteries he visited. The man was totally absorbed in his endless work as a cook and laughed out loud when Dogen asked him why he didn't spend more time in his final years practicing zazen and reading the sutras. In so many words the old cook replied, "If you think Zen practice consists only in those kinds of things, you haven't yet learned *anything*!" Dogen was deeply impressed by this cheerful old man and came to realize that the real evidence of enlightenment is loving service to others. Done in the right spirit, anything at all can be Zen practice. One's ordinary daily life can be a beautiful expression of Zen practice.

In his own opinion, the Dogen who returned from China in 1227 was a very different man from the one who had embarked on the journey of discovery four years earlier. His struggle for enlightenment had now matured, and as evidence he carried with him the Dharma seal of the master, Rujing. Here were his credentials, so to speak, which gave him the authority to found a monastic community in Japan that would be in the legitimate succession of the house of Caodao. Dogen made his way to Kyoto, where he established the new monastery of Kosho-ji in 1236. His teaching at Kosho-ji, naturally, placed great emphasis on the practice of zazen. Like those before him, Dogen earnestly hoped to heal the divisions within Buddhism in Japan, uniting all in the way of Caodao (Soto).

Before the China trip Dogen had been active in the Tendai community and also in the nascent Rinzai movement begun by Eisai. He hoped to absorb both of these—especially his former Rinzai fellow monks—into the Zen Buddhism that he was proclaiming. Quite possibly, Dogen imagined himself to be something of a messiah, the "one they were waiting for" who would unite all in a transcendent new movement based on his teachings. To his dismay, though, Dogen experienced only rivalry and criticism from the others. The Rinzai monks were particularly vociferous in their criticism, denouncing Dogen's attachment to sitting meditation. With their growing closeness to the imperial court, Rinzai opposition became an unendurable burden for Dogen. With a heavy heart, he finally gave up his great dream of reforming all of Japanese Buddhism under his banner and made the decision to abandon Kyoto altogether and go off to the wilds, where at least he and his monks could live in peace. He was further encouraged in this decision by remembering the words of his master, Rujing, to "shun cities and dwell deep in mountains and valleys."

In 1243, Dogen and his band of loyal disciples relocated to an out-of-the-way rural area about sixty miles northwest of Kyoto, not far from the desolate north coast of Honshu. There, on property given to them by a wealthy landowner, they founded the monastery of Eihei-ji (pronounced "Ay-hay-gee"). Dogen was to live another ten years, and it was during his time at Eihei-ji that he nailed down the particulars of his teaching, establishing the foundation of the school of Japanese Soto Zen. Most of his teaching is to be found in the collection of his writings known as the *Shobogenzo*.

The practice of sitting meditation was, of course, the heart of Dogen's discipline. And why should it not be central? Had not Buddha himself treasured meditation? It was the vehicle of his awakening. Moreover, throughout the evolution of Buddhism, great bodhisattvas had made a special place for meditation. Bodhidharma, for example, the titular founder of Zen, had spent nine long years in sitting meditation at Shaolinsi, and that was after his enlightenment.

The monks at Eihei-ji spent many hours in zazen; it was the core around which their daily routine was built. Normally, much of the day was also given over to other tasks, such as work projects and study, but at certain times of year all other activities were temporarily suspended so that the monks could devote almost all of their waking hours to zazen. Such a period of concentration came to be called a sesshin. At Eihei-ji, a sesshin lasted for seven days or more, and there were at least four of them, corresponding to the seasons of the year. Still very much a part of the Zen calendar, sesshin offers a special opportunity to make some kind of breakthrough in one's spiritual growth.

Dogen was precise about the way zazen was to be practiced. His method, fundamentally, is still the method practiced in Soto Zen. If we could enter his meditation hall, we would see rows of monks dressed in loose-fitting robes. Unlike a Rinzai meditation hall, in which the monks sit facing inward, Dogen's monks would be facing the wall. They would sit on low platforms, in the cross-legged posture, using only a mat and a small, firm cushion, known as a zafu, to sit on. Their posture would be upright, but not tense, and the hands would rest in the lap formed by the crossed legs. Dogen took exception to the traditional yogic practice of closing the eyes in meditation. His monks were to keep their eyes open, but downcast. The wall covering was bare straw mat or shoji screen, so there was nothing visual to catch the eye. Dogen emphasized the importance of regulated easy breathing, but only to help relax and center the body–mind. He had no interest in yogic breathing exercises in which the exercise was itself the meditation practice.

Chanting, repetition of a mantra, koan, and all other kinds of activity were ruled out in Dogen's method of zazen. They might have a place at other times, but not at the time specifically set aside for zazen. The meditator was to do one thing and one thing only; he was to completely focus his consciousness on the existential reality of the moment and *stay with that*. Thoughts, images, feelings of desire, and everything else were to be immediately dropped whenever they formed in consciousness, and the mind was to return gently to its focus on the present moment's fact of existence. This practice, which requires great energy and can be totally exhausting for the novice, is called *shikan-taza*; it is to fully grasp the moment. The dedicated practice of shikan-taza, so Dogen believed, was the way *par excellence* for "seeing into one's nature."

Dogen was in full accord with the tradition of Zen in emphasizing that "seeing into one's nature" is the very essence of Buddhism. One's nature *is* the Buddha-nature. There is nothing to be *acquired* in meditation; it remains only for the individual to see through the illusions of his own making that prevent him from knowing the truth of his own Buddha-nature. As Nagarjuna had so beautifully put it, "The meaning of the Buddha-nature is vast emptiness." Dogen was convinced that zazen was the royal road that could take one to the place where he or she was at last able and willing to let go completely of all attachments and accept the "vast emptiness" that is the ultimate nature of reality.

Although Dogen's primary concern was with the monastery and his immediate disciples, he was determined that Eihei-ji not become some sort of Buddhist ivory tower isolated from the common people of the area. All who lived within its environs were welcome to join in the life of the monastery, at least to some extent. Dogen himself often preached a simplified version of his discipline to the laypeople, encouraging them to make meditation and other Buddhist disciplines a part of their daily lives. The more typically "religious" elements of traditional Buddhism were emphasized where the common people were concerned, perhaps as a concession to the popularity of Pure Land Buddhism.

In addition to welcoming the neighboring people into the life of the monastery, Dogen encouraged his monks to go out to them, too. The monks of Eihei-ji were always available to help out in times of need. Dogen's monks were a familiar sight helping with the harvest, lending a hand at a barn raising, or joining a work party to repair a bridge. This close association with the common people set the pattern for Soto Zen communities that would eventually spread throughout Japan, and in this way Soto Zen came to permeate the lives of the ordinary men and women of Japan. As mentioned before, about fifty percent of modern Japanese people identify themselves as Buddhists, and a full half of these follow the Pure Land sect. The others are mostly Zen Buddhists, but well more than half of these follow Soto Zen. Rinzai accounts for only a relatively small minority, but then, Rinzai had been largely limited to the upper class, which was a much smaller proportion of the population to begin with.

To sum up, both Soto and Rinzai became firmly established in Japan during the thirteenth century. Their beautiful monasteries were being constructed at the same time that the great Gothic cathedrals were rising in distant Europe. It must be emphasized again that Rinzai and Soto were not so much antagonistic rivals as they were alternatives. Both were solidly grounded in the fundamentals of Zen Buddhism, growing from the Zen of the Patriarchs, as funneled through the teaching of Huineng. The basic character of each school had matured in China during the Tang and Song periods and had been transplanted to Japan, where a distinctively Japanese style had developed.

This difference in style was expressed primarily in three ways. First, of course, was the matter of social class. Speaking very generally, Rinzai was the Zen of the ruling class, and Soto was the Zen of the common people. This was broadly true, but there was room for lots of exceptions in both cases. The second difference concerns the place of meditation in Zen. Both Soto and Rinzai held zazen in high regard, but Soto emphasized the practice to a far greater degree than did Rinzai. In fact, Rinzai masters often gently (and sometimes not so gently) ridiculed Soto monks for their "excessive" love of sitting meditation. Of course, the Soto people returned the favor, chastising Rinzai for its attachment to the koan exercise. It was a case of "wall-gazing" versus "koan-gazing," "quiet illumination" versus "dynamic enlightenment." The word *dynamic* identifies the third difference. Rinzai took a dynamic, energetic approach to Zen, whereas Soto was more contemplative. A person might join a Rinzai community for a short period, but the Soto monastery was more likely to attract the dedicated person who wished to make the way of the monk his life's work.*

Rinzai and Soto became established in Japan during the thirteenth century. From that time to the present, both have continued to grow and develop; in modern times they have begun to take root in places far beyond the borders of Japan. Many important names have been added to the history of Zen Buddhism since the time of Eisai and Dogen, but one stands out in a special way, the name of Hakuin. Even in a broad survey such as this, it would be unthinkable not to pause and consider the enormously significant contribution of this man.

---

*In the Zen tradition, there is a wonderful way of describing the difference between Rinzai and Soto. A Rinzai monk wishes to get an apple on a limb that is just out of reach (a metaphorical way of describing enlightenment). He leaps and lunges until, finally, he snatches it. A Soto monk also wants the apple, but his method is simply to sit quietly beneath the tree and wait for the ripe fruit to drop into his lap.

Hakuin

Hakuin (pronounced "Hah-koo-in") was born in 1685, the same year as Johann Sebastian Bach, and lived until 1768. He died at the age of eighty-three, outliving his famous German contemporary by eighteen years. Hakuin never knew Bach, which is unfortunate, but he was well aware of the existence of European culture. For the first time in this story the civilizations of Europe and the Far East had begun to make contact and influence one another. Hakuin lived during the Tokugawa Period, often referred to as the Edo Period (1603–1867), a time in history when Japanese civilization had to adjust to the wrenching changes brought about by the coming of the Europeans. Eventually, the Japanese would deal with the challenge by barring all foreigners, exterminating the new growth of Christianity, and withdrawing into a self-imposed isolation that would have nearly devastating results. When Japan was persuaded to emerge from its isolation in the nineteenth century, the country was seriously behind the times with respect to the progress of technology. To say the least, though, Japan amazed the world with the speed with which it caught up. As a result, other than Thailand, Japan was the only Asian country never to be colonized and ruthlessly exploited by European empire builders. That, however, is another story. Back to Hakuin.

Hakuin is often said to represent the culmination of the development of Rinzai Zen in Japan. Although he was a Rinzai master and his contribution was directed specifically to the Rinzai tradition, his teaching has profoundly affected all of Zen Buddhism—in fact, all of Buddhism. Hakuin reaffirmed the fundamentals of Buddhism, but he did it in a new way.

Hakuin spent most of his life in the region of Shizuoka on the southern side of Honshu within sight of the great Mount Fuji. The ethereal beauty of snowcapped Fuji is truly awesome. Passengers on the train to Tokyo, even though they may make the trip regularly, always come alive and move toward the windows when Fuji first comes into view. Maybe the beauty of Fuji and the surrounding countryside worked its spell on the young Hakuin. His was an intense, deeply emotional personality. He loved beauty, and in addition to being a Zen philosopher, he was a gifted artist. Some of his work, such as the self-portrait and the portrait of Bodhidharma, have become masterpieces in the tradition of Zen art.

Hakuin was a true mystic. He longed for the joy of the transcendent experience, and he found myriad opportunities in the ordinary events of daily life. By his own account, Hakuin experienced rapture in such mundane things as the sound of gentle rain, the sight of freshly fallen snow, the song of a bird, or even the slow movement of a spider weaving its web. In other words, contact with *anything*, if the experience were entered into completely, could give rise to a transcendent moment. For Hakuin, these were the many gateways that opened the way to *kensho*, the experience of "seeing into one's nature."*

---

*Literally speaking, *kensho* is synonymous with *satori*. In customary usage, though, *kensho* refers to a "little satori," a powerful insight into the nature of reality, but one that is still short of full awakening.

Achieving kensho was all that mattered to Hakuin—achieving it and deepening it. That was his idea of a life well spent. It seems that in the earlier years of this life's quest, Hakuin was most affected by the deeply emotional experience. As his life matured, the intuitive experience came to be even more important. In this respect, he was very much like his European contemporary, Bach. Both men followed similar paths, and each gave expression to his discoveries in his own way, Bach in the language of the musical forms of his age and Hakuin in the language of Zen mysticism. What a profound influence they might have had on one another!

Hakuin was totally immersed in the Zen Buddhism of his age. He gave all of his time and energy to deepening the Zen experience, to understanding it in the marrow of his bones. This quest included a lifelong succession of pilgrimages to the numerous Rinzai monasteries of Japan in order to share the experience of many Zen Masters. Hakuin did not, however, travel beyond the islands of Japan. The sojourn to China, a nearly obligatory mission in an earlier age, was no longer seen as necessary. The vigor of Zen Buddhism had declined markedly in China since the golden age of Tang and Song, more than four centuries in the past by the time of Hakuin. The future of Zen Buddhism had passed from China to the hands of others—most notably, the Japanese.

As Hakuin's experience matured, he came to see a comprehensive order to it all, which became the basis of his teaching. He would focus on the fundamentals, just as Buddha himself had done. He would restate the essence of Buddha's teaching through the language and experience of Zen Buddhism. Hakuin began where Buddha began, with an assessment of the human condition in general, *sarvam dukkham.* To a very large degree, the general condition of humankind is fear, insecurity, and suffering. We start out in life as perfectly fine natural little beings, but something goes horrendously wrong. What *is it* that goes wrong? It is, Buddhism proclaims, the nearly irresistible tendency of the ego-centered human mind to create a prison of self-delusion. Once fashioned, this self-absorbed state of consciousness leads inevitably to the all-too-familiar human life of anxiety and dissatisfaction. But it doesn't have to be that way. Human life can be—and, in fact, *should* be—a state of abiding joy, the truly natural state for men and women; the more familiar alternative is an aberration.

It is possible for every person to free himself or herself from the prison of ego—to awaken to the real truth of one's nature and thus to know freedom from fear, the basis of abiding joy. Long ago, Buddha showed the way to freedom. The tradition that he founded preserved that teaching. But the way to freedom is very difficult; once hardened into our world of self-created delusions, we humans resist mightily any effort to change the situation. "Many are called, but few are chosen." Nonetheless, every person has at least the inner capacity to achieve liberation. The person who chooses to take up the great challenge must, as Buddha declared, become totally dedicated to the effort. Nothing short of total dedication can hope to succeed. A prisoner attempting an escape from jail doesn't dawdle along the way—at least, not those who make good the escape.

The quest for liberation is a process of total immersion. At the end of it is the great awakening to the truth of one's nature. It is the ultimate satori that sweeps away all delusions, opening consciousness to the clear knowledge of the "identity of one's own nature with all reality in an eternal now." In this state of freedom is found the abiding joy that is the natural fulfillment of human existence. But before that can occur, it is necessary that the unenlightened person experience a kind of death—a "Great Dying," as Hakuin put it. Satori, in fact, is the character of the "rebirth" that follows the act of finally letting go of everything, of "dying" to the old person, and being "reborn" as the new person. In the words of Hakuin: "If you wish to know the true self beyond ego, you must be prepared to let go your hold as if hanging from a sheer precipice, to die and return again to life."

The Great Dying is itself preceded, and in fact brought to fruition, by what Hakuin called the "Great Doubt." This is a matter of the most profound importance. Whatever the trials and tribulations of ordinary life may be, at least a person normally feels some measure of security regarding the things he believes in and takes for granted. Most of all, his strong sense of self seems solid, inflexible, enduring. There is comfort in this; it is at least a dependable home base. But when one "leaves home" to follow instead the path of Buddha, one truly becomes a homeless person in the deep, inner sense of the word. Whatever may be the pleasing initial experiences of this choice, the path must ultimately lead into a dark interior forest where the demons of fear reside. A genuine seeker of enlightenment has to face the fact that undreamed-of dreads—even terror—await the pilgrim who abandons the artificial comforts of ordinary life and ventures into the realm where that artificiality comes to be revealed. It is no easy matter to give up the deep-seated sense of substantiality that we unconsciously associate with familiar things, most of all with one's self. A growing sense of uncertainty and lack of control can result in a terrible anxiety, in some cases even leading to suicidal thoughts. And there's no turning back! In the Zen tradition, this familiar condition is referred to as the "Zen sickness." Given the normal character of human consciousness, it is to some degree the necessary and inevitable precondition of enlightenment. Hakuin called it the Great Doubt.

So what's to be done? Hakuin would answer that, first of all—and it is absolutely essential—the seeker must have the guidance of a genuinely enlightened teacher. Buddha could go it alone, and perhaps a few others have done so, but only a very few. The vast majority of men and women need the close and personal guidance of an already awakened teacher. But a Zen Master who employs only the techniques of meditation will not, in Hakuin's judgment, be successful. Hakuin fired many arrows at the Soto school. He denounced what he considered to be their excessive dependence on zazen. He called them tree stumps. Hakuin wanted a person to grapple with the Great Doubt in a dynamic way, to be like a blazing fire, not cold ashes:

> They foolishly take the dead teachings of no-thought and no-mind, where the mind is like dead ashes with wisdom obliterated, and make these into the essential doctrines of Zen. They practice silent, dead sitting as though they were incense burners in some old mausoleum and take this to be the treasure place of the true practice of the patriarchs.[1]

What, then, would Hakuin have the Zen Master do in properly guiding the student into and through the Great Doubt? He would have the Zen Master skillfully employ the koan exercise. In Hakuin's judgment, the koan exercise is the perfect solution, a wonderful tool that can be used in a series of stages to adroitly navigate the student into, and all the way through, the Great Doubt. After all, the Great Doubt is a product of the rational mind struggling hopelessly with new experiences that it can't comprehend. The special beauty of the koan exercise is that it produces a state of psychological tension that finally bursts through the blockage created by discursive thought, thus dissolving the Great Doubt. The solution of the koan clears one's consciousness of the rational mind's doubts and tension, thus opening the way to satori:

> When a person faces the Great Doubt, before him there is in all directions only a vast and empty land without birth and without death, like a huge plain of ice extending ten thousand miles. As though seated within a vase of lapis lazuli surrounded by absolute purity, without his senses he sits and forgets to stand, stands and forgets to sit. Within his heart there is not the slightest thought or emotion, only the single word *mu*. It is just as though he were standing in complete emptiness. At this time no fears arise, no thoughts creep in, and when he advances single-mindedly without retrogression, suddenly it will be as though a sheet of ice were broken or a jade tower had fallen. He will experience a great joy, one that never in forty years has he seen or heard.[2]

In the preceding passage, Hakuin is making reference to *Mu*, the famous response in Zhao Zhou's koan, "Does a dog have the Buddha-nature?" But many other koan would work just as well. Hakuin loved the koan, "What is the sound of one hand clapping?" Actually, this koan was formulated by the Chinese Zen Master Baiyin (Pai-*yin*), but Hakuin revived it and popularized it. Fully immersed in the traditions of Rinzai Zen, Hakuin was convinced that the koan exercise was the key to success in the quest for enlightenment. He reinvigorated the artful use of the koan, gathering together the best from the tradition and formulating a system that could be used by other Zen Masters. In Hakuin's system, the koan are hierarchically arranged in a series of gradations that correspond to the stages of growth that a Zen student will experience. The student starts at the beginning, usually with *Mu*, and then progressively moves through more and more difficult koan. Each solution produces a greater kensho experience, but thereby sets the stage for that much greater doubt, until finally the teacher guides the student into the koan exercise that results in perfect satori, the perfect "seeing into one's nature."

It's a wonderful ideal, and undoubtedly, in the hands of skillful Zen Masters Hakuin's system has produced impressive results over the centuries. Hakuin certainly did much to establish the koan exercise as an important and fundamental part of Zen Buddhism. As the modern Zen scholar D. T. Suzuki said, "To my mind it was the technique of the koan exercise that saved Zen as a unique heritage of Far Eastern culture." To the degree that that statement is accurate, Hakuin deserves much of the credit.

In addition to establishing the central place of the koan exercise in Rinzai discipline—and thus developing the orthodox line of Rinzai Zen—Hakuin did much to free Rinzai from its aristocratic exclusivity and bring it to the common people. Rinzai would never match Soto in this respect, but at least Hakuin began some movement in the direction of a universal appeal. Undoubtedly, his personal style had a lot to do with it.

We are told that he was a congenial and tolerant man who cared nothing about distinctions of rank and wealth.

Hakuin was a great Zen Master; his contribution would affect the course of Zen for all time to come. Hakuin in the Rinzai tradition and Dogen in the Soto tradition are the two tall mountains of the historical landscape of Zen Buddhism in Japan.

THE ZEN MONASTERY

The Zen monastery, like a Hindu ashram, is neither a specific place nor a group of buildings; it is a living organism. Specifically, a Zen monastery is a community of monks living and working together under the guidance of a roshi. They have come together in the belief that the communal way of living offers the richest possible environment within which to follow Buddha's path leading to enlightenment. The roshi, an already awakened man or woman, will oversee the life of the community and personally guide the development of each of the monks.

In China, Zen monasteries developed out of the monastic tradition of Buddhism generally, which in turn had its roots in the ashram tradition of India. When Zen became established in Japan, the Chinese monastic system was adopted and was gradually modified to fit the more characteristic Japanese way of life. In modern times, as Zen Buddhism takes root in the West, it is only natural that the Japanese monastic system is adopted and faithfully re-created, at least initially.* Already, though, significant adaptations can be discerned. For one thing, Zen communities in the West are generally referred to as "Zen centers," or "Zen practice centers," not monasteries.

Although a Zen monastery is a group of people, not a group of buildings, it is normal for the mind to think of a monastery in terms of its physical layout, the place where the community resides and practices the Zen way of life. A Zen monastery can be located in virtually any kind of environment. We ordinarily think of Zen monasteries, though, as being located in remote, out-of-the-way places—and usually that is the case—but many Zen centers are situated right in the heart of a busy city. The original Rinzai monasteries were clustered around the outskirts of Kyoto and were actively involved in the life of the capital. Even today, Zen centers are to be found in many urban areas of Japan, as well as in cities throughout the world. Often, though, urban-centered Zen communities will own, in addition to the city address, a remote location that offers a serene alternative.**

---

*Zen Buddhism has a long history in Korea and Vietnam as well as in Japan, and some Zen monasteries in the West are the products of these traditions, but the great majority are based on Japanese Zen Buddhism.

**This practice has become popular in the West. The Zen centers of San Francisco and Los Angeles, for example, are located right in the heart of their respective cities. Both, however, maintain fully developed monastic centers in remote locations. The San Francisco Zen center operates an excellent monastic retreat in a remote part of the coastal mountains near the Big Sur area, and the Los Angeles Zen center maintains a retreat high in the San Jacinto Mountains, southeast of the Los Angeles area urban sprawl. Many other urban Zen centers do the same sort of thing.

Still, for the most part, the founders of Zen monasteries have from the very beginning sought out relatively remote locations. Ideally, a Zen monastery would be found in an out-of-the-way place, far removed from the hustle and bustle of ordinary life, a place passed over by others where the environment has retained its natural character and beauty. In this serene and natural setting, the monastery can go about its daily life in a peaceful way, undisturbed by the usual distractions of human life. This, of course, is the description of an ideal; compromises often have to be made. Nevertheless, wherever it is located, the Zen monastery is a place of great tranquility and beauty. Whether it be large or small, richly endowed or humble, city centered or nestled in the farthest part of the mountains, a Zen monastery is one of the truly great achievements of the human spirit. To better understand its character, let's mentally visit a traditional country monastery and explore the parts that make up the whole.

Traditionally, the entry to a Zen monastery is through some sort of gateway. This is important, because the space that makes up the monastery grounds is a special place. It is distinctly set aside for the practice of Zen; in a way, it is a "sacred precinct." When one passes through the gateway, one has the feeling of entering another realm. The earliest monasteries in Japan, inspired by the Chinese model, had huge, elaborate gateways. They were ornate buildings in their own right, sometimes with several rooms. Examples of this type of architecture can still be seen at Nara. Over time, gateways became increasingly modest. (Some modern monasteries don't even have distinctive gateways at all, which seems to me to be an unfortunate omission.)

The grounds of a traditional Zen monastery are not left in a wild state; far from it, the grounds are cultivated into a gardenlike setting and are lovingly maintained. But everything—grounds, buildings, and other structures—fits together with the surrounding environment in perfect harmony. A traditional Zen monastery is not in conflict with its surroundings; it looks as if it had grown in that place along with the trees and the grass.

Within the grounds of the monastery precinct are a collection of buildings that serve the needs of the members of the community. The most important building by far is the Zendo. This structure, the core of the monastery, may serve several functions, but above all else, it is the place where the community gathers for zazen. In many cases the Zendo is used only for meditation, but it is not uncommon for it to have other uses as well. For example, the Zendo may double as a Buddha Hall, the place where "services" honoring Buddha are held. Monasteries that can afford it have a separate Buddha Hall, and not uncommonly, it is a very elaborate room. The Zendo, though, is the pride and joy of the community. Typically, the whole community will lavish its very best work on the construction and upkeep of the Zendo. Zendos represent some of the finest expressions of traditional Japanese architecture, and this tradition has spread to other parts of the world where Zen Buddhism has taken root.

In the early days, it was popular to arrange the buildings of the monastery, according to the Chinese custom, to conform loosely to the shape of a human body, the "body of Buddha." The Zendo, naturally, would be located at the position of the heart. This custom gradually died out, but the Zendo, wherever it may be located, remains the heart of the physical layout.

Every Zen monastery has a Zendo, but other buildings will vary widely from one monastery to another. One building likely to be found in modern times is a dormitory or residence hall for the monks. This is quite common today, but in the past it was often the custom, especially in Soto monasteries, for the monks to sleep and eat their meals right in the Zendo. The roshi, however, would not sleep with the rest. Typically, he would have a simple hut of some kind separate from the others. In the roshi's quarters would be found a small room where the monks could meet individually with him for dokusan, a private conversation that gives the roshi an opportunity to check and guide the progress of each member of the community.

A dining hall with an adjacent kitchen would be another commonly found building, and in connection with it would be some kind of barn or shed in which needed farming equipment could be stored. All traditional Zen monasteries—or at least, those located in a country setting—could be expected to have a large fruit and vegetable garden that would provide most of the food needs of the community. It is a distinctive feature of the Zen monastery that it strives to achieve the greatest possible degree of self-sufficiency. Work in the garden and in the kitchen is a major part of the productive activity of a Zen community.

Another building that is sure to be found in all of the monasteries of Japan is the bathhouse. The hot soaking tub is so deeply ingrained in Japanese culture that it was regarded as an indispensable part of monastery life as well. The Japanese bath is not for washing; it is for soaking the body in extremely hot water. Cleaning the body is a separate operation that precedes the bath. No soap ever reaches the soaking tub. (God help the person who makes this mistake!) It's probably not going too far to say that the locations of many Zen monasteries were chosen primarily because of their proximity to natural hot springs. The Japanese hot bath is a wonderful custom that, happy to say, has largely followed the migration of Zen Buddhism to other lands.

Several other buildings might be located within a Zen monastery, too—a monastery office, for example, an infirmary, or a library. Then, in addition to buildings, certain other structures are likely to be found. Ogane, the great monastery bell, ranks second only to the Zendo in the loving attention it receives. Every Zen monastic community—just like every Christian monastic community—yearns to have the special beauty of a great monastery bell marking out the divisions of the day. But this is one of the few things that the community cannot produce for itself. The craft of bronze casting became a specialized kind of work that was elevated to a fine art in Japan, just as it was in the West.

A great bell is a masterpiece of the bronzecaster's art; a Zen community might have to save for generations before being able to afford such a commission. But, great or small, some kind of bell would occupy an important place within the monastery grounds. By custom, it is usually placed near the Zendo and is hung from a large wooden scaffolding constructed specifically for this purpose. The Zen bell has no clapper; it is struck on the lower outside rim with a wooden piece that itself is ordinarily suspended by ropes. The sound of a Zen bell is typically very, very deep and resonating. It's more of a boom than a clang, the type of sound you feel as much as hear. The deep vibrating waves continue for a long time, finally trailing off to merge with the natural sounds of the environment. Usually, the bell is struck just once or twice. The sound is one that is never forgotten; in a way, the sound of a Zen bell ties together all of the disparate elements of the monastery.

Another thing certain to be found somewhere on the grounds of a traditional Zen monastery is a small shrine containing a statue of Shakyamuni Buddha. This, too, would probably represent a major purchase, but an indispensable one. The statue of Buddha is honored, not venerated in the usual religious sense. It is a visible and much-loved reminder of the founder and his teaching. The teaching of Buddha is, after all, what the monastery is all about. In addition to the statue of Shakyamuni Buddha, there may be other shrines as well, honoring, for example, esteemed bodhisattvas, such as Avalokiteshvara.

All of these things combined make up the fabric of a Zen monastery and are woven together in its gardenlike setting. The art of Japanese gardening reaches its finest expression in the grounds of some Zen monasteries. This is not formal gardening—nothing flamboyant or overstated. Although much care is given to detail, the grounds have a natural feel, very much in harmony with the surrounding environment. Through patient care and planting over many generations the gardeners have created a place of great tranquility and natural beauty. Everything about a Zen monastery is designed to promote serenity and the meditative state of mind. The Daoist love of nature is everywhere to be seen and heard. If you have an opportunity to visit a traditional Zen monastery, I'm sure that you will be struck by the many touches, some of them very humble, that give rise to feelings of beauty and harmony with nature. Let me mention just a couple of examples from my own experience.

Picture a small water basin made from natural rock. It is filled with clear stream water used for ritual cleaning. A long-handled bamboo cup rests on the rim of the rock. The water, diverted from a nearby rippling stream, trickles into a gourdlike structure to which is attached a short length of hollow bamboo. The gourd is fixed to a swivel, and when the water fills it, the increased weight tips the structure forward, spilling the water into the basin through the bamboo pipe. With the gourd now empty of water, a counterweight returns it to its original position, and the cycle begins again. At the end of each cycle, which lasts approximately one or two minutes, any nearby ear is treated to the sound of a hollow thwunk followed by a brief rush of spilling water. It might seem as if this would be distracting, but it's not at all. It's a beautiful sound, almost hypnotizing in a way. (And it also has the practical effect of keeping the deer from munching too much of the garden.) I suspect that a great many satori experiences have been triggered over the ages by such Zen garden sounds as this.

The same little stream that feeds the basin has been crossed by a large wooden beam similar to a railroad tie. The beam has been placed in the stream to help step it down from a higher to a lower level. The running water spills over the beam, making a wonderful rippling sound that never stops. In autumn, leaves falling into the stream back up behind the wooden beam, creating something of a tangled mass of wet leaves. One's first impulse might be to get a rake and clean it out, but what a mistake that would be! To the relaxed eye, the natural pattern of these many-colored leaves, shimmering in the dappled sunlight, becomes a sight of such great beauty as to be nearly overwhelming. This is the kind of experience that Hakuin and countless other lovers of Zen would want to cherish. These humble little "natural accidents" are filled with beauty and are capable of lifting the heart and the mind to a new and higher vision of reality.

A place of serene natural beauty, highly conducive to the meditative state of mind—that is the Zen monastery. The traditional arts of Japan have shown themselves to be very well suited to this environment. The physical layout of the monastery, however beautiful it may be, is, of course, only the setting for the practice of Zen; it is the community of monks that really makes it a monastery. The daily life the setting supports is what it's all about—and it matters not in the least whether the monastery be a fully developed center in a beautiful mountain setting or merely a converted warehouse in the middle of a modern city. The daily routine of the members of the community is the lifeblood of Zen Buddhism.

The daily routine of the Zen community has a grand simplicity about it. The cycle of the day begins before dawn and unfolds slowly and peacefully. There is never the feeling of hurry or anxiety that is so typical of modern life in general. Although there is room for much variation, daily life from one monastery to another is similar in quality. In very general terms, a typical day would begin early, well before dawn. The sounding of the great bell summons the community to the Zendo, where the day begins with the recitation of passages from the sutras. This is followed by a period of sitting meditation, typically about an hour. There may be an opportunity during the morning meditation period for dokusan, a brief private meeting with the roshi, whose experienced eye can quickly check on each person's progress. A simple breakfast (vegetarian, of course) would be served after zazen, and then the monks would spend about half an hour thoroughly sweeping and cleaning the entire monastery. The bulk of the day is given over to work or study, with a brief break for lunch. In the late afternoon, the monks are likely to gather again for recitation of the sutras, followed by the evening meal. The day closes with another session of sitting meditation, which again includes the opportunity for dokusan. The community retires around nine or ten o'clock. Sleep comes easily after a day such as this. Soon the morning bell will rouse them all for another turn of the cycle.

Clearly, the practice of zazen occupies a central place in the daily life of a Zen monastery. This is true in both Soto and Rinzai monasteries, although there is a greater emphasis on zazen in the Soto tradition. It's not uncommon for several hours of each day to be given to zazen, and this is just the *normal* daily routine. In addition to the normal routine, throughout the year there are times of intensive work known as "practice periods" or even more intense periods of work known as sesshins. During a sesshin, the normal routine is suspended, and the monks sit almost continuously in zazen. Twelve hours a day or more is not uncommon. In a Zen monastery, zazen is king.

Zazen is practiced in the Zendo, which is typically a large, airy room, or sometimes two or three rooms that open onto one another. In the traditional Japanese-style Zendo, the platformed sitting areas are covered with tatami mats and the walls are bare; doorways are sliding shoji screens. Its simplicity is the essence of the Zendo's beauty. In the central part of the room is an altarlike structure that holds a statue of Buddha and perhaps some other items, such as a floral arrangement and an incense burner. This is not an altar for the worship of a god in the customary religious sense. Again, it is a visible reminder of Buddha's teaching and one's link through that teaching to Buddha himself and all who have come after him.

Near the altar, one will likely find one or more bowl-shaped gongs resting on cushions. Next to these will be a wooden striker and perhaps other implements, such as wooden clappers. These are used by the senior monk who presides over the meditation session. In a large group, the senior monk may be assisted by one or two others.

The beginning of a meditation session is ordinarily announced by the striking of a wooden clapper that hangs just outside the Zendo. As the monks arrive they leave their shoes (or, more likely, sandals) in wooden cases designed for this purpose. No one ever walks in the Zendo with shoes on. In a traditional monastery, there is a ritual right way to do practically everything. One enters the Zendo slowly, in a dignified manner, stepping through the doorway with the left foot first. Upon leaving, it is the right foot first. The monk walks to his or her place and bows deeply before sitting down. The deep bow with the palms pressed together is called *gassho*. The monks sit in rows along the walls, unless the group is too large, in which case interior rows are also formed. Generally, each person sits facing the bare wall, although in the Rinzai tradition it is common to sit facing the interior of the room. Each monk sits on a firm, round, black cushion called a *zafu*, which is centered on a thin cloth mat that may be placed directly on the tatami floor covering or, as is more likely the case, on long wooden platforms built up about two feet from the floor. Unless one has some physical problem that prevents it, each person is expected to sit in the cross-legged posture, with the hands together above the lap. As mentioned before, there are variations to this posture so that almost everyone can master it in time. The great value of this posture is that, once mastered, it permits one to sit still for long periods of time without feeling the need to change the position. It is very solid and balanced and allows the blood to circulate freely and the breathing to be deep and easy. The spine is held upright, with the chin brought in toward the chest just a little. The eyes are open, but downcast, not focusing on anything.

So what's really going on here? Why is *so much* time given to simply sitting motionless? What are they *doing* when they practice zazen? These are legitimate questions. A person raised in the culture of the West can't help but find it puzzling, to say the least. And, as has been noted, there have been more than a few throughout the tradition of Zen itself who have criticized what they regarded to be an excessive affection for sitting meditation. The great Hakuin referred to the rows of sitting monks as tree stumps. Nonetheless, from the time of Buddha himself to the present day, sitting meditation has enjoyed a place of central importance in the tradition of Buddhism.

If nothing else, sitting meditation provides an excellent opportunity to set aside the usual distractions of life, turn inward for a little while to focus on the flow of consciousness, and thus, in a dispassionate way, get to know this ego self. There is great value in this. Growing intuitive self-knowledge can go far to loosen the grip of the ego-delusion. Also, sitting meditation, by emphasizing a concentration on the flow of the present moment, can have the effect of increasing one's sensitivity to the present—to the larger reality that one is always a part of, but often fails to perceive. In the Rinzai tradition, a sitting meditation period provides an ideal opportunity for one to concentrate on the present koan exercise.

The foregoing applications are all undeniably valuable, but there is something that many in Zen Buddhism, especially in the Soto tradition, hold to be vastly more valuable.

The art of sitting meditation, when mastered, holds forth the possibility of giving one the ability to enter into a state of consciousness in which the thinking mind is completely put to rest, the grip of ego is loosened, and the individual experiences, for a while at least, the unitive state. This is the state of being called *samadhi* in Sanskrit; *samadhi* becomes *zanmai* in Japanese. *Zanmai*, a glorious experience in its own right, is held by many to be a most fertile condition for the rising of satori, the perfect intuition of awakening in which one "sees the truth of one's nature." *Zanmai* does not cause satori—no one would argue that—but it may well provide an ideal condition for its spontaneous emergence.

Words become such frail things when we direct our attention to the nature of that which we call ultimate truth. One thing is certain, though; we must get out of our own way before we can be open to see the light. By this, I mean that we must be willing to let go of the way of the thinking mind. Learning to do this is one of the things that sitting meditation is all about.

Of course, developing skill in achieving the state of *zanmai* is no simple matter. Mastery of the art of meditation is essentially not different from mastery of a musical instrument—a violin, for instance. No one would expect to achieve mastery quickly; it takes many years and much hard work, and that is one reason why so many hours are given to zazen practice. One may develop skill in the *posture* of zazen relatively quickly. Thus, from the outside, the student may *appear* to be very calm, very "meditative." But inside it may well be a very different story; the tranquil exterior can often disguise the war going on inside. As Hakuin emphasized in his teaching, one must pass through various stages, especially the Great Doubt, on his or her journey to liberation. For many Zen students, meditation practice is the primary way in which this journey is walked, and that, once again, is why the continual guidance of an already enlightened roshi is essential.

Just as there are stages in the overall life of the Zen student, there are stages in each individual meditation session as well. Everyone has a contemporary "edge" (a "cutting edge"), which represents the farthest limit so far achieved in his or her progress toward experiencing the unitive state. Or maybe a better way of putting it is "the farthest limit so far achieved in being able and willing to totally let go." Real zazen is practiced "at the edge," but one cannot hope to sit down, assume the right posture, and immediately be at one's edge. It takes time to relax and become centered, to get past one's peculiar distractions—and everyone has his or her own personal collection of distractions. We could compare a meditation session to a diamond mine. Each time you go into the mine you must descend past the earlier levels and corridors before you reach the cutting face. This is why zazen sessions tend to be somewhat long. In a short session, too much of the time is spent just getting back to where the diamonds are.

There are many "schools" of meditation, and each one has its own collection of meditation techniques (ways of getting you to the diamonds). Traditional yoga meditation emphasizes the creation of a totally interiorized state of consciousness. Zen meditation, for the most part, emphasizes the practice of shikan-taza; fully experiencing the reality of the moment. No words, no thoughts—just a completely attentive concentration on the fact of existence just as it is at this moment. Doing this takes great power of concentration, and this power does not come quickly or easily. A novice in a Zen monastery will often be assigned the exercise of "counting the breath" while practicing zazen. In this exercise, the student concentrates his or her attention as fully as possible on the simple act of breathing. Each outbreath is silently given a number, usually only from one to ten and then repeated. "Counting the breath" is an excellent exercise for developing skill in centering and concentration.*

There is one little problem in the practice of sitting meditation that seems to plague everyone. If you have had experience with meditation, you'll know what I mean. It is the tendency, especially when sitting for a long time, to fall asleep. Some are bothered by this more than others—and perhaps a few rise above it altogether—but most meditators will sometimes know the experience. This is the chief reason why the drinking of tea became popular in Zen.

There is also another interesting way of dealing with this problem. In a traditional Zendo, a senior monk patrols the room during a meditation session. He carries with him the *kyosaku*, a long, thin stick flattened at the end. When he encounters a person who is slouching or who has fallen asleep, the kyosaku comes into play. As with everything else, this is a highly ritualized act. He will first lightly touch the person's shoulder with the kyosaku and then whack the same spot twice. Often, the blow will be administered on both sides of the neck. Don't let this shock you, and don't get the idea that it is violent, painful, or even embarrassing. It's none of these things. The kyosaku blow is not meant to hurt, but it does dramatically invigorate a body and mind that is much in need of some invigoration. It's not uncommon for a person to use a gesture to ask for a blow from the kyosaku. In a strange way, its occasional sound, far from being a distraction, actually adds to the meditative ambience of the Zendo and helps to keep everyone alert. Incidentally, when one is struck by the kyosaku, the only permitted response is to place the hands in gassho and bow respectfully. There are indeed some aspects of traditional Zen that seem somewhat violent to the modern world and have thus gradually disappeared. Perhaps, unfortunately, this is coming to include the use of the kyosaku. In many non-Japanese monasteries it has become merely a Zen ornament left to hang unused on the Zendo wall.

In addition to sleepiness of mind, there is the problem of sleepiness of body during a long meditation session. This is dealt with through the practice of *kin-hin*. After approximately an hour of sitting, a signal is given from a wooden clapper and everyone stands. The monks form a line and walk around the periphery of the room or outside the Zendo for about ten minutes. Naturally, this, too, is a highly ritualized affair. The line moves—in silence, of course—always in a clockwise direction. Soto monks walk very slowly; Rinzai monks walk relatively fast. But all Zen monks walk in a very distinctive way, holding the closed hands pressed against the solar plexus. When the time is up, the clapper is again sounded and everyone returns to the seated posture.

And so it goes, seemingly without end. The appearance of the monks seated in zazen seems so tranquil. The room seems to be the epitome of serenity. But each is

---

*Kobun Chino Otagawa Roshi, founder of Jikoji Zen Center in California, was once asked if counting the breath was a good practice. "Sure," he said, "One, one, one, . . ."

vividly absorbed in his or her own great adventure, and occasionally that adventure breaks through in the miracle of new vision. Consider this description by Kosen Imakita:

> One night as I sat absorbed in meditation, I suddenly fell into a strange state. It was as if I were dead and everything had been totally cut off. There was no longer a before or an after and both the object of my meditation and my Self had disappeared. The only remaining feeling was that my innermost Self was completely filled by and at one with everything above, below and around me. An infinite light shone within me. After a while I came back to myself like one risen from the dead. Seeing, hearing, speaking, movements and thoughts all seemed completely transformed from what they had previously been. As I tentatively pondered the truth of the world and tried to make sense of the inconceivable, everything was at once understood. It appeared to me clear and real. Without thinking about it, overjoyed, I began to throw my hands into the air and to dance around. Then suddenly I cried out: one million sutras are as but a single candle before the sun. Wonderful, truly wonderful.[3]

In the traditional Zen monastery, each member of the community meets privately from time to time with the roshi in dokusan. This does not necessarily occur every day; it may be very infrequent or no more often than once a week. After being admitted to the roshi's room, the student bows deeply and waits for the roshi's questions. Within the Zen community, it is believed that an experienced master can quickly and intuitively determine the state of mind of the student and can thus recommend exactly the right thing for that person to be working on. Dokusan is typically quite brief; two or three minutes is often sufficient, and seldom is more than ten minutes. This is not a "confession" period, nor is it meant to be a counseling session; it is simply an opportunity for the roshi to check each person's progress and recommend appropriate disciplines.

In the Rinzai tradition the usual purpose of dokusan is for the roshi to check the students' progress with their koan. The roshi will ask the student to explain the meaning of the koan he or she is currently working with. No amount of cleverness can ever fool an experienced roshi. If the response is not completely authentic and spontaneous, the student will be dismissed and told to work harder. In traditional Japanese monasteries, it would seem that it was customary for the roshi to affect a very gruff exterior manner. There are endless stories of roshis shouting at students, kicking them, or hitting them with a stick. The roshi might have said, for example, "All right, tell me now, what was your original face before your parents were born?" If the student's response did not show evidence of real Zen understanding, the master was likely to shout his disapproval, and the student might be driven from the room. This is a cultural difference that is simply incomprehensible to most of the modern world, and dokusan has correspondingly become a much more peaceful affair in today's Zen monasteries.

Zazen holds the place of central importance in the daily life of a Zen monk, occupying several hours of each day, and during periods of sesshin it takes up practically all of the monk's waking hours. But in a normal routine, zazen is far from being the only activity of the day. A number of other things are included, chief among which is *samu*. The word "samu" refers to the ongoing work of the monastery. Remember, a Zen community seeks to be as self-sufficient as it can be. Everyone works, and works hard, whether it be at manual labor or some other kind of useful work. This has always been the case. It was the eighth-century Chinese master Paijing, the creator of the basic monastic rule, who said, "A day without working is a day without eating." Later, Dogen, the founder of Japanese Soto Zen, elevated work to a place of profound importance by insisting that the real practice of Zen consists in loving service to others.

Samu is not to be thought of as toil or as a necessary evil. Work for the good of the community is an expression of the mutual support and love that the individual members share with one another. Seen in this way samu is a source of joy, and when entered into in the right spirit, it is a genuine form of meditation. In fact, samu is really the other side of zazen; together they form a whole. Both are ways of achieving the state of consciousness in which one transcends the delusion of the separated ego and experiences the undivided reality of being. Zazen is the physically passive side of this experience, in which one turns inward; samu is the physically active side of the experience. In a full Zen lifestyle each implies the other.

Although samu is concerned with physical activity, the mind can still be fully absorbed in the present moment. This all-important state of consciousness is called "mindfulness" in modern times. It is the wonderful skill of being able to enter fully into the being of this moment's activity: No distractions, no chattering thoughts about other things, no hurrying, no fretting about the clock's time—nothing but the undivided being of what exists, as it exists, here and now. If you are chopping lettuce, you chop lettuce; nothing more and nothing less. If you are raking the garden, you rake; you do not rake soil with the hands while raking old memories with the mind. Mindfulness is to samu what shikan-taza is to zazen. In a way, "mindfulness" is the bottom line of the life of Zen; it is the distinguishing characteristic of a Zen man and a Zen woman. A famous Zen saying puts it this way: "When you stand, stand. When you walk, walk. Just don't wobble."

Individual members of the community may have specialized skills, such as cooking, carpentry, or calligraphy, and will therefore usually work at these crafts during times of samu. But some things, such as general cleaning and helping in the kitchen, are shared by everyone. Work details are assigned by a senior monk delegated for this task by the roshi. It would be unthinkable that anyone would ever object or do less than his or her very best work. Once again, samu is not toil; it is an act of love. There is always work that needs to be done: gardening, fixing a leaky roof, preparing meals and washing dishes, tending to a sick person, paying the bills, shopping, chopping firewood, and on and on and on. I'm sure most of these things sound pretty familiar; the basic needs of life don't change much from one environment to another. But what could be thought of a drudgery in another context becomes a joy in the daily routine of a Zen monastery.

Samu, like its counterpart zazen, is meant to be done in silence. Outer silence helps to quiet the habitual inner chatter of the thinking mind. Speaking is not forbidden, but by mutual agreement talking is limited to only what is necessary. This, in fact, is true throughout the whole day in a Zen monastery. The usual background buzz of chattering voices is noticeably (and enjoyably) absent within a Zen community. Mindfulness and verbosity are mutually exclusive, and this applies equally to that inner verbosity that plagues almost all of us humans. Mindfulness is indeed a wonderful skill, but it is not acquired easily. The beginner must struggle against the habits of self-distracting thought. An experienced roshi knows this and keeps an eye on the novices; one can easily be overwhelmed both physically and mentally by the volcanolike power set free by the effort to adopt the Zen state of mind.

In the traditional Japanese monastery, afternoon was the customary time for samu. In the modern West it is more likely to be mornings or, depending on need, both mornings and afternoons. Other necessary activities compete with samu and are scheduled on a regular recurring basis, but not every day. One of these activities is the roshi's informal lecture to the community. Occasionally, the talk will be delivered by a senior monk or an honored guest, but usually it is the roshi himself (or herself, as is sometimes the case in modern times outside of Japan) who delivers the lecture. Zen Masters have always taken seriously their responsibility to educate their disciples in the deeper meaning of Zen. In this, the roshi is following the example of Buddha himself, who often called the sangha together and spoke to them from his own experience. The importance of this cannot be exaggerated. Zen tradition holds that, above all else, it is the special personal transmission from master to student that effects awakening. Recall that the fundamental gatha of Zen Buddhism states that enlightenment is "a special transmission outside of words and scriptures."

Personal transmission may be key, but words and scriptures are far from being unimportant. From the earliest times the Zen tradition has maintained a loving regard for its accumulated lore, especially the sutras. It has always been the expectation that Zen monks will be knowledgeable regarding this heritage of traditional wisdom. Consequently, periods of individual study have long had a place in the ongoing routine, perhaps not every day, but at least at frequent intervals. One excellent way of studying is to copy the text being studied by hand. In this way, Zen monks—just like their monastic counterparts in the West—have kept alive the literary treasures of the past. Even though the invention of printing ended the need for hand copying, the practice continues to some extent.

A brief general cleaning is done every morning, but by tradition, on certain days—days of the month with a 4 or a 9 in their number—a very thorough cleaning is scheduled. These days also include the much-loved hot bath. On "bath days," the bathhouse fire is stoked up, and the water in the soaking tub is raised to its customary nearly scorching temperature. Even the bath has its necessary ritual. Monks use the bathhouse in small groups according to rank, with the roshi going first. As a rule, there is a small statue of Batsudabara, the mythical god of the bath, somewhere near the entry. In the ultraorthodox tradition, each monk not only would bow in reverence to this statue, but would do three full prostrations in front of it before entering!

Bath days are also the days for shaving one another's heads, a task best performed by someone other than oneself. The shaved head, a universal badge of monkhood, is another of the changes occurring in modern times. It is still very popular, both in and out of Japan, but it is generally not required in Western monasteries and is by no means universal any longer.

One of the most profound changes concerns mendicancy, or begging. Until the time of Paijing, it was customary for monastic communities to support themselves almost entirely through begging. This was already a long-established tradition in India when Buddhism began to spread to China. The Rule of Paijing, though, stressed self-sufficiency. Mendicancy, however, continued to be practiced in Zen communities, but it became a ritualized activity with a higher purpose than merely acquiring the essentials of life from generous donors. In the traditional Japanese Zen monastery, mendicancy was preserved and became a regularly scheduled activity. The monks would leave the monastery in the morning and walk to the nearby villages. This is probably the reason for samu being an afternoon activity.

The ritual of medicancy was quite a spectacle! It can still be seen occasionally in rural parts of Japan, but is fast dying out in modern times and hardly exists at all any longer in Zen communities outside of Japan.* The monks would assemble dressed in the customary white inner kimono and black outer robe tied at the waist with a cord, straw sandals on the feet, and a broad, flat straw hat on the head or carried in the right hand. In addition, there was the cloth mendicant's bag slung around the neck. They would form a long line and, in a quiet and dignified manner, march off single file through the bamboo and rice fields to the villages where each would silently canvass a separate area. Townspeople considered it an honor to share something—perhaps some cooked rice or a small coin—with the monks of the local monastery. After about an hour or so, they would reassemble and return silently to the monastery. Undoubtedly, what they collected would be useful, but that was not the point of begging in a Zen community. Mendicancy was seen as a powerful exercise in humility; that was its real value. As the *Hoju Sutra* puts it, "If a man practice mendicancy, all arrogance will be destroyed."

These examples are just some of the more important activities that help to make up the daily routine. What ties it all together is the strong sense of community. A Zen monastery is, once again, a living organism made up of the men and women who have come together to share a way of life based on the teaching of Buddha and the long tradition of Zen Buddhism. The grounds of the monastery constitute the place the community calls home. That place is the matrix within which the community brings the teaching of Buddha to life. Although all Zen communities share the same tradition, each monastery is, of course, unique; each has its own special way of enlivening the teaching. For this reason, the custom of the pilgrimage has a long history in Zen.

It has always been the custom in Japan, especially in the Rinzai tradition, for the younger monks to enrich their practice by taking to the road from time to time in order to seek out other masters to study with for a while. Every monastery could expect to

---

*One unlikely place where the tradition of mendicancy is alive and well is the English village of West Sussex. A small group of Theravadin Buddhist monks from the nearby Chithurst Forest Monastery make their daily rounds. This very intersting center was described in a 1994 article written for a Buddhist periodical. (See Steven Batchelor, "A Thai Forest Tradition Grows in England," *Tricycle*, Summer 1994, p.39.)

have a certain number of "guest monks" among the community. This constant shuffling around undoubtedly helped to preserve a certain amount of uniformity within the tradition. It should come as no surprise that this, too, was a highly ritualized procedure—and how strange this particular ritual seems to the modern mind. The Zen Master Tsuguo Miyajima has given us a vivid description of what it was like.

The monk, traveling on foot, of course, would arrive at the gate of the monastery he hoped to visit. After making his request to enter, he would be kept waiting, usually for two whole days, in a little room near the entry. During this time he must show his sincerity and humility by remaining constantly in a kneeling position with his head bowed all the way to the floor, where it would rest on his small rucksack. His only break from this position would be for brief periods of eating and sleeping. Meanwhile, people would enter the room from time to time and heap abuse on him, telling him that he's not wanted and perhaps even attempting to throw him out physically. Of course, all parties know that this behavior is prescribed by tradition; nevertheless, the young monk had better not even for a minute cease to play the part expected of him, or he really will be thrown out. If he gets past this initial period, the visiting monk is allowed to enter another special room called the tankaryo, where he must ceaselessly practice zazen for as long as a week. He will be carefully watched, and if everyone is satisfied with his earnestness, the visitor will at last be allowed to join the community. How different it is today, but still, it is not uncommon to encounter at least a little ritual resistance at first. The discipline is demanding, to say the least, and not everyone is cut out for it. It's important to know that the person seeking admission does sincerely feel some measure of dedication.

I hope that this brief overview of the character of a Zen monastery helps to make it seem more real to you. I also hope that you haven't gotten the impression that a Zen monastery is too much of a formidable and serious sort of place. It's not that way at all. All of the members of the community are flesh-and-blood human beings who typically have an especially rich appreciation of the joy and humor of life.

Before we leave the monastery, there is one more thing to be aware of. It's not a part of all Zen monasteries, but it was a much-loved addition to the early ones, and when means permitted, it was included in many monasteries down through the ages. It is a unique masterpiece of Zen art with strong roots in the Daoist tradition. The Japanese name for it is *kare-sansui*, which, in English, means "dry—mountains and water," but it is usually referred to as a "rock and gravel garden." One will often hear it called a "sand garden." The kare-sansui has a spell binding beauty that no words can describe; it must be experienced. Fortunately, some of the greatest ones still exist, particularly in the Kyoto area, and are open to the public.

The special value of the kare-sansui lies in its having an unusual and potent influence on the meditative state of mind. Its beauty is something to be contemplated, slowly and quietly. Perhaps for this reason, the kare-sansui is usually located directly beside the Zendo. In fact, it is ordinarily attached to the Zendo by a low wall that encloses the garden on the three open sides. Just outside the wall, one would likely find a planting of ornamental trees. On the Zendo side, there is generally a long wooden veranda where people can sit and contemplate the garden scene.

Kare-sansui, Ryoan-ji Monastery; Kyoto, Japan. (P. Bresnan)

Each kare-sansui is a unique creation and can be any size and shape, but most are large rectangles. The masterpiece at Ryoan-ji, a monastery near Kyoto, is approximately one hundred feet by forty-six feet. Picture this broad, flat piece of ground completely carpeted with a deep layer of coarse, snow-white gravel, made from a special white rock found only in one mountainous part of Japan. Actually, if you look closely, you will see that the gravel pieces contain tiny flecks of black, but from a distance it has a snowy appearance. Gravel covers almost all of the surface, but a few small boulders have been carefully placed within it. These, too, have been chosen with great care; the eroded texture is especially beautiful and may appear to have a woodlike grain about it. Although the rock and gravel arrangement is most carefully selected, if it is done well the rock has a completely natural feeling about it, as if it had always been just there. A velvety green moss is allowed to grow on the surface of the rock and is the only vegetation to be found in this "garden." Nothing else will be included.

The most unique feature of the kare-sansui is the raking; this is what gives it its special beauty. Early every morning, one or two skilled monks have the highly honored task of "raking" the garden. This is done with a special wooden rake that has about six widely spaced, large wooden teeth. The monks use the rakes to create a fresh pattern of parallel rows in the gravel. For the most part, these rows are long, straight furrows that may stretch the entire length of the garden. In the vicinity of the boulders, though, the raking becomes more liquid and swirling, as if the lines of gravel were the waves of the ocean and the rocks were mountainous islands. Raking the whole garden this way is a high art and very much a Zen art. If the raking is to look right, it must be a completely spontaneous action, just like Zen painting or Zen archery.

The total effect of the kare-sansui is mesmerizing. The rational mind may at first try to interpret it in terms of symbolism—the way it first wrestles with a koan—but if one stays with it, the thinking mind eventually settles down and allows the deeper consciousness to enjoy it simply for what it is. Many visitors sit quietly for a very long time. The kare-sansui provides the setting for a fine meditation exercise.

From this description, you may get the impression that a kare-sansui is a static sort of thing. It's not static at all; the character of the garden is changing all the time, but in very subtle ways. Shadows play slowly across the surface—shadows from nearby trees and from passing clouds. Leaves occasionally drop onto the gravel surface. Far from being out of place, the leaves add a wonderful, very Daoist, touch to it all. Birds will come and go, leaving their footprints. All of this is perfectly natural and therefore perfectly in accord with the nature of a kare-sansui. But how ghastly it would be if a person walked across the gravel or left a beer can lying there. (No doubt this would be ugly, and yet, strangely enough, it could be just as natural as the bird. Perhaps it would be different if a baby got loose and toddled across the gravel.)

Beautiful as the kare-sansui is in the soft sunlight, it becomes even more enchanting in the moonlight. And when it's covered by a light snowfall, the beauty is indescribable. In fact, everything about it is indescribable; one must sit there for a while and personally experience it. To see the best of these gardens one must travel to the Zen monasteries of Japan. However, some excellent ones can be found outside of Japan. For example, a very beautiful kare-sansui is maintained on the grounds of the Huntington Library in southern California. For the most part, however, this delicate art form doesn't travel well beyond the limits of the monastery grounds.

ZEN AND THE ARTS

The kare-sansui may not have traveled well beyond the confines of the monastery, but the influence of Zen in general has traveled very well indeed beyond the monastery grounds. Japanese culture has been powerfully influenced by Zen Buddhism; it has affected all of the arts, including the humbler arts of practical, everyday things. It's a two-way street, of course. From the beginning, Zen in Japan has been shaped by the existing culture, but in return, Zen has also been a creative force, influencing in its own way the arts of Japanese life. We see this influence in the Japanece emphasis on simplicity and naturalness, as well as in that disciplined spontaneity which is the hallmark of Zen.

Nowhere is this more obvious than in the art of *sumi-e*, the wonderfully beautiful art that we often refer to simply as "Japanese ink painting." In a way, sumi-e is much like the art of kare-sansui; both depend on a sudden spontaneous expression that reveals the unspeakable "suchness" of the beauty of nature. Some of the finest kare-sansui were, in fact, created by renowned ink painters.

The sumi-e artist uses just three things: a finely tapered soft brush with a long wooden or bamboo handle, long pieces of finely made white paper (or, occasionally, white silk), and black ink that is mixed with water for different shades and textures. Sometimes, colored inks, such as pink, will be used, but in the pure tradition of sumi-e, only black ink on white paper is allowed. The ink starts out as a hard stick. A little water is poured into a flattish stone dish, and the ink stick is rubbed in the water until the desired consistency is achieved. The artist can create a great variety of shades by altering the amount of water in the ink.

The brush stroke must be completely spontaneous and without analytical thought. It is often the case that just a few well-executed strokes are all that the artist needs to capture the essence of the subject, whether it be a mountain, a face, or whatever. In sumi-e, the painting is not meant to be *about* nature; it is an *act of* nature. The artist, the subject, and the action of the brush are all one reality. There are many good stories that illustrate this point.

Once upon a time, the emperor wished to have a painting of a bamboo grove, so he called in his favorite court artist, and, paying the man his usual commission in advance, he asked the artist to produce such a work. Weeks stretched into months, and still there was no painting of bamboo. It began to look as if the artist had taken the money and fled. After three long years, he finally reappeared at court. "Where is my painting?" the emperor shouted. "After making me wait so long, it had better be good!"

"I haven't started it yet," the artist answered, but before anyone could react, he offered to do it right then and there. Supplies were brought to him, and in just a matter of seconds his fast brush strokes had finished the painting. Needless to say, it was perfect. The bamboo seemed to sway in the breeze.

The emperor was nonplussed. At last he spoke: "This is magnificent, and it took you only seconds. Why did you make me wait three long years?"

"I was not ready until now," the artist replied. "For the past three years, I have been living with the bamboo, feeling what the bamboo feels, thinking what bamboo thinks. At last I became bamboo myself. Only when I and the bamboo became one could I express its inner essence. Once that unity is achieved, it takes no time to do the painting."

The art of sumi-e, like Zen itself, came to Japan from China. It was already a highly developed art form in the Tang and Song periods. The Daoist love of nature was obvious from the beginning. Many sumi-e masterpieces have survived in museums and are familiar to us today. They are the large "nature paintings"—sometimes done on a series of folding panels—that display great landscapes, often including mist-shrouded mountains and plunging waterfalls. They were often done in a progression of scenes portraying the changing of the seasons. People are likely to be in the picture too, but you might not notice them at first. Instead of dominating the picture, as would be likely in traditional Western art, people fit into these great landscapes at the appropriate scale. They are a part of the whole; their activity is in harmony with the great scene of nature that they are a part of. By looking closely you might discover two or three figures standing on a small bridge or wending their way along a mountain trail. They fit into the scene as just one of its many elements. Again, this is not to say that human life was seen as unimportant—not at all—but what was *most important* was to show the grand harmony of nature, within which human life takes its meaning.

The art of Chinese landscape painting took root in Japan and flourished there. It became especially popular with Rinzai artists, who often decorated the walls of their Zendos with beautiful landscape murals. These paintings, some of which can still be seen, reveal that Japanese artists preferred an even sparer style than the Chinese masters, limiting their brush strokes to only what was essential. Beautiful though the landscape paintings may have been, the practice of decorating Zendo walls eventually died out in favor of leaving them simple and bare.

One of the most intriguing aspects of the sumi-e style is what it doesn't do. The artist feels no need to "fill the canvas." In fact, what the brush *does not do* is just as important as what it does do. "Painting by not painting" it is sometimes called. This can be disconcerting to a person raised in the Western tradition. Empty space—the creative reality of "emptiness"—plays a profoundly important role in the art of sumi-e. It's not uncommon for most of the paper to be left bare; sometimes the inked work occupies only one small corner. Far from appearing incomplete, though, this display of clean, white emptiness is very powerful, giving life and energy to whatever *is* portrayed. The effect is of a "marvelous void from which events suddenly appear." The art of sumi-e evolved as a visible expression of the Zen philosophy of emptiness. It is another way—another *potential* way—of grasping intuitively the perception of reality that is at the heart of Zen Buddhism.

Japanese artists, like the Chinese, favored scenes from nature in which the great harmony of nature is emphasized. The greatest of all the Japanese ink painters was the Zen master Sesshu Toyo (1420–1506). In his hands sumi-e landscape painting reached perfection. But he is also deservedly admired for his portraits, a side of sumi-e that was also inherited from the Chinese. Recall that Japanese Buddhist monks who studied in China often returned home with treasured portraits of their Chinese teachers. It is interesting to compare Sesshu's portrait of Bodhidharma with Da Vinci's Mona Lisa. Both are works of great genius; both are transcendent in that they really portray the universal rather than the particular. But what an infinite difference there is in technique! Da Vinci's creation was meticulously constructed over many months, with attention given to the tiniest details and the painting fills the whole canvas. Sesshu's portrait, by contrast, was probably completed in minutes; attention to detail would have ruined it. One is not better than the other because of this; they are simply different expressions of different philosophies. The brush stroke of a sumi-e master is Zen in action.

There is yet a third area of ink painting that the Japanese inherited from China, the art of calligraphy. In every way calligraphy is the equal of nature painting and portraiture. Chinese characters are such beautiful items in themselves; it must have been only natural to elevate the practice of writing to a fine art. When the Japanese adopted modified Chinese characters they understandably continued the tradition. To find any sort of parallel in the West we would have to go back to medieval times, when the production of illuminated manuscripts was a flourishing art. The invention of printing put an end to that tradition. How ironic it is that printing—movable type carved on wooden blocks—was invented in China so as to facilitate the reproduction of whole characters.

In China, though, printing did not lessen the love of the art of calligraphy. The Japanese certainly have shared this love; a paper panel containing only inked characters is seen as a fine piece of art in and of itself. Often, a much-admired scroll of this sort will be hung on the wall, to be appreciated for its artistic value in the same way that a painting or a flower arrangement would be.

The special thing about calligraphy, though, is that it *is* writing; not only is it beautiful to look at, but it also communicates the written thoughts of its creator. The art of calligraphy is thus ideally suited to unite with the art of poetry, in which Zen Buddhism found yet another magnificent vehicle for the expression of its essential spirit. This is especially true with regard to that unique style of Japanese poetry known as *haiku.*

A haiku is one short verse—only seventeen syllables long—that is meant to evoke a specific feeling or state of mind. It has been nicely described as "a pebble thrown into the pool of the listener's mind." The plop of the pebble creates a brief ripple of consciousness that is more intuitive than rational. It grasps the immediate "suchness" of an experience. Consider, for example, the following haiku:

> The old pond, ah!
> A frog jumps in:
> The water's sound.[4]

Do you see what I mean? Haiku does not aim to stimulate the thinking mind; rather, it evokes feelings and impressions from the memory:

> On a withered branch
> A crow is perched—
> Autumn evening.

How different this kind of poetry is from what became the traditional style in the West. The haiku is to traditional Western poetry what sumi-e is to traditional Western painting. Both, however, have profoundly influenced Western styles in modern times. Haiku is much like sumi-e. In haiku, the "brush strokes" are done with words or, more accurately, with sounds and rhythm. For this reason, haiku loses much in translation. But a well-done translation still preserves the essence of it:

> A fallen flower
> Returning to the branch?
> It was a butterfly.

Haiku generally focuses on very mundane things, the ordinary sights and sounds of daily life:

> The sound of the scouring
> of the saucepan blends
> With the tree-frog's voices.

The greatest name in haiku is Matsuo Basho, a Zen Master who lived during the latter half of the seventeenth century. (*Basho*, which means "banana tree" in Japanese, was his pen name.) Basho is to haiku what Sesshu is to sumi-e. It's tempting to imagine that Basho was inspired to verse by some of Sesshu's ink paintings.

Ishiyama no	White shines the stone
ishi yori shiroshi	Of the mountain rock; whiter yet
aki no kaze.	The autumn wind.

The spirit of Zen affects many of the arts of Japanese culture, and they all come together in the "Tea Ceremony," a sort of grand opera of all the elements influenced by Zen. What we know as the Tea Ceremony is called *Chado* in Japanese (the "way of tea"). Like the kare-sansui gardens, Chado is uniquely Japanese. Both art forms, so deep and filled with beauty, are difficult for the Western mind to understand. Both, however, have been honed to perfection over many centuries. When understood even a little they can easily be seen to be profound expressions of Japanese culture in general and Zen in particular.

The "cha" in Chado is tea, a plant known in botany as *camellia sinensis*, a bushy green shrub whose leaves contain small amounts of caffeine. It was first domesticated in the warm, hilly regions of southern China, and it became a highly popular drink with all classes of Chinese society. Tea keeps the mind alert, but without causing intoxication. Of course, the amount consumed *does* make a difference. Consider this comment by the Tang period poet Lo Dong (Lo-tung): "The first cup moistens my lips and throat, the second cup breaks my loneliness, the third cup searches my barren entrail but to find therein some five thousand volumes of odd ideographs. The fourth cup raises a slight perspiration—all the wrong of life passes away through my pores. At the fifth cup I am purified; the sixth cup calls me to the realms of immortals. The seventh cup—ah, but I could take no more!"[5] (And this is *tea* he's drinking!)

Lo Dong's comment is revealing. Tea was not just an early version of soda pop among the Chinese; they felt a deep affection for the mysterious beauty of tea in all of its aspects—not only the brewing and drinking of tea, but even the very appearance of the tea leaves. This point is made by another wonderful comment from the same time as Lo Dong's: According to the Tang poet Lu Wu, the best quality leaves must have "creases like the leather boot of Tartar horsemen, curl like the dewlap of a mighty bullock, unfold like a mist rising out of a ravine, gleam like a lake touched by a zephyr, and be wet and soft like fine earth newly swept by rain."[6]

Zen monks in particular were attracted to *tcha*, as the Chinese called it. The sipping of tea could ward off sleepiness during long hours of meditation practice. As a result, the ritual drinking of tea was introduced into the monastic routine. The origin of the Tea Ceremony is said to go back to Zen monasteries in China where monks would gather to sip tea before a portrait of Bodhidharma. Legend had it, you may remember, that the first tea plants grew from the eyelids (or eyebrows) of Bodhidharma when he tore them off and flung them on the ground. A certain amount of ritual grew up around this shared act of tea drinking, but it was still a rather modest affair when it was transported from Chinese to Japanese Zen monasteries. The ritual of the Tea Ceremony was transformed and perfected in the sixteenth century by Sen-no-Rikyu, the first great tea master of Japan. He was a counselor to Oda Nobunaga, a powerful military leader who unified the country. On the grounds of Nobunaga's estate, Sen-no-Rikyu constructed the first fully developed tea garden. The mature form of Chado created by Sen-no-Rikyu has been carefully preserved down to the present time, with only refinements being added.

Chado is a carefully designed ritual in which a small group of people participate. Every act, every movement, in Chado is prescribed by ritual. This may seem excessive to the uninitiated, but in fact it is very liberating; ritual permits the participants to temporarily set aside the role-playing of the ego. The procedure is led by a man (or woman) called a *teishu*, "master of tea," who prepares and serves tea to the others. But so much more is involved here than simply getting together to drink some tea. This is in no way a "tea party" in the conventional sense; it is a highly refined group activity in which each person plays an important role. In the course of the ceremony, *all* of the senses will be gently stimulated, creating an aesthetic experience of the highest order in the participants. Mindfulness, the Zen love of total immersion in the present moment, permeates the whole experience.

The ceremony of Chado can be conducted almost anywhere; a small room set off for the purpose can be perfectly adequate. Ideally, however, the ceremony of tea will have its own special setting: a teahouse, known as a *chashitsu*, set within a tea garden. By custom, a tea garden should be small and modest. The important thing, though, is that it promote a sense of naturalness and serenity and that it be separated from the ordinary environment of daily life.

The guests arrive at the *machiai*, which is just a simple little gathering place, perhaps a trellis-covered porch. When all are assembled, the teishu will summon them to the teahouse. Most likely, they will pause along the way and admire the beauty of the garden; its arrangement is meant to encourage a contemplative frame of mind. The path through the garden—the *roji*—signifies the first stage in the practice of meditation. The teahouse is simplicity itself, and therein lies its special beauty. It is a small, squarish building—a hut, really—ten feet on a side by tradition. The roof is likely to be straw thatch in the old rural style of Japan, overhanging the walls, which are made of bare lath and shoji paper. The building nestles into the garden in perfect harmony; it appears to have grown there.

Before entering the chashitsu each guest pauses at the *tsukubai*, the "stone water basin," to purify the inner self by ritually cleansing the hands and mouth. Certain guests may be especially honored, but all social rank is left outside. In the old days, the samurai had to leave their swords behind, the insignia of their class, when they entered the teahouse. Entry is made through a low sliding door. The doorway is deliberately made low so that one must bow or even kneel in the act of entering. Of course, all shoes are left outside. The interior of the teahouse is spotlessly clean and simple; there is a complete absence of clutter. Soft light filters into the room through the shoji-covered windows, and a subtle aroma of incense fills the air. The floor is covered in tatami mats, and near one end of the room is an opening in the floor for a small fire pit, where a charcoal fire will heat the water in a heavy cast-iron kettle. In one of the walls is an alcove called a *tokonoma*, where an object of art will be displayed, probably a hanging scroll with calligraphy, and on a shelf beneath it there is likely to be a naturally beautiful rock or a simple arrangement of flowers.

The display of natural objects, much influenced by the spirit of Zen, has been raised to a fine art in Japanese culture. Objects displayed in the teahouse are selected with great care. The tokonoma may hold a single flower or perhaps a small branch, and most likely, it will have been placed slightly off center on the shelf. In arranging the room, the tea master carefully avoids the clutter of repetition and the dullness of symmetry. "Uniformity of design is considered fatal to the freshness of the imagination." How different this is from a typical Western room in which the many things of the room are often methodically balanced and centered.

The guests sit directly on the tatami-covered floor, forming a small square or circle around the perimeter of the room. Cushions may be used, but Japanese people are more likely to prefer a posture called seiza, in which one kneels and then sits back on the heels. This is a very comfortable position when you get used to it. After the guests are seated, the tea master (the teishu) will enter the room and take his (or her) place near one end of the circle, beside the fire pit. While the teishu cleans the utensils the guests may chat among themselves. Silence is not required, but it is expected that conversation will be friendly and will be limited to appropriate subjects. Sports and politics would definitely be out of place. Particularly appropriate would be expressions of appreciation regarding the beauty of the things in the room. Everything has been selected with great care by the teishu. By no means are the guests merely passive receivers; Chado is a ritual event in which each participant plays an important role. There is an art to being a good guest. An atmosphere of relaxed formality characterizes the Tea Ceremony.

While they are waiting, the guests may take note of the beauty of the tokonoma or the tea utensils. At the same time, they enjoy the sound of the steaming water, which can be likened to wind passing through pine needles. Not infrequently, all will fall silent for a while in order to enjoy the sound. Other sounds, too, may be enjoyed, such as the song of a bird in the garden, the patter of lightly falling rain, or the wonderful sound of the wind in the trees just outside the teahouse.

Chado is a word with broad meaning. It refers not only to the Tea Ceremony, but to the whole philosophy behind it. The Tea Ceremony is a refined expression of a way of life based on tranquility and acceptance. Within the Tea Ceremony itself, the actual preparation and sipping of the tea is known by the name *temae*. The tea used in temae is a strong green tea that has been finely powdered. It has a rich aroma and an almost bitter taste. It is sipped, not from teacups, but from small ceramic bowls that are held lightly in both hands.

You might expect that only perfect and costly teaware would be used. In fact, it's quite the opposite. A person who attempts to impress his guests by showing off expensive items completely misses the point of Chado. The beauty of the humble and the natural is what is most appreciated. A tea master will search in unlikely places for his wares. He is looking for those wonderfully rare accidents that transform the ordinary into a masterpiece. Of course, such "flaws" may not be appreciated by everyone, but the experienced eye of a lover of Chado sees them easily. Prized tea bowls are often surprisingly humble pieces of ceramic. The glaze may drip unevenly, there may be a crack on one side, or the whole thing may even be misshapen, but the knowing guest will smile in appreciation. Ceramic tea caddies are delicate and sometimes are accidentally broken (and maybe, on occasion, not so accidentally). It is believed that the way the pieces are glued back together adds greatly to its beauty. This sense of seeing beauty in spontaneous "accidents" is very much in the spirit of Zen.

The tea is prepared one bowl at a time by the tea master. This ritual absorbs the full attention of the guests. Using a thin bamboo strip the teishu will spoon a measured amount of powdered tea into a bowl and add a little steaming water from the kettle. He then briskly stirs them together with a bamboo whisk until the mixture becomes "the froth of liquid jade." The bowl is then placed before one of the guests. Even this act is done in such a way as to show off the bowl's best appearance. What is regarded to be its most beautiful side will be placed facing the guest. Each guest lifts the bowl and courteously addresses those near him. Turning first to the person on his, or her, right the guest says, "Allow me to share tea with you." Then turning to the person on the left, he or she says, "Excuse me for going before you." Finally, addressing the tea master, the guest says, "Thank you for making tea." Only then does the guest begin to sip the wonderful concoction. At the first sip all of the taste buds will be stimulated to *full* attention.

The tea invigorates the senses. When the sipping is completed, it is customary to pass each of the implements around the circle so that they can be admired by the guests. No matter how humble its use, each utensil is a work of art. The whisk is a thing of simple beauty, and so is the bamboo dipping spoon, the small towel, and so on. This love of perfection in the most ordinary things of life is one of the distinguishing characteristics of Japanese culture in general. In the Tea Ceremony, it becomes the focus of attention. The Zen attitude of mindfulness is fully employed in Chado.

Temae does indeed refresh and stimulate all the senses, but it is a mistaken impression to see the Tea Ceremony as nothing more than a relaxing and pleasurable experience. It is that, of course, but it is much more as well. Above all else, the special appeal of Chado is to be found in the state of mind that it encourages. This is where the connection to Zen is most obvious and most profound. The ritual, the implements, and the sensory pleasures are the raw material out of which a particular state of consciousness is subtly constructed. Tradition identifies four aspects to this state of mind—principles that give definition to the Tea Ceremony. In Japanese, these four are known as *wa, kei, sei,* and *jaku.* It should come as no surprise that these words do not translate easily into English. *Wa* is usually rendered as "harmony," *kei* as "reverence," *sei* as "purity," and *jaku* as "tranquility." It is said that these four qualities bring together the spirit of Confucianism, of Daoism, and of Buddhism. The tea master seeks to use temae in the way a gifted musician *uses* an instrument: to create a state of mind in his guests that exemplifies the four virtues.

But there is still more, at least potentially. A gifted tea master brings it all together in a subtle, but transcendent, state of consciousness that cannot really be named. It has to be called something, though, and the Japanese use the word *wabi,* another word that defies translation, and maybe it's better that way. Let's be satisfied with saying only that wabi suggests a deep and serene state of mind that is in tune with the great beauty of emptiness. Wabi is sometimes called "poverty," but it is poverty in the sense of an acceptance of the fact that nothing is ever owned, nothing endures. Out of this kind of poverty can arise a deeply felt aesthetic appreciation of emptiness whose spirit is best expressed in poetry:

> In the woods, over there, deeply buried in snow,
> Last night a lone branch of the plum tree burst out in bloom.

All is fleeting; all is transitory; nothing endures. Everything emerges from emptiness and returns to emptiness. But, like the plum tree blossoming in the snow, every moment—if only we would stop and look—is filled with an awesome beauty that can lift the spirit to an experience of transcendent reality. The curling steam of the teakettle, the momentary scent of the incense, the fleeting taste of the tea—everything about temae is evanescent, transitory. And therein lies its excellence. In the hands of a true tea master, temae becomes a beautiful expression of the meaning of *shunyata*. There is a wonderful verse by the poet Rikyu that reveals the very heart of Chado:

> When tea is made with water drawn from the depths of mind,
> Whose bottom is beyond measure,
> We really have what is called cha-no-yu [Chado].

When the tea has been consumed and everything has been admired and put away, the teishu will invite everyone to return to the garden, where the guests will most graciously take their leave. For an hour or two they have set aside the usual responsibilities of ordinary life and entered the state of mind the Daoists called "the world of carefree hermits, wandering through the mountains like wind-blown clouds, with nothing to do but cultivate a row of vegetables, gaze at the drifting mist, and listen to the waterfalls."

Like all things, Buddhism, too, is transitory; it must be reborn each moment. Shakyamuni Buddha initiated a process, a wave of development that has known flourishing times and times of decline. Like a flowering plant, Buddhism in India blossomed and then declined. But by this time the seeds were in the ground outside of India. In China, a new flowering occurred, and then, too, began to decline. Again, though, the seeds had been carried to new lands. In Japan, Buddhism—especially Zen Buddhism—would experience yet another magnificent flowering, and alas, this was followed by still another period of decline.

By the beginning of the twentieth century it must have seemed to many that the golden age of Zen Buddhism in Japan was a thing of the past. But again, the flower had broadcast its seeds, this time very far afield. Seedlings were taking root in the most unlikely places. The ancient tradition of Buddhism had at last spread to the West. The new growth is strong and healthy. Yet another flowering—this time worldwide in scope—would seem certain to be an exciting part of the not-too-distant future.

Notes

1. Hakuin, as quoted in Heinrich Dumoulin, *Zen Buddhism: A History*, trans. James W. Hesig and Paul Knitter (New York: Macmillan, 1988), vol. 2, p. 384.
2. Hakuin, quoted in Dumoulin, p. 381.
3. Kosen Imakita, quoted in Dumoulin, p. 408.
4. All haiku are taken from R. H. Blyth, *Haiku* (Tokyo: Heian International Publishing, 1981).
5. Kakuzo Okakura, *The Book of Tea* (Tokyo: Kodansha, 1906; reprint 1989), p. 48.
6. *Ibid.*, p. 47.

Study Questions

1. How did Shinto influence the early development of Buddhism in Japan?
2. In what fundamental ways do Rinzai and Soto Zen differ?
3. What did Hakuin mean by the "Great Doubt" and the Great Dying"?
4. What do you understand to be the meaning of Suzuki's arresting statement; "To my mind it was the technique of koan exercise that saved Zen as a unique heritage of Far Eastern culture"?
5. Why does the practice of zazen play such an enormous role in the life of a Zen monastery?
6. Explain the character and purpose of the kare-sansui.
7. Speaking generally, how has Zen Buddhism influenced the traditional arts of Japanese culture? In particular, how is the influence of Zen revealed in sumi-e and haiku?
8. Wabi refers to "a transcendent state of consciousness that cannot really be named." How does wabi reveal the spirit of Zen working in the art of chado?

Index